ELEMENTS OF ARGUMENT

THIRD EDITION

ELEMENTS OF ARGUMENT

A Text and Reader

Annette T. Rottenberg
UNIVERSITY OF MASSACHUSETTS AT AMHERST

BEDFORD BOOKS OF ST. MARTIN'S PRESS
BOSTON

For Alex

For Bedford Books
Publisher: Charles H. Christensen
Associate Publisher: Joan E. Feinberg
Managing Editor: Elizabeth M. Schaaf
Developmental Editor: Stephen A. Scipione
Production Editor: Lori Chong
Copyeditor: Deborah Fogel
Text Design: Claire Seng-Niemoeller
Cover Design: Richard Emery
Cover Art: Honoré Daumier, *Lawyers and Justice* (L. Delteil No. 1343, April 24, 1845). Bequest of William P. Babcock. Courtesy, Museum of Fine Arts, Boston.

Library of Congress Catalog Card Number: 89–63931

Manufactured in the United States of America.

5 4 3 2 1 0

f e d c b a

For information, write: St. Martin's Press, Inc.
175 Fifth Avenue, New York, NY 10010
Editorial Offices: Bedford Books *of* St. Martin's Press,
29 Winchester Street, Boston, MA 02116

ISBN: 0–312–04059–8
Instructor's Edition ISBN: 0–312–04910–2

ACKNOWLEDGMENTS

Felicia Ackerman, "Not Everybody Wants to Sign a Living Will." From the *New York Times*, October 13, 1989. Copyright © 1989 by The New York Times Company. Reprinted by permission.

Gordon Allport, "The Nature of Prejudice." From the Seventeenth Claremont Reading Conference Yearbook, 1952. Reprinted by permission.

Acknowledgments and copyrights are continued at the back of the book on pages 631–636, which constitute an extension of the copyright page.

Preface for Instructors

PURPOSE

Argumentation as the basis of a composition course should need no defense, especially at a time of renewed pedagogical interest in critical thinking. A course in argumentation encourages practice in close analysis, use of supporting materials, and logical organization. It encompasses all the modes of development around which composition courses are often built. It teaches students to read and to listen with more than ordinary care. Not least, argument can engage the interest of students who have been indifferent or even hostile to required writing courses. Because the subject matter of argument can be found in every human activity, from the most trivial to the most elevated, both students and teachers can choose the materials that appeal to them. And those materials need not be masterpieces of the genre, as in courses based on literature; students can exercise their critical skills on flawed arguments that allow them to enjoy a well-earned superiority.

Composition courses using the materials of argument are, of course, not new. But the traditional methods of teaching argument through mastery of the formal processes of reasoning cannot account for the complexity of arguments in practice. Even more relevant to our purposes as teachers of composition is the tenuous relationship between learning about induction and deduction, however helpful in analysis, and the actual process of student composition. E. D. Hirsch, Jr., in *The Philosophy of Composition*, wrote, "I believe, as a practical matter, that instruction in logic is a very inefficient way to give instruction in writing."[1] The challenge has been to find a method of teaching argument that assists students in defending their claims as directly and efficiently as possible, a method that reflects the way people actually go about organizing and developing claims outside the classroom.

One such method, first adapted to classroom instruction by teachers of rhetoric and speech, uses a model of argument advanced by Stephen Toulmin in *The Uses of Argument*. Toulmin was interested in producing a description of the real *process* of argument. His model was the law. "Arguments," he said, "can be compared with law-suits, and the claims we make and argue for in extra-legal contexts with claims made in the courts."[2] Toulmin's model of argument was based on three principal elements: claim, evidence, and warrant. These elements answered the questions, "What are you trying to prove?" "What have you got to go on?" "How did you get from evidence to claim?" Needless to say, Toulmin's model of argument does not guarantee a classroom of skilled arguers, but his questions about the parts of an argument and their relationship are precisely the ones that students must ask and answer in writing their own essays and analyzing those of others. They lead students naturally into the formulation and development of their claims.

My experience in supervising hundreds of teaching assistants over a number of years has shown that they also respond to the Toulmin model with enthusiasm. They appreciate its clarity and directness and the mechanism it offers for organizing a syllabus.

In this text I have adapted — and greatly simplified — some of Toulmin's concepts and terminology for freshman students. I have also introduced two elements of argument with which Toulmin is not directly concerned. Most rhetoricians consider them indispensable, however, to discussion of what actually happens in the defense or rejection of a claim. One is motivational appeals — warrants based on appeals to the needs and values of an audience, designed to evoke emotional responses. A distinction between logic and emotion may be useful as an analytical tool, but in producing or attacking arguments human beings find it difficult, if not impossible, to make such a separation. In this text, therefore, persuasion through appeals to needs and values is treated as a legitimate element in the argumentative process.

---

[1] *The Philosophy of Composition* (Chicago: University of Chicago Press, 1977), p. 142.

[2] *The Uses of Argument* (Cambridge: Cambridge University Press, 1958), p. 7.

I have also stressed the significance of audience as a practical matter. In the rhetorical or audience-centered approach to argument, to which I subscribe in this text, success is defined as acceptance of the claim by an audience. Arguers in the real world recognize intuitively that their primary goal is not to demonstrate the purity of their logic, but to win the adherence of their audiences. To gain this adherence, students need to be reminded of the necessity for establishing themselves as credible sources for their readers.

ORGANIZATION

In Part One, after an introductory overview, a chapter each is devoted to the chief elements of argument — the claims that students make in their arguments (Chapter 2), the definitions and support they must supply for their claims (Chapters 3 and 4), the warrants that underlie their arguments (Chapter 5), the language that they use (Chapter 6). Popular fallacies, as well as induction and deduction, are treated in Chapter 7; because fallacies represent errors of the reasoning process, a knowledge of induction and deduction can make clear how and why fallacies occur.

I have tried to provide examples, readings, discussion questions, and writing suggestions that are both practical and stimulating. With the exception of several student dialogues, the examples are real, not invented; they have been taken from speeches, editorial opinions, letters to the editor, advertisements, interviews, and news reports. They reflect the liveliness and complexity that invented examples often suppress.

The readings in Part One support the discussions in several important ways. First, they illustrate the elements of argument; in each chapter, one or more essays have been analyzed to emphasize the chapter's principles of argument. Second, they are drawn from current publications and cover as many different subjects as possible to convince students that argument is a pervasive force in the world they read about and live in. Third, some of the essays are obviously flawed and thus enable students to identify the kinds of weaknesses they should avoid in their own essays.

Part Two takes up the processes of writing and researching. Chapter 8 explains how to find a topic, define the issues that it embraces, organize the information, and draft and revise an argument. Chapter 9 introduces students to the business of finding sources, mostly in the library, and using them effectively in research papers. Both chapters conclude with sample student papers; the annotated student research paper in Chapter 9 uses the MLA documentation system. (The MLA system is explained along with the APA system elsewhere in the chapter.)

Part Three, "Opposing Viewpoints," exhibits arguers in action, using informal and formal language, debating head-on. The subjects —

abortion, AIDS testing, animal rights, collegiate sports reform, environmental policy, euthanasia, freedom of speech, legalizing drugs, pornography — capture headlines every day. Despite their immediacy, these subjects are likely to arouse passions and remain controversial for a long time. Whether as matters of national policy or personal choice, they call for decisions based on familiarity with their competing views.

Finally, Part Four, "Classic Arguments," reprints eight selections that have stood the tests of both time and the classroom. Drawn from the works of Plato, Jonathan Swift, Henry David Thoreau, Elizabeth Cady Stanton, Virginia Woolf, George Orwell, and Martin Luther King, Jr., they are among the arguments that teachers find invaluable in any composition course.

The editor's notes provide additional suggestions for using the book, as well as for finding and using the enormous variety of materials available in a course on argument.

I hope this text will lead students to discover not only the practical and intellectual rewards of learning how to argue but the real excitement of engaging in civilized debate as well.

NEW TO THIS EDITION

Revising a successful textbook — the publisher says that *Elements of Argument* is now the bestselling book of its kind — presents both a challenge and an opportunity. The challenge is to avoid undoing features that have been well received in the earlier edition. The opportunity is to tap into the experiences of instructors and students who have used the earlier editions and to make use of their insights to improve what needs improvement. This is how we have approached this revision, and it accounts for all that we have done, and not done, in preparing the new edition.

The principles and concerns of the book have not changed. Rather, I have included a greater breadth of material to increase the book's usefulness as a teaching tool. Instructors who requested more explanation in Part One of warrants, induction, and deduction now have more, including sample analyses of inductive and deductive arguments and discussion of the relationship of warrants to other elements of argument. Instructor interest has also led me to add several advertisements to Part One for student analysis. Part Two is a substantial revision and enlargement of the second edition's appendix on writing arguments. Library research and writing from sources are now covered in more detail, and two sample student arguments (one of them an annotated research paper) are included; also new is a section on the APA documentation system to supplement the coverage of the MLA system. In Part Three, the number of "Opposing

Viewpoints" has increased from six to nine. The five most popular topics from the second edition — AIDS Testing, Animal Rights, Collegiate Sports Reform, Euthanasia, Pornography — have been retained and brought up to date, while four new topics that should appeal strongly to students have been added: Abortion, Environmental Policy, Freedom of Speech, and Legalizing Drugs. Part Four is now a separate anthology of classic arguments, perennial favorites of instructors and students. All told, the number of selections has grown from seventy-eight in the second edition to one hundred and seventeen in the third, with a corresponding increase in the number of debatable issues (and teaching options). Taken as a whole the changes in the third edition should enhance the versatility of the book, deepen students' awareness of how pervasive argument is, and increase their ability to think critically and communicate persuasively.

This book has profited from the critiques and suggestions of Patricia Bizzell, College of the Holy Cross; Richard Fulkerson, East Texas State University; William Hayes, California State College — Stanislaus; Marcia MacLennan, Kansas Wesleyan University; Lester Faigley, University of Texas at Austin; Cheryl W. Ruggiero, Virginia Polytechnic Institute; Michael Havens, University of California at Davis; Judith Kirscht, University of Michigan; Richard Katula, University of Rhode Island; Carolyn R. Miller, North Carolina State University at Raleigh; A. Leslie Harris, Georgia State University; Richard S. Hootman, University of Iowa; Donald McQuade, University of California at Berkeley; David L. Wagner; Ron Severson, Salt Lake Community College; Paul Knoke, East Carolina University; and Robert H. Bentley, Lansing Community College. The editor's notes are the better for the contributions of Gail Stygall, Miami University of Ohio.

Many instructors helped improve the book by responding to a questionnaire. I appreciate the thoughtful consideration given by: Timothy C. Alderman, Yvonne Alexander, William Arfin, Karen Arnold, Peter Banland, Carol A. Barnes, Don Beggs, Don Black, Kathleen Black, Stanley S. Blair, Laurel Boyd, Dianne Brehmer, Alan Brown, Paul L. Brown, W. K. Buckley, Alison A. Bulsterbaum, Clarence Bussinger, Gary T. Cage, Ruth A. Cameron, Barbara R. Carlson, Gail Chapman, Roland Christian, Dr. Thomas S. Costello, Mimi Dane, Judy Davidson, Philip E. Davis, Julia Dietrich, Marcia B. Dinnech, L. Leon Duke, P. Dunsmore, Bernard Earley, Carolyn L. Engdahl, David Estes, Kristina Faber, B. R. Fein, Delia Fisher, Evelyn Flores, Donald Forand, Mary A. Fortner, Leslye Friedberg, Diane Gabbard, Frieda Gardner, Gail Garloch, E. R. Gelber-Beechler, Scott Giantralley, Michael Patrick Gillespie, Paula Gillespie, Wallace Gober, Sara Gogol, Marilyn Hagans, Linda L. Hagge, Lee T. Hamilton, Phillip J. Hanse, Susan Harland, Carolyn G. Hartz, Anne Helms, Diane Price Herndl, Heidi Hobbs, William S. Hochman, Sharon E. Hockensmith, Joyce Hooker,

Clarence Hundley, Richard Ice, Mary Griffith Jackson, Ann S. Jagoe, Katherine James, Owen Jenkins, Ruth Y. Jenkins, Janet Jubnke, E. C. Juckett, George T. Karnezis, Mary Jane Kearny, Patricia Kellogg-Dennis, Joanne Kirkland, Nancy Klug, John H. Knight, Barbara Ladd, William Levine, Cynthia Lowenthal, Marjorie Lynn, Patrick McGuire, Ray McKerrow, Pamela J. McLagan, Christina M. McVay, D'Ann Madewell, Beth Madison, Susan Maloney, Barbara A. Manrigue, Joyce Marks, Charles May, Jean-Pierre Meterean, Lisa K. Miller, Logan D. Moon, Dennis D. Moore, Dan Morgan, Curt Mortenson, Philip A. Mottola, Thomas Mullen, Michael B. Naas, Joseph Nassar, Byron Nelson, Elizabeth Nist, Dr. Mary Jean Northcutt, Thomas O'Brien, James F. O'Neil, Richard D. Olson, Lori Jo Oswald, Leland S. Person, Steve Phelan, Teresa Marie Purvis, Barbara E. Rees, Pat Regel, Charles Reinhart, Janice M. Reynolds, Douglas F. Rice, Katherine M. Rogers, Judith Klinger Rose, Cathy Rosenfeld, Robert A. Rubin, Lori Ruediger, Joseph L. Sanders, Suzette Schlapkohl, Sybil Schlesinger, Richard Schneider, Lucy Sheehey, Sallye J. Sheppeard, Sally Bishop Shigley, John Shout, Thomas Simmons, Richard Singletary, Beth Slusser, Denzell Smith, Rebecca Smith, Elissa L. Stuchlik, Judy Szaho, Andrew Tadie, R. Terhorst, Marguerite B. Thompson, Arline R. Thorn, Mary Ann Trevathan, Whitney G. Vanderwerff, Jennie VerSteeg, Linda D. Warwick, Carol Adams Watson, Roger D. Watson, Karen Webb, Raymond E. Whelan, Betty E. White, Toby Widdicombe, Heywood Williams, and Alfred Wong.

I thank the people at Bedford Books whose efforts have made the progress of the third edition a thousand times lighter for me: Jane Betz, Frank Dumais, Deborah Fogel, Ellen Kuhl, Chris Rutigliano, and Elizabeth Schaaf. Most of all I thank Charles H. Christensen, Joan E. Feinberg, Lori Chong, and the editor with whom I have worked most closely for two editions, Steve Scipione.

Brief Contents

Preface for Instructors v

PART ONE

The Structure of Argument 1

1. *Introduction to Argument* 3
2. *Claims* 24
3. *Definition* 72
4. *Support* 104
5. *Warrants* 142
6. *Language and Thought* 175
7. *Induction, Deduction, and Logical Fallacies* 208

PART TWO

Writing and Researching Arguments 251

8. Writing an Argumentative Paper 253

9. Researching an Argumentative Paper 277

PART THREE

Opposing Viewpoints 311

10. Abortion 315

11. AIDS Testing 336

12. Animal Rights 362

13. Collegiate Sports Reform 397

14. Environmental Policy 419

15. Euthanasia 443

16. Freedom of Speech 472

17. Legalizing Drugs 503

18. Pornography 526

PART FOUR

Classic Arguments 553

Glossary and Index of Terms 637

Index of Authors and Titles 642

Contents

Preface for Instructors **v**

PART ONE

The Structure of Argument 1

1. Introduction to Argument **3**

The Nature of Argument **3**
Why Study Argument? **6**
Why Write? **8**
The Terms of Argument **9**
The Audience **13**

SAMPLE ANALYSIS

The Declaration of Independence
THOMAS JEFFERSON **18**

When revolutionaries resolved to throw off their king and form their own government, they turned to the eloquent Jefferson for a defense of their audacious plan.

EXERCISES FOR REVIEW **22**

2. Claims **24**

Claims of Fact **24**

SAMPLE ANALYSIS: CLAIM OF FACT

Cocaine Is Even Deadlier Than We Thought
LOUIS L. CREGLER and HERBERT MARK **30**

Two physicians examine the frightening and potentially lethal effects of cocaine abuse.

Claims of Value **31**

SAMPLE ANALYSIS: CLAIM OF VALUE

Kids in the Mall: Growing Up Controlled
WILLIAM SEVERINI KOWINSKI **35**

A journalist evaluates the lessons teens learn in "universities of suburban materialism."

Claims of Policy **39**

SAMPLE ANALYSIS: CLAIM OF POLICY

So That Nobody Has to Go to School If They Don't Want To
ROGER SIPHER **42**

A teacher argues that forcing unmotivated students to stay in school is a fruitless waste of energy and resources and a drag on those who truly want to learn.

READINGS FOR ANALYSIS

Homelessness in Colonial and Early America
PETER H. ROSSI **45**

A sociologist shows that, although the homeless today arouse sympathetic attention, they were in the past treated with indifference and even "contempt, fear, and loathing."

Discriminating Tastes: The Prejudice of Personal Preferences
VICTORIA A. SACKETT **50**

Our national tolerance of diversity has increased, writes an editor of *Public Opinion*; yet as individuals we are succumbing to a plague of petty prejudices.

In Support of Our Common Language . . .
U. S. ENGLISH **54**

A public interest group spells out why it is important that English be the official language of the United States.

Capital Punishment — An Idea Whose Time Has Come Again
J. A. PARKER **57**

A spokesman for a conservative African-American think tank musters evidence to show that opposition to capital punishment runs counter to our religious and legal tradition.

The Right to Bear Arms
WARREN E. BURGER **64**

A former chief justice of the United States examines the historical roots of the Second Amendment in order to construct an appeal for gun control.

The great American forest is closer than you think [advertisement] **68**

GE: The initials of a friend [advertisement] **69**

Nuclear energy can help America find a way out of our dangerous dependence on foreign oil [advertisement] **70**

EXERCISES FOR REVIEW **71**

3. Definition **72**

The Purposes of Definition **72**
Defining the Terms in Your Argument **74**
Methods for Defining Terms **77**
The Definition Essay **82**
Writing an Essay of Definition **82**

SAMPLE ANALYSIS

The Missing Element: Moral Courage
BARBARA TUCHMAN **84**

A historian argues that the ills of American society stem from our leaders' failure to stand up for values that any educated person should know are worth standing up for.

READINGS FOR ANALYSIS

The Nature of Prejudice
GORDON ALLPORT **92**

Identifying other people's prejudices is easy, observes a Harvard psychologist, but sometimes it takes careful definition to help us spot our own.

Saturday Night
SUSAN ORLEAN **94**

A reporter roams the United States to discover what Saturday night means to Americans.

Everything a good restaurant ought to be [advertisement] **102**

EXERCISES FOR REVIEW **103**

4. *Support* **104**

Types of Support: Evidence and Appeals to Needs and Values **104**

Evidence **106**

Evaluation of Evidence **112**

Appeals to Needs and Values **120**

Evaluation of Appeals to Needs and Values **126**

SAMPLE ANALYSIS

Lotto Is Financed by the Poor and Won by the States
PETER PASSELL **127**

Legalized lotteries are a "cash cow" state governments have learned to love, writes a *New York Times* reporter. But the data suggest that the public is being milked.

READINGS FOR ANALYSIS

Economic and Social Impact of Immigrants
STEPHEN MOORE **131**

The facts indicate that immigrants "do not just take jobs, but create jobs" through their consumption and initiative.

Playing Favorites
PATRICIA KEEGAN **135**

Men continue to outperform women academically, grants an educational analyst — but not because of innate intellectual superiority.

Gas heat makes me nervous [advertisement] **140**

EXERCISES FOR REVIEW **141**

5. *Warrants* **142**

Types of Warrants **148**

Evaluation of Warrants **156**

SAMPLE ANALYSIS

The Case for Torture
MICHAEL LEVIN **157**

A philosophy professor reasons that if torture is the only way to squeeze life-saving information from a kidnapper or terrorist, we should overcome our repugnance and apply the electrodes.

READINGS FOR ANALYSIS

A Proposal to Abolish Grading
PAUL GOODMAN **161**

The author of *Growing Up Absurd* argues that if the goal of higher education *is* education, we should use tests that foster learning, not competition.

Here Comes the Groom
ANDREW SULLIVAN **164**

A graduate student explains why allowing gays and lesbians to marry is not a "radical step" but a fair and practical advance of existing laws.

Death Penalty's False Promise: An Eye for an Eye
ANNA QUINDLEN **169**

A columnist for the *New York Times* pits her gut response to a mass murder against her intellectual opposition to the death penalty.

Success has its own rewards [advertisement] **172**

EXERCISES FOR REVIEW **173**

6. ***Language and Thought*** **175**

The Power of Words **175**
Connotation **177**
Slanting **179**
Picturesque Language **182**
Concrete and Abstract Language **184**
Short Cuts **188**

SAMPLE ANALYSIS

Nox Quondam, Nox Futura!
RICHARD MITCHELL **196**

A well-known word watcher castigates academics who predict that society won't suffer if most of the population in the future is illiterate.

READINGS FOR ANALYSIS

The Speech the Graduates Didn't Hear
JACOB NEUSNER **200**

A scholar's caustic commentary on student-faculty relations indicts college as a ludicrously inappropriate preparation for the unforgiving world outside.

Erasing the "R" Words
HELEN E. AND R. LYNN SAULS **202**

Passages from textbooks of three different eras illustrate the claim of two college professors that religion has become a taboo subject in the classroom.

Good taste comes naturally to women all over New England [advertisement] **206**

EXERCISES FOR REVIEW **207**

7. ***Induction, Deduction, and Logical Fallacies*** **208**

Induction **209**

SAMPLE ANALYSIS

The Silenced Majority
BARBARA EHRENREICH **211**

A social critic worries that media messages reflect a "parochialism" of the professional middle class, who are cut off from the lives and struggles of the American majority.

Deduction **214**

SAMPLE ANALYSIS

Women Know How to Fight
RUTH WESTHEIMER **219**

A psychologist argues that, as women in other countries are trained for and serve in combat, American women should have the right and the responsibility to do the same.

Common Fallacies **223**

READINGS FOR ANALYSIS

On Nation and Race
ADOLF HITLER **233**

This excerpt from *Mein Kampf* expounds the principles of Nazi racist ideology.

A Criminal Justifies Himself
TONY PARKER and ROBERT ALLERTON **239**

"So violence is wrong. . . . But on a day-to-day level, it just happens that it's a tool of my trade." A career felon discusses the nature of his vocation.

A trap can catch more than a mouse [advertisement] **247**

EXERCISES FOR REVIEW **248**

PART TWO

Writing and Researching Arguments **251**

8. ***Writing an Argumentative Paper*** **253**

Finding an Appropriate Topic **254**
Invention Strategies 254 *Evaluating Possible Topics 254*
To This Point 256

Defining the Issues **256**

Preparing an Initial Outline 256 Case Study: Coed Bathrooms 256

Organizing the Material **259**

Defending the Main Idea 260 Refuting the Opposing View 261 Presenting the Stock Issues 261 Ordering Material for Emphasis 262 Considering Scope and Audience 262 To This Point 264

Writing **264**

Beginning the Paper 264 Guidelines for Good Writing 267

Revising **270**

Preparing the Manuscript **271**

Review Checklist for Argumentative Papers **271**

A Short Student Argument **272**

The New Drinking Laws: A Sour Taste
CLEO BOYD **273**

9. *Researching an Argumentative Paper* 277

Getting Started **277**

Mapping Research: A Sample Outline **278**

Using Primary Sources **279**

Using Secondary Sources: The Library **280**

The Card Catalog and Catalog Access System 280 Encyclopedias 282 Indexes 283 Abstracts 284

Reading with a Purpose **285**

Taking Notes 285 Quoting 288 Paraphrasing 289 Summarizing 290 Avoiding Plagiarism 291 Keeping Research under Control 293 To This Point 293

MLA System for Citing Publications **294**

APA System for Citing Publications **298**

A Sample Research Paper **300**

Why We Don't Need Zoos
AMANDA REPP **301**

PART THREE

Opposing Viewpoints 311

***10. Abortion* 315**

Is Abortion Ever Equal to Murder?
HOWARD H. HIATT and CYRUS LEVINTHAL **316**

A physician and a professor of biology propose that fetal brain development ought to be the guideline for determining when life begins.

Abortion Is Not a Civil Right
GREG KEATH **318**

The president of Black Alliance for Family declares that African-Americans "cannot permit the public to continue to imagine that we are obediently following our national leaders in endorsing abortion on demand."

Nine Reasons Why Abortions Are Legal
PLANNED PARENTHOOD **320**

An advertisement outlines why abortion should be legal and rebuts the claims of anti-abortion groups.

Public Shouldn't Pay
E. L. PATTULLO **325**

A letter to the *New York Times* asks why, if abortion is a private matter, so many abortions are funded with public money.

Too Many Abortions
COMMONWEAL **325**

A Catholic journal argues that abortion represents a failure of that "exercise of autonomy, self-esteem, and responsibility" so crucial to feminists.

Parents Also Have Rights
RONNIE GUNNERSON **328**

A stepmother writes that if a pregnant teenager's parents are responsible for mother and child, they should have the right to decide whether the mother can keep her baby.

Abortion Consent Law Creates Support System
JULIET K. MOYNA **331**

A college student reasons that a parental consent law would "force society to wrestle with the same responsibilities that it has been forcing women to handle alone since the birth of the sexual revolution."

Parental Consent Could Justify Forced Abortion
ANGELA R. HOLDER **332**

A professor of pediatrics ponders the unreasonable powers a consent law would grant parents.

A Problem for Couples
ARTHUR B. SHOSTAK **333**

A sociology professor urges state lawmakers to enact "legislation that is both pro-choice and pro-couple."

THINKING AND WRITING ABOUT ABORTION **335**

11. AIDS Testing **336**

Don't Tell Me on Friday
THOMAS RICHARDS **337**

An actor who tested positive for AIDS antibodies tells why he thinks taking the test is a positive step.

AIDS: In Plagues, Civil Rights Aren't the Issue
RICHARD RESTAK **339**

A neurologist writes, "To take a position that the AIDS virus must be eradicated is not to make judgments on morals or lifestyles. It is to say the AIDS virus has no 'civil rights.' "

How* Not *to Control the AIDS Epidemic
MATHILDE KRIM **343**

Surveying the history of AIDS, a leading researcher concludes that mandatory testing is "clearly *not* the way to attempt to control this epidemic."

HIV Testing: Voluntary, Mandatory, or Routine?
THERESA L. CRENSHAW **347**

A doctor systematically addresses the objections to required testing and anticipates a time when "being tested for AIDS will become a way of life."

AIDS: What Is to Be Done?
HARPER'S FORUM **355**

A symposium of experts engages in a wide-ranging debate on the dilemmas of AIDS testing.

Discrimination Goes On
ROBERT H. COHEN **360**

A letter to the *New York Times* asserts the need for a national commitment to end discrimination against those with AIDS; otherwise those who suspect they are infected will never come forward to be tested.

THINKING AND WRITING ABOUT AIDS TESTING **361**

12. Animal Rights **362**

Animal Liberation
PETER SINGER **363**

Framing his case as a book review rather than as a partisan defense, a leading advocate of animal rights presents a chilling range of indictments of human "speciesism" and the suffering it inflicts on other living creatures.

Vivisection
C. S. LEWIS **375**

A Christian scholar reasons that if we dismiss the notion of "total difference between man and beast," it is inevitable that any argument for experimenting on animals can become an argument for experimenting on "inferior" men.

The Trials of Animals
CLEVELAND AMORY **379**

Let the public witness the atrocities committed on animals behind closed laboratory doors, urges an animal-rights activist; experimenters have been judge and jury long enough.

Vigilant Protocol
THOMAS E. HAMM, JR. **381**

A director at the Stanford University medical school details the stringent regulations his institution imposes on scientists before they are allowed to experiment upon animals.

Holding Human Health Hostage
MICHAEL E. DEBAKEY **383**

Asserting that major medical breakthroughs are unthinkable without animal experimentation, a pioneering heart surgeon questions whether the right of the sick to relief is of less importance than "the right of abandoned animals to die in a pound."

Alternatives to Animals
THE ECONOMIST **386**

This report balances the fiscal reasons for non-animal medical experimentation against the limits of its usefulness.

Animals and Sickness
THE WALL STREET JOURNAL **389**

An editorial lambastes the tactics and "professional activists" of the animal-rights movement, "a clear and present danger to the health of us all."

Breakthroughs Don't Require Torture
STEPHEN ZAWISTOWSKI, SUZANNE E. ROY, STEPHEN KAUFMAN, and MARJORIE CRAMER **391**

Readers take exception to the false claims and distortions they detect in the *Wall Street Journal* editorial.

In Defense of the Animals
MEG GREENFIELD **393**

A *Newsweek* columnist takes a stand in "the muddled, middling, inconsistent place" where some uses of animals are okay, and some aren't.

THINKING AND WRITING ABOUT ANIMAL RIGHTS **395**

13. Collegiate Sports Reform **397**

Should College Athletes Be Paid Salaries?
GEORGE SAGE and JOHN DAVIS **398**

A phys-ed professor and an NCAA official debate whether college athletes should become paid entertainers or remain unsalaried members of the university family.

What Can Be Done?
TED GUP **400**

A *Time* magazine correspondent's eight-point program for reforming college sports subordinates the role of athletics to the traditional educational function of the university.

College Basketball: Issues and Answers
BILLY PACKER **401**

A basketball analyst for *CBS Sports* sums up why Proposition 48's formula for athletic eligibility based on standardized test scores is a successful innovation.

Proposal 42 Closes the Door on the Poor
ACEL MOORE **402**

A sports editor explains why an amendment to Proposition 48 which would withhold scholarships from academically unprepared student-athletes is a bad idea.

The Case in Favor of Proposition 42
FREDERICK P. WHIDDON **403**

The president of the University of Southern Albama believes that Proposition 42 would not, in the long run, close the door on the poor.

Only Two Ways to Free College Sport
IRA BERKOW **405**

Accept that big-time college sports programs are purely profit-making entertainment, says this sportswriter. Then accept that there are but two choices for sports reform available to colleges.

Fair Play for College Athletes: Racism and NCAA Rules
HERBERT I. LONDON **407**

A former scholar-athlete recommends that coaches who cry foul over Proposition 42 should ask themselves "why their humanitarianism doesn't result in anything but cruel disappointment for the dropout."

Prop 48 Makes Athletes Study
CLIFF SJOGREN **410**

Proposition 48 is a proven success, writes the man who drafted it — but Proposition 42 is misguided legislation that *won't* make a good thing even better.

The Myth of the Student-Athlete
SHANNON BROWNLEE with NANCY S. LINNON **413**

U.S. News reports that "college sport has grown into an expensive circus, driven by an insatiable appetite for winning, and amateur athletes are getting neither the moral guidance nor the education they bargained for."

THINKING AND WRITING ABOUT COLLEGIATE SPORTS REFORM **418**

14. Environmental Policy **419**

Overview of the State of the Environment: Toward the Nineties
WILLIAM K. REILLY **420**

An official of the Conservation Foundation traces the factors that have complicated, and will complicate, the establishment of a successful environmental policy.

Nature Under Glass
JAMES R. UDALL **423**

An environmental reporter surveys the data that anticipate the effects of global warming, concluding that the planet's destiny is cradled in human hands.

Getting Warmer?
JANE S. SHAW and RICHARD L. STROUP **427**

Two associates at a Montana think tank argue that untrammeled free-market progress can prevent present and future environmental problems.

Rethinking the Greenhouse
THE ECONOMIST **432**

Although prophecies of a greenhouse-effect apocalypse are likely to fade, a benefit will be the adoption of policies "whose by-product will be a curb on greenhouse gases."

Hot Air in the Greenhouse Debate
GLENN T. WILSON **435**

A business school professor gives six reasons why global warming "is much less of a problem than painted by extremists."

Staggering Cost Is Foreseen to Curb Warming of Earth
PETER PASSELL **435**

A *New York Times* report charts the economic implications of controlling global warming.

Bottom-Line Thinking Won't Save Our Climate
PETER H. GLEICK **440**

The director of a global environmental program claims that waiting until cost-benefit reports are all in means "waiting until climatic changes are upon us."

THINKING AND WRITING ABOUT ENVIRONMENTAL POLICY **441**

15. Euthanasia 443

Death by Choice: Who Should Decide?
DANIEL C. MAGUIRE **444**

According to a professor of ethics, though few of us would grant a doctor, a family, or a panel of experts the moral right to end someone else's existence, we can't decide the question *whether* without considering *who.*

In Defense of Voluntary Euthanasia
SIDNEY HOOK **449**

Having survived a life-threatening illness during which he asked to be allowed to die, a philosopher explains why he still believes that his request should have been honored.

Euthanasia Is Not the Answer
MATTHEW E. CONOLLY **452**

Stop trying to secure patients the right to die, begs a physician. Instead help them to live out their last days in the relative comfort of hospices.

Consequences of Imposing the Quality of Life Ethic
EILEEN DOYLE **456**

In the attempts of euthanasia proponents to substitute a "quality of life" ethic for a "right to life" ethic, a nurse perceives a covert attack on cherished American principles.

Active and Passive Euthanasia
JAMES RACHELS **459**

The American Medical Association has condemned "mercy killing" but has condoned allowing a terminally ill patient to die. A philosopher of ethics asks whether it is truly kinder to watch someone yield to a slow and painful death than to hasten the patient's inevitable end.

That Right Belongs Only to the State
MORTIMER OSTOW **464**

A doctor argues that, just as no member of our society is entitled to take a life by murder or suicide, so the burden of making life-or-death decisions in medical cases should not fall on individuals.

A Living Will
CONCERN FOR DYING **466**

A document from a pro-euthanasia organization directs that a seriously ill patient be permitted to die rather than be kept alive by "medications, artificial means, or 'heroic measures.'"

Not Everybody Wants to Sign a Living Will
FELICIA ACKERMAN **468**

A philosophy professor decries the current tendency to perceive hopelessly ill people as blots on the lives of their long-suffering loved ones.

A Time to Die
THE ECONOMIST **469**

We should think of life in biographical rather than biological terms: "When a person (or his relatives) can see that a biography is finished, it is not for doctors to write a painful extra chapter."

THINKING AND WRITING ABOUT EUTHANASIA **471**

16. Freedom of Speech 472

In Praise of Censure
GARRY WILLS **473**

A political analyst reviews recent free-speech controversies to develop his point that censoriousness, not censorship, is an effective response to objectionable materials.

Interim Policy on Discrimination and Discriminatory Conduct by Students in the University Environment
THE UNIVERSITY OF MICHIGAN **478**

Should some speech be protected on campus and some not? Yes, said the University of Michigan, and provided guidelines and examples.

The Debate over Placing Limits on Racist Speech Must Not Ignore the Damage It Does to Its Victims
CHARLES R. LAWRENCE III **482**

A professor of law at Stanford University explains why racist speech does not deserve the protection of the First Amendment.

How to Handle Hate on Campus
THE NEW YORK TIMES **486**

A student's abuse of free speech at a public university requires careful handling, not summary expulsion of the student.

Free Speech on the Campus
NAT HENTOFF **487**

A "journalistic custodian of the First Amendment" asks, "If students are going to be 'protected' from bad ideas, how are they going to learn to identify and cope with them?"

Flag-Saving
MELVIN L. WULF **492**

A columnist in *The Nation* argues that "totemization of the flag is inconsistent with the concept of the First Amendment."

The Dynamics of Flag-Burning
JAMES M. WALL **494**

An editor of *Christian Century* writes that if we recognize the uniquely symbolic status of the flag, then we recognize that protecting it does not violate the First Amendment.

Legislating the Imagination
JON PARELES **497**

A music critic believes that well-intentioned efforts to warn consumers about potentially offensive music "is, in effect, an attempt to regulate the imagination."

Not Just a Few Prudes . . .
DAVID J. MELTZ **500**

A doctor objects to Pareles's blanket condemnation of warning stickers. "Labeling contents is not censorship, no matter how you make it try to fit that Procrustean bed."

THINKING AND WRITING ABOUT FREEDOM OF SPEECH **502**

17. Legalizing Drugs **503**

Drugs
GORE VIDAL **504**

A novelist contends that smoking marijuana or shooting heroin is the right of every citizen, should he or she choose to do it. Instead of putting our faith in government regulation, let's try trusting our own common sense.

Should Drugs Be Legalized?
WILLIAM J. BENNETT **506**

The nation's "drug czar" excoriates those who believe that "enforcing drug laws imposes greater costs on society than do drugs themselves."

Thinking about Drug Legalization
JAMES OSTROWSKI **511**

An attorney argues that though prohibition may decrease the use of illegal drugs, its negative consequences outweigh the beneficial effects of legalization.

We're Losing the Drug War because Prohibition Never Works
HODDING CARTER III **516**

A political commentator insists that drug prohibition "can't work, won't work, and has never worked." It will only undermine the criminal justice system and the integrity of government.

War on Drugs Falls through the Crack
GUY PIAZZA **518**

A letter notes that Carter's argument first goes astray when he equates alcohol abuse with hard drug abuse — and the fallacies don't stop there.

Legalize Drugs? Not on Your Life
CHARLES B. RANGEL **519**

A congressman dismisses arguments for legalization as "nonsensical talk." Americans must formulate a detailed national battle plan for the war on drugs and commit to it.

We Already Know the Folly of Decriminalized Drugs
ELIZABETH GESSNER **521**

Claiming that drug use underwent a "de facto decriminalization" two decades ago, a letter to the *New York Times* warns that we must try enforcing penalties for drug use "before we give up and turn our society into a drug bazaar."

We Can Control Drugs, but We Can't Ban Them
IRA GLASSER **523**

The director of the ACLU argues that generalizing about cocaine from its effects on pathological users is "like trying to infer the effects of alcohol at cocktail parties by looking only at skid-row alcoholics."

THINKING AND WRITING ABOUT LEGALIZING DRUGS **524**

18. Pornography **526**

Notes from a Free-Speech Junkie
SUSAN JACOBY **527**

A "First Amendment junkie" breaks ranks with those feminists who battle pornography yet defend other equally repellent forms of free expression.

Pornography: Anti-Female Propaganda
SUSAN BROWNMILLER **530**

This passage from the feminist classic *Against Our Will: Men, Women, and Rape* argues that pornography, far from freeing sensuality from "moralistic or parental inhibition," is a male invention that dehumanizes women and reduces the female to "an object of sexual access."

Sexual McCarthyism
HUGH HEFNER **534**

The publisher of *Playboy* magazine detects in a government report on the hazards of pornography a pervasive reliance on "deception, innuendo, and outright lies."

The Bitter Harvest of Pornography
HAVEN BRADFORD GOW **539**

An editor of *Police Times* cites data to support his contention that pornography "helps create a moral and social climate that is conducive to sexual abuse and exploitation."

Feminists Are Wrong about Pornography
AL GOLDSTEIN **540**

A publisher of erotica assails feminists and fundamentalists for their "hysterical" opposition to pornography.

Pornography on the March
BETTY WEIN **542**

An editor at Morality in the Media denounces pornography's ubiquitous encroachment on everyday life and urges her readers to take action against the flood of smut.

Pornography's Many Forms: Not All Bad
BARRY W. LYNN **546**

A spokesman for the ACLU writes that we must not mount a moral crusade against representations of sexual fantasies until we weigh the positive uses of sexual images.

The Place of Pornography
JEAN BETHKE ELSHTAIN **548**

What is the place of pornography? What is its function? Why is there so much of it today? A political scientist offers succinct answers to these questions.

Pornography Here and Abroad
ARYEH NEIER **549**

The "astounding level" of sexual violence in countries where pornography is banned leads a civil libertarian to believe that pornography's role in sexual abuse is insignificant.

THINKING AND WRITING ABOUT PORNOGRAPHY **550**

PART FOUR

Classic Arguments 553

***From* Crito**
PLATO **555**

Unjustly imprisoned in ancient Athens, the philosopher Socrates explains to an old friend why an individual is never justified in breaking the laws of a government, no matter how convinced he is that a law is wrong.

A Modest Proposal
JONATHAN SWIFT **560**

An eighteenth-century satirist concocts a chilling, ironic solution to the problems of Irish poverty and overpopulation.

Civil Disobedience
HENRY DAVID THOREAU **569**

The author of *Walden* explains why it is reasonable, and often imperative, to disobey laws that one believes to be unjust.

Declaration of Sentiments and Resolutions, Seneca Falls
ELIZABETH CADY STANTON **588**

This manifesto by the women of the 1848 Seneca Falls Convention adapts the language and structure of the Declaration of Independence to emphasize that half of America still waited to be freed from the chains of tyranny.

Professions for Women
VIRGINIA WOOLF **593**

A literary foremother of contemporary feminism argues in 1931 that two cultural obstacles prevent women from expressing themselves honestly as writers.

Politics and the English Language
GEORGE ORWELL **599**

In this 1946 essay, the author of *Nineteen Eighty-Four* suggests why the hand that pens a stale metaphor should not be trusted with the reins of government.

Letter from Birmingham Jail
MARTIN LUTHER KING, JR. **611**

In 1963, the imprisoned civil-rights leader argues that nonviolent victims of unjust laws have the right to break those laws so long as they use nonviolent tactics.

I Have a Dream
MARTIN LUTHER KING, JR. **626**

This stirring exhortation to marchers at a 1963 civil-rights rally rings out like a church bell with rhythm, imagery, joy, hope, and deep conviction. Don't just read the words — listen to the music!

Glossary and Index of Terms **637**

Index of Authors and Titles **642**

ELEMENTS OF ARGUMENT

PART ONE

THE STRUCTURE OF ARGUMENT

CHAPTER 1

Introduction to Argument

THE NATURE OF ARGUMENT

A conversation overheard in the school cafeteria:

"Hey, how come you didn't order the meat loaf special? It's pretty good today."

"Well, I read this book about vegetarianism, and I've decided to give up meat. The book says meat's unhealthy and vegetarians live longer."

"Don't be silly. Americans eat lots of meat, and we're living longer and longer."

"Listen, this book tells how much healthier the Danes were during World War II because they couldn't get meat."

"I don't believe it. A lot of these health books are written by quacks. It's pretty dumb to change your diet after reading one book."

These people are having what most of us would call an argument, one that sounds dangerously close to a quarrel. There are, however, significant differences between the colloquial meaning of argument as a quarrel and its definition as a process of reasoning and advancing proof, although even the exchange reported above exhibits some of the characteristics of formal argument. The kinds of arguments we deal with in this text are not quarrels. They often resemble ordinary discourse about controversial issues. You may, for example, overhear a conversation like this one:

> *"This morning while I was trying to eat breakfast I heard an announcer describing the execution of that guy in Texas who raped and murdered a teenaged couple. They gave him an injection, and it took him ten minutes to die. I almost lost my breakfast listening to it."*
>
> *"Well, he deserved it. He didn't show much pity for his victims, did he?"*
>
> *"Okay, but no matter what he did, capital punishment is really awful, barbaric. It's murder, even if the state does it."*
>
> *"No, I'd call it justice. I don't know what else we can do to show how we feel about a cruel, pointless murder of innocent people. The punishment ought to be as terrible as we can make it."*

Each speaker is defending a value judgment about an issue that tests ideas of good and evil, right and wrong, and that cannot be decided by facts.

In another kind of argument the speaker or writer proposes a solution for a specific problem. Two men, both aged twenty, are engaged in a conversation.

> *"I'm going to be broke this week after I pay my car insurance. I don't think it's fair for males under twenty to pay such high rates. I'm a good driver, much better than my older sister. Why not consider driving experience instead of age or sex?"*
>
> *"But I always thought that guys our age had the most accidents. How do you know that driving experience is the right standard to apply?"*
>
> *"Well, I read a report by the Highway Commission that said it's really driving experience that counts. So I think it's unfair for us to be discriminated against. The law's behind the times. They ought to change the insurance laws."*

In this case someone advocates a policy that appears to fulfill a desirable goal — making it impossible to discriminate against drivers just because they are young and male. Objections arise that the arguer must attempt to answer.

In these three dialogues, as well as in all the other arguments you will read in this book, human beings are engaged in explaining and defending their own actions and beliefs and opposing those of others. They do this for at least two reasons: to justify what they do and think both to themselves and to their opponents and, in the process, to solve problems and make decisions, especially those dependent on a consensus between conflicting views.

Unlike the examples cited so far, the arguments you will read and write will not usually take the form of dialogues, but arguments are implicit dialogues. Even when our audience is unknown, we write to persuade the unconvinced, to acquaint them with good reasons for changing their minds. As one definition has it, "Argumentation is the art of influencing others, through the medium of reasoned discourse, to believe or act as we wish them to believe or act."[1] This process is inherently dramatic; a good argument can create the kinds of tensions generated at sporting events. Who will win? What are the factors that enable a winner to emerge? One of the most popular and enduring situations on television is the courtroom debate, in which two lawyers (one, the defense attorney, the hero, unusually knowledgeable and persuasive; the other, the prosecuting attorney, bumbling and corrupt) confront each other before an audience of judge and jury that must render a heart-stopping verdict. Tensions are high because a life is in the balance. In the classroom the stakes are neither so intimidating nor so melodramatic, but even here a well-conducted argument can throw off sparks.

Most of the arguments in this book will deal with matters of public controversy, an area traditionally associated with the study of argument. As the word *public* suggests, these matters concern us as members of a community. "They are," according to one rhetorician, "the problems of war and peace, race and creed, poverty, wealth, and population, of democracy and communism. . . . Specific issues arise on which we must take decision from time to time. One day it is Suez, another Cuba. One week it is the Congo, another it is the plight of the American farmer or the railroads. . . . On these subjects the experts as well as the many take sides."[2] Today the issues are different from the issues that writers confronted more than twenty years ago. Today we are concerned about the nuclear freeze, unemployment, illegal immigration, bilingual education, gun control, homosexual rights, drug abuse, prayer in school, to name only a few.

Clearly, if all of us agreed about everything, if harmony prevailed everywhere, the need for argument would disappear. But given what we know about the restless, seeking, contentious nature of human beings and their conflicting interests, we should not be surprised that many controversial questions, some of them as old as human civilization itself, will not

---

[1] J. M. O'Neill, C. Laycock, and R. L. Scale, *Argumentation and Debate* (New York: Macmillan, 1925), p. 1.

[2] Karl R. Wallace, "Toward a Rationale for Teachers of Writing and Speaking," *English Journal*, September 1961, p. 386.

be settled nor will they vanish despite the energy we devote to settling them. Unresolved, they are submerged for a while and then reappear, sometimes in another form, sometimes virtually unchanged. Capital punishment is one such stubborn problem; abortion is another. Nevertheless, we value the argumentative process because it is indispensable to the preservation of a free society. In *Areopagitica*, his great defense of free speech, John Milton, the seventeenth-century poet, wrote, "I cannot praise a fugitive and cloistered virtue, unexercised and unbreathed, that never sallies out and sees her adversary." How can we know the truth, he asked, unless there is a "free and open encounter" between all ideas? "Give me the liberty to know, to utter, and to argue freely according to conscience, above all liberties."

WHY STUDY ARGUMENT?

Perhaps the question has already occurred to you: Why *study* argument? Since you've engaged in some form of the argumentative process all your life, is there anything to be learned that experience hasn't taught you? We think there is. If you've ever felt frustration in trying to decide what is wrong with an argument, either your own or someone else's, you might have wondered if there were rules to help in the analysis. If you've ever been dissatisfied with your attempt to prove a case, you might have wondered how good arguers, the ones who succeed in persuading people, construct their cases. Good arguers do, in fact, know and follow rules. Studying and practicing these rules can provide you with some of the same skills.

You will find yourself using these skills in a variety of situations, not only in arguing important public issues. You will use them, for example, in your academic career. Whatever your major field of study — the humanities, the social sciences, the physical sciences, business — you will be required to defend views about materials you have read and studied.

Humanities. Why have some of the greatest novels resisted translation into great films?

Social Science. What is the evidence that upward social mobility continues to be a positive force in American life?

Physical Science. What will happen to the world climate as the amount of carbon dioxide in the atmosphere increases?

Business. Are the new tax laws beneficial or disadvantageous to the real estate investor?

For all these assignments, different as they may be, you would use the same kinds of analysis, research techniques, and evaluation. The conventions or rules for reporting results might differ from one field of study to another, but for the most part the rules for defining terms, evaluating evidence, and arriving at conclusions cross disciplinary lines. Many employers, not surprisingly, are aware of this. One sheriff in Arizona advertised for an assistant with a degree in philosophy. He had discovered, he said, that the methods used by philosophers to solve problems were remarkably similar to the methods used in law enforcement.

Whether or not you are interested in serving as a sheriff's assistant, you will encounter situations in the workplace that call for the same analytical and argumentative skills employed by philosophers and law enforcement personnel. Almost everywhere — in the smallest businesses as well as the largest corporations — a worker who can articulate his or her views clearly and forcefully has an important advantage in gaining access to positions of greater interest and challenge. Even when they are primarily informative, the memorandums, reports, instructions, questions, and explanations that issue from offices and factories obey the rules of argumentative discourse.

You may not anticipate doing the kind of writing or speaking at your job that you will practice in your academic work. It is probably true that in some careers, writing constitutes a negligible part of a person's duties. But outside the office, the studio, and the salesroom, you will be called on to exhibit argumentative skills as a citizen, as a member of a community, and as a consumer of leisure. In these capacities you can contribute to decision making if you are knowledgeable and prepared. By writing or speaking to the appropriate authorities, you can argue for a change in the meal ticket plan at your school or the release of pornographic films at the neighborhood theater or against a change in automobile insurance rates. Most of us are painfully aware of opportunities we lost because we were uncertain of how to proceed, even in matters that affected us deeply.

A course in argumentation offers another invaluable dividend: It can help you to cope with the bewildering confusion of voices in the world around you. It can give you tools for distinguishing between what is true and what is false, what is valid and what is invalid, in the claims of politicians, promoters of causes, newscasters, advertisers, salespeople, teachers, parents and siblings, employers and employees, neighbors, friends, and lovers, any of whom may be engaged at some time in attempting to persuade you to accept a belief or adopt a course of action. It can even offer strategies for arguing with yourself about a personal dilemma.

So far we have treated argument as an essentially pragmatic activity that benefits the individual. But choosing argument over force or evasion has clear moral benefits for society as well. We can, in fact, defend the study of argumentation for the same reasons that we defend universal education despite its high cost and sometimes controversial results. In a democracy, widespread literacy ultimately benefits all the members of society, not only those who are the immediate beneficiaries of education, because only an informed citizenry can make responsible choices. One distinguished writer explains that "democracy depends on a citizenry that can reason for themselves, on men who know whether a case has been proved, or at least made probable."[3]

It is not too much to say that argument is a civilizing influence, the very basis of democratic order. In totalitarian countries, coercion, which may express itself in a number of reprehensible forms — censorship, imprisonment, exile, torture, or execution — is a favored means of removing opposition to establishment "truth." In free societies, argument and debate remain the preeminent means of arriving at consensus.

Of course, rational discourse in a democracy can and does break down. Confrontations with police at nuclear power plants, shouting and heckling at a meeting to prevent a speaker from being heard, student sit-ins in college administrators' offices — such actions have become common in recent years. The demands of the demonstrators are often passionately and sincerely held, and the protesters sometimes succeed through force or intimidation in influencing policy changes. When this happens, however, we cannot be sure that the changes are justified. History and experience teach us that reason, to a far greater degree than other methods of persuasion, ultimately determines the rightness or wrongness of our actions.

A piece of folk wisdom sums up the superiority of reasoned argument as a vehicle of persuasion: "A man convinced against his will is of the same opinion still." Those who accept a position after engaging in a dialogue offering good reasons on both sides will think and act with greater willingness and conviction than those who have been coerced or denied the privilege of participating in the decision.

WHY WRITE?

If we agree that studying argumentation provides important critical tools, one last question remains: Why *write?* Isn't it possible to learn the rules by reading and talking about the qualities of good and bad arguments? Not quite. All writers, both experienced and inexperienced, will

---

[3] Wayne C. Booth, "Boring from Within: The Art of the Freshman Essay," adapted from a speech delivered to the Illinois Council of College Teachers of English in May 1963.

probably confess that looking at what they have written, even after long thought, can produce a startled disclaimer: But that isn't what I meant to say! They know that more analysis and more hard thinking are in order. Writers are also aware that words on paper have an authority and a permanency that invite more than casual deliberation. It is one thing to make an assertion, to express an idea or a strong feeling in conversation, and perhaps even to deny it later; it is quite another to write out an extended defense of your own position or an attack on someone else's that will be read and perhaps criticized by people unsympathetic to your views.

Students are often told that they must become better thinkers if they are to become better writers. It works the other way, too. In the effort to produce a clear and convincing argument, a writer matures as a thinker and a critic. The very process of writing calls for skills that make us better thinkers. An authority on language, the British etymologist Eric Partridge, put it this way.

> Good — that is, clear, effective, entirely adequate — speaking and writing will ease and smooth the passage of general thought and the conveyance of a particular thought or impression in statement or question or command. Bad speaking and writing do just the opposite and, worse, set up doubt and ambiguity.[4]

In sum, writing argumentative essays tests and enlarges important mental abilities — developing and organizing ideas, evaluating evidence, observing logical consistency, expressing ourselves clearly and economically — that we need to exercise all our lives in our various social roles, whether or not we continue to write after college.

THE TERMS OF ARGUMENT

One definition of argument, emphasizing audience, has been given earlier: "Argumentation is the art of influencing others, through the medium of reasoned discourse, to believe or act as we wish them to believe or act." A distinction is sometimes made between argument and persuasion. Argument, according to most authorities, gives primary importance to logical appeals. Persuasion introduces the element of ethical and emotional appeals. The difference is one of emphasis. In real-life arguments about social policy, the distinction is hard to measure. In this book we use the term *argument* to represent forms of discourse that attempt to persuade readers or listeners to accept a claim, whether acceptance is based

---

[4] "Speaking of Books: Degraded Language," *New York Times Book Review*, September 18, 1966, p. 2.

on logical or emotional appeals or, as is usually the case, on both. The following brief definition includes other elements: *An argument is a statement or statements offering support for a claim.*

An argument is composed of at least three parts: the claim, the support, and the warrant.[5]

The Claim

The claim (also called a *proposition*) answers the question "What are you trying to prove?" It may appear as the thesis statement of your essay, although in some arguments it may not be stated directly. There are three principal kinds of claim (discussed more fully in Chapter 2): claims of fact, of value, and of policy. (The three dialogues at the beginning of this chapter represent these three kinds of claim respectively.) *Claims of fact* assert that a condition has existed, exists, or will exist and are based on facts or data that the audience will accept as being objectively verifiable:

> The present cocaine epidemic is not unique. From 1885 to the 1920s, cocaine was as widely used as it is today.
>
> Horse racing is the most dangerous sport.
>
> California will experience colder, stormier weather for the next ten years.

All these claims must be supported by data. Although the last example is an inference or an educated guess about the future, a reader will probably find the prediction credible if the data seem authoritative.

Claims of value attempt to prove that some things are more or less desirable than others. They express approval or disapproval of standards of taste and morality. Advertisements and reviews of cultural events are one common source of value claims, but such claims emerge whenever people argue about what is good or bad, beautiful or ugly.

> One look and Crane [writing paper] says you have a tasteful writing style.
>
> *Tannhäuser* provides a splendid viewing as well as listening experience.
>
> Football is one of the most dehumanizing experiences a person can face. — Dave Meggyesy
>
> Ending a patient's life intentionally is absolutely forbidden on moral grounds. — Presidential Commission on Medical Ethics, 1983

---

[5] Some of the terms and analyses used in this text are adapted from Stephen Toulmin's *The Uses of Argument* (Cambridge: Cambridge University Press, 1958).

Claims of policy assert that specific policies should be instituted as solutions to problems. The expression *should, must,* or *ought to* usually appears in the statement.

> Prisons should be abolished because they are crime-manufacturing concerns.
>
> Our first step must be to immediately establish and advertise drastic policies designed to bring our own population under control. — Paul Ehrlich, biologist
>
> The New York City Board of Education should make sure that qualified women appear on any new list [of candidates for Chancellor of Education].

Policy claims call for analysis of both fact and value. (A full discussion of claims follows in Chapter 2.)

The Support

Support consists of the materials used by the arguer to convince an audience that his or her claim is sound. These materials include *evidence* and *motivational appeals.* The evidence or data consist of facts, statistics, and testimony from experts. The motivational appeals are the ones that the arguer makes to the values and attitudes of the audience to win support for the claim. The word *motivational* points out that these appeals are the reasons that move an audience to accept a belief or adopt a course of action. For example, in his argument advocating population control, Ehrlich first offered statistical evidence to prove the magnitude of the population explosion. But he also made a strong appeal to the generosity of his audience to persuade them to sacrifice their own immediate interests to those of future generations. (See Chapter 4 for detailed coverage of support.)

The Warrant

The warrant is an inference or an assumption, a belief or principle that is taken for granted. A warrant is a guarantee of reliability; in argument it guarantees the soundness of the relationship between the support and the claim. It allows the reader to make the connection between the support and the claim.

Warrants or assumptions underlie all the claims we make. They may be stated or unstated. If the arguer believes that the audience shares his assumption, he may feel it unnecessary to express it. But if he thinks that the audience is doubtful or hostile, he may decide to state the assumption in order to emphasize its importance or argue for its validity.

This is how the warrant works. In the dialogue beginning this chapter, one speaker made the claim that vegetarianism was more healthful than a diet containing meat. As support he offered the evidence that the authors of a book he had read recommended vegetarianism for greater health and longer life. He did not state his warrant — that the authors of the book were trustworthy guides to theories of healthful diet. In outline form the argument looks like this:

CLAIM: Adoption of a vegetarian diet leads to healthier and longer life.

SUPPORT: The authors of *Becoming a Vegetarian Family* say so.

WARRANT: The authors of *Becoming a Vegetarian Family* are reliable sources of information on diet.

A writer or speaker may also need to offer support for the warrant. In the case cited above, the second speaker is reluctant to accept the unstated warrant, suggesting that the authors may be quacks. The first speaker will need to provide support for the assumption that the authors are trustworthy, perhaps by introducing proof of their credentials in science and medicine. Notice that although the second speaker accepts the evidence, he cannot agree that the claim has been proved unless he also accepts the warrant. If he fails to accept the warrant — that is, if he refuses to believe that the authors are credible sources of information about diet — then the evidence cannot support the claim.

The following example demonstrates how a different kind of warrant, based on values, can also lead an audience to accept a claim.

CLAIM: Laws making marijuana illegal should be repealed.

SUPPORT: People should have the right to use any substance they wish.

WARRANT: No laws should prevent citizens from exercising their rights.

Support for repeal of the marijuana laws often consists of medical evidence that marijuana is harmless. Here, however, the arguer contends that an important ethical principle is at work: Nothing should prevent people from exercising their rights, including the right to use any substance, no matter how harmful. Let us suppose that the reader agrees with the supporting statement, that individuals should have the right to use any substance. But in order to accept the claim, the reader must also agree with the principle expressed in the warrant, that government should not interfere with the individual's right. He or she can then agree that laws making marijuana illegal should be repealed. Notice that this warrant, like all warrants, certifies that the relationship between the support and the claim is sound.

One more element of argument remains to be considered — *definition.* Definition, of course, is important in all forms of exposition, but it can be crucial in argument. For this reason we've devoted a whole chapter to it in this text. Many of the controversial questions you will encounter in your reading about public affairs are primarily arguments about the definition of terms. Such terms as *abortion, pornography, equality, poverty,* and *insanity* must be defined before useful public policies about them can be formulated. (For more on warrants, see Chapter 5.)

THE AUDIENCE

All arguments are composed with an audience in mind. We have already pointed out that an argument is an implicit dialogue or exchange. Often the writer of an argument about a public issue is responding to another writer or speaker who has made a claim that needs to be supported or opposed. In writing your own arguments, you should assume that there is a reader who may not agree with you. Throughout this book, we will continue to refer to ways of reaching such a reader.

Speechmakers are usually better informed than writers about their audience. Some writers, however, are familiar with the specific persons or groups who will read their arguments; advertising copywriters are a conspicuous example. They discover their audiences through sophisticated polling and marketing techniques and direct their messages to a well-targeted group of prospective buyers. Other professionals may be required to submit reports to persuade a specific and clearly defined audience of certain beliefs or courses of action: An engineer may be asked by an environmental interest group to defend his plans for the building of a sewage treatment plant; or a town planner may be called on to tell the town council why she believes that rent control may not work; or a sales manager may find it necessary to explain to his superior why a new product should be launched in the Midwest rather than the South.

In such cases the writer asks some or all of the following questions about the audience:

Why has this audience requested this report? What do they want to get out of it?

How much do they already know about the subject?

Are they divided or agreed on the subject?

What is their emotional involvement with the issues?

Assessing Credibility

Providing abundant evidence and making logical connections between the parts of an argument may not be enough to win agreement from an audience. In fact, success in convincing an audience is almost always inseparable from the writer's credibility, or the audience's belief in the writer's trustworthiness. Aristotle, the Greek philosopher who wrote a treatise on argument that has influenced its study and practice for more than two thousand years, considered credibility — what he called *ethos* — the most important element in the arguer's ability to persuade the audience to accept his or her claim.

Aristotle named "intelligence, character, and good will" as the attributes that produce credibility. Today we might describe these qualities somewhat differently, but the criteria for judging a writer's credibility remain essentially the same. First, the writer must convince the audience that he is knowledgeable, that he is as well informed as possible about the subject. Second, he must persuade his audience that he is not only truthful in the presentation of his evidence but also morally upright and dependable. Third, he must show that, as an arguer with good intentions, he has considered the interests and needs of others as well as his own.

As an example in which the credibility of the arguer is at stake, consider a wealthy Sierra Club member who lives on ten acres of a magnificent oceanside estate and who appears before a community planning board to argue against future development of the area. His claim is that more building will destroy the delicate ecological balance of the area. The board, acting in the interests of all the citizens of the community, will ask themselves: Has the arguer proved that his information about environmental impact is complete and accurate? Has he demonstrated that he sincerely desires to preserve the wilderness, not merely his own privacy and space? And has he also made clear that he has considered the needs and desires of those who might want to live in a housing development by the ocean? If the answers to all these questions are yes, then the board will hear the arguer with respect, and the arguer will have begun to establish his credibility.

A reputation for intelligence, character, and goodwill is not often won overnight. And it can be lost more quickly than it is won. Once a writer or speaker has betrayed an audience's belief in her character or judgment, she may find it difficult to persuade an audience to accept subsequent claims, no matter how sound her data and reasoning are. "We give no credit to a liar," said Cicero, "even when he speaks the truth."

Political life is full of examples of lost and squandered credibility. After it was discovered that President Lyndon Johnson had deceived the American public about U.S. conduct in the Vietnam War, he could not regain his popularity. After Senator Edward Kennedy failed to persuade the public that he had behaved honorably at Chappaquiddick, his influence and power in the Democratic party declined. After President Gerald Ford pardoned former President Richard Nixon for his complicity in the Watergate scandal, Ford was no longer a serious candidate for reelection.

We can see the practical consequences when an audience realizes that an arguer has been guilty of a deception — misusing facts and authority, suppressing evidence, distorting statistics, violating the rules of logic. But suppose the arguer is successful in concealing his or her manipulation of the data and can persuade an uninformed audience to take the action or adopt the idea that he or she recommends. Even supposing that the argument promotes a "good" cause, is the arguer justified in using evasive or misleading tactics?

The answer is no. To encourage another person to make a decision on the basis of incomplete or dishonestly used data is profoundly unethical. It indicates lack of respect for the rights of others — their right to know at least as much as you do about the subject, to be allowed to judge and compare, to disagree with you if they challenge your own interests. If the moral implications are still not clear, try to imagine yourself not as the perpetrator of the lie but as the victim.

There is also a danger in measuring success wholly by the degree to which audiences accept our arguments. Both as writers and readers, we must be able to respect the claim, or proposition, and what it tries to demonstrate. Toulmin has said: "To conclude that a proposition is true, it is not enough to know that this man or that finds it 'credible': the proposition itself must be *worthy* of credence."[6]

Acquiring Credibility

You may wonder how you can acquire credibility. You are not yet an expert in many of the subjects you will deal with in assignments, although you are knowledgeable about many other things, including your cultural and social activities. But there are several ways in which you can create confidence by your treatment of topics derived from academic disciplines, such as politics, psychology, economics, sociology, and art, on which most assignments will be based.

First, you can submit evidence of careful research, demonstrating that you have been conscientious in finding the best authorities, giving credit, and attempting to arrive at the truth. Second, you can adopt a

---

[6] *An Examination of the Place of Reason in Ethics* (Cambridge: Cambridge University Press, 1964), p. 71.

thoughtful and judicious tone that reflects a desire to be fair in your conclusion. Tone expresses the attitude of the writer toward his or her subject. When the writer feels strongly about the subject and adopts a belligerent or complaining tone, for example, he or she forgets that readers who feel differently may find the tone disagreeable and unconvincing. In the following excerpt a student expresses his feelings about standard grading, that is, grading by letter or number on a scale that applies to a whole group.

> You go to school to learn, not to earn grades. To be educated, that's what they tell you. "He's educated, he graduated Magna Cum Laude." What makes a Magna Cum Laude man so much better than a man that graduates with a C? They are both still educated, aren't they? No one has a right to call someone less educated because they got a C instead of an A. Let's take both men and put them in front of a car. Each car has something wrong with it. Each man must fix his broken car. Our C man goes right to work while our Magna Cum Laude man hasn't got the slightest idea where to begin. Who's more educated now?

Probably a reader who disagreed with the claim — that standard grading should not be used — would find the tone, if not the evidence itself, unpersuasive. The writer sounds as if he is defending his own ability to do something that an honors graduate can't do, while ignoring the acknowledged purposes of standard grading in academic subjects. He sounds, moreover, as if he's angry because someone has done him an injury. Compare the preceding passage to the following one, written by a student on the same subject.

> Grades are the play money in a university Monopoly game. As long as the tokens are offered, the temptation will be largely irresistible to play for them. Students are so busy taking notes, doing tests, and getting tokens that they have forgotten to ask: Of what worth is all this? Or perhaps they ask and the grade is their answer.
>
> One certainly learns something in the passive lecture-note-read-note-test process: how to do it all more efficiently next time (in the hope of eventually owning Boardwalk and Park Place). As Marshall McLuhan has said, we learn what we do. In this process most students come to view learning as studying and remembering what other people have learned. They assume that knowledge is logically and for practical reasons divided up into discrete pieces called "disciplines" and that the highest knowledge is achieved by specializing in a discipline. By getting good grades in a lot of disciplines they conclude they have learned a lot. They have indeed, and it is too bad.[7]

---

[7] Roy E. Terry in "Does Standard Grading Encourage Excessive Competitiveness?" *Change*, September 1974, p. 45.

Most readers would consider this writer more credible, in part because he has adopted a tone that seems moderate and impersonal. That is, he does not convey the impression that he is interested only in defending his own grades. Notice also that the language of this passage suggests a higher level of learning and research.

Sometimes, of course, an expression of anger or even outrage is appropriate and morally justified. But if readers do not share your sense of outrage, you must try to reach them through a more moderate approach. In his autobiography, Benjamin Franklin recounted his attempts to acquire the habit of temperate language in argument:

> Retaining . . . the habit of expressing myself in terms of modest diffidence; . . . never using, when I advanced anything that may possibly be disputed, the words "*certainly, undoubtedly,*" or any others that give the air of positiveness to an opinion; but rather say, I conceive or apprehend a thing to be so and so; it appears to me, *I should think it is so or so*, for such and such reasons; or *I imagine it to be so*; or *it is so, if I am not mistaken*. This habit, I believe, has been of great advantage to me when I have had occasion to inculcate my opinions, and persuade men into measures that I have been from time to time engaged in promoting.[8]

This is not to say that the writer must hedge his or her opinions or confess uncertainty at every point. Franklin suggests that the writer must recognize that other opinions may also have validity and that, although the writer may disagree, he or she respects the other opinions. Such an attitude will also dispose the reader to be more generous in evaluating the writer's argument.

A final method of establishing credibility is to produce a clean, literate, well-organized paper, with evidence of care in writing and proofreading. Such a paper will help persuade the reader to take your efforts seriously.

---

[8] *The Autobiography of Benjamin Franklin* (New York: Pocket Library, 1954), pp. 22–23.

SAMPLE ANALYSIS

The Declaration of Independence

THOMAS JEFFERSON

When in the course of human events, it becomes necessary for one 1
people to dissolve the political bands which have connected them with another, and to assume among the Powers of the earth, the separate and equal station to which the Laws of Nature and Nature's God entitle them, a decent respect to the opinions of mankind requires that they should declare the causes which impel them to the separation.

We hold these truths to be self-evident, that all men are created 2
equal, that they are endowed by their Creator with certain unalienable Rights, that among these are Life, Liberty and the pursuit of Happiness.

That to secure these rights, Governments are instituted among Men, 3
deriving their just powers from the consent of the governed.

That whenever any Form of Government becomes destructive of 4
these ends, it is the Right of the People to alter or to abolish it, and to institute a new Government laying its foundation on such principles and organizing its powers in such form, as to them shall seem most likely to effect their Safety and Happiness. Prudence, indeed, will dictate that Governments long established should not be changed for light and transient causes; and accordingly all experience hath shown that mankind are more disposed to suffer, while evils are sufferable, than to right themselves by abolishing the forms to which they are accustomed. But when a long train of abuses and usurpations pursuing invariably the same Object evinces a design to reduce them under absolute Despotism, it is their right, it is their duty, to throw off such government, and to provide new Guards for their future security.

Such has been the patient sufferance of these Colonies; and such is 5
now the necessity which constrains them to alter their former Systems of Government. The history of the present King of Great Britain is a history of repeated injuries and usurpations, all having in direct object the establishment of an absolute Tyranny over these States. To prove this, let Facts be submitted to a candid world.

He has refused his Assent to laws, the most wholesome and necessary 6
for the public good.

He has forbidden his Governors to pass Laws of immediate and press- 7
ing importance, unless suspended in their operation till his Assent should

be obtained; and when so suspended, he has utterly neglected to attend to them.

8 He has refused to pass other Laws for the accommodation of large districts of people, unless those people would relinquish the right of Representation in the Legislature, a right inestimable to them and formidable to tyrants only.

9 He has called together legislative bodies at places unusual, uncomfortable, and distant from the depository of their Public Records, for the sole purpose of fatiguing them into compliance with his measures.

10 He has dissolved Representative Houses repeatedly, for opposing with manly firmness his invasions on the rights of the people.

11 He has refused for a long time, after such dissolutions, to cause others to be elected; whereby the Legislative Powers, incapable of Annihilation, have returned to the People at large for their exercise; the State remaining in the mean time exposed to all the danger of invasion from without, and convulsions within.

12 He has endeavored to prevent the population of these States; for that purpose obstructing the Laws of Naturalization of Foreigners; refusing to pass others to encourage their migration hither, and raising the conditions of new Appropriations of Lands.

13 He has obstructed the Administration of Justice, by refusing his Assent to Laws for establishing Judiciary Powers.

14 He has made Judges dependent on his Will alone, for the tenure of their offices, and the amount and payment of their salaries.

15 He has erected a multitude of New Offices, and sent hither swarms of Officers to harass our People, and eat out their substance.

16 He has kept among us, in time of peace, Standing Armies without the consent of our Legislature.

17 He has affected to render the Military independent of and superior to the Civil Power.

18 He has combined with others to subject us to jurisdictions foreign to our constitution, and unacknowledged by our laws; giving his Assent to their acts of pretended Legislation:

19 For quartering large bodies of armed troops among us:

20 For protecting them, by a mock Trial, from Punishment for any Murders which they should commit on the Inhabitants of these States:

21 For cutting off our Trade with all parts of the world:

22 For imposing Taxes on us without our Consent:

23 For depriving us in many cases, of the benefits of Trial by Jury:

24 For transporting us beyond Seas to be tried for pretended offenses:

25 For abolishing the free System of English Laws in a Neighbouring Province, establishing therein an Arbitrary government, and enlarging its

boundaries so as to render it at once an example and fit instrument for introducing the same absolute rule into these Colonies:

For taking away our Charters, abolishing our most valuable Laws, and altering fundamentally the Forms of our Governments: 26

For suspending our own legislatures, and declaring themselves invested with Power to legislate for us in all cases whatsoever. 27

He has abdicated Government here, by declaring us out of his Protection and waging War against us. 28

He has plundered our seas, ravaged our Coasts, burnt our towns and destroyed the Lives of our people. 29

He is at this time transporting large Armies of foreign Mercenaries to compleat the works of death, desolation and tyranny, already begun with circumstances of Cruelty & perfidy scarcely paralleled in the most barbarous ages, and totally unworthy the Head of a civilized nation. 30

He has constrained our fellow Citizens taken Captive on the high Seas to bear Arms against their Country, to become the executioners of their friends and Brethren, or to fall themselves by their Hands. 31

He has excited domestic insurrections amongst us, and has endeavored to bring on the inhabitants of our frontiers, the merciless Indian Savages, whose known rule of warfare is an undistinguished destruction of all ages, sexes, and conditions. 32

In every stage of these Oppressions We Have Petitioned for Redress in the most humble terms. Our repeated petitions have been answered only by repeated injury. A Prince, whose character is thus marked by every act which may define a Tyrant, is unfit to be the ruler of a free People. 33

Not have We been wanting in attention to our British brethren. We have warned them from time to time of attempts by their legislature to extend an unwarrantable jurisdiction over us. We have reminded them of the circumstances of our emigration and settlement here. We have appealed to their native justice and magnanimity and we have conjured them by the ties of our common kindred to disavow these usurpations, which would inevitably interrupt our connections and correspondence. They too have been deaf to the voice of justice and of consanguinity. We must, therefore, acquiesce in the necessity, which denounces our Separation, and hold them, as we hold the rest of mankind, Enemies in War, in Peace Friends. 34

We, therefore, the Representatives of the United States of America, in General Congress, Assembled, appealing to the Supreme Judge of the world for the rectitude of our intentions, do, in the Name, and by Authority of the good People of these Colonies, solemnly publish and declare, That these United Colonies are, and of Right ought to be, Free and Independent States; that they are Absolved from all Allegiance to the British 35

Crown, and that all political connection between them and the State of Great Britain, is and ought to be totally dissolved; and that as Free and Independent States, they have full power to levy War, conclude Peace, contract Alliances, establish Commerce, and to do all other Acts and Things which Independent States may of right do. And for the support of this Declaration, with a firm reliance on the protection of Divine Providence, we mutually pledge to each other our lives, our Fortunes and our sacred Honor.

Analysis

Claim: What is Jefferson trying to prove? *The American colonies are justified in declaring their independence from British rule.* Jefferson and his fellow signers might have issued a simple statement such as appears in the last paragraph, announcing the freedom and independence of these United Colonies. Instead, however, they chose to justify their right to do so.

Support: What does Jefferson have to go on? The Declaration of Independence bases its claim on two kinds of support: *factual evidence* and *motivational appeals* or appeals to the values of the audience.

Factual Evidence: Jefferson presents a long list of specific acts of tyranny by George III, beginning with "He has refused his Assent to Laws, the most wholesome and necessary for the public good." This list constitutes more than half the text. Notice how Jefferson introduces these grievances: "The history of the present King of Great Britain is a history of repeated injuries and usurpations, all having in direct object the establishment of an absolute Tyranny over these States. *To prove this, let Facts be submitted to a candid world*" (italics added). Jefferson hopes that a recital of these specific acts will convince an honest audience that the United Colonies have indeed been the victims of an intolerable tyranny.

Appeal to Values: Jefferson also invokes the moral values underlying the formation of a democratic state. These values are referred to throughout. In the second and third paragraphs he speaks of equality, "Life, Liberty and the pursuit of Happiness," "Just powers," "Consent of the governed," and safety. In the last paragraph he refers to freedom and independence. Jefferson believes that the people who read his appeal will, or should, share these fundamental values. Audience acceptance of these values constitutes the most important part of the support. Some historians have called the specific acts of oppression cited by Jefferson trivial, inconsequential, or distorted. Clearly, however, Jefferson felt that the list of specific grievances was vital to definition of the abstract terms in which values are always expressed.

Warrant: How does Jefferson get from support to claim? *People have a right to revolution in order to free themselves from oppression.* This warrant is explicit: "But when a long train of abuses and usurpations pursuing invariably the same Object evinces a design to reduce them under absolute Despotism, it is their right, it is their duty, to throw off such government, and to provide new Guards for their future security." Some members of Jefferson's audience, especially those whom he accuses of oppressive acts, will reject the principle that any subject people have earned the right to revolt. But Jefferson believes that the decent opinion of mankind will accept this assumption. Many of his readers will also be aware that the warrant is supported by seventeenth-century political philosophy, which defines government as a social compact between the government and the governed.

If Jefferson's readers do, in fact, accept the warrant and if they also believe in the accuracy of the factual evidence and share his moral values, then they will conclude that his claim has been proved, that Jefferson has justified the right of the colonies to separate themselves from Great Britain.

Audience: The Declaration of Independence is addressed to several audiences: to the American colonists; to the British people; to the British Parliament; to the British king, George III; and to mankind or a universal audience.

Not all the American colonists were convinced by Jefferson's argument. Large numbers remained loyal to the King and for various reasons opposed an independent nation. In the next-to-the-last paragraph, Jefferson refers to previous addresses to the British people. Not surprisingly, most of the British citizenry as well as the King also rejected the claims of the Declaration. But the universal audience, the decent opinion of mankind, found Jefferson's argument overwhelmingly persuasive. Many of the liberal reform movements of the eighteenth and nineteenth centuries were inspired by the Declaration. In basing his claim on universal principles of justice and equality, Jefferson was certainly aware that he was addressing future generations.

EXERCISES FOR REVIEW

1. From the following list of claims, select the ones you consider most controversial. Tell why they are difficult to resolve. Are the underlying assumptions controversial? Is support hard to find or disputed? Can you think of circumstances under which some of these claims might be resolved?

a. Congress should endorse the right-to-life amendment.
b. Solar power can supply 20 percent of the energy needs now satisfied by fossil and nuclear power.
c. Homosexuals should have the same job rights as heterosexuals.
d. Rapists should be treated as mentally ill rather than depraved.
e. Whale hunting should be banned by international law.
f. Violence on television produces violent behavior in children who watch more than four hours a day.
g. Both creationism and evolutionary theory should be taught in the public schools.
h. Mentally defective men and women should be sterilized or otherwise prevented from producing children.
i. History will pronounce Reggie Jackson a greater all-round baseball player than Joe DiMaggio.
j. Bilingual instruction should not be permitted in the public schools.
k. Some forms of cancer are caused by a virus.
l. Dogs are smarter than horses.
m. Curfews for teenagers will reduce the abuse of alcohol and drugs.
n. The federal government should impose a drinking age of twenty-one.
o. The United States should proceed with unilateral disarmament.
p. Security precautions at airports are out of proportion to the dangers of terrorism.
q. Bodybuilding cannot be defined as a sport; it is a form of exhibitionism.

2. Report on an argument you have heard recently. Identify the parts of that argument — claim, support, warrant — as they are defined in this chapter. What were the strengths and weaknesses in the argument you heard?
3. Choose one of the more controversial claims in the previous list and explain the reasons it is controversial. Is support lacking or in doubt? Are the warrants unacceptable to many people? Try to go as deeply as you can, exploring, if possible, systems of belief, traditions, societal customs. You may confine your discussion to personal experience with the problem in your community or group. If there has been a change over the years in the public attitude toward the claim, offer what you think may be an explanation for the change.
4. Write your own argument for or against the value of standard grading in college.
5. Discuss an occasion when a controversy arose that the opponents could not settle. Describe the problem and tell why you think the disagreement was not settled.

CHAPTER 2

Claims

Claims, or propositions, represent answers to the question: "What are you trying to prove?" Although they are the conclusions of your arguments, they often appear as thesis statements. Claims can be classified as *claims of fact, claims of value,* and *claims of policy.*

CLAIMS OF FACT

Claims of fact assert that a condition has existed, exists, or will exist and their support consists of factual information — that is, information such as statistics, examples, and testimony that most responsible observers assume can be verified.

Many facts are not matters for argument: Our own senses can confirm them, and other observers will agree about them. We can agree that a certain number of students were in the classroom at a particular time, that lions make a louder sound than kittens, and that apples are sweeter than potatoes.

We can also agree about information that most of us can rarely confirm for ourselves — information in reference books, such as atlases, almanacs, and telephone directories; data from scientific resources about the physical world; and happenings reported in the media. We can agree on the reliability of such information because we trust the observers who report it.

However, the factual map is constantly being redrawn by new data in such fields as history and science that cause us to reevaluate our conclusions. For example, the discovery of the Dead Sea Scrolls in 1947 revealed that some books of the Bible — *Isaiah*, for one — were far older than we had thought. Researchers at New York Hospital–Cornell Medical Center say that many symptoms previously thought inevitable in the aging process are now believed to be treatable and reversible symptoms of depression.[1]

In your conversations with other students you probably generate claims of fact every day, some of which can be verified without much effort, others of which are more difficult to substantiate.

> **CLAIM:** Most of the students in this class come from towns within fifty miles of Boston.

To prove this the arguer would need only to ask the students in the class where they come from.

> **CLAIM:** Students who take their courses Pass/Fail make lower grades than those who take them for specific grades.

In this case the arguer would need to have access to student records showing the specific grades given by instructors. (In most schools the instructor awards a letter grade, which is then recorded as a Pass or a Fail if the student has elected this option.)

> **CLAIM:** The Red Sox will win the pennant this year.

This claim is different from the others because it is an opinion about what will happen in the future. But it can be verified (in the future) and is therefore classified as a claim of fact.

More complex factual claims about political and scientific matters remain controversial because proof on which all or most observers will agree is difficult or impossible to obtain.

> **CLAIM:** The nuclear arsenal of the Soviet Union exceeds that of the United States.
>
> **CLAIM:** The only life in the universe exists on this planet.

---

[1] *New York Times*, February 20, 1983, Sec. 22, p. 4.

Not all claims are so neatly stated or make such unambiguous assertions. Because we recognize that there are exceptions to most generalizations, we often qualify our claims with words such as *generally, usually, probably, as a rule.* It would not be true to state flatly, for example, "College graduates earn more than high school graduates." This statement is generally true, but we know that some high school graduates who are electricians or city bus drivers or sanitation workers earn more than college graduates who are schoolteachers or nurses or social workers. In making such a claim, therefore, the writer should qualify it with a word that limits the claim.

To support a claim of fact, the writer needs to produce sufficient and appropriate data, that is, examples, statistics, and testimony from reliable sources. Provided this requirement is met, the task of establishing a factual claim would seem to be relatively straightforward. But as you have probably already discovered in ordinary conversation, finding convincing support for factual claims can pose a number of problems. Whenever you try to establish a claim of fact, you will need to ask at least three questions about the material you plan to use: What are sufficient and appropriate data? Who are the reliable authorities? and Have I made clear whether my statements are facts or inferences?

Sufficient and Appropriate Data

The amount and kind of data for a particular argument depend on the importance and complexity of the subject. The more controversial the subject, the more facts and testimony you will need to supply. Consider the claim "The nuclear arsenal of the Soviet Union is greater than that of the United States." If you want to prove the truth of this claim, obviously you will have to provide a larger quantity of data than for a claim that says, "By following three steps, you can train your dog to sit and heel in fifteen minutes." In examining your facts and opinions, an alert reader will want to know if they are accurate, current, and typical of other facts and opinions that you have not mentioned.

The reader will also look for testimony from more than one authority, although there may be cases where only one or two experts, because they have achieved a unique breakthrough in their field, will be sufficient. These cases would probably occur most frequently in the physical sciences. The Nobel Prize winners James Watson and Francis Crick, who first discovered the structure of the DNA molecule, are an example of such experts. However, in the case of the so-called Hitler diaries that surfaced in 1983, at least a dozen experts — journalists, historians, bibliographers who could verify the age of the paper and the ink — were needed to establish that they were forgeries.

Reliable Authorities

Not all those who pronounce themselves experts are trustworthy. Your own experience has probably taught you that you cannot always believe the reports of an event by a single witness. The witness may be poorly trained to make accurate observations — about the size of a crowd, the speed of a vehicle, his distance from an object. Or his own physical conditions — illness, intoxication, disability — may prevent him from seeing or hearing or smelling accurately. The circumstances under which he observes the event — darkness, confusion, noise — may also impair his observation. In addition, the witness may be biased for or against the outcome of the event, as in a hotly contested baseball game, where the observer sees the play that he wants to see. You will find the problems associated with the biases of witnesses to be relevant to your work as a reader and writer of argumentative essays.

You will undoubtedly want to quote authors in some of your arguments. In most cases you will not be familiar with the authors. But there are guidelines for determining their reliability: the rank or title of the experts, the acceptance of their publications by other experts, their association with reputable universities, research centers, or think tanks. For example, for a paper on euthanasia, you might decide to quote from an article by Paul Ramsey, identified as the Harrington Spear Paine Professor of Religion at Princeton University. For a paper on prison reform you might want to use material supplied by Tom Murton, a professional penologist, formerly superintendent in the Arkansas prison system, now professor of criminology at the University of Minnesota. Most readers of your arguments would agree that these authors have impressive credentials in their fields.

What if several respectable sources are in conflict? What if the experts disagree? After a preliminary investigation of a controversial subject, you may decide that you have sufficient material to support your claim. But if you read further, you may discover that other material presented by equally qualified experts contradicts your original claim. In such circumstances you will find it impossible to make a definitive claim. (On pages 119–120, in the treatment of support of a claim by evidence, you will find a more elaborate discussion of this vexing problem.)

Facts or Inferences

We have defined a fact as a statement that can be verified. An inference is "a statement about the unknown on the basis of the known."[2] The

---

[2] S. I. Hayakawa, *Language in Thought and Action* (New York: Harcourt, Brace, Jovanovich, 1978), p. 35.

difference between facts and inferences is important to you as the writer of an argument because an inference is an *interpretation*, or an opinion reached after informed evaluation of evidence. As you and your classmates wait in your classroom on the first day of the semester, a middle-aged woman wearing a tweed jacket and a corduroy skirt appears and stands in front of the room. You don't know who this woman is. However, based on what you do know about the appearance of many college teachers and the fact that teachers usually stand in front of the classroom, you may *infer* that this woman is your teacher. You will probably be right. But you cannot be certain until you have more information. Perhaps you will find out that this woman has come from the department office to tell you that your teacher is sick and cannot meet the class today.

You have probably come across a statement such as the following in a newspaper or magazine: "Excessive television viewing has caused the steady decline in the reading ability of children and teenagers." Presented this way, the statement is clearly intended to be read as a factual claim that has been or can be proved. But it is an inference. The facts, which can be, and have been, verified, are (1) the reading ability of children and teenagers has declined and (2) the average child views television for six or more hours a day. (Whether this amount of time is "excessive" is also an opinion.) The cause-effect relation between the two facts is an interpretation of the investigator who has examined both the reading scores and the amount of time spent in front of the television set and *inferred* that one is the cause of the other. The causes of the decline in reading scores are probably more complex than the original statement indicates. Since we can seldom or never create laboratory conditions for testing the influence of television separate from other influences in the family and the community, any statement about the connection between reading scores and television viewing can only be a guess.

By definition, no inference can ever do more than suggest probabilities. Of course, some inferences are much more reliable than others and afford a high degree of probability. Almost all claims in science are based on inferences, interpretations of data on which most scientists agree. Paleontologists find a few ancient bones from which they make inferences about an animal that might have been alive millions of years ago. We can never be absolutely certain that the reconstruction of the dinosaur in the museum is an exact copy of the animal it is supposed to represent, but the probability is fairly high because no other interpretation works so well to explain all the observable data — the existence of the bones in a particular place, their age, their relation to other fossils, and their resemblance to the bones of existing animals with which the paleontologist is familiar.

Inferences are profoundly important, and most arguments could not proceed very far without them. But an inference is not a fact. The writer of an argument must make it clear when he or she offers an inference, an interpretation, or an opinion that it is not a fact.

Defending a Claim of Fact

Here is a summary of the guidelines that should help you to defend a factual claim. (We'll say more about support of factual claims in Chapter 4.)

1. Be sure that the claim — what you are trying to prove — is clearly stated, preferably at the beginning of your paper.
2. Define terms that may be controversial or ambiguous. For example, in trying to prove that "radicals" had captured the student government, you would have to define "radicals," distinguishing them from "liberals" or members of other ideological groups, so that your readers would understand exactly what you meant.
3. As far as possible, make sure that your evidence — facts and opinions, or interpretations of the facts — fulfills the appropriate criteria. The data should be sufficient, accurate, recent, typical; the authorities should be reliable.
4. Make clear when conclusions about the data are inferences or interpretations, not facts. For example, you might write, "The series of lectures, 'Modern Architecture,' sponsored by our fraternity, was poorly attended because the students at this college aren't interested in discussions of art." What proof could you offer that this *was* the reason, that your statement was a *fact*? Perhaps there were other reasons that you hadn't considered.
5. Arrange your evidence in order to emphasize what is most important. Place it at the beginning or the end, the most emphatic positions in an essay, and devote more space to it.

SAMPLE ANALYSIS: CLAIM OF FACT

Cocaine Is Even Deadlier Than We Thought

LOUIS L. CREGLER and HERBERT MARK

To the Editor:

In his July 3 letter about recreational cocaine use, Dr. Carl C. Pfeiffer notes that some of the toxic effects of cocaine on the heart have long been known to those versed in pharmacology. We wish to point out that cardiologists and neurologists are seeing additional complications not previously known. Indeed, little information on the cardiovascular effects of cocaine appeared until recently. 1

As Dr. Pfeiffer says, cocaine sensitizes the heart to the normal stimulant effects of the body's adrenaline. This ordinarily makes the heart beat much faster and increases blood pressure significantly. Cocaine abuse has also been associated with strokes, heart attacks (acute myocardial infarctions) and sudden deaths. Individuals with weak blood vessels (aneurysms or arteriovenous malformations) in the head are at greatest risk of having a stroke. With the sudden surge in blood pressure, a blood vessel can burst. Cocaine can also cause blood vessels supplying the heart muscle itself to undergo vasoconstriction (coronary spasm), and this can produce a heart attack. 2

Deaths have been reported after administration of cocaine by all routes. Most such deaths are attributed to cocaine intoxication, leading to generalized convulsions, respiratory failure, and cardiac arrhythmias, minutes to hours after administration. Much of this information is so new that it has not found its way into the medical literature or standard textbooks. 3

Cocaine abuse continues to escalate in American society. It is estimated that 30 million Americans have used it, and some 5 million use it regularly. As cocaine has become less expensive, its availability and purity are increasing. It has evolved from a minor problem into a major threat to public health. And as use has increased, greater numbers of emergency-room visits, cocaine-related heart problems, and sudden 4

Louis L. Cregler, M.D., is assistant chief of medicine and Herbert Mark, M.D., is chief of medicine at the Bronx Veterans Administration Medical Center. This article appeared in the *New York Times* on July 30, 1986.

deaths have been reported. With so many people using cocaine, it is not unexpected that more strokes, heart attacks, and sudden cardiac deaths will be taking place.

— Louis L. Cregler, M.D.
Herbert Mark, M.D.

Analysis

The authors of this letter supply data to prove that the deadly effects of cocaine exceed those that are already well known in medicine and pharmacology. Four aspects of this factual claim are noteworthy. First, it is a response to a letter that, according to the authors, ignored significant new evidence. Many factual claims originate in just this way — as answers to previous claims. Second, the authors, both physicians at a large medical center, apparently have expert knowledge of the scientific data they report. Third, the effects of cocaine use are precisely and vividly described. It is, in fact, these specific references to the damage done to heart and blood vessels that make the claim particularly convincing. Finally, the authors make this claim in order to promote a change in our attitudes toward the use of cocaine; they do not call on their readers to abstain from cocaine. This use of a factual claim as a first step in calling for changes in attitude and behavior is a familiar and often effective argumentative strategy.

CLAIMS OF VALUE

Unlike claims of fact, which attempt to prove that something is true and which can be validated by reference to the data, claims of value make a judgment. They express approval or disapproval. They attempt to prove that some action, belief, or condition is right or wrong, good or bad, beautiful or ugly, worthwhile or undesirable.

CLAIM: Democracy is superior to any other form of government.

CLAIM: Killing animals for sport is wrong.

CLAIM: The Sam Rayburn Building in Washington is an aesthetic failure.

Some claims of value are simply expressions of tastes, likes and dislikes, or preferences and prejudices. The Latin proverb "De gustibus non est disputandum" states that we cannot dispute about tastes. Suppose you express a preference for chocolate over vanilla. If your listener should ask why you prefer this flavor, you cannot refer to an outside authority or produce data or appeal to her moral sense to convince her that your preference is justified.

Many claims of value, however, can be defended or attacked on the basis of standards that measure the worth of an action, a belief, or an object. As far as possible, our personal likes and dislikes should be supported by reference to these standards. Value judgments occur in any area of human experience, but whatever the area, the analysis will be the same. We ask the arguer who is defending a claim of value: *What are the standards or criteria for deciding that this action, this belief, or this object is good or bad, beautiful or ugly, desirable or undesirable? Does the thing you are defending fulfill these criteria?*

There are two general areas in which people often disagree about matters of value: aesthetics and morality. They are also the areas that offer the greatest challenge to the writer. What follows is a discussion of some of the elements of analysis that you should consider in defending a claim of value in these areas.

Aesthetics is the study of beauty and the fine arts. Controversies over works of art — the aesthetic value of books, paintings, sculpture, architecture, dance, drama, and movies — rage fiercely among experts and laypeople alike. They may disagree on the standards for judging or, even if they agree, may disagree about how successfully the art object under discussion has met these standards.

Consider a discussion about popular music. Hearing someone praise the singing of a well-known vocalist, Sheila Jordan, you might ask why she is so highly regarded. You expect Jordan's fan to say more than "I like her" or "Man, she's great." You expect the fan to give reasons to support his claim. "She's unique," he says. He shows you a short review from a widely read newspaper that says, "Her singing is filled with fascinating phrasings, twists, and turns, and she's been compared with Billie Holiday for her emotional intensity. . . . She can be so heart-wrenching that conversations stop cold." Her fan agrees with the criteria for judging a singer given by the author of the review: uniqueness, fascinating phrasings, emotional intensity.

You may not agree that these are the only standards or even the significant ones for judging a singer. But the establishment of standards itself offers material for a discussion or an argument. You may argue about the relevance of the criteria, or, agreeing on the criteria, you may argue about the success of the singer in meeting them. Perhaps you prefer cool singers to intense ones. Or, even if you choose intensity over coolness, you may not think Sheila Jordan can be described as "expressive." Moreover, in any arguments about criteria, differences in experience and preparation acquire importance. You would probably take for granted that a writer with formal musical training who has listened carefully to dozens of singers over a period of years, who has read a good deal of musical criticism and discussed musical matters with other knowledgeable people would be a more reliable critic than someone who lacked these qualifications.

It is probably not surprising then, that, despite wide differences in taste, professional critics more often than not agree on criteria and whether an art object has met the criteria. For example, almost all movie critics agreed that *Citizen Kane* and *Gone with the Wind* were superior films. They also agreed that *A Tomato Ate My Sister*, a horror film, was terrible.

Value claims about morality express judgments about the rightness or wrongness of conduct or belief. Here disagreements are as wide and deep as in the arts. The first two examples on page 31 reveal how controversial such claims can be. Although you and your reader may share many values, among them a belief in democracy, a respect for learning, and a desire for peace, you may also disagree, even profoundly, about other values. The subject of divorce, for example, despite its prevalence in our society, can produce a conflict between differing moral standards. Some people may insist on adherence to absolute standards, arguing that the values they hold are based on immutable religious precepts derived from God and Scripture. Since marriage is sacred, divorce is always wrong, they say, whether or not the conditions of society change. Other people may argue that values are relative, based on the changing needs of societies in different places and at different times. Since marriage is an institution created by human beings at a particular time in history to serve particular social needs, they may say, it can also be dissolved when other social needs arise. The same conflicts between moral values might occur in discussions of abortion or suicide.

As a writer you cannot always know what system of values is held by your reader. Yet it might be possible to find a rule on which almost all readers agree. One such rule was expressed by the eighteenth-century German philosopher Immanuel Kant: "Man and, in general, every rational being exists as an end in itself and not merely as a means to be arbitrarily used by this or that will." Kant's prescription urges us not to subject any creature to a condition that it has not freely chosen. In other words, we cannot use other creatures, as in slavery, for our own purposes. (Some philosophers would extend this rule to the treatment of animals by human beings.) This standard of judgment has, in fact, been invoked in recent years against medical experimentation on human beings in prisons and hospitals without their consent and against the sterilization of poor or mentally defective women without their knowledge of the decision.

Nevertheless, even where there is agreement about standards for measuring behavior, you should be aware that a majority preference is not enough to confer moral value. If in a certain neighborhood a majority of heterosexual men decide to harass a few gay men and lesbians, that consensus does not make their action right. In formulating value claims, you should be prepared to ask and answer questions about the way in which your value claims and those of others have been arrived at. Lionel Ruby, an American philosopher, sums it up in these words: "The law of rationality tells us that we ought to justify our beliefs by evidence and reasons, instead of asserting them dogmatically."[3]

Of course, you will not always be able to persuade those with whom you argue that your values are superior to theirs and that they should therefore change their attitudes. Nor, on the other hand, would you want to compromise your values or pretend that they were different in order to win an argument. What you can and should do, however, as Lionel Ruby advises, is give *good reasons* why you think one thing is better than another. If as a child you asked why it was wrong to take your brother's toys, you might have been told by an exasperated parent, "Because I say so." Some adults still give such answers in defending their judgments, but such answers are not arguments and do nothing to win the agreement of others.

Defending a Claim of Value

The following suggestions are a preliminary guide to the defense of a value claim. (We discuss value claims further in Chapter 4.)

1. Try to make clear that the values or principles you are defending should have priority on any scale of values. Keep in mind that you and your readers may differ about their relative importance. For example, although your readers may agree with you that brilliant photography is important in a film, they may think that a well-written script is even more crucial to its success. And although they may agree that freedom of the press is a mainstay of democracy, they may regard the right to privacy as even more fundamental.
2. Suggest that adherence to the values you are defending will bring about good results in some specific situation or bad results if respect for the values is ignored. You might argue, for example, that a belief in freedom of the press will make citizens better informed and the country stronger while a failure to protect this freedom will strengthen the forces of authoritarianism.
3. Since value terms are abstract, use examples and illustrations to clarify meanings and make distinctions. Comparisons and contrasts are especially helpful. If you are using the term *heroism*, can you provide

[3] *The Art of Making Sense* (New York: Lippincott, 1968), p. 271.

examples to differentiate between *heroism* and *foolhardiness* or *exhibitionism*?

4. Use testimony of others to prove that knowledgeable or highly regarded people share your values.

SAMPLE ANALYSIS: CLAIM OF VALUE

Kids in the Mall: Growing Up Controlled

WILLIAM SEVERINI KOWINSKI

> Butch heaved himself up and loomed over the group. "Like it was different for me," he piped. "My folks used to drop me off at the shopping mall every morning and leave me all day. It was like a big free baby-sitter, you know? One night they never came back for me. Maybe they moved away. Maybe there's some kind of a Bureau of Missing Parents I could check with."
>
> Richard Peck
> *Secrets of the Shopping Mall,*
> a novel for teenagers

From his sister at Swarthmore, I'd heard about a kid in Florida whose mother picked him up after school every day, drove him straight to the mall, and left him there until it closed — all at his insistence. I'd heard about a boy in Washington who, when his family moved from one suburb to another, pedaled his bicycle five miles every day to get back to his old mall, where he once belonged. 1

These stories aren't unusual. The mall is a common experience for the majority of American youth; they have probably been going there all their lives. Some ran within their first large open space, saw their first fountain, bought their first toy, and read their first book in a mall. They may have smoked their first cigarette or first joint, or turned them down, had their first kiss or lost their virginity in the mall parking lot. Teenagers in America now spend more time in the mall than anywhere else but home and school. Mostly it is their choice, but some of that mall time is put in as the result of two-paycheck and single-parent households, and 2

William Severini Kowinski is a free-lance writer who has been the book review editor and managing arts editor of the *Boston Phoenix*. This excerpt is from his book *The Malling of America: An Inside Look at the Great Consumer Paradise* (1985).

the lack of other viable alternatives. But are these kids being harmed by the mall?

3 I wondered first of all what difference it makes for adolescents to experience so many important moments in the mall. They are, after all, at play in the fields of its little world and they learn its ways; they adapt to it and make it adapt to them. It's here that these kids get their street sense, only it's mall sense. They are learning the ways of a large-scale, artificial environment; its subtleties and flexibilities, its particular pleasures and resonances, and the attitudes it fosters.

4 The presence of so many teenagers for so much time was not something mall developers planned on. In fact, it came as a big surprise. But kids became a fact of mall life very easily, and the International Council of Shopping Centers found it necessary to commission a study, which they published along with a guide to mall managers on how to handle the teenage incursion.

5 The study found that "teenagers in suburban centers are bored and come to the shopping centers mainly as a place to go. Teenagers in suburban centers spent more time fighting, drinking, littering and walking than did their urban counterparts, but presented fewer overall problems." The report observed that "adolescents congregated in groups of two to four and predominantly at locations selected by them rather than management." This probably had something to do with the decision to install game arcades, which allow management to channel these restless adolescents into naturally contained areas away from major traffic points of adult shoppers.

6 The guide concluded that mall management should tolerate and even encourage the teenage presence because, in the words of the report, "The vast majority support the same set of values as does shopping center management." *The same set of values* means simply that mall kids are already preprogrammed to be consumers and that the mall can put the finishing touches to them as hard-core, lifelong shoppers just like everybody else. That, after all, is what the mall is about. So it shouldn't be surprising that in spending a lot of time there, adolescents find little that challenges the assumption that the goal of life is to make money and buy products, or that just about everything else in life is to be used to serve those ends.

7 Growing up in a high-consumption society already adds inestimable pressure to kids' lives. Clothes consciousness has invaded the grade schools, and popularity is linked with having the best, newest clothes in the currently acceptable styles. Even what they read has been affected. "Miss [Nancy] Drew wasn't obsessed with her wardrobe," noted the *Wall Street Journal*. "But today the mystery in teen fiction for girls is what outfit the heroine will wear next." Shopping has become a survival skill and there is certainly no better place to learn it than the mall, where its importance is powerfully reinforced and certainly never questioned.

The mall as a university of suburban materialism, where Valley Girls and Boys from coast to coast are educated in consumption, has its other lessons in this era of change in family life and sexual mores and their economic and social ramifications. The plethora of products in the mall, plus the pressure on teens to buy them, may contribute to the phenomenon that psychologist David Elkind calls "the hurried child": kids who are exposed to too much of the adult world too quickly and must respond with a sophistication that belies their still-tender emotional development. Certainly the adult products marketed for children — form-fitting designer jeans, sexy tops for preteen girls — add to the social pressure to look like an adult, along with the home-grown need to understand adult finances (why mothers must work) and adult emotions (when parents divorce). 8

Kids spend so much time at the mall partly because their parents allow it and even encourage it. The mall is safe, doesn't seem to harbor any unsavory activities, and there is adult supervision; it is, after all, a controlled environment. So the temptation, especially for working parents, is to let the mall be their baby-sitter. At least the kids aren't watching TV. But the mall's role as a surrogate mother may be more extensive and more profound. 9

Karen Lansky, a writer living in Los Angeles, has looked into the subject, and she told me some of her conclusions about the effects on its teenaged denizens of the mall's controlled and controlling environment. "Structure is the dominant idea, since true 'mall rats' lack just that in their home lives," she said, "and adolescents about to make the big leap into growing up crave more structure than our modern society cares to acknowledge." Karen pointed out some of the elements malls supply that kids used to get from their families, like warmth (Strawberry Shortcake dolls and similar cute and cuddly merchandise), old-fashioned mothering ("We do it all for you," the fast-food slogan), and even home cooking (the "homemade" treats at the food court). 10

The problem in all this, as Karen Lansky sees it, is that while families nurture children by encouraging growth through the assumption of responsibility and then by letting them rest in the bosom of the family from the rigors of growing up, the mall as a structural mother encourages passivity and consumption, as long as the kid doesn't make trouble. Therefore all they learn about becoming adults is how to act and how to consume. 11

Kids are in the mall not only in the passive role of shoppers — they also work there, especially as fast-food outlets infiltrate the mall's enclosure. There they learn how to hold a job and take responsibility, but still within the same value context. When *CBS Reports* went to Oak Park Mall in suburban Kansas City, Kansas, to tape part of their hour-long consideration of malls, "After the Dream Comes True," they interviewed a teenaged girl who worked in a fast-food outlet there. In a sequence that didn't 12 make the final program, she described the major goal of her present life, which was to perfect the curl on top of the ice-cream cones that were her store's specialty. If she could do that, she would be moved from the lowly soft-drink dispenser to the more prestigious ice-cream division, the curl on top of the status ladder at her restaurant. These are the achievements that are important at the mall.

Other benefits of such jobs may also be overrated, according to Laurence D. Steinberg of the University of California at Irvine's social ecology department, who did a study on teenage employment. Their jobs, he found, are generally simple, mindlessly repetitive and boring. They don't really learn anything, and the jobs don't lead anywhere. Teenagers also work primarily with other teenagers; even their supervisors are often just a little older than they are. "Kids need to spend time with adults," Steinberg told me. "Although they get benefits from peer relationships, without parents and other adults it's one-sided socialization. They hang out with each other, have age-segregated jobs, and watch TV." 13

Perhaps much of this is not so terrible or even so terribly different. Now that they have so much more to contend with in their lives, adolescents probably need more time to spend with other adolescents without adult impositions, just to sort things out. Though it is more concentrated in the mall (and therefore perhaps a clearer target), the value system there is really the dominant one of the whole society. Attitudes about curiosity, initiative, self-expression, empathy, and disinterested learning aren't necessarily made in the mall; they are mirrored there, perhaps a bit more intensely — as through a glass brightly. 14

Besides, the mall is not without its educational opportunities. There are bookstores, where there is at least a short shelf of classics at great prices, and other books from which it is possible to learn more than how to do sit-ups. There are tools, from hammers to VCRs, and products, from clothes to records, that can help the young find and express themselves. There are older people with stories, and places to be alone or to talk one-on-one with a kindred spirit. And there is always the passing show. 15

The mall itself may very well be an education about the future. I was struck with the realization, as early as my first forays into Greengate, that the mall is only one of a number of enclosed and controlled environments that are part of the lives of today's young. The mall is just an extension, say, of those large suburban schools — only there's Karmelkorn instead of chem lab, the ice rink instead of the gym: It's high school without the impertinence of classes. 16

Growing up, moving from home to school to the mall — from enclosure to enclosure, transported in cars — is a curiously continuous process, without much in the way of contrast or contact with unenclosed reality. Places must tend to blur into one another. But whatever differences and dangers there are in this, the skills these adolescents are learning may 17 turn out to be useful in their later lives. For we seem to be moving inexorably into an age of preplanned and regulated environments, and this is the world they will inherit.

Still, it might be better if they had more of a choice. One teenaged girl 18
confessed to *CBS Reports* that she sometimes felt she was missing something by hanging out at the mall so much. "But I'm here," she said, "and this is what I have."

Analysis

Kowinski has chosen to evaluate one aspect of an extraordinarily successful economic and cultural phenomenon — the commercial mall. He asks whether the influence of the mall on adolescents is good or bad. The answer seems to be a little of both. The good values may be described as exposure to a variety of experiences, a protective structure for adolescents who often live in unstable environments, and immersion in a world that may well serve as an introduction to adulthood. But the bad values, which Kowinski thinks are more influential (as the title suggests) are those of the shoppers' paradise, a society that believes in acquisiton and consumption of goods as ultimate goals, and too much control over the choices available to adolescents. The tone of the judgment, however, is moderate and reflects a balanced, even scholarly, attitude. More than other arguments, the treatment of values requires such a voice, one which respects differences of opinion among readers. But serious doesn't mean heavy. His style is formal but highly readable, brightened by interesting examples and precise details. The opening paragraph is a strikingly effective lead.

Some of his observations are personal, but others are derived from studies by professional researchers, from *CBS Reports* to a well-known writer on childhood. These studies give weight and authority to his conclusions. Here and there we detect an appealing sympathy for the adolescents in their controlled environment.

Like any thoughtful social commentator, Kowinski casts a wide net. He sees the mall not only as a hangout for teens but as a good deal more, an institution that offers insights into family life and work, the changing urban culture, the nature of contemporary entertainment, even glimpses of a somewhat forbidding future.

CLAIMS OF POLICY

Claims of policy argue that certain conditions should exist. As the name suggests, they advocate adoption of policies or courses of action because problems have arisen that call for solution. Almost always *should* or *ought to* or *must* is expressed or implied in the claim.

CLAIM: Voluntary prayer should be permitted in public schools.

CLAIM: A dress code should be introduced for all public high schools.

CLAIM: A law should permit sixteen-year-olds and parents to "divorce" each other in cases of extreme incompatibility.

CLAIM: Mandatory jail terms should be imposed for drunk driving violations.

In defending such claims of policy you may find that you must first convince your audience that a problem exists. This will require that, as part of your longer argument, you make a factual claim, offering data to prove that present conditions are unsatisfactory. You may also find it necessary to refer to the values that support your claim. Then you will be ready to introduce your policy, to persuade your audience that the solution you propose will solve the problem.

We will examine a policy claim in which all these parts are at work. The claim can be stated as follows: "The time required for an undergraduate degree should be extended to five years." Immediate agreement with this policy among student readers would certainly not be universal. Some students would not recognize a problem. They would say, "The college curriculum we have now is fine. There's no need for a change. Besides, we don't want to spend more time in school." First, then, the arguer would have to persuade a skeptical audience that there is a problem, that four years of college are no longer enough because the stock of knowledge in almost all fields of study continues to increase. The arguer would provide data to show how many more choices in history, literature, and science students have now compared to the choices in those fields a generation ago. She would also find it necessary to emphasize the value of greater knowledge and more schooling compared to the value of other goods the audience cherishes, such as earlier independence. Finally, the arguer would offer a plan for putting her policy into effect. Her plan would have to take into consideration initial psychological resistance, revision of the curriculum, the costs of more instruction, and the costs of lost production in the work force. Most important, she would point out the benefits for both individuals and society if this policy were adopted.

In this example, we assumed that the reader would disagree that a problem existed. In many cases, however, the reader may agree that there is a problem but disagree with the arguer about the way of solving it. Most of us, no doubt, will agree that we want to reduce or eliminate the following problems: misbehavior and vandalism in schools, drunk driving, crime on the streets, child abuse, pornography, pollution. But how shall we go about solving those problems? What public policy will give us well-behaved, diligent students who never destroy school property? Safe streets where no one is ever robbed or assaulted? Loving homes where no child is ever mistreated? Some members of society would choose to introduce rules or laws that punish infractions so severely that wrongdoers would be unwilling or unable to repeat their offenses. Other members of society would prefer policies that attempt to rehabilitate or reeducate offenders through training, therapy, counseling, and new opportunities.

Defending a Claim of Policy

The following steps will help you organize arguments for a claim of policy.

1. Make your proposal clear. The terms in the proposal should be precisely defined.
2. If necessary, establish that there is a need for a change. If changes have been ignored or resisted, there may be good or at least understandable reasons why this is so. (It is often wrongly assumed that people cling to cultural practices long after their significance and necessity have eroded. But rational human beings do not continue to observe practices unless those practices serve a purpose. The fact that you and I may see no value or purpose in the activities of another is irrelevant.)
3. Consider the opposing arguments. You may want to state the opposing arguments in a brief paragraph in order to answer them in the body of your argument.
4. Devote the major part of your essay to proving that your proposal is an answer to the opposing arguments and that there are distinct benefits for your readers in adopting your proposal.
5. Support your proposal with solid data, but don't neglect the moral considerations and the common-sense reasons, which may be even more persuasive.

SAMPLE ANALYSIS: CLAIM OF POLICY

So That Nobody Has to Go to School If They Don't Want To

ROGER SIPHER

A decline in standardized test scores is but the most recent indicator 1
that American education is in trouble.

One reason for the crisis is that present mandatory-attendance laws 2
force many to attend school who have no wish to be there. Such children have little desire to learn and are so antagonistic to school that neither they nor more highly motivated students receive the quality education that is the birthright of every American.

The solution to this problem is simple: Abolish compulsory-attend- 3
ance laws and allow only those who are committed to getting an education to attend.

This will not end public education. Contrary to conventional belief, 4
legislators enacted compulsory-attendance laws to legalize what already existed. William Landes and Lewis Solomon, economists, found little evidence that mandatory-attendance laws increased the number of children in school. They found, too, that school systems have never effectively enforced such laws, usually because of the expense involved.

There is no contradiction between the assertion that compulsory at- 5
tendance has had little effect on the number of children attending school and the argument that repeal would be a positive step toward improving education. Most parents want a high school education for their children. Unfortunately, compulsory attendance hampers the ability of public school officials to enforce legitimate educational and disciplinary policies and thereby make the education a good one.

Private schools have no such problem. They can fail or dismiss stu- 6
dents, knowing such students can attend public school. Without compulsory attendance, public schools would be freer to oust students whose academic or personal behavior undermines the educational mission of the institution.

Roger Sipher is associate professor of history at the State University of New York at Cortland. This article appeared in the *New York Times* on December 22, 1977.

Has not the noble experiment of a formal education for everyone failed? While we pay homage to the homily, "You can lead a horse to water but you can't make him drink," we have pretended it is not true in education. 7

Ask high school teachers if recalcitrant students learn anything of value. Ask teachers if these students do any homework. Ask if the threat of low grades motivates them. Quite the contrary, these students know they will be passed from grade to grade until they are old enough to quit or until, as is more likely, they receive a high school diploma. At the point when students could legally quit, most choose to remain since they know they are likely to be allowed to graduate whether they do acceptable work or not. 8

Abolition of archaic attendance laws would produce enormous dividends. 9

First, it would alert everyone that school is a serious place where one goes to learn. Schools are neither day-care centers nor indoor street corners. Young people who resist learning should stay away; indeed, an end to compulsory schooling would require them to stay away. 10

Second, students opposed to learning would not be able to pollute the educational atmosphere for those who want to learn. Teachers could stop policing recalcitrant students and start educating. 11

Third, grades would show what they are supposed to: how well a student is learning. Parents could again read report cards and know if their children were making progress. 12

Fourth, public esteem for schools would increase. People would stop regarding them as way stations for adolescents and start thinking of them as institutions for educating America's youth. 13

Fifth, elementary schools would change because students would find out early that they had better learn something or risk flunking out later. Elementary teachers would no longer have to pass their failures on to junior high and high school. 14

Sixth, the cost of enforcing compulsory education would be eliminated. Despite enforcement efforts, nearly 15 percent of the school-age children in our largest cities are almost permanently absent from school. 15

Communities could use these savings to support institutions to deal with young people not in school. If, in the long run, these institutions prove more costly, at least we would not confuse their mission with that of schools. 16

Schools should be for education. At present, they are only tangentially so. They have attempted to serve an all-encompassing social function, trying to be all things to all people. In the process they have failed miserably at what they were originally formed to accomplish. 17

Analysis

Roger Sipher's article offers a straightforward solution to a distressing educational problem. Following a clear and familiar pattern of organization, the author begins by referring to the problem and the need for change that has induced him to present this solution. He seems sure that his readers will recognize the disciplinary problems arising from compulsory attendance, and he therefore alludes to them but omits any specific mention of them. Instead he concentrates on the unfortunate educational consequences of compulsory attendance. In the third paragraph he states his thesis directly: "Abolish compulsory-attendance laws and allow only those who are committed to getting an education to attend."

Sipher is no doubt aware that his proposal will strike many readers as a radical departure from conventional solutions, perhaps more damaging than the problem itself. He moves at once to dispel the fear that public education will suffer if mandatory attendance laws are repealed. He offers as proof a study by two economists who conclude that compulsory attendance has little effect on the actual number of students who attend school. But in this part of the discussion Sipher is guilty of a seeming contradiction. The reader may ask, "If compulsory-attendance laws make little difference — that is, if students attend in the same numbers regardless of the laws — why abolish them?" Later in the essay Sipher points out that in some large cities almost 15 percent of school-age children are permanently absent. If they are absent, they cannot be the ones who are "polluting the educational atmosphere." Apparently, then, the author is referring to a small number of students uninterested in learning who continue to come to school because they are compelled to do so.

In the middle section Sipher elaborates on the difficulties of teaching those who are uninterested in learning. The use of the imperative mode, of speaking directly to the reader — "Ask high school teachers if recalcitrant students learn anything of value" — is effective. Here, too, however, some readers may want to know if Sipher is aware of the alternative programs introduced into many city schools for reaching unwilling students or whether he knows about them but regards them as unsuccessful.

The strongest part of the argument appears in the last third of the essay, where the author lists six advantages that will follow the repeal of compulsory attendance laws. He also seems to recognize that some readers will have another question: "What will become of the young people who are required to leave school?" His answer — "institutions" — is vague. But since the burden of his proposal is to offer ways of improving the quality of education, Sipher may consider that he is justified in declining to answer this question more fully.

The strengths of Sipher's argument are clear, direct organization, readable language, and listing of the specific dividends that would follow implementation of his proposal. Equally important is the novelty of the proposal, which will outrage some readers and delight others. In either case the proposal will arouse attention and initiate discussion.

However, the orginality of the solution may also constitute a weakness. The more original the solution to a problem, the more likely it is to encounter initial resistance. Sipher's argument is too short to answer the many questions his readers might have about possible disadvantages. This argument, in other words, should be considered an introduction to any attempt to solve the problem, a limitation of which Sipher was probably aware.

READINGS FOR ANALYSIS

Homelessness in Colonial and Early America

PETER H. ROSSI

If there is no mystery about the sympathetic attention paid to the problem of homelessness in America over the past decade, there certainly *is* a mystery concerning why comparable attention and sympathy were not extended to the homeless in the past. Homelessness has waxed and waned throughout our history, but America has always had a goodly complement of homeless people.[1] Nevertheless, compared with the scale of contemporary popular concern, throughout most of our history the homeless have been regarded at least with indifference and often with contempt, fear, and loathing (Hopper 1987). . . . 1

Concern about homelessness can be discerned in the minutes of seventeenth-century New England town meetings. Under the Elizabethan 2

Peter H. Rossi is a sociologist. This excerpt is from his study *Down and Out in America: The Origins of Homelessness* (1989).

[1] In this respect our history is no different from those of other countries. Literal homelessness has existed throughout the world and is especially prevalent now in the large cities of developing countries.

poor laws that governed colonial New England towns, each town shouldered responsibility for the care of its own poor. A critical distinction was made between what must be done for "settled" persons, whose households were members of the town, and everyone else, especially newcomers. Those with settlement rights, acquired by being accepted by vote as a town member or by being born into an accepted family, were entitled to help from the town when in adversity. The town had no responsibility for nonmembers.

3 Newcomers could petition the selectmen and the town meeting for permission to settle in the town. Many of the applicants for membership considered at town meetings were by definition homeless and often without resources, raising a concern whether they would mean additional tax burdens for the town. As a consequence, those who had some promise to be self-supporting stood a better chance of being accepted. Nonmembers likely to become town charges, especially widows and children as well as disabled or aged adults, were often "warned" to leave town. There thus arose a kind of transient poor, shunted from community to community because in place after place they were denied settlement rights.[2]

4 Local responsibility for the unfortunate may have benefited town members and their families when misfortunes fell, but it must have made life miserable for those not on town rolls. The town meeting minutes are silent about what happened to the men, women, and children who were warned out of town: Did some community take them in, or did they wander endlessly from place to place?

5 The colonial preoccupation with rights of settlement and the benefit entitlements accompanying them has persisted throughout most of our history, placing a good proportion of the indigent and needy who were migrants in a kind of geopolitical limbo where no jurisdiction was responsible for their care. Throughout the nineteenth century and most of the twentieth, in most states welfare legislation made clear distinctions between the settled and the transient poor, with benefits reserved mainly for the former. Some states even distinguished between county and state settlement rights, with different benefit schedules for those who qualified as residents of each. Settlement rights were dependent on length of residence (usually one or more years of uninterrupted time).

---

[2] This raises the question how such people managed to survive. Some hint of coping methods can be gleaned from the town meeting minutes. Many became squatters, living on unused land and hoping the town would not notice them. In addition, some must have found their way to the larger settlements, such as Boston, where their presence might be more easily overlooked. Most historical studies on the treatment of the poor in colonial New England have concerned small communities that were primarily rural: It may well be that larger places were more tolerant of outsiders.

Correspondingly, the "local" homeless were treated in a variety of 6
ways ranging from receiving small support payments to being settled in poorhouses. The transient homeless were either left in limbo or urged, sometimes forcibly, to move on. As in colonial times, those who did not have settlement rights (or could not document uninterrupted residence of the required duration) were often transported to the jurisdiction boundary. Indeed, during the early years of the Great Depression, in some years more money was spent in New York on "Greyhound relief" (bus tickets to bordering states) than on direct benefits (Crouse 1986).

The settlement issue in public welfare was ended only twenty years 7
ago by a 1969 Supreme Court decision that declared unconstitutional the length-of-residence restrictions that states and local communities ordinarily placed on eligibility for benefits.[3]

Nineteenth-century Americans were no more sympathetic to the 8
homeless than were their ancestors. The post–Civil War period saw a considerable increase in homelessness and transience. The construction of the railroads, their subsequent continual maintenance needs, and the rise of large-scale commercial agriculture created a strong demand for transient workers who could supply seasonal and episodic labor. The skills needed were often based on strength and endurance. The demand was met by restless discharged Civil War veterans, immigrant laborers, and other young males, often recruited by labor agents — middlemen commissioned to recruit workers. These transient homeless of the post–Civil War period were predominantly young, unattached men with low levels of education and job skills. Their employment took them all over the country: Some settled far from where they started as recruits.

A bit more can be learned about the local homeless of the nineteenth 9
century because of the records kept by local community relief officials. Katz (1986) provides a detailed account of how the indigent poor were treated in New York State. Policies vacillated between providing small monetary stipends (outdoor relief) and maintaining poorhouses (indoor relief), and there was a protracted debate over which was less expensive. Alongside this controversy was another debate over whether outdoor relief encouraged the lazy and immoral to look to the public treasury for support rather than to earn their living, a point that favored poorhouses, since they were unlikely to attract those seeking subsidized loafing. You may recognize this last theme as a variant on the perennial issue of how best to help the "deserving poor" without subsidizing the undeserving.

---

[3] Voting privileges in most jurisdictions are still predicated on establishing some minimum period of residence, thus disfranchising a sizable number of voters, perhaps as many as the 20 percent who change residence over a year's time.

10 In the second half of the nineteenth century there were several severe economic downturns, each accompanied by surges in homelessness and the demand for public relief. Homelessness per se was not so much the central concern as was the general need for food, fuel, and clothing.

11 The relief burdens of counties and municipalities also varied seasonally: When wintry conditions reduced the demand for unskilled labor, the need for poor relief grew. How frequently indigence led to literal homelessness is not discussed, although the literature is full of references to using police station lockups and local jails as temporary housing for the poor. For example, anyone could approach a New York City police station and be given lodging for the night without being arrested and booked for any offense. The New York City police reported in 1890 that over the previous decade the department had provided lodging in jails and lockups to 150,000 persons annually (making it the largest lodging supplier in the city).[4] How many of the homeless people they housed were transient and how many were local is not known. There are also references to the nineteenth-century shantytowns that grew up on the periphery of settled urban areas.[5] Building houses on unused land out of scrap materials has always been one of the solutions the poor resorted to before the time of zoning laws and when much vacant land was held by absentee owners speculating on price increases. Indeed, the impetus for many of the urban monuments of today came out of nineteenth-century urban renewal efforts to remove the eyesores of shantytowns. Such motives played a part in the construction of New York's Central Park, Chicago's Grant Park, and the filling in of Boston's Back Bay, all built on land that had been occupied by shantytowns built by poor squatters.

12 Despite the important role they played in constructing the infrastructure of late nineteenth-century industrial development, the transient homeless scarcely had any respected place in American society. These transient workers were characterized as tramps, hoboes, and bums and were often warned to leave town when there was no demand for their labor. Police departments solved many crimes by attributing them to tramps and bums. Mark Twain ended one of his stories by advertising to medical schools that he had the bodies of several tramps in his basement to sell as teaching cadavers.

13 The prevailing lack of sympathy in the nineteenth century for the homeless and the transient is all the more puzzling because the absence

---

[4] In the 1890s the major police departments were relieved of their role as housing supplier of last resort. Most cities established municipal lodging houses, charging token sums for beds in dormitory arrangements to all who applied.

[5] The term "shanty Irish" undoubtedly had its origins in the shantytowns built by poor Irish immigrants on the urban fringes.

of any significant safety net of social welfare programs meant that almost every household had a good chance of suffering catastrophic declines in standard of living through unemployment, illness, and death and hence of becoming impoverished and homeless. Katz's (1975) detailed longitudinal study of the census records of Hamilton, Ontario, found many families that plummeted from middle-class, homeowning status to indigence when catastrophic illness struck down a main breadwinner. The imposing sizes of nineteenth-century orphanages also testify how frequently death broke up families. That a widespread fear of the economic consequences of illness persisted into the 1930s is shown in the Lynds' classic studies of Muncie, Indiana (Lynd and Lynd 1929, 1937).

References

Crouse, Joan M. *The Homeless Transient in the Great Depression: New York State, 1929–1941.* Albany, NY: SUNY Press, 1986.

Hopper, Kim. The Public Response to Homelessness in New York City: The Last Hundred Years. In *On Being Homeless: Historical Perspectives*, ed. Rick Beard. New York: Museum of the City of New York, 1987.

Katz, Michael B. *The People of Hamilton, Canada West.* Cambridge, MA: Harvard University Press, 1975.

______. *In the Shadow of the Poorhouse.* New York: Basic Books, 1986.

Lynd, Robert A., and Helen M. Lynd. *Middletown.* New York: Harcourt, Brace, 1929.

______. *Middletown in Transition.* New York: Harcourt, Brace, 1937.

Discussion Questions

1. Explain the distinctions that were made in colonial and early America between various applicants for poor relief. How did these distinctions affect migrants?
2. What factors contributed to the increase in homelessness after the Civil War?
3. How does Rossi explain the significance for modern cities of the shantytowns of the nineteenth century?

Writing Suggestions

1. Rossi says that there is a mystery concerning the cruel treatment of the homeless in the past. Can you speculate on possible reasons? Can the reasons be justified? (You can find some clues in Rossi's discussion.)

2. Do some research into the causes of present-day homelessness in America. (These are discussed in subsequent chapters in Rossi's book, but magazines and newspapers in recent years have been full of articles on the subject.) Compare causes of present-day homelessness with those of the past. Do any striking differences emerge? If so, how can we account for them?

Discriminating Tastes: The Prejudice of Personal Preferences

VICTORIA A. SACKETT

The nation is suffering from a plague. It has nothing to do with our immune systems or cicadas or controlled substances or insider trading. But it is just as damaging to our individual well-being and our social fabric. We've developed a persistent low-grade fever of intolerance that's sapping our strength and making us all behave like cranky, spoiled brats. 1

This is not major-league prejudice, the kind we've seen in decades past leveled at ethnic groups and scary new ideas. This is a common, everyday strain of irritability whose target is Anyone who does Anything that we find vaguely Unpleasant. 2

The disease progresses in three distinct stages: 3

Primary intolerance: You begin to suspect that everyone else has the symptoms. You will be dismayed and irked by other people's impatience. Suddenly the world will seem to be populated with fast-food clerks who grow surly if a customer requests a napkin; cab drivers who shower invective upon riders going anyplace but the airport; friends who say, "Will you *please* get to the point?" instead of listening politely to your too-long stories; and women who smite stopped trucks with their umbrellas if the rear tires overlap a crosswalk.

Secondary intolerance: Behavior in others that never bothered you in the past begins to give you all the symptoms of a neurological or myocardial incident — muscles twitch, heart pounds, respiration rate accelerates, vision tunnels, head throbs. In the presence of whatever annoys

Victoria A. Sackett is the deputy managing editor at *Public Opinion* magazine, where this column appeared in the July/August 1987 issue.

you — gum-chewing, ice-crunching, high-pitched giggling, foot-shuffling, finger-drumming, toe-tapping — you will be unable to hear, see, smell, or think about anything but that which you would most like to avoid. You will take indirect action: glaring, sighing heavily, twisting in your seat, and glaring harder. You will begin to commit thought crimes — adrenaline-fed dreams of slapping, yelling, and smiting with your umbrella.

Tertiary intolerance: You give in to your fantasies and frustration and take direct action to ease your discomfort. You speak to the offender. "Would you mind not doing that? It bothers me," is the favored beginner's phrase. It means quite simply, "Stop doing things the way you want to and do them the way I want you to."

Once you've shushed your first talkative movie viewer, you know 4
that the virus has entered your bloodstream. All the antibodies built up by your mother's fine teachings of patience have proven unequal to their task. This can be life-threatening. One young man at a recent Laurel, Maryland, showing of *The Untouchables*, for example, asked a noisy neighbor to be quiet once too often and was beaten unconscious by the talker and nine companions.

The Pathology

The cruelty of this particular ailment is that efforts to alleviate the 5
symptoms make it worse. The more vexations that you attempt to control, the more easily you will be vexed. Victory over one provocation just lowers your resistance to another; once you begin to suspect that you *can* get people to behave according to your specifications, chances are you will be unwilling to let them get away with much of anything. We've hardly noticed it happening, but this is what has turned small-time intolerance into a countrywide epidemic.

The irony is that, as the nation has grown more tolerant and welcom- 6
ing of all kinds of ethnic and other diversity, individuals succumbing to their petty prejudices now comprise veritable lynch mobs. Their targets are the newly beleaguered minorities: cholesterol eaters (watch what happens at a family dinner when you ask for butter *and* sour cream *and* bacon bits for your potato. Someone will describe for you in clinical detail just what saturated fat does to your innards), perfume wearers (Ann Landers published the seat number of a subscription ticket holder at the Arena stage who wore a scent that bothered someone near her), and smokers of any variety (I have one friend of otherwise saintly patience who can't *bear* the smell of fake logs burning. He was able to get his neighbors to stop).

Antismokers are the most contagious group. It begins in childhood. Every three-year-old holds his or her nose, waves a fat little arm in the air, and says "That stinks" when an adult lights up. It's always been this way, even before the surgeon general frightened us. But in the olden days, mothers and fathers used this behavior as an opportunity to teach one of life's most valuable lessons: It's rude to boss people around, and you can't always have everything the way you want it. 7

Now these children are congratulated for their wisdom and adults imitate *them*. It is true that both the small ones and the big ones have arguments in their favor. They can insist that it's their health and not their whim that is being indulged, but this is open to doubt. If smoking smelled good, chances are the investigations into its ill effects would have stopped with the damage it did to the smoker. 8

These days, smoke-haters are armed with a doctor's excuse for their own intolerance. There's no such thing as being rude to a smoker. And 90 percent of the people who are snarling at the addict, driving him out of restaurants, workplaces, and entire communities, throwing pitchers of water at him, and teaching their children to say "That's disgusting" to him are less concerned about being infected by his cigars or cigarettes than they are concerned with manifesting the symptoms of their own disease — final-stage intolerance. 9

The Causes

Expanded to a global scale, tertiary intolerance could add up to something serious. Other than making each of us — the irritable as well as the irritating — less happy than we were when we could take things in stride, this plague of intolerance could threaten the fate of the world. What if our president, for instance, decided to take the advice of all the actresses and junior high school students who've been telling him that the Russians are just like us, so we should all lay down arms and be good friends? Then what if we found out that the Soviets were like us, but weren't what we liked — they smoke cigars, say, or shuffle their feet, or chew gum in movie theaters? Peace wouldn't have a chance. 10

Why have we become so testy? One explanation could well be the trend toward later marriage. People who live by themselves for prolonged periods tend to expect the world to be far more within their control than those who are constantly disrupted by the demands of spouses or offspring. Or, the other side of that, people who marry later tend to be those who enjoy the control they have over their own lives. Either way, there are more of them around, and they may be having their effect on the collective tolerance level. 11

The other culprit has to be assertiveness training. Since politeness came to be identified as meekness and repression, there have been no holds barred on expressing oneself. To avoid stating your wishes is to invite psychological damage, professional dead ends, and lack of respect from others. Few schools of thought have been swallowed so unquestioningly and with such exasperating results. 12

Widespread irritability may just be one more irritation that we have to deal with in late twentieth-century America. Maybe human nature requires a certain irreducible minimum of intolerance, the way the human body requires minute quantities of "trace minerals" that keep everything from going haywire. If we chase prejudice out of one part of our souls, it pops up somewhere else. Legislation and enlightenment have accustomed us to large-scale diversity, so now we fuss about petty differences. This is still an exhausting and unpleasant state of mind, but it may be as close as we can come to conquering intolerance altogether. We can't, after all, always have everything the way we want it. 13

Discussion Questions

1. Define the "plague" from which the nation is suffering.
2. Explain the three stages of the disease. Do any of these symptoms sound familiar?
3. What are the causes of this new intolerance? Do they seem like reasonable explanations?

Writing Suggestions

1. Since Sackett wrote this essay, new symptoms of the disease have appeared. One is the intolerance of fur garments. People who wear them have been attacked on the street by animal-rights activists. Is this conduct defensible? Is it analogous to antismoking attacks? Write an essay arguing that some discriminatory practices may be justified. Make clear which attacks are not defensible.
2. Sackett mentions two or three causes for this intolerance. Can you think of others?

In Support of Our Common Language . . .

U.S. ENGLISH

English, Our Common Bond

Throughout its history, the United States has been enriched by the 1
cultural contributions of immigrants from many traditions, but blessed with one common language that has united a diverse nation and fostered harmony among its people.

As much by accident as by design, that language is English. Given our 2
country's history of immigration and the geography of immigrant settlements, it might have been Dutch, or Spanish, or German; or it might have been two languages, as is the case in Canada, our neighbor to the north.

But English prevailed, and it has served us well. Its eloquence shines 3
in our Declaration of Independence and in our Constitution. It is the living carrier of our democratic ideals.

English is a world language which we share with many other nations. 4
It is the most popular medium of international communication.

The Spread of Language Segregation

The United States has been spared the bitter conflicts that plague so 5
many countries whose citizens do not share a common tongue. Historic forces made English the language of all Americans, though nothing in our laws designated it the official language of the nation.

But now English is under attack, and we must take affirmative steps 6
to guarantee that it continues to be our common heritage. Failure to do so may well lead to institutionalized language segregation and a gradual loss of national unity.

The erosion of English and the rise of other languages in public life 7
have several causes:

- Some spokesmen for ethnic groups reject the "melting pot" ideal; they label assimilation a betrayal of their native cultures and demand government funding to maintain separate ethnic institutions.

U.S. English is a national organization, based in Washington, D.C., founded to "defend the public interest in the growing debate on bilingualism and biculturalism." This text is taken from one of their brochures.

- Well-intentioned but unproven theories have led to extensive government-funded bilingual education programs, ranging from preschool through college.
- New civil-rights assertions have yielded bilingual and multilingual ballots, voting instructions, election site counselors, and government-funded voter registration campaigns aimed solely at speakers of foreign languages.
- Record immigration, concentrated in fewer language groups, is reinforcing language segregation and retarding language assimilation.
- The availability of foreign language electronic media, with a full range of news and entertainment, is a new disincentive to the learning of English.

U.S. ENGLISH: A Timely Public Response

In 1981, Senator S. I. Hayakawa, himself an immigrant and distin- 8
guished scholar of semantics, proposed a constitutional amendment designating English as the official language of the United States. Senator Hayakawa helped found U.S. ENGLISH in 1983 to organize and support a citizens' movement to maintain our common linguistic heritage.

U.S. ENGLISH is committed to promoting the use of English in the po- 9
litical, economic, and intellectual life of the nation. It operates squarely within the American political mainstream and rejects all manifestations of cultural or linguistic chauvinism.

Our Guiding Principles

Our goal is to maintain the blessing of a common language — English 10
— for the people of the United States.

These principles guide us: 11

- In a pluralistic nation such as ours, government should foster the similarities that unite us rather than the differences that separate us.
- The nation's public schools have a special responsibility to help students who don't speak English to learn the language as quickly as possible.
- Quality teaching of English should be part of every student's curriculum, at every academic level.
- The study of foreign languages should be strongly encouraged, both as an academic discipline and for practical, economic, and foreign-policy considerations.

- *All* candidates for U.S. citizenship should be required to demonstrate the ability to understand, speak, read, and write simple English, and demonstrate basic understanding of our system of government.
- The rights of individuals and groups to use other languages and to establish *privately funded* institutions for the maintenance of diverse languages and cultures must be respected in a pluralistic society.

Our Action Program

U.S. ENGLISH actively works to reverse the spread of foreign language usage in the nation's official life. Our program calls for: 12

- Adoption of a constitutional amendment to establish English as the official language of the United States.
- Repeal of laws mandating multilingual ballots and voting materials.
- Restriction of government funding for bilingual education to short-term transitional programs only.
- Universal enforcement of the English language and civics requirement for naturalization.
- Expansion of opportunities for learning English.

Towards these ends, U.S. ENGLISH serves as a national center for consultation and cooperation on ways to defend English as the sole official language of the United States. It directs its efforts to leading a public discussion on the best language policies for our multiethnic society; educating opinion leaders on the long-term implications of language segregation; encouraging research on improved methods of teaching English; and promoting effective programs of English language instruction. 13

We Need Your Help

U.S. ENGLISH welcomes to membership all who are concerned about the prospect of entrenched language segregation and the possibility of losing our strongest national bond. 14

We hope that you will join us and defend our common language against misguided policies that threaten our national unity. 15

Discussion Questions

1. What are the reasons for the apparent erosion of English? Are some reasons more convincing than others? Explain.
2. How would foreign languages be encouraged if English became the official language? Does the solution seem practical and fair?

3. According to this announcement, what advantages will result from adoption of U.S. English? What are the dangers if U.S. English does not become law?

Writing Suggestions

1. The article says that bilingual education programs are based on "well-intentioned but unproven theories." Write a paper that either supports or refutes this allegation. Use expert opinion as your primary sources, but include your own experience or that of someone you know if it is relevant.
2. Some critics see in this movement a revival of *nativism*, or a rejection of recent immigrants from Asia and South America. Analyze the view of English only as a reflection of prejudice.

Capital Punishment — An Idea Whose Time Has Come Again

J. A. PARKER

Capital punishment has been the subject of increasing debate in the 1
American society in recent days.

In recent years, few murderers have been executed. In 1957, when 2
65 executions took place, the nation witnessed 8,060 murders. In 1981, when 1 execution occurred, there were 22,520 murders.

Our murder rate is the highest in the industrial world. It is even 3
higher than the rate of death by violence in certain war zones.

In Northern Ireland, for example, there were 8.8 deaths per 100,000 4
population in the years 1968–74. In 1980, in the United States, there were 10.2 deaths per 100,000 by murder.

Similarly, during the German bombardment of London in the years 5
1940–45, there were 21.7 deaths per 100,000 as a result. In Detroit, from the years 1972–78, there were 42.4 deaths per hundred thousand from murder.

While there may be disagreement about the element of cause and 6
effect, it is clear that as we have departed from capital punishment our society has seen an epidemic of murder.

J.A. Parker is the editor of *The Lincoln Review*, the journal of an African-American think tank, where this essay appeared in the summer of 1986.

Between 1966 and 1972, no death penalties were carried out. In 1972, in the case of *Furman v. Georgia*, the Supreme Court invalidated the death sentence in both state and federal courts. The grounds of the decision were sweeping — that without specific legislative guidelines, the death penalty was automatically an arbitrary punishment. The vote, however, was narrow, 5–4. 7

Following this decision, state legislatures passed laws clearly setting forth procedures for judging when death was the appropriate punishment. Thirty-eight states adopted this approach. As crimes were committed and sentences passed, the issue once again was litigated in the courts. As a result, from 1972 to 1976, no cases reached the Supreme Court and no executions occurred. 8

From 1976 to 1981, the Supreme Court used various procedural arguments to invalidate specific death sentences. A judgment in an Ohio case, for example, was thrown out on the grounds that the lower courts had not given sufficient consideration to mitigating factors before invoking the death penalty. An Alabama ruling was invalidated on grounds that the jury was not given an opportunity to find that the crime was not premeditated. 9

Finally, in 1981, with Justice Potter Stewart having retired and been replaced by Sandra Day O'Connor, the court began to decline to interpose procedural objections to capital punishment, and once again the death penalty has been applied. 10

At the present time, there is only one major challenge to capital punishment laws (the subject of an article in this issue by George C. Smith and Daniel J. Popeo). That challenge is based on statistical studies showing racial disparities in imposition of the death sentence. The Georgia death penalty is being challenged on behalf of a black man sentenced to death for killing a white police officer. The evidence includes a study showing that those who killed whites in Georgia were eleven times more likely to receive the death penalty than those who killed blacks. A Federal appellate court rejected the appeal, but the Supreme Court has decided to hear the case in its next session. 11

In this case, Warren McCleskey, a black male recidivist, was tried and convicted in 1979 of murdering a police officer, plus two counts of armed robbery. The jury found two statutory aggravating factors — murder in the course of a robbery, plus killing a police officer performing his official duties — and therefore sentenced McCleskey to death. The Eleventh Circuit firmly rejected McCleskey's discrimination arguments by a 9–3 vote. 12

The theory in the McCleskey case — that the race of the victim rather than the perpetrator of the crime is a key element in determining which murderers are executed and which are not — is viewed by authors Smith and Popeo as revealing that the advocates of such a theory "simply lack 13 the facts to press the more direct case they would much prefer — i.e., a straightforward claim that the death penalty is disproportionately imposed on black defendants." As a result of the Justice Department's 1985 survey of sentencing outcomes, it is now documented that, "Whereas 12 blacks were sent to death row for every 1,000 blacks arrested for murder and non-negligent homicide, a significantly higher ratio of 16 out of 1,000 whites arrested for those same crimes were sent to death row. That means a 33 percent greater probability of receiving the death sentence for the white murderer. . . . Whereas only 1.1 percent of black death-row inmates were actually executed, 1.7 percent of white death-row inmates were executed. The white inmate thus has a 55 percent greater likelihood of actual execution than his black counterpart."

Since the facts contradict the notion that race is a primary factor in their convictions or executions, the notion that the victim's race is a key element appears particularly strained. Placing racial considerations aside, however, the debate over the morality and deterrent effect of capital punishment is likely to continue for some time. 14

Is it, somehow, "immoral" to execute murderers? At the present time, there are some in the religious community and elsewhere in the American society who argue that it is. In the Judeo-Christian tradition, however, the weight of evidence may be found on the opposite side. 15

The distinguished Christian writer C. S. Lewis argued that, "We can rest contentedly in our sins and in our stupidities . . . but pain insists on being attended to. God whispers to us in our pleasures, speaks in our conscience, but shouts in our pains: It is His megaphone to rouse a deaf world. A bad man, happy, is a man without the least inkling that his actions do not 'answer,' that they are not in accord with the laws of the universe. A perception of this truth lies at the back of the universal human feeling that bad men ought to suffer. It is no use turning up our noses at this feeling, as if it were wholly base. . . . Some enlightened people would like to banish all conceptions of retribution or desert from their theory of punishment and place its value wholly in the deterrence of others or the reform of the criminal himself. They do not see that by doing so they render all punishment unjust. What can be more immoral than to inflict suffering on me for the sake of deterring others if I do not *deserve* it? And if I do deserve it, you are admitting the claims of 'retribution.' And what can be more outrageous than to catch me and submit me to a disagreeable process of moral improvement without my consent, unless (once more) I *deserve* it?" 16

The Sixth Commandment, it is widely recognized, is correctly translated from the Hebrew as "Thou shalt not murder." The Mosaic Code, in fact, provided the death penalty for murder and for many other crimes, most of which would not be considered capital offenses today. Christian 17 forgiveness, while a mandate for individuals, is not such for duly constituted governmental authority. St. Paul wrote that government "does not bear the sword in vain" but is appointed by God "to execute His wrath on the wrongdoer." The dictum of Jesus that, "All who take the sword will perish by the sword" may be seen as a declaration that the death penalty for murder is indeed just.

Some critics of capital punishment argue that it violates the Eighth Amendment, which forbids cruel and unusual punishments. Yet, they forget that the Eighth Amendment was made part of the Constitution in 1791 at a time when governments throughout the world had established methods of execution which were intended to inflict maximum suffering such as burning, drawing and quartering, impalement, and pressing. It is such actions which were viewed as "cruel and unusual," not the act of executing a murderer. Indeed, capital punishment existed in the United States before the adoption of the Bill of Rights — and has continued to exist for more than two hundred years. 18

Yet another argument presented by critics of capital punishment is that, placing the moral and constitutional questions aside, it simply does not deter crime. In this instance, while some data seems to support the critics' assessment, the burden of the evidence would lead to an opposite conclusion. 19

Professor Isaac Ehrlich of the University of Chicago has concluded that over the period 1933–1969, "an additional execution per year . . . may have resulted on the average in seven or eight fewer murders." Dr. Ehrlich has shown that previous investigations, which did not find deterrent effects of the death penalty, suffer from fatal defects. He believes that it is possible to demonstrate the marginal deterrent effect of the death penalty statistically. 20

What we know with certainty is that as executions for murder have declined, murder itself has dramatically increased. Those who argue that life imprisonment is a sufficient deterrent to protect society overlook the fact that most of the killers sentenced to life in prison are back on the streets in approximately fourteen years. "Today, there is no true life sentence," declared Robert Johnson, assistant professor of justice at American University's School of Justice. "It all depends on individual parole boards, but on a first-degree murder conviction a realistic minimum term served would be between seven and fourteen years." In New York, prisoners serving life sentences become eligible for parole in just nineteen months. 21

To the argument that capital punishment degrades the condemned and the executioner equally, New York City's Mayor Edward Koch responds: "Let me ask you to consider which one of the following cases disgraces and outrages human dignity more. One Lemuel Smith was con- 22 victed last year in Dutchess County for murder. He had already been convicted in Schenectady for a kidnapping and rape, for which he received two twenty-five-years-to-life sentences. He had also already been convicted of murder in Albany, for which he received another twenty-five-years-to-life sentence. While serving these three life sentences in Green Haven Prison, Smith lured a woman corrections officer . . . into the Catholic chaplain's office and there strangled her to death and mutilated her body. . . . A fourth life sentence is meaningless. The status of the law in New York has effectively given him a license to kill. . . . "

Mayor Koch argues that, "Only moral ciphers could equate the infliction of a supremely just legal penalty with the horrifying ordeals that . . . innocent human beings . . . endured. And this says nothing of the endless grief visited upon those who loved them. . . . Murder is sui generis in the realm of social and moral evil. The sanctity of human life cannot credibly be proclaimed without capital punishment. . . . Capital punishment must be endorsed and, in the appropriate cases, applied, if we are to have a truly civilized society." 23

The distinguished English legal philosopher Sir James Stephen declared that, "The fact that men are hanged for murder is one great reason why murder is considered so dreadful a crime." 24

It is the simple justice of capital punishment which has been clear throughout history to most observers. In a debate on the subject more than a decade ago, the late Senator John McClellan (D-Ark.) asked: "What other punishment is 'just' for a man, found to be sane, who would stab, strangle, and mutilate eight student nurses? What other punishment is 'just' for men who would invade the home of members of a rival religious sect and shoot to death men, women, and children, after forcing a mother to watch as her three young children were drowned before her eyes? What other punishment is 'just' for a band of social misfits who would invade the homes of people they had never even met and stab and hack to death a woman eight and a half months pregnant and her guests?" 25

The overwhelming majority of the American people support capital punishment. Recent polls indicate that 72 percent of Americans favored executing murderers, the highest percentage since 1936. Support for the death penalty has risen sharply since 1966, when 42 percent of those interviewed favored the death penalty. A majority of all groups — men and women, whites and blacks — supported capital punishment. 26

Justice Oliver Wendell Holmes wrote, in "The Common Law," that, "The first requirement of a sound body of law is that it should correspond with the actual feelings and demands of the community. . . . " 27

It is high time that we rejected the notion that sadistic murderers can be "rehabilitated." The job of society and those who act in its name is to remove murderers from our midst, not provide them with an opportunity 28 to kill again. Beyond this, retribution is a legitimate function of society. Professor Walter Berns notes that, "We in the United States have always recognized the legitimacy of retribution. We have schedules of punishment in every criminal code according to which punishments are designed to fit the crime and not simply to fit what social science tells us about deterrence and rehabilitation; the worse the crime, the more severe the punishment. Justice requires criminals (as well as the rest of us) to get what they (and we) deserve, and what criminals deserve depends on what they have done."

It is a misreading of our religious tradition to believe that men are not responsible for the consequences of their actions and that it is in violation of our moral teachings to execute murderers. "Whoso sheddeth man's blood, by man shall his blood be shed," states Genesis (9:6). In the Bible (Exodus 21:12), exactly twenty-five verses after the Sixth Commandment, "Thou shalt not kill," the Law says, "He that smiteth a man so that he die, shall be surely put to death." This sentiment is repeated in Leviticus (24:17) which states, "He who kills a man shall be put to death." Again, in Numbers (35:30–31) it is said: "If anyone kills a person, the murderer shall be put to death on the evidence of witnesses. . . . Moreover, you shall accept no ransom for the life of a murderer who is guilty of death; but he shall be put to death." 29

The philosophical position of opponents of capital punishment contradicts not only our religious and legal tradition, but common sense as well. Florida's Governor Graham, who has signed nearly fifty death warrants, cites the case of a restaurant robbery seen by a customer. "Afterward," recounts Graham, "he was the only witness. So the two guys took him out to the Everglades and shot him in the back of the head. If they had felt that being convicted of robbery and first-degree murder was sufficiently different, they might have had second thoughts." 30

Indeed, those critics of capital punishment who argue that it is not, in fact, a deterrent, are, in mose cases, opposed to executing murderers regardless of the deterrent effect. 31

In this connection, Professor Ernest van den Haag writes: "Common sense, lately bolstered by statistics, tells us that the death penalty will deter murder, if anything can. People fear nothing more than death. Therefore, nothing will deter a criminal more than the fear of death. Death is final. But where there is life there is hope. Wherefore, life in prison is less feared. Murderers clearly prefer it to execution — otherwise, they would not try to be sentenced to life in prison instead of death (only an infinitesimal percentage of murderers are suicidal). Therefore, a life sentence must be less deterrent than a death sentence. And we must execute murderers as long as it is merely possible that their execution protects citizens from future murder. . . . I have occasionally asked abolitionists if they would fa- 32 vor the death penalty were it shown that every execution deters, say, five hundred murders. The answer to this admittedly hypothetical question, after some dodging, has always been no. . . . Abolitionists want to abolish the death penalty regardless of whether it deters. The nondeterrence argument they use is a sham. . . . It is fair to conclude that they would rather save the life of a convicted murderer than that of any number of innocent victims. In their eyes, the sanctity of the life of the murderer exceeds that of any future murder victims."

Given our escalating murder rate, and the intellectual and moral bankruptcy of the arguments of those who have opposed the execution of murderers, it seems clear that capital punishment is an idea whose time has come — again. 33

Discussion Questions

1. List the objections to capital punishment that Parker attempts to refute (there are at least eight). Which of his rebuttals is the most convincing? Which is the least convincing? Explain.
2. Does the fact that Parker is black affect our acceptance of his argument?
3. Explain the comment by Sir James Stephen: "The fact that men are hanged for murder is one great reason why murder is considered so dreadful a crime."
4. Explain Walter Berns's opinion of *rehabilitation.*
5. Would Anna Quindlen (see "Death Penalty's False Promise: An Eye for an Eye," p. 169) take a favorable view of Parker's arguments?

Writing Suggestions

1. Choose one or two of Parker's issues and develop an opposing view. You may need to support your claim with statistics, expert opinion, and examples of noteworthy cases. (Notice how Quindlen uses the case of Ted Bundy.)
2. Try to explain the views of abolitionists who "want to abolish the death penalty regardless of whether it deters."

The Right to Bear Arms

WARREN E. BURGER

Our metropolitan centers, and some suburban communities of America, are setting new records for homicides by handguns. Many of our large centers have up to ten times the murder rate of all of Western Europe. In 1988, there were 9,000 handgun murders in America. Last year, Washington, D.C., alone had more than 400 homicides — setting a new record for our capital. 1

The Constitution of the United States, in its Second Amendment, guarantees a "right of the people to keep and bear arms." However, the meaning of this clause cannot be understood except by looking to the purpose, the setting, and the objectives of the draftsmen. The first ten amendments — the Bill of Rights — were not drafted at Philadelphia in 1787; that document came two years later than the Constitution. Most of the states already had bills of rights, but the Constitution might not have been ratified in 1788 if the states had not had assurances that a national Bill of Rights would soon be added. 2

People of that day were apprehensive about the new "monster" national government presented to them, and this helps explain the language and purpose of the Second Amendment. A few lines after the First Amendment's guarantees — against "establishment of religion," "free exercise" of religion, free speech and free press — came a guarantee that grew out of the deep-seated fear of a "national" or "standing" army. The same First Congress that approved the right to keep and bear arms also limited the national army to 840 men; Congress in the Second Amendment then provided: 3

> A well regulated Militia, being necessary to the security of a free State, the right of the people to keep and bear Arms, shall not be infringed.

In the 1789 debate in Congress on James Madison's proposed Bill of Rights, Elbridge Gerry argued that a state militia was necessary: 4

> . . . to prevent the establishment of a standing army, the bane of liberty . . . Whenever governments mean to invade the rights and liberties of the people, they always attempt to destroy the militia in order to raise an army upon their ruins.

Warren E. Burger was Chief Justice of the United States from 1969 to 1986. This article is from the January 14, 1990 issue of *Parade* magazine.

5 We see that the need for a state militia was the predicate of the "right" guaranteed; in short, it was declared "necessary" in order to have a state military force to protect the security of the state. That Second Amendment clause must be read as though the word "because" was the opening word of the guarantee. Today, of course, the "state militia" serves a very different purpose. A huge national defense establishment has taken over the role of the militia of 200 years ago.

6 Some have exploited these ancient concerns, blurring sporting guns — rifles, shotguns, and even machine pistols — with all firearms, including what are now called "Saturday night specials." There is, of course, a great different between sporting guns and handguns. Some regulation of handguns has long been accepted as imperative; laws relating to "concealed weapons" are common. That we may be "overregulated" in some areas of life has never held us back from more regulation of automobiles, airplanes, motorboats, and "concealed weapons."

7 Let's look at the history.

8 First, many of the 3.5 million people living in the thirteen original Colonies depended on wild game for food, and a good many of them required firearms for their defense from marauding Indians — and later from the French and English. Underlying all these needs was an important concept that each able-bodied man in each of the thirteen independent states had to help or defend his state.

9 The early opposition to the idea of national or standing armies was maintained under the Articles of Confederation; that confederation had no standing army and wanted none. The state militia — essentially a part-time citizen army, as in Switzerland today — was the only kind of "army" they wanted. From the time of the Declaration of Independence through the victory at Yorktown in 1781, George Washington, as the commander in chief of these volunteer-militia armies, had to depend upon the states to send those volunteers.

10 When a company of New Jersey militia volunteers reported for duty to Washington at Valley Forge, the men initially declined to take an oath to "the United States," maintaining, "Our country is New Jersey." Massachusetts Bay men, Virginians, and others felt the same way. To the American of the eighteenth century, his state was his country, and his freedom was defended by his militia.

11 The victory at Yorktown — and the ratification of the Bill of Rights a decade later — did not change people's attitudes about a national army. They had lived for years under the notion that each state would maintain its own military establishment, and the seaboard states had their own navies as well. These people, and their fathers and grandfathers before them, remembered how monarchs had used standing armies to oppress their ancestors in Europe. Americans wanted no part of this. A state

militia, like a rifle and powder horn, was as much a part of life as the automobile is today; pistols were largely for officers, aristocrats — and dueling.

Against this background, it was not surprising that the provision concerning firearms emerged in very simple terms with the significant predicate — basing the right on the *necessity* for a "well regulated militia," a state army. 12

In the two centuries since then — with two world wars and some lesser ones — it has become clear, sadly, that we have no choice but to maintain a standing national army while still maintaining a "militia" by way of the National Guard, which can be swiftly integrated into the national defense forces. 13

Americans also have a right to defend their homes, and we need not challenge that. Nor does anyone seriously question that the Constitution protects the right of hunters to own and keep sporting guns for hunting game any more than anyone would challenge the right to own and keep fishing rods and other equipment for fishing — or to own automobiles. To "keep and bear arms" for hunting today is essentially a recreational activity and not an imperative of survival, as it was 200 years ago; "Saturday night specials" and machine guns are not recreational weapons and surely are as much in need of regulation as motor vehicles. 14

Americans should ask themselves a few questions. The Constitution does not mention automobiles or motorboats, but the right to keep and own an automobile is beyond question; equally beyond question is the power of the state to regulate the purchase or the transfer of such a vehicle and the right to license the vehicle and the driver with reasonable standards. In some places, even a bicycle must be registered, as must some household dogs. 15

If we are to stop this mindless homicidal carnage, is it unreasonable: 16

1. to provide that, to acquire a firearm, an application be made reciting age, residence, employment, and any prior criminal convictions?
2. to require that this application lie on the table for ten days (absent a showing for urgent need) before the license would be issued?
3. that the transfer of a firearm be made essentially as that of a motor vehicle?
4. to have a "ballistic fingerprint" of the firearm made by the manufacturer and filed with the license record so that, if a bullet is found in a victim's body, law enforcement might be helped in finding the culprit?

These are the kinds of questions the American people must answer if we are to preserve the "domestic tranquility" promised in the Constitution. 17

Discussion Questions

1. Why does Burger recount the history of the Second Amendment so fully? Explain his reason for arguing that the Second Amendment does not guarantee the right of individuals to "bear arms."
2. Burger also uses history to argue that there is a difference between legislation against sporting guns and legislation against handguns. Summarize his argument.
3. How effective is his analogy between licensing vehicles and licensing handguns?

Writing Suggestions

1. Other people interpret "the right to bear arms" differently. Look at some of their arguments and write an essay summarizing their interpretations and defending them.
2. Burger outlines a policy for registration of handguns that would prevent criminal use. But at least one sociologist has pointed out that most guns used by criminals are obtained illegally. Examine and evaluate some of the arguments claiming that registration is generally ineffective.
3. Analyze arguments of the National Rifle Association, the nation's largest gun lobby. Do they answer Burger's claims?

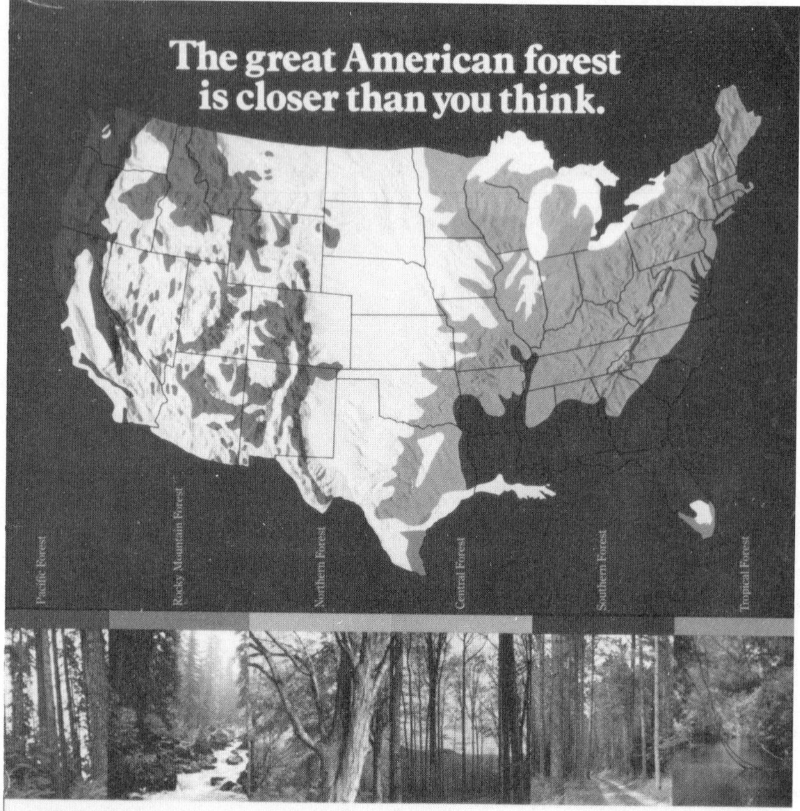

Wherever you are.

Because after giving up land to build our cities and highways, after meeting our constantly growing demands for wood and paper products, we still have three-fourths as much forestland as we had when Columbus landed.

Even more surprising, this 761 *million* acres is still widely distributed all across the country—it's not all just "out West" or "down South." 51% of New York State is forest. 65% of Rhode Island. And 51% of New Jersey—the most densely populated state. As a matter of fact, more than half of the forest in the continental United States is located in the eastern part of the country.

Because America's forest is truly an *American* forest, growing in many different elevations and rainfalls and temperatures and soils, its six distinct natural regions provide us with a constant variety, too, from the Douglas firs of the Northwest to the hardwoods of the Northeast.

Much of the forest has been harvested and regrown three or four times. And, public or private, government or individually owned, much of it is available for hunting and fishing, picnicking and camping—as millions of outdoorsmen from Maine to California can tell you. So if you haven't seen it lately, why wait?

It's right there in your backyard, keeping America green—and growing.

For the whole story on America's forest today, get "Forests USA." For your copy of this full-color, 16 page booklet, send 25¢ to AFI, 1619 Massachusetts Avenue, N.W., Washington, D.C. 20036

Name

Address

City

State Zip

American Forest Institute

Discussion Questions

1. What fears does this ad respond to? Does it succeed in reassuring the reader? If so, how?
2. How does the advertiser go beyond the facts to reach the audience?

The initials of a friend
You will find these letters on many tools by which electricity works. They are on great generators used by electric light and power companies; and on lamps that light millions of homes.
They are on big motors that pull railway trains; and on tiny motors that make hard housework easy.
By such tools electricity dispels the dark and lifts heavy burdens from human shoulders. Hence the letters G-E are more than a trademark. They are an emblem of service—the initials of a friend.
GENERAL ELECTRIC

This advertisement first appeared in 1923. Today, you'll find our initials on many more things — from appliances, plastics, motors and lighting to financial services and medical equipment. Wherever you see our initials, we want them to mean the same thing to you — the initials of a friend.

We bring good things to life.

Discussion Questions

1. To what need does the ad make an appeal?
2. What devices in the ad — both objects and the choice of objects to discuss — contribute to the effectiveness of the message?
3. How does the company's present-day slogan compare?

Nuclear energy can help America find a way out of our dangerous dependence on foreign oil

Oil imports are increasing to dangerous levels. As the uncertainty in the Persian Gulf continues, the ability to rely on America's nuclear energy becomes more important than ever.

During the 1973 embargo, when we were importing 35% of our oil, prices skyrocketed as supply nose-dived. In the last 18 months, America's dependence on OPEC oil has increased dramatically. We're even more dependent now than we were in 1973. Oil imports have risen by over 25% while domestic oil production has fallen nearly 10%. Looking to the future, the situation is even worse.

In fact, if projections from the Department of Energy are correct, America may be importing as much as 50% of our oil by 1990. That would seriously jeopardize our national energy security.

Nuclear Energy Saves Oil

Electricity generated from America's 108 commercial nuclear electric plants saves us over 750,000 barrels of oil a day. Every day. Without nuclear energy's contribution, we would need to import even more foreign oil than we already do.

Nuclear Energy for the Future

America's use of electricity has been growing steadily to fuel our growing economy. At current growth rates, electricity demand will overtake supply in the early 1990s.

New nuclear electric plants should be in planning *now*. But they are not, despite the fact that most Americans believe that nuclear energy is important and that we will need more.

Too many financial, political, licensing, and regulatory uncertainties stand in the way of America's being able to fully utilize its nuclear energy resources. For example, it has taken some plants as long as 12 years to be completed. If nothing changes, that means that a plant begun now might not be operating before the year 2000.

As America's economy continues to grow, America must find ways to keep pace with its growing electricity needs. Nuclear energy can play a major role in meeting those needs as well as keeping us less dependent on foreign oil.

For a free booklet on energy independence, write to the U.S. Council for Energy Awareness, P.O. Box 66103, Dept. NS02, Washington, D.C. 20035. Please allow 2-3 weeks for delivery.

Information about energy America can count on
U.S. COUNCIL FOR ENERGY AWARENESS

©1988 USCEA

As seen in March 1988 issues of Reader's Digest, National Geographic, Newsweek, U.S. News & World Report, The Economist, and State Legislatures and in April 1988 issues of National Geographic, TIME, Newsweek, Sports Illustrated, U.S. News & World Report, Smithsonian, Forbes, Scientific American, Natural History, National Journal, and State Legislatures.

Discussion Questions

1. How does the format of the ad affect the message?
2. What words in the headline are meant to rouse an emotional response in the reader?
3. How are the objections to nuclear energy handled?
4. Is this a successful policy claim?

EXERCISES FOR REVIEW

1. Look for personal advertisements (in which men and women advertise for various kinds of companionship) in a local or national paper or magazine. (The *Village Voice*, a New York paper, is an outstanding source.) What inferences can you draw about the people who place these particular ads? About the "facts" they choose to provide? How did you come to these conclusions? You might also try to infer the reasons that more men than women place ads and why this might be changing.
2. "I like Colonel Sanders" is the title of an article that praises ugly architecture, shopping malls, laundromats, and other symbols of "plastic" America. The author claims that these aspects of the American scene have unique and positive values. Defend or refute his claim by pointing out what the values of these things might be, giving reasons for your own assessments.
3. A psychiatrist says that in pro football personality traits determine the positions of the players. Write an essay developing this idea and providing adequate evidence for your claim. Or make inferences about the relationship between the personalities of the players and another sport that you know well.
4. At least one city in the world — Reykjavik, the capital of Iceland — bans dogs from the city. Defend or attack this policy by using both facts and values to support your claim.
5. Write a review of a movie, play, television program, concert, restaurant, or book. Make clear your criteria for judgment and their order of importance.
6. The controversy concerning seat belts and air bags in automobiles has generated a variety of proposals, one of which is mandatory use of seat belts in all the states. Make your own policy claim regarding laws about safety devices (the wearing of motorcycle helmets is another thorny subject), and defend it by using both facts and values — facts about safety, values concerning individual freedom and responsibility.
7. Select a ritual with which you are familiar and argue for or against the value it represents. *Examples*: the high school prom, Christmas gift-giving, a fraternity initiation, a wedding, a confirmation or bar mitzvah, a funeral ceremony, a Fourth of July celebration.
8. Choose a recommended policy — from the school newspaper or elsewhere — and argue that it will or will not work to produce beneficial changes. *Examples*: expansion of core requirements, comprehensive tests as a graduation requirement, reinstitution of a physical education requirement, removal of junk food from vending machines.

CHAPTER 3

Definition

THE PURPOSES OF DEFINITION

Before we examine the other elements of argument, we need to consider definition, a component you may have to deal with early in writing an essay. Definition may be used in two ways: to clarify the meanings of vague or ambiguous terms or as a method of development for the whole essay. In some arguments your claims will contain words that need explanation before you can proceed with any discussion. But you may also want to devote an entire essay to the elaboration of a broad concept or experience that cannot be adequately defined in a shorter space.

The Roman statesman Cicero said, "Every rational discussion of anything whatsoever should begin with a definition in order to make clear what is the subject of dispute." You have probably already discovered the importance of definition in argument. If you have ever had a disagreement with your parents about using the car or drinking or dyeing your hair or going away for a weekend or staying out till three in the morning, you know that you were really arguing about the meaning of the term "adolescent freedom."

Arguments often revolve around definitions of crucial terms. For example, how does one define *democracy*? Does a democracy guarantee freedom of the press, freedom of worship, freedom of assembly, freedom of movement? In the United States, we would argue that such freedoms are essential to any definition of *democracy*. But countries in which these freedoms are nonexistent also represent themselves as democracies or governments of the people. In the words of Senator Daniel J. Moynihan, "For years now the most brutal totalitarian regimes have called themselves 'people's' or 'democratic' republics." Rulers in such governments are aware that defining their regimes as democratic may win the approval of people who would otherwise condemn them. In his formidable attack on totalitarianism, *Nineteen Eighty-Four*, George Orwell coined the slogans "War Is Peace" and "Slavery Is Freedom," phrases that represent the corrupt use of definition to distort reality.

But even where there is no intention to deceive, the snares of definition are difficult to avoid. How do you define *abortion*? Is it "termination of pregnancy"? Or is it "murder of an unborn child"? During a celebrated trial in 1975 of a physician who performed an abortion and was accused of manslaughter, the prosecution often used the word *baby* to refer to the fetus, but the defense referred to "the products of conception." These definitions of *fetus* reflected the differing judgments of those on opposite sides. Not only do judgments create definitions; definitions influence judgments. In the abortion trial, the definitions of *fetus* used by both sides were meant to promote either approval or disapproval of the doctor's action.

Definitions can indeed change the nature of an event or a "fact." How many farms are there in the state of New York? The answer to the question depends on the definition of *farm*. In 1979 the *New York Times* reported:

> Because of a change in the official definition of the word "farm," New York lost 20 percent of its farms on January 1, with numbers dropping from 56,000 to 45,000. . . .
>
> Before the change, a farm was defined as "any place from which $250 or more of agricultural products is sold" yearly or "any place of 10 acres or more from which $50 or more of agricultural products is sold" yearly. Now a farm is "any place from which $1,000 or more of agricultural products is sold" in a year.[1]

A change in the definition of poverty can have similar results. An article in the *New York Times*, whose headline reads, "Who's in Poverty? Depends on Definition," makes this clear.

[1] *New York Times*, March 4, 1979, Sec. 1, p. 40.

> The official poverty definition includes money income only. According to this definition 13.5 percent of Americans . . . were below the poverty threshold in 1987. [But] including the value of noncash benefits, such as food stamps, subsidized housing, and Medicare . . . reduces the general poverty level to 8.5 percent.[2]

The differences in the numbers are wholly a matter of definition, as the editorial writer recognizes by inserting the phrase, "According to this definition." Such differences can, of course, have serious personal consequences for those who are being defined.

In fact, local and federal courts almost every day redefine traditional concepts that can have a direct impact on our everyday lives. The definition of the family, for example, has undergone significant changes that acknowledge the existence of new relationships. (See "Here Comes the Groom" on page 164.) In January 1990 the New Jersey Supreme Court ruled that a family may be defined as "one or more persons occupying a dwelling unit as a single nonprofit housekeeping unit, who are living together as a stable and permanent living unit, being a traditional family unit or the *functional equivalent* thereof" (italics added). This meant that ten Glassboro State College students, unrelated by blood, could continue to occupy a single-family house despite the objection of the borough of Glassboro.[3]

DEFINING THE TERMS IN YOUR ARGUMENT

In some of your arguments you will introduce terms that require definition. We've pointed out that a definition of poverty is crucial to any debate on the existence of poverty in the United States. The same may be true in a debate about the legality of euthanasia, or mercy killing. Are the arguers referring to passive euthanasia, that is, the withdrawal of life-support systems, or to active euthanasia, in which death is hastened through the direct administration of drugs?

It is not uncommon, in fact, for arguments about controversial questions to turn into arguments about the definition of terms. If, for example, you wanted to argue in favor of the regulation of religious cults, you would first have to define *cult*. In so doing, you might discover that it is not easy to distinguish clearly between conventional religions and cults. Then you would have to define *regulation*, spelling out the legal restric-

---

[2] *New York Times*, November 2, 1988, Sec. B, p. 1.

[3] *New York Times*, February 1, 1990, Sec. B, p. 5.

tions you favored so as to make them apply only to cults, not to established religions. An argument on the subject might end almost before it began if writer and reader could not agree on definitions of these terms. While clear definitions do not guarantee agreement, they do ensure that all parties understand the nature of the argument.

Defining Vague and Ambiguous Terms

You will need to define other terms in addition to those in your claim. If you use words and phrases that have two or more meanings, they may appear vague and ambiguous to your reader. In arguments of value and policy abstract terms such as *freedom, justice, patriotism*, and *equality* require clarification. Despite their vagueness, however, they are among the most important in the language because they represent the ideals that shape our laws. When conflicts arise, the courts must define these terms to establish the legality of certain practices. Is the Ku Klux Klan permitted to make disparaging public statements about ethnic and racial groups? That depends on the court's definition of "free speech." Can execution for some crimes be considered "cruel and unusual punishment"? That, too, depends on the court's definition of "cruel and unusual punishment." In addition, such terms as *happiness*, *mental health*, *success*, and *creativity* often defy precise definition because they reflect the differing values within a society or a culture.

The definition of *success*, for example, varies not only among social groups but also among individuals within the group. One scientist has postulated five signs by which to judge the measure of success: wealth (including health), security (confidence in retaining the wealth), reputation, performance, and contentment.[4] Consider whether all of these are necessary to your own definition of *success*. If not, which may be omitted? Do you think others should be added? Notice that one of the signs — reputation — depends on definition by the community; another — contentment — can be measured only by the individual. The assessment of performance probably owes something to both the group and the individual.

Christopher Atkins, a young actor, gave an interviewer an example of an externalized definition of success, that is, a definition based on the standards imposed by other people:

> Success to me is judged through the eyes of others. I mean, if you're walking around saying, "I own a green Porsche," you might meet somebody who says, "Hey, that's no big deal, I own a green Porsche and a house." So all of a sudden, you don't feel so successful. Really, it's in the eyes of others.[5]

---

[4] Gwynn Nettler, *Social Concerns* (New York: McGraw-Hill, 1976), pp. 196–197.
[5] *New York Times*, August 6, 1982, Sec. III, p. 8.

So difficult is the formulation of a universally accepted measure for success that some scholars regard the concept as meaningless. Nevertheless, we continue to use the word as if it represented a definable concept because the idea of success, however defined, is important for the identity and development of the individual and the group. It is clear, however, that when crossing subcultural boundaries, even within a small group, we need to be aware of differences in the use of the word. If "contentment" — that is, the satisfaction of achieving a small personal goal — is enough, then a person lying under a palm tree subsisting on handouts from picnickers may be a success. But you should not expect all your readers to agree that these criteria are enough to define *success*.

In arguing about aesthetic matters, whose vocabulary is almost always abstract, the criteria for judgment must be revealed, either directly or indirectly, and then the abstract terms that represent the criteria must be defined. If you want to say that a film is distinguished by great acting, have you made clear what you mean by *great*? That we do not always understand or agree on the definition of *great* is apparent, say, on the morning after the Oscar winners have been announced.

Even subjects that you feel sure you can identify may offer surprising insights when you rethink them for an extended definition. One critic, defining rock music, argued that the distinguishing characteristic of rock music was *noise* — not the beat, not the harmonies, not the lyrics, not the vocal style, but noise, "nasty, discordant, irritating noise — or, to its practitioners, unfettered, liberating, expressive noise."[6] In producing this definition, the author had to give a number of examples to prove that he was justified in rejecting the most familiar criteria.

Robert Sommer, an architect who is critical of the "hard" architecture of prison cells, dormitory rooms, and public facilities such as picnic tables and restrooms, explains the meaning of *hard* by setting down its characteristics: strength, resistance to human imprint, lack of permeability between inside and out. He defines the last term by giving details.

> Often this [lack of permeability] means an absence of windows, a style referred to in Berkeley as post-revolutionary architecture. At first glance the Bank of America on Berkeley's Telegraph Avenue seems to have windows but these are really reflecting metal surfaces. The new postal center in Oakland, with its tiny slit windows, looks as if it were intended for urban guerrilla warfare. Older buildings that still have plate glass use steel shutters and gates that can be drawn across the exterior in a matter of minutes. Some corpora-

---

[6] Jon Pareles, "Noise Evokes Modern Chaos for a Band," *New York Times*, March 9, 1986, Sec. H., p. 26.

tions are moving their data-processing machinery underground where they are less vulnerable to attack.[7]

References to other matters of taste outside the arts — food, fashion, cars — also require definition of criteria if arguer and reader are to understand one another. How does the reviewer define "very good" for the restaurant to which she awards two stars? How does the wearer define Jordache jeans as "better" than Wrangler jeans? How does the maker of a Mercedes-Benz define its car as "superior" to a BMW?

METHODS FOR DEFINING TERMS

The following strategies for defining terms in an argument are by no means mutually exclusive. You may use all of them in a single argumentative essay.

Dictionary Definition

Giving a dictionary definition is the simplest and most obvious way to define a term. An unabridged dictionary is the best source because it usually gives examples of the way a word can be used in a sentence; that is, it furnishes the proper context.

In many cases, the dictionary definition alone is not sufficient. It may be too broad or too narrow for your purpose. Suppose, in an argument about pornography, you wanted to define the word *obscene. Webster's New International Dictionary* (third edition, unabridged) gives the definition of *obscene* as "offensive to taste; foul; loathsome; disgusting." But these synonyms do not tell you what qualities make an object or an event or an action "foul," "loathsome," and "disgusting." In 1973 the Supreme Court, attempting to narrow the definition of *obscenity*, ruled that obscenity was to be determined by the community in accordance with local standards. One person's obscenity, as numerous cases have demonstrated, may be another person's art. The celebrated trials in the early twentieth century about the distribution of novels regarded as pornographic — D. H. Lawrence's *Lady Chatterley's Lover* and James Joyce's *Ulysses* — emphasized the problems of defining obscenity.

Another dictionary definition may strike you as too narrow. *Patriotism*, for example, is defined in one dictionary as "love and loyal or zealous

---

[7] Robert Sommer, *Tight Spaces: Hard Architecture and How to Humanize It* (Englewood Cliffs, NJ: Prentice-Hall, 1974), p. 7.

support of one's country, especially in all matters involving other countries." Some readers may want to include an unwillingness to support government policies they consider wrong.

Stipulation

In stipulating the meaning of a term, the writer asks the reader to accept a definition that may be different from the conventional one. He or she does this in order to limit or control the argument. Someone has said, "Part of the task of keeping definitions in our civilization clear and pure is to keep a firm democratic rein on those with the power, or craving the power, to stipulate meaning." Perhaps this writer was thinking of a term like *national security*, which can be defined by a nation's leaders in such a way as to sanction persecution of citizens and reckless military adventures. Likewise, a term such as *liberation* can be appropriated by terrorist groups whose activities often lead to oppression rather than liberation.

Religion is usually defined as a belief in a supernatural power to be obeyed and worshiped. But in an article entitled "Civil Religion in America," a sociologist offers a different meaning.

> While some have argued that Christianity is the national faith, and others that church and synagogue celebrate only the generalized religion of "the American way of life," few have realized that there actually exists alongside of and rather clearly differentiated from the churches an elaborate and well-institutionalized civil religion in America. This article argues not only that there is such a thing, but also that this religion . . . has its own seriousness and integrity and requires the same care in understanding that any other religion does.[8]

When the author adds, "This religion — there seems no other word for it — was neither sectarian nor in any specific sense Christian," he emphasizes that he is distinguishing his definition of religion from definitions that associate religion and church.

Even the word *violence*, which the dictionary defines as "physical force used so as to injure or damage" and whose meaning seems so clear and uncompromising, can be manipulated to produce a definition different from the one normally understood by most people. Some pacifists refer to conditions in which "people are deprived of choices in a systematic way" as "institutionalized quiet violence." Even where no physical force is employed, this lack of choice in the schools, in the workplace, in the black ghettos is defined as violence.[9]

---

[8] Robert N. Bellah, "Civil Religion in America," *Daedalus*, Winter 1967, p. 1.

[9] Newton Garver, "What Violence Is," in *Moral Choices*, edited by James Rachels (New York: Harper and Row, 1971), pp. 248–249.

In *Through the Looking-Glass* Alice asked Humpty Dumpty "whether you can make words mean so many different things."

"When I use a word," Humpty Dumpty said scornfully, "it means just what I choose it to mean, neither more nor less."[10]

A writer, however, is not free to invent definitions that no one will recognize or that create rather than solve problems between writer and reader.

Negation

To avoid confusion it is sometimes helpful to tell the reader what a term is *not*. In discussing euthanasia, a writer might say, "By euthanasia I do not mean active intervention to hasten the death of the patient."

A negative definition may be more extensive, depending on the complexity of the term and the writer's ingenuity. The critic of rock music quoted earlier in this chapter arrived at his definition by rejecting attributes that seemed misleading. The ex-Communist Whittaker Chambers, in a foreword to a book on the spy trial of Alger Hiss, defined communism this way:

> First, let me try to say what Communism is not. It is not simply a vicious plot hatched by wicked men in a subcellar. It is not just the writings of Marx and Lenin, dialectical materialism, the Politburo, the labor theory of value, the theory of the general strike, the Red Army secret police, labor camps, underground conspiracy, the dictatorship of the proletariat, the technique of the coup d'état. It is not even those chanting, bannered millions that stream periodically, like disorganized armies, through the heart of the world's capitals: Moscow, New York, Tokyo, Paris, Rome. These are expressions, but they are not what Communism is about.[11]

This, of course, is only part of the definition. Any writer beginning a definition in the negative must go on to define what the term *is*.

Examples

One of the most effective ways of defining terms in an argument is the use of examples. Both real and hypothetical examples can bring life to abstract and ambiguous terms. The writer in the following passage defines *preferred categories* (classes of people who are meant to benefit from affirmative action policies) by invoking specific cases:

---

[10] Lewis Carroll, *Alice in Wonderland and Through the Looking-Glass* (New York: Grosset and Dunlap, 1948), p. 238.

[11] *Witness* (New York: Random House, 1952), p. 8.

The absence of definitions points up one of the problems with preferred categories. . . . These preferred categories take no account of family wealth or educational advantages. A black whose father is a judge or physician deserves preferential treatment over any nonminority applicant. The latter might have fought his way out of the grinding poverty of Appalachia, or might be the first member of an Italian-American or a Polish-American family to complete high school. But no matter.[12]

Insanity is a word that has been used and misused to describe a variety of conditions. Even psychiatrists are in dispute about its meaning. In the following anecdote, examples narrow and refine the definition.

Dr. Zilboorg says that present-day psychiatry does not possess any satisfactory definition of mental illness or neurosis. To illustrate, he told a story: A psychiatrist was recently asked for a definition of a "well-adjusted person" (not even slightly peculiar). The definition: "A person who feels in harmony with himself and who is not in conflict with his environment." It sounded fine, but up popped a heckler. "Would you then consider an anti-Nazi working in the underground against Hitler a maladjusted person?" "Well," the psychiatrist hemmed, "I withdraw the latter part of my definition." Dr. Zilboorg withdrew the first half for him. Many persons in perfect harmony with themselves, he pointed out, are in "distinctly pathological states."[13]

Extended Definition

When we speak of an extended definition, we usually refer not only to length but also to the variety of methods for developing the definition. Let's take the word *materialism*. A dictionary entry offers the following sentence fragments as definitions: "1. the doctrine that comfort, pleasure, and wealth are the only or highest goals or values. 2. the tendency to be more concerned with material than with spiritual goals or values." But the term *materialism* has acquired so many additional meanings, especially emotional ones, that an extended definition serves a useful purpose in clarifying the many different ideas surrounding our understanding of the term.

Below is a much longer definition of *materialism*, which appears at the beginning of an essay entitled "People and Things: Reflections on Materialism."[14]

There are two contemporary usages of the term, materialism, and it is important to distinguish between them. On the one hand we can talk about

---

[12] Anthony Lombardo, "Quotas Work Both Ways," *U.S. Catholic*, February 1974, p. 39.

[13] Quoted in *The Art of Making Sense*, p. 48.

[14] Mihaly Csikszentmihalyi and Eugene Rochberg-Halton, "People and Things: Reflections on Materialism," *University of Chicago Magazine*, Spring 1978, pp. 7–8.

> *instrumental materialism*, or the use of material objects to make life longer, safer, more enjoyable. By instrumental, we mean that objects act as essential means for discovering and furthering personal values and goals of life, so that the objects are instruments used to realize and further those goals. There is little negative connotation attached to this meaning of the word, since one would think that it is perfectly sensible to use things for such purposes. While it is true that the United States is the epitome of materialism in this sense, it is also true that most people in every society aspire to reach our level of instrumental materialism.
>
> On the other hand the term has a more negative connotation, which might be conveyed by the phrase *terminal materialism*. This is the sense critics use when they apply the term to Americans. What they mean is that we not only use our material resources as instruments to make life more manageable, but that we reduce our ultimate goals to the possession of things. They believe that we don't just use our cars to get from place to place, but that we consider the ownership of expensive cars one of the central values in life. Terminal materialism means that the object is valued only because it indicates an end in itself, a possession. In instrumental materialism there is a sense of directionality, in which a person's goals may be furthered through the interactions with the object. A book, for example, can reveal new possibilities or widen a person's view of the world, or an old photograph can be cherished because it embodies a relationship. But in terminal materialism, there is no sense of reciprocal interaction in the relation between the object and the end. The end is valued as final, not as itself a means to further ends. And quite often it is only the status label or image associated with the object that is valued, rather than the actual object.

In the essay from which this passage is taken, the authors distinguish between two kinds of materialism and provide an extended explanation, using contrast and examples as methods of development. They are aware that the common perception of materialism, the love of things for their own sake, is a negative one. But this view, according to the authors, doesn't fully account for the attitudes of many Americans toward the things they own. There is, in fact, another more positive meaning that the authors call *instrumental materialism*. You will recognize that the authors are *stipulating* a meaning with which their readers might not be familiar. In their essay they distinguish between *terminal materialism*, in which "the object is valued only because it indicates an end in itself" and *instrumental materialism*, "the use of material objects to make life longer, safer, more enjoyable." Since *instrumental materialism* is the less familiar definition, the essay provides a great number of examples that show how people of three different generations value photographs, furniture, musical instruments, plants, and other objects for their memories and personal associations rather than as proof of the owners' ability to acquire the objects or win the approval of others.

THE DEFINITION ESSAY

The argumentative essay can take the form of an extended definition. An example of such an essay is the one from which we've just quoted, as well as the three essays at the end of this chapter. The definition essay is appropriate when the idea under consideration is so controversial or so heavy with historical connotations that even a paragraph or two cannot make clear exactly what the arguer wants his or her readers to understand. For example, if you were preparing a definition of patriotism, you would want to answer some or all of the following questions. You would probably use a number of methods to develop your definition: personal narrative, examples, stipulation, comparison and contrast, and cause and effect analysis.

1. *Dictionary Definition.* Is the dictionary definition the one I will elaborate on? Do I need to stipulate other meanings?
2. *Personal History.* Where did I first acquire my notions of patriotism? What was taught? How and by whom was it taught?
3. *Cultural Context.* Has my patriotic feeling changed in the last few years? Why or why not? Does my own patriotism reflect the mood of the country or the group to which I belong?
4. *Values.* What is the value of patriotism? Does it make me more humane, more civilized? Is patriotism consistent with tolerance of other systems and cultures? Is patriotism the highest duty of a citizen? Do any other values take precedence? What was the meaning of President Kennedy's injunction: "Ask not what your country can do for you; ask rather what you can do for your country"?
5. *Behavior.* How do I express my patriotism (or lack of it)? Can it be expressed through dissent? What sacrifice, if any, would I make for my country?

WRITING AN ESSAY OF DEFINITION

The following list suggests several important steps to be taken in writing an essay of definition.

1. Choose a term that needs definition because it is controversial or ambiguous, or because you want to offer a personal definition that differs from the accepted interpretation. Explain why an extended definition is necessary. Or choose an experience that lends itself to treatment in an extended definition. One student defined "culture shock" as she

had experienced it while studying abroad in Hawaii among students of a different ethnic background.

2. Decide on the thesis — the point of view you wish to develop about the term you are defining. If you want to define "heroism," for example, you may choose to develop the idea that this quality depends on motivation and awareness of danger rather than on the specific act performed by the hero.
3. Begin by consulting the dictionary for the conventional definition, the one with which most readers will be familiar. Make clear whether you want to elaborate on the dictionary definition or take issue with it because you think it is misleading or inadequate.
4. Distinguish wherever possible between the term you are defining and other terms with which it might be confused. If you are defining "love," can you make a clear distinction between the different kinds of emotional attachments contained in the word?
5. Try to think of several methods of developing the definition — using examples, comparison and contrast, analogy, cause and effect analysis. However, you may discover that one method alone — say, use of examples — will suffice to narrow and refine your definition. See the sample essay "The Nature of Prejudice" on page 92 for an example of such a development.
6. Arrange your supporting material in an order that gives emphasis to the most important ideas.

SAMPLE ANALYSIS

The Missing Element: Moral Courage

BARBARA TUCHMAN

What I want to say is concerned less with leadership than with its absence, that is, with the evasion of leadership. Not in the physical sense, for we have, if anything, a superabundance of leaders — hundreds of Pied Pipers, or would-be Pied Pipers, running about, ready and anxious to lead the population. They are scurrying around, collecting consensus, gathering as wide an acceptance as possible. But what they are *not* doing, very notably, is standing still and saying, "*This is* what I believe. This I will do and that I will not do. This is my code of behavior and that is outside it. This is excellent and that is trash." There is an abdication of moral leadership in the sense of a general unwillingness to state standards. 1

Of all the ills that our poor criticized, analyzed, sociologized society is heir to, the focal one, it seems to me, from which so much of our uneasiness and confusion derive is the absence of standards. We are too unsure of ourselves to assert them, to stick by them, or if necessary, in the case of persons who occupy positions of authority, to impose them. We seem to be afflicted by a widespread and eroding reluctance to take any stand on any values, moral, behavioral, or aesthetic. 2

Everyone is afraid to call anything wrong, or vulgar, or fraudulent, or just bad taste or bad manners. Congress, for example, pussyfooted for months (following years of apathy) before taking action on a member convicted by the courts of illegalities; and when they finally got around to unseating him, one suspects they did it for the wrong motives. In 1922, in England, a man called Horatio Bottomley, a rather flamboyant character and popular demagogue — very similar in type, by the way, to Adam Clayton Powell, with similarly elastic financial ethics — who founded a paper called *John Bull* and got himself elected to Parliament, was found guilty of misappropriating the funds which his readers subscribed to victory bonds and other causes promoted by his paper. The day after the verdict, he was expelled from the House of Commons, with no fuss and 3

Barbara Tuchman (1912–1989) was a historian and the author of many popular, prize-winning books including *The Guns of August* (1962), *A Distant Mirror: The Calamitous 14th Century* (1978), *The March of Folly* (1984), and *The First Salute: A View of the American Revolution* (1988).

very little debate, except for a few friendly farewells, as he was rather an engaging fellow. But no member thought the House had any other course to consider: Out he went. I do not suggest that this represents a difference between British and American morality; the difference is in the *times.*

Our time is one of disillusion in our species and a resulting lack of self-confidence — for good historical reasons. Man's recent record has not been reassuring. After engaging in the Great War with all its mud and blood and ravaged ground, its disease, destruction, and death, we allowed ourselves a bare twenty years before going at it all over again. And the second time was accompanied by an episode of man's inhumanity to man of such enormity that its implications for all of us have not yet, I think, been fully measured. A historian has recently stated that for such a phenomenon as the planned and nearly accomplished extermination of a people to take place, one of three preconditions necessary was public indifference. 4

Since then the human species has been busy overbreeding, polluting the air, destroying the balance of nature, and bungling in a variety of directions so that it is no wonder we have begun to doubt man's capacity for good judgment. It is hardly surprising that the self-confidence of the nineteenth century and its belief in human progress has been dissipated. "Every great civilization," said Secretary Gardner last year, "has been characterized by confidence in itself." At mid-twentieth century, the supply is low. As a result, we tend to shy away from all judgments. We hesitate to label anything wrong, and therefore hesitate to require the individual to bear moral responsibility for his acts. 5

We have become afraid to fix blame. Murderers and rapists and muggers and persons who beat up old men and engage in other forms of assault are not guilty; society is guilty; society has wronged them; society beats its breast and says *mea culpa* — it is our fault, not the wrongdoer's. The wrongdoer, poor fellow, could not help himself. 6

I find this very puzzling because I always ask myself, in these cases, what about the many neighbors of the wrongdoer, equally poor, equally disadvantaged, equally sufferers from society's neglect, who nevertheless maintain certain standards of social behavior, who do *not* commit crimes, who do not murder for money or rape for kicks. How does it happen that they know the difference between right and wrong, and how long will they abide by the difference if the leaders and opinion-makers and pace-setters continue to shy away from bringing home responsibility to the delinquent? 7

Admittedly, the reluctance to condemn stems partly from a worthy instinct — *tout comprendre, c'est tout pardonner* — and from a rejection of what was often the hypocrisy of Victorian moral standards. True, there was a large component of hypocrisy in nineteenth-century morality. 8

Since the advent of Freud, we know more, we understand more about human behavior, we are more reluctant to cast the first stone — to condemn — which is a good thing; but the pendulum has swung to the point where we are now afraid to place moral responsibility at all. Society, that large amorphous, nonspecific scapegoat, must carry the burden for each of us, relieving us of guilt. We have become so indoctrinated by the terrors lurking in the dark corridors of the guilt complex that guilt has acquired a very bad name. Yet a little guilt is not a dangerous thing; it has a certain social utility.

When it comes to guilt, a respected writer — respected in some circles — has told us, as her considered verdict on the Nazi program, that evil is banal — a word that means something so ordinary that you are not bothered by it; the dictionary definition is "commonplace and hackneyed." Somehow that conclusion does not seem adequate or even apt. *Of course*, evil is commonplace; *of course* we all partake of it. Does that mean that we must withhold disapproval, and that when evil appears in dangerous degree or vicious form we must not condemn but only understand? That may be very Christian in intent, but in reality it is an escape from the necessity of exercising judgment — which exercise, I believe, is a prime function of leadership. 9

What it requires is courage — just a little, not very much — the courage to be independent and stand up for the standard values one believes in. That kind of courage is the quality most conspicuously missing, I think, in current life. I don't mean the courage to protest and walk around with picket signs or boo Secretary McNamara which, though it may stem from the right instinct, is a group thing that does not require any very stout spirit. I did it myself for Sacco and Vanzetti when I was about twelve and picketed in some now forgotten labor dispute when I was a freshman and even got arrested. There is nothing to that; if you don't do that sort of thing when you are eighteen, then there is something wrong with you. I mean, rather, a kind of lonely moral courage, the quality that attracted me to that odd character, Czar Reed, and to Lord Salisbury, neither of whom cared a rap for the opinion of the public or would have altered his conduct a hair to adapt to it. It is the quality someone said of Lord Palmerston was his "you-be-damnedness." That is the mood we need a little more of. 10

Standards of taste, as well as morality, need continued reaffirmation to stay alive, as liberty needs eternal vigilance. To recognize and to proclaim the difference between the good and the shoddy, the true and the fake, as well as between right and wrong, or what we believe at a given time to be right and wrong, is the obligation, I think, of persons who presume to lead, or are thrust into leadership, or hold positions of authority. That includes — whether they asked for it or not — all educators and even, I regret to say, writers. 11

For educators it has become increasingly the habit in the difficult circumstances of college administration today to find out what the students want in the matter of curriculum and deportment and then give it to them. This seems to me another form of abdication, another example of the prevailing reluctance to state a standard and expect, not to say require, performance in accord with it. The permissiveness, the yielding of decision to the student, does not — from what I can tell — promote responsibility in the young so much as uneasiness and a kind of anger at *not* being told what is expected of them, a resentment of their elders' unwillingness to take a position. Recently a student psychiatric patient of the Harvard Health Services was quoted by the director, Dr. Dana Farnsworth, as complaining, "My parents never tell me what to do. They never stop me from doing anything." That is the unheard wail, I think, extended beyond parents to the general absence of a guiding, reassuring pattern, which is behind much of society's current uneasiness. 12

It is human nature to want patterns and standards and a structure of behavior. A pattern to conform to is a kind of shelter. You see it in kindergarten and primary school, at least in those schools where the children when leaving the classroom are required to fall into line. When the teacher gives the signal, they fall in with alacrity; they know where they belong and they instinctively like to *be* where they belong. They like the feeling of being in line. 13

Most people need a structure, not only to fall into but to fall out of. The rebel with a cause is better off than the one without. At least he knows what he is "agin." He is not lost. He does not suffer from an identity crisis. It occurs to me that much of the student protest now may be a testing of authority, a search for that line to fall out of, and when it isn't there students become angrier because they feel more lost, more abandoned than ever. In the late turmoil at Berkeley, at least as regards the filthy speech demonstration, there was a missed opportunity, I think (however great my respect for Clark Kerr) for a hearty, emphatic, and unmistakable "No!" backed up by sanctions. Why? Because the act, even if intended as a demonstration of principle, was in this case, like any indecent exposure, simply offensive, and what is offensive to the greater part of society is antisocial, and what is antisocial, so long as we live in social groups and not each of us on his own island, must be curtailed, like Peeping Toms or obscene telephone calls, as a public nuisance. The issue is really not complicated or difficult but, if we would only look at it with more self-confidence, quite simple. 14

So, it seems to me, is the problem of the CIA. You will say that in this case people have taken a stand, opinion-makers have worked themselves into a moral frenzy. Indeed they have, but over a false issue. The CIA is not, after all, the Viet Cong or the Schutzstaffel in black shirts. Its initials do not stand for Criminal Indiscretions of America. It is an arm of the 15

American government, our elected, representative government (whatever may be one's feelings toward that body at the moment). Virtually every government in the world subsidizes youth groups, especially in the international relations, not to mention in athletic competitions. (I do not know if the CIA is subsidizing our Equestrian Team, but I know personally a number of people who would be only too delighted if it were.) The difficulty here is simply that the support was clandestine in the first place and not the proper job of the CIA in the second. An intelligence agency should be restricted to the gathering of intelligence and not extend itself into operations. In armies the two functions are distinct: intelligence is G2 and operations is G3. If our government could manage its functions with a little more precision and perform openly those functions that are perfectly respectable, there would be no issue. The recent excitement only shows how easily we succumb when reliable patterns or codes of conduct are absent, to a confusion of values.

A similar confusion exists, I think, with regard to the omnipresent 16
pornography that surrounds us like smog. A year ago the organization of my own profession, the Authors League, filed a brief *amicus curiae* in the appeal of Ralph Ginzburg, the publisher of a periodical called *Eros* and other items, who had been convicted of disseminating obscenity through the mails. The League's action was taken on the issue of censorship to which all good liberals automatically respond like Pavlov's dogs. Since at this stage in our culture pornography has so far gotten the upper hand that to do battle in its behalf against the dragon Censorship is rather like doing battle today against the bustle in behalf of short skirts, and since I believe that the proliferation of pornography in its sadistic forms is a greater social danger at the moment than censorship, and since Mr. Ginzburg was not an author anyway but a commercial promoter, I raised an objection, as a member of the Council, to the Authors League's spending its funds in the Ginzburg case. I was, of course, outvoted; in fact, there was no vote. Everyone around the table just sat and looked at me in cold disapproval. Later, after my objection was printed in the *Bulletin*, at my request, two distinguished authors wrote privately to me to express their agreement but did not go so far as to say so publicly.

Thereafter, when the Supreme Court upheld Mr. Ginzburg's convic- 17
tion, everyone in the intellectual community raised a hullaballoo about censorship advancing upon us like some sort of Frankenstein's monster. This seems to me another case of getting excited about the wrong thing. The cause of pornography is *not* the same as the cause of free speech. There *is* a difference. Ralph Ginzburg is *not* Theodore Dreiser and this is not the 1920s. If one looks around at the movies, especially the movie advertisements, and the novels and the pulp magazines glorifying perversion, and the paperbacks that make de Sade available to schoolchildren,

one does not get the impression that in the 1960s we are being stifled in the Puritan grip of Anthony Comstock. Here again, leaders — in this case authors and critics — seem too unsure of values or too afraid of being unpopular to stand up and assert the perfectly obvious difference between smut and free speech, or to say "Such and such is offensive and can be harmful." Happily, there are signs of awakening. In a *Times* review of a book called *On Iniquity* by Pamela Hansford Johnson, which related pornography to the Moors murders in England, the reviewer concluded that "this may be the opening of a discussion that must come, the opening shot."

In the realm of art, no less important than morals, the abdication of 18
judgment is almost a disease. Last fall when the Lincoln Center opened its glittering new opera house with a glittering new opera on the tragedy of Antony and Cleopatra, the curtain rose on a gaudy crowd engaged in energetic revels around a gold box in the shape of a pyramid, up whose sides (conveniently fitted with toe-holds, I suppose) several sinuous and reasonably nude slave girls were chased by lecherous guards left over from "Aida." When these preliminaries quieted down, the front of the gold box suddenly dropped open, and guess who was inside? No, it was not Cleopatra; it was Antony, looking, I thought, rather bewildered. What he was doing inside the box was never made clear. Thereafter everything happened — and in crescendos of gold and spangles and sequins, silks and gauzes, feathers, fans, jewels, brocades, and such a quantity of glitter that one began to laugh, thinking that the spectacle was intended as a parody of the old Shubert revue. But no, this was the Metropolitan Opera in the vaunted splendor of its most publicized opening since the Hippodrome. I gather it was Mr. Bing's idea of giving the first-night customers a fine splash. What he achieved was simply vulgarity, as at least some reviewers had the courage to say next day. Now, I cannot believe that Mr. Bing and his colleagues do not know the difference between honest artistry in stage design and pretentious ostentation. If they know better, why do they allow themselves to do worse? As leaders in their field of endeavor, they should have been setting standards of beauty and creative design, not debasing them.

One finds the same peculiarities in the visual arts. Non-art, as its prac- 19
titioners describe it — the blob school, the all-black canvasses, the paper cutouts and Campbell soup tins and plastic hamburgers and pieces of old carpet — is treated as art, not only by dealers whose motive is understandable (they have discovered that shock value sells); not only by a gullible pseudocultural section of the public who are not interested in art but in being "in" and wouldn't, to quote an old joke, know a Renoir from a Jaguar; but also, which I find mystifying, by the museums and the critics. I am sure they know the difference between the genuine and the hoax. But

not trusting their own judgment, they seem afraid to say no to anything, for fear, I suppose, of making a mistake and turning down what may be next decade's Matisse.

For the museums to exhibit the plastic hamburgers and twists of scrap iron is one thing, but for them to *buy* them for their permanent collection puts an imprimatur on what is fraudulent. Museum curators, too, are leaders who have an obligation to distinguish — I will not say the good from the bad in art because that is an elusive and subjective matter dependent on the eye of the time — but at least honest expression from phony. Most of what fills the galleries on Madison Avenue is simply stuff designed to take advantage of current fads and does not come from an artist's vision or an honest creative impulse. The dealers know it; the critics know it; the purveyors themselves know it; the public suspects it; but no one dares say it because that would be committing oneself to a standard of values and even, heaven forbid, exposing oneself to being called square. 20

In the fairy story, it required a child to cry out that the Emperor was naked. Let us not leave that task to the children. It should be the task of leaders to recognize and state the truth as they see it. It is their task not to be afraid of absolutes. 21

If the educated man is not willing to express standards, if he cannot show that he has them and applies them, what then is education for? Its purpose, I take it, is to form the civilized man, whom I would define as the person capable of the informed exercise of judgment, taste and values. If at maturity he is not willing to express judgment on matters of policy or taste or morals, if at fifty he does not believe that he has acquired more wisdom and informed experience than is possessed by the student at twenty, then he is saying in effect that education has been a failure. 22

Analysis

Tuchman defines moral courage as the willingness to stand up and defend one's principles. In the late 1960s, when she delivered this speech, she saw a failure of this kind of courage among our leaders as well as ourselves. Most troubling was the reluctance to define standards of value — moral, behavioral, or aesthetic.

The opening sentence indicates that this was an oral presentation. Speeches require clear, careful organization because the hearers cannot go back and consult the text if they misunderstand. Tuchman is aware of this imperative. She discusses in turn the three areas she has listed above with impeccable transitions from one subject to another.

Speeches also demand a development that can capture and retain the attention of the audience. (It goes without saying that written essays, too, benefit from these attributes.) Moreover, we know that no definition of an abstract term, such as moral courage, can succeed without a wide variety of examples in which the term is seen to function. These Tuchman has provided in abundance, some from the early twentieth century, but most from the sixties — the decline of discipline, student protests against the traditional curriculum and the Vietnam War, censorship, visual art. These cases bring the speech to life. They are not sketched but fully realized. Notice the development of the case against pornography and the description of the Metropolitan Opera scene. As a distinguished historian, Tuchman can also interpret these events. And whether or not we agree with the interpretations, we can respect them as the products of an informed analysis.

Even if readers miss some of the references (and they are well worth looking up), the essay doesn't lose power. In large part this is because many of the problems of more than twenty years ago are still alive: "murderers and rapists and muggers" who are judged "not guilty"; student protests against the curriculum (now often in the form of a reaction against so-called Eurocentrism); protests against pornography; distaste for "phony" modern art.

Obviously Tuchman's is not a neutral definition, one that merely names, describes, or differentiates. It expresses a personal point of view, that of an intensely committed advocate of what some readers may think of as "old-fashioned" values. Definitions of this kind are common in the social sciences and humanities. And Tuchman's essay does what such definitions should do: It encourages readers to reflect on the events of the past and to measure them against present-day values. In the process readers will be defining their own moral, behavioral, and aesthetic principles and asking if they and their leaders exhibit the missing element in the 1990s.

READINGS FOR ANALYSIS

The Nature of Prejudice

GORDON ALLPORT

Before I attempt to define prejudice, let us have in mind four in- 1
stances that I think we all would agree are prejudice.

The first is the case of the Cambridge University student who said, "I 2
despise all Americans. But," he added, a bit puzzled, "I've never met one that I didn't like."

The second is the case of another Englishman, who said to an Ameri- 3
can, "I think you're awfully unfair in your treatment of Negroes. How *do* Americans feel about Negroes?" The American replied, "Well, I suppose some Americans feel about Negroes just the way you feel about the Irish." The Englishman said, "Oh, come now. The Negroes are human beings."

Then there's the incident that occasionally takes place in various parts 4
of the world (in the West Indies, for example, I'm told). When an American walks down the street the natives conspicuously hold their noses till the American goes by. The case of odor is always interesting. Odor gets mixed up with prejudice because odor has great associative power. We know that some Chinese deplore the odor of Americans. Some white people think Negroes have a distinctive smell and vice versa. An intrepid psychologist recently did an experiment; it went as follows. He brought to a gymnasium an equal number of white and colored students and had them take shower baths. When they were nice and clean he had them exercise vigorously for fifteen minutes. Then he brought his judges in, and each went to the sheeted figures and sniffed. They were to say "white" or "black," guessing at the identity of the subject. The experiment seemed to prove that when we are sweaty we all smell the same way. It's good to have experimental demonstration of the fact.

The fourth example I'd like to bring before you is a piece of writing 5
that I quote. Please ask yourselves who, in your judgment, wrote it. It's a passage about the Jews.

Gordon Allport (1897–1967) was a psychologist who taught at Harvard University from 1924 until his death. He was author of numerous books, among them *Personality: A Psychological Interpretation* (1937). Allport delivered "The Nature of Prejudice" at the Seventeenth Claremont Reading Conference in 1952.

> The synagogue is worse than a brothel. It's a den of scoundrels. It's a criminal assembly of Jews, a place of meeting for the assassins of Christ, a den of thieves, a house of ill fame, a dwelling of iniquity. Whatever name more horrible to be found, it could never be worse than the synagogue deserves.
>
> I would say the same things about their souls. Debauchery and drunkenness have brought them to the level of lusty goat and pig. They know only one thing: to satisfy their stomachs and get drunk, kill, and beat each other up. Why should we salute them? We should not even have the slightest converse with them. They are lustful, rapacious, greedy, perfidious robbers.

Now who wrote that? Perhaps you say Hilter, or Goebbels, or one of our local anti-Semites? No, it was written by Saint John Chrysostom, in the fourth century A.D. Saint John Chrysostom, as you know, gave us the first liturgy in the Christian church still used in the Orthodox churches today. From it all services of the Holy Communion derive. Episcopalians will recognize him also as the author of that exalted prayer that closes the offices of both matins and evensong in the *Book of Common Prayer.* I include this incident to show how complex the problem is. Religious people are by no means necessarily free from prejudice. In this regard be patient even with our saints. 6

What do these four instances have in common? You notice that all of them indicate that somebody is "down" on somebody else — a feeling of rejection, or hostility. But also, in all these four instances, there is indication that the person is not "up" on his subject — not really informed about Americans, Irish, Jews, or bodily odors. 7

So I would offer, first a slang definition of prejudice: *Prejudice is being down on somebody you're not up on.* If you dislike slang, let me offer the same thought in the style of St. Thomas Aquinas. Thomists have defined prejudice as *thinking ill of others without sufficient warrant.* 8

You notice that both definitions, as well as the examples I gave, specify two ingredients of prejudice. First there is some sort of faulty generalization in thinking about a group. I'll call this the process of *categorization.* Then there is the negative, rejective, or hostile ingredient, a *feeling* tone. "Being down on something" is the hostile ingredient; "that you're not up on" is the categorization ingredient; "thinking ill of others" is the hostile ingredient; "without sufficient warrant" is the faulty categorization. 9

Parenthetically I should say that of course there is such a thing as *positive* prejudice. We can be just as prejudiced *in favor of* as we are *against.* We can be biased in favor of our children, our neighborhood or our college. Spinoza makes the distinction neatly. He says that *love prejudice* is "thinking well of others, through love, more than is right." *Hate prejudice,* he says, is "thinking ill of others, through hate, more than is right." 10

Discussion Questions

1. This was a speech, obviously not delivered extemporaneously but read to the audience. What characteristics suggest an oral presentation?
2. Allport has arranged his anecdotes carefully. What principle of organization has he used?
3. This essay was written in 1952. Are there any references or examples that seem dated? Why or why not?

Writing Suggestions

1. Some media critics claim that negative prejudice exists in the treatment of certain groups in movies and television. (For example, see Barbara Ehrenreich's "The Silenced Majority" on page 211, which argues that the working class is invisible in the media.) If you agree, select a group that seems to you to be the object of prejudice in these media, and offer evidence of the prejudice and the probable reasons for it. Or disagree with the media critics and provide evidence that certain groups are *not* the object of prejudice.
2. Can you think of examples of what Allport calls *positive prejudice*? Perhaps you can find instances which are less obvious than the ones Allport mentions. Explain in what way these prejudices represent a love that is "more than is right."

Saturday Night

SUSAN ORLEAN

Saturday night is different from any other. On Saturday night, people get together, go dancing, bowling, drinking, out to dinner, get drunk, get killed, kill other people, go out on dates, visit friends, go to parties, listen to music, sleep, gamble, watch television, go cruising, and sometimes fall in love — just as they do every other night of the week. But on Saturday night they do all these things more often and with more passion and intent. Even having nothing to do on Saturday night is different from having nothing to do on, say, Thursday afternoon, and being alone on Saturday night is different from being alone on any other night of the week. 1

For most people Saturday is the one night that neither follows nor precedes work, when they expect to have a nice time, when they want to 2

Susan Orlean is a New York–based writer whose work has appeared in *The New Yorker, Rolling Stone*, and *Vogue*. This article, from the February 11, 1990 issue of the *New York Times Magazine*, is adapted from her first book, *Saturday Night in America* (1990).

be with their friends and lovers and not with their bosses, employees, teachers, landlords, or relatives — unless those categories happen to include friends or lovers. Saturday night is when you want to do what you want to do and not what you have to do. In the extreme, this leads to what I think of as the Fun Imperative: the sensation that a Saturday night not devoted to having a good time is a major human failure and evidence of a possible character flaw. The particularly acute loneliness you can feel only on Saturday night is the Fun Imperative unrequited. But most of the time Saturday night is a medium of enjoyment.

For the last few years, I have traveled around the country and spent Saturday nights with a variety of people in a variety of situations, with the intention not to define Saturday night but to illustrate it. When I wanted to know about Saturday night was not so much what is fun to do with your spare time as what, given some spare time and no directives or obligations, people do. 3

Distinguishing Saturday night from the rest of the week began around 700 B.C. with the introduction in Assyria of once-a-week "evil days," and it has remained constant throughout human history, including but not ending with *Saturday Night Fever*. I don't know of anything else that has social significance spanning ancient Babylonia and Babylon, L.I. 4

The origin of Saturday night's distinctiveness was religious — one day each week set aside as sacred, to contrast with the six others that were profane — and over time became economic (a day of rest versus a day of labor). Before this century, days of rest were permitted mainly so that laborers could restore — "recreate," in Victorian terms — their strength and then return to another six days of hard work. 5

Eventually, as affluence and easy credit spread through the American middle class after World War II, weekend "recreation" became an end in itself. Fun was viewed as an entitlement of the middle class rather than an exclusive right of the rich and elite. The satisfying life, after the war, included an imperative to have fun, and Saturday night was the center of it. 6

How is Saturday night different now from the past? There is no doubt that AIDS has quashed some of the abandon that Saturday night both symbolized and contained — not just in gay nightclubs, but in all bars and clubs and parties. There are other ways social behavior and Saturday night have changed in tandem. A sex researcher told me he believed many people used to have sex only on Saturday nights, in some cases because it was their only chance, and in others because an unconscious sense of guilt made them feel it was improper on "regular" nights of the week. He also ventured that having sex on Saturday night was titillating for some people because it was only hours before they would go to church. Sexual liberation, the researcher concluded, has probably 7 changed that. Then there's the effect of indoor plumbing on Saturday night: When baths were once-a-week events at the neighborhood bathhouse, Saturday had the distinction of being bath night for most people.

Saturday night happens to be when most people take part in whatever is the current entertainment trend. They might watch a break-dance contest one month, and a lip-synching contest the next, and a lambada-dance demonstration the one after that. I began to think of this aspect of Saturday night culture as the Palace of Social Meteors. Every city I've ever visited seems to have a bar or nightclub called the Palace, the local showcase for whatever the current public diversion happens to be. I made a practice of avoiding the Palaces and all study of Social Meteors. Bar life is certainly a constant of the American Saturday night, but the ancillary activities that take place in them, I'm convinced, are mostly new ways to get people to spend money on drinks, and their evanescence proves only that people get bored with the ways they keep busy in bars. 8

It's hard to think about Saturday night without realizing that chronological time itself is something of an anachronism these days. Schedules are less rigid now than in the past. When I was a kid, grocery stores closed at six and were never open on Sundays. I still remember the first time I went to a twenty-four-hour grocery at four in the morning, thinking that something fundamental had changed forever. You used to be out of luck for money on the weekend if you didn't get to the bank by three on Friday. Now most people I know don't even know when banks are open because they use twenty-four-hour automatic-teller machines. Most stores are now open every day, since blue laws were repealed. 9

The way we perceive time changed when the American economy shifted from agriculture to industry. On a farm, the significant unit of time is a season. On an assembly line, though, you're inside all the time and you work all year round and you have no interaction with the natural physical world, so seasons no longer matter. What matters is the week, and you know that if you're annoyed to be back at work, it's probably Monday, and if you just got paid and feel more cheerful, it's Friday, and if you're happy, it's the weekend. 10

Now, as manufacturing, with its regular hours and rigid schedules, is displaced by a service and high-tech economy that runs incessantly, night and day, the convention of the five-day work week and the two-day weekend is coming apart. Many workers have unusual schedules — swing shifts, night work, three-day weekends. They also have their pay deposited electronically, bank by phone, shop at midnight, and tape *The Tonight Show* and watch it at breakfast. The idea of having to get to a bank by three on Friday or to watch Johnny Carson at midnight seems, in the 1990s, nostalgic. 11

Murray Melbin, a sociologist at Boston University, recently wrote that we have run out of land to colonize, so we are now colonizing nighttime, operating businesses twenty-four hours a day, and setting up services to obviate the importance of time. Many people work from their homes via computer work stations and modem hookups and don't have work schedules. Soon, the week as we know it won't mean anything. Some people see this as liberation. Other people — I'm inclined to include myself in this camp — think it sounds awful. Maybe it would eliminate the problems of getting to work on time, but that's only because it means you're at work all the time. And the more the structure of the week disappears, the less extraordinary and special Saturday night will be. 12

I am not an enthusiast of the seamless week. I think the Assyrians had it right when they decided it was comforting to divide infinity into comprehensible, repeating units of time with distinct qualities. In particular, I would consider losing the singular nature of Saturday night — one night set aside to be off-limits to obligations — kind of a shame. 13

Not long ago, I spent an interesting Saturday night in Elkhart, Ind. I had gone there to write about a local imbroglio that pitted the Mayor, a young man with conservative tastes, against a group of people who liked to spend their Saturday evenings cruising in fancy cars through downtown. The Mayor saw the issue as a traffic problem; the cruisers saw his efforts as an infringement on their inalienable right to have fun on weekends. I saw it as a chance to see how seriously people take Saturday night. 14

I arranged to meet the cruisers at nine o'clock, so I could ride with them on Main Street. At seven, I went to an Italian restaurant someone had recommended. I hoped the restaurant would be a quiet hole-in-the-wall. It was not. It was the sort of place that attracts every birthday celebration, first date, last date, prom date, anniversary party, engagement celebration, and stag party within a 200-mile radius. I am not unaccustomed to being alone in a crowd, but this was the first time in my life I had dined alone at a restaurant — let alone a restaurant preferred by big, ostentatiously convivial groups of people — on a Saturday night. It was a largely disagreeable sensation. 15

I noticed that I was being noticed by the people seated near me. I decided that the best defense was to look busy, but reading the label on the aspirin bottle in my purse took only a minute. Next, I read the menu. Then I turned to the place mat, which had only a photograph of a beach — I never thought I would see the day when I would miss place mats with puzzles on them. I wondered whether I could leave without being too obvious, and if I left, whether I could get a more secluded dinner somewhere else. 16

My musing was interrupted by my waitress, a tall woman with curly brown hair, a high forehead and a voice that could cut through dry wall. Her name tag said MARIAN. She greeted me and asked if I was meeting someone. I said I wasn't. "Here on vacation?" she asked. When I said I was in town doing work, she gave me a long look full of pity. At that point, all I wanted was to get a quick dinner and get out. Marian, however, dawdled. After she took my order, she tidied my place setting and filled my water glass. She checked my salt and pepper shakers. I began to suspect that in her eyes I was a statistical freak — in the category of customers, a Fourth of July snowstorm. Finally, she grabbed a waitress passing by, turned her so she could get a good look at me, and said in a loud, clear voice, "Just look at her! My God! All by herself and working on Saturday night!" 17

After that dinner, and after I had gone cruising, I set out to see how Americans spend Saturday night. Is it regional? Is it a matter of age and marital status? Relative wealth? Urban versus suburban versus rural? Is there such a thing as a typical Southern Saturday night, or a middle-aged Saturday night, or a working-class Saturday night? Is there some place that has sprung up to replace the vanished town squares and bars and bowling alleys where people used to gather when they wanted to get together and had no particular place to go? 18

This task had a few challenges. For one thing, many people, including me, often spend Saturday night at home. For a reporter, this is a tough world to infiltrate. And judging by many of the Saturday nights I've spent this way, their pleasures are too self-referential to bear description. It is also true that in the era of disaster news, people have come to expect to be written about only when something exceptional takes place in their lives. Quite often, people would ask me to come back when the town was having its jazz festival or mariachi festival or rodeo. That wasn't what I was after. I had this notion that Saturday night itself was a good enough subject. I liked the contrariness of examining leisure in an era that is career-crazy, and average citizens in an era that celebrates celebrity. 19

There were a few things about Saturday night I wanted to figure out. For instance, even though Saturday night is itself a democratic occasion, I wondered if most people choose to spend it undemocratically — that is, to spend it around people just like themselves. Some Saturday night situations don't appear to have any social parameters. One Saturday night, I hung around the emergency room of a large veterinary hospital in New York City. I'd heard there were certain animal accidents (cats falling out of windows, especially) that seemed to happen mostly on Saturday nights, and I wanted to find out why. I also wondered whether there was any similarity to the people who ended up at such a place on Saturday night when they didn't have an emergency. Some flattened cats did come in (it was a 20 hot night, and a lot of people had probably left their windows open) but there were also a lot of people who just chose that night to have their dogs' teeth cleaned or their sick parakeets put to sleep. Except for sharing a somewhat unconventional notion of pet care, these people apparently had nothing in common. The animal emergency center aside, I saw some white people at a black church social I went to, and some black kids and a few upper-middle-class white kids hanging around the white, blue-collar Elkhart cruising crowd. But generally, it seems that Saturday night acts as a subset intensifier.

The possibility of a dateless, hourless, calendarless future notwithstanding, I was happy to discover that Saturday night still does have a distinct personality and effect on most people. People still act differently on Saturday night for no reason other than it's Saturday night. For instance, there are fewer long-distance calls made Saturday night than any other night of the week. What is it about Saturday night that inhibits the urge to make calls? Is it that so many people are out, or that those who happen to be at home assume that anyone they want to call is out? Or does it just feel weird? 21

On Saturday night, there are the fewest airplane flights, the most murders, most taped radio shows, fewest television viewers, most visits to the emergency room, fewest suicides, most scheduled showings of *The Rocky Horror Picture Show*, most people breaking their diets, most liquor sold by the glass, the fewest number of calls to businesses offering products on television, and the highest number of reported incidents of cow-toppling in rural Pennsylvania. These might at first seem like weird specifics — information dead ends, like knowing that 75 percent of all Iowans think Scotch tape is the best modern invention — but they really add up to a picture of what Saturday night in America is like. 22

It is a time when people listen to prerecorded radio shows, are too busy to watch television, have accidents, don't feel like killing themselves, go out for the evening and forget to close their windows and own curious cats with bad depth perception, feel like seeing campy movies, are in the mood to eat with abandon, drink in bars, aren't in the mood to order the five-volume set of Slim Whitman's greatest hits or aren't home to fall victim to the ad, see cows sleeping in pastures and are inspired to tip them over just for fun. It's in keeping with what the Assyrians had in mind when they first established the seven-day week. 23

For the last few years, while considering the nature of Saturday night, I have kept a clipping from the *Chicago Tribune* wire service over my desk, headlined: "Leisure Time Shrinks By 32 Percent." The article says: "Since 1973, the median number of hours worked by Americans has 24 increased by 20 percent, while the amount of leisure time available to the average person has dropped by 32 percent. The difference between the rise in working hours and the drop in leisure time has been the time that people spend on work around the house and other responsibilities that do not qualify as work. The trend toward less and less leisure time has been steady and inexorable, according to a Harris Survey."

If the law of supply and demand is universally true, the shrinking of 25
leisure time could only serve to make Saturday night more valuable. In a world with 32 percent less leisure time, wouldn't a night imbued with pleasure and abandon remain an important and welcome tonic, no matter how irrelevant the conventional notion of time may come to be?

That equation seemed especially evident to me in Elkhart. It is a clas- 26
sic working-class town — more than half of its residents are employed at building, servicing, selling, or outfitting recreational vehicles and customized vans — and the people I met there are probably among those Americans whose leisure time is shrinking the fastest. Accordingly, they considered Saturday night a matter of enormous consequence. "The week is just something I get through until Saturday night," one man told me.

When Mayor James Perron banned cruising on Main Street, it set off 27
three years of furious public debate. The superficial concern was traffic flow. What really got everyone roiled up was the idea that the city was legislating their leisure time. "I'm a working man and I pay my taxes," the same man said, "but no one's going to tell me how to spend my weekend. That's all mine."

I also have posted over my desk something I found buried in a survey 28
about leisure-time activity. It says: "Fifty-four percent of those surveyed have sex at least once a week but ranked it below gardening and visiting relatives as regular activities."

For a year or so, I didn't really know why I was so taken with this 29
piece of arcane data except for its innate comic value. I went to spend Saturday night in a few dozen different places around the country. Time and time again I saw that Saturday night was indeed something special — a time when people are most at ease with themselves. Surveys and statistics of any sort began to seem less important once I realized that Saturday night is mostly mythic: larger than life, more meaningful the less closely it is examined, romantic in the purest way, more an idea than an event.

At last I figured out why that survey seemed to have a particular con- 30
nection to my interest in Saturday night. According to the survey, most people have sex less often than they garden or visit their relatives, but I'm positive that they still consider sex the larger, more mystical, more mythic, more important, more noteworthy experience. That is how I finally feel about Saturday night. It is a matter of quality over quantity. If you add them up, there are many more weekdays in our lives than there are Saturday nights, but Saturday night is the one worth living for.

Discussion Questions

1. How does the origin of Saturday night distinguish it even today from other nights of the week? (Although Orlean says her intention was "not to define Saturday night but to illustrate it," her essay is clearly a definition. It answers the question, "What is it?" It describes, isolates, differentiates, compares and contrasts, examines origins, all significant elements of definition.)
2. How does a changed perception of chronological time influence the meaning of Saturday night for us?
3. What is Orlean trying to prove in the account of her dinner at the Italian restaurant?
4. What specifics about Saturday night prove to her that it has a "distinct personality"?

Writing Suggestions

1. "Saturday night," says Orlean, "is the one worth living for." If this is true for you, explain why.
2. Orlean asks:

    > Is [Saturday night] regional? Is it a matter of age and marital status? Relative wealth? Urban versus suburban versus rural? Is there such a thing as a typical Southern Saturday night, or a middle-aged Saturday night, or a working-class Saturday night? Is there some place that has sprung up to replace the vanished town squares and bars and bowling alleys where people used to gather when they wanted to get together and had no particular place to go?

    Choose one or more of these questions and elaborate on them. Show how these criteria do or do not influence our activities on Saturday night. Your own experiences in your family and your community — including college — may be good starting points.

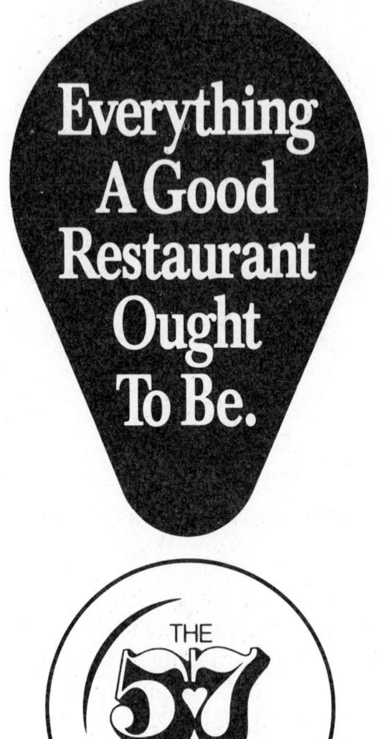

Everything
A Good
Restaurant
Ought
To Be.
THE
57
RESTAURANT
Good food. Good service. Good prices. Good
atmosphere. Good entertainment.
On premises parking. And a great location.
Open every day for luncheon and dinner from
11:30 AM to 11:30 PM. Lounge open until 2 AM.
Private dining rooms, meeting rooms
and complete function facilities available.
All credit cards welcome.
For reservations: (617) 423-5700.
Go ahead, be good to yourself.
200 Stuart Street, Boston, MA 02116

Discussion Questions

1. Look back at the discussion about popular music on page 32. Does this advertisement make clear what is meant by a *good* restaurant?
2. To what extent do you think readers would agree on the definitions of *good* in evaluating the food, service, prices, atmosphere, and entertainment?

EXERCISES FOR REVIEW

1. Choose one of the following statements and define the italicized term. Make the context as specific as possible (for example, by referring to the Declaration of Independence or your own experience).
   a. All men are created *equal.*
   b. I believe in *God.*
   c. This school doesn't offer a *liberal education.*
   d. The marine corps needs *good men.*
   e. *Roseanne* is a *better* television show than *Cosby.*
2. Many recent controversial movements and causes are identified by terms that have come to mean different things to different people. Choose one of the following and define it, explaining both the favorable and unfavorable connotations of the term. Use examples to clarify the meaning.
   a. comparative worth
   b. Palestinian homeland
   c. affirmative action
   d. assertiveness training
   e. nationalism
3. Choose two words that are sometimes confused and define them to make their differences clear. *Examples*: authoritarianism and totalitarianism; envy and jealousy; sympathy and pity; cult and established church; justice and equality; liberal and radical; agnostic and atheist.
4. Define a good parent, a good teacher, a good husband or wife. Try to uncover the assumptions on which your definition is based. (For example, in defining a good teacher, students sometimes mention the ability of the teacher to maintain order. Does this mean that the teacher alone is responsible for classroom order?)
5. Define any popular form of entertainment, such as the soap opera, western, detective story, or science fiction story or film. Support your definition with references to specific shows or books. *Or* define an idealized type from fiction, film, the stage, advertising, or television, describing the chief attributes of that type and the principal reasons for its popularity.
6. From your own experience write an essay describing a serious misunderstanding that arose because two people had different meanings for a term they were using.
7. Write about an important or widely used term whose meaning has changed since you first learned it. Such terms often come from the slang of particular groups: teenagers, drug users, rock music fans, musicians, athletes.
8. Define the differences between *necessities, comforts*, and *luxuries*. Consider how they have changed over time.

CHAPTER 4

Support

TYPES OF SUPPORT: EVIDENCE AND APPEALS TO NEEDS AND VALUES

All the claims you make — whether of fact, of value, or of policy — must be supported. Support for a claim represents the answer to the question, "What have you got to go on?"[1] There are two basic kinds of support in an argument: evidence and appeals to needs and values.

Evidence, as one dictionary defines it, is "something that tends to prove; ground for belief." When you provide evidence, you use facts, including statistics, and opinions, or interpretations of facts, both your own and those of experts. In the following conversation, the first speaker offers facts and the opinion of an expert to convince the second speaker that robots are exceptional machines.

> *"You know, robots do a lot more than work on assembly lines in factories."*
>
> *"Like what?"*

---

[1] Stephen Toulmin, *The Uses of Argument* (Cambridge: Cambridge University Press, 1958), p. 98.

"They shear sheep, pick citrus fruit, and even assist in neurosurgery. And by the end of the century, every house will have a robot slave."

"No kidding. Who says so?"

"An engineer who's the head of the world's largest manufacturer of industrial robots."

A writer often appeals to readers' needs, that is, requirements for physical and psychological survival and well-being, and values, or standards for right and wrong, good and bad. In the following conversation, the first speaker makes an appeal to the universal need for self-esteem and to the principle of helping others, a value the second speaker probably shares.

"I think you ought to come help us at the nursing home. We need an extra hand."

"I'd like to, but I really don't have the time."

"You could give us an hour a week, couldn't you? Think how good you'd feel about helping out, and the old people would be so grateful. Some of them are very lonely."

Although they use the same kinds of support, conversations are less rigorous than arguments addressed to larger audiences in academic or public situations. In the debates on public policy that appear in the media and in the courts, the quality of support can be crucial in settling urgent matters. The following summary of a well-known court case demonstrates the critical use of both evidence and value appeals in the support of opposing claims.

On March 30, 1981, President Ronald Reagan and three other men were shot by John W. Hinckley, Jr., a young drifter from a wealthy Colorado family. Hinckley was arrested at the scene of the shooting. In his trial the factual evidence was presented first: There were dozens of reliable witnesses who had seen the shooting at close range. Hinckley's diaries, letters, and poems revealed that he had planned the shooting to impress actress Jodie Foster. Opinions, consisting of testimony by experts, were introduced by both the defense and the prosecution. This evidence was contradictory. Defense attorneys produced several psychiatrists who defined Hinckley as insane. If this interpretation of his conduct convinced the jury, then Hinckley would be confined to a mental hospital rather than a prison. The prosecution introduced psychiatrists who interpreted Hinckley's motives and actions as those of a man who knew what he was doing and knew it was wrong. They claimed he was *not* insane by legal definition. The fact that experts can make differing conclusions about the meaning of the same information indicates that interpretations are less reliable than other kinds of support.

Finally, the defense made an appeal to the moral values of the jury. Under the law, criminals judged to be insane are not to be punished as harshly as criminals judged to be sane. The laws assume that criminals who cannot be held responsible for their actions are entitled to more compassionate treatment, confinement to a mental hospital rather than prison. The jury accepted the interpretive evidence supporting the claim of the defense, and Hinckley was pronounced not guilty by reason of insanity. Clearly the moral concern for the rights of the insane proved to be decisive.

In your arguments you will advance your claims, not unlike a lawyer, with these same kinds of support. But before you begin, you should ask two questions: Which kind of support should I use in convincing an audience to accept my claim? and How do I decide that each item of support is valid and worthy of acceptance? This chapter presents the different types of evidence and appeals you can use to support your claim and examines the criteria by which you can evaluate the soundness of that support.

EVIDENCE

Factual Evidence

In Chapter 2, we defined facts as "statements possessing a high degree of public acceptance." In theory, facts can be verified by experience alone. Eating too much will make us sick; we can get from Hopkinton to Boston in a half hour by car; in the Northern Hemisphere it is colder in December than in July. The experience of any individual is limited in both time and space, so we must accept as fact thousands of assertions about the world that we ourselves can never verify. Thus we accept the report that human beings landed on the moon in 1969 because we trust those who can verify it. (Country people in Morocco, however, received the news with disbelief because they had no reason to trust the reporters of the event. They insisted on trusting their senses instead. One man said, "I can see the moon very clearly. If a man were walking around up there, wouldn't I be able to see him?")

Factual evidence appears most frequently as examples and statistics, which are a numerical form of examples.

Examples

Examples are the most familiar kind of factual evidence. In addition to providing support for the truth of a generalization, examples can enliven otherwise dense or monotonous prose.

In the following paragraph the writer supports the claim in the topic sentence by offering a series of specific examples. (The article claims that most airport security is useless.)

> Meanwhile, seven hijacking incidents occurred last year (twenty-one in 1980 and eleven the year before), despite the security system. Two involved the use of flammable liquids. . . . In four other cases, hijackers claimed to have flammables or explosives but turned out to be bluffing. In the only incident involving a gun, a man brushed past the security system and brandished the weapon on the plane before being wrestled to the ground. One other hijacking was aborted on the ground, and the remaining five were concluded after some expense, fright, and delay — but no injuries or deaths.[2]

Hypothetical examples, which create imaginary situations for the audience and encourage them to visualize what might happen under certain circumstances, can also be effective. The following paragraph, taken from the same article as the preceding paragraph, illustrates the use of hypothetical examples.

> But weapons can get through nonetheless. Some are simply overlooked; imagine being one of those 10,000 "screeners" staring at X-rayed baggage, day in and day out. Besides, a gun can be broken down into unrecognizable parts and reassembled past the checkpoint. A hand grenade can be hidden in an aerosol shaving-cream can or a photographer's lens case. The ingredients of a Molotov cocktail can be carried on quite openly; any bottle of, say, duty-free liquor or perfume can be emptied and refilled with gasoline. And the possibilities for bluffing should not be forgotten; once on board, anyone could claim that a bottle of water was really a Molotov cocktail, or that a paper bag contained a bomb.[3]

All claims about vague or abstract terms would be boring or unintelligible without examples to illuminate them. For example, if you claim that a movie contains "unusual sound effects," you will certainly have to describe some of the effects to convince the reader that your generalization can be trusted.

Statistics

Statistics express information in numbers. In the following example statistics have been used to express raw data in numerical form.

> Surveys have shown that almost half of all male high school seniors — and nearly 20 percent of all ninth grade boys — can be called "problem

---

[2] Patrick Brogan, "The $310 Million Paranoia Subsidy," *Harper's*, September 1982, p. 18.

[3] Ibid.

> drinkers." . . . Over 5,000 teenagers are killed yearly in auto accidents due to drunken driving.[4]

These grim numbers probably have meaning for you, partly because you already know that alcoholism exists even among young teenagers and partly because your own experience enables you to evaluate the numbers. But if you are unfamiliar with the subject, such numbers may be difficult or impossible to understand. Statistics, therefore, are more effective in comparisons that indicate whether a quantity is relatively large or small and sometimes even whether a reader should interpret the result as gratifying or disappointing. For example, if a novice gambler were told that for every dollar wagered in a state lottery, 50 percent goes back to the players as prizes, would the gambler be able to conclude that the percentage is high or low? Would he be able to choose between playing the state lottery and playing a casino game? Unless he had more information, probably not. But if he were informed that in casino games, the return to the players is over 90 percent and in slot machines and racetracks the return is around 80 percent, the comparison would enable him to evaluate the meaning of the 50 percent return in the state lottery and even to make a decision about where to gamble his money.[5]

Comparative statistics are also useful for measurements over time. A national survey by The Institute for Social Research of the University of Michigan, in which 17,000 of the nation's 2.7 million high school seniors were questioned about their use of drugs, revealed a continuing downward trend.

> . . . 50.9 percent of those questioned in 1989 reported that they had at least tried an illicit drug like marijuana or cocaine, as against 53.9 percent in 1988 and 56.6 percent in 1987.[6]

Diagrams, tables, charts, and graphs can make clear the relations among many sets of numbers. Such charts and diagrams allow readers to grasp the information more easily than if it were presented in paragraph form. The bar graph[7] that is shown on page 109 summarizes the information produced by a poll on gambling habits. A pie chart[8] such as the one on page 110 can also clarify lists of data.

---

4 "The Kinds of Drugs Kids Are Getting Into" (Spring House, PA: McNeil Pharmaceutical, n.d.).

5 Curt Suphee, "Lotto Baloney," *Harper's*, July 1983, p. 20

6 *New York Times*, February 14, 1990, Sec. A, p. 16.

7 *New York Times*, May 28, 1989, p. 24.

8 *Wall Street Journal*, February 2, 1990, Sec. B, p. 1.

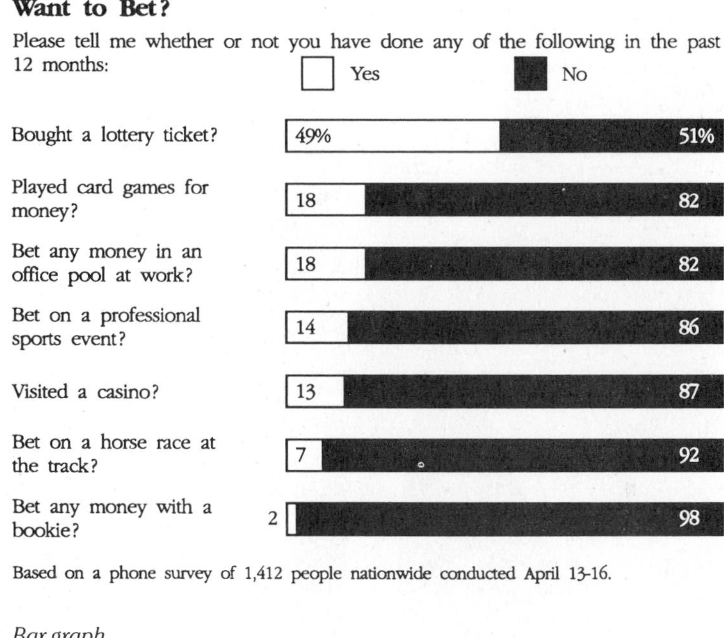

Bar graph

Opinions: Interpretations of the Facts

We have seen how opinions of experts influenced the verdict in the trial of John Hinckley. Facts alone were not enough to substantiate the claim that Hinckley was guilty of attempted assassination. Both the defense and the prosecution relied on experts — psychiatrists — to interpret the facts. Opinions or interpretations about the facts are the inferences discussed in Chapter 2. They are an indispensable source of support for your claims.

Suppose a disco for teenagers — Studio 44: A Young Adult Dance Club — has opened in your town. That is a fact. What is the significance of it? Is the disco's existence good or bad? What consequences will it have for the community? Some parents oppose the idea of a disco, fearing that it may allow teenagers to escape from parental control and engage in dangerous activities. Other parents approve of a disco, hoping that it will serve as a substitute for unsupervised congregation in the streets. The importance of these interpretations is that they, not the fact itself, help people decide what actions they should take. If the community accepts the interpretation that Studio 44 is a source of delinquency, they may decide to revoke the owner's license and close the disco. As one writer puts it, "The interpretation of data becomes a struggle over power."

Plastic that Goes to Waste

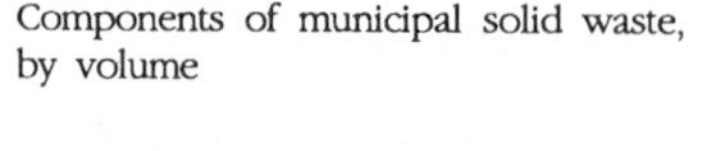
Components of municipal solid waste, by volume
Types of plastic in municipal solid waste, by weight
Paper and cardboard
38%
Plastics
18%
13%
14%
4%
11%
Metals
Glass 2%
Yard waste
Food waste
Other
47% Polyethylene. Includes milk jugs, garbage bags, and most liquid soap and detergent bottles.
16% Polypropylene. Includes some electric appliances, videocassette cases, drinking straws, and screw-on tops.
16% Polystyrene. Includes foam cups, plates and hamburger containers; plastic utensils; and radio and TV cabinets.
6.5% Polyvinyl chloride. Includes plastic wrap and clear containers such as some peanut butter jars and dishwashing liquid bottles.
5% Polyethylene tereph-thalate. Includes soda bottles and other clear bottles such as some cooking oil containers.
5% Polyurethane. Includes foam for insulation and furniture.
4.5% Other plastics.

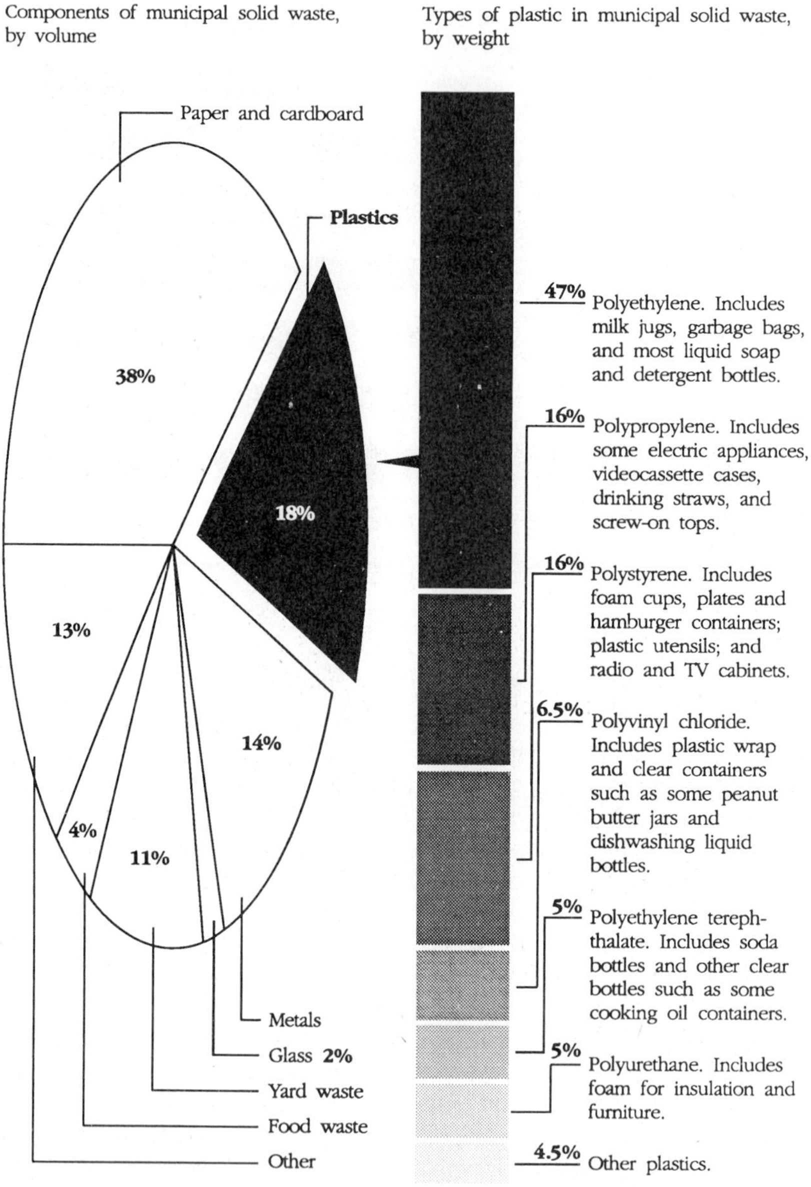

Source: Franklin Associates Ltd.

Pie chart

Opinions or interpretations of facts generally take three forms: (1) They may suggest a causal connection between two sets of data or the cause for a condition; (2) they may offer predictions about the future; (3) they may suggest solutions to a problem.

1. Causal Connection

Anorexia is a serious, sometimes fatal, disease, characterized by self-starvation. It is found largely among young women. Physicians, psychologists, and social scientists have speculated about the causes, which remain unclear. A leading researcher in the field, Hilde Bruch, believes that food refusal expresses a desire to postpone sexual development. Another authority, Joan Blumberg, believes that one cause may be biological, a nervous dysfunction of the hypothalamus. Still others infer that the causes are cultural, a response to the admiration of the thin female body.[9]

2. Predictions about the Future

In the fall and winter of 1989–90 extraordinary events shook Eastern Europe, toppling Communist regimes and raising more popular forms of government. Politicians and scholars offered predictions about future changes in the region. One expert, Zbigniew Brzezinski, former national security adviser under President Carter, concluded that the changes for the Soviet Union might be destructive.

> It would be a mistake to see the recent decisions as marking a breakthrough for democracy. Much more likely is a prolonged period of democratizing chaos. One will see the rise in the Soviet Union of increasingly irreconcilable conflicts between varying national political and social aspirations, all united by a shared hatred for the existing Communist nomenklatura. One is also likely to see a flashback of a nationalist type among the Great Russians, fearful of the prospective breakup of the existing Great Russian empire.[10]

3. Solutions to Problems

How shall we solve the problems caused by young people in our cities "who commit crimes and create the staggering statistics in teenage pregnancies and the high abortion rate"? The minister emeritus of the Abyssinian Baptist Church proposes establishment of a national youth academy with fifty campuses on inactive military bases. "It is a 'parenting'

---

[9] Phyllis Rose, "Hunger Artists," *Harper's*, July 1988, p. 82.
[10] *New York Times*, February 9, 1990, Sec. A, p. 13.

institution. . . . It is not a penal institution, not a prep school, not a Job Corps Center, not a Civilian Conservation Camp, but it borrows from them." Although such an institution has not been tried before, the author of the proposal thinks that it would represent an effort "to provide for the academic, moral, and social development of young people, to cause them to become responsible and productive citizens."[11]

Expert Opinion

For many of the subjects you discuss and write about, you will find it necessary to accept and use the opinions of experts. Based on their reading of the facts, experts express opinions on a variety of controversial subjects: whether capital punishment is a deterrent to crime; whether legalization of marijuana will lead to an increase in its use; whether children, if left untaught, will grow up honest and cooperative; whether sex education courses will result in less sexual activity and fewer illegitimate births. The interpretations of the data are often profoundly important because they influence social policy and affect our lives directly and indirectly.

For the problems mentioned above, the opinions of people recognized as authorities are more reliable than those of people who have neither thought about nor done research on the subject. But opinions may also be offered by student writers in areas in which they are knowledgeable. If you were asked, for example, to defend or refute the statement that work has advantages for teenagers, you could call on your own experience and that of your friends to support your claim. You can also draw on your experience to write convincingly about your special interests.

One opinion, however, is not as good as another. The value of any opinion depends on the quality of the evidence and the trustworthiness of the person offering it.

EVALUATION OF EVIDENCE

Before you begin to write, you must determine whether the facts and opinions you have chosen to support your claim are sound. Can they convince your readers? A distinction between the evaluation of facts and the evaluation of opinions is somewhat artificial because many facts are verified by expert opinion, but for our analysis we discuss them separately.

---

[11] Samuel D. Proctor, "To the Rescue: A National Youth Academy," *New York Times*, September 16, 1989, Sec. A, p. 27.

Evaluation of Factual Evidence

As you evaluate factual evidence, you should keep in mind the following questions:

1. Is the evidence up to date? The importance of up-to-date information depends on the subject. If you are defending the claim that suicide is immoral, you will not need to examine new data. For many of the subjects you write about, recent research and scholarship will be important, even decisive, in proving the soundness of your data. "New" does not always mean "best," but in fields where research is ongoing — education, psychology, technology, medicine, and all the natural and physical sciences — you should be sensitive to the dates of the research.

In writing a paper a few years ago warning about the health hazards of air pollution, you would have used data referring only to outdoor pollution produced by automobile and factory emissions. But writing about air pollution today, you would have to take into account new data about indoor pollution, which has become a serious problem as a result of attempts to conserve energy. Because research studies in indoor pollution are continually being updated, recent evidence will probably be more accurate than past research.

2. Is the evidence sufficient? The amount of evidence you need depends on the complexity of the subject and the length of your paper. Given the relative brevity of most of your assignments, you will need to be selective. For the claim that indoor pollution is a serious problem, one example would obviously not be enough. For a 750-to-1,000-word paper, three or four examples would probably be sufficient. The choice of examples should reflect different aspects of the problem: in this case, different sources of indoor pollution — gas stoves, fireplaces, kerosene heaters, insulation — and the consequences for health.

Indoor pollution is a fairly limited subject for which the evidence is clear. But more complex problems require more evidence. A common fault in argument is generalization based on insufficient evidence. In a 1,000-word paper you could not adequately treat the causes of unrest in the Middle East; you could not develop workable solutions for the health-care crisis; you could not predict the development of education in the next century. In choosing a subject for a brief paper, determine whether you can produce sufficient evidence to convince a reader who may not agree with you. If not, the subject may be too large for a brief paper.

3. Is the evidence relevant? All the evidence should, of course, contribute to the development of your argument. Sometimes the arguer loses sight of the subject and introduces examples that are wide of the claim. In defending a national health care plan, one student offered examples of the success of health maintenance organizations, but such organizations, although subsidized by the federal government, are not the structure favored by sponsors of a national health-care plan. The examples were interesting but irrelevant.

Also keep in mind that not all readers will agree on what is relevant. Is the unsavory private life of a politician relevant to his or her performance in office? If you want to prove that a politician is unfit to serve because of his or her private activities, you may first have to convince some members of the audience that private activities are relevant to public service.

4. Are the examples representative? This question emphasizes your responsibility to choose examples that are typical of all the examples you do not use. Suppose you offered Vermont's experience to support your claim that passage of a bottle bill would reduce litter. Is the experience of Vermont typical of what is happening or may happen in other states? Or is Vermont, a small, mostly rural New England state, different enough from other states to make the example unrepresentative?

5. Are the examples consistent with the experience of the audience? The members of your audience use their own experiences to judge the soundness of your evidence. If your examples are unfamiliar or extreme, they will probably reject your conclusion. Consider the following excerpt from a flyer distributed on a university campus by the Revolutionary Communist Party.

> What is growing up female in a capitalist society? Growing up to Laverne and Shirley and the idea that female means scatterbrained broad? Being chained to the kitchen and let out on a leash to do cheap labor? Overburdened by the hardships of trying to raise children in this putrid, degenerate society — with or without husbands?

If most members of the audience find such a characterization of female experience inconsistent with their own, they will probably question the validity of the claim.

Evaluation of Statistics

The questions you must ask about examples also apply to statistics. Are they recent? Are they sufficient? Are they relevant? Are they typical? Are they consistent with the experience of the audience? But there are additional questions directed specifically to evaluation of statistics.

1. Do the statistics come from trustworthy sources? Perhaps you have read newspaper accounts of very old people, some reported to be as old as 135, living in the Caucasus or the Andes, nourished by yogurt and hard work. But these statistics are hearsay; no birth records or other official documents exist to verify them. Now two anthropologists have concluded that the numbers were part of a rural mythology and that the ages of the people were actually within the normal range for human populations elsewhere.[12]

Hearsay statistics should be treated with the same skepticism accorded to gossip or rumor. Sampling a population to gather statistical information is a sophisticated science; you should ask whether the reporter of the statistics is qualified and likely to be free of bias. Among the generally reliable sources are polling organizations such as Gallup, Roper, and Louis Harris and agencies of the U.S. government such as the Census Bureau and the Bureau of Labor Statistics. Other qualified sources are well-known research foundations, university centers, and insurance companies that prepare actuarial tables. Statistics from underdeveloped countries are less reliable for obvious reasons: lack of funds, lack of trained statisticians, lack of communication and transportation facilities to carry out accurate censuses.

2. Are the terms clearly defined? In an example in Chapter 3, the reference to "poverty" (p. 73) made clear that any statistics would be meaningless unless we knew exactly how "poverty" was defined by the user. "Unemployment" is another term for which statistics will be difficult to read if the definition varies from one user to another. For example, are seasonal workers "employed" or "unemployed" during the off-season? Are part-time workers "employed"? (In Russia they are "unemployed.") Are workers on government projects "employed"? (During the 1930s they were considered "employed" by the Germans and "unemployed" by the Americans.) The more abstract or controversial the term, the greater the necessity for clear definition.

3. Are the comparisons between comparable things? Folk wisdom warns us that we cannot compare apples and oranges. Population statistics for the world's largest city, for example, should indicate the units being compared. Greater London is defined in one way; greater New York in another; and greater Tokyo in still another. The population numbers will mean little unless you can be sure that the same geographical units are being compared.

---

[12] Richard B. Mazess and Sylvia H. Forman, "Longevity and Age Exaggeration in Vilcabamba, Ecuador," *Journal of Gerontology*, 1979, pp. 94–98.

4. Has any significant information been omitted? *The Plain Truth*, a magazine published by the World-Wide Church of God, advertises itself as follows:

> *The Plain Truth* has now topped 5,000,000 copies per issue. It is now the fastest-growing magazine in the world and one of the widest circulated mass-circulation magazines on earth. Our circulation is now greater than *Newsweek*. New subscribers are coming in at the rate of around 40,000 per week.

What the magazine neglects to mention is that it is *free*. There is no subscription fee, and the magazine is widely distributed free in drugstores, supermarkets, and airports. *Newsweek* is sold on newsstands and by subscription. The comparison therefore omits significant information.

Evaluation of Opinions

When you evaluate the reliability of opinions in subjects with which you are not familiar, you will be dealing almost exclusively with opinions of experts. Most of the following questions are directed to an evaluation of authoritative sources. But you can also ask these questions of students or of others with opinions based on their own experience and research.

1. Is the source of the opinion qualified to give an opinion on the subject? The discussion on credibility in Chapter 1 (pp. 14–17) pointed out that certain achievements by the interpreter of the data — publications, acceptance by colleagues — can tell us something about his or her competence. Although these standards are by no means foolproof — people of outstanding reputations have been known to falsify their data — nevertheless they offer assurance that the source is generally trustworthy. The answers to questions you must ask are not hard to find: Is the source qualified by education? Is the source associated with a reputable institution — a university or a research organization? Is the source credited with having made contributions to the field — books, articles, research studies? Suppose in writing a paper recommending relaxation of rules on prescription drugs you came across an article by Michael J. Halberstam. He is identified as follows:

> Michael J. Halberstam, M.D., is a practicing cardiologist, associate clinical professor of medicine at George Washington University School of Medicine, and editor-in-chief of *Modern Medicine*. He is also a member of the advisory committee of the Center for Health Policy Research at the American Enterprise Institute.[13]

---

[13] Michael Halberstam, "Too Many Drugs?" (Washington, DC: Center for Policy Health Research, 1979), inside cover.

These credentials would suggest to almost any reader that Halberstam is a reliable source of information about prescription drugs.

If the source is not so clearly identified, you should treat the data with caution. Such advice is especially relevant when you are dealing with popular works about such subjects as miracle diets, formulas for instant wealth, and sightings of monsters and UFOs. Do not use such data until you can verify them from other, more authoritative sources.

In addition, you should question the identity of any source listed as "spokesperson" or "reliable source" or "an unidentified authority." The mass media are especially fond of this type of attribution. Sometimes the sources are people in public life who plant stories anonymously or off the record for purposes they prefer to keep hidden.

Even when the identification is clear and genuine, you should ask if the credentials are relevant to the field in which the authority claims expertise. So specialized are areas of scientific study today that scientists in one field may not be competent to make judgments in another. William Shockley is a distinguished engineer, a Nobel Prize winner for his contribution to the invention of the electronic transistor. But when he made the claim, based on his own research, that blacks are genetically inferior to whites, geneticists accused Shockley of venturing into a field where he was unqualified to make judgments. Similarly, advertisers invite stars from the entertainment world to express opinions about products with which they are probably less familiar than members of their audience. All citizens have the right to express their views, but this does not mean that all views are equally credible or worthy of attention.

2. Is the source biased for or against his or her interpretation? Even authorities who satisfy the criteria for expertise may be guilty of bias. Bias arises as a result of economic reward, religious affiliation, political loyalty, and other interests. The expert may not be aware of the bias; even an expert can fall into the trap of ignoring evidence that contradicts his or her own intellectual preferences. A British psychologist has said:

> The search for meaning in data is bound to involve all of us in distortion to greater or lesser degree. . . . Transgression consists not so much in a clear break with professional ethics, as in an unusually high-handed, extreme or self-deceptive attempt to promote one particular view of reality at the expense of all others.[14]

Before accepting the interpretation of an expert, you should ask: Is there some reason why I should suspect the motives of this particular source?

---

[14] Liam Hudson, *The Cult of the Fact* (New York: Harper and Row, 1972), p. 125.

Consider, for example, an advertisement claiming that sweetened breakfast cereals are nutritious. The advertisement, placed by the manufacturer of the cereal, provides impeccable references from scientific sources to support its claims. But since you are aware of the economic interest of the company in promoting sales, you may wonder if they have reproduced only facts that favor their claims. Are there other facts that might prove the opposite? As a careful researcher you would certainly want to look further for data about the advantages and disadvantages of sugar in our diets.

It is harder to determine bias in the research done by scientists and university members even when the research is funded by companies interested in a favorable review of their products. If you discover that a respected biologist who advocates the use of sugar in baby food receives a consultant's fee from a sugar company, should you conclude that the research is slanted and that the scientist has ignored contrary evidence? Not necessarily. The truth may be that the scientist arrived at conclusions about the use of sugar legitimately through experiments that no other scientist would question. But it would probably occur to you that a critical reader might ask about the connection between the results of the research and the payment by a company that profits from the research. In this case you would be wise to read further to find confirmation or rejection of the claim by other scientists.

The most difficult evaluations concern ideological bias. Early in our lives we learn to discount the special interest that makes a small child brag, "My mother (or father) is the greatest!" Later we become aware that the claims of people who are avowed Democrats or Republicans or Marxists or Yankee fans or zealous San Franciscans or joggers must be examined somewhat more carefully than those of people who have no special commitment to a cause or a place or an activity. This is not to say that all partisan claims lack support. They may, in fact, be based on the best available support. But whenever special interest is apparent, there is always the danger that an argument will reflect this bias.

3. Has the source bolstered the claim with sufficient and appropriate evidence? In an article attacking pornography, one author wrote, "Statistics prove that the recent proliferation of porno is directly related to the increasing number of rapes and assaults upon women."[15] But the author gave no further information — neither statistics nor proof that a cause-effect relation exists between pornography and violence against women.

---

[15] Charlotte Allen, "Exploitation for Profit," *Daily Collegian* [University of Massachusetts], October 5, 1976, p. 2.

The critical reader will ask, "What are the numbers? Who compiled them?"

Even those who are reputed to be experts in the subjects they discuss must do more than simply allege that a claim is valid or that the data exist. They must provide facts to support their interpretations.

When Experts Disagree

Authoritative sources can disagree. Such disagreement is probably most common in the social sciences. They are called the "soft" sciences precisely because a consensus about conclusions in these areas is more difficult to arrive at than in the natural and physical sciences. Consider the influence of television viewing on children, an issue that has divided the experts for more than a generation. Dr. William Dietz, chairman of an American Academy of Pediatrics subcommittee on children's television, deplores the effect of TV watching on children. He has said, "I have to wonder whether our children wouldn't be better off spending that time bored rather than watching television. . . . Boredom generates creativity and self-reliance." However, a recent study for the Department of Education by Daniel R. Anderson, a professor of psychology at the University of Massachusetts, and Patricia A. Collins — "The Impact of Children's Education: Television's Influence on Cognitive Development" — finds little or no evidence that television "stifles a child's imagination or has a negative effect on school performance."[16] The resolution of this issue is complicated by the difficulty of controlling all the factors that affect human behavior.

But even in the natural and physical sciences, where the results of observation and experiment are more conclusive, we encounter heated differences of opinion. A popular argument concerns the extinction of the dinosaurs. Was it the effect of a comet striking the earth? Or widespread volcanic activity? Or a cooling of the planet? All these theories have their champions among the experts. A debate of more immediate relevance concerns the possible dangers in experiments with the AIDS virus. Dr. Robert Gallo and his colleagues at the National Cancer Institute have published a warning that "laboratory experiments involving the growing of AIDS viruses in cells that are infected with mouse viruses could generate more pathogenic AIDS viruses," which might find new routes of transmission through the air. But two experts, Dr. Stephen Goff, a molecular biologist at the College of Physicians and Surgeons at Columbia University, and Dr. Mark Feinberg, a molecular biologist at the Whitehead Institute for

---

[16] *Wall Street Journal*, June 13, 1989, Sec. A, p. 13.

Biomedical Research in Cambridge, Massachusetts, are not alarmed. Dr. Feinberg says that there is no proof that "new and more deadly AIDS virus strains are being produced."[17]

An argument of even wider interest to the public has emerged on the extent of global warming and proposals for solving the problem. The section entitled "Environmental Policy" in Part Three of this book provides a wide range of opinions by scientists.

How can you choose between authorities who disagree? If you have applied the tests discussed so far and discovered that one source is less qualified by training and experience or makes claims with little support or appears to be biased in favor of one interpretation, you will have no difficulty in rejecting that person's opinion. If conflicting sources prove, as in the case above, to be equally reliable in all respects, then continue reading other authorities to determine whether a greater number of experts support one opinion rather than another. Although numbers alone, even of experts, don't guarantee the truth, nonexperts have little choice but to accept the authority of the greater number until evidence to the contrary is forthcoming. Finally, if you are unable to decide between competing sources of evidence, you may conclude that the argument must remain unsettled. Such an admission is not a failure; after all, such questions are considered controversial because even the experts cannot agree, and such questions are often the most interesting to consider and argue about. This book contains a section (Part Three) on several long-standing, highly controversial questions, some of them very old and still unresolved.

APPEALS TO NEEDS AND VALUES

Good factual evidence is usually enough to convince an audience that your factual claim is sound. Using examples, statistics, and expert opinion, you can prove, for example, that women do not earn as much as men for the same work. But even good evidence may not be enough to convince your audience that unequal pay is wrong or that something should be done about it. In making value and policy claims, an appeal to the needs and values of your audience is absolutely essential to the success of your argument. If you want to persuade the audience to change their minds or adopt a course of action — in this case, to demand legalization of equal pay for equal work — you will have to show that assent to your claim will bring about what they want and care deeply about.

---

[17] *New York Times*, February 16, 1990, Sec. A, p. 19.

As a writer, you cannot always know who your audience is; it's impossible, for example, to predict exactly who will read a letter you write to a newspaper. Even in the classroom, you have only partial knowledge of your readers. You may not always know or be able to infer what the goals and principles of your audience are. You may not know how they feel about big government, the draft, private school education, feminism, environmental protection, homosexuality, religion, or any of the other subjects you might write about. If the audience concludes that the things you care about are very different from what they care about, if they cannot identify with your goals and principles, they may treat your argument with indifference, even hostility, and finally reject it. But you can hope that decent and reasonable people will share many of the needs and values that underlie your claims.

Appeals to Needs

Suppose that you are trying to persuade Joan Doakes, a friend who is still undecided, to attend college. In your reading you have come across a report about the benefits of a college education written by Howard Bowen, a former professor of economics at Claremont (California) Graduate School, former president of Grinnell College, and a specialist in the economics of higher education. Armed with this testimony, you write to Joan. As support for your claim that she should attend college, you offer evidence that (1) college graduates earn more throughout their lifetime than high school graduates; (2) college graduates are more active and exert greater influence in their communities than high school graduates; and (3) college graduates achieve greater success as partners in marriage and as thoughtful and caring parents.[18]

Joan writes back that she is impressed with the evidence you've provided — the statistics, the testimony of economists and psychologists — and announces that she will probably enroll in college instead of accepting a job offer.

How did you succeed with Joan Doakes? If you know your friend pretty well, the answer is not difficult. Joan has needs that can be satisfied by material success; more money will enable her to enjoy the comforts and luxuries that are important to her. She also needs the esteem of her peers and the sense of achievement that political activity and service to others will give her. Finally, she needs the rootedness to be found in close and lasting family connections.

---

[18] "The Residue of Academic Learning," *Chronicle of Higher Education*, November 14, 1977, p. 13.

Encouraged by your success with Joan Doakes, you write the same letter to another friend, Fred Fox, who has also declined to apply for admission to college. This time, however, your argument fails. Fred, too, is impressed with your research and evidence. But college is not for him, and he repeats that he has decided not to become a student.

Why such a different response? The reason, it turns out, is that you don't know what Fred really wants. Fred Fox dreams of going to Alaska to live alone in the wilderness. Money means little to him, influence in the community is irrelevant to his goals, and at present he feels no desire to become a member of a loving family.

Perhaps if you had known Fred better, you would have offered different evidence to show that you recognized what he needed and wanted. You could have told him that Bowen's study also points out that "college-educated persons are healthier than are others," that "they also have better ability to adjust to changing times and vocations," that "going to college enhances self-discovery" and enlarges mental resources, which encourage college graduates to go on learning for the rest of their lives. This information might have persuaded Fred that college would also satisfy some of his needs.

As this example demonstrates, you have a better chance of persuading your reader to accept your claim if you know what he or she wants and what importance he or she assigns to the needs that we all share. Your reader must, in other words, see some connection between your evidence and his or her needs.

The needs to which you appealed in your letters to Joan and Fred are the requirements for physiological or psychological well-being. The most familiar classification of needs was developed by the psychologist Abraham H. Maslow in 1954.[19] These needs, said Maslow, motivate human thought and action. In satisfying our needs, we attain both long- and short-term goals. Because Maslow believed that some needs are more important than others, he arranged them in hierarchical order from the most urgent biological needs to the psychological needs that are related to our roles as members of a society.

Physiological Needs. Basic bodily requirements: food and drink; health; sex

Safety Needs. Security; freedom from harm; order and stability

Belongingness and Love Needs. Love within a family and among friends; roots within a group or a community

---

[19] *Motivation and Personality* (New York: Harper and Row, 1954), pp. 80–92.

Esteem Needs. Material success; achievement; power, status, and recognition by others

Self-actualization Needs. Fulfillment in realizing one's potential

For most of your arguments you won't have to address the audience's basic physiological needs for nourishment or shelter. The desire for health, however, now receives extraordinary attention. Appeals to buy health foods, vitamin supplements, drugs, exercise and diet courses, and health books are all around us. Many of the claims are supported by little or no evidence, but readers are so eager to satisfy the need for good health that they often overlook the lack of facts or authoritative opinion. The desire for physical well-being, however, is not so simple as it seems; it is strongly related to our need for self-esteem and love.

Appeals to our needs to feel safe from harm, to be assured of order and stability in our lives are also common. Insurance companies, politicians who promise to rid our streets of crime, and companies that offer security services all appeal to this profound and nearly universal need. (We say "nearly" because some people are apparently attracted to risk and danger.) At this writing the nuclear freeze movement has attempted both to arouse fears for our safety and to suggest ways of removing the dangers that make us fearful.

The last three needs in Maslow's hierarchy are the ones you will find most challenging to appeal to in your arguments. It is clear that these needs arise out of human relationships and participation in society. Advertisers make much use of appeals to these needs.

Belongingness and Love Needs.
"Whether you are young or old, the need for companionship is universal." (ad for dating service)
"Share the Fun of High School with Your Little Girl!" (ad for a Barbie Doll)

Esteem Needs.
"Enrich your home with the distinction of an Oxford library."
"Apply your expertise to more challenges and more opportunities. Here are outstanding opportunities for challenge, achievement, and growth." (Perkin-Elmer Co.)

Self-actualization Needs.
"Be all that you can be." (U.S. Army)
"Are you demanding enough? Somewhere beyond the cortex is a small voice whose mere whisper can silence an army of arguments. It goes by many names: integrity, excellence, standards. And it stands alone in final judgment as to whether we have de-

> manded enough of ourselves and, by that example, have inspired the best in those around us." (*New York Times*)

Of course, it is not only advertisers who use these appeals. We hear them from family and friends, from teachers, from employers, from editorials and letters to the editor, from people in public life.

Appeals to Values

Needs give rise to values. If we feel the need to belong to a group, we learn to value commitment, sacrifice, and sharing. And we then respond to arguments that promise to protect our values. It is hardly surprising that values, the principles by which we judge what is good or bad, beautiful or ugly, worthwhile or undesirable, should exercise a profound influence on our behavior. Virtually all claims, even those that seem to be purely factual, contain expressed or unexpressed judgments. The two scientists quoted in Chapter 2 (pp. 29–30) who presented evidence that cocaine was "deadlier than we thought," did so not for academic reasons but because they hoped to persuade people that using the drug was bad.

For our study of argument, we will speak of groups or systems of values because any single value is usually related to others. People and institutions are often defined by such systems of values. We can distinguish, for example, between those who think of themselves as traditional and those who think of themselves as modern by listing their differing values. One writer contrasts such values in this way:

> Among the values of traditionalism are: merit, accomplishment, competition, and success; self-restraint, self-discipline, and the postponement of gratification; the stability of the family; and a belief in certain moral universals. The modernist ethos scorns the pursuit of success; is egalitarian and redistributionist in emphasis; tolerates or encourages sensual gratification; values self-expression as against self-restraint; accepts alternative or deviant forms of the family; and emphasizes ethical relativism.[20]

Systems of values are neither so rigid nor so distinct from one another as this list suggests. Some people who are traditional in their advocacy of competition and success may also accept the modernist values of self-expression and alternative family structures. One editorial writer explained the popularity of the governor of New York, Mario Cuomo:

> He embodies that rare combination of an old-fashioned liberal who has traditional, conservative family values — calling for compassion for the

[20] Joseph Adelson, "What Happened to the Schools," *Commentary*, March 1981, p. 37.

needy and afflicted while inveighing against a lack of discipline in American life.[21]

Values, like needs, are arranged in a hierarchy; that is, some are clearly more important than others to the people who hold them. Moreover, the arrangement may shift over time or as a result of new experiences. In 1962, for example, two speech teachers prepared a list of what they called "Relatively Unchanging Values Shared by Most Americans."[22] Included were "puritan and pioneer standards of morality" and "perennial optimism about the future." More than twenty years later, an appeal to these values might fall on a number of deaf ears.

You should also be aware of not only changes over time but also different or competing value systems that reflect a multitude of subcultures in our country. Differences in age, sex, race, ethnic background, social environment, religion, even in the personalities and characters of its members define the groups we belong to. Such terms as "honor," "loyalty," "justice," "patriotism," "duty," "responsibility," "equality," "freedom," and "courage" will be interpreted very differently by different groups.

All of us belong to more than one group, and the values of the several groups may be in conflict. If one group to which you belong, say, peers of your own age and class, is generally uninterested in and even scornful of religion, you may nevertheless hold to the values of your family and continue to place a high value on religious belief.

How can a knowledge of your readers' values enable you to make a more effective appeal? Suppose you want to argue in favor of a sex education program in the junior high school you attended. The program you support would not only give students information about contraception and venereal disease but also teach them about the pleasures of sex, the importance of small families, and alternatives to heterosexuality. If the readers of your argument are your classmates or your peers, you can be fairly sure that their agreement will be easier to obtain than that of their parents, especially if their parents think of themselves as conservative. Your peers are more likely to value experimentation, tolerance of alternative sexual practices, freedom, and novelty. Their parents are more likely to value restraint, conformity to conventional sexual practices, obedience to family rules, and foresight in planning for the future.

Knowing that your peers share your values and your goals will mean that you need not spell out the values supporting your claim; they are

---

[21] *New York Times*, June 21, 1983, Sec. I, p. 29.

[22] Edward Steele and W. Charles Redding, "The American Value System: Premises for Persuasion," *Western Speech*, Vol. 26, Spring 1962, pp. 83–91.

understood by your readers. Convincing their parents, however, who think that freedom, tolerance, and experimentation have been abused by their children, will be a far more challenging task. In one written piece you have little chance of changing their values, a result that might be achieved only over a longer period of time. So you might first attempt to reduce their hostility by suggesting that, even if a community-wide program were adopted, students would need parental permission to enroll. This might convince some parents that you share their values regarding parental authority and primacy of the family. Second, you might look for other values to which the parents subscribe and to which you can make an appeal. Do they prize maturity, self-reliance, responsibility in their children? If so, you could attempt to prove, with authoritative evidence, that the sex education program would promote these qualities in students who took the course.

But familiarity with the value systems of prospective readers may also lead you to conclude that winning assent to your argument will be impossible. It would probably be fruitless to attempt to persuade a group of lifelong pacifists to endorse the use of nuclear weapons. The beliefs, attitudes, and habits that support their value systems are too fundamental to yield to one or two attempts at persuasion.

EVALUATION OF APPEALS TO NEEDS AND VALUES

If your argument is based on an appeal to the needs and values of your audience, the following questions will help you evaluate the soundness of your appeal.

1. Have the values been clearly defined? If you are appealing to the patriotism of your readers, can you be sure that they agree with your definition? Does patriotism mean "Our country, right or wrong!" or does it mean dissent, even violent dissent, if you think your country is wrong? Because value terms are abstractions, you must make their meaning explicit by placing them in context and providing examples.

2. Are the needs and values to which you appeal prominent in the reader's hierarchy at the time you are writing? An affluent community, fearful of further erosion of quiet and open countryside, might resist an appeal to allow establishment of a high-technology firm, even though the firm would bring increased prosperity to the area.

3. Is the evidence in your argument clearly related to the needs and values to which you appeal? Remember that the reader must see some connection between your evidence and his or her goals. Suppose you were writing an argument to persuade a group of people to vote in an upcoming election. You could provide evidence to prove that only 20 percent of the town voted in the last election. But this evidence would not motivate your audience to vote unless you could provide other evidence to show that their needs were not being served by such a low turnout.

SAMPLE ANALYSIS

Lotto Is Financed by the Poor and Won by the States

PETER PASSELL

The happiest person in Pennsylvania last month may have been Alverta Handel, a housekeeper from the town of Portage who beat 9.6 million-to-one odds to win an $8.2 million share of the record-breaking $115 million lotto jackpot. But the biggest winner by far in Pennsylvania's lottery is the state treasury, which last year netted $593 million from ticket sales. 1

Boosted by ultra-high-stakes lotto games, lotteries have been transformed from a small-change alternative to illegal numbers games into a $16 billion cash cow for financially pressed states. From Maine to California, legislators have stopped worrying about the wages of sin and learned to love the tax that millions wait patiently in line to pay each day. 2

Even the Bible Belt is succumbing to the lure of easy government revenue. Last September, Virginia became the twenty-eighth state to go into the lottery business. And just last month opponents of a property and gasoline tax increase in Louisiana convinced the voters that a lottery could fill the gap left by evaporating oil royalties. 3

Not everyone, though, believes that this form of revenue-gathering is painless. In a book to be published this fall, two Duke University economists, Charles Clotfelter and Philip Cook, offer evidence that the states' share of the lottery amounts to a heavy tax, levied in part on people who can ill afford to pay it. And they raise less tangible, but arguably more troubling questions about the impact of state-sponsored lotteries on public attitudes toward work and thrift. 4

This article by economist Peter Passell appeared in the *New York Times* on May 21, 1989.

Last year 48 cents of every dollar bet on the state lotteries went for 5
prizes, while another 15 cents covered the cost of promotion, sales, and administration. That left 37 percent of the $16 billion pot, or $5.7 billion, for government.

To grateful state officials, the 37 percent is a free lunch. To econo- 6
mists, it is a levy on a product that people plainly want and can only buy legally from the government. The fact that so many people prefer to pay the premium rather than do without the product makes it no more voluntary than the tax on airline tickets.

Moreover, unlike the tax on air travel, the tax on lottery tickets is 7
sharply regressive. According to Mr. Clotfelter and Mr. Cook's study of the Maryland lottery, people earning less than $10,000 buy more tickets than any other income group.

Even in states like California, where evidence suggests that the rich 8
and poor spend roughly the same amount on lottery tickets, those at the low end of the income scale spend a far higher percentage of their incomes on lottery games. And though almost anyone can afford the occasional $1 flyer, some people bet far more. While the average Californian shelled out just $75 last year for lottery tickets, a 1986 poll by the *Los Angeles Times* showed that just 10 percent of adults made 65 percent of the wagers.

Taxes on alcohol and tobacco are almost as regressive as the lottery 9
tax, Mr. Clotfelter and Mr. Cook point out. But the tax rates on these products are generally much lower. In any case, taxes on drinking and smoking are usually justified as a means of discouraging consumption or covering the costs of related, antisocial behavior like drunken driving.

"A Dollar and a Dream"

But if the states still view gambling as an antisocial activity to be dis- 10
couraged through taxation, the message is not getting through to lottery managers. Most lotteries advertise heavily ("All you need is a dollar and a dream"). And most aggressively market the product, tinkering with the frequency of drawings and the mechanics of the game to maintain a sense of novelty and excitement. When it became clear, for example, that huge payouts were the key to lotto's success, New York increased the odds against winning from 1 in 6 million to 1 in 12.9 million.

Of course, it would hardly matter who bought tickets if the lottery 11
merely diverted revenues and profits from illegal gambling to worthy government activities. The daily three-digit games may indeed be displacing some betting on illegal numbers. But Mr. Clotfelter and Mr. Cook find no evidence of such substitution in the high-stakes lotto games, which

now absorb almost half of all lottery dollars. Lotto fever, it seems, is a brand new disease.

Nor is it always clear that lottery earnings are financing good government. Where states earmark lottery revenues for specific purposes, it may be possible to figure out who actually benefits. Kansas, for example, uses the lottery to finance technical assistance to small businesses. 12

Where the Money Goes

More typically, the money amounts to seasoning in the stewpot of ever-changing state appropriations and taxes, leaving each observer free to speculate about how budget priorities would be altered if the lottery lagniappe were to vanish. As Bill Honig, California's public school superintendent, complained to an *Atlanta Constitution* reporter, "For every $5 the lottery gives to the schools, the state takes away $4." 13

Betting on the lotteries is still modest compared to sports and casino wagering, and it is probably less regressive and poses fewer temptations to problem gamblers. 14

But these are private (and often illegal) activities, tolerated by government. The fact that states promote and celebrate the lottery games may increase their impact on public attitudes to work and saving. 15

A survey of Southern California high school students found that the percentage who participate in any form of gambling went up by 40 percent after the state lottery was introduced in 1985. And according to an article in *Forbes* magazine last October, many manufacturers of supermarket products are abandoning "cents-off" coupons for big-prize sweepstakes promotions. 16

To Mr. Clotfelter and Mr. Cook, the lottery is "a risky experiment to determine whether a system that allocates rewards on the basis of luck will undermine a parallel system that allocates . . . on the basis of effort and skill." For many people, however, it remains the only imaginable way to become filthy rich. 17

Analysis

This article offers both kinds of support — factual evidence supplied by experts and an appeal to values — to prove that state-supported lotteries are unfair and socially risky. The author has based his claim largely on the arguments in a book by two Duke University economists. All three writers — Passell, Clotfelter, and Cook — attempt to disprove major misconceptions about legal gambling: (1) that such gambling diverts funds to worthy government enterprises like education; (2) that legal gambling reduces the amount of illegal gambling; (3) that both rich and poor are being fairly "taxed," the tax being the share taken by the states. According to the data, lottery revenues are regressive, that is, the poor invest far more heavily than the rich in the lottery and derive few monetary benefits. Although the chances of winning are very small, the advertising of state lotteries encourages the gambler to think otherwise. In addition, lottery earnings don't necessarily finance good government. They mostly contribute to "ever changing" state budget priorities. The examples and details make a good case for the claim that the lotteries are deceptive and unfair.

The appeal to values rests on the assumption that the work ethic serves a useful social purpose. If people believe that they can achieve windfall profits without working for them, the importance of effort and skill may be undermined. And the fact that lotto games are advertised by the government seems to reinforce these ideas.

Since the three writers are economists, most readers will accept both their data and their interpretations of the data. (Of course, other economists may dispute them.) Their appeal to values is on less solid ground. Obviously not all readers will agree with the authors' assumption that relying on luck for a reward is morally suspect. A more exhaustive argument would provide backing for the belief that gambling reduces willingness to work hard. But given the widespread love of gambling, even among hard workers, and the difficulty of making causal connections in human affairs, such backing might not be easy to find.

READINGS FOR ANALYSIS

Economic and Social Impact of Immigrants

STEPHEN MOORE

Before Congress can establish a pro-family, pro-growth immigration policy, it must know what impact immigrants have on the nation's economy and social fabric. Most research has found that immigrants benefit U.S. citizens economically and socially.[1] 1

A 1986 survey of thirty of America's most distinguished economic scholars found that eight out of ten polled believe that twentieth-century immigration has had a "very favorable effect on the nation's economic growth."[2] Today, a disproportionate share of America's Nobel Prize winners, high school valedictorians, inventors, Ph.D. scientists and engineers, and business entrepreneurs are foreign born.[3] The U.S. Council of Economic Advisers concluded its 1986 study of the economic impact of immigrants: "For much of the nation's history, U.S. immigration policy has been based on the premise that immigrants have a favorable effect on the overall standard of living and on economic development. Analysis of recent migrant flows bears this out."[4] Added former U.S. Ambassador to the United Nations Jeane Kirkpatrick during the 100th Anniversary of the Statue of Liberty: "What gives resonance to our Republic is its continual 2

Stephen Moore, director of an immigration research organization in the nation's capital, was for many years a fellow at the Heritage Foundation in Washington, DC. This excerpt is from the November 6, 1989 *Backgrounder*, published by the Heritage Foundation.

[1] A comprehensive review of studies on the economic benefits of immigration is contained in Julian L. Simon, *How Do Immigrants Affect Us Economically?*, Center for Immigration Policy and Refugee Assistance, Georgetown University, 1985. For an examination of the social/cultural consequences of the "new immigrants," see James Fallows, "Immigration: How It's Affecting Us," *The Atlantic Monthly*, November 1983, pp. 45–106.

[2] Stephen Moore, "Social Scientists' Views on Immigrants and U.S. Immigration Policy: A Postscript," *Annals of the American Academy of Political and Social Sciences*, September 1986, pp. 213–217.

[3] Roy Lerner, "Numbers, Origins, Economic Value and Quality of Technically Trained Immigrants into the United States," *Scientometrics*, Vol. 6, No. 4, 1983, pp. 243–259.

[4] U.S. Council of Economic Advisers, "The Economic Effects of Immigration," *The Economic Report of the President*, 1986, pp. 213–232.

renewal by new citizens who bring to us a special sense of the importance of freedom."[5]

Careful research discredits most of the common objections to immi- 3
grants: that they take jobs from American workers and drive down their wages; that they strain the nation's natural resources and infrastructure; that they are welfare abusers; and that they fail to integrate into American society.[6] On balance, whether they come to reunite with families in the United States, to fill skill gaps in the U.S. labor market, or to start new businesses, immigrants are valuable assets, not liabilities, to the nation.

Labor Market Impact of Immigrants

Immigrants do not just take jobs, they create jobs through their con- 4
sumption, their propensity for starting new businesses, and their contribution in keeping U.S. businesses internationally competitive.

The U.S. Department of Labor this year completed an exhaustive 5
study on the effects of immigrants on job opportunities and wages for native-born Americans. The study concludes: "The presence of immigrants in the U.S. labor market benefits employers, consumers, and the U.S. international economic position. . . . Neither U.S. workers nor most minority workers appear to be adversely affected by immigration — especially during periods of economic expansion such as those we have been experiencing in recent years.[7]

Increasing Workers' Income. The U.S. Council of Economic Advisers 6
reached a similar conclusion in its 1986 analysis of the impact of immigrants. The report finds: "Arguments supporting the restriction of immigration to protect American jobs are similar to those favoring protectionism in international trade. Limiting the entry of immigrant labor may increase the demand for some groups of native-born workers, but it will impose costs on consumers, investors and other workers." The report emphasized that "the net effect of an increase in labor supply due to immigration is to increase the aggregate income of native workers."[8]

---

[5] Jeane Kirkpatrick, "We Need the Immigrants," *Washington Post*, June 30, 1986, p. A-11.

[6] These objections are enumerated in: Richard Lamm and Gary Imhoff, *The Immigration Time Bomb: The Fragmenting of America* (New York: Truman Talley Books, 1985).

[7] U.S. Department of Labor, *The Effects of Immigration on the U.S. Economy and Labor Market*, Immigration Policy and Research Report #1, 1989.

[8] U.S. Council of Economic Advisers, "The Economic Effects of Immigration," *The Economic Report of the President*, 1986, pp. 213–232.

Impact on Taxes and Public Services

Immigrants generally come to the United States to work and improve their economic condition, not to collect welfare. A 1985 study by Ellen Sehgal, of the U.S. Bureau of Labor Statistics, examines Census Bureau data to compare the use of public assistance by the U.S. native-born population with that by the foreign born who entered the United States before 1982. Sehgal finds that, contrary to what seem to be widespread perceptions, "the foreign born do not seem more likely than the U.S. born to be recipients of government benefits."[9] Indeed, the share of foreign born collecting public assistance — including unemployment compensation, food stamps, Supplemental Security Income, and Aid to Families with Dependent Children (AFDC) — was 12.8 percent versus 13.9 percent for the native born. 7

After about fifteen years in the United States, immigrants' earnings generally exceed those of native-born workers. The result: Most immigrant cohorts pay more in taxes over their lifetime than they receive in government benefits, thus resulting in a net fiscal benefit to the U.S. Treasury. One study has estimated that the average immigrant pays $12,000 to $20,000 (in 1975 dollars) more in lifetime taxes than he or she receives in government benefits.[10] The biggest fiscal windfall to U.S.-born citizens is through the large contributions immigrants make to the Social Security system. Immigrants pay Social Security taxes during their working life, even though they do not have parents who are collecting benefits, thus causing a one-time windfall to the retirement system's trust fund. By the time the immigrants collect Social Security themselves, their children are paying into the system. 8

Public Assistance for Refugees

Because of the large recent influx of Soviet Jews to the United States, much public attention has been focused on the taxpayer cost of admitting refugees. Unlike economic immigrants, who must prove that they are "not likely to become a public charge" before they can come to the United States, refugees are, under current law, entitled to about $5,000 in public assistance. These costs cover such short-term readjustment expenses as transportation to the United States, English language training, job placement, medical checkups, and access to U.S. public aid programs. 9

---

[9] Ellen Sehgal, "Foreign Born in the U.S. Labor Market: The Results of a Special Survey," *Monthly Labor Review*, July 1985, pp. 18–24.

[10] Julian L. Simon, *op. cit.*, p. 15.

Paying More Taxes. Yet, as with immigrants, refugees make rapid economic progress within a few years in the United States. A 1984 study by the Church World Service, called "Making It on Their Own," examined the economic progress of 4,500 recent Indochinese refugee families. The study found that, after three years in the United States, only 7 percent were collecting AFDC or other cash assistance, and less than 20 percent were collecting food stamps.[11] A study by Rita Simon on Soviet Jewish refugees and immigrants concluded that after only two years in the United States, these newcomers were contributing more in taxes than they were collecting in public benefits.[12] 10

Given the economic success of most refugees coming to the United States, Congress should stop treating new Americans as welfare recipients and should consider converting federal refugee resettlement aid programs into a loan program. Instead of giving each refugee the $5,000 in readjustment services, that amount would be loaned to the refugee. Modeled after the college student loan program, the refugees would be entitled to a low-interest federal loan or loan guarantee for their first two years in the United States. They would be expected to pay back this money after five years in the United States, provided their income had risen above 120 percent of the poverty level. Loan repayments would be placed in a fund to finance new waves of refugees. This program would reduce, or even eliminate entirely, the budgetary cost of refugee resettlement programs and thereby provide more room in America for refugees fleeing persecution. 11

Discussion Questions

1. What "common objections to immigrants" does the author refute?
2. Does he provide convincing support in his rebuttals? Were you surprised by any of his conclusions? Explain.
3. Based on his research, what policy does the author suggest for new Americans to reduce the cost of resettlement? Does his analogy of the college loan program make the policy more plausible?

Writing Suggestions

1. If you are familiar with the experience of recent immigrants in your community, tell how it proves or disproves the claims in Moore's article. Use several examples to avoid hasty generalization.

---

[11] Church World Service, "Making It on Their Own: From Refugee Sponsorship to Self-Sufficiency," New York, 1983.

[12] Rita J. Simon, *New Lives: The Adjustment of Soviet Jewish Immigrants in the United States and Israel* (Lexington, MA: Lexington Books, 1984).

2. Elsewhere the author urges changes in immigration policy that would favor family immigration over immigration of individuals. Do some research and use your own powers of inference to decide whether favoring immigration of whole families rather than individuals would benefit American society.

Playing Favorites

PATRICIA KEEGAN

There is strong evidence today that nurture — in the role of parents, teachers, and a society still influenced by sex stereotypes — plays an important part in determining how and what boys and girls learn. There is even stronger evidence that, particularly since the advent of the computer, the American education system is geared more closely to boys' learning styles than to those of girls. It is a bias that a growing number of projects are aiming to correct. 1

Studies of school and college classrooms have helped broadly define gender differences in learning. Boys, for example, are competitive, girls cooperative. Boys often prefer individual work, girls do better in groups. Boys seek leadership roles, girls are more willing to be led. Boys believe that they earn high grades, while girls more often attribute their success to luck. "How we treat boys and girls obviously affects the way they learn and what they learn," said Dr. Myra Sadker, acting dean of the school of education at American University in Washington, D.C. 2

Dr. Sadker and her husband, Dr. David Sadker, also a professor of education at American University, have studied classroom interactions in all levels for more than a decade. In one study financed by the National Institute of Education, field researchers who observed more than one hundred fourth-, sixth- and eighth-grade classrooms in four states and the District of Columbia found that male students received more attention from teachers and were given more time to talk in class. 3

While boys are more assertive than girls — they are eight times more likely to call out answers — the Sadkers found that teachers also called on boys more often and gave them more positive feedback than girls. Boys also received more precise feedback from teachers — praise, criticism or help with the answers they gave in class; girls, the Sadkers said, more often received bland and diffuse responses, such as "O.K." and "uh-huh." 4

Patricia Keegan is a free-lance writer based in New York State who specializes in writing about education. This selection is from the Education Life supplement in the *New York Times*, August 16, 1989.

Most of the researchers in this and other studies found that boys got more attention whether the teachers were male or female.

Parents also affect how and what their children learn. According to 5
Dr. Jacquelynne Eccles, who is both a professor of psychology at the University of Colorado and senior research scientist at the University of Michigan, parents — particularly mothers — believe in sex-stereotyped ability more strongly today than they did in the mid-1970s when she began her research.

"Parents, teachers, and kids think boys have more ability in mathe- 6
matics and sports and girls slightly more in English and music," said Dr. Eccles, who surveyed 1,000 Michigan families with school-age children. She reinterviewed one hundred families after news stories appeared on research showing that boys were genetically better in math. About half the families had read the stories. Among those who had, the parents, particularly the mothers, had lowered their opinions of their daughters' math ability.

"Their attitudes have more of an impact on kids' confidence than 7
grades, but certainly affect the likelihood that kids will spend more time on those subjects," Dr. Eccles said.

In response to the continuing low number of girls entering technical 8
fields, some schools have begun programs to encourage them to take math and science courses. For example, in seventh- and eighth-grade science classes at the Montgomery Middle School, just outside Princeton, N.J., female students act as group leaders and teach lessons to their male and female classmates. Their teachers find that assigning girls leadership roles that most would not take on their own, and setting up small groups, builds the girls' self-confidence and interest in these fields.

Proponents of women's colleges take these findings a step further, ar- 9
guing that their environment — in which, in the absence of men, women must assume leadership positions — encourages women to enter male-dominated fields such as science and math. A 1985 study by the Women's College Coalition, which represents most of the nation's ninety-four womens' colleges, found that 5.4 percent of its graduates earned degrees in biology compared with 3.6 percent of women at coeducational colleges. In physics, the figures were 1.7 percent compared with 1.2 percent and in math, 2.3 percent compared with 1.5 percent.

The different treatment of students based on their gender has been 10
observed at all levels. In a 1975 study of classroom interaction in Suffolk County, New York, involving more than 200 children in nursery schools, two psychologists then affiliated with the State University of New York at Stony Brook, Lisa Serbin and K. Daniel O'Leary, found that teachers showed boys how to staple pieces of construction paper together for a

crafts project, then let the boys do their own stapling. But the teachers did the stapling for the girls.

"Girls Taught to Be Dependent"

Although no studies of the same children have been done over the long term, Dr. O'Leary said, "The findings would suggest that girls are taught to be more dependent and boys more independent." Dr. Serbin said that in this study and in later studies of nursery-school children, she found that girls "tend to remain close to the teacher while boys are more comfortable exploring on their own, working independently without teacher structure." 11

Similarly, in colleges and graduate schools, professors show male students how to use equipment and perform lab experiments, while they did the work for female students. 12

After looking at many of the studies on college-classroom interactions, the Association of American Colleges concluded that male students also receive more eye contact and far more of the professor's attention than do female students. 13

The classroom climate obviously affects women's learning and intellectual self-esteem. "Women students are much less likely than their male classmates to feel confident about their preparation for and their ability to do graduate work," according to the association's 1982 report. 14

Yet at least one recent study shows that things can change over time. Research among 4,500 adult learners at Empire State College of the State University of New York found that the women's perception of learning ability jumps ahead of the men's in their late twenties and continues higher through the early retirement years. In the midlife transition phase, between ages thirty-seven and forty-three, men think their academic acumen is significantly below that of midlife women. 15

Follow-up interviews, explained Dr. Timothy Lehmann, associate vice president for research and evaluation, indicate that: "By reentering college, women students more than men clearly recognize they are at a transition point. They go on to have a greater graduation rate than men." 16

One instrument that has provided researchers with a rich opportunity to study gender-related learning differences is the computer. In a 1987 survey of and interviews with forty-four fifth-graders, Dr. Lise Motherwell of the Massachusetts Institute of Technology found that 75 percent of the boys thought the computer was more like a machine and 60 percent of the girls said it was more like a person. "Computers have become the erector sets and doll houses of the eighties," Dr. Motherwell writes in a paper soon to be published by the National Organization for Women. 17

What Computers Are to Girls and Boys

A federally funded study to encourage girls' use of computers, conducted by the Women's Action Alliance, a national nonprofit organization furthering equality for women, based in New York City, yielded similar findings in its final report in 1986, titled, "The Neuter Computer: Computers for Boys and Girls." It read, "While many boys seem to enjoy the computer for its own sake — playing around with it just to see what it can do — many girls seem to value the computer for how it can help them do what they want or have to do. In other words, computers are often means for girls but ends for boys." 18

A 1984 survey by the Alliance as part of the same study, which examined 700 seventh- and eighth-grade students in California, Nebraska, and Vermont, found boys far more likely than girls to use the computer in school during free time and more likely to have a home computer and use it. 19

Hoping to reduce the disparity, the Women's Action Alliance, with money from the National Science Foundation, is sponsoring what it calls a computer-equity project involving six school districts in New York State. One of these, Orchard Park Middle School, in a suburb of Buffalo, started a computer club just for girls. The female students liked choosing their own computer activities, instead of the militaristic, competitive games usually chosen by the boys, according to Barbara Chmura, district computer coordinator. Once the girls developed more confidence about using computers, they were more likely to take part in joint projects with boys, she said. 20

Recent evidence indicates that gender-related differences in attitudes toward computers and technology continue through adulthood, even among those who use computers in their careers. 21

The Center for Children and Technology of the Bank Street College of Education in New York City interviewed more than seventy men and women in technological fields including architecture, engineering, computer programming, and video production. "Women in technological fields want their work to be useful, helpful, and empower others," said Dr. Margaret Honey, senior research scientist at the center. "Men don't talk that way." 22

When the subjects were asked to create a perfect technological instrument, women proposed ways to humanize the computer, Dr. Honey said, while men "believed the computer has the goods and they want to be connected to it." 23

The ongoing Bank Street project, financed by the Spencer Foundation, now is interviewing adolescent boys and girls to find out how they view technology. The goal, as with the other programs, is to develop al- 24 ternate learning programs so that girls will feel more comfortable choosing careers in technological fields still dominated by men.

Discussion Questions

1. What is the principal kind of support Keegan uses to establish her claim that parents and teachers treat boys more favorably than they treat girls? Is it convincing? Why or why not?
2. List some of the differences in the treatment of male and female students. How can they be explained? Mention some of the consequences for learners.
3. Keegan points out that "things can change over time." Discuss some of the changes and their causes.

Writing Suggestions

1. Does your own experience with parents and teachers confirm or deny Keegan's conclusion? Are girls favored in some ways not treated in the article? Whether you agree or disagree with Keegan, make clear in your essay that your argument is based on limited experience.
2. Some feminists have argued that men and women perceive and react to the world differently. Keegan refers to a few of these differences in the use of computers. Are there advantages to the individual and society in reducing the differences? Are there also disadvantages?

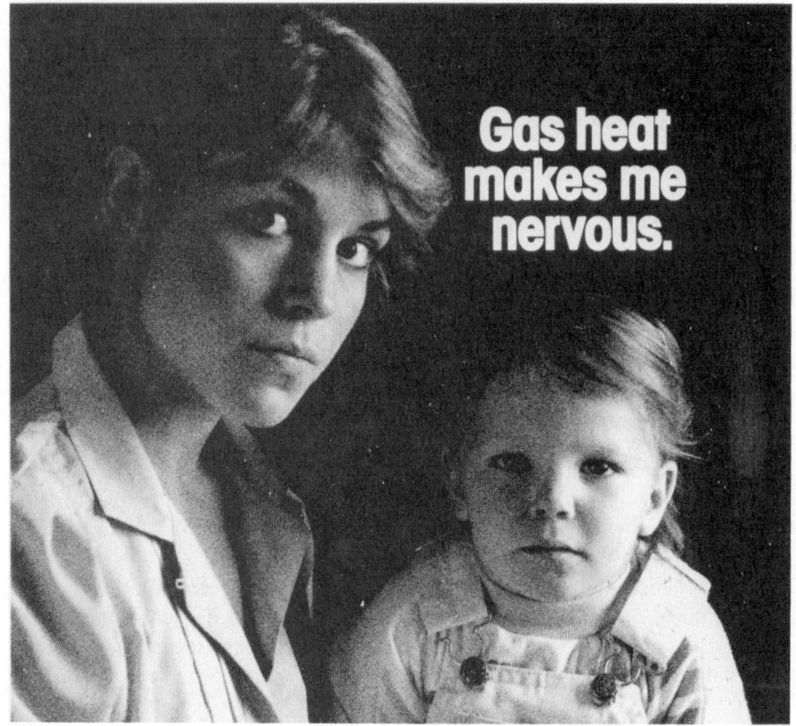

Gas comes from the big utility.
They don't know my name.
They don't know my family.

If you need prompt service from them,
you have to say, "I smell gas."

That's what scares me most. I think gas heat
is dangerous . . . too dangerous
for my home, my kids.

I heat with oil.

66 Morris Ave., P.O. Box 359, Springfield, NJ 07081 • (201) 379-1100

Discussion Questions

1. What strong emotional appeal does the ad make? Is it justified?
2. How would you verify the validity of the appeal?

EXERCISES FOR REVIEW

1. What kind of evidence would you offer to prove to a skeptic that the moon landings — or any other space ventures — have actually occurred? What objections would you anticipate?
2. A group of heterosexual people in a middle-class community who define themselves as devout Christians have organized to keep a group of homosexuals from joining their church. What kind of support would you offer for your claim that the homosexuals should be welcomed into the church? Address your argument to the heterosexuals unwilling to admit the group of homosexuals.
3. In the summer of 1983, after an alarming rise in the juvenile crime rate, the mayor of Detroit instituted a curfew for young people under the age of eighteen. What kind of support can you provide for or against such a curfew?
4. "Racism [or sexism] is [not] a major problem on this campus for home town or neighborhood]." Produce evidence to support your claim.
5. Write a full-page advertisement to solicit support for a project or cause that you believe in.
6. How do you account for the large and growing interest in science fiction films and literature? In addition to their entertainment value, are there other less obvious reasons for their popularity?
7. According to some researchers soap operas are influential in transmitting values, life-styles, and sexual information to youthful viewers. Do you agree? If so, what values and information are being transmitted? Be specific.
8. Choose one of the following stereotypical ideas and argue that it is true or false or partly both. Discuss the reasons for the existence of the stereotype.
   a. Jocks are stupid.
   b. The country is better than the city for bringing up children.
   c. TV is justly called "the boob tube."
   d. A dog is man's best friend.
   e. Beauty contests are degrading to women.
9. Defend or refute the view that organized sports build character.
10. The philosopher Bertrand Russell said, "Most of the work that most people have to do is not in itself interesting, but even such work has certain advantages." Defend or refute this assertion. Use your own experience as support.

CHAPTER 5

Warrants

We now come to the third element in the structure of the argument — the warrant. In the first chapter we defined the warrant as an assumption, a belief we take for granted, or a general principle. Claim and support, the other major elements we have discussed, are more familiar in ordinary discourse, but there is nothing mysterious or unusual about the warrant. All our claims, both formal and informal, are grounded in warrants or assumptions that the audience must share with us if our claims are to prove acceptable.

These warrants reflect our observations, our personal experience, and our participation in a culture. But because these observations, experiences, and cultural associations will vary, the audience may not always agree with the warrants or assumptions of the writer. The British philosopher Stephen Toulmin refers to warrants as "general, hypothetical statements, which can act as bridges" and "entitle one to draw conclusions or make claims."[1] The word *bridges* to denote the action of the warrant is crucial. One dictionary defines warrant as a "guarantee or justification."

---

[1] Stephen Toulmin, *The Uses of Argument* (Cambridge: Cambridge University Press, 1958), p. 98.

We use the word *warrant* to emphasize that in an argument it guarantees a connecting link — a bridge — between the claim and the support. This means that even if a reader agrees that the support is sound, the support cannot prove the validity of the claim unless the reader also agrees with the underlying warrant. Recall the sample argument outlined in Chapter 1 (p. 12):

CLAIM: Adoption of a vegetarian diet leads to healthier and longer life.

SUPPORT: The authors of *Becoming a Vegetarian Family* say so.

WARRANT: The authors of *Becoming a Vegetarian Family* are reliable sources of information on diet.

Notice that the reader must agree with the assumption that the testimony of experts is trustworthy before he or she arrives at the conclusion that a vegetarian diet is healthy. Simply providing evidence that the authors say so is not enough to prove the claim.

The following dialogue offers another example of the relationship between the warrant and the other elements of the argument.

"I don't think that Larry can do the job. He's pretty dumb."

"Really? I thought he was smart. What makes you say he's dumb?"

"Did you know that he's illiterate — can't read above third-grade level? In my book that makes him dumb."

If we put this into outline form, the warrant or assumption in the argument becomes clear.

CLAIM: Larry is pretty dumb.

EVIDENCE: He can't read above third-grade level.

WARRANT: Anybody who can't read above third-grade level must be dumb.

We can also represent the argument in diagram form, which shows the warrant as a bridge between the claim and the support.

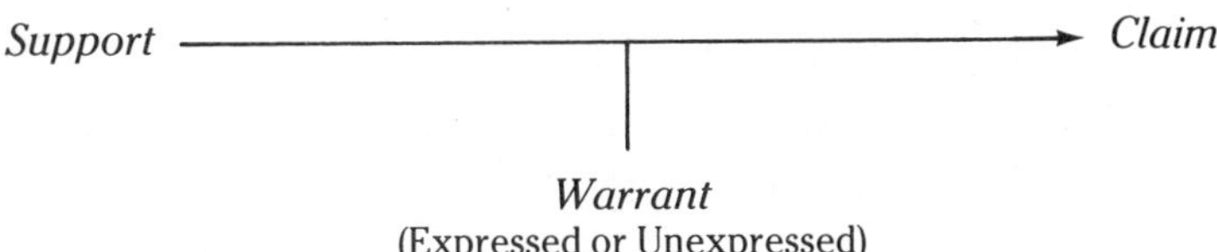

The argument above can then be written like this:

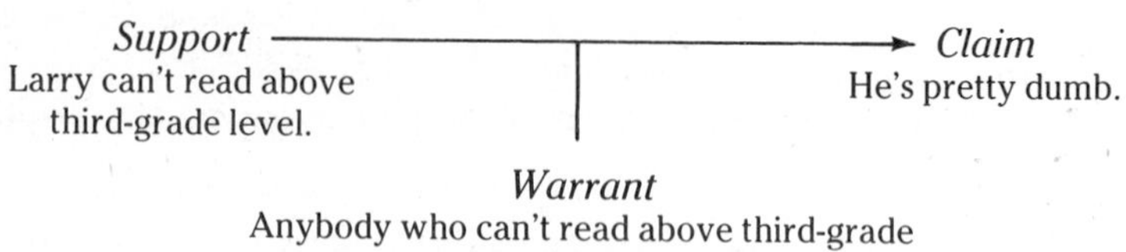

Is this warrant valid? We cannot answer this question until we consider the *backing*. Every warrant or assumption rests on something else that gives it authority; this is what we call backing. Backing or authority for the warrant in this example would consist of research data that prove a relationship between stupidity and illiteracy. This particular warrant, we would discover, lacks backing because we know that the failure to learn to read may be due to a number of things unrelated to intelligence. So, if the warrant is unprovable, the claim — that Larry is dumb — is also unprovable, even if the evidence is true. In this case, then, the evidence does not guarantee the soundness of the claim.

Now consider this example of a somewhat more complicated warrant: The beautiful and unspoiled Eastern Shore of Maryland is being discovered by thousands of tourists, vacationers, and developers who will, according to the residents, change the landscape and the way of life, which is now based largely on fishing and farming. In a few years the Eastern Shore may become a noisy, crowded string of resorts. Mrs. Walkup, the Kent County commissioner, says,

> Catering to the wealthy puts property back on the tax rolls, but it's going to make the Eastern Shore look like the rest of the country. Everything that made our way of life so special is being eroded. We are a fragile area. The Eastern Shore is still special, but it is feeling pressure from all directions. Lots of people don't seem to appreciate the fact that God made us to need a little peace and quiet now and then.[2]

In simplified form the argument of those opposed to development would be outlined this way:

---

[2] Michael Wright, "The Changing Chesapeake," *New York Times Magazine*, July 10, 1983, p. 27.

CLAIM: Development will bring undesirable changes to the present way of life on the Eastern Shore, a life of farming and fishing, peace and quiet.

SUPPORT: Developers will build express highways, condominiums, casinos, and nightclubs.

WARRANT: A pastoral life of fishing and farming is superior to the way of life brought by expensive, fast-paced modern development.

Notice that the warrant is a broad generalization that can apply to a number of different situations, while the claim is about a specific place and time. It should be added that in other arguments the warrant may not be stated in such general terms. However, even in arguments in which the warrant makes a more specific reference to the claim, the reader can infer an extension of the warrant to other similar arguments. In both the vegetarian diet example (p. 3, outlined on p. 12) and the example of the authority warrant below (p. 149), the warrants mention specific authors. But it is clear that such warrants can be generalized to apply to other arguments in which we accept a claim based on the credibility of the sources.

To be convinced of the validity of Mrs. Walkup's claim, you must first find that the support is true, that the developers plan to introduce drastic changes that will destroy the pastoral life of the Eastern Shore. You may, however, believe that the support is not entirely sound, that the development will be much more modest than residents fear, and that the Eastern Shore will not be seriously altered. Next, you may want to see more justification for the warrant. Is pastoral life superior to the life that will result from large-scale development? Perhaps you have always thought that a life of fishing and farming means poverty and limited opportunities for the majority of the residents. Although the superiority of a way of life is largely a matter of taste and therefore difficult to prove, Mrs. Walkup may need to produce backing for her belief that the present way of life is more desirable than one based on developing the area for new residents and summer visitors. If you find either the support or the warrant unconvincing, you cannot accept the claim.

Remember that a claim is often modified by one or more qualifiers, which limit the claim. Mrs. Walkup might have said, "Development will *probably* destroy *some aspects of* the present way of life on the Eastern Shore." Warrants can also be modified or limited by *reservations*, which remind the reader that there are conditions under which the warrants will not be relevant. Mrs. Walkup might have added, ". . . unless increased prosperity and exposure to the outside world brought by development improve some aspects of our lives."

A diagram of Mrs. Walkup's argument shows the additional elements:

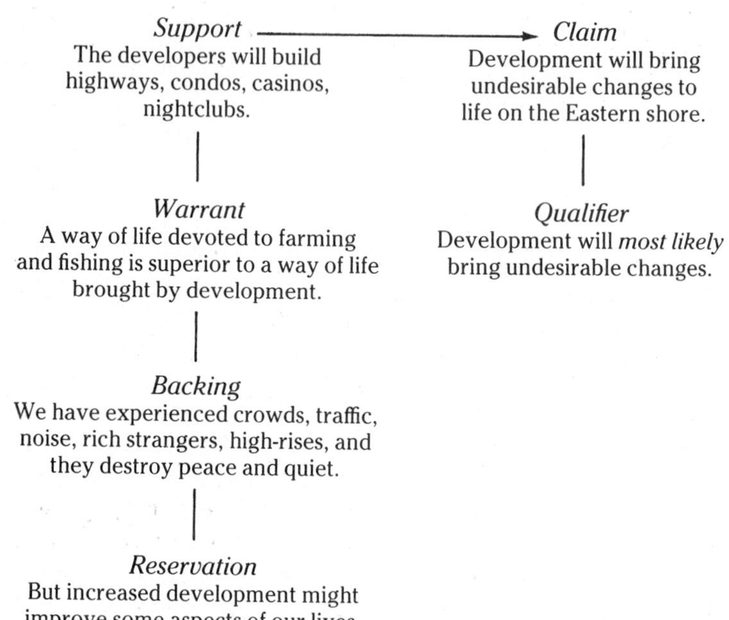
Support
The developers will build highways, condos, casinos, nightclubs.
Claim
Development will bring undesirable changes to life on the Eastern shore.
Warrant
A way of life devoted to farming and fishing is superior to a way of life brought by development.
Qualifier
Development will *most likely* bring undesirable changes.
Backing
We have experienced crowds, traffic, noise, rich strangers, high-rises, and they destroy peace and quiet.
Reservation
But increased development might improve some aspects of our lives.

Claim and support (or lack of support) are relatively easy to uncover in most arguments. One thing that makes the warrant different is that it is often unexpressed and therefore unexamined by both writer and reader because they take it for granted. In the argument about Larry's intelligence, the warrant was stated. But in the argument about development on the Eastern Shore, Mrs. Walkup did not state her warrant directly, although her meaning is perfectly clear. She probably felt that it was not necessary to be more explicit because her readers would understand and supply the warrant.

Arguers will often neglect to state their warrants for one of two reasons: First, like Mrs. Walkup, they may believe that the warrant is obvious and need not be expressed; second, they may want to conceal the warrant in the hope that the reader will overlook its weakness.

What kinds of warrants are so obvious that they need not be expressed? Here are a few that will probably sound familiar.

Mothers love their children.

The more expensive the product, the more satisfactory it will be.

A good harvest will result in lower prices for produce.

First come, first served.

These statements seem to embody beliefs that most of us would share and that might be unnecessary to make explicit in an argument. The last statement, for example, is taken as axiomatic, an article of faith that we seldom question in ordinary circumstances. Suppose you hear someone make the claim, "I deserve to get the last ticket to the concert." If you ask why he is entitled to a ticket that you also would like to have, he may answer in support of his claim, "Because I was here first." No doubt you accept his claim without further argument because you understand and agree with the warrant that is not expressed: "If you arrive first, you deserve to be served before those who come later." Your acceptance of the warrant probably also takes into account the unexpressed backing that is based on a belief in justice: "It is only fair that those who sacrifice time and comfort to be first in line should be rewarded for their trouble."

In this case it may not be necessary to expose the warrant and examine it. Indeed, as Stephen Toulmin tells us, "If we demanded the credentials of all warrants at sight and never let one pass unchallenged, argument could scarcely begin."[3]

But even those warrants that seem to express universal truths invite analysis if we can think of claims for which these warrants might not, after all, be relevant. "First in line," for example, may justify the claim of a person who wants a concert ticket, but it cannot in itself justify the claim of someone who wants a vital medication that is in short supply. Moreover, offering a rebuttal to a long-held but unexamined warrant can often produce an interesting and original argument. If someone exclaims, "All this buying of gifts! I think people have forgotten that Christmas celebrates the birth of Christ," she need not express the assumption — that the buying of gifts violates what ought to be a religious celebration. It goes unstated by the speaker because it has been uttered so often that she knows the hearer will supply it. But one writer, in an essay titled "Let's Keep Christmas Commercial," argued that, contrary to popular belief, the purchase of gifts, which means the expenditure of time, money, and thought on others rather than oneself, is not a violation but an affirmation of the Christmas spirit.[4]

The second reason for refusal to state the warrant lies in the arguer's intention to disarm or deceive the reader, although the arguer may not be aware of this. For instance, failure to state the warrant is common in advertising and politics, where the desire to sell a product or an idea may outweigh the responsibility to argue explicitly. The following advertisement is famous not only for what it says but for what it does not say:

---

[3] *The Uses of Argument* (Cambridge: Cambridge University Press, 1958), p. 106.

[4] April Oursler Armstrong, *Saturday Evening Post*, December 18, 1965, p. 8.

In 1918 Leona Currie scandalized a New Jersey beach with a bathing suit cut above her knees. And to irk the establishment even more, she smoked a cigarette. Leona Currie was promptly arrested.

Oh, how Leona would smile if she could see you today.

You've come a long way, baby. *Virginia Slims.* The taste for today's woman.

What is the unstated warrant? The manufacturer of Virginia Slims hopes we will agree that being permitted to smoke cigarettes is a significant sign of female liberation. But many readers would insist that proving "You've come a long way, baby" requires more evidence than women's freedom to smoke (or wear short bathing suits.) The shaky warrant weakens the claim.

Politicians, too, conceal warrants that may not survive close scrutiny. In the 1983 mayoral election in Chicago, one candidate revealed that his opponent had undergone psychiatric treatment. He did not have to state the warrant supporting his claim. He knew that many in his audience would assume that anyone who had undergone psychiatric treatment was unfit to hold public office. This same assumption contributed to the withdrawal of a vice-presidential candidate from the 1972 campaign.

TYPES OF WARRANTS

In this section we show how arguments may be classified according to the types of warrants offered as proof. Because warrants represent the reasoning process by which we establish the relationship between support and claim, analysis of warrants enables us to see the whole argument as a sum of its parts.

Warrants may be organized into three categories: "*authoritative, substantive,* and *motivational*."[5] We have already given examples of these types of warrants in this chapter and in Chapter 1. The *authoritative warrant* (see p. 12) is based on the credibility or trustworthiness of the source. If we assume that the source of the data is authoritative, then we find that the support justifies the claim. A *substantive warrant* is based on beliefs about reliability of factual evidence. In the example on page 143 the speaker assumes, although mistakenly, that the relationship between illiteracy and stupidity is a verifiable datum, one that can be proved by objective research. A *motivational warrant*, on the other hand, is based on the needs and values of the audience. For example, the warrant on page 12

[5] D. Ehninger and W. Brockriede, *Decision by Debate* (New York: Dodd, Mead, 1953).

reflects a preference for individual freedom, a value that would cause a reader who held it to agree that laws against marijuana should be repealed.

Seven types of warrants in these categories are examined below. Authority, of course, represents the authoritative warrant. Generalization, sign, cause and effect, comparison, and analogy are substantive warrants, based on relationships between facts in the external world. Under values you will find examples of motivational warrants, which are subjective, or a reflection of feelings and attitudes.

There are at least two good reasons for summarizing the types of warrants. First, reading these summaries will give you a number of additional examples of warrants as they work (or don't work) to justify claims. Second, it will become clear as you examine them that each type of warrant requires a different set of questions for testing its soundness. At the end of this discussion on pages 156–157 a list of questions will help you to decide whether a particular kind of warrant is valid and can justify a particular claim. The list is not exhaustive, and you may be able to think of other criteria for evaluating warrants.

Authority

Arguments from authority depend on the credibility of their sources, as in this example.

> [Benjamin] Bloom maintains that most children can learn everything that is taught them with complete competence.[6]

Because Benjamin Bloom is a professor of education at the University of Chicago and a widely respected authority on educational psychology, his statement about the educability of children carries considerable weight. Notice that Professor Bloom has qualified his claim by asserting that "most" children, but not all, can learn everything. The reader might also recognize the limits of the warrant — the authority could be mistaken, or there could be disagreement among authorities.

CLAIM: Most children can learn everything that is taught them with complete competence.

SUPPORT: Professor Bloom attests that this is so.

WARRANT: Professor Bloom's testimony is sufficient because he is an accepted authority on educational achievement.

RESERVATIONS: Unless the data for his studies were inaccurate, unless his criteria for evaluation were flawed, and so on.

---

[6] Michael Alper, "All Our Children Can Learn," *University of Chicago Magazine*, Summer 1982, p. 3.

Generalization

Arguments from generalization are based on the belief that we can derive a general principle from a series of examples. But these warrants are credible only if the examples are representative of the whole group being described and not too many contradictory examples have been ignored. In the following excerpt the author documents the tragic effects for children born "unnaturally" (outside the mother's womb) or without knowledge of their fathers.

> For years I've collected bits of data about certain unfortunate people in the news: Son of Sam, the Hillside strangler, the Pennsylvania shoemaker who raped and brutalized several women, a Florida man who killed at least thirty-four women, the man sought in connection with the Tylenol scare. All of them grew up not knowing at least one of their natural parents; most knew neither.[7]

In outline the argument takes this form:

CLAIM: People brought up without a sense of identity with their natural parents will respond to the world with rage and violence.

SUPPORT: Son of Sam, the Hillside strangler, the Pennsylvania shoemaker, the Florida murderer, the man in the Tylenol scare responded to the world with rage and violence.

WARRANT: What is true of this sample is true for others in this class.

RESERVATION: Unless this sample is too small or exceptions have been ignored.

Sign

As their name suggests, in arguments based on sign the arguer offers an observable datum as an indicator of a condition. The warrant that a sign is convincing can be accepted only if the sign is appropriate, if it is sufficient, and if other indicators do not dispute it. We have already examined one such argument, in which the enjoyment of Virginia Slims is presented as a sign of female liberation. In the following example the warrant is stated:

> There are other signs of a gradual demoting of the professions to the level of ordinary trades and businesses. The right of lawyers and physicians

[7] Lorraine Dusky, "Brave New Babies?" *Newsweek*, December 6, 1982, p. 30.

to advertise, so as to reintroduce money competition and break down the "standard practices," is being granted. Architects are being allowed to act as contractors. Teachers have been unionized.[8]

Here, too, a reservation is in order.

CLAIM: Professions are being demoted to the level of ordinary trades and businesses.

SUPPORT: Lawyers and physicians advertise, architects act as contractors, teachers have been unionized.

WARRANT: These business practices are signs of the demotion of the professions.

RESERVATION: Unless these practices are not widespread.

Cause and Effect

Causal reasoning assumes that one event or condition can bring about another. We can reason from the cause to the effect or from the effect to the cause. The following is an example of reasoning from effect (the claim) to cause (the warrant). The quotation is taken from the famous Supreme Court decision of 1954, *Brown v. Board of Education*, which mandated the desegregation of public schools throughout the United States.

> Segregation of white and colored children in public schools has a detrimental effect upon the colored children. The impact is greater when it has the sanction of the law; for the policy of separating the races is usually interpreted as denoting the inferiority of the Negro group. A sense of inferiority affects the motivation of a child to learn. Segregation with the sanction of law, therefore, has a tendency to [retard] the educational and mental development of Negro children and to deprive them of some of the benefits they would receive in a racial[ly] integrated school system.[9]

The outline of the argument would take this form:

CLAIM: (EFFECT) Colored children have suffered mental and emotional damage in legally segregated schools.

SUPPORT: They suffer from feelings of inferiority, which retard their ability to learn. They are being deprived of important social and educational benefits.

---

[8] Jacques Barzun, "The Professions Under Siege," *Harper's*, October 1978, p. 66.

[9] *Brown v. Board of Education of Topeka*, 347 U.S. 487–496 (May 17, 1954).

WARRANT: Legal segregation has a tendency to retard the emo-
(CAUSE) tional and mental development of Negro children.

In cause-effect arguments the reasoning may be more complicated than an outline suggests. For one thing, events and conditions in the world are not always the result of single causes, nor does a cause necessarily produce a single result. It is probably more realistic to speak of chains of causes as well as chains of effects. A recent headline emphasizes this form of reasoning: "Experts Fear That Unpredictable Chain of Events Could Bring Nuclear War." The article points to the shooting of the Archduke Francis Ferdinand of Austria-Hungary in the Bosnian city of Sarajevo in 1914, which "set in motion a series of events that the world's most powerful leaders could not stop" — that is, World War I.

Or, as another example, opinion polls a few years ago indicated Americans' unwillingness to "approve any bellicose activity, unless U.S. interests are seen as truly vital and are clearly defined."[10] The immediate cause of this isolationism is usually attributed to the "Vietnam syndrome," the relic of a bitter experience in an unpopular war. But this single cause, according to some students of the problem, is insufficient to explain the current mood. History, they say, reveals "decades of similar American resistance to foreign involvements."

Causes can also be either *necessary* or *sufficient*. That is, to contract tuberculosis, it is necessary to be exposed to the bacillus, but this exposure in itself may not be sufficient to bring on the disease. However, if the victim's immune system is depressed for some reason, exposure to the bacillus will be sufficient to cause the illness. Or, to take an example from law and politics: To reduce the incidence of drunk driving, it would be necessary to enact legislation that penalized the drunk driver. But that would not be sufficient unless the police and the courts were diligent in making arrests and imposing sentences.

If you are aware of the intricate relations between causes and effects, you will be cautious about proposing simple explanations or inferring simple results from some of the complex subjects you examine.

Comparison

In some arguments we compare characteristics and circumstances in two or more cases to prove that what is true in one case ought to be true in another. Unlike the elements in analogies, which we will discuss next, the things being matched in comparisons belong to the same class. The following is a familiar argument based on a comparison of similar activi-

---

[10] *Public Opinion*, April–May 1982, p. 16.

ties in different countries at different times. On the basis of these apparent similarities the author makes a judgment about America's future.

> Perhaps I'm wrong, but the auguries seem to me threatening. Like the bourgeoisie of pre–World War I in Europe, we are retreating into our well-furnished houses, hoping the storm, when it comes, will strike someone else, preferably the poor. Our narcissistic passion for sports and fitness reminds me of Germany in the twenties and early thirties, when the entire nation turned to hiking, sun-bathing and the worship of the body beautiful, in part so as not to see what was happening to German politics — not to speak of the family next door. The belief that gold in the garden is more important than government helped to bring France to defeat in 1940 and near civil war in the 1950s. When the middle class stops believing in government or in the future, it's all over, time truly to sew the diamonds in the lining of your coat and make a run for it.[11]

This is the argument in outline form:

CLAIM: The behavior of many middle-class Americans today threatens our future.

SUPPORT: The same kind of behavior by the Germans in the twenties and thirties and by the French in the thirties and forties led to disaster.

WARRANT: Because such behavior brought disaster to Germany and France, it will bring disaster to America.

But is this warrant believable? Are the dissimilarities between our country now and these European countries in earlier decades greater than the similarities? For example, if our present passion for sports and fitness is caused by very different social forces than those that operated in Germany in the twenties and thirties, then the comparison warrant is too weak to support the author's claim.

Analogy

An analogy warrant assumes a resemblance in some characteristics between dissimilar things. Analogies differ in their power to persuade. Some are explanatory; others are merely descriptive. Those that describe are less likely to be useful in a serious argument. In conversation we often liken human beings to other animals — cows, pigs, rats, chickens. Or we compare life and happiness to a variety of objects: "Life is a cabaret," "Life is just a bowl of cherries," "Happiness is a warm puppy." But such metaphorical uses are more colorful than precise. In those examples one

---

[11] Michael Korda, "The New Pessimism," *Newsweek*, June 14, 1982, p. 20.

quality is abstracted from all the others, leaving us with two objects that remain essentially dissimilar. Descriptive analogies promise immediate access to the reader, as do paintings or photographs. For this reason you may find the idea of such short cuts tempting, but descriptive analogies are seldom enough to support a claim. Consider the following example, which appears in a speech by Malcolm X, the black civil-rights leader, criticizing the participation by whites in the march on Washington in 1962 for black rights and employment:

> It's just like when you've got some coffee that's too black, which means it's too strong. What do you do? You integrate it with cream, you make it weak. But if you pour too much cream in it, you won't even know you ever had coffee.[12]

This is the outline of the argument:

CLAIM: Integration of black and white people in the march on Washington weakened the black movement for rights and jobs.

SUPPORT: Putting white cream into black coffee weakens the coffee.

WARRANT: Weakening coffee with cream is analogous to weakening the black rights movement by allowing white people to participate.

The imagery is vivid, but the analogy does not represent convincing proof. The dissimilarities between whitening coffee with cream and integrating a political movement are too great to convince the reader of the damaging effects of integration. Moreover, words like *strong* and *weak* as they apply to a civil-rights movement need careful definition. To make a convincing case, the author would have to offer not imagery but facts and authoritative opinion.

The following analogy is more successful because it is explanatory rather than descriptive. The elements on both sides of the analogy are weapons and a contest of arms. These remarks were made by Representative Jim Leach, Republican of Iowa, to the House of Representatives in support of a freeze on nuclear arms, March 16, 1983:

> In a world of nuclear overkill and redundance, the United States and the Soviet Union are like two rivals locked in a small room in a duel to the death where one has 1,400 pistols and the other 1,200. The one with 1,400 has no

[12] "Message to the Grass Roots," *Roots of Rebellion*, edited by Richard P. Young (New York: Harper and Row, 1970), p. 357.

advantage when one or both of the parties are likely to be killed or maimed with the first pistol shot.[13]

Representative Leach's argument may be outlined like this:

CLAIM: In enlarging their nuclear arsenals the United States and the Soviet Union are engaged in a duel that neither can win.

SUPPORT: A duelist in a locked room with 1,400 pistols could probably not win against a duelist with 1,200 pistols.

WARRANT: A pistol duel is analogous to the nuclear arms rivalry between the United States and the Soviet Union.

This analogy, however, also suffers from the weakness of all analogies — dissimilarities exist between the objects being compared. In arguing for a nuclear freeze, Representative Leach would have had to offer substantive proof of the dangers of the arms race itself based on a knowledge of history, diplomatic relations, and other circumstances that influence the conduct of the superpowers.

Values

Warrants may also reflect needs and values, and readers accept or reject the claim to the extent that they find the warrants relevant to their own goals and standards. Mrs. Walkup and others based their opposition to development of the Eastern Shore on a value warrant: Rural life is superior to the way of life being introduced by developers. Clearly, numbers of outsiders who valued a more sophisticated way of life did not agree.

The persuasive appeal of advertisements, as we know, leans heavily on value warrants, which are often unstated. Sometimes they include almost no printed message, except the name of the product accompanied by a picture. The advertisers expect us to assume that if we use their product, we can acquire the desirable characteristics of the attractive people shown using it.

Value warrants are indispensable in arguments on public policy. In the following excerpt from a radio debate, a professor of statistics at Berkeley argues in favor of affirmative action policies to promote the hiring of women faculty. Her claim has been made earlier, but her warrant and any reservations remain unstated. This is her supporting material.

> 6.9 percent is [a] very tiny proportion of the faculty. You still have to go a long ways to see a woman teaching in this university. Most all of the

---

[13] *New York Times*, March 2, 1984.

students go to this university and never, ever have a woman professor, a woman associate professor, even a woman assistant professor teaching them. There's a lack of role models, there's a lack of teaching, and it brings a lack of breadth into the teaching.[14]

CLAIM: The proportion of women on the Berkeley faculty should be increased.

SUPPORT: Because women are only 6.9 percent of the faculty, most students never have a woman teacher.

WARRANT: Exposure of students to women faculty is a desirable educational goal.

RESERVATION: Unless individual women faculty members are significantly less competent than men.

EVALUATION OF WARRANTS

We've pointed out that the warrant underlying your claim will define the kind of argument you are making. Answering the following questions about warrants, whether expressed or unexpressed, will help you to judge the soundness of your arguments.

1. *Authority.*
   Is the authority sufficiently respected to make a credible claim?
   Do other equally reputable authorities agree with the authority cited?
   Are there equally reputable authorities who disagree?

2. *Generalization.*
   Are sufficient examples given to convince us that a general statement is justified? That is, are the examples given representative of the whole community?
   Are there sufficient negative instances to weaken the generalization?

3. *Sign.*
   Is the sign used appropriate as an indicator?
   Is the sign sufficient to account for the claim?
   Are negative signs — that is, other indicators — available that might contradict the claim?

---

[14] Elizabeth Scott, quoted in *Affirmative Action: Not a Black and White Issue*, National Public Radio, week of April 25, 1977, p. 7.

4. *Cause and Effect.*
   Does the cause given seem to account entirely for the effect?
   Are other possible causes equally important as explanations for the effect?
   Is it possible to prove that the stated cause produced the effect?

5. *Comparison.*
   Are the similarities between the two situations greater than the differences?
   Have all or only a few of the important characteristics been compared? Have some important dissimilarities been overlooked?

6. *Analogy.*
   Is the analogy explanatory or simply descriptive?
   Are there sufficient similarities between the two elements to make the analogy appropriate?

7. *Values.*
   Is the value one that the audience will regard as important?
   Is the value relevant to the claim?

SAMPLE ANALYSIS

The Case for Torture

MICHAEL LEVIN

It is generally assumed that torture is impermissible, a throwback to a more brutal age. Enlightened societies reject it outright, and regimes suspected of using it risk the wrath of the United States. 1

I believe this attitude is unwise. There are situations in which torture is not merely permissible but morally mandatory. Moreover, these situations are moving from the realm of imagination to fact. 2

Suppose a terrorist has hidden an atomic bomb on Manhattan Island which will detonate at noon on July 4 unless . . . (here follow the usual demands for money and release of his friends from jail). Suppose, further, that he is caught at 10 A.M. of the fateful day, but — preferring death to 3

Michael Levin is a professor of philosophy at the City College of New York. This essay is reprinted from the June 7, 1982 issue of *Newsweek*.

failure — won't disclose where the bomb is. What do we do? If we follow due process — wait for his lawyer, arraign him — millions of people will die. If the only way to save those lives is to subject the terrorist to the most excruciating possible pain, what grounds can there be for not doing so? I suggest there are none. In any case, I ask you to face the question with an open mind.

Torturing the terrorist is unconstitutional? Probably. But millions of lives surely outweigh constitutionality. Torture is barbaric? Mass murder is far more barbaric. Indeed, letting millions of innocents die in deference to one who flaunts his guilt is moral cowardice, an unwillingness to dirty one's hands. If *you* caught the terrorist, could you sleep nights knowing that millions died because you couldn't bring yourself to apply the electrodes? 4

Once you concede that torture is justified in extreme cases, you have admitted that the decision to use torture is a matter of balancing innocent lives against the means needed to save them. You must now face more realistic cases involving more modest numbers. Someone plants a bomb on a jumbo jet. He alone can disarm it, and his demands cannot be met (or if they can, we refuse to set a precedent by yielding to his threats). Surely we can, we must, do anything to the extortionist to save the passengers. How can we tell 300, or 100, or 10 people who never asked to be put in danger, "I'm sorry, you'll have to die in agony, we just couldn't bring ourselves to. . . ." 5

Here are the results of an informal poll about a third, hypothetical, case. Suppose a terrorist group kidnapped a newborn baby from a hospital. I asked four mothers if they would approve of torturing kidnappers if that were necessary to get their own newborns back. All said yes, the most "liberal" adding that she would administer it herself. 6

I am not advocating torture as punishment. Punishment is addressed to deeds irrevocably past. Rather, I am advocating torture as an acceptable measure for preventing future evils. So understood, it is far less objectionable than many extant punishments. Opponents of the death penalty, for example, are forever insisting that executing a murderer will not bring back his victim (as if the purpose of capital punishment were supposed to be resurrection, not deterrence or retribution). But torture, in the cases described, is intended not to bring anyone back but to keep innocents from being dispatched. The most powerful argument against using torture as a punishment or to secure confessions is that such practices disregard the rights of the individual. Well, if the individual is all that important — and he is — it is correspondingly important to protect the rights of individuals threatened by terrorists. If life is so valuable that it must never be taken, the lives of the innocents must be saved even at the price of hurting the one who endangers them. 7

Better precedents for torture are assassination and preemptive attack. No Allied leader would have flinched at assassinating Hitler, had that been possible. (The Allies did assassinate Heydrich.) Americans would be angered to learn that Roosevelt could have had Hitler killed in 1943 — thereby shortening the war and saving millions of lives — but refused on moral grounds. Similarly, if nation A learns that nation B is about to launch an unprovoked attack, A has a right to save itself by destroying B's military capability first. In the same way, if the police can by torture save those who would otherwise die at the hands of kidnappers or terrorists, they must. 8

There is an important difference between terrorists and their victims that should mute talk of the terrorists' "rights." The terrorist's victims are at risk unintentionally, not having asked to be endangered. But the terrorist knowingly initiated his actions. Unlike his victims, he volunteered for the risks of his deed. By threatening to kill for profit or idealism, he renounces civilized standards, and he can have no complaint if civilization tries to thwart him by whatever means necessary. 9

Just as torture is justified only to save lives (not extort confessions or recantations), it is justifiably administered only to those *known* to hold innocent lives in their hands. Ah, but how can the authorities ever be sure they have the right malefactor? Isn't there a danger of error and abuse? Won't We turn into Them? 10

Questions like these are disingenuous in a world in which terrorists proclaim themselves and perform for television. The name of their game is public recognition. After all, you can't very well intimidate a government into releasing your freedom fighters unless you announce that it is your group that has seized its embassy. "Clear guilt" is difficult to define, but when 40 million people see a group of masked gunmen seize an airplane on the evening news, there is not much question about who the perpetrators are. There will be hard cases where the situation is murkier. Nonetheless, a line demarcating the legitimate use of torture can be drawn. Torture only the obviously guilty, and only for the sake of saving innocents, and the line between Us and Them will remain clear. 11

There is little danger that the Western democracies will lose their way if they choose to inflict pain as one way of preserving order. Paralysis in the face of evil is the greater danger. Some day soon a terrorist will threaten tens of thousands of lives, and torture will be the only way to save them. We had better start thinking about this. 12

Analysis

Levin's controversial essay attacks a popular assumption which most people have never thought to question — that torture is impermissible under any circumstances. Levin argues that in extreme cases torture is morally justified in order to bring about a greater good than the rights of the individual who is tortured.

Against the initial resistance that most readers may feel, Levin makes a strong case. Its strength lies in the backing he provides for the warrant that torture is sometimes necessary. This backing consists in the use of two effective argumentative strategies. One is the anticipation of objections. Unprecedented? No. Unconstitutional? No. Barbaric? No. Second, and more important, are the hypothetical examples that compel readers to rethink their positions and possibly arrive at agreement with the author. Levin chooses extreme examples — kidnapping of a newborn child, planting a bomb on a jumbo jet, detonating an atomic bomb in Manhattan — that draw a line between clear and murky cases and make agreement easier. And he bolsters his moral position by insisting that torture is not to be used as punishment or revenge but only in order to save innocent lives.

To support such an unpopular assumption the writer must convey the impression that he is a reasonable man, and this Levin attempts to do by a searching definition of terms, the careful organization and development of his argument, including references to the opinions of other people, and the expression of compassion for innocent lives.

Another strength of the article is its readability — the use of contractions, informal questions, conversational locutions. This easy, familiar style is disarming; the reader doesn't feel threatened by heavy admonitions from a writer who affects a superior, moral attitude.

Notice that Levin's opening words, "It is generally assumed . . . " are the same as Orwell's in the opening sentence of "Politics and the English Language" (page 599), another essay that attacks a popular assumption.

READINGS FOR ANALYSIS

A Proposal to Abolish Grading

PAUL GOODMAN

Let half a dozen of the prestigious Universities — Chicago, Stanford, 1
the Ivy League — abolish grading, and use testing only and entirely for pedagogic purposes as teachers see fit.

Anyone who knows the frantic temper of the present schools will un- 2
derstand the transvaluation of values that would be effected by this modest innovation. For most of the students, the competitive grade has come to be the essence. The naive teacher points to the beauty of the subject and the ingenuity of the research; the shrewd student asks if he is responsible for that on the final exam.

Let me at once dispose of an objection whose unanimity is quite fasci- 3
nating. I think that the great majority of professors agree that grading hinders teaching and creates a bad spirit, going as far as cheating and plagiarizing. I have before me the collection of essays, *Examining in Harvard College*, and this is the consensus. It is uniformly asserted, however, that the grading is inevitable; for how else will the graduate schools, the foundations, the corporations *know* whom to accept, reward, hire? How will the talent scouts know whom to tap?

By testing the applicants, of course, according to the specific task- 4
requirements of the inducting institution, just as applicants for the Civil Service or for licenses in medicine, law, and architecture are tested. Why should Harvard professors do the testing *for* corporations and graduate schools?

The objection is ludicrous. Dean Whitla, of the Harvard Office of 5
Tests, points out that the scholastic-aptitude and achievement tests used for *admission* to Harvard are a super-excellent index for all-around Harvard performance, better than high-school grades or particular Harvard course-grades. Presumably, these college-entrance tests are tailored for what Harvard and similar institutions want. By the same logic, would not an employer do far better to apply his own job-aptitude test rather than to rely on the vagaries of Harvard section-men? Indeed, I doubt that many employers bother to look at such grades; they are more likely to be

---

Paul Goodman (1911–1972) was a college professor and writer whose outspoken views were popular with students during the 1960s. This essay is from *Compulsory Miseducation* (1964).

interested merely in the fact of a Harvard diploma, whatever that connotes to them. The grades have most of their weight with the graduate schools — here, as elsewhere, the system runs mainly for its own sake.

It is really necessary to remind our academics of the ancient history of Examination. In the medieval university, the whole point of the grueling trial of the candidate was whether or not to accept him as a peer. His disputation and lecture for the Master's was just that, a masterpiece to enter the guild. It was not to make comparative evaluations. It was not to weed out and select for an extramural licensor or employer. It was certainly not to pit one young fellow against another in an ugly competition. My philosophic impression is that the medievals thought they knew what a good job of work was and that we are competitive because we do not know. But the more status is achieved by largely irrelevant competitive evaluation, the less will we ever know. 6

(Of course, our American examinations never did have this purely guild orientation, just as our faculties have rarely had absolute autonomy; the examining was to satisfy Overseers, Elders, distant Regents — and they as paternal superiors have always doted on giving grades, rather than accepting peers. But I submit that this set-up itself makes it impossible for the student to *become* a master, to *have* grown up, and to commence on his own. He will always be making A or B for some overseer. And in the present atmosphere, he will always be climbing on his friend's neck.) 7

Perhaps the chief objectors to abolishing grading would be the students and their parents. The parents should be simply disregarded; their anxiety has done enough damage already. For the students, it seems to me that a primary duty of the university is to deprive them of their props, their dependence on extrinsic valuation and motivation, and to force them to confront the difficult enterprise itself and finally lose themselves in it. 8

A miserable effect of grading is to nullify the various uses of testing. Testing, for both student and teacher, is a means of structuring, and also of finding out what is blank or wrong and what has been assimilated and can be taken for granted. Review — including high-pressure review — is a means of bringing together the fragments, so that there are flashes of synoptic insight. 9

There are several good reasons for testing, and kinds of test. But if the aim is to discover weakness, what is the point of down-grading and punishing it, and thereby inviting the student to conceal his weakness, by faking and bulling, if not cheating? The natural conclusion of synthesis is the insight itself, not a grade for having had it. For the important purpose of placement, if one can establish in the student the belief that one is testing *not* to grade and make invidious comparisons but for his own advantage, the student should normally seek his own level, where he is chal- 10 lenged and yet capable, rather than trying to get by. If the student dares to accept himself as he is, a teacher's grade is a crude instrument compared with a student's self-awareness. But it is rare in our universities that students are encouraged to notice objectively their vast confusion. Unlike Socrates, our teachers rely on power-drives rather than shame and ingenuous idealism.

Many students are lazy, so teachers try to goad or threaten them by grading. In the long run this must do more harm than good. Laziness is a character-defense. It may be a way of avoiding learning, in order to protect the conceit that one is already perfect (deeper, the despair that one *never* can be). It may be a way of avoiding just the risk of failing and being down-graded. Sometimes it is a way of politely saying, "I won't." But since it is the authoritarian grown-up demands that have created such attitudes in the first place, why repeat the trauma? There comes a time when we must treat people as adult, laziness and all. It is one thing courageously to fire a do-nothing out of your class; it is quite another thing to evaluate him with a lordly F. 11

Most important of all, it is often obvious that balking in doing the work, especially among bright young people who get to great universities, means exactly what it says: The work does not suit me, not this subject, or not at this time, or not in this school, or not in school altogether. The student might not be bookish; he might be school-tired; perhaps his development ought now to take another direction. Yet unfortunately, if such a student is intelligent and is not sure of himself, he *can* be bullied into passing, and this obscures everything. My hunch is that I am describing a common situation. What a grim waste of young life and teacherly effort! Such a student will retain nothing of what he has "passed" in. Sometimes he must get mononucleosis to tell his story and be believed. 12

And ironically, the converse is also probably commonly true. A student flunks and is mechanically weeded out, who is really ready and eager to learn in a scholastic setting, but he has not quite caught on. A good teacher can recognize the situation, but the computer wreaks its will. 13

Discussion Questions

1. Why do you think Goodman calls on "half a dozen of the prestigious Universities" instead of all universities to abolish grading?
2. Where does the author reveal the purposes of his proposal?
3. Most professors, Goodman argues, think that grading hinders teaching. Why, then, do they continue to give grades? How does Goodman reply to their objections?
4. What does Goodman think the real purpose of testing should be? How does grading "nullify the various uses of testing"?

Writing Suggestions

1. Do you agree that grading prevents you from learning? If so, write an essay in which you support Goodman's thesis by reporting what your own experience has been.
2. If you disagree with Goodman, write an essay that outlines the benefits of grading.
3. Is there a better way than grading to evaluate the work of students — a way that would achieve the goals of education Goodman values? Suggest a method and explain why it would be superior to grading.

Here Comes the Groom

ANDREW SULLIVAN

A (Conservative) Case for Gay Marriage

Last month in New York, a court ruled that a gay lover had the right to stay in his deceased partner's rent-control apartment because the lover qualified as a member of the deceased's family. The ruling deftly annoyed almost everybody. Conservatives saw judicial activism in favor of gay rent control: three reasons to be appalled. Chastened liberals (such as the *New York Times* editorial page), while endorsing the recognition of gay relationships, also worried about the abuse of already stretched entitlements that the ruling threatened. What neither side quite contemplated is that they both might be right, and that the way to tackle the issue of unconventional relationships in conventional society is to try something both more radical and more conservative than putting courts in the business of deciding what is and is not a family. That alternative is the legalization of civil gay marriage. 1

The New York rent-control case did not go anywhere near that far, which is the problem. The rent-control regulations merely stipulated that a "family" member had the right to remain in the apartment. The judge ruled that to all intents and purposes a gay lover is part of his lover's family, inasmuch as a "family" merely means an interwoven social life, emotional commitment, and some level of financial interdependence. 2

A doctoral candidate in government at Harvard University, Andrew Sullivan was formerly an associate editor at *The New Republic*, where this essay appeared on August 28, 1989.

It's a principle now well established around the country. Several cities have "domestic partnership" laws, which allow relationships that do not fit into the category of heterosexual marriage to be registered with the city and qualify for benefits that up till now have been reserved for straight married couples. San Francisco, Berkeley, Madison, and Los Angeles all have legislation, as does the politically correct Washington, DC, suburb, Takoma Park. In these cities, a variety of interpersonal arrangements qualify for health insurance, bereavement leave, insurance, annuity and pension rights, housing rights (such as rent-control apartments), adoption and inheritance rights. Eventually, according to gay lobby groups, the aim is to include federal income tax and veterans' benefits as well. A recent case even involved the right to use a family member's accumulated frequent-flier points. Gays are not the only beneficiaries; heterosexual "live-togethers" also qualify. 3

There's an argument, of course, that the current legal advantages extended to married people unfairly discriminate against people who've shaped their lives in less conventional arrangements. But it doesn't take a genius to see that enshrining in the law a vague principle like "domestic partnership" is an invitation to qualify at little personal cost for a vast array of entitlements otherwise kept crudely under control. 4

To be sure, potential DPs have to prove financial interdependence, shared living arrangements, and a commitment to mutual caring. But they don't need to have a sexual relationship or even closely mirror old-style marriage. In principle, an elderly woman and her live-in nurse could qualify. A couple of uneuphemistically confirmed bachelors could be DPs. So could two close college students, a pair of seminarians, or a couple of frat buddies. Left as it is, the concept of domestic partnership could open a Pandora's box of litigation and subjective judicial decision-making about who qualifies. You either are or are not married; it's not a complex question. Whether you are in a "domestic partnership" is not so clear. 5

More important, the concept of domestic partnership chips away at the prestige of traditional relationships and undermines the priority we give them. This priority is not necessarily a product of heterosexism. Consider heterosexual couples. Society has good reason to extend legal advantages to heterosexuals who choose the formal sanction of marriage over simply living together. They make a deeper commitment to one another and to society; in exchange, society extends certain benefits to them. Marriage provides an anchor, if an arbitrary and weak one, in the chaos of sex and relationships to which we are all prone. It provides a mechanism for emotional stability, economic security, and the healthy rearing of the next generation. We rig the law in its favor not because we disparage all forms of relationships other than the nuclear family, but because we recognize that not to promote marriage would be to ask too 6 much of human virtue. In the context of the weakened family's effect upon the poor, it might also invite social disintegration. One of the worst products of the New Right's "family values" campaign is that its extremism and hatred of diversity has disguised this more measured and more convincing case for the importance of the marital bond.

The concept of domestic partnership ignores these concerns, indeed directly attacks them. This is a pity, since one of its most important objectives — providing some civil recognition for gay relationships — is a noble cause and one completely compatible with the defense of the family. But the way to go about it is not to undermine straight marriage; it is to legalize old-style marriage for gays. 7

The gay movement has ducked this issue primarily out of fear of division. Much of the gay leadership clings to notions of gay life as essentially outsider, antibourgeois, radical. Marriage, for them, is co-optation into straight society. For the Stonewall generation, it is hard to see how this vision of conflict will ever fundamentally change. But for many other gays — my guess, a majority — while they don't deny the importance of rebellion twenty years ago and are grateful for what was done, there's now the sense of a new opportunity. A need to rebel has quietly ceded to a desire to belong. To be gay and to be bourgeois no longer seems such an absurd proposition. Certainly since AIDS, to be gay and to be responsible has become a necessity. 8

Gay marriage squares several circles at the heart of the domestic partnership debate. Unlike domestic partnership, it allows for recognition of gay relationships, while casting no aspersions on traditional marrige. It merely asks that gays be allowed to join in. Unlike domestic partnership, it doesn't open up avenues for heterosexuals to get benefits without the responsibilities of marriage, or a nightmare of definitional litigation. And unlike domestic partnership, it harnesses to an already established social convention the yearnings for stability and acceptance among a fast-maturing gay community. 9

Gay marriage also places more responsibilities upon gays: It says for the first time that gay relationships are not better or worse than straight relationships, and that the same is expected of them. And it's clear and dignified. There's a legal benefit to a clear, common symbol of commitment. There's also a personal benefit. One of the ironies of domestic partnership is that it's not only more complicated than marriage, it's more demanding, requiring an elaborate statement of intent to qualify. It amounts to a substantial invasion of privacy. Why, after all, should gays be required to prove commitment before they get married in a way we would never dream of asking of straights? 10

Legalizing gay marriage would offer homosexuals the same deal society now offers heterosexuals: general social approval and specific legal advantages in exchange for a deeper and harder-to-extract-yourself-from commitment to another human being. Like straight marriage, it would foster social cohesion, emotional security, and economic prudence. Since there's no reason gays should not be allowed to adopt or be foster parents, it could also help nurture children. And its introduction would not be some sort of radical break with social custom. As it has become more acceptable for gay people to acknowledge their loves publicly, more and more have committed themselves to one another for life in full view of their families and their friends. A law institutionalizing gay marriage would merely reinforce a healthy social trend. It would also, in the wake of AIDS, qualify as a genuine public health measure. Those conservatives who deplore promiscuity among some homosexuals should be among the first to support it. Burke could have written a powerful case for it. 11

The argument that gay marriage would subtly undermine the unique legitimacy of straight marriage is based upon a fallacy. For heterosexuals, straight marriage would remain the most significant — and only legal — social bond. Gay marriage could only delegitimize straight marriage if it were a real alternative to it, and this is clearly not true. To put it bluntly, there's precious little evidence that straights could be persuaded by any law to have sex with — let alone marry — someone of their own sex. The only possible effect of this sort would be to persuade gay men and women who force themselves into heterosexual marriage (often at appalling cost to themselves and their families) to find a focus for their family instincts in a more personally positive environment. But this is clearly a plus, not a minus: Gay marriage could both avoid a lot of tortured families and create the possibility for many happier ones. It is not, in short, a denial of family values. It's an extension of them. 12

Of course, some would claim that any legal recognition of homosexuality is a de facto attack upon heterosexuality. But even the most hardened conservatives recognize that gays are a permanent minority and aren't likely to go away. Since persecution is not an option in a civilized society, why not coax gays into traditional values rather than rail incoherently against them? 13

There's a less elaborate argument for gay marriage: It's good for gays. It provides role models for young gay people who, after the exhilaration of coming out, can easily lapse into short-term relationships and insecurity with no tangible goal in sight. My own guess is that most gays would embrace such a goal with as much (if not more) commitment as straights. Even in our society as it is, many lesbian relationships are 14 virtual textbook cases of monogamous commitment. Legal gay marriage could also help bridge the gulf often found between gays and their parents. It could bring the essence of gay life — a gay couple — into the heart of the traditional straight family in a way the family can most understand and the gay offspring can most easily acknowledge. It could do as much to heal the gay-straight rift as any amount of gay rights legislation.

If these arguments sound socially conservative, that's no accident. It's 15
one of the richest ironies of our society's blind spot toward gays that essentially conservative social goals should have the appearance of being so radical. But gay marriage is not a radical step. It avoids the mess of domestic partnership; it is humane; it is conservative in the best sense of the word. It's also practical. Given the fact that we already allow legal gay relationships, what possible social goal is advanced by framing the law to encourage those relationships to be unfaithful, undeveloped, and insecure?

Discussion Questions

1. Explain the court ruling that prompted this essay. In what way, according to Sullivan, did it fail to go far enough?
2. What are Sullivan's objections to "domestic partnership"? Why is a legal marriage superior to a "domestic partnership"?
3. Why is the gay movement divided on the issue of marriage?
4. How would gay marriage benefit heterosexuals? Is Sullivan's argument persuasive?
5. What is the irony in the phrase, "A (Conservative) Case for Gay Marriage" that announces the essay?

Writing Suggestions

1. Defend or attack the principle of "domestic partnership" laws. (See Sullivan's definition in the third paragraph of his essay.) Do they strengthen or threaten social stability?
2. What opposition might arise to attempts to enact gay marriage laws? Evaluate the objections and the reasons that guide them.

Death Penalty's False Promise: An Eye for an Eye

ANNA QUINDLEN

Ted Bundy and I go back a long way, to a time when there was a series of unsolved murders in Washington State known only as the Ted murders. Like a lot of reporters, I'm something of a crime buff. But the Washington Ted murders — and the ones that followed in Utah, Colorado and finally in Florida, where Ted Bundy was convicted and sentenced to die — fascinated me because I could see myself as one of the victims. I looked at the studio photographs of young women with long hair, pierced ears, easy smiles, and I read the descriptions: polite, friendly, quick to help, eager to please. I thought about being approached by a handsome young man asking for help, and I knew if I had been in the wrong place at the wrong time I would have been a goner. 1

By the time Ted finished up in Florida, law enforcement authorities suspected he had murdered dozens of young women. He and the death penalty seemed made for each other. 2

The death penalty and I, on the other hand, seem to have nothing in common. But Ted Bundy has made me think about it all over again, now that the outlines of my sixties liberalism have been filled in with a decade as a reporter covering some of the worst back alleys in New York City and three years as a mother who, like most, would lay down her life for her kids. 3

Simply put, I am opposed to the death penalty. I would tell that to any judge or lawyer undertaking the voir dire of jury candidates in a state in which the death penalty can be imposed. That is why I would be excused from such a jury. In a rational, completely cerebral way, I think the killing of one human being as punishment for the killing of another makes no sense and is inherently immoral. 4

But whenever my response to an important subject is rational and completely cerebral, I know there is something wrong with it — and so it is here. I have always been governed by my gut, and my gut says I am hypocritical about the death penalty. That is, I do not in theory think that Ted Bundy, or others like him, should be put to death. But if my daughter had been the one clubbed to death as she slept in a Tallahassee sorority 5

Anna Quindlen is a regular columnist for the Sunday *New York Times*. For several years she authored "Life in the 30s," a weekly column in the same newspaper where this article appeared on September 17, 1986.

house, and if the bite mark left in her buttocks had been one of the prime pieces of evidence against the young man charged with her murder, I would with the greatest pleasure kill him myself.

The State of Florida will not permit the parents of Bundy's victims to do that, and, in a way, that is the problem with an emotional response to capital punishment. The only reason for a death penalty is to exact retribution. Is there anyone who really thinks that it is a deterrent, that there are considerable numbers of criminals out there who think twice about committing crimes because of the sentence involved? The ones I have met in the course of my professional duties have either sneered at the justice system, where they can exchange one charge for another with more ease than they could return a shirt to a clothing store, or they have simply believed that it is the other guy who will get caught, get convicted, get the stiffest sentence. Of course, the death penalty would act as a deterrent by eliminating recidivism, but then so would life without parole, albeit at greater taxpayer expense. 6

I don't believe deterrence is what most proponents seek from the death penalty anyhow. Our most profound emotional response is to want criminals to suffer as their victims did. When a man is accused of throwing a child from a high-rise terrace, my emotional — some might say hysterical — response is that he should be given an opportunity to see how endless the seconds are from the thirty-first story to the ground. In a civilized society that will never happen. And so what many people want from the death penalty, they will never get. 7

Death is death, you may say, and you would be right. But anyone who has seen someone die suddenly of a heart attack and someone else slip slowly into the clutches of cancer knows that there are gradations of dying. 8

I watched a television reenactment one night of an execution by lethal injection. It was well done; it was horrible. The methodical approach, people standing around the gurney waiting, made it more awful. One moment there was a man in a prone position; the next moment that man was gone. On another night I watched a television movie about a little boy named Adam Walsh, who disappeared from a shopping center in Florida. There was a reenactment of Adam's parents coming to New York, where they appeared on morning talk shows begging for their son's return, and in their hotel room, where they received a call from the police saying that Adam had been found: not all of Adam, actually, just his severed head, discovered in the waters of a Florida canal. There is nothing anyone could do that is bad enough for an adult who took a six-year-old boy away from his parents, perhaps tortured, then murdered, him and cut off his head. Nothing at all. Lethal injection? The electric chair? Bah. 9

And so I come back to the position that the death penalty is wrong, 10
not only because it consists of stooping to the level of the killers, but also because it is not what it seems. Just before Ted Bundy's most recent execution date was postponed, pending further appeals, the father of his last known victim, a twelve-year-old girl, said what almost every father in his situation must feel. "I wish they'd bring him back to Lake City," said Tom Leach of the town where Kimberly Leach lived and died, "and let us all have at him." But the death penalty does not let us all have at him in the way Mr. Leach seems to mean. What he wants is for something as horrifying as what happened to his child to happen to Ted Bundy. And that is impossible.

Discussion Questions

1. "An eye for an eye" is a biblical injunction that is often misunderstood. What kind of vengeance does it prescribe?
2. What claim does Quindlen defend in this essay? (The title of the essay is a clue.) Is it explicitly stated anywhere?
3. What conflict in herself is Quindlen trying to resolve? How does she respond to the conventional arguments against capital punishment?
4. Why does she use Ted Bundy throughout as an example of the criminal condemned to death? Is his example an effective one? Explain your answer.
5. What personal references contribute most strongly to her argument?

Writing Suggestions

1. If you disagree with Quindlen's claim about capital punishment, offer a rebuttal to her argument.
2. Although it isn't always easy to make a clear distinction, we all make decisions based on both reason and emotion. Think of an important decision — choosing a lover or a marriage partner, deciding to have children, selecting a career, choosing to commit (or not commit) an illegal act — and explain how you came or would come to a conclusion based on a compromise between reason and emotion or a rejection of one in favor of the other.

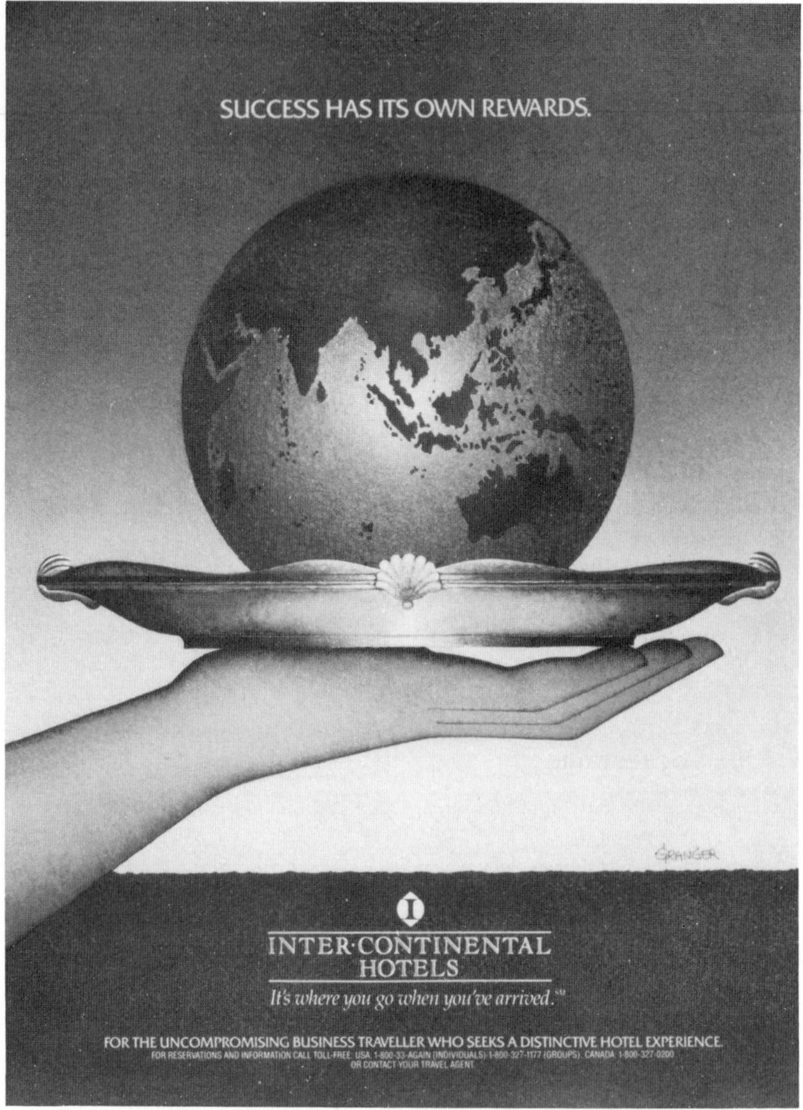

Discussion Questions

1. Which of the warrants is represented by this ad? (Think of the connection between "success" and "reward" and the hotel as the reward.) Is the warrant valid?
2. To what extent is the globe in the picture important?
3. How would you describe the values to which this ad appeals? What kinds of people are likely to respond to this ad?

EXERCISES FOR REVIEW

1. What are some of the assumptions underlying the preference for *natural* foods and medicines? Can *natural* be clearly defined? Is this preference part of a broader philosophy? Try to evaluate the validity of the assumption.
2. Is plagiarism wrong? What assumptions about education are relevant to the issue of plagiarism? (Some students defend it. What kinds of arguments do they provide?)
3. Choose an advertisement and examine the warrants on which the advertiser's claim is based.
4. "Religious beliefs are (or are not) necessary to a satisfactory life." Explain the warrants underlying your claim. Define any ambiguous terms.
5. Should students be given a direct voice in the hiring of faculty members? On what warrants about education do you base your answer?
6. Discuss the validity of the warrant in this statement from *The Watch Tower* (a publication of the Jehovah's Witnesses) about genital herpes: "The sexually loose are indeed 'receiving in themselves the full recompense, which was due for their error' (Romans 1:27)."
7. Read the following passage about suicide by the Greek philosopher Aristotle (adapted from his *Ethics*). Then defend or attack his argument, being careful to make clear both Aristotle's and your own warrants.

> Just as a murderer does not have the right to take a mother from her family or a child from her parents and simultaneously to deny society the use of a productive citizen, so the suicide, even though he or she freely chooses to be his or her own victim, does not possess the right to thus diminish the welfare of so many others.

8. In view of the increasing attention to health in general, and nutrition and exercise in particular, do you think that universities and colleges should impose physical education requirements? If so, what form should they take? If not, why not? Defend your reasons.
9. In recent years both state and federal governments have been embroiled in controversies concerning the rights of citizens to engage in harmful practices. In Massachusetts, for example, a mandatory seat belt law was repealed by rebellious voters who considered the law an infringement of their freedom. What principles do you think ought to guide government regulation of dangerous practices?
10. The author of the following passage, Katherine Butler Hathaway, became a hunchback as a result of a childhood illness. Here she writes about the relationship between love and beauty from the point of view of someone who is deformed. Discuss the warrants on which the author bases her conclusion.

> I could secretly pretend that I had a lover . . . but I could never risk showing that I thought such a thing was possible for me . . . with any man. Because of my repeated encounters with the mirror and my irrepressible

tendency to forget what I had seen, I had begun to force myself to believe and to remember, and especially to remember, that I would never be chosen for what I imagined to be the supreme and most intimate of all experience. I thought of sexual love as an honor that was too great and too beautiful for the body in which I was doomed to live.

CHAPTER 6

Language and Thought

THE POWER OF WORDS

Words play such a critical role in argument that they deserve special treatment. Elsewhere we have referred directly and indirectly to language: Chapter 3 discusses definitions and Part Two discusses style — the choice and arrangement of words and sentences — and shows how successful writers express arguments in language that is clear, vivid, and thoughtful. An important part of these writers' equipment is a large and active vocabulary, but no single chapter in a book can give this to you; only reading and study can widen your range of word choices. Even in a brief chapter, however, we can point out how words influence the feelings and attitudes of an audience, both favorably and unfavorably.

One kind of language responsible for shaping attitudes and feelings is *emotive language*, language that expresses and arouses emotions. Understanding it and using it effectively is indispensable to the arguer who wants to move an audience to accept a point of view or undertake an action.

Long before you thought about writing your first argument, you learned that words had the power to affect you. Endearments and affectionate and flattering nicknames evoked good feelings about the speaker and yourself. Insulting nicknames and slurs produced dislike for the speaker and bad feelings about yourself. Perhaps you were told, "Sticks and stones may break your bones, but words will never hurt you." But even to a small child it is clear that ugly words are as painful as sticks and stones and that the injuries are sometimes more lasting.

Nowhere is the power of words more obvious and more familiar than in advertising, where the success of a product may depend on the feelings that certain words produce in the prospective buyer. Even the names of products may have emotive significance. In recent years a new industry, composed of consultants who supply names for products, has emerged. Although most manufacturers agree that a good name won't save a poor product, they also recognize that the right name can catch the attention of the public and persuade people to buy a product at least once. According to an article in the *Wall Street Journal*, a product name not only should be memorable but also should "remind people of emotional or physical experiences." One consultant created the name Magnum for a malt liquor from Miller Brewing Company: "The product is aimed at students, minorities, and lower-income customers." The president of the consulting firm says that Magnum "implies strength, masculinity, and more bang for your buck."[1]

It is not hard to see the connection between the use of words in conversation and advertising and the use of emotive language in the more formal arguments you will be writing. Emotive language reveals your approval or disapproval, assigns praise or blame — in other words, makes a judgment about the subject. Keep in mind that unless you are writing purely factual statements, such as scientists write, you will find it hard to avoid expressing judgments. Neutrality does not come easily, even where it may be desirable, as in news stories or reports of historical events. For this reason you need to attend carefully to the statements in your argument, making sure that you have not disguised judgments as statements of fact. Of course, in attempting to prove a claim, you will not be neutral. You will be revealing your judgment about the subject, first in the selection of facts and opinions and the emphasis you give to them and second in the selection of words.

Like the choice of facts and opinions, the choice of words can be effective or ineffective in advancing your argument, moral or immoral in the honesty with which you exercise it. The following discussions offer some insights into recognizing and evaluating the use of emotive language in the arguments you read, as well as into using such language in

---

[1] *Wall Street Journal*, August 5, 1982, p. 19.

your own arguments where it is appropriate and avoiding it where it is not.

CONNOTATION

The connotations of a word are the meanings we attach to it apart from its explicit definition. Because these added meanings derive from our feelings, connotations are one form of emotive language. For example, the word *rat* denotes or points to a kind of rodent, but the attached meanings of "selfish person," "evil-doer," "betrayer," and "traitor" reflect the feelings that have accumulated around the word.

In Chapter 3 we observed that definitions of controversial terms, such as *poverty* and *unemployment*, may vary so widely that writer and reader cannot always be sure that they are thinking of the same thing. A similar problem arises when a writer assumes that the reader shares his or her emotional response to a word. Emotive meanings originate partly in personal experience. The word *home*, defined merely as "a family's place of residence," may suggest love, warmth, and security to one person; it may suggest friction, violence, and alienation to another. The values of the groups to which we belong also influence meaning. Writers and speakers count on cultural associations when they refer to our country, our flag, and heroes and enemies we have never seen. The arguer must also be aware that some apparently neutral words trigger different responses from different groups — words such as *cult, revolution, police, beauty contest,* and *corporation*.

Various reform movements have recognized that words with unfavorable connotations have the power not only to reflect but also to shape our perceptions of things. The words *Negro* and *colored* were rejected by the civil-rights movement in the 1960s because they bore painful associations with slavery and discrimination. Instead, the word *black*, which was free from such associations, became the accepted designation; more recently, the Reverend Jesse Jackson suggested another change, African-American, to reflect ethnic origins. The women's liberation movement also insisted on changes that would bring about improved attitudes toward women. The movement condemned the use of *girl* for a female over the age of eighteen and the use in news stories of descriptive adjectives that emphasized the physical appearance of women. And the homosexual community succeeded in reintroducing the word *gay*, a word current centuries ago, as a substitute for words they considered offensive.

Members of certain occupations have invented terms to confer greater respectability on their work. The work does not change, but the workers hope that public perceptions will change if janitors are called custodians, garbage collectors are called sanitation engineers, if undertakers are called morticians, if people who sell makeup are called cosmetologists. Events considered unpleasant or unmentionable are sometimes disguised by polite terms, called *euphemisms*. Many people refuse to use the word *died* and choose *passed away* instead. Some psychologists and physicians use the phrase "negative patient care outcome" for what most of us would call "death." Even when referring to their pets, some people cannot bring themselves to say "put to death" but substitute "put to sleep" or "put down." In place of a term to describe an act of sexual intercourse, some people use "slept together" or "went to bed together" or "had an affair."

Polite words are not always so harmless. If a euphemism disguises a shameful event or condition, it is morally irresponsible to use it to mislead the reader into believing that the shameful condition does not exist. In his powerful essay "Politics and the English Language" (reprinted in Part Four), George Orwell pointed out that politicians and reporters have sometimes used terms like "pacification" or "rectification of frontiers" to conceal acts that result in torture and death for millions of people. An example of such usage was cited by a member of Amnesty International, a group monitoring human rights violations throughout the world. He objected to a news report describing camps in which the Chinese were promoting "reeducation through labor." This term, he wrote, "makes these institutions seem like a cross between Police Athletic League and Civilian Conservation Corps camps." On the contrary, he went on, the reality of "reeducation through labor" was that the victims were confined to "rather unpleasant prison camps." The details he offered about the conditions under which people lived and worked gave substance to his claim.[2]

Perhaps the most striking examples of the way that connotations influence our perceptions of reality occur when people are asked to respond to questions of poll-takers. Sociologists and students of poll-taking know that the phrasing of a question, or the choice of words, can affect the answers and even undermine the validity of the poll. In one case poll-takers first asked a selected group of people if they favored continuing the welfare system. The majority answered no. But when the poll-takers asked if they favored government aid to the poor, the majority answered yes. Although the terms "welfare" and "government aid to the poor" refer to essentially the same forms of government assistance, "welfare" has acquired for many people negative connotations of corruption and shiftless recipients.

---

[2] Letter to the *New York Times*, August 30, 1982, p. 25.

The *New York Times* reports the result of another poll in which "a random sample of Americans were asked about their views of abortion in several different ways." The first question was phrased this way: "Do you think there should be an amendment to the Constitution prohibiting abortion, or shouldn't there be such an amendment?" The respondents were solidly opposed — 62 percent — to such an amendment. But when the question read, "Do you believe there should be an amendment to the Constitution protecting the life of the unborn child, or shouldn't there be such an amendment?" only 50 percent were in favor. "Fully one-third of those who opposed the amendment when it was presented as 'prohibiting abortions' supported it when it was presented as 'protecting the life of the unborn child.'" As the headline concluded, "Wording of a Question Makes a Big Difference."[3]

The wording of an argument is crucial. Since readers may interpret the words you use on the basis of feelings different from your own, you must support your word choices with definitions and evidence that allows readers to determine how and why you made them.

SLANTING

Slanting, says one dictionary, is "interpreting or presenting in line with a special interest." The term is almost always used in a negative sense. It means that the arguer has selected facts and words with favorable or unfavorable connotations to create the impression that no alternative view exists or can be defended. For some questions it is true that no alternative view is worthy of presentation, and emotionally charged language to defend or attack a position that is clearly right or wrong would be entirely appropriate. We aren't neutral, nor should we be, about the tragic abuse of human rights anywhere in the world or even about less serious infractions of the law, such as drunk driving or vandalism, and we should use strong language to express our disapproval of these practices.

Most of your arguments, however, will concern controversial questions about which people of goodwill can argue on both sides. In such cases, your own judgments should be restrained. Slanting will suggest a prejudice — that is, a judgment made without regard to all the facts. Unfortunately, you may not always be aware of your bias or special interest; you may believe that your position is the only correct one. You may also feel the need to communicate a passionate belief about a serious problem. But if you are interested in persuading a reader to accept your belief and

---

[3] *New York Times*, August 18, 1980, p. 15.

to act on it, you must also ask: If the reader is not sympathetic, how will he or she respond? Will he or she perceive my words as "loaded" — one-sided and prejudicial — and my view as slanted?

R. D. Laing, a Scottish psychiatrist, defined prayer in this way: "Someone is gibbering away on his knees, talking to someone who is not there."[4] This description probably reflects a sincerely held belief. Laing also clearly intended it for an audience that already agreed with him. But the phrases "gibbering away" and "someone who is not there" would be offensive to people for whom prayer is sacred.

The following remark by an editor of *Penthouse* appeared in a debate on women's liberation.

> I haven't noticed that there is such a thing as a rise in the women's liberation movement. It seems to me that it's a lot of minor sound and a tiny fury. There are some bitty bitty groups of some disappointed ladies who have some objective or other.[5]

An unfriendly audience would resent the use of language intended to diminish the importance of the movement: "minor sound," "tiny fury," "bitty bitty group of some disappointed ladies," "some objective or other." But even audiences sympathetic to the claim may be repelled or embarrassed by intense, colorful, obviously loaded words. In 1970, Senators George McGovern and Mark Hatfield introduced an amendment to enforce America's withdrawal from the Vietnam War. A New York newspaper, violently opposed to the amendment, named it the "White Flag Amendment." An editorial called it a "bug-out scheme" designed to "sucker fence-sitting senators," "a simple and simple-minded solution" supported by "defeatists and Reds," a "cheap way out" that would reveal "the jelly content of America's spine," a "skedaddle scheme." Most readers, including those who agreed with the claim, might feel that the name-calling, slang, and exaggeration revealed a lack of dignity inappropriate to the cause they were defending. Such language is better suited to informal conversation than to serious argument.

We find slanting everywhere, not only in advertising and propaganda, where we expect to find it, but in news stories, which should be strictly neutral in their recounting of events, and in textbooks. In the field of history, for example, it is often difficult for scholars to remain impartial about significant events. Like the rest of us, they may approve or disapprove, and their choice of words will reflect their judgments.

---

4 "The Obvious," in *The Dialectics of Liberation*, edited by David Cooper (Penguin Books, 1968), p. 17.

5 "Women's Liberation: A Debate" (Penthouse International Ltd., 1970).

The following passage by a distinguished Catholic historian describes the events surrounding the momentous decision by Henry VIII, king of England, to break with the Roman Catholic Church in 1534, in part because of the Pope's refusal to grant him a divorce from the Catholic princess Catherine of Aragon so that he could marry Anne Boleyn.

> The *protracted* delay in receiving an annulment was very *irritating* to the *impulsive* English king. . . . Gradually Henry's former *effusive* loyalty to Rome gave way to a settled conviction of the tyranny of the papal power, and there *rushed* to his mind the recollections of efforts of earlier English rulers to restrict that power. A few *salutary* enactments against the Church might *compel* a favorable decision from the Pope.
>
> Henry seriously opened his campaign against the Roman Church in 1531, when he *frightened* the clergy into paying a fine of over half a million dollars for violating an *obsolete* statute . . . and in the same year he *forced* the clergy to recognize himself as supreme head of the Church. . . .
>
> His *subservient* Parliament then empowered him to stop the payments of annates to the Pope and to appoint bishops in England without recourse to the papacy. *Without waiting longer* for the decision from Rome, he had Cranmer, *one of his own creatures*, whom he had just named Archbishop of Canterbury, declare his marriage null and void. . . .
>
> Yet Henry VIII encountered considerable *opposition* from the *higher clergy*, from the monks, and from many *intellectual leaders*. . . . A *popular uprising* — the Pilgrimage of Grace — was *sternly* suppressed, and such men as the *brilliant* Sir Thomas More and John Fisher, the *aged* and *saintly* bishop of Rochester, were beheaded because they retained their former belief in papal supremacy.[6] [Italics added]

In the first paragraph the italicized words help make the following points: that Henry was rash, impulsive, and insincere and that he was intent on punishing the church (the word *salutary* means healthful or beneficial and is used sarcastically). In the second paragraph the choice of words stresses Henry's use of force and the cowardly submission of his followers. In the third paragraph the adjectives describing the opposition to Henry's campaign and those who were executed emphasize Henry's cruelty and despotism. Within the limits of this brief passage the author has offered support for his strong indictment of Henry VIII's actions, both in defining the statute as obsolete and in describing the popular opposition. In a longer exposition you would expect to find a more elaborate justification with facts and authoritative opinion from other sources.

The advocate of a position in an argument, unlike the reporter or the historian, must express a judgment, but the preceding examples

---

[6] Carlton J. H. Hayes, *A Political and Cultural History of Modern Europe*, Vol. 1 (New York: Macmillan Company, 1933), pp. 172–173.

demonstrate how the arguer should use language to avoid or minimize slanting and to persuade readers that he or she has come to a conclusion after careful analysis. The careful arguer must not conceal his or her judgments by presenting them as if they were statements of fact, but must offer convincing support for his or her choice of words and respect the audience's feelings and attitudes by using temperate language.

Depending on the circumstances, *exaggeration* can be defined, in the words of one writer, as "a form of lying." An essay in *Time* magazine, "Watching Out for Loaded Words," points to the danger for the arguer in relying on exaggerated language as an essential part of the argument.

> The trouble with loaded words is they tend to short-circuit thought. While they may describe something, they simultaneously try to seduce the mind into accepting a prefabricated opinion about the something described.[7]

PICTURESQUE LANGUAGE

Picturesque language consists of words that produce images in the mind of the reader. Students sometimes assume that vivid picture-making language is the exclusive instrument of novelists and poets, but writers of arguments can also avail themselves of such devices to heighten the impact of their messages.

Picturesque language can do more than render a scene. It shares with other kinds of emotive language the power to express and arouse deep feelings. Like a fine painting or photograph, it can draw readers into the picture where they partake of the writer's experience as if they were also present. Such power may be used to delight, to instruct, or to horrify. In 1741 the Puritan preacher Jonathan Edwards delivered his sermon "Sinners in the Hands of an Angry God," in which people were likened to repulsive spiders hanging over the flames of Hell to be dropped into the fire whenever a wrathful God was pleased to release them. The congregation's reaction to Edwards's picture of the everlasting horrors to be suffered in the netherworld included panic, fainting, hysteria, and convulsions. Subsequently Edwards lost his pulpit in Massachusetts, in part as a consequence of his success at provoking such uncontrollable terror among his congregation.

Language as intense and vivid as Edwards's emerges from very strong emotion about a deeply felt cause. In an argument against abor-

---

[7] *Time*, May 24, 1982, p. 86.

tion, a surgeon recounts a horrifying experience as if it were a scene in a movie.

> You walk toward the bus stop. . . . It is all so familiar. All at once you step on something soft. You feel it with your foot. Even through your shoe you may have the sense of something unusual, something marked by a special "give." It is a foreignness upon the pavement. Instinct pulls your foot away in an awkward little movement. You look down, and you see . . . a tiny naked body, its arms and legs flung apart, its head thrown back, its mouth agape, its face serious. A bird, you think, fallen from the nest. But there is no nest here on 73rd Street, no bird so big. It is rubber, then. A model, a . . . a joke. And you bend to see. Because you must. And it is no joke. Such a gray softness can be but one thing. It is a baby, and dead. You cover your mouth, your eyes. You are fixed. Horror has found its chink and crawled in, and you will never be the same as you were. Years later you will step from a sidewalk to a lawn, and you will start at its softness and think of that upon which you have just trod.[8]

Here the use of the pronoun *you* serves to draw readers into the scene and intensify their experience.

The rules governing the use of picturesque language are the same as those governing other kinds of emotive language. Is the language appropriate? Is it too strong, too colorful for the purpose of the message? Does it result in slanting or distortion? What will its impact be on a hostile or indifferent audience? Will they be angered, repelled? Will they cease to read or listen if the imagery is too disturbing?

We expect strong language in arguments about life and death. For subjects about which your feelings are not so passionate, your choice of words will be more moderate. The excerpt below, from an article arguing against repeal of Sunday closing laws, creates a sympathetic picture of a market-free Sunday. Most readers, even those who oppose Sunday closing laws, would enjoy the picture and perhaps react more favorably to the argument.

> Think of waking in the city on Sunday. Although most people no longer worship in the morning, the city itself has a reverential air. It comes to life slowly, even reluctantly, as traffic lights blink their orders to empty streets. Next, joggers venture forth, people out to get the paper, families going to church or grandma's. Soon the city is its Sunday self: People cavort with their children, discuss, make repairs, go to museums, gambol. Few people go to

---

[8] Richard Selzer, *Mortal Lessons: Notes on the Art of Surgery* (New York: Simon and Schuster, 1974), pp. 153–154.

work, and any shopping is incidental. The city on Sunday is a place outside the market. Play dominates, not the economy.[9]

CONCRETE AND ABSTRACT LANGUAGE

Writers of argument need to be aware of another use of language — the distinction between concrete and abstract. Concrete words point to real objects and real experiences. Abstract words express qualities apart from particular things and events. *Beautiful roses* is concrete; we can see, touch, and smell them. *Beauty* in the eye of the beholder is abstract; we can speak of the quality of beauty without reference to a particular object or event. *Returning money found in the street to the owner, although no one has seen the discovery* is concrete. *Honesty* is abstract. In abstracting we separate a quality shared by a number of objects or events, however different from each other the individual objects or events may be.

Writing that describes or tells a story leans heavily on concrete language. Although arguments also rely on the vividness of concrete language, they use abstract terms far more extensively than other kinds of writing. Using abstractions effectively, especially in arguments of value and policy, is important for two reasons: (1) Abstractions represent the qualities, characteristics, and values that the writer is explaining, defending, or attacking; and (2) they enable the writer to make generalizations about his or her data. Equally important is knowing when to avoid abstractions that obscure the message.

In some textbook discussions of language, abstractions are treated as inferior to concrete and specific words, but such a distinction is misleading. Abstractions allow us to make sense of our experience, to come to conclusions about the meaning of the bewildering variety of emotions and events we confront throughout a lifetime. One writer summarized his early history as follows: "My elementary school had the effect of *destroying* any *intellectual motivation*, of *stifling* all *creativity*, of *inhibiting personal relationships* with either my teachers or my peers" (italics added). Writing in the humanities and in some social and physical sciences would be impossible without recourse to abstractions that express qualities, values, and conditions.

You should not, however, expect abstract terms alone to carry the emotional content of your message. The effect of even the most suggestive words can be enhanced by details, examples, and anecdotes. One

---

[9] Robert K. Manoff, "New York City, It Is Argued, Faces 'Sunday Imperialism,' " *New York Times*, January 2, 1977, Sec. IV, p. 13.

mode of expression is not superior to the other; both abstractions and concrete detail work together to produce clear, persuasive argument. This is especially true when the meanings assigned to abstract terms vary from reader to reader.

In establishing claims based on the support of values, for example, you may use such abstract terms as *religion, duty, freedom, peace, progress, justice, equality, democracy,* and *pursuit of happiness.* You can assume that some of these words are associated with the same ideas and emotions for almost all readers; others require further explanation. Suppose you write, "We have made great progress in the last fifty years." One dictionary defines *progress* as "a gradual betterment," another abstraction. How will you define "gradual betterment" for your readers? Can you be sure that they have in mind the same references for progress that you do? If not, misunderstandings are inevitable. You may offer examples: supersonic planes, computers, shopping malls, nuclear energy. Many of your readers will react favorably to the mention of these innovations, which to them represent progress; others, for whom these inventions represent change but not progress, will react unfavorably. You may not be able to convince all of your readers that "we have made great progress," but all of them will now understand what you mean by "progress." And intelligent disagreement is preferable to misunderstanding.

Abstractions tell us what conclusions we have arrived at; details tell us how we got there. But there are dangers in either too many details or too many abstractions. For example, a writer may present only concrete data without telling readers what conclusions are to be drawn from them. Suppose you read the following:

> To Chinese road-users, traffic police are part of the grass . . . and neither they nor the rules they're supposed to enforce are paid the least attention. . . . Ignoring traffic-lights is only one peculiarity of Chinese traffic. It's normal for a pedestrian to walk straight out into a stream of cars without so much as lifting his head; and goodness knows how many Chinese cyclists I've almost killed as they have shot blindly in front of me across busy main roads.[10]

These details would constitute no more than interesting gossip until we read, "It's not so much a sign of ignorance or recklessness . . . but of fatalism." The details of specific behavior have now acquired a significance expressed in the abstraction *fatalism.*

A more common problem, however, in using abstractions is omission of details. Either the writer is not a skilled observer and cannot provide the details, or he or she feels that such details are too small and quiet

---

[10] Philip Short, "The Chinese and the Russians," *The Listener*, April 8, 1982, p. 6.

compared to the grand sounds made by abstract terms. These grand sounds, unfortunately, cannot compensate for the lack of clarity and liveliness. Lacking detailed support, abstract words may be misinterpreted. They may also represent ideas that are so vague as to be meaningless. Sometimes they function illegitimately as short cuts (discussed on pp. 188–195), arousing emotions but unaccompanied by good reasons for their use. The following paragraph exhibits some of these common faults. How would you translate it into clear English?

> We respectively petition, request and entreat that due and adequate provision be made, this day and the date hereinafter subscribed, for the satisfying of these petitioners' nutritional requirements and for the organizing of such methods of allocation and distribution as may be deemed necessary and proper to assure the reception by and for said petitioners of such quantities of baked cereal products as shall, in the judgment of the aforesaid petitioners, constitute a sufficient supply thereof.[11]

If you had trouble decoding this, it was because there were almost no concrete references — the homely words *baked* and *cereal* leap out of the paragraph like English signposts in a foreign country — and too many long words or words of Latin origin when simple words would do: *requirements* instead of *needs, petition* instead of *ask*. An absence of concrete references and an excess of long Latinate words can have a depressing effect on both writer and reader. The writer may be in danger of losing the thread of the argument, the reader at a loss to discover the message.

The paragraph above, according to James B. Minor, a lawyer who teaches courses in legal drafting, is "how a federal regulation writer would probably write, 'Give us this day our daily bread.' " This brief sentence with its short, familiar words and its origin in the Lord's Prayer has a deep emotional effect. The paragraph composed by Minor deadens any emotional impact because of its preponderance of abstract terms and its lack of connection with the world of our senses.

That passage was invented to educate writers in the government bureaucracy to avoid inflated prose. But writing of this kind is not uncommon among professional writers, including academics. If the subject matter is unfamiliar and the writer an acknowledged expert, you may have to expend a special effort in penetrating the language. But you may also rightly wonder if the writer is making unreasonable demands on you.

> The human race is now entering upon a new phase of evolutionary consciousness and progress, a phase in which, impelled by the forces of evolution itself, it must converge upon itself and convert itself into one single hu-

---

[11] *New York Times*, May 10, 1977, p. 35.

man organism infused by a reconciliation of knowing and being in their inner unity and destined to make a qualitative leap into a higher form of consciousness as we know it, or otherwise destroy itself. For the entire universe is one vast field, potential for incarnation, and achieving incandescence here and there of reason and spirit. And in the whole world of *quality* with which by the nature of our minds we necessarily make contact, we here and there apprehend preeminent value. This can be achieved only if we recognize that we are unable to focus our attention on the particulars of the whole, without diminishing our comprehension of the whole, and of course, conversely, we can focus on the whole only by diminishing our comprehension of the particulars which constitute the whole.[12]

You probably found this paragraph even more baffling than the previous example. Although there is some glimmer of meaning here — that mankind must attain a higher level of consciousness, or perish — you should ask whether the extraordinary overload of abstract terms is justified. In fact, most readers would be disinclined to sit still for an argument with so little reference to the real world. One critic of social science prose maintains that if preeminent thinkers like Bertrand Russell can make themselves clear but social scientists continue to be obscure, "then you can justifiably suspect that it might all be nonsense."[13]

Finally, there are the moral implications of using abstractions that conceal a disagreeable reality. George Orwell pointed them out more than forty years ago in "Politics and the English Language." Another essayist, Joseph Wood Krutch, in criticizing the attitude that cheating "doesn't really hurt anybody," observed, " 'It really doesn't hurt anybody' means it doesn't do that abstraction called society any harm." The following news story reports a proposal with which Orwell and Krutch might have agreed. His intention, says the author, is to "slow the hand of any President who might be tempted to unleash a nuclear attack."

It has long been feared that a President could be making his fateful decision while at a "psychological distance" from the victims of a nuclear barrage; that he would be in a clean, air-conditioned room, surrounded by well-scrubbed aides, all talking in abstract terms about appropriate military responses in an international crisis, and that he might well push to the back of his mind the realization that hundreds of millions of people would be exterminated.

So Roger Fisher, professor of law at Harvard University, offers a simple suggestion to make the stakes more real. He would put the codes needed to

---

[12] Ruth Nanda Anshen, "Credo Perspectives," introduction to *Two Modes of Thought* by James Bryant Conant (New York: Simon and Schuster, 1964), p. x.

[13] Stanisslav Andreski, *Social Sciences as Sorcery* (New York: St. Martin's Press, 1972), p. 86.

> fire nuclear weapons in a little capsule, and implant the capsule next to the heart of a volunteer, who would carry a big butcher knife as he accompanied the President everywhere. If the President ever wanted to fire nuclear weapons, he would first have to kill, with his own hands, that human being.
>
> He has to look at someone and realize what death is — what an innocent death is. "It's reality brought home," says Professor Fisher.[14]

The moral lesson is clear: It is much easier to do harm if we convince ourselves that the object of the injury is only an abstraction.

SHORT CUTS

Short cuts are arguments that depend on readers' responses to words. Short cuts, like other devices we have discussed so far, are a common use of emotive language but are often mistaken for valid argument.

Although they have power to move us, these abbreviated substitutes for argument avoid the hard work necessary to provide facts, expert opinion, and analysis of warrants. Even experts, however, can be guilty of using short cuts, and the writer who consults an authority should be alert to that authority's use of language. Two of the most common uses of short cuts are clichés and slogans.

Clichés

"I'm against sloppy, emotional thinking. I'm against fashionable thinking. I'm against the whole cliché of the moment."[15] This statement by the late Herman Kahn, the founder of the Hudson Institute, a famous think tank, serves as the text for this section. A cliché is an expression or idea grown stale through overuse. Clichés in language are tired expressions that have faded like old photographs; readers no longer see anything when clichés are placed before them. Clichés include phrases like "cradle of civilization," "few and far between," "rude awakening," "follow in the footsteps of," "fly in the ointment."

But more important to recognize and avoid are clichés of thought. A cliché of thought may be likened to a formula, which one dictionary defines as "any conventional rule or method for doing something, especially when used, applied or repeated without thought." Clichés of thought represent ready-made answers to questions, stereotyped solutions to problems, "knee-jerk" reactions. Two writers who call these

---

[14] *New York Times*, September 7, 1982, Sec. C, p. 1.

[15] *New York Times*, July 8, 1983, Sec. B, p. 1.

forms of expression "mass language" describe it this way: "Mass language is language which presents the reader with a response he is expected to make without giving him adequate reason for having this response."[16] These "clichés of the moment" are often expressed in single words or phrases. For example, the phrase "the Me generation" has been repeated so often that it has come to represent an indisputable truth for many people, one they no longer question. The acceptance of this cliché, however, conceals the fact that millions of very different kinds of people from ages eighteen to thirty-five are being thoughtlessly lumped together as selfish and materialistic.

Certain cultural attitudes encourage the use of clichés. The liberal American tradition has been governed by hopeful assumptions about our ability to solve problems. A professor of communications says that "we tell our students that for every problem there must be a solution."[17] But real solutions are hard to come by. In our haste to provide them, to prove that we can be decisive, we may be tempted to produce familiar responses that resemble solutions.

History teaches us that a solution to an old and serious problem is almost always accompanied by unexpected drawbacks. As the writer quoted in the previous paragraph warns us, "Life is not that simple. There is no one answer to a given problem. There are multiple solutions, all with advantages and disadvantages." By solving one problem, we often create another. Automobiles, advanced medical techniques, industrialization, and liberal divorce laws have all contributed to the solution of age-old problems: lack of mobility, disease, poverty, domestic unhappiness. We now see that these solutions bring with them new problems that we nevertheless elect to live with because the advantages seem greater than the disadvantages. A well-known economist puts it this way: "I don't look for solutions; I look for trade-offs. I think the person who asks, 'What is the solution to this problem?' has a fundamental misconception of the way the world works. We have trade-offs, and that's all we have."[18]

This means that we should be skeptical of solutions promising everything and ignoring limitations and criticism. Such solutions have probably gone around many times. Having heard them so often, we are inclined to believe that they have been tried and proven. Thus they escape serious analysis.

---

[16] Richard E. Hughes and P. Albert Duhamel, *Rhetoric: Principles and Usage* (Englewood Cliffs, NJ: Prentice-Hall, 1962), p. 161.

[17] Malcolm O. Sillars, "The New Conservatism and the Teacher of Speech," *Southern Speech Journal* 21 (1956), p. 240.

[18] Thomas Sowell, "Manhattan Report" (edited transcript of *Meet the Press*) (New York: International Center for Economic Policy Studies, 1981), p. 10.

Some of these problems and their solutions represent the fashionable thinking to which Kahn objected. They confront us everywhere, like the public personalities who gaze at us week after week from the covers of magazines and tabloid newspapers at the checkout counter in the supermarket. Alarms about the failures of public education, about drug addiction or danger to the environment or teenage pregnancy are sounded throughout the media continuously. The same solutions are advocated again and again: "Back to basics"; "Impose harsher sentences"; "Offer sex education." Their popularity, however, should not prevent us from asking: Are the problems as urgent as their prominence in the media suggests? Are the solutions workable? Does sufficient evidence exist to justify their adoption?

Your arguments will not always propose solutions. They will sometimes provide interpretations of or reasons for social phenomena, especially for recurrent problems. Some explanations have acquired the status of folk wisdom, like proverbs, and careless arguers will offer them as if they needed no further support. One object of stereotyped responses is the problem of juvenile delinquency, which liberals attribute to poverty, lack of community services, meaningless education, and violence on TV. Conservatives blame parental permissiveness, decline in religious influence, lack of individual responsibility, lenient courts. Notice that the interpretations of the cause of juvenile delinquency are related to an ideology, to a particular view of the world that may prevent the arguer from recognizing any other way of examining the problem. Other stereotyped explanations for a range of social problems include inequality, competition, self-indulgence, alienation, discrimination, technology, lack of patriotism, excessive governmental regulation, and lack of sufficient governmental regulation. All of these explanations are worthy of consideration, but they must be defined and supported if they are to be used in a thoughtful, well-constructed argument.

Although formulas change with the times, some are unexpectedly hardy and survive long after critics have revealed their weaknesses. Overpopulation is an often-cited cause of poverty, disease, and war. It can be found in the writing of the ancient Greeks 2,500 years ago. "That perspective," says the editor of *Food Monitor*, a journal published by World Hunger Year, Inc., "is so pervasive that most Americans have simply stopped thinking about population and resort to inane clucking of tongues."[19] If the writer offering overpopulation as an explanation for poverty were to look further, he or she would discover that the explanation rested on shaky data. The Netherlands, the most densely populated

---

[19] Letter to the *New York Times*, October 4, 1982, Sec. A, p. 18.

country in the world (931 persons per square mile) is also one of the richest ($13,065 per capita income per year). Chad, one of the most sparsely populated (11 persons per square mile) is also one of the poorest ($158 per capita income per year).[20] Strictly defined, overpopulation may serve to explain some instances of poverty; obviously it cannot serve as a blanket to cover all or even most instances. "By repeating stock phrases," one columnist reminds us, "we lose the ability, finally, to hear what we are saying."

Clichés sometimes appear in less familiar guise. In summer 1983 Nigeria elected a new government, an important, peaceful event that received less media attention than violent events of much more trivial significance. An editorial in the *Wall Street Journal* attributed this lack of interest to our inability to look beyond cherished clichés:

> Let's be frank about this: An awful lot of people in the industrialized West just can't take seriously the idea of these underdeveloped countries conducting their own affairs in any sensible or civilized way. The cliché on the right is that you're lucky if someone imposes stability on the country long enough to let a proper mix of economic policies take hold. And the left thinks that elections aren't as important as a government that will force a presumably more equal restructuring of the nation's wealth.[21]

Slogans

> I have always been rather impressed by those people who wear badges stating where they stand on certain issues. The badges have to be small, and therefore the message has to be small, concise, and without elaboration. So it comes out as "I hate something" or "I love something," or ban this or ban that. There isn't space for argument, and I therefore envy the badge-wearer who is so clear-cut about his or her opinions.[22]

The word *slogan* has a picturesque origin. A slogan was the war cry or rallying cry of a Scottish or Irish clan. From that early use it has come to mean a "catchword or rallying motto distinctly associated with a political party or other group" as well as a "catch phrase used to advertise a product."

Slogans, like clichés, are short, undeveloped arguments. They represent abbreviated responses to often complex questions. As a reader you

---

[20] *World Almanac and Book of Facts 1990* (New York: World Almanac, 1990), pp. 737, 698.

[21] *Wall Street Journal*, August 15, 1983, p. 16.

[22] Anthony Smith, "Nuclear Power — Why Not?" *The Listener*, October 22, 1981, p. 463.

need to be aware that slogans merely call attention to a problem; they cannot offer persuasive proof for a claim in a dozen words or less. As a writer you should avoid the use of slogans that evoke an emotional response "without giving [the reader] adequate reason for having this response."

Advertising slogans are the most familiar. Some of them are probably better known than nursery rhymes: "Reach out and touch someone," "It costs more, but I'm worth it," "Don't leave home without it." Advertisements may, of course, rely for their effectiveness on more than slogans. They may also give us interesting and valuable information about products, but most advertisements give us slogans that ignore proof — short cuts substituting for argument.

The persuasive appeal of advertising slogans is heavily dependent on the connotations associated with products. In Chapter 4 (see "Appeals to Needs and Values"), we discussed the way in which advertisements promise to satisfy our needs and protect our values. Wherever evidence is scarce or nonexistent, the advertiser must persuade us through skillful choice of words and phrases (as well as pictures), especially those that produce pleasurable feelings. "Coke — it's the real thing." "Real" — as opposed to artificial or unnatural — sounds like a desirable quality. But what is "real" about Coke? Probably even the advertiser would find it hard to define the "realness" of Coke. Another familiar slogan — "Noxzema, clean makeup" — also emphasizes a quality that we approve of, but what is "clean" makeup? Since the advertisers are silent, we are left with warm feelings about the word and not much more.

Advertising slogans are persuasive because their witty phrasing and punchy rhythms produce an automatic "yes" response. We react to them as we might react to the lyrics of popular songs, and we treat them far less critically than we treat more straightforward and elaborate arguments. Still, the consequences of failing to analyze the slogans of advertisers are usually not serious. You may be tempted to buy a product because you were fascinated by a brilliant slogan, but if the product doesn't satisfy, you can abandon it without much loss. However, ignoring ideological slogans, coined by political parties or special interest groups, may carry an enormous price, and the results are not so easily undone.

Ideological slogans, like advertising slogans, depend on the power of connotation, the emotional associations aroused by a word or phrase. In the 1960s and 1970s, a period of well-advertised social change, slogans flourished; they appeared by the hundreds of thousands on buttons, T-shirts, and bumper stickers. One of them read, "Student Power!" To some readers of the slogan, distrustful of young people and worried about student unrest on campuses and in the streets, the suggestion was frightening. To others, mostly students, the idea of power, however undefined, was intoxicating. Notice that "Student Power!" is not an argument; it is only a claim. (It might also represent a warrant.) As a claim, for example, it might take this form: Students at this school should have the power to select the faculty. Of course, the arguer would need to provide the kinds of proof that support his or her claim, something the slogan by itself cannot do. Many people, whether they accepted or rejected the claim, supplied the rest of the argument without knowing exactly what the issues were and how a developed argument would proceed. They were accepting or rejecting the slogan largely on the basis of emotional reaction to words.

American political history is, in fact, a repository of slogans. Leaf through a history of the United States and you will come across "Tippecanoe and Tyler, too," "manifest destiny," "fifty-four forty or fight," "make the world safe for democracy," "the silent majority," "the domino theory," "the missile gap," "the window of vulnerability." Each administration tries to capture the attention and allegiance of the public by coining catchy phrases. Roosevelt's New Deal in 1932 was followed by the Square Deal and the New Frontier. Today, slogans must be carefully selected to avoid offending groups that are sensitive to the ways in which words affect their interests. In 1983 Senator John Glenn, announcing his candidacy for president, talked about bringing "old values and new horizons" to the White House. "New horizons" apparently carried positive connotations. His staff, however, worried that "old values" might suggest racism and sexism to minorities and women.

A professor of politics and international affairs at Princeton University explains why public officials use slogans, despite their obvious shortcomings:

> Officials long have tried to capture complicated events and to dominate public discussion of foreign policy by using simple phrases and slogans. They engage in phrase-making in order to reach wide audiences. . . .
>
> Slogans and metaphors often express the tendencies of officials and academics who have a common wish to be at once sweeping, unequivocal, easily understood and persuasive. The desire to capture complicated phenomena through slogans stems also from impatience with the particular and unwillingness or inability to master interrelationships.[23]

Over a period of time slogans, like clichés, can acquire a life of their own and, if they are repeated often enough, come to represent an unchanging truth we no longer need to examine. "Dangerously," says the writer

[23] Henry Bienen, "Slogans Aren't the World," *New York Times*, January 16, 1983, Sec. IV, p. 19.

quoted above, "policy makers become prisoners of the slogans they popularize."

The arguments you write will not, of course, be one-sentence slogans. Unfortunately, many longer arguments amount to little more than sloganeering or series of suggestive phrases strung together to imitate the process of argumentation. Following are two examples. The first is taken from a full-page magazine advertisement in 1983, urging the formation of a new political party. The second is part of the second inaugural address of George C. Wallace, governor of Alabama, in 1971. These extracts are typical of the full advertisement and the full speech.

> We can't dislodge big money from its domination over the two old parties, but we can offer the country something better: a new party that represents the people and responds to their needs. . . . How can we solve any problem without correcting the cause — the structure of the Dem/Rep machine and the power of the military-industrial establishment? . . . The power of the people could be a commanding force if only we could get together — Labor, public-interest organizations, blacks, women, antinuclear groups, and all the others.[24]

> The people of the South and those who think like the South, represent the majority viewpoint within our constitutional democracy, but they are not organized and do not speak with a loud voice. Until the day arrives when the voice of the people of the South and those who think like us is, within the law, thrust into the face of the bureaucrats, only then can the "people's power" express itself legally and ethically and get results. . . . Too long, oh, too long, has the voice of the people been silenced by their own disruptive government — by governmental bribery in quasi-governmental handouts such as H.E.W. and others that exist in America today! An aroused people can save this nation from those evil forces who seek our destruction. The choice is yours. The hour is growing late![25]

Whatever power these recommendations might have if their proposals were more clearly formulated, as they stand they are collections of slogans and loaded words. (Even the language falters; can the voice of the people be thrust into the face of the bureaucrats?) We can visualize some of the slogans as brightly colored banners: "Dislodge Big Money!" "Power of the People!" "Save This Nation from Evil Forces!" "The Choice Is Yours!" Do all the groups mentioned share identical interests? If so, what are they? Given the vagueness of the terms, it is not surprising that arguers on opposite sides of the political spectrum — loosely characterized as liberal and conservative — sometimes resort to the same clichés and slo-

---

[24] *The Progressive*, September 1983, p. 38.

[25] Second Inaugural Address as Governor of Alabama, January 18, 1971.

gans: the language of populism, or a belief in the virtues of the "common people" in these examples.

Slogans have numerous shortcomings as substitutes for the development of an argument. First, their brevity presents serious disadvantages. Slogans necessarily ignore exceptions or negative instances that might qualify a claim. They usually speak in absolute terms without describing the circumstances in which a principle or idea might not work. Their claims therefore seem shrill and exaggerated. In addition, brevity prevents the sloganeer from revealing how he or she arrived at conclusions.

Second, slogans may conceal unexamined warrants. When Japanese cars were beginning to compete with American cars, the slogan "Made in America by Americans" appeared on the bumpers of thousands of American-made cars. A thoughtful reader would have discovered in this slogan several implied warrants: American cars are better than Japanese cars; the American economy will improve if we buy American; patriotism can be expressed by buying American goods. If the reader were to ask a few probing questions, he or she might find these warrants unconvincing.

Silent warrants that express values hide in other popular and influential slogans. "Pro-life," the slogan of those who oppose abortion, assumes that the fetus is a living being entitled to the same rights as individuals already born. "Pro-choice," the slogan of those who favor abortion, suggests that the freedom of the pregnant woman to choose is the foremost or only consideration. The words *life* and *choice* have been carefully selected to reflect desirable qualities, but the words are only the beginning of the argument.

Third, although slogans may express admirable sentiments, they often fail to tell us how to achieve their objectives. They address us in the imperative mode, ordering us to take an action or refrain from it. But the means of achieving the objectives may be nonexistent or very costly. If the sloganeer cannot offer workable means for implementing his or her goals, he or she risks alienating the audience.

Sloganeering is one of the recognizable attributes of propaganda. Propaganda for both good and bad purposes is a form of slanting, of selecting language and facts to persuade an audience to take a certain action. Even a good cause may be weakened by an unsatisfactory slogan. The slogans of some organizations devoted to fundraising for the physically handicapped have come under attack for depicting the handicapped as helpless. According to one critic, the popular slogan "Jerry's kids" promotes the idea that Jerry Lewis is the sole support of children afflicted with muscular dystrophy. Perhaps increased sensitivity to the needs of the handicapped will produce new words and new slogans. If you assume that your audience is sophisticated and alert, you will probably write your strongest arguments, devoid of clichés and slogans.

SAMPLE ANALYSIS

Nox Quondam, Nox Futura!

RICHARD MITCHELL

> Students do not read, write, and do arithmetic as well as they used to because they can get along quite nicely without these skills. . . . Americans are finding that they need to rely less and less on "basic skills" to find out what they want to know and what they want to do. Our basic skills are declining precisely because we need them less.
>
> Peter Wagschal, Futurist,
> University of Massachusetts

Yeah. And that's not all! Just you take a good look at the standard 1
American dogs and cats. They live pretty damn well, toiling not, neither spinning, and they've never even *heard* of stuff like reading, writing, and arithmetic. They "do quite nicely without those skills," and so do tropical fish and baboons. And so, too, did black slaves and Russian serfs, and all those marvelously skillful and industrious ancestors of us all who gathered nuts and roots and killed small rodents with sticks. They all knew everything they needed to know.

We would probably never have heard of Peter Wagschal, or of his 2
neato Ouija Board Studies Program, if it hadn't been for one Larry Zenke, a pretty neato guy himself. Zenke is Superintendent of Schools in Tulsa, Oklahoma, where men are still men. Did he quail when the national achievement test scores, which used to be quite good in that prosperous and orderly city, hit new lows last fall? Nosirree. When taxpayers grumbled, did he ignominiously promise to do better? And when the *Tulsa Tribune* started shooting off its editorial mouth about "fads" and "anti-academic garbage," did Zenke tiptoe away into the piloting of experiential remediation enhancement parameters?

No way. Not in Oklahoma. In the finest frontier fashion, he stood up 3
tall in the middle of Main Street at high noon and told the unruly rabble that maybe they'd like to talk it over, before doing anything hasty, with his pal, Pete (The Persuader) Wagschal, who somehow just happened to drift into town. True grit.

A professor of classics at Glassboro State College, Richard Mitchell is the editor and publisher of the *Underground Grammarian*, a one-person review of the follies of academic discourse (and, in general, academia). This piece is from his collection *The Leaning Tower of Babel* (1984).

Then, having (by proxy) brought light to the benighted fuddy-duddies of Tulsa, Zenke, who obviously knows more than he lets on, laid a little groundwork for the defense of *next* year's test scores: "Wagschal even suggests that fifty years from now we could be the smartest, most knowledgeable society that has ever existed, *and yet be largely illiterate.*" 4

The italics are Zenke's, not ours, and we're grateful for them. We have often wondered what kind of an idea it would take to make a school superintendent excited about the life of the intellect. 5

And a dandy idea it is, especially for all those much misunderstood "educators," saddled (for now) with the thankless (and difficult) task of teaching what no one will need to know when the bright age dawns. All that burnout and stress! And for what? For nothing more than an arcane and elitist social grace no more necessary in a truly "knowledgeable society" than the ability to play polo, or the lute. 6

And how, you ask, will people who are "largely illiterate" come to amass all that knowledge? Well, don't you worry, bless your heart. Someone will probably be quite willing to tell them what to know, even if it means all the trouble and expense of attaching loudspeakers to every lamp-post in America. 7

The teachers, then, will be liberated to do what the teacher academies train them to do. Zenke foretells: 8

> Teachers, for example, will no longer be disseminators of cognitive information — machines will do that. Teachers will be program developers and/or facilitators of group membership, helping students develop interaction skills. Some educators, of course, will be found too rigid to survive this metamorphosis, but those who do will find excitement and fulfillment in their new "teaching roles."

And that will be just dandy too. Happy, happy, the teachers of tomorrow, at long last fulfilled and excited! Freed forever from the stern constraints of the tiny smatterings of mere information still incongruously expected of teachers, the facilitator-trainees of the future won't have to take *any* of those dull and irrelevant "subjects" that now impede their growth as *professionals* and their group membership development. They'll be able to spend *all* their time in the enhancement of their interaction skills, so that they can go forth and facilitate the same for little children. (Those cunning tots, of course, *do* have to be *educated*, you know, so that they will sit quietly in organized groups when it's time to hear some knowledge from the loudspeaker.) And the training program for superintendents of schools will be even more exciting and fulfilling. There's just no counting the skills that *they* can get along nicely without. 9

Which is it you've lost, Tulsans, your spirit or your minds? Could it be both? Do you lie awake in the still watches of the night worrying about 10 those godless communists who are panting to nationalize oil? Do you fear that bleeding hearts will take away the guns by which you fancy that you won and may yet preserve your liberty? Pooh, Tulsans, pooh.

The most dangerous threat to your liberty, the one that has by far the 11
best chance of turning you all into docile clods, is right there in Tulsa. Think, dammit! Do you imagine that foreign enemies of this nation could devise for your children a more hideous and revolting destiny than the one so blithely envisioned — and as an *exoneration*, no less — by the superintendent of schools? Do you yawn and turn to the sports section, citizens of Tulsa, when the man whom you have hired to oversee the growth of understanding and judgment in your children airily tells you that in a palmier day they will have no need of the literacy that alone can give those powers? Do you shrug when he tells you that the children will be spared the burden of whatever "cognitive information" they don't actually need, which must obviously, since the children will have no powers of judgment, be chosen by someone like Zenke? Do you, like Zenke, dream of the day when no one will be able to *read* our Constitution, but it won't matter, because the machines provided by the government schools will tell us all we really need to know about it? Can you think of something to say to those teachers, and superintendents, who are *not* excited and fulfilled with leading young minds into the ways of understanding and thoughful discretion, and who are *un*rigid enough, flaccid and limp enough, not only to survive but to hail as liberation their metamorphosis into developers and facilitators? Does it not occur to you that the inculcation of "interaction skills" for the purpose of "group development" is exactly the opposite of an education, by which a mind can find its way *out* of group-think and the pet promulgations of collectivisms? And in short, Tulsans, what are those strange black boxes we see on *your* lamp-posts? What soothing message have they recited, even as you slept? How is it, O Pioneers, that you are not mad as hell?

Oklahoma is much changed, but the descendants of the settlers still 12
like to watch the hawk making lazy circles in the sky. Their bird-lore, however, is not what it was. In fact, there's hardly a damn one of them that can tell a hawk from a vulture nowadays.

Analysis

The Latin title means "Night (or Darkness) in the Past, Night in the Future," a meaning that becomes clear when we read the quotation from Wagschal. Mitchell has probably used a Latin phrase, whose translation may not be readily apparent, precisely to distance himself from the half-educated who are the object of his attack.

Mitchell is attacking a serious idea, that it won't matter much in the future if we're illiterate or not. The weapon of attack is satire, and the depth of his anger and scorn is reflected in his language. Like other satirists — Swift, the author of "A Modest Proposal" (p. 560), is the most famous — Mitchell at some points assumes an invented *persona*. In fact, he assumes several fictitious personalities, each of whom speaks a different language of sarcasm and insult.

In the first two paragraphs he expresses withering scorn with examples of animals and cavemen that reduce the futurist's prediction to absurdity. We notice his use of "Yeah," "Just you take a good look," "damn well," "neato," "Nosirree," the slangy speech of a tough guy who pretends to be in agreement with Wagschal. At the same time he satirizes the meaningless and inflated jargon of education: "experiential remediation enhancement parameters."

In the third paragraph Mitchell makes fun of the Tulsa superintendent who agrees with the futurist by portraying him as a character in a Western shoot-out. There is more colloquial talk — "No way," "Well, don't you worry, bless your heart," "And that will be just dandy too," "Pooh, Tulsans, pooh" — that contrasts sharply with the serious, angry, scholarly expression of the real Richard Mitchell, a teacher and grammarian, whose views are stated most directly in the next to last paragraph. In his great essay Swift, too, while adopting the language and ideas of a reasonable and compassionate man for most of the essay, becomes himself for a few paragraphs near the end, the bitter social critic enraged by conditions in Ireland.

This kind of satire is not easy to do. It depends on finding words that establish a distance between the author's real argument and the argument of the person he is pretending to be, without confusing the reader. (Even Swift's essay was misunderstood by some eighteenth-century readers, who regarded his proposal as the work of a monster.) Mitchell handles this strategy with great skill and icy humor. In the paragraph beginning, "And that will be just dandy, too," his sarcastic predictions make clear what he really fears. After all, no serious person ought to find this scenario acceptable. He has even italicized six words in the paragraph to underscore his contempt for the futurist and his apostles.

READINGS FOR ANALYSIS

The Speech the Graduates Didn't Hear

JACOB NEUSNER

We the faculty take no pride in our educational achievements with you. We have prepared you for a world that does not exist, indeed, that cannot exist. You have spent four years supposing that failure leaves no record. You have learned at Brown that when your work goes poorly, the painless solution is to drop out. But starting now, in the world to which you go, failure marks you. Confronting difficulty by quitting leaves you changed. Outside Brown, quitters are no heroes. 1

With us you could argue about why your errors were not errors, why mediocre work really was excellent, why you could take pride in routine and slipshod presentation. Most of you, after all, can look back on honor grades for most of what you have done. So, here grades can have meant little in distinguishing the excellent from the ordinary. But tomorrow, in the world to which you go, you had best not defend errors but learn from them. You will be ill-advised to demand praise for what does not deserve it, and abuse those who do not give it. 2

For four years we created an altogether forgiving world, in which whatever slight effort you gave was all that was demanded. When you did not keep appointments, we made new ones. When your work came in beyond the deadline, we pretended not to care. 3

Worse still, when you were boring, we acted as if you were saying something important. When you were garrulous and talked to hear yourself talk, we listened as if it mattered. When you tossed on our desks writing upon which you had not labored, we read it and even responded, as though you earned a response. When you were dull, we pretended you were smart. When you were predictable, unimaginative, and routine, we listened as if to new and wonderful things. When you demanded free lunch, we served it. And all this why? 4

Despite your fantasies, it was not even that we wanted to be liked by you. It was that we did not want to be bothered, and the easy way out was pretense: smiles and easy Bs. 5

Jacob Neusner is university professor and distinguished scholar of Judaic studies at Brown University. His speech appeared in Brown's *The Daily Herald* on June 12, 1983.

It is conventional to quote in addresses such as these. Let me quote someone you've never heard of: Professor Carter A. Daniel, Rutgers University (*Chronicle of Higher Education*, May 7, 1979): 6

"College has spoiled you by reading papers that don't deserve to be read, listening to comments that don't deserve a hearing, paying attention even to the lazy, ill-informed, and rude. We had to do it, for the sake of education. But nobody will ever do it again. College has deprived you of adequate preparation for the last fifty years. It has failed you by being easy, free, forgiving, attentive, comfortable, interesting, unchallenging fun. Good luck tomorrow." 7

That is why, on this commencement day, we have nothing in which to take much pride. 8

Oh, yes, there is one more thing. Try not to act toward your coworkers and bosses as you have acted toward us. I mean, when they give you what you want but have not earned, don't abuse them, insult them, act out with them your parlous relationships with your parents. This too we have tolerated. It was, as I said, not to be liked. Few professors actually care whether or not they are liked by peer-paralyzed adolescents, fools so shallow as to imagine professors care not about education but about popularity. It was, again, to be rid of you. So go, unlearn the lies we taught you. To Life! 9

Discussion Questions

1. Pick out some of the words and phrases — especially adjectives and verbs — used by Neusner to characterize both students and teachers. Do you think these terms are loaded? Explain.
2. Has Neusner chosen "facts" to slant his article? If so, point out where slanting occurs. If not, point out where the article seems to be truthful.
3. As a student you will probably object to Neusner's accusations. How would you defend your behavior as a student in answer to his specific charges?

Writing Suggestions

1. Rewrite Neusner's article with the same "facts" — or others from your experience — using temperate language and a tone of sadness rather than anger.
2. Write a letter to Neusner responding to his attack. Support or attack his argument by providing evidence from your own experience.
3. Write your own short commencement address. Do some things need to be said that commencement speakers seldom or never express?
4. Write an essay using the same kind of strong language as Neusner uses about some aspect of your education of which you disapprove. Or write a letter to a teacher using the same form as "The Speech the Graduates Didn't Hear."

Erasing the "R" Words

HELEN E. AND R. LYNN SAULS

1 R words seldom appear in social studies and history textbooks anymore. The G word is practically gone. The P word is rare. So are the B word and the C word.

2 Writers and publishers have virtually eradicated from textbooks *God, prayer, Bible, church* — in short, religion — as a force in American life.

3 This is the conclusion of three studies conducted independently during the mid-1980s. Funded through a federal grant from the Department of Education, Paul C. Vitz, a New York University professor, completed the first one. People of the American Way — a Washington group founded by Norman Lear to monitor the Religious Right — and Americans United for Separation of Church and State conducted the other two studies.

4 Vitz analyzed line by line sixty elementary social studies textbooks and eight high school American history textbooks. The elementary texts included those adopted by California, Texas, and fifteen other states — textbooks used by 60 to 70 percent of the nation's children. The high school texts included those that appeared most frequently on state adoption lists — textbooks used by more than 50 percent of the nation's high school students taking U.S. history.

5 Vitz completed his study in 1985. It became available as a paperback in 1986 under the title *Censorship: Evidence of Bias in Our Children's Textbooks.*[1] . . .

[The following excerpts are from textbooks used in 1871, 1921, and 1982.]

On the Pilgrims

From an 1871 "Common School Textbook."[2] Look for these R words: religious sect, church, religious independence, religious persecution, God-fearing, and Christians. Keep in mind that the author attempted "a tone of treatment free from partisan bias of sectionalism, politics, or religion — a tone of treatment as completely as possible American."

Helen E. and R. Lynn Sauls are professors of education and journalism, respectively, at Southern College of Seventh-Day Adventists in Tennessee. These excerpts are from their article in the May/June 1989 issue of *Liberty*.

[1] Ann Arbor, MI: Servant Books, 1986.

[2] William Swinton, *A Condensed School History of the United States*, rev. ed. (New York: Ivison, Blakeman, Taylor, 1871), pp. 39–41.

The Pilgrim Fathers belonged to a religious sect that had separated or seceded from the Established Church of England. On this account they were sometimes called Separatists. They were Puritans; but they went further than most of the Puritans in favor of religious independence. . . .

It is always very noble when men do or suffer anything for the sake of principle; and we must admire the self-sacrifice and courage of the Pilgrims.

In 1620 this band . . . took ship in a vessel named the *Mayflower*. . . . The *Mayflower* reached the coast of Massachusetts, and the Pilgrim band made a landing at the place marked on Captain Smith's map as Plymouth. . . .

The Pilgrims and their descendants were a quiet, thrifty, God-fearing people. They were, for the age, liberal Christians, and were never guilty of that religious persecution for which the Puritans of Massachusetts Bay Colony have been much blamed.

From a 1921 Elementary School Textbook.[3] Look for these R words; hymns, anthem, faith, shrine, holy ground, worship, God.

Landing of the Pilgrim Fathers
By Felicia Dorothea Hemans

The breaking waves dashed high
On a stern and rock-bound coast,
And the woods against a stormy sky
Their giant branches tossed;

And the heavy night hung dark,
The hills and waters o'er,
When a band of exiles moored their bark
On the wild New England shore.

What sought they thus afar?
Bright jewels of the mine?
The wealth of seas, the spoils of war?—
They sought a faith's pure shrine!

Ay, call it holy ground,
The soil where first they trod:
They have left unstained what there they found—
Freedom to worship God.

---

[3] *McGuffey's Sixth Eclectic Reader*, rev. ed. (New York: American Book Co., 1921), pp. 227, 228. NOTE: The *McGuffey Readers* were among the first books published in the United States to reach a mass audience. They held and shaped the minds of generations of Americans from the 1830s until the 1920s, when their popularity began to decline. Felicia Hemans's "Landing of the Pilgrim Fathers" was included in nearly all editions of *McGuffey's Sixth Reader*. Many schoolchildren had to learn it "by heart."

From a 1982 Elementary School Textbook.[4] As you read these few pages from a thirty-two page unit on the Pilgrims from a second-grade social studies textbook, don't look for any R words. There aren't any. Not a single word related to religion occurs in the whole thirty-two page section. On the basis of this reading, to whom would you think the Pilgrims were thankful on that first Thanksgiving if you were a second grader and didn't know better?

> . . . The Pilgrims had a very hard time that first winter. There was not enough food. Many people were sick. Some people died.
>
> In the spring, Americans came to Plymouth. They lived nearby. . . .
>
> The Pilgrims met an American named Squanto. He became their good friend. Squanto taught them many things.
>
> He showed them how to plant corn. He told them where the wild berries and plants grew.
>
> Squanto showed the Pilgrims the best way to fish. He told them where to hunt for turkey and deer.
>
> Everyone worked hard all summer. People worked in the fields. They worked in the woods, in the gardens, and in the homes.
>
> That fall the Pilgrims had enough food to eat. They had houses to live in. They had wood for their fires.
>
> The Pilgrims wanted to give thanks for all they had. So they made plans for a feast. They asked their American friends to share their food.
>
> They asked them to play in their games. What do people call this feast today?

Discussion Questions

1. Do the Saulses succeed in presenting themselves as scholarly advocates? Find places in the article that support your answer.
2. Is the evidence concerning the absence of religion persuasive? Explain.
3. What major reason do they give for proposing textbook treatment of religious events? Do they try to answer the objections of those who disagree with them?
4. Compare the three textbook excerpts from 1871, 1921, and 1982. Summarize the emphasis in each passage.

Writing Suggestions

1. Select a major religious event in American history which interests you, and argue that it was a significant event and merits treatment in a history textbook.

---

[4] *Here We Are*, Grade 2 of the Riverside Social Studies Program (Chicago: Riverside Pub. Co., 1982), pp. 34, 35.

2. The article does not explore the reasons for the omission of the R words. Try to infer the reasons and the attitudes that produced them. You might find it easier to discuss only the 1982 text.
3. If you agree with the authors, write a further defense of their position, offering other reasons for coverage of religion in textbooks. If you disagree — that is, if you think the absence of religion is justified — write a defense of your position.

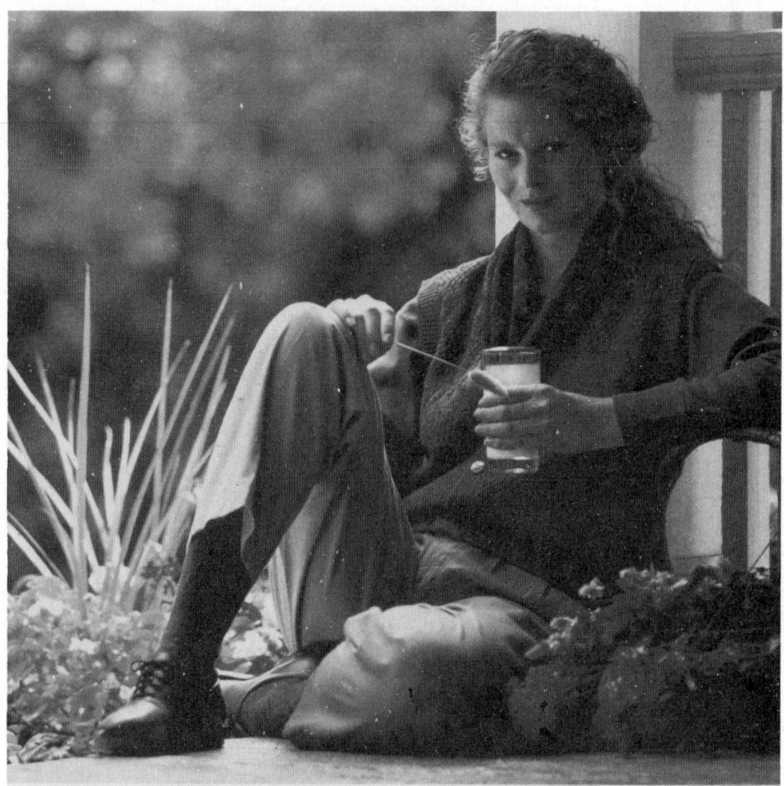

Good taste comes naturally to women all over New England.

Good taste is a part of everything Julie Morton does. You can see it in her style, her home, and even in the milk she drinks. That's why she buys Nuform Milk from Hood.® She knows that Hood has taken out most of the fat, while adding healthy protein and vitamins. She also knows that it has the taste that she insists upon. So, when it comes to good taste and good health, Julie Morton wants the best. Nuform Milk from Hood.

Discussion Questions

1. Look for a shift in the use of a word, which makes nonsense of the message. Explain why.
2. What sort of *visual* connotations does the image of the woman convey?

EXERCISES FOR REVIEW

1. Select one or two related bumper stickers visible in your neighborhood. Examine the hidden warrants on which they are based and assess their validity.
2. For a slogan found on a bumper sticker or elsewhere, supply the evidence to support the claim in the slogan. Or find evidence that disproves the claim.
3. Examine a few periodicals from fifty or more years ago. Select either an advertising or a political slogan contained in them and relate it to beliefs or events of the period. Or tell why the slogan is no longer relevant.
4. Discuss the origin of a cliché or slogan. Describe, as far as possible, the backgrounds and motives of its users.
5. Make up your own slogan for a cause that you support. Explain and defend your slogan.
6. Discuss the appeal to needs and values of some popular advertising or political slogan.
7. Choose a cliché and find evidence to support or refute it. Examples: People were much happier in the past. Mother knows best. Life was much simpler in the past. Money can't buy happiness.
8. Choose one of the statements in exercise 7 or another statement and write a paper telling why you think such a statement has persisted as an explanation.
9. Select a passage, perhaps from a textbook, written largely in abstractions, and rewrite it using simpler and more concrete language.

CHAPTER 7

Induction, Deduction, and Logical Fallacies

Throughout the book we have pointed out the weaknesses that cause arguments to break down. In the vast majority of cases these weaknesses represent breakdowns in logic or the reasoning process. We call such weaknesses *fallacies*, a term derived from the Latin. Sometimes these false or erroneous arguments are deliberate; in fact, the Latin word *fallere* means to deceive. But more often these arguments are either carelessly or unintentionally constructed. Thoughtful readers learn to recognize them; thoughtful writers learn to avoid them.

The reasoning process was first given formal expression by Aristotle, the Greek philosopher, almost 2,500 years ago. In his famous treatises, he described the way we try to discover the truth — observing the world, selecting impressions, making inferences, generalizing. In this process Aristotle identified two forms of reasoning: *induction* and *deduction*. Both forms, he realized, are subject to error. Our observations may be incorrect or insufficient, and our conclusions may be faulty because they have violated the rules governing the relationship between statements. The terms we've introduced may be unfamiliar, but the processes of reasoning, as well as the fallacies that violate these processes, are not. Induction and deduction are not reserved only for formal arguments about important problems; they also represent our everyday thinking about the most ordinary matters. As for the fallacies, they, too, unfortunately, may crop up anywhere, whenever we are careless in our use of the reasoning process.

In this chapter we will examine some of the most common fallacies. First, however, a closer look at induction and deduction will make clear what happens when fallacies occur.

INDUCTION

Induction is the form of reasoning in which we come to conclusions about the whole on the basis of observations of particular instances. If you notice that prices on the four items you bought in the campus bookstore are higher than similar items in the bookstore in town, you may come to the conclusion that the campus store is a more expensive place to shop. If you also noticed that all three of the instructors you saw on the first day of school were wearing faded jeans and sandals, you might say that your teachers are generally informal in their dress. In both cases you have made an *inductive leap,* reasoning from what you have learned about a few examples to what you think is true of a whole class of things.

How safe are you in coming to these conclusions? As we've noticed in discussing data and generalization warrants, the reliability of your conclusion depends on the quantity and quality of your observations. Were four items out of the thousands available in the campus store a sufficiently large sample? Would you come to the same conclusion if you chose fifty items? Might another selection have produced a different conclusion? As for the casually dressed instructors, perhaps further investigation would disclose that the teachers wearing jeans were all teaching assistants and that associate and full professors usually wore business clothes. Or the difference might lie in the academic discipline; anthropology teachers might turn out to dress less formally than business school teachers.

In these two situations, you could come closer to verifying your conclusions by further observation and experience, that is, by buying more items at both stores over a longer period of time and by coming into contact with a greater number of professors during a whole semester. Even without pricing every item in both stores or encountering every instructor on campus, you would be more confident of your generalization as the quality and quantity of your samples increased.

In some cases you can observe all the instances in a particular situation. For example, by acquiring information about the religious beliefs of all the residents of the dormitory, you can arrive at an accurate assessment of the number of Buddhists. But since our ability to make definitive observations about everything is limited, we must also make an inductive leap about categories of things that we ourselves can never encounter in their entirety. For some generalizations, as we have learned about evidence, we rely on the testimony of reliable witnesses who report that they have experienced or observed many more instances of the phenomenon. A television documentary may give us information about unwed teenage mothers in a city neighborhood; four girls are interviewed and followed for several days by the reporter. Are these girls typical of thousands of others? A sociologist on the program assures us that, in fact, they are. She herself has consulted with hundreds of other young mothers and can vouch for the fact that a conclusion about them, based on our observation of the four, will be sound. Obviously, though, our conclusion can only be probable, not certain. The sociologist's sample is large, but she can account only for hundreds, not thousands, and there may be unexamined cases that will seriously weaken our conclusions.

In other cases, we may rely on a principle known in science as "the uniformity of nature." We assume that certain conclusions about oak trees in the temperate zone of North America, for example, will also be true for oak trees growing elsewhere under similar climatic conditions. We also use this principle in attempting to explain the causes of behavior in human beings. If we discover that institutionalization of some children from infancy results in severe emotional retardation, we think it safe to conclude that under the same circumstances all children would suffer the same consequences. As in the previous example, we are aware that certainty about every case of institutionalization is impossible. With rare exceptions, the process of induction can offer only probability, not certain truth.

SAMPLE ANALYSIS: AN INDUCTIVE ARGUMENT

The Silenced Majority

BARBARA EHRENREICH

It is possible for a middle-class person today to read the papers, watch television, even go to college, without suspecting that America has any inhabitants other than white-collar people — and, of course, the annoyingly persistent "black underclass." The average American has disappeared — from the media, from intellectual concern, and from the mind of the American middle class. The producers of public affairs talk shows do not blush to serve up four upper-income professionals (all, incidentally, white, male, and conservative) to ponder the minimum wage or the possible need for national health insurance. Never, needless to say, an uninsured breadwinner or an actual recipient of the minimum wage. Working-class people are likely to cross the screen only as witnesses to crimes or sports events, never as commentators or — even when their own lives are under discussion — as "experts." 1

A quick definition: By "working class" I mean not only industrial workers in hard hats, but all those people who are not professionals, managers, or entrepreneurs; who work for wages rather than salaries; and who spend their working hours variously lifting, bending, driving, monitoring, typing, keyboarding, cleaning, providing physical care for others, loading, unloading, cooking, serving, etc. The working class so defined makes up 60 to 70 percent of the U.S. population. 2

By "middle class" I really mean the "professional middle class," or the "professional-managerial class." This group includes the journalists, professors, media executives, etc. who are responsible, in a day-to-day sense, for what we do or do not see or read about in the media. By this definition, the middle class amounts to no more than 20 percent of the U.S. population. 3

So when I say the working class is disappearing, I do not mean just a particular minority group favored, for theoretical reasons, by leftists. I mean the American majority. And I am laying the blame not only on the 4

Barbara Ehrenreich is a feminist writer and social critic whose writings appear frequently in magazines such as *Mother Jones* and *Ms.* "The Silenced Majority" first appeared in the September 1989 issue of *Zeta*; this excerpt was reprinted in January/February 1990 issue of the *UTNE Reader*.

corporate sponsors of the media, but on many less wealthy and powerful people. Media people for example. People who are, by virtue of their lifestyles and expectations, not too different from me, and possibly also you.

5 The disappearance of the working class reflects — and reinforces — the long-standing cultural insularity of the professional middle class. Compared to, say, a decade ago, the classes are less likely to mix in college (due to the decline of financial aid), in residential neighborhoods (due to the rise in real estate prices), or even in the malls (due to the now almost universal segmentation of the retail industry into upscale and downscale components).

6 In the absence of real contact or communication, stereotypes march on unchallenged; prejudices easily substitute for knowledge. The most intractable stereotype is of the working class (which is, in imagination, only white) as a collection of reactionaries and bigots — reflected, for example, in the use of the terms "hard hat" or "redneck" as class slurs. Even people who call themselves progressives are not immune to this prejudice.

7 The truth is that, statistically and collectively, the working class is far more reliably liberal than the professional middle class. It was more, not less, opposed to the war in Vietnam. It is more, not less, disposed to vote for a Democrat for president. And thanks to the careful, quantitative studies of Canadian historian Richard F. Hamilton, we know that the white working class (at least outside the South) is no more racist, and by some measures less so, than the white professional class.

8 Even deeper-rooted than the stereotype of the hard-hat bigot is the middle-class suspicion that the working class is dumb, inarticulate, and mindlessly loyal to old-fashioned values. In the entertainment media, for example, the working class is usually portrayed by macho exhibitionism (from *Saturday Night Fever* to *Working Girl*) or mental inferiority (*Married . . . with Children*). Mainstream sociologists have reinforced this prejudice with their emphasis on working class "parochialism," as illustrated by this quote from a 1976 beginning sociology textbook: "Their limited education, reading habits and associations isolate the lower class . . . , and this ignorance, together with their class position, makes them suspicious of [the] middle- and upper-class 'experts' and 'do-gooders'. . . ."

9 Finally, there is a level of prejudice that grows out of middle-class moralism about matters of taste and lifestyle. All privileged classes seek to differentiate themselves from the less-privileged through the ways they dress, eat, entertain themselves, and so on, and tend to see their own choices in these matters as inherently wiser, better, and more aesthetically inspired. In middle-class stereotype, the white working class, for example, is addicted to cigarettes, Budweiser, polyester, and network television. (In part this is true, and it is true in part because Bud is cheaper than

Dos Equis and polyester is cheaper than linen.) Furthermore, in the middle-class view, polyester and the like are "tacky" — a common code word for "lower class." Health concerns, plus a certain reverence for the "natural" in food and fiber, infuse these middle-class prejudices with a high-minded tone of moral indignation.

10 But I am alarmed by what seems to me to be the growing parochialism of the professional middle class — living in its own social and residential enclaves, condemned to hear only the opinions of its own members (or, of course, of the truly rich), and cut off from the lives and struggles and insights of the American majority. This middle-class parochialism is insidiously self-reinforcing: The less "we" know about "them," the more likely "we" are to cling to our stereotypes — or forget "them" altogether.

Analysis

An inductive argument proceeds by examining particulars and arriving at a generalization that represents a probable truth. In this lively essay Ehrenreich has come to the conclusion, based on her observations, that the working class as she defines it is conspicuously absent from television, newspapers, and even college. The "professional middle class," she says, regards the working classes as dumb, illiberal, and vulgar and cuts itself off from any real contact with them. Her generalization is value-laden; she believes that the refusal of the middle classes to see and communicate with the working class is a dangerous moral and social lapse. The title, in fact, suggests that the majority is not only silent or unheard but *silenced* by some sinister and repressive force.

The power of any inductive generalization rests on the truth and number of its examples. Ehrenreich has provided support from history, movies and television, a sociology text, and her own experiences. Some of the material is vivid and precise. Notice the examples of the insularity of the middle class and their prejudices in paragraphs 8 and 9.

Some readers, however, may ask if the author has been too selective in her proof. They may be able to supply examples of contradictory evidence from their own reading and observation, examples that would reduce the force of her claim.

We know that the author of any inductive argument can never examine all the details necessary to prove a claim. That is why we say that inductive arguments can arrive only at probability, not certainty. That is the reason for qualifying the claim. With the words "It is possible" in her introductory sentence Ehrenreich seems to acknowledge that her claim is not absolute, although elsewhere in the essay her language is less restrained.

DEDUCTION

While induction attempts to arrive at the truth, deduction guarantees sound relationships between statements. If each of a series of statements, called *premises,* is true, deductive logic tells us that the conclusion must also be true. Unlike the conclusions from induction, which are only probable, the conclusions from deduction are certain. The simplest deductive argument consists of two premises and a conclusion. In outline such an argument looks like this:

MAJOR PREMISE: All students with 3.5 averages and above for three years are invited to become members of Kappa Gamma Pi, the honor society.

MINOR PREMISE: George has had a 3.8 average for over three years.

CONCLUSION: Therefore, he will be invited to join Kappa Gamma Pi.

This deductive conclusion is *valid* or logically consistent because it follows necessarily from the premises. No other conclusion is possible. Validity, however, refers only to the form of the argument. The argument itself may not be satisfactory if the premises are not true — if Kappa Gamma Pi has imposed other conditions or if George has only a 3.4 average. The difference between truth and validity is important because it alerts us to the necessity for examining the truth of the premises before we decide that the conclusion is sound.

One way of discovering how the deductive process works is to look at the methods used by Sherlock Holmes, that most famous of literary detectives, in solving his mysteries. His reasoning process followed a familiar pattern. Through the inductive process, that is, observing the particulars of the world, he came to certain conclusions about those particulars. Then he applied deductive reasoning to come to a conclusion about a particular person or event.

On one occasion Holmes observed that a man sitting opposite him on a train had chalk dust on his fingers. From this observation Holmes deduced that the man was a schoolteacher. If his thinking were outlined, it would take the form of the syllogism, the classic form of deductive reasoning:

MAJOR PREMISE: All men with chalk dust on their fingers are schoolteachers.

MINOR PREMISE: This man has chalk dust on his fingers.

CONCLUSION: Therefore, this man is a schoolteacher.

One dictionary defines the syllogism as "a formula of argument consisting of three propositions." The first proposition is called the major premise and offers a generalization about a large group or class. This generalization has been arrived at through inductive reasoning or observation of particulars. The second proposition is called the minor premise, and it makes a statement about a member of that group or class. The third proposition is the conclusion, which links the other two propositions, in much the same way that the warrant links the support and the claim.

If we look back at the syllogism that summarizes Holmes's thinking, we see how it represents the deductive process. The major premise, the first statement, is an inductive generalization, a statement arrived at after observation of a number of men with chalk on their fingers. The minor premise, the second statement, assigns a particular member, the man on the train, to the general class of those who have dust on their fingers.

But although the argument may be logical, it is faulty. The deductive argument is only as strong as its premises. As Lionel Ruby pointed out, Sherlock Holmes was often wrong.[1] Holmes once deduced from the size of a large hat found in the street that the owner was intelligent. He obviously believed that a large head meant a large brain and that a large brain indicated intelligence. Had he lived one hundred years later, new information about the relationship of brain size to intelligence would have enabled him to come to a different and better conclusion.

In this case, we might first object to the major premise, the generalization that all men with chalk dust on their fingers are schoolteachers. Is it true? Perhaps all the men with dusty fingers whom Holmes had so far observed had turned out to be schoolteachers, but was his sample sufficiently large to allow him to conclude that all dust-fingered men, even those with whom he might never have contact, were teachers? Were there no other vocations or situations that might require the use of chalk? Draftsmen or carpenters or tailors or artists might have fingers just as white as those of schoolteachers. In other words, Holmes may have ascertained that all schoolteachers have chalk dust on their fingers, but he had not determined that *only* schoolteachers can be thus identified. Sometimes it is helpful to draw circles representing the various groups in their relation to the whole.

If the large circle (see top figure, p. 216) represents all those who have chalk dust on their fingers, we see that several different groups may be contained in this universe. To be safe, Holmes should have deduced that the man on the train *might* have been a schoolteacher; he was not safe in deducing more than that. Obviously, if the inductive generalization or major premise is false, the conclusion of the particular argument is also false or invalid.

---

[1] *The Art of Making Sense* (Philadelphia, PA: Lippincott, 1954), chap. 17.

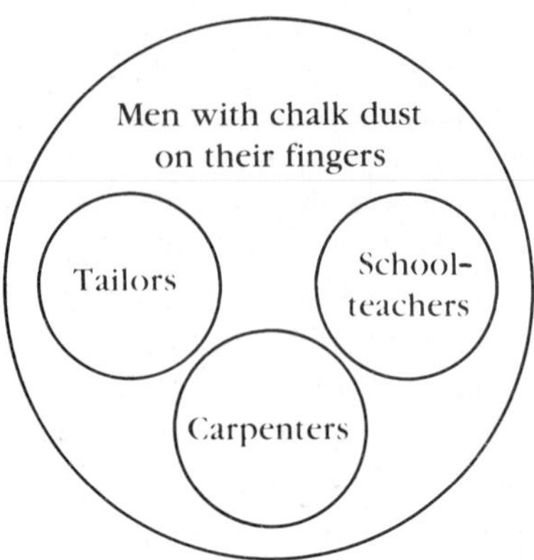

The deductive argument may also go wrong elsewhere. What if the minor premise is untrue? Could Holmes have mistaken the source of the white powder on the man's fingers? Suppose it was not chalk dust but flour or confectioner's sugar or talcum or heroin? Any of these possibilities would weaken or invalidate his conclusion.

Another example, closer to the kinds of arguments you will examine, reveals the flaw in the deductive process.

MAJOR PREMISE: All Communists oppose organized religion.

MINOR PREMISE: Robert Roe opposes organized religion.

CONCLUSION: Therefore, Robert Roe is a Communist.

The common name for this fallacy is "guilt by association." The fact that two things share an attribute does not mean that they are the same thing. As in the first example, the diagram makes clear that Robert Roe and Communists do not necessarily share all attributes.

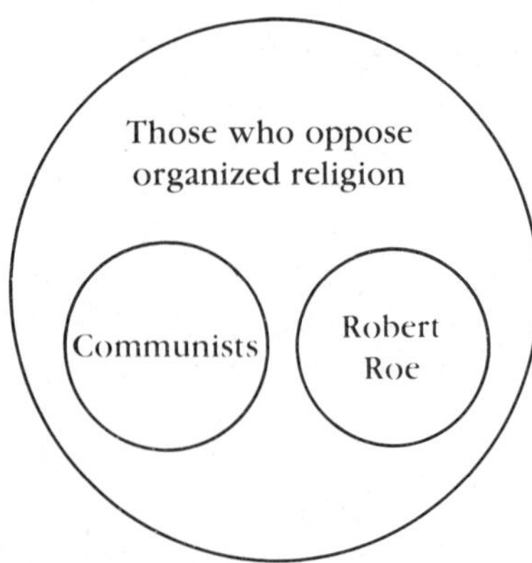

Remembering that Holmes may have misinterpreted the signs of chalk on the traveler's fingers, we may also want to question whether Robert Roe's opposition to organized religion has been misinterpreted.

An example from history shows us how such an argument may be used. In a campaign speech during the summer of 1952, Senator Joseph McCarthy, who had made a reputation as a tireless enemy of communism, said, "I do not tell you that Schlesinger, Stevenson's number one man, number one braintrust, I don't tell you he's a Communist. I have no information on that point. But I do know that if he were a Communist he would also ridicule religion as Schlesinger has done."[2] This is an argument based on a sign warrant. Clearly the sign referred to by Senator McCarthy, ridicule of religion, would not be sufficient to characterize someone as a Communist.

Some deductive arguments give trouble because one of the premises, usually the major premise, is omitted. As in the warrants we examined in Chapter 5, a failure to evaluate the truth of the unexpressed premise may lead to an invalid conclusion. When only two parts of the syllogism appear, we call the resulting form an *enthymeme.* Suppose we overhear the following snatch of conversation:

> *"Did you hear about Jean's father? He had a heart attack last week."*
>
> *"That's too bad. But I'm not surprised. I know he always refused to go for his annual physical checkups."*

The second speaker has used an unexpressed major premise, the cause-effect warrant "If you have annual physical checkups, you can avoid heart attacks." He does not express it because he assumes that it is unnecessary to do so. The first speaker recognizes the unspoken warrant and may agree with it. Or the first speaker may produce evidence from reputable sources that such a generalization is by no means universally true, in which case the conclusion of the second speaker is suspect.

A knowledge of the deductive process can help guide you toward an evaluation of the soundness of your reasoning in an argument you are constructing. The syllogism is often clearer than an outline in establishing the relations between the different parts of an argument.

Suppose you wanted to argue that your former high school should introduce a dress code. You might begin by asking these questions: What would be the purpose of such a regulation? How would a dress code fulfill that purpose? What reasons could you provide to support your claim?

---

[2] Joseph R. McCarthy, "The Red-Tinted Washington Crowd," speech delivered to a Republican campaign meeting at Appleton, Wisconsin, November 3, 1952.

Then you might set down part of your argument like this:

> Dressing in different styles makes students more aware of social differences among themselves.
>
> The students in this school dress in many different styles.
>
> Therefore, they are more aware of differences in social status among the student body.

As you diagram this first part of the argument, you should ask two sets of questions:

1. Is the major premise true? Do differences in dress cause awareness of differences in social status? Has my experience confirmed this?
2. Is the minor premise true? Has my observation confirmed this?

The conclusion, of course, represents something that you don't have to observe. You can deduce with certainty that it is true if both the major and minor premises are true.

So far the testing of your argument has been relatively easy because you have been concerned with the testing of observation and experience. Now you must examine something that does not appear in the syllogism. You have determined certain facts about perceptions of social status, but you have not arrived at the policy you want to recommend: that a dress code should be mandated. Notice that the dress code argument is based on acceptance of a moral value.

> Reducing awareness of social differences is a desirable goal for the school.
>
> A uniform dress code would help to achieve that goal.
>
> Therefore, students should be required to dress uniformly.

The major premise in this syllogism is clearly different from the previous one. While the premise in the previous syllogism can be tested by examining sufficient examples to determine probability, this statement, about the desirability of the goal, is a value judgment and cannot be proved by counting examples. Whether equality of social status is a desirable goal depends on an appeal to other more basic values.

Setting down your own or someone else's argument in this form will not necessarily give you the answers to questions about how to support your claim, but it should clearly indicate what your claims are and, above all, what logical connections exist between your statements.

SAMPLE ANALYSIS: A DEDUCTIVE ARGUMENT

Women Know How to Fight

RUTH WESTHEIMER

As Americans, we can count ourselves lucky that in this century the wars we have engaged in have barely touched our soil. But in all wars, there is at least one country that has to endure its ravages, and the women and children of that land face nearly the same hardships as the men who do the actual fighting. 1

Since women don't escape war, and the nature of combat has changed so that the need for upper body strength is no longer preeminent, all that is keeping women out of combat is the same discrimination we've faced breaking into every other male-dominated position. 2

I come to this conclusion from my own experiences. At the age of sixteen I immigrated to Palestine from Europe, where I became a member of the Haganah, the main underground army of the Jews. I learned to assemble a rifle in the dark and was trained as a sniper so that I could hit the center of the target time after time. As it happened, I never did get into actual combat, but that didn't prevent my being severely wounded. I almost lost both my feet as a result of a bombing attack on Jerusalem. 3

Now were it up to me, I would abolish all warfare. But having lost my family at the hands of the Nazis, I know that we need our armed forces in order to protect our freedoms. And there is no reason why our troops have to be composed only of one sex. 4

My daughter, Miriam, lived in Israel for six years and underwent the same rigorous training as a member of the Israeli Army as the men. Not only was it something she wanted to do for Israel, but she also gained a lot from her experience. She shared in the warmth of the army's esprit de corps and tested herself in ways she never would have done in America. 5

When the first armies were formed, the course of battle took courage, which women share equally with men, and strength, which we do not. But though I am only 4 feet 7 inches tall, with a gun in my hand I am the equal of a soldier who's 6 feet 7 — and perhaps even at a slight advantage, as I make a smaller target. 6

Ruth Westheimer is a psychosexual therapist and the host of a cable television show. This essay was published in the *New York Times* on February 11, 1990.

This is not to say hand-to-hand fighting is a thing of the past, but it is no longer the predominant method. That a general would want the biggest, strongest men in the front lines goes without question, but it is also true that women could fill many, many other roles — from driving a tank to dropping a bomb to firing a cannon to acting as snipers. A fighting spirit is the most important ingredient in the makeup of a fighter. 7

Of course, there are those men who say women don't belong on the battlefield for the same reasons they said we didn't belong in the corporate board room, the assembly line, the police force, or the executive mansion. They're worried that the battle of the sexes will affect the outcome of the battle. While I'm a romantic who likes it when a man offers me flowers, when I'm wearing my hat as psychologist or interviewer or whatever, I can be as tough as the next guy — and if you don't believe me, just ask anyone I've gone up against. 8

Women are demanding equal rights, and most deservedly are getting them. But with those rights come equal responsibilities. Until these, too, are conferred, I don't believe men will ever consider women their true equals. 9

Analysis

A deductive argument proceeds from a general statement that the writer assumes to be true to a conclusion that is more specific. Deductive reasoning is commonplace, but it is seldom so pure as the definition suggests. The essay by Westheimer, though brief, is more complex than it appears. And it is flawed for the most ordinary of reasons — a failure to examine carefully the validity of the major premises or warrants.

The title of the essay is misleading. "Women know how to fight" is only part of the argument, not the conclusion. The claim is that women should be allowed to engage in combat. To support this claim Westheimer must first address the objections of those who believe that women are incapable of fighting. That is, she must first prove that women know how to fight. Her evidence is represented by an account of her own experience and that of her daughter. This is hardly convincing proof. One of the most elementary errors in inductive reasoning is to draw a general conclusion from a very limited sample. In addition she was *trained* to fight but never engaged in combat. (Contrary to her implication, women in the Israeli army, although conscripted, do not fight.)

Let us assume, however, that she has proved that women know how to fight. How does she proceed from that premise to the conclusion that women should therefore be allowed to engage in combat? In the form of a syllogism the argument is this:

ments in the argument and suppresses the third, makes analyzing the relationship even more difficult.

On the other hand, the use of the term *warrant* indicates that the validity of the proposition must be established in order to *guarantee* the claim, or make the crossing from support to claim. It makes clear that the arguer must ask *why* such advertising must be banned.

Nor is the term *minor premise* as useful to the arguer as "support." The word *support* instructs the arguer that he or she must take steps to provide the claim with factual evidence or an appeal to values.

Secondly, while the syllogism is essentially static, with all three parts logically locked into place, the Toulmin model suggests that an argument is a *movement* from support to claim by way of the warrant, which acts as a bridge. Remember that Toulmin introduced the concept of warrant by asking "How do you get there?" (His first two questions, introducing the claim and support, were, "What are you trying to prove?" and "What have you got to go on?")

Lastly, recall that in addition to the three basic elements, the Toulmin model offers supplementary elements of argument. The *qualifier*, in the form of words like "probably" or "more likely," shows that the claim is not absolute. The *backing* offers support for the validity of the warrant. The *reservation* suggests that the validity of the warrant may be limited. These additional elements, which refine and expand the argument itself, reflect the real flexibility and complexity of the argumentative process.

COMMON FALLACIES

In this necessarily brief review it would be impossible to discuss all the fallacies listed by logicians, but we can examine the ones most likely to be found in the arguments you will read and write. Fallacies are difficult to classify, first, because there are literally dozens of systems for classifying, and second, because under any system there is always a good deal of overlap. Our discussion of the reasoning process, however, tells us where faulty reasoning occurs.

Inductive fallacies, as we know, result from the wrong use of evidence: That is, the arguer leaps to a conclusion on the basis of an insufficient sample, ignoring evidence that might have altered his or her conclusion. Deductive fallacies, on the other hand, result from a failure to follow the logic of a series of statements. Here the arguer neglects to make a clear connection between the parts of his or her argument. One of the commonest strategies is the introduction of an irrelevant issue, one that has little or no direct bearing on the development of the claim and serves only to distract the reader.

It's helpful to remember that, even if you cannot name the particular fallacy, you can learn to recognize it and not only refute it in the arguments of others but avoid it in your own as well.

1. Hasty Generalization

In Chapter 4 (see pp. 113–114) we discussed the dangers in drawing conclusions on the basis of insufficient evidence. Many of our prejudices are a result of hasty generalization. A prejudice is literally a judgment made before the facts are in. On the basis of experience with two or three members of an ethnic group, for example, we may form the prejudice that all members of the group share the characteristics that we have attributed to the two or three in our experience. (See Gordon Allport, "The Nature of Prejudice," on p. 92.)

Superstitions are also based in part on hasty generalization. As a result of a very small number of experiences with black cats, broken mirrors, Friday the thirteenth, or spilled salt, some people will assume a cause-effect relation between these signs and misfortunes. Superstition has been defined as "a notion maintained despite evidence to the contrary." The evidence would certainly show that, contrary to the superstitious belief, in a lifetime hundreds of such "unlucky" signs are not followed by unfortunate events. To generalize about a connection is therefore unjustified.

2. Faulty Use of Authority

The attempt to bolster claims by citing the opinions of experts was discussed in Chapter 4. Both writers and readers need to be especially aware of the testimony of authorities who may disagree with those cited. In circumstances where experts disagree, you are encouraged to undertake a careful evaluation and comparison of credentials.

3. *Post Hoc* or Doubtful Cause

The entire Latin term for this fallacy is *post hoc, ergo propter hoc*, meaning, "After this, therefore because of this." The arguer infers that because one event follows another event, the first event must be the cause of the second. But proximity of events or conditions does not guarantee a causal relation. The rooster crows every morning at 5:00 and, seeing the sun rise immediately after, decides that his crowing has caused the sun to rise. A month after A-bomb tests are concluded, tornadoes damage the area where the tests were held, and residents decide that the tests caused the tornadoes. After the school principal suspends daily prayers in the classroom, acts of vandalism increase, and some parents are convinced that failure to conduct prayer is responsible for the rise in vandalism. In each of these cases, the fact that one event follows another does not prove a causal connection. The two events may be coincidental, or the first event may be only one, and an insignificant one, of many causes that have produced the second event. The reader or writer of causal arguments must determine whether another more plausible explanation exists and whether several causes have combined to produce the effect. Perhaps the suspension of prayer was only one of a number of related causes: a decline in disciplinary action, a relaxation of academic standards, a change in school administration, and changes in family structure in the school community.

In the previous section we pointed out that superstitions are the result not only of hasty generalization but also of the willingness to find a cause-effect connection in the juxtaposition of two events. A belief in astrological signs also derives from erroneous inferences about cause and effect. Only a very few of the millions of people who consult the astrology charts every day in newspapers and magazines have submitted the predictions to statistical analysis. A curious reader might try this strategy: Save the columns, usually at the beginning or end of the year, in which astrologers and clairvoyants make predictions for events in the coming year, allegedly based on their reading of the stars and other signs. At the end of the year evaluate the percentage of predictions that were fulfilled. The number will be very small. But even if some of the predictions prove true, there may be other less fanciful explanations for their accuracy.

In defending simple explanations against complex ones, philosophers and scientists often refer to a maxim called *Occam's razor,* a principle of the medieval philosopher and theologian William of Occam. A modern science writer says this principle "urges a preference for the simplest hypothesis that does all we want it to do."[4] Bertrand Russell, the twentieth-century British philosopher, explained it this way:

> It is vain to do with more what can be done with fewer. That is to say, if everything in some science can be interpreted without assuming this or that hypothetical entity, there is no ground for assuming it. I have myself found this a most fruitful principle in logical analysis.[5]

In other words, choose the simpler, more credible explanation wherever possible.

---

[4] Martin Gardner, *The Whys of a Philosophical Scrivener* (New York: Quill, 1983), p. 174.

[5] *Dictionary of Mind, Matter and Morals* (New York: Philosophical Library, 1952), p. 166.

We all share the belief that scientific experimentation and research can answer questions about a wide range of natural and social phenomena: evolutionary development, hurricanes, disease, crime, poverty. It is true that repeated experiments in controlled situations can establish what seem to be solid relations suggesting cause and effect. But even scientists prefer to talk not about cause but about an extremely high probability that under controlled conditions one event will follow another.

In the social sciences cause-effect relations are especially susceptible to challenge. Human experiences can seldom be subjected to laboratory conditions. In addition, the complexity of the social environment makes it difficult, even impossible, to extract one cause from among the many that influence human behavior.

4. False Analogy

Problems in the use of analogy have been treated in Chapter 5. Many analogies are merely descriptive — like the analogy used by Malcolm X — and offer no proof of the connection between the two things being compared.

Historians are fond of using analogical arguments to demonstrate that particular circumstances prevailing in the past are being reproduced in the present. They therefore feel safe in predicting that the present course of history will follow that of the past. British historian Arnold Toynbee argues by analogy that humans' tenure on earth may be limited.

> On the evidence of the past history of life on this planet, even the extinction of the human race is not entirely unlikely. After all, the reign of man on the Earth, if we are right in thinking that man established his present ascendancy in the middle paleolithic age, is so far only about 100,000 years old, and what is that compared to the 500 million or 900 million years during which life has been in existence on the surface of this planet? In the past, other forms of life have enjoyed reigns which have lasted for almost inconceivably longer periods — and which yet at last have come to an end.[6]

Toynbee finds similarities between the limited reigns of other animal species and the possible disappearance of the human race. For this analogy, however, we need to ask whether the conditions of the past, so far as we know them, at all resemble the conditions under which human existence on earth might be terminated. Is the fact that human beings are also members of the animal kingdom sufficient support for this comparison?

---

[6] *Civilization on Trial* (New York: Oxford University Press, 1948), pp. 162–163.

5. *Ad Hominem*

The Latin term *ad hominem* means "against the man" and refers to an attack on the person rather than on the argument or the issue. The assumption in such a fallacy is that if the speaker proves to be unacceptable in some way, his or her statements must also be judged unacceptable. Attacking the author of the statement is a strategy of diversion that prevents the reader from giving attention where it is due — to the issue under discussion.

You might hear someone complain, "What can the priest tell us about marriage? He's never been married himself." This accusation ignores the validity of the advice the priest might offer. In the same way an overweight patient might reject the advice on diet by an overweight physician. In politics it is not uncommon for antagonists to attack each other for personal characteristics that may not be relevant to the tasks they will be elected to perform. They may be accused of infidelity to their partners, homosexuality, atheism, or a flamboyant social life. Even if certain accusations should be proved true, voters should not ignore the substance of what politicians do and say in their public offices.

This confusion of private life with professional record also exists in literature and the other arts. According to their biographers, the American writers Thomas Wolfe, Robert Frost, and William Saroyan — to name only a few — and numbers of film stars, including Charlie Chaplin, Joan Crawford, and Bing Crosby, made life miserable for those closest to them. Having read about their unpleasant personal characteristics, some people find it hard to separate the artist from his or her creation, although the personality and character of the artist are often irrelevant to the content of the work.

Accusations against the person do *not* constitute a fallacy if the characteristics under attack are relevant to the argument. If the politician is irresponsible and dishonest in the conduct of his or her personal life, we may be justified in thinking that the person will also behave irresponsibly and dishonestly in public office.

6. False Dilemma

As the name tells us, the false dilemma, sometimes called the black-white fallacy, poses an either/or situation. The arguer suggests that only two alternatives exist, although there may be other explanations of or solutions to the problem under discussion. The false dilemma reflects the simplification of a complex problem. Sometimes it is offered out of ignorance or laziness, sometimes to divert attention from the real explanation or solution that the arguer rejects for doubtful reasons.

You may encounter the either/or situation in dilemmas about personal choices. "At the University of Georgia," says one writer, "the measure of a man was football. You either played it or worshiped those who did, and there was no middle ground."[7] Clearly this dilemma — "Love football or you're not a man" — ignores other measures of manhood.

Politics and government offer a wealth of examples. In an interview with the *New York Times* in 1975, the Shah of Iran was asked why he could not introduce into his authoritarian regime greater freedom for his subjects. His reply was, "What's wrong with authority? Is anarchy better?" Apparently he considered that only two paths were open to him — authoritarianism or anarchy. Of course, democracy was also an option, which, perhaps fatally, he declined to consider.

In this country some advocates of unilateral nuclear disarmament by the United States assume that only two alternatives exist as an end to the nuclear arms race — unilateral disarmament or nuclear war. Other possibilities, however, may exist, at least one of which is the preservation of the status quo between the superpowers. In this argument the stakes are so high that the advocate needs to reassure the audience that he or she has examined the largest number of possible outcomes before proposing a solution.

7. Slippery Slope

If an arguer predicts that taking a first step will lead inevitably to a second usually undesirable step, he or she must provide evidence that this will happen. Otherwise, the arguer is guilty of a slippery slope fallacy.

Asked by an inquiring photographer on the street how he felt about censorship of a pornographic magazine, a man replied, "I don't think any publication should be banned. It's a slippery slope when you start making decisions on what people should be permitted to read. . . . It's a dangerous precedent." Perhaps. But if questioned further, the man should have offered evidence that a ban on some things leads inevitably to a ban on everything.

Predictions based on the danger inherent in taking the first step are commonplace:

> Legalization of abortion will lead to murder of the old and the physically and mentally handicapped.
>
> The Connecticut law allowing sixteen-year-olds and their parents to divorce each other will mean the death of the family.

---

[7] Phil Gailey, "A Nonsports Fan," *New York Times Magazine*, December 18, 1983, Sec. VI, p. 96.

> If we ban handguns, we will end up banning rifles and other hunting weapons.

Distinguishing between probable and improbable predictions — that is, recognizing the slippery slope fallacy — poses special problems because only future developments can verify or refute predictions. For example, in 1941 the imposition of military conscription aroused some opponents to predict that the draft was a precursor of fascism in this country. Only after the war, when ten million draftees were demobilized, did it become clear that the draft had been an insufficient sign for a prediction of fascism. In this case the slippery slope prediction of fascism might have been avoided if closer attention had been paid to other influences pointing to the strength of democracy.

Slippery slope predictions are simplistic. They ignore not only the dissimilarities between first and last steps but also the complexity of the developments in any long chain of events.

8. Begging the Question

If the writer makes a statement that assumes that the very question being argued has already been proved, the writer is guilty of begging the question. In a letter to the editor of a college newspaper protesting the failure of the majority of students to meet the writing requirement because they had failed an exemption test, the writer said, "Not exempting all students who honestly qualify for exemption is an insult." But whether the students are honestly qualified is precisely the question that the exemption test was supposed to resolve. The writer has not proved that the students who failed the writing test were qualified for exemption. She has only made an assertion *as if* she had already proved it.

In an effort to raise standards of teaching, some politicians and educators have urged that "master teachers" be awarded higher salaries. Opponents have argued that such a proposal begs the question because it assumes that the term "master teachers" can be or has already been defined.

Circular reasoning is an extreme example of begging the question: "Women should not be permitted to join men's clubs because the clubs are for men only." The question to be resolved first, of course, is whether clubs for men only should continue to exist.

9. Straw Man

This fallacy consists of an attack on a view similar to but not the same as the one your opponent holds. It is a familiar diversionary tactic. The name probably derives from an old game in which a straw man was set up to divert attention from the real target that a contestant was supposed to knock down.

One of the outstanding examples of the straw man fallacy occurred in the famous Checkers speech of Senator Richard Nixon. In 1952 during his vice-presidential campaign, Nixon was accused of having appropriated $18,000 in campaign funds for his personal use. At one point in the radio and television speech in which he defended his reputation, he said:

> One other thing I probably should tell you, because if I don't they will probably be saying this about me, too. We did get something, a gift, after the election.
>
> A man down in Texas heard Pat on the radio mention the fact that our two youngsters would like to have a dog, and, believe it or not, the day before we left on this campaign trip we got a message from Union Station in Baltimore saying they had a package for us. We went down to get it. You know what it was?
>
> It was a little cocker spaniel dog, in a crate that he had sent all the way from Texas, black and white, spotted, and our little girl, Tricia, the six-year-old, named it Checkers.
>
> And, you know, the kids, like all kids, loved the dog, and I just want to say this, right now, that regardless of what they say about it, we are going to keep it.[8]

Of course, Nixon knew that the issue was the alleged misappropriation of funds, not the ownership of the dog, which no one had asked him to return.

10. Two Wrongs Make a Right

This is another example of the way in which attention may be diverted from the question at issue.

After a speech by President Jimmy Carter in March 1977 attacking the human rights record of the Soviet Union, Russian officials responded:

> As for the present state of human rights in the United States, it is characterized by the following eloquent facts: millions of unemployed, racial discrimination, social inequality of women, infringement of citizens' personal freedom, the growth of crime and so on.[9]

---

[8] Radio and television address of Senator Nixon from Los Angeles on September 23, 1952.

[9] *New York Times*, March 3, 1977, p. 1.

The Russians made no attempt to deny the failure of *their* human rights record; instead they attacked by pointing out that the Americans are not blameless either.

11. *Non Sequitur*

The Latin term *non sequitur,* which means "it does not follow," is another fallacy of irrelevance. An advertisement for a book, *Worlds in Collision,* whose theories about the origin of the earth and evolutionary development have been challenged by almost all reputable scientists, states:

> Once rejected as "preposterous!" Critics called it an outrage! It aroused incredible antagonism in scientific and literary circles. Yet half a million copies were sold and for twenty-seven years it remained an outstanding bestseller.

We know, of course, that the popularity of a book does not bestow scientific respectability. The number of sales, therefore, is irrelevant to proof of the book's theoretical soundness.

12. *Ad Populum*

Arguers guilty of this fallacy make an appeal to the prejudices of the people (*populum* in Latin). They assume that their claim can be adequately defended without further support if they emphasize a belief or attitude that the audience shares with them. One common form of *ad populum* is an appeal to patriotism, which may allow arguers to omit evidence that the audience needs for proper evaluation of the claim. In the following advertisement the makers of *Zippo* lighters made such an appeal in urging readers to buy their product.

> It's a grand old lighter. Zippo — the grand old lighter that's made right here in the good old U. S. A.
>
> We truly make an all-American product. The raw materials used in making a Zippo lighter are all right from this great land of ours.
>
> Zippo windproof lighters are proud to be Americans.

13. Appeal to Tradition

In making an appeal to tradition, the arguer assumes that what has existed for a long time and has therefore become a tradition should continue to exist *because* it is a tradition. If the arguer avoids telling his or her reader *why* the tradition should be preserved, he or she may be accused of failing to meet the real issue.

The following statement appeared in a letter defending the membership policy of the Century Club, an all-male club established in New York City in 1847 that is now under pressure to admit women. The writer is a Presbyterian minister who opposed the admission of women.

> I am totally opposed to a proposal which would radically change the nature of the Century. . . . A club creates an ethos of its own over the years, and I would deeply deplore a step that would inevitably create an entirely different kind of place.
>
> A club like the Century should surely be unaffected by fashionable whims . . . [10]

14. Faulty Emotional Appeals

In some discussions of fallacies, appeals to the emotions of the audience are treated as illegitimate or "counterfeit proofs." All such appeals, however, are *not* illegitimate. As we saw in Chapter 4 on support, appeals to the values and emotions of an audience are an appropriate form of persuasion. You can recognize fallacious appeals if (1) they are irrelevant to the argument or draw attention from the issues being argued or (2) they appear to conceal another purpose. Here we treat two of the most popular appeals — to pity and to fear.

Appeals to pity, compassion, and natural willingness to help the unfortunate are particularly hard to resist. The requests for aid by most charitable organizations — for hungry children, victims of disaster, stray animals — offer examples of legitimate appeals. But these appeals to our sympathetic feelings should not divert us from considering other issues in a particular case. It would be wrong, for example, to allow a multiple murderer to escape punishment because he or she had experienced a wretched childhood. Likewise, if you are asked to contribute to a charitable cause, you should try to learn how many unfortunate people or animals are being helped and what percentage of the contribution will be allocated to maintaining the organization and its officers. In some cases the financial records are closed to public review, and only a small share of the contribution will reach the alleged beneficiaries.

Appeals to fear are likely to be even more effective. But they must be based on evidence that fear is an appropriate response to the issues and that it can move an audience toward a solution to the problem. (Fear can also have the adverse effect of preventing people from taking a necessary action.) Insurance companies, for example, make appeals to our fears of destitution for ourselves and our families as a result of injury, unemploy-

---

[10] David H. C. Read, letter to the *New York Times*, January 13, 1983, p. 14.

ment, sickness, and death. These appeals are justified if the possibilities of such destitution are real and if the insurance will provide relief. It would also be legitimate to arouse fear of the consequences of drunk driving, provided, again, that the descriptions were accurate. On the other hand, it would be wrong to induce fear that fluoridation of public water supplies causes cancer without presenting sound evidence of the probability. It would also be wrong to instill a fear of school integration unless convincing proof were offered of undesirable social consequences.

An emotional response by itself is not always the soundest basis for making decisions. Your own experience has probably taught you that in the grip of a strong emotion like love or hate or anger you often overlook good reasons for making different and better choices. Like you, your readers want to be given the opportunity to consider all the available kinds of support for an argument.

READINGS FOR ANALYSIS

On Nation and Race

ADOLF HITLER

There are some truths which are so obvious that for this very reason 1
they are not seen or at least not recognized by ordinary people. They sometimes pass by such truisms as though blind and are most astonished when someone suddenly discovers what everyone really ought to know. Columbus's eggs lie around by the hundreds of thousands, but Columbuses are met with less frequency.

Thus men without exception wander about in the garden of Nature; 2
they imagine that they know practically everything and yet with few exceptions pass blindly by one of the most patent principles of Nature's rule: the inner segregation of the species of all living beings on this earth.

Even the most superficial observation shows that Nature's restricted 3
form of propagation and increase is an almost rigid basic law of all the innumerable forms of expression of her vital urge. Every animal mates only with a member of the same species. The titmouse seeks the titmouse, the

---

Adolf Hitler (1889–1945) became the Nazi dictator of Germany in the mid-1930s. "On Nation and Race" (editor's title) begins the eleventh chapter of *Mein Kampf (My Struggle)*, vol. 1, published in 1925.

finch the finch, the stork the stork, the field mouse the field mouse, the dormouse the dormouse, the wolf the she-wolf, etc.

Only unusual circumstances can change this, primarily the compul- 4
sion of captivity or any other cause that makes it impossible to mate within the same species. But then Nature begins to resist this with all possible means, and her most visible protest consists either in refusing further capacity for propagation to bastards or in limiting the fertility of later offspring; in most cases, however, she takes away the power of resistance to disease or hostile attacks.

This is only too natural. 5

Any crossing of two beings not at exactly the same level produces a 6
medium between the level of the two parents. This means: The offspring will probably stand higher than the racially lower parent, but not as high as the higher one. Consequently, it will later succumb in the struggle against the higher level. Such mating is contrary to the will of Nature for a higher breeding of all life. The precondition for this does not lie in associating superior and inferior, but in the total victory of the former. The stronger must dominate and not blend with the weaker, thus sacrificing his own greatness. Only the born weakling can view this as cruel, but he after all is only a weak and limited man; for if this law did not prevail, any conceivable higher development of organic living beings would be unthinkable.

The consequence of this racial purity, universally valid in Nature, is 7
not only the sharp outward delimitation of the various races, but their uniform character in themselves. The fox is always a fox, the goose a goose, the tiger a tiger, etc., and the difference can lie at most in the varying measure of force, strength, intelligence, dexterity, endurance, etc., of the individual specimens. But you will never find a fox who in his inner attitude might, for example, show humanitarian tendencies toward geese, as similarly there is no cat with a friendly inclination toward mice.

Therefore, here, too, the struggle among themselves arises less from 8
inner aversion than from hunger and love. In both cases, Nature looks on calmly, with satisfaction, in fact. In the struggle for daily bread all those who are weak and sickly or less determined succumb, while the struggle of the males for the female grants the right or opportunity to propagate only to the healthiest. And struggle is always a means for improving a species' health and power of resistance and, therefore, a cause of its higher development.

If the process were different, all further and higher development 9
would cease and the opposite would occur. For, since the inferior always predominates numerically over the best, if both had the same possibility of preserving life and propagating, the inferior would multiply so much more rapidly that in the end the best would inevitably be driven into the

background, unless a correction of this state of affairs were undertaken. Nature does just this by subjecting the weaker part to such severe living conditions that by them alone the number is limited, and by not permitting the remainder to increase promiscuously, but making a new and ruthless choice according to strength and health.

10 No more than Nature desires the mating of weaker with stronger individuals, even less does she desire the blending of a higher with a lower race, since, if she did, her whole work of higher breeding, over perhaps hundreds of thousands of years, might be ruined with one blow.

11 Historical experience offers countless proofs of this. It shows with terrifying clarity that in every mingling of Aryan blood with that of lower peoples the result was the end of the cultured people. North America, whose population consists in by far the largest part of Germanic elements who mixed but little with the lower colored peoples, shows a different humanity and culture from Central and South America, where the predominantly Latin immigrants often mixed with the aborigines on a large scale. By this one example, we can clearly and distinctly recognize the effect of racial mixture. The Germanic inhabitant of the American continent, who has remained racially pure and unmixed, rose to be master of the continent; he will remain the master as long as he does not fall a victim to defilement of the blood.

12 The result of all racial crossing is therefore in brief always the following:

13 (a) Lowering of the level of the higher race;

14 (b) Physical and intellectual regression and hence the beginning of a slowly but surely progressing sickness.

15 To bring about such a development is, then, nothing else but to sin against the will of the eternal creator.

16 And as a sin this act is rewarded.

17 When man attempts to rebel against the iron logic of Nature, he comes into struggle with the principles to which he himself owes his existence as a man. And this attack must lead to his own doom.

18 Here, of course, we encounter the objection of the modern pacifist, as truly Jewish in its effrontery as it is stupid! "Man's role is to overcome Nature!"

19 Millions thoughtlessly parrot this Jewish nonsense and end up by really imagining that they themselves represent a kind of conqueror of Nature; though in this they dispose of no other weapon than an idea, and at that such a miserable one, that if it were true no world at all would be conceivable.

20 But quite aside from the fact that man has never yet conquered Nature in anything, but at most has caught hold of and tried to lift one or another corner of her immense gigantic veil of eternal riddles and secrets,

that in reality he invents nothing but only discovers everything, that he does not dominate Nature, but has only risen on the basis of his knowledge of various laws and secrets of Nature to be lord over those other living creatures who lack this knowledge — quite aside from all this, an idea cannot overcome the preconditions for the development and being of humanity, since the idea itself depends only on man. Without human beings there is no human idea in this world; therefore, the idea as such is always conditioned by the presence of human beings and hence of all the laws which created the precondition for their existence.

And not only that! Certain ideas are even tied up with certain men. 21
This applies most of all to those ideas whose content originates, not in an exact scientific truth, but in the world of emotion, or, as it is so beautifully and clearly expressed today, reflects an "inner experience." All these ideas, which have nothing to do with cold logic as such, but represent only pure expressions of feeling, ethical conceptions, etc., are chained to the existence of men, to whose intellectual imagination and creative power they owe to their existence. Precisely in this case the preservation of these definite races and men is the precondition for the existence of these ideas. Anyone, for example, who really desired the victory of the pacifistic idea in this world with all his heart would have to fight with all the means at his disposal for the conquest of the world by the Germans; for, if the opposite should occur, the last pacifist would die out with the last German, since the rest of the world has never fallen so deeply as our own people, unfortunately, has for this nonsense so contrary to Nature and reason. Then, if we were serious, whether we liked it or not, we would have to wage wars in order to arrive at pacifism. This and nothing else was what Wilson, the American world savior, intended, or so at least our German visionaries believed — and thereby his purpose was fulfilled.

In actual fact the pacifistic-humane idea is perfectly all right perhaps 22
when the highest type of man has previously conquered and subjected the world to an extent that makes him the sole ruler of this earth. Then this idea lacks the power of producing evil effects in exact proportion as its practical application becomes rare and finally impossible. Therefore, first struggle and then we shall see what can be done. Otherwise mankind has passed the high point of its development and the end is not the domination of any ethical idea but barbarism and consequently chaos. At this point someone or other may laugh, but this planet once moved through the ether for millions of years without human beings and it can do so again some day if men forget that they owe their higher existence, not to the ideas of a few crazy ideologists, but to the knowledge and ruthless application of Nature's stern and rigid laws.

Everything we admire on this earth today — science and art, technol- 23
ogy and inventions — is only the creative product of a few peoples and

originally perhaps of *one* race. On them depends the existence of this whole culture. If they perish, the beauty of this earth will sink into the grave with them.

However much the soil, for example, can influence men, the result of 24
the influence will always be different depending on the races in question. The low fertility of a living space may spur the one race to the highest achievements; in others it will only be the cause of bitterest poverty and final undernourishment with all its consequences. The inner nature of peoples is always determining for the manner in which outward influences will be effective. What leads the one to starvation trains the other to hard work.

All great cultures of the past perished only because the originally cre- 25
ative race died out from blood poisoning.

The ultimate cause of such a decline was their forgetting that all cul- 26
ture depends on men and conversely; hence that to preserve a certain culture the man who creates it must be preserved. This preservation is bound up with the rigid law of necessity and the right to victory of the best and stronger in this world.

Those who want to live, let them fight, and those who do not want to 27
fight in this world of eternal struggle do not deserve to live.

Even if this were hard — that is how it is! Assuredly, however, by far 28
the harder fate is that which strikes the man who thinks he can overcome Nature, but in the last analysis only mocks her. Distress, misfortune, and diseases are her answer.

The man who misjudges and disregards the racial laws actually for- 29
feits the happiness that seems destined to be his. He thwarts the triumphal march of the best race and hence also the precondition for all human progress, and remains, in consequence, burdened with all the sensibility of man, in the animal realm of helpless misery.

It is idle to argue which race or races were the original representative 30
of human culture and hence the real founders of all that we sum up under the word "humanity." It is simpler to raise the question with regard to the present, and here an easy, clear answer results. All the human culture, all the results of art, science, and technology that we see before us today, are almost exclusively the creative product of the Aryan. This very fact admits of the not unfounded inference that he alone was the founder of all higher humanity, therefore representing the prototype of all that we understand by the word "man." He is the Prometheus of mankind from whose bright forehead the divine spark of genius has sprung at all times, forever kindling anew that fire of knowledge which illumined the night of silent mysteries and thus caused man to climb the path to mastery over the other beings of this earth. Exclude him — and perhaps after a few

thousand years darkness will again descend on the earth, human culture will pass, and the world turn to a desert.

Discussion Questions

1. In explaining his ideology, how does Hitler misinterpret the statement that "Every animal mates only with a member of the same species"? How would you characterize this fallacy?
2. Hitler uses the theory of evolution and his interpretation of the "survival of the fittest" to justify his racial philosophy. Find the places in the text where Hitler reveals that he misunderstands the theory in its application to human beings.
3. What false evidence about race does Hitler use in his assessment of the racial experience in North America? Examine carefully the last sentence of paragraph 11: "The Germanic inhabitant of the American continent, who has remained racially pure and unmixed, rose to be master of the continent; he will remain the master as long as he does not fall a victim to defilement of the blood."
4. What criticism of Jews does Hitler offer? How does this criticism help to explain Hitler's pathological hatred of Jews?
5. Hitler believes that pacifism is a violation of "Nature and reason." Would modern scientists agree that the laws of Nature require unremitting struggle and conflict between human beings — until the master race conquers?

Writing Suggestion

Do some research in early human history to discover the degree of truth in this statement: "All human culture, all the results of art, science, and technology that we see before us today, are almost exclusively the creative product of the Aryan." You may want to limit your discussion to one area of human culture.

A Criminal Justifies Himself

TONY PARKER and ROBERT ALLERTON

My first question is this: If you were to describe yourself in one word, 1
would the description invariably be "a criminal"?

Yes, definitely. That's what I am, I never think of myself in any other 2
way.

And have you any intention of changing, of going straight or re- 3
forming?

None whatsoever. There's one thing, though, I'd like to make clear 4
right at the start — and that is, I don't want to try and pass myself off as a "master criminal" or anything like that. I'm not. I've had successes and failures in life like everyone else, and I'm nothing out of the ordinary as far as criminals go. I don't consider myself cleverer than most, or even cleverer than the police, for example: sometimes I have been, and quite obviously sometimes not. On the whole I'd say I was just the ordinary run of professional criminal, similar to — well, let's say to a bank clerk from Surbiton in the straight world. But having said that, still definitely "a criminal," yes . . .

Is there any particular form of crime, or criminal activity, which you 5
wouldn't commit?

A year or two ago I used to think I'd never go in for drug-trafficking, 6
but now I'm not so sure about that. I've never actually done it yet, but as I get older I seem to be losing my inhibitions, I don't feel as strongly about it as I used to. There's only one thing I still feel I could never do, and that's poncing.[1] To me it's the worst thing of the lot, I'd never stoop to it — or at least I hope I wouldn't. Maybe I'm old-fashioned, or sentimental about women or something — I just can't stomach the idea of poncing at all. I've nothing but contempt, real, deep contempt, for ponces.

There's no other limit you'd set yourself? 7

No, I'll go as far as necessary, whatever it is. 8

What does that mean, exactly? 9

What it says. If it was ever necessary to kill somebody, well, I'd go up 10
to and including that. I'd kill somebody in a fit of temper, I'm quite capable of that — or if they were trying to stop me getting something I'd really made up my mind to have. Or if they were holding me down, and there

---

Tony Parker is a British sociologist who has written several books on crime and prisons, including *The Courage of His Convictions* (1962), from which this interview with career criminal Robert Allerton is excerpted.

[1] Pimping.—ED.

was so much at stake that I'd just got to get away. But I think most people have it in them to do murder at some time in their lives, under certain circumstances.

The thing that I find most difficult to understand about you is that you're apparently quite undeterred by your repeated prison sentences. You've now reached the stage, with your record, that when you're caught next time it's more than likely you'll get about eight years' preventive detention. I don't understand how you can be prepared to face that. 11

I'm not prepared. This is the thing which people like you can never grasp. I'm no more "prepared" to do eight years' P.D. than you're prepared to knock somebody down in your car tomorrow. I don't think too much about the one more than you do about the other. It's an ever-present risk but one doesn't dwell on it — do you see what I mean? . . . 12

I don't want to do eight years, no — but if I have to I have to, and that's all there is to it. If you're a criminal, what's the alternative to the risk of going to prison? Coal-miners don't spend their time worrying about the risk they might get killed by a fall at the coal-face either. Prison's an occupational risk, that's all — and one I'm quite prepared to take. I'll willingly gamble away a third of my life in prison, so long as I can live the way I want for the other two-thirds. After all, it's my life, and that's how I feel about it. The alternative — the prospect of vegetating the rest of my life away in a steady job, catching the 8:13 to work in the morning, and the 5:50 back again at night, all for ten or fifteen quid[2] a week — now that really does terrify me, far more than the thought of a few years in the nick. 13

You don't think, then, that there's anything wrong in not working for your living? 14

But I do work for my living. Most crime — unless it's the senseless, petty-thieving sort — is quite hard work, you know. Planning a job, working out all the details of the best way to do it — and then carrying it out, under a lot of nervous strain and tension — and having to run round afterwards, if it's goods, fencing the stuff, getting a good price for it, delivering it to the fence, and so on — all this needs a lot of thinking and effort and concentration. It certainly is "work," don't kid yourself about that. 15

But anyway this whole point's not all that simple. A lot of other people don't "work" for their living, in the way you mean — but nobody goes on at them like they do at criminals. Quite a large proportion of the "upper classes," for instance. You can see them any day round Piccadilly, Vigo Street, Savile Row — nattily dressed half-wits who've never done a stroke of work in their lives, popping in and out of Fortnum's or Scott's, 16

[2] Ten or fifteen pounds sterling.—ED.

spending all their time trying to get rid of the money their fathers and grandfathers and great-grandfathers left them. And usually it's that sort who get fiercest about people like me, saying we ought to be caned and whipped and flogged because we never do an honest day's work.

I can steal from people like that without the faintest compunction at all, in fact I'm delighted to do it. I remember once screwing the town house of the Duke of . . . well, I'd better not say who, because I didn't get caught for it. The inside of the house was the most beautiful place I've ever been in in my life — gorgeous curtains and furnishings, antique furniture, silver bowls and vases all over the place, exquisite miniatures on the walls — it was a fabulous place. My only regret was I hadn't got a furniture van so I could strip it from top to bottom. His Lordship I suppose was up in Scotland shooting wild birds, or some other civilized hobby, and his house was just standing unused until he chose to come back and live in it again. 17

I remember after I'd come out I passed an old man in rags, standing on the street-corner scraping at a violin to try and earn himself a few coppers, and I thought: "You mug, why don't you go in there and at least get yourself a good sleep in one of his Lordship's unused beds for a night." 18

All the things that were in that house, all those beautiful possessions, the duke had got for himself without the faintest effort of any kind. Most of them had been handed down to him, and all he'd ever had to do to get the others was write out a check — and he probably didn't even do that for himself but had a flunkey to do it. Never in his whole life had he known what it was like to be short of anything. Well, I had, and I don't think it was wrong to steal enough from him to subsidize me for a bit. 19

And those people, when they have something nicked, they've got it all insured anyway, so they don't suffer. Sometimes they advertise for its return — you know, "Sentimental value" and all that. I'm sure I'd feel sentimental, too, about losing something worth a few hundred quid, only I'd be a bit more honest about it. 20

And the stuff I pinched from that particular house I appreciated, I did really. In fact, if it hadn't been too dangerous, I'd gladly have kept a lot of it to have around my own place, because it was so beautiful. But I never felt bad about taking it — why should I? I feel terrific. He'd got no cause for complaint, because it was taken, after all, by someone who could really appreciate its artistic merit, not one of those insensitive thugs who couldn't differentiate between Royal Worcester and a Woolworth's chamber-pot. . . . 21

What about wages-snatches? 22

. . . All right, wages-snatches. I'll try and take it from the beginning. 23

If I can see a chance of earning myself — or making myself, if you prefer it — a few thousand quid all at one go, naturally I'll do it. It's only what people, millions of them, are trying to do on the football pools every 24 week. You could say: "Yes, but they're trying to do it honestly" — to which I'd reply: "It depends on your definition of honest, because while they're trying to get themselves several thousand of someone else's money for the outlay of a few shillings and no work. I'm trying to get it by some careful thinking and plotting, some bloody hard effort, and the risk of my own liberty into the bargain."

So who's doing more to earn the money — me or the pools "inves- 25
tors," as they're called? (By the promoters, of course. It's the old con-man's trick of persuading a mug you're going to give him something for nothing, playing on people's natural avarice and greed.) The "investors" trust to luck to bring them a lot of money — well, I bank on my own efforts.

But there's a difference. Pools winnings come out of what the "inves- 26
tors" hand over voluntarily, so those who lose have no complaint. Workers don't hand over their wages voluntarily for you to steal.

I'll say they don't. But look, don't try to break my heart. Who loses on 27
a wages-snatch — the workers? Of course not. It's the company — and they can usually stand it. It's the same with banks — if I have a few thousand from a bank, theoretically it's their customers' money I've taken. But you never hear of a bank apportioning the losses round their customers, do you? "We're so sorry, Major Bloodworthy, somebody blew our safe last night and took ten thousand quid — and it was your ten thousand that was in there!" Mind you, I'm not saying they shouldn't; to me it's quite an attractive idea.

No, let's face it, most of these people are insured against robberies, so 28
it's only the insurance companies who pay up.

But this doesn't in any way defend the use of violence to get it, does it, 29
by coshing[3] *the man carrying the wages-bag for instance? . . .*

Bob . . . 30

Yes, all right. So violence is wrong, on a fundamental level, I admit 31
that. But on a day-to-day level it just happens that it's a tool of my trade and I use it — like an engineer uses a slide-rule, or a bus-driver the handbrake, or a dentist the drill. Only when necessary, and only when it can't be avoided. If I've got to whack a bloke with an iron bar to make him let go of the wages-bag he's carrying, O.K., so I'll whack him. If he lets go without any trouble, I don't. That's all.

I don't indulge in it, you know, for the sheer pleasure of the thing. I'm 32
no sadist. This has always been my theory, that I'll take whatever job comes along. If there's a vanload of stuff to be pulled, I'll pull it; a screwing

[3] Hitting with a blackjack.—ED.

job, I'll screw it; a safe-blowing, I'll blow it — and so on. And if it's a coshing job, well then, I'll use a cosh. . . .

I can remember the first time quite clearly, I was only a kid, sixteen or seventeen, and thought myself a real tearaway of course. There was an old woman, a pawnbroker I think she was, lived in a little house just off Cable Street somewhere. Me and a couple of my mates heard that on Saturday nights she always had a bomb in there. Money was short and we decided to have it. 33

We went along about nine o'clock one Saturday night with shooters, banging on the door and shouting out: "Mrs. Rosenbloom, Mrs. Rosenbloom!" or whatever her name was. "Let us in, it's urgent, we've got to talk to you." She opened the door, and seeing we were only kids she let us in. When we were inside we shoved her back into her kitchen and knocked her into a chair, telling her to keep quiet while we turned the place inside out looking for the money. 34

So of course she starts screaming and raving like a mad woman. Before we went in it'd been decided it was going to be my job to keep her quiet. I rammed my shooter up against her ear and said: "Belt up, you old faggot, or I'll pull the trigger." 35

It made not a blind bit of difference, she just yelled all the louder for help. The other two were tearing everything to bits trying to find where she'd hidden her money, and this racket she was making was really getting on their nerves, so one of them said: "Oh, for Christ's sake hit the old bag, can't you? If you don't lay her out she'll have the whole neighborhood on us." 36

And I just couldn't do it. All I could do was stand there bleating: "Shut up, will you! I'm warning you, I'll pull the trigger." Naturally it didn't stop her. Finally one of the other two walked over, took the gun out of my hand, and belted her unconscious. He put the gun back in my hand, really angry, and he said: "It's her or us, you silly bastard, can't you see that?" 37

It taught me the lesson, and after that I was all right. . . . 38

Not long after that there was another job, in a warehouse in Islington: And this one got rid of the last of my scruples about violence. While we were in the place the night watchman heard us moving about and he came up the stairs to the floor we were on, to see what was going on. On the landing were a couple of five-gallon oil drums. When I saw him coming towards us, I lifted one of them right over my head and let him have it. It knocked him back all the way downstairs, but he lay at the bottom yelling blue murder, so I took a fire extinguisher off the wall and went down and laid him out with it. I didn't try to batter him to death or anything, just put him out and stop his noise. I didn't feel angry, savage, anything like that — I don't think I felt anything, just dispassionate about it, knowing it'd 39 got to be done, because he was threatening us and our safety with his noise.

You felt no compunction at all about hitting him like that? 40

No, none. I feel if someone takes a job as night watchman he's got to 41
be prepared to be hit if he tries to make a hero of himself. I wouldn't have touched him if he'd left us alone, but since he tried to stop us he got what he earned. Personally I think he was stupid, he should have kept quiet and kept his nose out of it. What was he trying to do, win himself a medal? And what was he hoping to get from it, anyway — a pat on the shoulder from the guv'nor, "Good fella, Jim," a gold watch when he retired? Anyone who takes a job like that wants his brains testing, to me he does. Perhaps I'm missing something, but I can't see anything admirable in it at all, these heroes trying to win themselves medals for about nine-pounds-ten a week. You read it in the papers sometimes — "Last night Mr. Jim Smith tried to tackle some bandits and he's now in hospital recovering from concussion." It always gives me a laugh, if it was a job I was on that it's referring to. O.K., so the bloke's a hero and got his name in the paper. So what's he got for it? Concussion. And what have I got? What I went for, which is what I would have got anyway, and he needn't have got his concussion trying to stop me.

But it's fortunate not everybody uses your methods, isn't it, or else 42
we'd all be living in the jungle?

But we *are* living in a jungle. You've put your finger on it with that 43
word, though, because that's all it is, a question of method. Lots of people take money off others, but they use other ways of doing it. Some of them are considered respectable. Personally I don't think they are — but it's a matter of opinion, that's all.

A landlord gets money out of people when he puts their rents up, by 44
extortion, by playing on the fact they've got nowhere else to live. And the Law upholds him in doing it. Yet really all he's doing is stealing money from people. But if I go along and steal that money from him he screams to the Law, and they come after me to try and get his money back for him. If his tenant screams to the police that his landlord's robbing him, they do nothing of course. No: He perpetrates his crime upheld by all the respectability of society, without any risk on his part of going to prison. Well, personally, I think my method's a lot more straightforward and honest than his is. And I don't pretend to be doing anything other than what I am — stealing. But the landlord does. And, what's more, I don't go in for robbing poor people, either, like he does. Thieving off your own kind, that's terrible.

Or take the case of a jeweller. He's a business man, and he's in the 45
game to make money. O.K., so I'm a business man too, and I'm also out to make money. We just use different methods. The jeweller makes a profit

— and often a very big profit — out of what he sells. On top of that he fiddles the income tax and the purchase tax, and even the customs duty as well if he can get away with it. That's considered all right by him and others like him, and if he makes enough to buy himself a big house and a posh car everyone looks up to him as a clever fellow, a shrewd business man. But how's he got his money? By rooking people, taking advantage of soft young couples getting engaged to sell them a more expensive ring than they can afford, and fiddling the authorities whenever he can. But at least he didn't steal it. Well, what's in a name? Tell me exactly where the line is between thieving and "shrewd business" and I might believe it. What's more, the jeweller can insure himself against people like me going and pinching his stock. But I can't insure against the police nicking me, can I? The Law's on one side only, the side of the pretenders, that's all.

It's funny, there's a few criminals, you do meet them from time to 46
time, who won't do any violence. A firm I was with once, there was three of them besides me, we were discussing some job we had in view — a wages-snatch I think it was — where it was obvious we'd have to whack someone to get what we wanted. One of the three was one of these humanitarian types, you know, had what you might call a conscientious objection to using violence altogether. He went on about it so long the other two started to dither as well. We had a long argument about it, and my line was the one I've already explained: If violence needs doing, then you've got to do it. Some people won't hand over to you what you want just like that, so you've got to whack them. Well, this whole job fell through because they didn't look at it my way at all, they were scared about the thing. Once you start drawing lines here, there, and everywhere about what you will do, and what you won't, you might as well give up villainy altogether. It's amateurism — and the amateur's the curse of thieving like he is of any other game. The only approach I can go along with is to be a professional, and get on with whatever comes.

Discussion Questions

1. Do you detect fallacious reasoning in the following statements? Examine the statements that precede or follow them in the interview in order to understand the context.
   a. " . . . I think most people have it in them to do murder at some time in their lives, under certain circumstances."
   b. "A lot of other people don't 'work' for their living, in the way you mean — but nobody goes on at them like they do at criminals."
   c. "Never in his whole life had he known what it was like to be short of anything. Well, I had, and I don't think it was wrong to steal enough from him to subsidize me for a bit."

d. "He [the Duke]'d got no cause for complaint, because it was taken, after all, by someone who could really appreciate its artistic merit, not one of those insensitive thugs who couldn't differentiate between Royal Worcester and a Woolworth's chamber-pot."

e. "So violence is wrong, on a fundamental level, I admit that. But on a day-to-day level it just happens that it's a tool of my trade and I use it — like an engineer uses a slide-rule, or a bus-driver the handbrake, or a dentist the drill."

2. How does Robert Allerton justify his use of violence against the old woman pawnbroker and the night watchman at the warehouse? Is there any weakness in his defense?
3. Are his analogies between burglar and landlord and burglar and jeweller sound?

Writing Suggestions

1. The introduction to this interview says: "An English career criminal discusses the philosophy of his occupation." Write a letter to the criminal, summarizing your principal criticisms of the reasoning he uses to justify his occupation. Name specific fallacies, if possible. If some of his arguments seem valid, point these out as well.
2. Invent an occupation for yourself (such as mercenary soldier, phony doctor or lawyer, smuggler of contraband goods, drug dealer) that might be regarded dubiously by most people, and write an essay in which you defend your work. Invite your classmates to discover any fallacies.

A TRAP CAN CATCH MORE THAN A MOUSE.

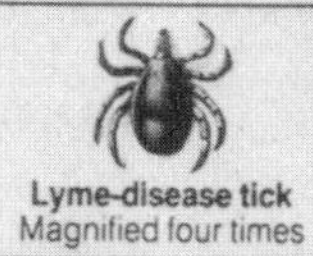

Lyme-disease tick
Magnified four times

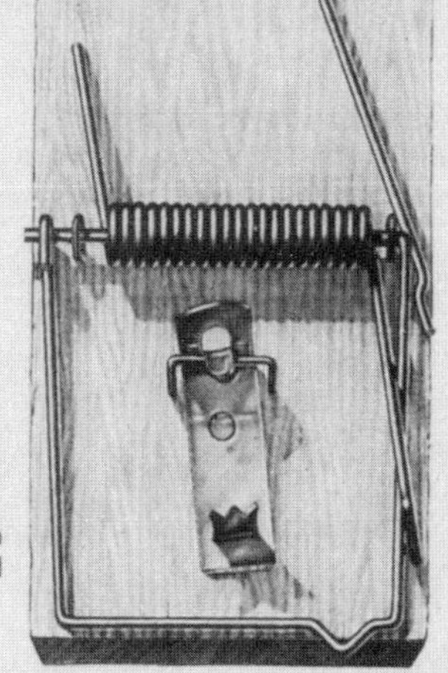

Mice can carry ticks that carry disease. Even dead mice.

When you pick up a trap, wherever it's been set, you may be picking up more than a dead mouse. There may also be disease-carrying ticks. And fleas. And mites. These parasites can carry serious diseases such as Rocky Mountain Spotted Fever, Colorado Tick Fever, Tularemia, Typhus.

Recently, you may have read about Lyme-disease ticks carried by the white-footed field mouse. People bitten by the Lyme-disease tick can suffer temporary paralysis of the facial nerves, pain in the joints, and even severe neurological problems similar to multiple sclerosis.

So if you're a homeowner, be careful in your garage or in any barns or outbuildings you may have. While the mouse that carries Lyme-disease ticks has not been shown to enter homes, the ordinary mice found indoors can carry ticks that also may be as threatening.

Why use traps?

If a trap happens to catch a mouse, the only way for you to dispose of it is to go near it. And that may increase your risk of being exposed to ticks, fleas or mites that can remain alive —even on a dead mouse! Why take chances?

With d-CON bait products, you never go near a mouse.

If you have mice in your home, you'll feel more secure using d-CON bait products instead of traps.

All you do is set out the bait. Mice eat it, then leave and go off to die, without you ever having to touch them. Without you ever having to go near them. Or the ticks they can carry.

d-CON makes Mouse Prufe II—which can kill mice in just one feeding. d-CON also makes Ready Mixed and Pellets, which kill both mice and rats.

d-CON helps you in other ways.

We at d-CON understand that you might want more information about how to get rid of mice. Please write us at: d-CON, P.O. Box 4130-I, Westbury, NY 11592. We'll be happy to send you our brochure.

© 1989
The d-CON Company, Inc.

Because mice are more than just pests.

Discussion Question

Can you uncover a gap in the reasoning? What was the advertiser trying to do?

EXERCISES FOR REVIEW

Decide whether the reasoning in the following examples is faulty. Explain your answers.

1. The presiding judge of a revolutionary tribunal, on being asked why people were being executed without trial: "Why should we put them on trial when we know that they're guilty?"
2. Since good nutrition is essential to the health of its citizens, the government should punish people who eat junk food.
3. A research study demonstrated that children who watched the *Cosby Show* rather than *Miami Vice* received higher grades in school. So it must be true that the *Cosby Show* is more educational than *Miami Vice.*
4. The meteorologist was wrong in predicting the amount of rain for May. Obviously the meteorologist is unreliable.
5. Women ought to be permitted to serve in combat. Why should men be the only ones to face death and danger?
6. If Bruce Willis drinks Seagram's Wine Cooler, it must taste best.
7. People will gamble anyway, so why not legalize gambling in this state?
8. Because so much money was spent on public education in the last decade while educational achievement declined, more money to improve education can't be the answer to reversing the decline.
9. He's a columnist for the campus newspaper, so he must be a pretty good writer.
10. We tend to exaggerate the need for standard English. You don't need much standard English for most jobs in this country.
11. It's discriminatory to mandate that police officers must conform to certain height and weight.
12. A doctor can consult books to make a diagnosis, so a medical student should be able to consult books when being tested.
13. Because this soft drink contains so many chemicals, it must be unsafe.
14. Core requirements should be eliminated. After all, students are paying for their education so they should be able to earn a diploma by choosing the courses they want.
15. We should encourage a return to arranged marriages in this country since marriages based on romantic love haven't been very successful.
16. I know three red-heads who have terrible tempers, and since Annabel has red hair, I'll bet she has a terrible temper, too.
17. Supreme Court Justice Byron White was an All-American football player while at college, so how can you say that athletes are dumb?
18. Benjamin H. Sasway, a student at Humboldt State University in California, was indicted for failure to register for possible conscription. Barry Lynn, president of Draft Action, an antidraft group, said, "It is disgraceful that this Administration is embarking on an effort to fill the prisons with men of conscience and moral commitment."
19. You know Jane Fonda's exercise books must be worth the money. Look at the great shape she's in at age fifty-three.

20. James A. Harris, former president of the National Education Association: "Twenty-three percent of schoolchildren are failing to graduate, and another large segment graduate as functional illiterates. If 23 percent of anything else failed — 23 percent of automobiles didn't run, 23 percent of the buildings fell down, 23 percent of stuffed ham spoiled — we'd look at the producer."
21. A professor at Rutgers University: "The arrest rate for women is rising three times as fast as that of men. Women, inflamed by the doctrines of feminism, are pursuing criminal careers with the same zeal as business and the professions."
22. Physical education should be required because physical activity is healthful.
23. George Meany, former president of the AFL-CIO, in 1968: "To these people who constantly say you have got to listen to these younger people, they have got something to say, I just don't buy that at all. They smoke more pot than we do and if the younger generation are the hundred thousand kids that lay around a field up in Woodstock, New York, I am not going to trust the destiny of the country to that group."
24. That candidate was poor as a child, so he will certainly be sympathetic to the poor if he's elected.
25. When the federal government sent troops into Little Rock, Arkansas, to enforce integration of the public school system, the governor of Arkansas attacked the action, saying that it was as brutal an act of intervention as Russia's sending troops into Hungary to squelch the Hungarians' rebellion. In both cases, the governor said, the rights of a freedom-loving, independent people were being violated.
26. Governor Jones was elected two years ago. Since that time constant examples of corruption and subversion have been unearthed. It is time to get rid of the man responsible for this kind of corrupt government.
27. Are we going to vote a pay increase for our teachers or are we going to allow our schools to deteriorate into substandard custodial institutions?
28. You see, the priests were right. After we threw those virgins into the volcano, it quit erupting.
29. The people of Rome lost their vitality and desire for freedom when their emperors decided that the way to keep them happy was to provide them with bread and circuses. What can we expect of our own country now that the government gives people free food and there is a constant round of entertainment provided by television?
30. From Mark Clifton, "The Dread Tomato Affliction" (proving that eating tomatoes is dangerous and even deadly): "Ninety-two point four percent of juvenile delinquents have eaten tomatoes. Fifty-seven point one percent of the adult criminals in penitentiaries throughout the United States have eaten tomatoes. Eighty-four percent of all people killed in automobile accidents during the year have eaten tomatoes."
31. "But can you doubt that air has weight when you have the clear testimony of Aristotle affirming that all elements have weight, including air, and excepting only fire?" (From Galileo, *Dialogues Concerning Two New Sciences*)
32. Robert Brustein, artistic director of the American Repertory Theatre, commenting on a threat by Congress in 1989 to withhold funding from an offen-

sive art show: "Once we allow lawmakers to become art critics, we take the first step into the world of Ayatollah Khomeini, whose murderous review of *The Satanic Verses* still chills the heart of everyone committed to free expression." (The Ayatollah Khomeini called for the death of the author, Salman Rushdie, because he had allegedly committed blasphemy against Islam in his novel.)

PART TWO

WRITING ARGUMENTS

CHAPTER 8

Writing an Argumentative Paper

The person who understands how arguments are constructed has an important advantage in today's world. Television commercials, political speeches, newspaper editorials, and magazine advertisements, as well as many communications between individuals, all draw on the principles we have examined in the preceding chapters. By now you should be fairly adept at picking out claims, support, and warrants (explicit or unstated) in these presentations. The next step is to apply your skills to writing an argument of your own. The process of using what you have learned will enhance your ability to analyze critically the marketing efforts with which we are all bombarded every day. Mastering the writing of arguments also gives you a valuable tool for communicating with other people in school, on the job, and even at home.

In this chapter we will move through the various stages involved in creating an argumentative paper: choosing a topic, defining the issues, organizing the material, writing the essay, and revising. We will also consider the more general question of how to use the principles already discussed in order to convince a real audience. The more carefully you follow the guidelines set out here and the more thought you give to your work at each point, the better you will be able to utilize the art of argument when this course is over.

FINDING AN APPROPRIATE TOPIC

An old British recipe for jugged hare is said to begin, "First, catch your hare." To write an argumentative paper, you first must choose your topic. This is a relatively easy task for someone writing an argument as part of his or her job — a lawyer defending a client, for example, or an advertising executive presenting a campaign. For a student, however, it can be daunting. Which of the many ideas in the world worth debating would make a good subject?

Several guidelines can help you evaluate the possibilities. Perhaps your assignment limits your choices. If you have been asked to write a research paper, you obviously must find a topic on which research is available. If your assignment is more open-ended, you need a topic that is worth the time and effort you expect to invest in it. In either case, your subject should be one that interests you. Don't feel you have to write about what you know — very often finding out what you don't know will turn out to be more satisfying. You should, however, choose a subject that is familiar enough for you to argue about without fearing you're in over your head.

Invention Strategies

As a starting point, think of conversations you've had in the past few days or weeks that have involved defending a position. Is there some current political issue you're concerned about? Some dispute with friends that would make a valid paper topic? One of the best sources is controversies in the media. Keep your project in mind as you watch TV, read, or listen to the radio. You may even run into a potential subject in your course reading assignments or classroom discussions. The "Opposing Viewpoints" in this book and the research topics that follow them will also provide ideas. Fortunately for the would-be writer, nearly every human activity includes its share of disagreement.

As you consider possible topics, write them down. One that looks unlikely at first glance may suggest others or may have more appeal when you come back to it later. Further, simply putting words on paper has a way of stimulating the thought processes involved in writing. Even if your ideas are tentative, the act of converting them into phrases or sentences can often help in developing them.

Evaluating Possible Topics

Besides interesting you, your topic must interest your audience. Who is the audience? For a lawyer it is usually a judge or jury; for a columnist, anyone who reads the newspaper in which his or her column appears.

For the student writer, the audience is to some extent hypothetical. You should assume that your paper is directed at readers who are reasonably intelligent and well informed, but who have no specific knowledge of the subject. It may be useful to imagine you are writing for a local or school publication — this may be the case if your paper turns out well.

Be sure, too, that you choose a topic with two sides. The purpose of an argument is to defend or refute a thesis, which means the thesis must be debatable. In evaluating a subject that looks promising, ask yourself: Can a case be made for the opposing view? If not, you have no workable ground for building your own case.

Finally, check the scope of your thesis. Consider how long your paper will be, and whether you can do justice to your topic in that amount of space. For example, suppose you want to argue in favor of worldwide nuclear disarmament. Is this a thesis you can support persuasively in a short paper? One way to find out is by listing the potential issues or points about which arguers might disagree. Consider the thesis: "The future of the world is in danger as long as nuclear weapons exist." Obviously this statement is too general. You would have to specify what you mean by the future of the world (the continuation of human life? of all life? of the earth itself?) and exactly how nuclear weapons endanger it before the claim would hold up. You could narrow it down: "Human beings are error-prone; therefore as long as nuclear weapons exist there is the chance that a large number of people will be killed accidentally." Though this statement is more specific and includes an important warrant, it still depends on other unstated warrants: that one human being (or a small group) is in the position to discharge a nuclear weapon capable of killing a large number of people; that such a weapon could, in fact, be discharged by mistake, given current safety systems. Can you expect to show sufficient evidence for these assumptions in the space available to you?

By now it should be apparent that arguing in favor of nuclear disarmament is too broad an undertaking. A more workable approach might be to defend or refute one of the disarmament proposals under consideration by the U.S. Congress, or to show that nuclear weapons pose some specific danger (such as long-term water pollution) that is sufficient reason to strive for disarmament.

Can a thesis be too narrow? Certainly. If this is true of the one you have chosen, you probably realized it when you asked yourself whether the topic was debatable. If you can prove your point convincingly in a paragraph, or even a page, you need a broader thesis.

At this preliminary stage, don't worry if you don't know exactly how to word your thesis. It's useful to write down a few possible phrasings to be sure your topic is one you can work with, but you need not be precise. The information you unearth as you do research will help you to formulate your ideas. Also, stating a thesis in final terms is premature until you know the organization and tone of your paper.

To This Point

Let's assume you have surveyed a range of possible topics and chosen one that provides you with a suitable thesis for your paper. Before you go on, check your thesis against the following questions:

1. Is this topic one that will interest both me and my audience?
2. Is the topic debatable?
3. Is my thesis appropriate in scope for a paper of this length?
4. Do I know enough about my thesis to have a rough idea of what ideas to use in supporting it and how to go about finding evidence to back up these ideas?

DEFINING THE ISSUES

Preparing an Initial Outline

An outline, like an accounting system or a computer program, is a practical device for organizing information. Nearly every elementary and high school student learns how to make an outline. What will you gain if you outline your argument? Time and an overview of your subject. The minutes you spend organizing your subject at the outset generally save at least double the time later, when you have few minutes to spare. An outline also enables you to see the whole argument at a glance.

Your preliminary outline establishes an order of priority for your argument. Which supporting points are issues to be defended, which are warrants, and which are evidence? Which supporting points are most persuasive? By constructing a map of your territory, you can identify the research routes that are likely to be most productive. You can also pinpoint any gaps in your reasoning.

List each issue as a main heading in your outline. Next, write below it any relevant support (or sources of support) that you are aware of. Then reexamine the list and consider which issues appear likely to offer the strongest support for your argument. You should number these in order of importance.

Case Study: Coed Bathrooms

To see how we raise and evaluate issues in a specific context, let's look at a controversy that surfaced recently at a large university. Students living in coed dorms elected to retain their coed bathrooms. The university administration, however, withdrew its approval, in part because of growing protests from parents and alumni.

The students raised these issues:

1. The rights of students to choose their living arrangements
2. The absence of coercion on those who did not wish to participate
3. The increase in civility between the sexes as a result of sharing accommodations
4. The practicality of coed bathrooms, which preclude the necessity for members of one sex to travel to a one-sex bathroom on another floor
5. The success of the experiment so far

On the other side, the administration introduced the following issues:

1. The role of the university *in loco parentis*
2. The necessity for the administration to retain the goodwill of parents and alumni
3. The dissatisfaction of some students with the arrangement
4. The inability of immature students to respect the rights of others and resist the temptation of sexual activity

Now let's analyze these issues, comparing their strengths and weaknesses.

1. It was clear that not all the issues in this dispute were equally important. The arguers decided, therefore, to give greater emphasis to the issues that were most likely to be ultimately persuasive to their audiences and less attention to those that were difficult to prove or narrower in their appeal. The issue of convenience, for example, seemed a minor point. How much cost is imposed in being required to walk up or down a flight of stairs?

2. It was also clear that, as in several of the other cases we have examined, the support consisted of both factual data and appeals to values. In regard to the factual data, each side reported evidence to prove that

a. The experiment was or was not a success
b. Civility had or had not increased
c. The majority of students did or did not favor the plan
d. Coercion had or had not been applied

The factual data were important. If the administration could prove that the interests of some students had been injured, then the student case for coed bathrooms would be weakened.

But let us assume that the factual claims either were settled or remained in abeyance. We now turn our attention to a second set of issues, a contest over the values to be served.

3. Both sides claimed adherence to the highest principles of university life. Here the issues, while no easier to resolve, offered greater opportunity for serious and fruitful discussion.

The first question to be resolved was that of democratic control. The students asserted, "We should be permitted to have coed bathrooms because we can prove that the majority of us want them." The students hoped that the university community would agree with the implied analogy: that the university community should resemble a political democracy and that students should have full rights as citizens of that community. (This is an argument also made in regard to other areas of university life.)

The university denied that it was a democracy in which students had equal rights and insisted that it should not be. The administration offered its own analogical proof: Students are not permitted to hire their own teachers or to choose their manner of instruction, their courses of study, their grades, or the rules of admission. The university, they insisted, represented a different kind of community, like a home, in which the experienced are required to lead and instruct the inexperienced.

Students responded by pointing out that coed bathrooms or any other aspect of their living arrangements were areas in which *they* were experts and that freedom to choose living arrangements was not to be confused with a demand for equal participation in academic matters. Moreover, it was also true that in recent years the verdict had increasingly been rendered in favor of rights of special groups as against those of institutions. Students' rights have been among those that have benefited from the movement toward freedom of choice.

4. The second issue was related to the first but introduced a practical consideration, namely, the well-being of the university. The administration argued that more important than the wishes of the students in this essentially minor dispute was the necessity for retaining the support and goodwill of parents and alumni, who are ultimately responsible for the very existence of the university.

The students agreed that this support was necessary but felt that parents and alumni could be persuaded to consider the good reasons in the students' argument. Some students were inclined to carry the argument over goals even further. They insisted that if the university could maintain its existence only at the cost of sacrificing principles of democracy and freedom, then perhaps the university had forfeited its right to exist.

In making our way through this debate, we have summarized a procedure for tackling the issues in any controversial problem.

1. Raise the relevant issues and arrange them in order of importance. Plan to devote more time and space to issues you regard as crucial.

2. Produce the strongest evidence you can to support your factual claims, knowing that the opposing side or critical readers may try to produce conflicting evidence.
3. Defend your value claims by finding support in the fundamental principles with which most people in your audience would agree.
4. Argue with yourself. Try to foresee what kinds of refutation are possible. Try to anticipate and meet the opposing arguments.

ORGANIZING THE MATERIAL

Once you are satisfied that you have identified all the issues that will appear in your paper, you should begin to determine what kind of organization will be most effective for your argument. Now is the time to organize the results of your thinking into a logical and persuasive form. If you have read about your topic, answered questions, and acquired some evidence, you may already have decided on ways to approach your subject. If not, you should look closely at your outline now, recalling your purposes when you began your investigation, and develop a strategy for using the information you have gathered to achieve those purposes.

The first point to establish is what type of thesis you plan to present. Is your intention to make readers aware of some problem? To offer a solution to the problem? To defend a position? To refute a position held by others? The way you organize your material will depend to a great extent on your goal. With that goal in mind, look over your outline and reevaluate the relative importance of your issues. Which ones are most convincing? Which are backed up by the strongest support? Which ones relate to facts, and which concern values?

With these points in mind, let us look at various ways of organizing an argumentative paper. It would be foolish to decide in advance how many paragraphs a paper ought to have; however, you can and should choose a general strategy before you begin writing. If your thesis presents an opinion or recommends some course of action, you may choose simply to state your main idea and then defend it. If your thesis argues against an opposing view, you probably will want to mention that view and then refute it. Both these organizations introduce the thesis in the first or second paragraph (called the *thesis paragraph*). A third possibility is to start establishing that a problem exists and then introduce your thesis as the solution; this method is called *presenting the stock issues.* Although these three approaches sometimes overlap in practice, examining each one individually can help you structure your paper. Let's take a look at each arrangement.

Defending the Main Idea

All forms of organization will require you to defend your main idea, but one way of doing this is simple and direct. Early in the paper state the main idea that you will defend throughout your argument. You can also indicate here the two or three points you intend to develop in support of your claim; or you can raise these later as they come up. Suppose your thesis is that widespread vegetarianism would solve a number of problems. You could phrase it this way: "If the majority of people in this country adopted a vegetarian diet, we would see improvements in the economy, in the health of our people, and in moral sensitivity." You would then develop each of the claims in your list with appropriate data and warrants. Notice that the thesis statement in the first (thesis) paragraph has already outlined your organizational pattern.

Defending the main idea is effective for factual claims as well as policy claims, in which you urge the adoption of a certain policy and give the reasons for its adoption. It is most appropriate when your thesis is straightforward and can be readily supported by direct statements.

Refuting the Opposing View

Refuting an opposing view means to attack it in order to weaken, invalidate, or make it less credible to a reader. Since all arguments are dialogues or debates — even when the opponent is only imaginary — refutation of the other point of view is always implicit in your arguments. As you write, keep in mind the issues that an opponent may raise. You will be looking at your own argument as an unsympathetic reader may look at it, asking yourself the same kinds of critical questions and trying to find its weaknesses in order to correct them. In this way every argument you write becomes a form of refutation.

How do you plan a refutation? Here are some general guidelines.

1. If you want to refute the argument in a specific essay or article, read the argument carefully, noting all the points with which you disagree. This advice may seem obvious, but it cannot be too strongly emphasized. If your refutation does not indicate scrupulous familiarity with your opponent's argument, he or she has the right to say, and often does, "You haven't really read what I wrote. You haven't really answered my argument."

2. If you think that your readers are sympathetic to the opposing view or are not familiar with it, summarize it at the beginning of your paper, providing enough information to give readers an understanding of ex-

actly what you plan to refute. When you summarize, it's important to be respectful of the opposition's views. You don't want to alienate readers who might not agree with you at first. (In this book, Richard Restak's "AIDS: In Plagues, Civil Rights Aren't the Issue" on p. 339 and George Orwell's "Politics and the English Language" on p. 599 are entirely devoted to refuting arguments, and begin with summaries of the arguments with which they disagree.)

3. If your argument is long and complex, choose only the most important points to refute. Otherwise the reader who does not have the original argument on hand may find a detailed refutation hard to follow. If the argument is short and relatively simple — a claim supported by only two or three points — you may decide to refute all of them, devoting more space to the most important ones.

4. Attack the principal elements in the argument of your opponent.

a. Question the evidence. (See pp. 112–119 in the text.) Question whether your opponent has proved that a problem exists.
b. Attack the warrants or assumptions that underlie the claim. (See pp. 156–157 in the text.)
c. Attack the logic or reasoning of the opposing view. (Refer to the discussion of fallacious reasoning on pp. 223–233 in the text.)
d. Attack the proposed solution to a problem, pointing out that it will not work.

5. Be prepared to do more than attack the opposing view. Supply evidence and good reasons in support of your own claim.

Presenting the Stock Issues

Presenting the stock issues, or stating the problem before the solution, is a type of organization borrowed from traditional debate format. It works for policy claims when an audience must be convinced that a need exists for changing the status quo (present conditions) and for introducing plans to solve the problem. You begin by establishing that a problem exists (need). You then propose a solution (plan), which is your thesis. Finally, you show reasons for adopting the plan (advantages). These three elements — need, plan, and advantages — are called the stock issues.

For example, suppose you wanted to argue that measures for reducing acid rain should be introduced at once. You would first have to establish a need for such measures by defining the problem and providing evidence of damage. Then you would produce your thesis, a means for improving conditions. Finally you would suggest the benefits that would follow from implementation of your plan. Notice that in this organization your thesis paragraph usually appears toward the middle of your paper, although it may also appear at the beginning.

Ordering Material for Emphasis

Whichever way you choose to work, you should revise your outline to reflect the order in which you intend to present your thesis and supporting ideas. Not only the placement of your thesis paragraph but also the wording and arrangement of your ideas will determine what points in your paper receive the most emphasis.

Suppose your purpose is to convince the reader that cigarette smoking is a bad habit. You might decide to concentrate on three unpleasant attributes of cigarette smoking: (1) it is unhealthy; (2) it is dirty; (3) it is expensive. Obviously, these are not equally important as possible deterrents. You would no doubt consider the first reason the most compelling, accompanied by evidence to prove the relationship between cigarette smoking and cancer, heart disease, emphysema, and other diseases. This issue, therefore, should be given greater emphasis than the others.

There are several ways to achieve emphasis. One is to make the explicit statement that you consider a certain issue the most important.

> Finally, and *most importantly,* human culture is often able to neutralize or reverse what might otherwise be genetically advantageous consequences of selfish behavior.[1]

This quotation also reveals a second way — placing the material to be emphasized in an emphatic position, either first or last in the paper. The end position, however, is generally more emphatic.

A third way to achieve emphasis is to elaborate on the material to be emphasized, treating it at greater length, offering more data and reasons for it than you give for the other issues.

Considering Scope and Audience

With a working outline in hand that indicates the order of your thesis and claims, you are almost ready to begin turning your notes into prose. First, however, it is useful to review the limits on your paper to be sure your writing time will be used to the best possible advantage.

The first limit involves scope. As mentioned earlier, your thesis should introduce a claim that can be adequately supported in the space

---

[1] Peter Singer, *The Expanding Circle* (New York: New American Library, 1982), p. 171.

available to you. If your research has opened up more aspects than you anticipated, you may want to narrow your thesis to one major subtopic. Or you could emphasize only the most persuasive arguments for your position (assuming these are sufficient to make your case) and omit the others. In a brief paper (three or four pages), three issues are probably all you have room to develop. On the other hand, if you suspect your thesis can be proved in one or two pages, look for ways to expand it. What additional issues might be brought in to bolster your argument? Alternatively, is there a larger issue for which your thesis could become a supporting idea?

Other limits on your paper are imposed by the need to make your points in a way that will be persuasive to an audience. The style and tone you choose depend not only on the nature of the subject, but also on how you can best convince readers that you are a credible source. *Style* in this context refers to the elements of your prose — simple versus complex sentences, active versus passive verbs, metaphors, analogies, and other literary devices. *Tone* is the approach you take to your topic — solemn or humorous, detached or sympathetic. Style and tone together compose your voice as a writer.

Many students assume that every writer has only one voice. In fact, a writer typically adapts his or her voice to the material and the audience. Perhaps the easiest way to appreciate this is to think of two or three works by the same author that are written in different voices. Contrast, for instance, Martin Luther King, Jr.'s "I Have a Dream" (p. 626) with his "Letter from Birmingham Jail" (p. 611). Or compare the speeches of two different characters in the same story, novel, or film. Every writer has individual talents and inclinations that appear in most or all of his or her work. A good writer, however, is able to amplify some stylistic elements and diminish others, as well as to change tone, by choice.

It is usually appropriate in a short paper to choose an *expository* style, which emphasizes the elements of your argument rather than your personality. You many want to appeal to your readers' emotions as well as their intellects, but keep in mind that sympathy is most effectively gained when it is supported by believable evidence. If you press your point stridently, your audience is likely to be suspicious rather than receptive. If you sprinkle your prose with jokes or metaphors, you may diminish your credibility by detracting from the substance of your case. Both humor and analogy can be useful tools, but they should be used with discretion.

You can discover some helpful pointers on essay style by reading the editorials in newspapers such as the *New York Times*, the *Washington Post*, or the *Wall Street Journal*. The authors are typically addressing a mixed audience comparable to the hypothetical readers of your own paper. Though their approaches vary, each writer is attempting to portray himself or herself as an objective analyst whose argument deserves careful attention.

Again, remember your goals. You are trying to convince your audience of something; an argument is, by its nature, directed at people who may not initially agree with its thesis. Therefore, your voice as well as the claims you make must be convincing.

To This Point

The organizing steps that come between preparation and writing are often neglected. Careful planning at this stage, however, can save much time and effort later. As you prepare to start writing, you should be able to answer the following questions:

1. Is the purpose of my paper to persuade readers to accept a potentially controversial idea, to refute someone else's position, or to propose a solution to a problem?
2. Have I decided on an organization that is likely to accomplish this purpose?
3. Does my outline arrange my thesis and issues in an appropriate order to emphasize the most important issues?
4. Does my outline show an argument whose scope suits the needs of this paper?
5. What questions of style and tone do I need to keep in mind as I write to ensure that my argument will be persuasive?

WRITING

Beginning the Paper

Having found a claim you can defend and the voice you will adopt toward your audience, you must now think about how to begin. An introduction to your subject should consist of more than just the first paragraph of your paper. It should invite the reader to give attention to what you have to say. It should also point you in the direction you will take in developing your argument. You may want to begin the actual writing of your paper with the thesis paragraph. It is useful to consider the whole paragraph rather than simply the thesis statement for two reasons. First, not all theses are effectively expressed in a single sentence. Second, the rest of the paragraph will be closely related to your statement of the main idea. You may show why you have chosen this topic or why your audience will benefit from reading your paper. You may introduce your warrant, qualify your claim, and in other ways prepare for the body of your argument. Because readers will perceive the whole paragraph as a unit, it makes sense to approach it that way.

Consider first the kind of argument you intend to present. Does your paper make a factual claim? Does it address values? Does it recommend a policy or action? Is it a rebuttal of some current policy or belief? The answers to those questions will influence the way you introduce the subject.

If your thesis makes a factual claim, you may be able to summarize it in one or two opening sentences. "Whether we like it or not, money is obsolete. The currency of today is not paper or coin, but plastic." Refutations are easy to introduce in a brief statement: "Contrary to popular views on the subject, the institution of marriage is as sound today as it was a generation ago."

A thesis that defends a value is usually best preceded by an explanatory introduction. "Some wars are morally defensible" is a thesis that can be stated as a simple declarative opening sentence. However, readers who disagree may not read any further than the first line. Someone defending this claim is likely to be more persuasive if he or she first gives an example of a situation in which war is or was preferable to peace or presents the thesis less directly.

One way to keep such a thesis from alienating the audience is to phrase it as a question. "Are all wars morally indefensible?" Still better would be to prepare for the question:

> Few if any of us favor war as a solution to international problems. We are too vividly aware of the human suffering imposed by armed conflict, as well as the political and financial turmoil that inevitably result. Yet can we honestly agree that no war is ever morally defensible?

Notice that this paragraph gains appeal from use of the first person *we*. The author implies that he or she shares the readers' feelings but has good reasons for believing those feelings are not sufficient grounds for condemning all wars. Even if readers are skeptical, the conciliatory phrasing of the thesis should encourage them to continue reading.

For any subject that is highly controversial or emotionally charged, especially one that strongly condemns an existing situation or belief, you may sometimes want to express your indignation directly. Of course, you must be sure that your indignation can be justified. The author of the following introduction, a physician and writer, openly admits that he is about to make a case that may offend readers.

> Is there any polite way to introduce today's subject? I'm afraid not. It must be said plainly that the media have done about as sorry and dishonest a

job of covering health news as is humanly possible, and that when the media do not fail from bias and mendacity, they fail from ignorance and laziness.[2]

If your thesis advocates a policy or makes a recommendation, it may be a good idea, as in a value claim, to provide a short background. The following paragraph introduces an argument favoring relaxation of controls in high schools.

> "Free the New York City 275,000" read a button worn by many young New Yorkers some years ago. The number was roughly the total of students enrolled in the City's high schools.
>
> The condition of un-freedom which is described was not, however, unique to the schools of one city. According to the Carnegie Commission's comprehensive study of American public education, *Crisis in the Classroom,* public schools across the country share a common characteristic, namely, "preoccupation with order and control." The result is that students find themselves the victims of "oppressive and petty rules which give their schools a repressive, almost prison-like atmosphere."[3]

There are also other ways to introduce your subject. One is to begin with an appropriate quotation.

> "Reading makes a full man, conversation makes a ready man, and writing makes an exact man." So Francis Bacon told us around 1600. Recently I have been wondering how Bacon's formula might apply to present-day college students.[4]

Or you may begin with an anecdote. In the following introduction to an article about the relation between cancer and mental attitude, the author recounts a personal experience.

> Shortly after I moved to California, a new acquaintance sat in my San Francisco living room drinking rose-hip tea and chainsmoking. Like so many residents of the Golden West, Cecil was "into" all things healthy, from jogging to *shiatsu* massage to kelp. Tobacco didn't seem to fit, but he told me confidently that there was no contradiction. "It all has to with energy," he said. "Unless you have a lot of negative energy about smoking cigarettes, there's no way they can hurt you; you won't get cancer."[5]

---

[2] Michael Halberstam, "TV's Unhealthy Approach to Health News," *TV Guide,* September 20–26, 1980, p. 24

[3] Alan Levine and Eve Carey, *The Rights of Students* (New York: Avon Books, 1977), p. 11.

[4] William Aiken, "The Conversation on Campus Today Is, Uh . . . ", *Wall Street Journal,* May 4, 1982, p. 18.

[5] Joel Guerin, "Cancer and the Mind," *Harvard Magazine,* November–December 1978, p. 11.

Finally, you may introduce yourself as the author of the claim.

> I wish to argue an unpopular cause: the cause of the old, free elective system in the academic world, or the untrammeled right of the undergraduate to make his own mistakes.[6]
>
> My subject is the world of Hamlet. I do not of course mean Denmark, except as Denmark is given a body by the play; and I do not mean Elizabethan England, though this is necessarily close behind the scenes. I mean simply the imaginative environment that the play asks us to enter when we read it or go to see it.[7]

You should, however, use such introductions with care. They suggest an authority about the subject that you shouldn't attempt to assume unless you can demonstrate that you are entitled to it.

Guidelines for Good Writing

In general, the writer of an argument follows the same rules that govern any form of expository writing. Your style should be clear and readable, your organization logical, your ideas connected by transitional phrases and sentences, your paragraphs coherent. The main difference between an argument and other kinds of expository writing, as noted earlier, is the need to persuade an audience to adopt a belief or take an action. You should assume your readers will be critical rather than neutral or sympathetic. Therefore, you must be equally critical of your own work. Any apparent gap in reasoning or ambiguity in presentation is likely to weaken the argument.

As you read the essays in this book and elsewhere, you will discover that good style in argumentative writing shares several characteristics:

- Variety in sentence structure: a mixture of both long and short sentences, different sentence beginnings
- Rich but standard vocabulary: avoidance of specialized terms unless they are fully explained, word choice appropriate to a thoughtful argument
- Use of details and examples to illustrate and clarify abstract terms, principles, and generalizations

---

[6] Howard Mumford Jones, "Undergraduates on Apron Strings," *Atlantic Monthly,* October 1955, p. 45.

[7] Maynard Mack, "The World of Hamlet," *Yale Review,* June 1952, p. 502.

You should take care to avoid the following:

- Unnecessary repetition: making the same point without new data or interpretation
- Exaggeration or stridency, which can create suspicion of your fairness and powers of observation
- Short paragraphs of one or two sentences, which are common in advertising and newspaper writing to get the reader's attention but are inappropriate in a thoughtful essay

In addition to these stylistic principles, seven general points are worth keeping in mind:

1. Although *you*, like *I*, should be used judiciously, it can be found even in the treatment of weighty subjects. Here is an example from an essay by the distinguished British mathematician and philosopher, Bertrand Russell.

> Suppose you are a scientific pioneer and you make some discovery of great scientific importance and suppose you say to yourself, "I am afraid this discovery will do harm": you know that other people are likely to make the same discovery if they are allowed suitable opportunities for research; you must therefore, if you do not wish the discovery to become public, either discourage your sort of research or control publication by a board of censors.[8]

Don't be afraid to use *you* or *I* when it is useful to emphasize the presence of the person making the argument.

2. Don't pad. This point should be obvious; the word *pad* suggests the addition of unnecessary material. Many writers find it tempting, however, to enlarge a discussion even when they have little more to say. It is never wise to introduce more words into a paper that has already made its point. If the paper turns out to be shorter than you had hoped, it may mean that you have not sufficiently developed the subject or that the subject was less substantial than you thought when you selected it. Padding, which is easy to detect in its repetition and sentences empty of content, weakens the writer's credibility.

3. For any absolute generalization — a statement containing words such as *all* or *every* — consider the possibility that there may be at least one example that will weaken the generalization. Such a precaution means that you won't have to backtrack and admit that your generalization is not, after all, universal. A student who was arguing against capital punishment for the reason that all killing was wrong suddenly paused in her presentation and added, "On the other hand, if given the chance, I'd

---

[8] "Science and Human Life," in *What Is Science?* edited by James R. Newman (New York: Simon and Schuster, 1955), p.12.

probably have been willing to kill Hitler." This admission meant that she recognized important exceptions to her rule and that she would have to qualify her generalization in some significant way.

4. When offering an explanation, especially one that is complicated or extraordinary, look first for a cause that is easier to accept, one that doesn't strain credibility. (In Chapter 7, we called attention to this principle. See p. 225.) For example, a few years ago a great many people were bemused by reports about the mysterious Bermuda Triangle, which had apparently swallowed up ships and planes since the mid-nineteenth century. The forces at work were variously described as space-time warps, UFOs that transported earthlings to other planets, and sea monsters seeking revenge. But a careful investigation revealed familiar, natural causes. A reasonable person interested in the truth would have searched for more conventional explanations before accepting the bizarre stories of extraterrestrial creatures. He or she would also exercise caution when confronted by conspiracy theories that try to account for controversial political events, such as the assassination of John Kennedy.

5. Check carefully for questionable warrants. Your outline should specify your warrants. When necessary, these should be included in your paper to link claims with support. Many an argument has failed because it depended on an unstated warrant with which the reader did not agree. If you were arguing for a physical education requirement at your school, you might make a good case for all the physical and psychological benefits of such a requirement. But you would certainly need to introduce and develop the warrant on which your claim was based — that it is the proper function of a college or university to provide the benefits of a physical education. Many readers would agree that physical education is valuable, but they might question the assumption that an academic institution should introduce a nonintellectual enterprise into the curriculum. At any point where you draw a controversial or tenuous conclusion, be sure your reasoning is clear and logical.

6. Avoid conclusions that are merely summaries. Summaries may be needed in long technical papers, but in brief arguments they create endings that are without force or interest. In the closing paragraph you should find a new idea that emerges naturally from the development of the whole argument.

7. Strive for a paper that is unified, coherent, and emphatic where appropriate. A *unified* paper stays focused on its goal and directs each claim, warrant, and piece of evidence toward that goal. Extraneous information or unsupported claims impair unity. *Coherence* means that all ideas are fully explained and adequately connected by transitions. To ensure coherence, give especially close attention to the beginnings and ends of your paragraphs: Is each new concept introduced in a way that shows it following naturally from the one that preceded it? *Emphasis*, as we have

mentioned, is a function partly of structure and partly of language. Your most important claims should be placed where they are certain of receiving the reader's attention: key sentences at the beginning or end of a paragraph, key paragraphs at the beginning or end of your paper. Sentence structure can also be used for emphasis. If you have used several long, complex sentences, you can emphasize a significant point by stating it briefly and simply. You can also create emphasis with verbal flags, such as "The primary issue to consider . . ." or "Finally, we cannot ignore . . ."

All clear expository prose will exhibit the qualities of unity, coherence, and emphasis. But the success of an argumentative paper is especially dependent on these qualities because the reader may have to follow a line of reasoning that is both complicated and unfamiliar. Moreover, a paper that is unified, coherent, and properly emphatic will be more readable, the first requisite of an effective argument.

REVISING

The final stage in writing an argumentative paper is revising. The first step is to read through what you have written for mistakes. Next, check your work against the guidelines listed under "Organizing the Material" and "Writing." Have you omitted any of the issues, warrants, or supporting evidence on your outline? Is each paragraph coherent in itself? Do your paragraphs work together to create a coherent paper? All the elements of the argument — the issues raised, the underlying assumptions, and the supporting material — should contribute to the development of the claim in your thesis statement. Any material that is interesting but irrelevant to that claim should be cut. Finally, does your paper reach a clear conclusion that reinforces your thesis?

Be sure, too, that the style and tone of your paper are appropriate for the topic and the audience. Remember that people choose to read an argument because they want the answer to a troubling question or the solution to a recurrent problem. Besides stating your thesis in a way that invites the reader to join you in your investigation, you must retain your audience's interest through a discussion that may be unfamiliar or contrary to their convictions. The outstanding qualities of argumentative prose style, therefore, are clarity and readability.

Style is obviously harder to evaluate in your own writing than organization. Your outline provides a map against which to check the structure of your paper. Clarity and readability, by comparison, are somewhat abstract qualities. Two procedures may be helpful. The first is to read two or three (or more) essays by authors whose style you admire and then turn back to your own writing. Awkward spots in your prose are sometimes easier to see if you get away from it and respond to someone else's perspective than if you simply keep rereading your own writing.

The second method is to read aloud. If you have never tried it, you are likely to be surprised at how valuable this can be. Again, start with someone else's work that you feel is clearly written, and practice until you achieve a smooth rhythmic delivery that satisfies you. And listen to what you are reading. Your objective is to absorb the patterns of English structure that characterize the clearest, most readable prose. Then read your paper aloud and listen to the construction of your sentences. Are they also clear and readable? Do they say what you want them to say? How would they sound to a reader? According to one theory, you can learn the rhythm and phrasing of a language as you learn the rhythm and phrasing of a melody. And you will often *hear* a mistake or a clumsy construction in your writing that has escaped your eye in proofreading.

PREPARING THE MANUSCRIPT

Type on one side of 8½-by-11-inch 20-pound white typing paper, double-spacing throughout. Leave margins of 1 to 1½ inches on all sides and indent each paragraph five spaces. Unless a formal outline is part of the paper, a separate title page is unnecessary. Instead, beginning about one inch from the top of the first page and flush with the left margin, type your name, the instructor's name, the course title, and the date, each on a separate line; then double-space and type the title, capitalizing the first letter of the first and last words of the title and all other words except articles, prepositions, and conjunctions. Quadruple-space and type the body of the paper.

Number all but the first page at the top right corner, typing your last name before each page number in case pages are mislaid. If an outline is included, number its pages with lowercase roman numerals.

Proofread the paper carefully for mistakes in grammar, spelling, and punctuation. Make corrections with liquid correction fluid or, if there are only a few mistakes, cross them out and neatly write the correction above the line.

REVIEW CHECKLIST FOR ARGUMENTATIVE PAPERS

A successful argumentative paper meets the following criteria:

1. It presents a thesis that is of interest to both the writer and the audience, is debatable, and can be defended in the amount of space available.

2. Each statement offered in support of the thesis is backed up with enough evidence to give it credibility. Data cited in the paper come from a variety of sources. All quotations and direct references to primary or secondary sources are fully documented.
3. The warrants linking claims to support are either specified or implicit in the author's data and line of reasoning. No claim should depend on an unstated warrant with which skeptical readers might disagree.
4. The thesis is clearly presented and adequately introduced in a thesis paragraph, which indicates the purpose of the paper.
5. Supporting statements and data are organized in a way that builds the argument, emphasizes the author's main ideas, and justifies the paper's conclusions.
6. All possible opposing arguments are anticipated and refuted.
7. The paper is written in a style and tone appropriate to the topic and the intended audience. The author's prose is clear and readable.
8. The manuscript is clean, carefully proofed, and typed in an acceptable format.

A SHORT STUDENT ARGUMENT

Cleo Boyd wrote the following paper arguing against the legal drinking age for her English 107 course. She chose to start with an anecdote that points out the existence of a problem and to end with a short reference to that anecdote. Although most of Boyd's paper is dedicated to refuting opposing views, she does offer some suggestions of her own for keeping people from drinking irresponsibly. Because the argument is tied to her own experience, Boyd decided to write her paper in the first person.

As you read this paper, try to think of ways that you would revise it. What warrants underlie Boyd's claims? Are her analogies sound? What kinds of support does she offer? Are there any weaknesses in the support? Can you think of any important opposing arguments that Boyd does not address?

Cleo Boyd

Professor Gordon

English 107

March 16, 1990

The New Drinking Laws: A Sour Taste

All I wanted was an Amaretto sour. To get it, I had to have the little black stamp on the back of my hand that told the bartender I was at least twenty-one. I was only twenty and a half. So there I sat at a North Carolina nightspot with my brother and his girlfriend Debbie, sipping a soda. Six months made the difference between a watery Coke and a taste of liquor.

Debbie had a solution. She led me back to the ladies' room, licked the black stamp on the back of her hand, and pressed it onto my hand. It was light, so I darkened it with black eyeliner.

"It's backwards, but they won't notice," Debbie assured me. "It's dark in here."

Well, the bartender did notice, and I didn't get the Amaretto sour. "This is a fake," he said. "You have to come with me." He walked around to my side of the bar, grabbed my arm, and led me to a small office at the front of the bar. There, he took a bottle of rubbing alcohol out of the desk, wet a piece of cotton with it, and wiped the stamp from my hand. "Now get out of here," he said.

At first, I wanted to cry. But as I walked to the car with Debbie and Grant, I became angry. I was a responsible person, and I had never taken a drink and gotten behind the wheel. I rarely had

Boyd 2

more than two drinks at a time. Sure, I had skirted the law, but the law was unfair.

Now young people across the country are getting a taste of that unfairness. Under pressure from special-interest groups and a federal government that has threatened to take away their highway funds, every state in the country has raised the legal age for buying and drinking alcohol to twenty-one. I argue that, in raising the drinking age, states have violated the rights of a large group of people. Further, I believe that increasing the age is not the best way to deter drunken driving and reduce traffic fatalities.

Supporters of the current drinking laws question the ability of eighteen-year-olds to drink responsibly. These people need to take a look at the other responsibilities that rest with eighteen-year-olds now. Under United States law, an eighteen-year-old can vote, go to war, get married, and have a family, but cannot legally enjoy a beer. The implication is that people who are under the age of twenty-one are mature enough to assume the responsibilities of adulthood but are not responsible enough to enjoy its pleasures. I find this judgment arbitrary and unfair. Once we have decided what the age of majority should be (and we seem to have decided on the age of eighteen for most activities) we should apply that standard uniformly.

Other supporters of new laws argue that when drinking ages go up, traffic fatalities go down. In

Boyd 3

fact, studies <u>have</u> indicated that in states where the drinking age has been increased, fatalities have dropped by as much as 10 percent. This is good news, but it does not prove that the new drinking laws are entirely responsible for the drop in traffic fatalities. Tougher drunk driving laws and stepped-up efforts to educate the public about the dangers of drinking and driving could also have been major factors in the drop in fatalities.

In the last several years, drunk driving laws and penalties have been made tougher throughout the nation. That is good: Rigorous enforcement of these laws is what we need. Also, education is always a positive force. The better the general public understands the damage that irresponsible drinking can do to individuals and society, the better off everyone will be. There are problem drinkers in all age groups. The law should go after them instead of using an arbitrary age limit that restricts the rights of citizens.

Finally, I do not believe that the higher drinking age will deter people under the age of twenty-one from drinking. Those under the legal age have always found ways to skirt the law and get their hands on alcohol, and they will continue to do so. The quest for the pleasure of intoxication is part of our nature. Restricting the supply of alcohol might make it harder for eighteen-year-olds to get, but it will not make it less desirable.

I wasn't deterred from drinking the night that

Boyd 4

I got kicked out of that bar in North Carolina. After leaving there, we drove a few miles down the road to another bar, and my brother bought me my Amaretto sour. It might have been more satisfying had it been legal.

CHAPTER 9

Researching an Argumentative Paper

The success of any argument, short or long, depends in large part on the quantity and quality of the support behind it. Research, therefore, can be crucial for any argument outside your own experience. Some papers will benefit from research in the library and elsewhere because development of the claim requires facts, example, statistics, and informed opinions that are available only from experts. This chapter offers information and advice to help you work through the steps of writing a research paper, from getting started to preparing the finished product.

GETTING STARTED

The following guidelines will help you keep your research on track:

1. Focus your investigation on building your argument, not merely on collecting information about the topic. Do follow any promising leads that turn up from the sources you consult, but don't be diverted into general reading that has no direct bearing on your thesis.

2. Look for at least two pieces of evidence to support each point you make. If you cannot find sufficient evidence, you may need to revise or abandon the point.

3. Use a variety of sources. Check not only different publications but information drawn from different fields as well.

4. Be sure your sources are authoritative. We have already pointed out elsewhere the necessity for examining the credentials of sources. Although it may be difficult or impossible for those outside the field to conclude that one authority is more trustworthy than another, some guidelines are available. Articles and essays in scholarly journals are probably more authoritative than articles in college newspapers. Authors whose credentials include many publications and years of study at reputable institutions are probably more reliable than newspaper columnists and the so-called man in the street. However, we can judge reliability much more easily if we are dealing with facts and inferences than with values and emotions.

5. Don't let your sources' opinions outweigh your own. Your paper should demonstrate that the thesis and ideas you present are yours, arrived at after careful reflection and supported by research. The thesis need not be original, but your paper should be more than a collection of quotations or a report of the facts and opinions you have been reading. It should be clear to the reader that the quotations and other materials support *your* claim and that *you* have been responsible for finding and emphasizing the important issues, examining the data, and choosing between strong and weak opinions.

MAPPING RESEARCH: A SAMPLE OUTLINE

To explore a range of research activities, let's suppose that you are preparing a research paper, six to ten pages long. You have chosen to defend the following thesis: *Conventional zoos should be abolished because they are cruel to animals and cannot provide the benefits to the public that they promise.* To keep your material under control and give directions to your reading, you would sketch a preliminary outline, which might look like this:

Why We Don't Need Zoos

I. Moral Objection: Animals have fundamental right to liberty
   A. Must prove animals are negatively affected by captivity
      1. research?
      2. research?
   B. Must refute claims that captivity is not detrimental to animals
      1. Brownlee's description of dolphin: "seeming stupor"; eating "half-heartedly"; not behaving like wild dolphins

2. Personal experience: watching leopards running in circles in cages for hours

II. Practical Objection: Zoos can't accomplish what they claim to be their goals
   A. "Educational benefits" zoo provides are inaccurate at best: public is not learning about wild animals at all but about domesticated descendants of same (support with research from [I.A] above)
   B. Conservation programs at zoos are ineffective
      1. It's difficult to breed animals in zoos
      2. Resultant offspring, when there is any, is victim of inbreeding. Leads to inferior stock that will eventually die out (research?)

There are two general ways to gather support for your argument. The first is to collect your data from primary sources. A *primary source* is raw information not already compiled or interpreted. It is most useful when your topic relates to a local issue, one involving your school or town. The second way is to find data provided by scholars and investigators who have studied the subject and reported their findings in books, magazines, and newspapers. In some cases reports present an original argument; in other cases, the argument has a purely factual basis. For example, the Census Bureau compiles statistical data on the population of the United States. These statistics can then be used by demographers and sociologists to interpret population trends and make predictions or by a writer who needs to know the nation's current population, perhaps as a basis for an inference about the family. Usually the best place to find this type of information, known as *secondary sources*, is the library.

USING PRIMARY SOURCES

Suppose you decide to investigate the food services on campus, about which you have heard numerous complaints. You may have one or two purposes in mind: First, you may want to establish the fact that a problem exists, because you think that not all members of the community are sufficiently aware of it. In this case, then, having determined that the problem is real, you may want to propose a solution. You can go directly to primary sources without consulting books or journals.

After talking informally with students about their reactions to the food in the dining commons, the coffee shops, the snack bars, and elsewhere, you might distribute a questionnaire to a selected group to get information about the specific grounds for complaint — nutritional value, cost, variety, quantity of food, quality of service. Eliciting useful information from a questionnaire is not, however, as simple as it seems, and you should probably consult a sociologist or psychologist on campus to find the most reliable sample of students and the most appropriate questions for your particular study.

You will also, of course, want to ask questions of those in charge of the food service to discover their view of the problem. If they agree with the students that the service is unsatisfactory, perhaps they can offer reasons that they consider beyond their control. Or they may disagree and point out the injustice of the students' complaints.

The answers to these questions might then lead you to interview university officials and to consult records about food purchases and budgets, it they are accessible. And even an investigation into a local problem can benefit from library research and a look at journal articles about the ways other schools have solved, or failed to solve, the same problems.

USING SECONDARY SOURCES: THE LIBRARY

If you were going to write a research paper on why we don't need zoos, you would probably want to rely on secondary sources for most of your evidence. Although you could collect some primary evidence by visiting a zoo yourself (as the author of the paper at the end of this chapter has), expert opinions will carry more weight in your argument. Having drawn up a preliminary outline to help map out your reading, how can you most effectively use the library to research the fate of wild animals in captivity?

It's a good idea to consult the librarian before starting your research; he or she will be able to direct you to specific reference works relevant to your subject, which could save you a lot of time. Your library also contains useful systems for recovering material of all kinds, including the card catalog or catalog access system; dictionaries and encyclopedias; magazine, newspaper, and specialized indexes; and abstracting services.

The Card Catalog and Catalog Access System

The card catalog is an alphabetical listing of books arranged by title, author, and subject. Usually the title and author cards are found in one file, and the subject cards are found in another. The information on all three types of cards is the same. Every card in the file will tell you a book's title, author, and publisher, the city and date of publication, the book's size and length, and whether the book contains illustrations, an introduction, a bibliography, or an index. The call number appears in the upper left corner of the card or at the bottom of the card.

Subject Card

	ANIMALS, TREATMENT OF -- MORAL AND ETHICAL ASPECTS
HV 4711 .A56 1976	Singer, Peter. Animal rights and human obligations / edited by Tom Regan and Peter Singer. -- Englewood Cliffs, N. J. : Prentice Hall. 1976. 250 p. ; 23 cm. Includes bibliography. ISBN 0-13-037523-3 1. Animals, Treatment of. 2. Animals, Treatment of -- Moral and ethical aspects. I. Regan, Tom. II. Singer, Peter.

Author Card

HV 4711 .A56 1976	Singer, Peter. Animal rights and human obligations / edited by Tom Regan and Peter Singer. -- Englewood Cliffs, N. J. : Prentice Hall, 1976. 250 p. ; 23 cm. Includes bibliography. ISBN 0-13-037523-3 1. Animals, Treatment of. 2. Animals, Treatment of -- Moral and ethical aspects. I. Regan, Tom. II. Singer, Peter.

Title Card

HV 4711 .A56 1976	Animal rights and human obligations Singer, Peter. Animal rights and human obligations / edited by Tom Regan and Peter Singer. -- Englewood Cliffs, N. J. : Prentice Hall, 1976. 250 p. ; 23 cm. Includes bibliography. ISBN 0-13-037523-3 1. Animals, Treatment of. 2. Animals, Treatment of -- Moral and ethical aspects. I. Regan, Tom. II. Singer, Peter.

Unless you already know of specific authors and titles you wish to look up, you will probably begin with the subject file. No matter what your subject, keep an open mind: You may have to use your imagination to find the listings you need. For example, the entry for "Zoo" reads "See Zoological gardens," but the books under that topic are mainly descriptive and therefore not very useful. You might look next under "Animals," and then "Animals, treatment of." Preliminary reading may also have suggested the key words and phrases "Endangered species," "Conservation," and "Preservation." If you're having trouble finding the specific heading for the subject you want to research, the *Library of Congress Subject Headings* can help you determine the heading you need. These large red books are usually kept near the catalog.

When you find a citation for a book that interests you, copy down the complete call number. Most libraries have a great many books with almost identical call numbers, so if you don't write the number down, or if you write down a shortened form of the call number, you could search the stacks for hours without finding the book you want.

Some libraries have replaced their card catalogs with microfilm or on-line computer catalogs. Both of these systems allow a large amount of material to be stored in a much smaller space than the standard card catalog allows. Some libraries also subscribe to database services that list sources available at libraries throughout the United States and Canada. If your library subscribes to a database, you might be able to use it yourself, or you might have to ask the librarian to print out a listing of materials for you (usually for a price). Specialized databases exist for almost any discipline you would want to search, but you should find out which databases your library subscribes to before you decide to consult any one of them. Some of the most popular databases are:

ERIC (Educational Research Information Center)

DIALOG (which includes over 250 databases)

BRS (Bibliographical Retrieval Services)

RLIN (Research Libraries Information Network)

OCLC (Online Computer Library Center)

Encyclopedias

When beginning your research, you will find that general encyclopedias can provide a useful overview of your subject and also suggest related terms under which you might look. Two general encyclopedias that are probably on the shelves of your library are the *Encyclopedia Americana* and the *Encyclopedia Britannica*. You will also find many specialized encyclopedias in the research section of your library. Some encyclopedias you might find useful include:

Britannica Encyclopedia of American Art
Cassell's Encyclopedia of World Literature
Encyclopedia of Biological Sciences
Encyclopedia of Education
Encyclopedia of Environmental Science
Encyclopedia of Philosophy
Encyclopedia of Physics
International Encyclopedia of the Social Sciences
McGraw-Hill Encyclopedia of Science and Technology
New Illustrated Encyclopedia of World History

For a list of specialized encyclopedias in your library, consult the subject file of the card catalog under "Encyclopedias."

Indexes

Magazine indexes. The Reader's Guide to Periodical Literature is likely to be useful if your subject is particularly timely. While there may not be any books published yet on your topic, you will probably find some articles. The *Readers' Guide* lists articles published in over one hundred of the best-known magazines in the country in volumes arranged by year. As in the card catalog, entries are organized by the author's name, title of the article, or subject of the article. For a contoversial or timely subject, it makes sense to start with the most recent volumes and work backward. (If you are researching a specific event, you should start with the year in which it took place.) If your library does not carry the periodicals you need, the librarian will be able to direct you to a library that does.

Newspaper indexes. Newspaper indexes are an excellent source for articles on current events. While books can contain detailed analyses of events that occurred years ago and magazines can give you a thorough discussion of the events of last week or last month, newspapers cover the stories that are in the news right now. Like the *Readers' Guide*, newspaper indexes are arranged by year, with entries organized according to author, title, and subject.

The most popular newspaper index is the *New York Times Index*. Indexes also exist for the *Wall Street Journal* and the *Christian Science Monitor*, and the *National Newspaper Index* includes indexes for the *Chicago*

Tribune, the *Los Angeles Times*, the *New Orleans Times-Picayune*, and the *Washington Post*.

Specialized indexes. Most college libraries carry specialized indexes citing more sophisticated articles from scholarly and professional journals and magazines. The articles listed in these indexes will be more difficult to read than the articles listed in the *Readers' Guide*, but they will also be more substantial and authoritative. Your paper might give you reason to consult one of these specialized indexes:

Applied Science and Technology Index
Art Index
Biological and Agricultural Index
Business Periodicals Index
Education Index
Humanities Index
Index to Legal Periodicals
Music Index
Philosopher's Index
Social Sciences Index

Abstracts

If you want to know the main points of a book or article before you take the time to read it, then you might want to consult an abstract. Collections of abstracts index books and articles on a particular subject and summarize them briefly. Abstracting services include:

Abstracts in Anthropology
Biological Abstracts
Book Review Digest
Chemical Abstracts
Congressional Abstracts
Historical Abstracts
Physics Abstracts
Psychological Abstracts
Sociological Abstracts
Women's Studies Abstracts

READING WITH A PURPOSE

When you begin studying your sources, read first to acquire general familiarity with your subject. Make sure that you are covering both sides of the question — in this case arguments both for and against the existence of zoos — as well as facts and opinions from a variety of sources. In investigating this subject, you will encounter data from biologists, ecologists, zoo directors, anthropologists, animal-rights activists, and ethical philosophers; their varied points of view will contribute to the strength of your claim.

As you read, look for what seem to be the major issues. They will probably be represented in all or most of your sources. For the claim about zoos the major issues may be summarized as follows: (1) the fundamental right wild animals have to liberty; (2) the harm done to animals who are denied this right and kept in captivity. On the other side, these issues will emerge: (1) the lack of concrete evidence that animals suffer or are harmed by being in zoos; (2) the benefits, in terms of entertainment, education, and conservation efforts that the public derives from zoos. The latter two, of course, are the issues you will have to refute. Your note taking should emphasize these important issues.

Write down questions as they occur to you in your reading. Why do zoos exist? What are their major goals, and how well do they meet them? What happens to animals who are removed from the wild and placed in zoos? What happens to animals born and reared in captivity? How do these groups compare with their wild counterparts, who are free to live in their natural habitats? Do animals really have a right to liberty? What are the consequences of denying them this right? Are there consequences to humanity?

Taking Notes

While everyone has his or her own method for taking notes, here are a few suggestions that should be useful to any writer.

Summarize instead of quoting long passages, unless you feel the quotation is more effective than anything you can write and can provide crucial support for your argument. Summarizing as you read can save you a great deal of time.

When you do quote, make sure to quote exactly. Copy the material word for word, leaving all punctuation exactly as it appears and inserting ellipsis points if you delete material. Make sure to enclose all quotations in quotation marks and to copy complete information about your source, including page numbers and publishing information as well as the author's

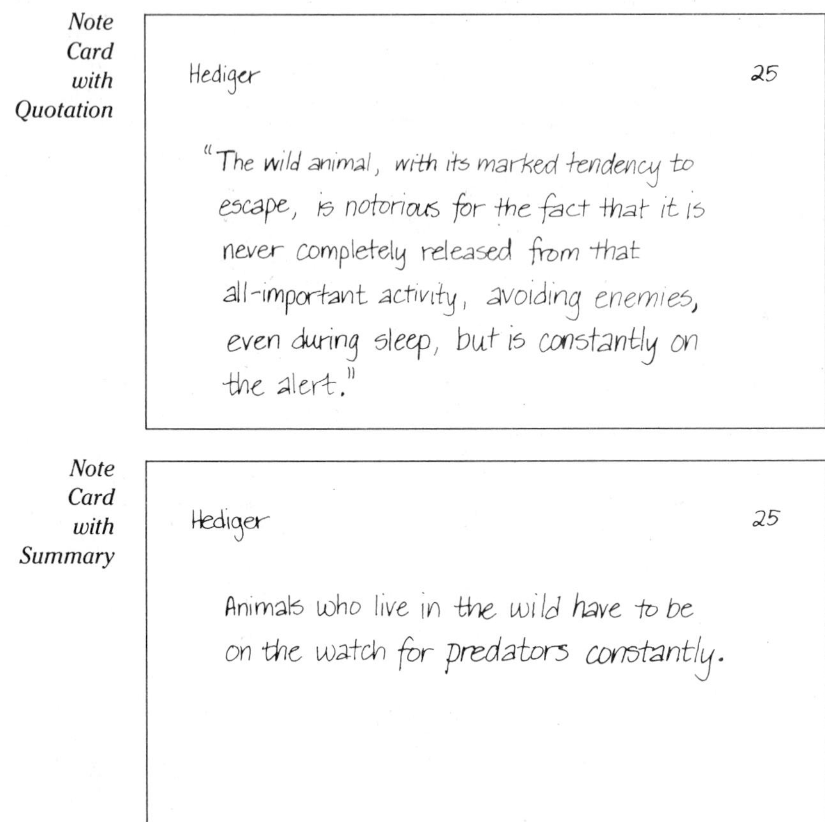

name and the title of the book or article. If you quote an article that appears in an anthology or collection, make sure you record complete information about the book itself.

Note Card with Quotation
Hediger
25
"The wild animal, with its marked tendency to escape, is notorious for the fact that it is never completely released from that all-important activity, avoiding enemies, even during sleep, but is constantly on the alert."
Note Card with Summary
Hediger
25
Animals who live in the wild have to be on the watch for predators constantly.

Keep index cards for each source you use, and write down complete bibliographical information for each source *as you use it.* That way you will have all the information necessary to document your paper when you need it. Some people find it useful to keep two sets of note cards: one set for the bibliographical information and one set for the notes themselves. Each source appears on one card by itself, ready to be arranged in alphabetical order for the Works Cited or References page of the paper.

As you take notes, refer to your outline frequently to ensure that you are acquiring sufficient data to support all the points you intend to use. You will also be revising your outline during the course of your research,

Note Card with Statistics

Reiger 32

By end of decade, worldwide extinction rate will be one species per hour.

Other statistics, too, in Reiger, "The Wages of Growth," Field and Stream, July 1981: 32.

Bibliography Note Card

Hediger, Heini. The Psychology and Behavior of Animals in Zoos and Circuses. Trans. Geoffrey Sircom. New York: Dover, 1968.

as issues are clarified and new ones emerge. Keeping close track of your outline will prevent you from recording material that is interesting but not relevant. If you aren't sure whether you will want to use a certain piece of information later, don't copy the whole passage. Instead, make a note for future reference so that you can find it again if you need it. Taking too many notes is, however, preferable to taking too few, a problem that will force you to go back to the library for missing information. For the ideas and quotations in your notes, you should always take down enough information to enable you to find the references again as quickly as possible.

When researching your topic, you will find words and ideas put together by other people, that you will want to use in your paper. Relying on the knowledge of others is an important part of doing research; expert opinions and eloquent arguments will help support your claims when your own expertise is limited. But remember, this is your paper. Your ideas and your insights into other people's ideas are just as important as the information you uncover at the library. Try to achieve a balance between solid information and original interpretation.

Quoting

You may want to quote passages or phrases from your sources if they express an idea in words more effective than your own. In this particular project, you might come across a statement that provides succinct, irrefutable evidence for an issue you wish to support. If the author of this statement is a professional in his or her field, someone with a great deal of authority on the subject, it would be appropriate to quote that author. Suppose, during the course of your research for the zoo paper, you find that many sources agree that zoos don't have the money or space necessary to maintain large enough animal populations to ensure successful captive breeding programs. But so far you only have opinions to that effect. You have been unable to find any concrete documentation of this fact until you come across Ulysses S. Seal's address to the National Zoological Park Symposia for the Public, September 1982. Here is how you could use Seal's words in your paper:

> Bear in mind that "none of these [zoo] budgets is allocated specifically for species preservation. Zoos have been established primarily as recreational institutions and are only secondarily developing programs in conservation, education and research" (Seal 74).

Notice the use of brackets (not parentheses) in the first sentence, which enclose material that did not appear in the original source but is necessary for clarification. Brackets must be used to indicate any such changes in quoted material.

Quotations should be introduced logically and gracefully in your text. Make sure that the quoted material either supports or illustrates the point you have just made or the point you are about to make and that your writing remains grammmatically correct once the quotation is introduced.

Quotations are an important tool for establishing your claims, but it is important not to overuse them. If you cannot say most of what you want to say in your own words, you probably haven't thought hard enough about what it is you want to say.

Paraphrasing

Paraphrasing involves restating the content of an original source in your own words. It is most useful when the material from your source is too long for your paper, can be made clearer to the reader by rephrasing, or is written in a style markedly different from your own.

A paraphrase should be as true to the original source as you can make it: Do not change the tone or the ideas, or even the order in which the ideas are presented. Take care not to allow your own opinions to creep into your paraphrase of someone else's argument. Your readers should always be aware of which arguments belong to you and which belong to outside sources.

Like a quotation, a paraphrase must *always* include documentation, or you will be guilty of plagiarism. Even though you are using your own words, the ideas in a paraphrase belong to someone else, and that person deserves credit for them. One final caveat: When putting a long passage into your own words, beware of picking up certain expressions and turns of phrase from your source. If you do end up using your source's exact words, make sure to enclose them in quotation marks.

Below is a passage from Shannon Brownlee's "First It Was 'Save the Whales,' now it's 'Free the Dolphins'" (*Discover* Dec. 1986: 70–72), along with a good paraphrase of the passage and two unacceptable paraphrases.

ORIGINAL PASSAGE:

But are we being good caretakers by holding a dolphin or a sea lion in a tank? Yes, if two conditions are met: that they're given the best treatment possible and, no less important, that they're displayed in a way that educates and informs us. Captive animals must be allowed to serve as ambassadors for their species (72).

A PARAPHRASE THAT PLAGIARIZES:

In "First It Was 'Save the Whales,' Now It's 'Free the Dolphins,' " Shannon Brownlee argues that it's all right for people to hold animals in captivity as long as (1) the animals are treated as well as possible, and (2) the animals are displayed in a way that educates the public. Brownlee insists that animals be allowed to serve as "ambassadors for their species" (72).

A PARAPHRASE THAT ALTERS THE MEANING OF THE ORIGINAL PASSAGE:

According to Shannon Brownlee, a captive animal is being treated fairly as long as it's kept alive and its captivity gives people pleasure. In her essay, "First It Was 'Save the Whales,' Now It's 'Free the Dolphins,' " she argues that people who keep animals in cages are responsible to the animals in only two ways: (1) they should treat their captives as well as possible (even if a small tank is all that can be provided), and (2) they should make sure that the spectators enjoy watching them (72).

A GOOD PARAPHRASE:

Shannon Brownlee holds that two criteria are necessary in order for the captivity of wild animals to be considered worthwhile. First, the animals should be treated as well as possible. Second, their captivity should have educational value for the people who come to look at them. "Captive animals," Brownlee claims, "must be allowed to serve as ambassadors for their species" (72).

Summarizing

A summary is like a paraphrase, but it involves shortening the original passage as well as putting it in your own words. It gives the gist of the passage. Summarizing is useful when the material from your source is too long for the purposes of your paper. As with a paraphrase, a summary should not alter the meaning of the original passage.

In the paper at the end of this chapter, for instance, the statement, "It is generally acknowledged that there is a great deal of difficulty involved in breeding zoo animals" is not a direct quotation, but the idea comes from Jon Luoma's article in *Audubon*. The statement in the paper is both a summary and a paraphrase. Returning to the source makes it clear that neither quoting nor paraphrasing would have been suitable choices in this instance, since for the writer's purposes it was possible to reduce the following passage from Luoma's article to one sentence.

> But the successful propagation of entire captive species poses awesome management problems. . . . Sanford Friedman, the Minnesota Zoo's director of biological programs, had explained to me that long-term maintenance of a species in captivity demands solutions to these fundamental problems. "First, we have to learn *how* to breed them. Second, we have to decide *who* to breed. And third, we have to figure out *what* to do with them and their offspring once we've bred them."

This passage is far too long to include in a brief research paper, but it is easily summarized without losing any of its effectiveness.

Avoiding Plagiarism

Plagiarism is the use of someone else's words or ideas without adequate acknowledgment — that is, presenting such words or ideas as your own. Putting something in your own words is not in itself a defense against plagiarism; the source of the ideas must be identified as well. Giving credit to the sources you use serves three important purposes: (1) It reflects your own honesty and seriousness as a researcher; (2) it enables the reader to find the source of the reference and read further, sometimes to verify that the source has been correctly used; and (3) it adds the authority of experts to your argument. Deliberate plagiarism is nothing less than cheating and theft, and it is an offense that deserves serious punishment. Accidental plagiarism can be avoided if you take a little care when researching and writing your papers.

The writer of the zoo paper, for instance, uses and correctly introduces the following direct quotation by James Rachels:

> In his essay, "Do Animals Have a Right to Liberty?" James Rachels writes:
>
> > Humans have a right to liberty because they have various other interests that will suffer if their freedom is unduly restricted. The right to liberty--the right to be free of external constraints on one's actions--may then be seen as derived from a more basic right not to have one's interests needlessly harmed (210).

If the writer of the zoo paper had chosen to state this idea more briefly, in her own words, the result might have been something like this: "Human beings believe in their fundamental right to liberty because they all agree that they would suffer without it. The right to liberty, then, stems from the right not to suffer unnecessarily." Although the wording has been significantly altered, if this statement appeared as is, undocumented, the author of the paper would be guilty of plagiarism because the ideas are not original. To avoid plagiarism, the author needs to include a reference to James Rachels at the beginning of the summary and a citation of the page number at the end. Taking care to document sources is an obvious way to avoid plagiarism. You should also be careful in taking notes and, when writing your paper, in indicating where your ideas end and someone else's ideas begin.

When taking notes, make sure either to quote word-for-word *or* to paraphrase: one or the other, not a little bit of both. If you quote, enclose any language that you borrow from other sources in quotation marks. That way, when you look back at your note cards weeks later, you won't mistakenly assume that the language is your own. If you know that you aren't going to use a particular writer's exact words in your paper, then take the time to summarize that person's ideas right away. That will save you time and trouble later.

When using someone else's ideas in your paper, always let the reader know where that person's ideas begin and end. Here is an example from the zoo paper:

> When zoo animals do mate successfully, the offspring is often weakened by inbreeding. According to geneticists, this is because a population of 150 breeder animals is necessary in order to "assure the more or less permanent survival of a species in captivity" (Ehrlich 211).

The phrase "according to geneticists" indicates that the material to follow comes from another source, cited as "Ehrlich 211" at the end of the borrowed material. If the student had not included the phrase "according to geneticists," it might look as if she only borrowed the passage in quotation marks, and not the information that precedes that passage.

Material that is considered common knowledge — that is, familiar or at least accessible to the general public — does not have to be documented. The author of *Hamlet*, the date the Declaration of Independence was signed, or the definition of *misfeasance*, while open to dispute (some scholars, for example, claim that William Shakespeare did not write *Hamlet*) are indisputably considered to be common knowledge in our culture. Unfortunately, it is not always clear whether a particular fact *is* common knowledge. The author of the zoo paper, for instance, suspected it was *probably* safe to assume that everyone had heard of Hsing Hsing and Ling Ling, the National Zoo's giant pandas. Ultimately, however, she questioned her initial assumption and decided to provide documentation to be on the safe side. Although too much documentation can clutter a paper and distract the reader, it's still better to cite too many sources than to cite too few and risk being accused of dishonesty. In general, if you are unsure whether or not to give your source credit, you should document the material.

Keeping Research under Control

Your preliminary outline provides guideposts for your research. You will need to revise it as you go along to make room for new ideas and evidence and for the questions that come up as you read. Rather than try to fit each new piece of information into your outline, you can use the numbering or lettering system in your outline to cross-reference your notebooks or file cards.

As much as possible, keep all materials related to the same point in the same place. You might do this by making a separate pile of file cards for each point and its support and questions or by reserving several pages in your notebook for information bearing on each point.

How do you know when you have done enough research? If you have kept your outline updated, you have a visual record of your progress. Check this against the guidelines on pages 277–278: Is each point backed by at least two pieces of support? Do your sources represent a range of authors and of types of data? If a large proportion of your support comes from one book, or if most of your references are to newspaper articles, you probably need to keep working. On the other hand, if your notes cite five different authorities making essentially the same point, you may have collected more data than you need. It can be useful to point out that more than one authority holds a given view and to make notes of examples that are notably different from one another. But it is not necessary to take down all the passages or examples expressing the same idea.

To This Point

Before you leave the library or your primary sources for your typewriter, check to make sure your research is complete.

1. Does your working outline show any gaps in your argument?
2. Have you found adequate data to support your claim?
3. Have you identified the warrants linking your claim with data and ensured that these warrants too are adequately documented?
4. If you intend to quote or paraphrase sources in your paper, do your notes include exact copies of all statements you may want to use and complete references?
5. Have you answered all the relevant questions that have come up during your research?
6. Do you have enough information about your sources to document your paper?

MLA SYSTEM FOR CITING PUBLICATIONS

One of the simplest methods of crediting sources is the MLA in-text system, which is used in the research paper at the end of this chapter. In the text of your paper, immediately after any quotation, paraphrase, or anything else you wish to document, simply insert a parenthetical mention of the author's last name and the page number on which the material appeared. You don't need a comma after the author's name or an abbreviation of the word "page." For example, the following sentence appears in the zoo paper:

> It is generally acknowledged that there is a great deal of difficulty involved in breeding zoo animals (Luoma 104).

The parenthetical reference tells the reader that the information in this sentence came from page 104 of the book or article by Jon Luoma that appears in Works Cited, after the last page of the paper. The complete reference on the Works Cited page provides all the information readers need to refer to the original source:

> Luoma, Jon. "Prison or Ark?" Audubon Nov. 1982: 102-109.

If the author's name is mentioned in the same sentence, it is also acceptable to place only the page number in parentheses; it is not necessary to repeat the author's name. For example:

> As Luoma tells us, it is generally acknowledged that there is a great deal of difficulty involved in breeding zoo animals (104).

The list of works cited includes all material you have used to write your research paper. This list appears at the end of your paper and always starts on a new page. Center the title Works Cited, double-space between the title and the first entry, and begin your list, which should be arranged alphabetically by author. Each entry should start at the left margin; indent all subsequent lines of the entry five spaces. Number each page, and double-space throughout.

Following are examples of the citation forms you are most likely to need as you document your research. In general, for both books and magazines, information should appear in the following order: author, title, and publication information. Each item should be followed by a period. When using as a source an essay that appears in this book, follow the citation model for "Material reprinted from another source," unless your instructor indicates otherwise. Consult the third edition of the *MLA Handbook for Writers of Research Papers* by Joseph Gibaldi and Walter S. Achert (New York: Modern Language Association of America, 1988) for other documentation models and a list of acceptable shortened forms of publishers.

A BOOK BY A SINGLE AUTHOR

Kinder, Chuck. The Silver Ghost. New York: Harcourt, 1979.

AN ANTHOLOGY OR COMPILATION

Abrahams, William, ed. Prize Stories 1980: The O. Henry Awards. Garden City: Doubleday, 1980.

A BOOK BY TWO AUTHORS

Danzig, Richard, and Peter Szanton. National Service: What Would It Mean? Lexington: Lexington, 1986.

Note: This form is followed even for two authors with the same last name.

Ehrlich, Paul, and Anne Ehrlich. Extinction: The Causes and Consequences of the Disappearance of Species. New York: Random, 1981.

A BOOK BY TWO OR MORE AUTHORS

Heffernan, William A., Mark Johnston, and Frank Hodgins. Literature: Art and Artifact. San Diego: Harcourt, 1987.

If there are more than three authors, name only the first and add: "et al." (and others).

A BOOK BY A CORPORATE AUTHOR

Poets & Writers, Inc. The Writing Business: A Poets & Writers Handbook. New York: Poets & Writers, 1985.

A WORK IN AN ANTHOLOGY

Morton, Eugene S. "The Realities of Reintroducing Species to the Wild." Animal Extinctions: What Everyone Should Know. Ed. J. R. Hoage. National Zoological Park Symposia for the Public Series. Washington: Smithsonian Institution, 1985. 71-95.

AN INTRODUCTION, PREFACE, FOREWORD, OR AFTERWORD

Borges, Jorge Luis. Preface. New Islands. By Maria Luisa Bombal. Trans. Richard and Lucia Cunningham. New York: Farrar, 1982.

MATERIAL REPRINTED FROM ANOTHER SOURCE

Sullivan, Andrew. "Here Comes the Groom." The New Republic 28 Aug. 1989: 20-22. Rpt. in Elements of Argument: A Text and Reader. Ed. Annette T. Rottenberg. 3rd ed. New York: Bedford-St. Martin's, 1991. 164-68.

A MULTIVOLUME WORK

Skotheim, Robert Allen, and Michael McGiffert, eds. Since the Civil War. Vol. 2 of American Social Thought: Sources and Interpretations. 2 vols. Reading: Addison, 1972.

AN EDITION OTHER THAN THE FIRST

Cassill, R.V., ed. The Norton Anthology of Short Fiction, 2nd ed. New York: Norton, 1985.

A TRANSLATION

Allende, Isabel. The House of the Spirits. Trans. Magda Bogin. New York: Knopf, 1985.

A REPUBLISHED BOOK

Weesner, Theodore. The Car Thief. 1972. New York: Vintage-Random, 1987.

Note: The only information about original publication you need to provide is the publication date, which appears immediately after the title.

A BOOK IN A SERIES

Eady, Cornelius. Victims of the Latest Dance Craze. Omnation Press Dialogues on Dance Series 5. Chicago: Omnation, 1985.

ARTICLE FROM A DAILY NEWSPAPER

Dudar, Helen. "James Earl Jones at Bat." New York Times 22 Mar. 1987, sec. 2: 1+.

ARTICLE FROM A PERIODICAL

O'Brien, Conor Cruise. "God and Man in Nicaragua." Atlantic Monthly Aug. 1986: 50-72.

UNSIGNED EDITORIAL

"Medium, Message." Editorial. Nation 28 Mar. 1987: 383-84.

ARTICLE IN A JOURNAL WITH CONTINUOUS PAGINATION THROUGHOUT VOLUME

McCafferty, Janey. "The Shadders Go Away." New England Review and Bread Loaf Quarterly 9 (1987): 332-42.

Note that the issue number is not mentioned here; because the volume has continuous pagination throughout the year, only the volume number (9) is needed.

A REVIEW

Walker, David. Rev. of A Wave, by John Ashbery. Field 32 (1985): 63-71.

AN INTERVIEW

Hines, Gregory. Interview. With D. C. Denison. The Boston Globe Magazine 29 Mar. 1987: 2.

Note: An interview conducted by the author of the paper would be documented as follows:

Hines, Gregory. Personal interview. 29 Mar. 1987.

AN ARTICLE IN A REFERENCE WORK

"Bylina." The Princeton Encyclopedia of Poetry and Poetics. Ed. Alex Preminger. Enlarged ed. Princeton: Princeton UP, 1974.

APA SYSTEM FOR CITING PUBLICATIONS

Instructors in the social sciences might prefer the citation system of the American Psychological Association (APA). Like the MLA system, the APA system calls for parenthetical citation in the text of the paper. Unlike the MLA system, the APA system includes the year of publication in the parenthetical reference. Here is an example:

> Even though many South American countries rely on the drug trade for their economic survival, the majority of South Americans disapprove of drug use (Gorriti, 1989, 72).

The complete publication information for Gorriti's article will appear at the end of your paper, on a page titled "References." (Sample citations for the "References" page appear below.)

If your list of references includes more than one work written by the same author in the same year, cite the first work as *a* and the second as *b*. For example, Gorriti's second article of 1989 would be cited in your paper as (Gorriti, 1989b).

Following are examples of the citation forms you are most likely to use. If you need the format for a type of publication not listed here, consult the third edition of the *Publication Manual of the American Psychological Association* (1983).

A BOOK BY A SINGLE AUTHOR

Briggs, J. (1988). Fire in the crucible: The alchemy of creative genius. New York: St. Martin's Press.

AN ANTHOLOGY OR COMPILATION

Gioseffi, D. (Ed.). (1988). Women on war. New York: Simon & Schuster.

A BOOK BY TWO OR MORE AUTHORS OR EDITORS

Colombo, G., Cullen, R., & Lisle, B. (Eds.). (1989). Rereading America: Cultural contexts for critical thinking and writing. New York: Bedford Books/St. Martin's Press.

Note: List the names of *all* the authors or editors, no matter how many.

A BOOK BY A CORPORATE AUTHOR

International Advertising Association. (1977). *Controversy advertising: How advertisers present points of view on public affairs*. New York: Hastings House.

WORK IN AN ANTHOLOGY

Mukherjee, B. (1988). The colonization of the mind. In Gioseffi, D. (Ed.). *Women on war* (pp. 140-142). New York: Simon & Schuster.

AN INTRODUCTION, PREFACE, FOREWORD, OR AFTERWORD

Hemenway, R. (1984). Introduction. In Z. N. Hurston, *Dust tracks on a road*. Urbana: University of Illinois Press, ix-xxxix.

AN EDITION OTHER THAN THE FIRST

Gumpert, G., & Cathcart, R. (Eds.). (1986). *Inter/media: Interpersonal communication in a media world*. (3rd ed.). New York: Oxford University Press.

A TRANSLATION

Sartre, J. P. (1962). *Literature and existentialism*. (B. Frechtman, Trans.) New York: Citadel Press. (Original work published 1949).

A REPUBLISHED BOOK

James, W. (1969). *The varieties of religious experience: A study in human nature*. London: Collier Books. (Original work published 1961).

A BOOK IN A SERIES

Berthrong, D. J. (1976). *The Cheyenne and Arapaho ordeal: Reservation and agency life in the Indian territory, 1875-1907. Vol. 136 The civilization of the American Indian series*. Norman: University of Oklahoma Press.

ARTICLE FROM A DAILY NEWSPAPER

Hottelet, R. C. (1990, March 15). Germany: Why it can't happen again. Christian Science Monitor, p. 19.

ARTICLE FROM A PERIODICAL

Gorriti, G. A. (1989, July). How to fight the drug war. Atlantic Monthly, pp. 70-76.

ARTICLE IN A JOURNAL WITH CONTINUOUS PAGINATION THROUGHOUT VOLUME

Cockburn, A. (1989). British justice, Irish victims. The Nation, 249, 554-555.

GOVERNMENT PUBLICATION

United States. Dept. of Health, Education, and Welfare. (1973). Current ethical issues in mental health. Washington, DC: U.S. Government Printing Office.

A PERSONAL INTERVIEW

Wagner, Helen. Personal Interview. April 7, 1990.

Note: The name that appears is the name of the person interviewed.

A SAMPLE RESEARCH PAPER

The following paper urges a change in our attitudes toward zoos. Arguing the value claim that it is morally wrong for humans to exploit animals for our own selfish entertainment, the student writer deftly combines expert opinion gathered through research with her own thoughtful interpretations of evidence. Throughout she is careful to anticipate and represent the claims of the opposition before going on to refute them point by point. Although we may not ultimately accept her recommendations, we are likely to find ourselves unable to look at animals in cages as pleasurably, or as indifferently, as we did before reading her paper.

The paper uses the MLA citation system.

1″

Amanda Repp

Professor Kennedy

English 2-G

April 6, 1987

Double space

Why We Don't Need Zoos

Sensible, descriptive title prepares readers for the paper's topic

Zoos have come a long way from their grim beginnings. Once full of tiny cement-block cages lined with steel bars, the larger zoos now boast simulated jungles, veldts, steppes, and rain forests, all in an attempt to replicate the animals' natural habitat. The attempt is admirable, but it's not enough. No amount of replication, no matter how convincing, is enough to make up for denying these creatures their freedom.

First paragraph eases readers into the thesis

Thesis at end of first paragraph

1″

These cosmetic changes skirt the real issue at hand: Namely, that it is morally wrong to keep wild animals in captivity. "A wild animal's life is spent in finding food, avoiding enemies, sleeping, and in mating or other family activities," writes Peter Batten in his book, Living Trophies. "Intelligent people are aware that deprivation of any of these fundamentals results in irreparable damage to the individual" (1). The argument is simple: The fact that we are stronger or smarter than animals does not give us the right to ambush and exploit them solely for the purposes of our own entertainment.

A quotation with the author's name cited in the text and the page number in parentheses

We humans take our own freedom quite seriously. Indeed, we consider liberty one of our inalienable rights. But too many of us apparently feel no obligation to grant that same right to animals, who,

1″

Repp 2

because they have no defense against our sophisticated methods of capture, and because they do not speak our language, cannot claim it for themselves.

But the right to liberty is not based on the ability to claim it, or even on the ability to understand what it is. In his essay, "Do Animals Have a Right to Liberty?" James Rachels writes:

Long quotation begins on a new line and is indented

> Humans have a right to liberty because they have various other interests that will suffer if their freedom is unduly restricted. The right to liberty--the right to be free of external constraints on one's actions--may then be seen as derived from a more basic right not to have one's interests needlessly harmed (210).

We do not <u>need</u> to look at animals in a zoo. And animals have interests that are harmed if they are kept in captivity: They are separated from their families and prevented from behaving according to their natural instincts by being removed from the lives they know, which are the lives they were meant to lead.

Summary of an opposing argument

There are those who argue that animals' interests are <u>not</u> being harmed when they're kept in a zoo or an aquarium; that, contrary to Mr. Batten's claim, no damage at all is being done to the individual. Dr. Heini Hediger of the Zurich Zoo, for instance, protests "the absurdity of attributing human qualities to animals" at all. Hediger

Direct quotation worked into the text of the paper

Repp 3

Student's name and page number

claims: "Wild animals in the zoo rather resemble estate owners. Far from desiring to escape and regain their freedom, they are only bent on defending the space they inhabit and keeping it safe from invasion" (9).

Refutation of Hediger's argument

But if Dr. Hediger is right, how can he explain the leopards and cheetahs I have seen executing figure eights off the walls and floors of their cages for hours on end? I have watched this performance countless times, spellbound by the beauty and grace of the huge cat leaping from one wall of his cage to the floor to the opposite wall, turning in midair only to spring from the floor to the far wall again and again. I have watched spellbound, but also horrified; it is impossible for me to believe that this animal doesn't want his freedom. An estate owner would not spend his time running frantically around the perimeters of his property. This cat knows he's not lord of any estate. The senseless repetition of his action suggests he knows that he is caged, and that there's no one to defend his space against, and that there will be no intrusion --for he is caged alone.

Evidence from personal experience

Shannon Brownlee, in "First It Was 'Save the Whales,' Now It's 'Free the Dolphins' " (264), also believes that there is no concrete evidence that animals in captivity are suffering or unhappy. But she weakens her own case by describing Jackie as a dolphin who "spends the day in a seeming stupor" and "chews on the mackerel half-heartedly" at

Summary of a second opposing argument

Student points out a weakness in Brownlee's argument

Repp 4

feeding time. Clearly there <u>is</u> something wrong with Jackie; this becomes apparent when Brownlee contrasts Jackie's behavior with that of the wild dolphins in the bay, who are "leaping, chasing fish, riding the bow waves of boats, scrapping with each other, having sex (a favorite activity among this species)."

Student questions an unstated warrant in Brownlee's argument

The author points out that although Jackie knows there is a hole in his enclosure, he has never tried to leave. The fact that Jackie doesn't try to escape is not necessarily an indication that he likes it where he is. It is more likely a manifestation of a broken spirit (the most important, and admittedly least tangible, result of keeping an animal in captivity), possessed by an animal who either no longer remembers, or no longer cares, what his earlier days were like. Granted we have no way of knowing what this animal is really feeling, but does that give us the right to <u>assume</u> that he isn't feeling anything?

Analogy

In all fairness to Brownlee, she doesn't go quite that far. The author allows Jackie one emotional state: She attributes Jackie's malaise to the fact that he's "just bored." But the adjective "just" belies Brownlee's sensitivity to Jackie's plight. Perhaps if the author were removed from all members of her family, as well as all other members of her species, and prevented from engaging in the activities that most mattered to her, she would recognize Jackie's problems as something more than boredom. And even if Jackie were "just bored," any human knows that boredom can be a very depressing state. Why should we inflict that experience on Jackie, or any other animal, just because we happen to have the means to do so?

Having registered my basic objections to zoos --that keeping any creature in captivity is a fundamental infringement on that creature's right to liberty and dignity--I want to take a closer look at the zoo as an institution, in order to fairly assess its goals and how it tries to meet them. Most zoo professionals today maintain that zoos exist for two main reasons: to educate humans and to conserve animal species. These are both admirable goals, certainly, but "none of these [zoo] budgets is allocated specifically for species preservation. Zoos have been established primarily as recreational institutions and are only secondarily developing programs in conservation, education and research" (Seal 74). The fact is, most zoos don't have the money, space, or equipment required to make significant contributions in these areas. The bulk of their money goes to the upkeep of the animals and exhibits--that is, to put it crudely, to the displays.

Student shifts to the second half of her argument

Clarifier in brackets

On behalf of the education a zoo provides, a common argument is that there's nothing like seeing the real thing. But what you see in the zoo is not the real thing at all. Many zoo and aquarium animals, like Jackie the dolphin, have been domesti-

Another opposing argument, with refutation

Repp 6

cated to the point of lethargy, in large part because they are being exhibited alone or with only one other member of their species, when what they are used to is traveling in groups and finding their own food, instead of being fed. Anyone who wants to see the real thing would be better off watching some of the excellent programming about nature and wildlife that appears on public television.

Summaries of two experts' arguments that zoos do not help preserve endangered species

As for conservation, it is clearly a worthwhile effort, but representing zoos as being front-runners in this field is quite misleading. It is generally acknowledged that there is a great deal of difficulty involved in breeding zoo animals (Luoma 104). They often don't reproduce at all--quite possibly because of the artificial, and consequently unsettling, circumstances in which they live. One of the most publicized instances of this problem involved the National Zoo's repeatedly unsuccessful attempt to mate the giant pandas Hsing Hsing and Ling Ling. After five years, the keepers finally resorted to artificial insemination (Ehrlich 211).

When zoo animals do mate successfully, the offspring is often weakened by inbreeding. According to geneticists, this is because a population of 150 breeder animals is necessary in order to "assure the more or less permanent survival of a species in captivity" (Ehrlich 211). Few zoos have the resources to maintain populations that size. When zoos rely on smaller populations for breeding (as many do), the species' gene pool becomes more

Repp 7

and more limited, "vigor and fecundity tend to decline" (Ehrlich 212), and this can eventually lead to extinction. In other words, we aren't doing these animals any favors by trying to conserve them in zoos. Reserves and preservations, which have room for the larger populations necessary for successful conservation efforts and which can concentrate on breeding animals rather than on displaying them, are much more suitable for these purposes.

For what purposes, then, are zoos suitable? Are they even necessary? For the time being, they must house the many generations of animals that have been bred there, since these animals have no place else to go. Most animals in captivity cannot go back to the wild for one of two reasons. The first is that the creatures would be unable to survive there, since their instincts for finding their own food and protecting themselves from predators, or even the weather, have been greatly diminished during their time spent in captivity (Morton 155). Perhaps this is why Jackie the dolphin chooses to remain in his enclosure.

Paraphrase with source cited in parentheses

The other reason animals can't return to the wild is an even sadder one: In many cases, their natural habitats are no longer there. Thanks to deforesting and clearing of land for homes, highways, factories, and shopping malls--which are continually being built with no regard for the plant and animal life around them--ecosystems are destroyed constantly, driving increasing numbers of

Repp 8

species from their homes. Air and water pollution and toxic waste, results of the ever-increasing urbanization and industrialization throughout the world, are just some of the agents of this damning change. It is this problem I wish to address in closing.

Student closes by proposing a solution of her own

If zoos were to leave breeding programs to more appropriate organizations and to stop collecting animals, the zoo as an institution would eventually be phased out. Animals would cease to be exhibits and could resume being animals, and the money previously used to run zoos could be put to much better use. Ideally it would be used to help investigate the reasons endangered species _are_ endangered, and why so many of the original habitats of these species _have_ disappeared. Most importantly, it could be used to explore how we can change our habits and reorient our behavior, attitudes, and priorities, so we can begin to address these issues.

The problem of endangered species does not exist in a vacuum; it is a symptom of a much greater predicament. Humankind is responsible for this predicament, and it is up to us to recognize this before it's too late. Saving a selected species here and there will do none of us any good if those species can only exist in isolated, artificial environments, where they will eventually breed themselves into extinction. The money that has been concentrated on such efforts should be devoted instead to educating the public about the endangered

Repp 9

planet--not just its animals--or, like the animals, none of us will have any place to go.

Works Cited

Batten, Peter. Living Trophies. New York: Crowell, 1976.

Brownlee, Shannon. "First It Was 'Save the Whales,' Now It's 'Free the Dolphins.' " Discover Dec. 1986: 70-72.

Ehrlich, Paul, and Anne Ehrlich. Extinction: The Causes and Consequences of the Disappearance of Species. New York: Random, 1981.

Hediger, Heini. "From Cage to Territory." The World of Zoos; A Survey and Gazetteer. Ed. Dr. Rosl Kirchschofer. New York: Viking, 1968. 9-20.

Luoma, Jon. "Prison or Ark?" Audubon Nov. 1982: 102-109.

Morton, Eugene S. "The Realities of Reintroducing Species to the Wild." Animal Extinctions: What Everyone Should Know. Ed. J. R. Hoage. National Zoological Park Symposia for the Public Series. Washington: Smithsonian Institution, 1985. 71-95.

Rachels, James. "Do Animals Have a Right to Liberty?" Animal Rights and Human Obligations. Eds. Tom Regan and Peter Singer. Englewood Cliffs: Prentice, 1976. 205-23.

Indent five spaces

A book with two authors

A work in an anthology

An article from a periodical

Publisher's name is abbreviated

Repp 10

Seal, Ulysses S. "The Realities of Preserving Species in Captivity." Animal Extinctions: What Everyone Should Know. Ed. J. R. Hoage. National Zoological Park Symposia for the Public Series. Washington: Smithsonian Institution, 1985. 147-58.

PART THREE

OPPOSING VIEWPOINTS

THE FOLLOWING SECTION contains a variety of opposing viewpoints on nine controversial questions. These questions generate conflict among experts and laypeople alike for two principal reasons. First, even when the facts are not in dispute, they may be interpreted differently by opposing sides. Example: Do the statistics prove that capital punishment is or is not a deterrent to crime? Second, and certainly more difficult to resolve, equally worthwhile values may be in conflict. Example: In dealing with harmful substances, should we decide in favor of the freedom of the individual to choose or the responsibility of the government to protect?

"Opposing Viewpoints" lends itself to classroom debates, both formal and informal. It can also serve as a useful source of informed opinions which can lead to further research. First, read all of the articles in one of the "Opposing Viewpoints." Then select a topic for your research paper, either one suggested in this book (see "Topics for Research" at the end of each chapter) or another approved by your teacher. You may wish to begin your research by choosing material to support your claim from two or three articles in the text.

In reading, analyzing, and preparing your own responses to the opposing viewpoints, you should ask the following questions about each controversy:

1. Are there two — or more — different points of view on the subject? Do both sides make clear what they are trying to prove? Summarize their claims.
2. Do both sides share the same goals? If not, how are they different?
3. How important is definition of key terms? Do both sides agree on the definitions? If so, what are they? If not, how do they differ? Does definition become a significant issue in the controversy?
4. How important is factual and opinion evidence in support of the claims? Does the support fulfill the appropriate criteria? If not, what are its weaknesses? Is the support conflicting? Do the authorities — both the arguers and the experts they quote — have convincing credentials?
5. Do the arguers base any part of their arguments on needs and values that their readers are expected to share? What are they? Do the arguers provide examples of the ways these values

function? Are these values implicit or explicit in the arguments? Is there a conflict of values? If so, which seem more important?

6. What warrants or assumptions underlie the claims? Are they implicit or explicit? Do the arguers examine them for the reader? Are the warrants acceptable? If not, point out their weaknesses.
7. What are the main issues? Is there a genuine debate — that is, does each side try to respond to arguments on the other side?
8. Do the arguers propose solutions to a problem? Are the advantages of their proposals clear? Are there obvious disadvantages to implementation of their solutions?
9. Does each argument follow a clear and orderly organization, one that lends itself to a good outline? If not, what are the weaknesses?
10. Does language play a part in the argument? Are there any examples of misuse of language — slanted or loaded words, clichés, slogans, euphemisms, or other short cuts?
11. Do the arguers show an awareness of audience? How would you describe the audience(s) for whom the various arguments are presented?
12. Do you think that one side won the argument? Explain your answer in detail.

CHAPTER 10

Abortion

In 1973 the Supreme Court of the United States ruled that a woman's right to an abortion is protected by the Constitution. This decision, *Roe v. Wade*, did not, however, put an end to the controversy over the morality — or the legality — of this right. In the intervening years probably no social issue has ignited so much passion and political activity on both sides. In 1989 (*Webster v. Reproductive Health Services, Inc.*) the Supreme Court voted to allow state legislatures to restrict abortion by imposing limits on the circumstances under which abortion might be performed. Although most Americans favor a woman's right to an abortion, they also favor new legal restrictions on that right — for example, a denial of abortions after viability of the fetus has been established. In other words, abortion should be available but harder to get.

In the argument about the morality of abortion, the definition of the fetus, whether or not it is a child entitled to all the rights of a human being, remains crucial. But other, equally divisive issues have arisen on which the courts will rule. One is the question of parental consent for an abortion for a girl under eighteen years of age. According to one poll, 71 percent of those interviewed favor such a restriction, and several states have already enacted legislation requiring consent. Other states require only notification or the consent of a judge. In June 1990 the Supreme Court ruled that states may require a pregnant girl to notify at least one parent before having an abortion as long as the law also provides the alternative of a judicial hearing. Another issue concerns the rights of prospective fathers to prohibit an abortion. One judge has ruled in favor of the father, likening the argument to a battle over custody rights. In addition, many Americans who are not morally opposed to abortion do, however, object to public funding of abortion.

Opponents are now grouping for another battle, which may change the struggle in still unforeseen ways. This new struggle will be centered on the proposed introduction of an abortion pill that will eliminate the need for a surgical procedure in suitable cases.

Is Abortion Ever Equal to Murder?

HOWARD H. HIATT and CYRUS LEVINTHAL

1 When does life begin? That value-laden question will come to the forefront of the abortion debate this year, when the Supreme Court is scheduled to take up the case of *Webster v. Reproductive Health Services.*

2 That case concerns a 1986 Missouri anti-abortion law that declared in its preamble that the "life of each human being begins at conception." In large part, the outcome of *Webster* will hinge on what the Court decides about that assertion. Let's consider some of its implications.

3 After penetration of the egg by the sperm, the DNA of the egg and the sperm join to form the chromosomes of the fertilized egg, which then begins to divide. As many as half of the fertilized eggs have chromosomal anomalies that will cause them to abort spontaneously early in pregnancy. Some anomalies, such as Down's syndrome, do not always lead to spontaneous abortion. The Down's chromosome can be recognized within weeks of conception, permitting parents to decide whether to abort the defective fetus.

4 Some would preclude this option by endowing a fertilized egg with full legal rights. At the other extreme are a few who deny that even a fully developed fetus just before birth is entitled to full protection. Most pro-choice advocates feel that full rights exist at some time between conception and birth. But when?

5 Before looking at the possibilities, it helps to think about when life ends. Consider the following.

6 A two-week-old infant is hospitalized with massive brain injury

---

Howard H. Hiatt is a professor of medicine at Harvard Medical School. Cyrus Levinthal is a professor of biology at Columbia University. Their article appeared in the *New York Times* on February 18, 1989.

suffered in an automobile accident. Despite heroic measures, no electrical or other brain activity can be detected during the next two days and he is pronounced dead.

But life for his body parts may continue after his death, as after the death of every person of whatever age. Hair and nails will grow for days. Kidneys, heart, liver, and other organs may go on living for years if transplanted into another individual. Cells taken soon after death and cultured in a laboratory might live well beyond the seventy-two or more years this infant might have lived. But the life of the infant has ended. The conclusion reached in this case — that death of the brain means the end of life — is generally accepted by physicians, courts, and the public. 7

Returning to the question of when life begins, it is true that the DNA of the fertilized egg has the information necessary to form an individual. But so does virtually every other cell in the body. And nobody would claim full rights for the living cells of the infant killed in the accident, although each has a complete library of DNA. Nor would they for the thousands of living skin cells we lose every time we wash our hands and faces. 8

Is there some stage in the development of the brain that is critical? Or is it the time at which the fetus can survive outside the womb, either unassisted or with the full support of medical technology? Or should we revert to a criterion used for many years, the time of quickening, when one can feel the fetus moving? 9

Since none of these criteria can be considered a scientific basis for when life begins, the courts are asked to decide when the products of conception should be endowed with rights. As one considers the relative rights of the pregnant woman and the fetus, three propositions seem reasonable. First, the rights of the fetus for some time before birth are no less than those of the infant immediately following. A fetus born prematurely, as early as the twenty-fourth week, may survive. Technology could shorten that period further. Therefore, thinking should be flexible about what constitutes the period of viability. 10

Second, as the Supreme Court ruled in the landmark *Roe v. Wade* case of 1973, there is no justification for state interference with the rights of pregnant women in the first three months of a pregnancy, when brain development is still primitive. 11

Third, after about three months, there should be a gradual increase in fetal rights relative to the rights of the pregnant woman. Some women will choose to bear, for example, a deformed or diseased infant, but others will not. Most will likely wish to terminate pregnancies that result from rape or incest. 12

In pregnancies beyond three months, the woman considering abortion might turn for advice to groups similar to the multidisciplinary committees that now exist in many hospitals to help advise patients on ethical matters. 13

The assertion that life begins at conception can be made only on religious, not medical, grounds. No one can prove that the soul does not enter the egg with the DNA from the sperm. However, just as life ends with brain death, so a strong case can be made that human awareness and consciousness emerge only when the brain is well on the way to full development. Since the question of when that occurs cannot now be answered by science or, under our Constitution, by religion, we believe that for abortion decisions in the latter part of pregnancy, the courts should give the states leeway to set guidelines. 14

Abortion Is Not a Civil Right

GREG KEATH

The battle around the abortion issue has raged for years with the understanding that the major combatants involved are either white liberals, white evangelical Protestants, or white Catholics. Meanwhile, black America — which is affected more profoundly by abortion than is any other group in society — has experienced its own sharp internal division. While most black leaders have favored abortion rights, opinion surveys have found mainstream blacks to be among those most strongly opposed to abortion on demand. 1

Where does black America really stand on the issue? Statistics from the Department of Health and Human Services suggest that black women are more than twice as likely to abort their children as white women. For every three black babies born, two are aborted. Forty-three percent of all abortions in the United States are performed on black women. From figures supplied by the federal government and the Alan Guttmacher Institute, Richard D. Glasow of National Right to Life has estimated that some 400,000 black pregnancies are aborted each year. At the same time, according to a 1988 poll taken by the National Opinion Research Center, 62 percent of blacks said abortion should be illegal under all circumstances. 2

How can blacks consistently tell pollsters they oppose abortion while we exercise that right proportionately more than any other group in America? In part, black abortion rates reflect the pressure of social service and private welfare agencies in our communities. A black teenager told me she had asked Planned Parenthood in Detroit for help in carrying 3

Greg Keath is the founder and president of Black Alliance for Family. His argument is from the September 27, 1989 issue of the *Wall Street Journal.*

her baby to term and putting it up for adoption. But because the baby's father was white, a clinician advised her to abort the baby because, "No one wants to adopt a zebra." Better-educated black women are pushed toward abortion by different forces: the threat to educational hopes or aspirations to economic independence.

As these women struggle with their profound moral choices, many national black leaders have ceased to look at abortion as a moral problem with moral consequences, and have come to see it instead as an opportunity for forging political alliances. At the March for Life rally in 1977 Jesse Jackson said, "The solution to a [crisis pregnancy] is not to kill the innocent baby but to deal with [the mother's] values and her attitudes toward life." Twelve years later, he spoke to the enormous April 1989 abortion rights march in Washington. 4

The black leadership has succumbed to the temptation to present abortion as a civil-rights issue. By this reasoning, abortion is to women in the 1980s what desegregation was to blacks in the 1960s. Any erosion of abortion rights would accelerate the "move to the right" that black leaders say threatens black progress. At a news conference earlier this year sponsored by Planned Parenthood, Jesse Jackson, Andrew Young, and Julian Bond issued a statement denouncing Operation Rescue, comparing those who participate in abortion clinic sit-ins to "the segregationists who fought desperately to block black Americans from access to their rights." 5

But many blacks wonder whether black civil rights and abortion fit so neatly together. Black pregnancies have historically been the target of social engineers such as Margaret Sanger, founder of Planned Parenthood. Sanger was convinced that blacks, Jews, Eastern Europeans, and other non-Aryan groups were detracting from the creative intellectual and social potential of America, and she wanted those groups' numbers reduced. In her first book, *Pivot of Civilization*, she warned of free maternity care for the poor: "Instead of decreasing and aiming to eliminate the stocks that are most detrimental to the future of the race and the world it tends to render them to a menacing degree dominant." 6

In the late 1930s Sanger instituted the Negro Project, a program to gain the backing of black ministers, physicians, and political leaders for birth control and sterilization in the black community. Sanger wrote, "The most successful education approach to the Negro is through a religious appeal. We do not want word to go out that we want to exterminate the Negro population, and the minister is the man who can straighten out that idea if it ever occurs to any of their more rebellious members." 7

There are disturbing indications that this state of mind has not vanished. Even now, 70 percent of the clinics operated by Planned Parenthood — the operator of the largest chain of abortion facilities in the nation — are in black and Hispanic neighborhoods. The schools in which their school-based clinics are located are substantially nonwhite. In a March 8

1939 letter, Sanger explained why clinics had to be located where the "dysgenic" races lived: "The birth control clinics all over the country are doing their utmost to reach the lower strata of our population . . . but we must realize that there are hundreds of thousands of women who never leave their own vicinity."

Blacks must no longer keep silent on this issue. We cannot permit the 9
public to continue to imagine that we are obediently following our national leaders in endorsing abortion on demand and we must resist the forces that drive black women to seek abortion. The black community in cities such as Baltimore, Chicago, Detroit, and Washington, D.C., has started crisis pregnancy centers to help these women. We are already besieged by homicide, drugs, AIDS, and an alarmingly high infant mortality rate. We do not need to reenact the sterilization programs of the 1930s and 1940s.

Nine Reasons Why Abortions Are Legal

PLANNED PARENTHOOD

I wonder if young women today can fully identify with the situation only two decades ago. When I was a young doctor at a New York hospital, there would scarcely be a week go by that some woman wouldn't be brought to the emergency room near death from an illegal abortion. I saw some wonderful women die, and others reproductively crippled. Then, I too became pregnant, by accident, and though I was a doctor I could not ask any other doctor for help. In those days, if known, it would have cost us both our jobs. So I drove secretly to a Pennsylvania coal-mining town and was led to a secret location. I was lucky. I wasn't injured. But I'm so glad that times have changed. I have five daughters and a son now. I hope they never have to make the agonizing decision about abortion, but if they do, I would hate for them to have to act like criminals and to risk their lives to do what they feel is right for their future.

Elaine Shaw, M.D., San Francisco, California

I have been married for thirty-five years. I'm the mother of five children, grandmother of three. In the mid-1950s I was brutally raped and left for dead. I later discovered I was pregnant. I was horrified. I would not have that child. Our family doctor couldn't help. An abortion could have cost him and me twenty years in prison. I tried home remedies—like scalding

---

This advertisement from Planned Parenthood, a national pro-choice organization, appeared in the *New York Times* on October 17, 1988.

myself and falling down stairs—but they didn't work. Finally I found a local abortionist. I will always remember walking up those dark stairs. The incredible filth. The man had a whiskey glass in one hand and a knife in the other. The pain was the worst I have ever felt, but the humiliation was even worse. Hemorrhaging and hospitalization followed. I thought I would never be with my family again. I had no choice, but I resent what I had to go through to terminate that pregnancy. And I resent the people who now say that women should be forced to endure such experiences.

Sherry Matulis, Peoria, Illinois

Abortion is never an easy decision, but women have been making 1 that choice for thousands of years, for many good reasons. Whenever a society has sought to outlaw abortions, it has only driven them into back alleys where they became dangerous, expensive, and humiliating. Amazingly, this was the case in the United States until 1973 when abortion was legalized nationwide. Thousands of American women died. Thousands more were maimed. For this reason and others, women and men fought for and achieved women's legal right to make their own decisions about abortion.

However, there are people in our society who still won't accept this. 2 Some argue that even the victims of rape or incest should be forced to bear the child. And now, having failed to convince the public or the lawmakers, certain of these people have become violent extremists, engaging in a campaign of intimidation and terror aimed at women seeking abortions and the health professionals who work at family planning clinics.

Some say these acts will stop abortions, but that is ridiculous. When 3 the smoke clears, the same urgent reasons will exist for safe, legal abortions as have always existed. No nation committed to individual liberty could seriously consider returning to the days of back alley abortions; to the revolting specter of a government forcing women to bear children against their will. Still, amid such attacks, it is worthwhile to repeat a few of the reasons *why* our society trusts each woman to make the abortion decision herself.

1. Laws Against Abortion Kill Women

To prohibit abortions does not stop them. When women feel it is ab- 4 solutely necessary, they will choose to have abortions, even in secret, without medical care, in dangerous circumstances. In the two decades before abortion was legal in the United States it's been estimated that *nearly a million women per year* sought out illegal abortions. Thousands died. Tens of thousands were mutilated. All were forced to behave as if they were criminals.

2. Legal Abortions Protect Women's Health

Legal abortion not only protects women's lives, it also protects their 5
health. For tens of thousands of women with heart disease, kidney disease, severe hypertension, sickle-cell anemia, severe diabetes, and other illnesses that can be life-threatening, the availability of legal abortion has helped avert serious medical complications that could have resulted from childbirth. Before legal abortion, such women's choices were limited to dangerous illegal abortion or dangerous childbirth.

3. A Woman Is More than a Fetus

There's an argument these days that a fetus is a "person" that is "in- 6
distinguishable from the rest of us" and that it deserves rights equal to women's. On this question there is a tremendous spectrum of religious, philosophical, scientific, and medical opinion. It's been argued for centuries. Fortunately, our society has recognized that each woman must be able to make this decision, based on her own conscience. To impose a law defining a fetus as a "person," granting it rights equal to or superior to a woman's — a thinking, feeling conscious human being — is arrogant and absurd. It only serves to diminish women.

4. Being a Mother Is Just One Option for Women

Many hard battles have been fought to win political and economic 7
equality for women. These gains will not be worth much if reproductive choice is denied. To be able to choose a safe, legal abortion makes many other options possible. Otherwise an accident or a rape can end a woman's economic and personal freedom.

5. Outlawing Abortion Is Discriminatory

Anti-abortion laws discriminate against low-income women, who are 8
driven to dangerous self-induced or back-alley abortions. That is all they can afford. But the rich can travel wherever necessary to obtain a safe abortion.

6. Compulsory Pregnancy Laws Are Incompatible with a Free Society

If there is any matter which is personal and private, then pregnancy 9
is it. There can be no more extreme invasion of privacy than requiring a woman to carry an unwanted pregnancy to term. If government is per-

mitted to compel a woman to bear a child, where will government stop? The concept is morally repugnant. It violates traditional American ideas of individual rights and freedoms.

7. Outlaw Abortion, and More Children Will Bear Children

Forty percent of fourteen-year-old girls will become pregnant before they turn twenty. This could happen to your daughter or someone else close to you. Here are the critical questions: Should the penalty for lack of knowledge or even for a moment's carelessness be enforced pregnancy and child-rearing? Or dangerous illegal abortion? Should we consign a teenager to a life sentence of joblessness, hopelessness, and dependency? 10

8. "Every Child a Wanted Child."

If women are forced to carry unwanted pregnancies to term, the result is unwanted children. Everyone knows they are among society's most tragic cases, often uncared for, unloved, brutalized, and abandoned. When they grow up, these children are often seriously disadvantaged, and sometimes inclined toward brutal behavior to others. This is not good for children, for families, or for the country. Children need love and families who want and will care for them. 11

9. Choice Is Good for Families

Even when precautions are taken, accidents can and do happen. For some families, this is not a problem. But for others, such an event can be catastrophic. An unintended pregnancy can increase tensions, disrupt stability, and push people below the line of economic survival. *Family planning* is the answer. All options must be open. 12

Bombings and Harrassment

There has been a growing number of arsons and bombings at family planning and abortion clinics as the anti-abortion extremists escalate their campaign of intimidation and terror: Since 1977, over one hundred clinic bombings, arsons, and attempts have occurred. Just as insidious is the harassment inflicted on women attempting to enter these clinics. 13

At the most basic level, the abortion issue is not really about abortion. It is about the value of women in society. Should women make their own decisions about family, career, and how to live their lives? Or should gov- 14 ernment do that for them? Do women have the option of deciding when or whether to have children? Or is *that* a government decision?

The anti-abortion leaders really have a larger purpose. They oppose 15
most ideas and programs which can help women achieve equality and freedom. They also oppose programs which protect the health and well-being of women *and* their children.

Anti-abortion leaders claim to act "in defense of life." If so, why have 16
they worked to destroy programs which *serve* life, including prenatal care and nutrition programs for dependent pregnant women? Is this respect for life?

Anti-abortion leaders also say they are trying to save children, but 17
they have fought against health and nutrition programs for children once they are born. The anti-abortion groups seem to believe life begins at conception, but it ends at birth. Is this respect for life?

Then there are programs which diminish the number of unwanted 18
pregnancies *before* they occur: family planning counseling, sex education, and contraception for those who wish it. Anti-abortion leaders oppose those too. And clinics providing such services have been bombed. Is this respect for life?

Such stances reveal the ultimate cynicism of the compulsory preg- 19
nancy movement. "Life" is not what they're fighting for. What they want is a return to the days when a woman had few choices in controlling her future. They think that the abortion option gives too much freedom. That even contraception is too liberating. That women cannot be trusted to make their own decisions.

Americans today don't accept that. Women can now select their own 20
paths in society, including when and whether to have children. Family planning, contraception and, if need be, legal abortion are critical to sustaining women's freedom. There is no going back.

If you agree with this, you can help. Circulate this statement among 21
your friends, and support our work by contacting Planned Parenthood in your area. Thank you.

Public Shouldn't Pay

E. L. PATTULLO

To the Editor:

In "Bush and the Zealots" (column, October 19), Anthony Lewis can find no moral basis on which George Bush can deny "the right" to abortion "to poor victims of violence," while allowing it for others. The President denies nothing to the poor that he would grant to the rich; he simply opposes federal financing of abortion in the circumstances concerned. 1

Lest this seem justice of the kind that gives rich and poor equal freedom to sleep under bridges, Mr. Lewis should examine the economics of the matter. According to ABC's *World News Tonight* of October 25, rape and incest are responsible for about 16,000 pregnancies each year. The average cost of an abortion, the report added, is $190. Though it would not be necessary — rape and incest not being limited to the poor — only $3.04 million would provide abortions for all these women. Raising such a sum annually would be a minor task for Planned Parenthood and other pro-choice groups. One can only conclude that their concern is not to succor the victims but to score a political victory. 2

It is not hypocritical for the President and others who reluctantly concede that abortion is sometimes the lesser evil to reject government financing of it. If there be moral fault, it lies with those — is "zealots" too strong a word? — who insist that abortion is a private matter, while denouncing as opportunistic political leaders who resist making the public pay for it. 3

— E. L. Pattullo

Too Many Abortions

COMMONWEAL

One-and-a-half million abortions a year is a national scandal. Most of these abortions fall outside even the broadest reading of our prevailing ethic that allows taking the life of an assailant in self-defense or the defense of another, that condemns to death individuals guilty of capital crimes, or that authorizes the killing of combatants in time of war or a just 1

E. L. Pattullo's letter appeared in the *New York Times* on November 17, 1989.

This editorial is from the August 11, 1989 issue of the Roman Catholic magazine *Commonweal.*

revolution. That much we allow the police, the courts, and the armed forces. Physicians and women are allowed greater latitude when it comes to the fetus. That's the law; but it is not moral.

The law rests on the Supreme Court's 1973 decision in *Roe v. Wade*, 2 which ruled that most state laws restricting abortion were a violation of the personal liberty protected by the due process clause of the Fourteenth Amendment. Almost without exception subsequent Court decisions offered the broadest possible interpretation favoring abortion and limiting restrictions. Now many people think the Court's latest abortion decision, *Webster v. Reproductive Health Services*, will shift the balance in the opposite direction.

We are not so sure. First, the Court has not dismantled *Roe*. Second, 3 whatever the law, there is an abortion ethic so deeply rooted in our culture that overturning or narrowing *Roe* may have minimal effect on the number of abortions. What was once unthinkable has become thinkable; indeed, as time passes, the abortion decision is increasingly treated as one almost not worth thinking about at all. A change in law will mean little without a transformation of minds and hearts.

One might argue that *Roe* engendered this abortion ethic — this 4 unique exception to our general prohibition of killing innocent others. But in rereading *Roe*, it is hard to find the hard-edged thinking or absolutist language that has come to characterize the way we now speak individually and as a polity on the subject. For example, "abortion on demand" and "the absolute right to privacy" are catchphrases we hear often and loudly, phrases pro-choicers defend and against which pro-lifers rail. But back in 1973, the Court wrote: "Appellants . . . argue that the woman's right is absolute and that she is entitled to terminate her pregnancy at whatever time, in whatever way, and for whatever reason she alone chooses. With this we do not agree." The Court went on: "[T]he right of personal privacy includes the abortion decision, but . . . this right is not unqualified and must be considered against important state interests in regulation." Nor was the decision the woman's alone: "All these are factors [in the abortion decision] the woman and her responsible physician necessarily will consider in consultation." It is not hard to find in these words justification for viability testing at twenty weeks as the Court did in upholding the Missouri law, or, for that matter, for upholding certain counseling and informed consent procedures that were not at issue in *Webster*.

We do not return to *Roe* in order to defend it; its usurpation of the po- 5 litical process in 1973 in favor of judicial fiat is indefensible. And if *Webster* is the prelude to a full, rational, political consideration of abortion at the state level, it is indeed welcome. But we harbor an unhappy premonition that it is not. While the Supreme Court teases the nation with a patchwork process of allowing some restrictions and turning down others, the acrimonious scramble for influence in fifty state houses and state legislatures by pro-life and pro-choice forces will be poisonous to our whole political system. Even worse, as we have suggested above, it is unlikely to help restore a moral perspective of a kind that will help actually to reduce the number of abortions, some of which, under the new dispensation, will be performed illegally. It is indeed a struggle for the minds and hearts of women — and men.

The best, but most difficult, place to begin is with the claim that the 6
fetus is not nothing. *Roe* concluded that the fetus is not considered a "person" under the Fourteenth Amendment, and further on it declined to "resolve the difficult question of when life begins." In most adult humans there arises a sound intuition that somewhere between the period of conception and implantation and a later period when the developing fetus has every aspect of a human being, this is a human being, a human being worthy of protection — and perhaps that sense is nowhere more fully developed than in the pregnant woman herself. Most of us would offer a seat on a crowded train to a pregnant woman; many would offer help if she collapsed on a street or rush to her aid if she was endangered by a speeding car or threatened with a beating. It is not just her comfort or her life that is at stake, but the life of another, our immediate sense is not of one human being deserving of protection, but two. The more obviously pregnant a woman is, the more surely we draw that conclusion. The fetus is something.

But so is the woman. And it is the woman contemplating an abortion 7
who must be convinced that the fetus is something, indeed at a certain point becomes someone. Implanting and supporting this conviction has two possible starting points. The most immediate: A pregnant woman considering abortion should receive counseling that fully describes for her what we now know about fetuses and their development; if it is to be an abortion at eight weeks or at twelve weeks, she should see what such a fetus looks like and know its stage of development. Responsible counseling would also offer viable alternatives to the woman if she cannot raise the child; indeed a positive ethic of adoption and the ability of social workers to provide a woman with a serious adoption plan ought to be part of the counseling process. Does that unduly burden the abortion decision as the Court has previously ruled? Perhaps. But it is a burden that the gravity of an abortion decision warrants.

Another and more distant starting point for building the conviction 8
that the fetus deserves maternal consideration and protection lies with a fuller development of the feminist insight that women themselves must take responsibility for their lives, the choices they make, their relationships with others — parallel to the kind of responsibility men must also exercise. Moral agency entails a kind of autonomy, self-esteem, and responsibility in which women and men act instead of merely being acted upon.

Feminist thought has generally treated the abortion decision as part and parcel of that exercise of autonomy, self-esteem, and responsibility, but the decision for abortion can be read in the opposite way.

9 Except in extreme cases, the decision to have an abortion can simply be the end point in a series of events in which a woman has failed to take responsibility for her sexual life and become pregnant in a situation in which no family life is possible, or she has allowed herself to be sexually exploited by a man who has no intention of sharing in the care of a child. This starting point for stemming the number of abortions depends on women becoming reproductively responsible moral agents by either saying no to men who will not or cannot share the responsibilities of parenthood or by women becoming effective users of contraception. This is not an ethic that fully expresses the Christian vision of human love, or the care that men and women should express toward one another. But it is a better ethic than the one now expressed in one-and-a-half million abortions. Pro-choice and pro-life advocates, at their best and most sensitive, recognize this: They see that along with the unborn no less victims of this dismal ethic are the women who have abortions. If the coming political struggle can be built on the sense that there are too many abortions, that women and fetuses alike are victims of a shabby ethic, then it will be a struggle that will end not only in better laws, but in a more tolerable moral standard.

Parents Also Have Rights

RONNIE GUNNERSON

1 What's a parent to do?" is the punch line to many a joke on the perils of raising children. But what a parent does when a teenager gets pregnant is far from a joke; it's a soul-searching, heart-wrenching condition with responses as diverse as the families affected.

2 In an era besotted with concern for both the emotional and social welfare of teenage mothers and their babies, anger seems to be forbidden. Yet how many parents can deny anger when circumstances over which they have no control force them into untenable situations?

3 And untenable they are. What I discovered after my sixteen-year-old stepdaughter became pregnant shocked me. Parents have no rights. We could neither demand she give the baby up for adoption, nor insist on an abortion. The choice belongs to the teenage mother, who is still a child

---

Ronnie Gunnerson is managing editor of Vidmar Communications in Hollywood, California. This article appeared in *Newsweek*, March 2, 1987.

herself and far from capable of understanding the lifelong ramifications of whatever choice she makes.

At the same time, homes for unwed mothers, at least the two we checked in Los Angeles, where we live, will house the teenager at no cost to the family, but they will not admit her unless her parents sign a statement agreeing to pick up both her and her baby from a designated maternity hospital. Parents may sit out the pregnancy if they so desire, but when all is said and done, they're stuck with both mother and baby whether they like it or not. 4

In essence, then, the pregnant teenager can choose whether or not to have her baby and whether or not to keep it. The parents, who have the legal responsibility for both the teenage mother and her child, have no say in the matter. The costs of a teenage pregnancy are high; yes, the teenager's life is forever changed by her untimely pregnancy and childbirth. But life is forever changed for the rest of her family as well, and I am tired of the do-gooders who haven't walked a yard, let alone a mile, in my shoes shouting their sympathy for the "victimized" teen. 5

What about the victimized parents? Are we supposed to accept the popular notion that we failed this child and that therefore we are to blame for her lack of either scruples or responsibility? Not when we spend endless hours and thousands of dollars in therapy trying to help a girl whose behavior has been rebellious since the age of thirteen. Not when we have heart-to-heart talks until the wee hours of the morning which we learn are the butt of jokes between her and her friends. And not when we continually trust her only to think afterward that she's repeatedly lied to us about everything there is to lie about. 6

Yes, the teenager is a victim — a victim of illusions fostered by a society that gives her the right to decide whether or not to have an illegitimate baby, no matter what her parents say. Many believe it is feelings of rejection that motivate girls to have babies; they want human beings of their own to love and be loved by. I wouldn't disagree, but another motive may be at work as well: the ultimate rebellion. Parents are forced to cope with feelings more devastating than adolescent confusion. And I'm not talking about the superficial, what-will-the-Joneses-think attitudes. I mean gut-gripping questions that undermine brutally the self-confidence it can take adults years to develop. 7

We can all write off to immaturity mistakes made in adolescence. To what do we attribute our perceived parental failures at forty or fifty? Even as I proclaim our innocence in my stepdaughter's folly, I will carry to my grave, as I know my husband will, the nagging fear that we could have prevented it *if only* we'd been *better* parents. 8

And I will carry forevermore the sad realization that I'm not the compassionate person I'd tried so hard to be and actually thought I was. My reaction to my stepdaughter's pregnancy horrified me. I was consumed 9 with hatred and anger. Any concern I felt for her was overridden by the feeling that I'd been had. I'd befriended this child, housed her and counseled her for years, and what did I get in return? Not knowing her whereabouts that culminated in her getting pregnant with a boy we didn't even know. At first I felt like a fool. When I discovered how blatantly society's rules favor the rule breaker, I felt like a raving maniac.

Resentment and Rage

It took more hours of counseling for me to accept my anger than it 10
did for my stepdaughter to deal with her pregnancy. But then, she had the support of a teenage subculture that reveres motherhood among its own and a news-media culture that fusses and frets over adolescent mothers. Few ears were willing to hear what my husband and I were feeling. While I can't speak for my husband, I can say that today, a year after the baby's birth, he still turns to ice when his daughter is around. Smitten as he is with his first grandchild, he hasn't forgotten that the joy of the boy's birth was overshadowed by resentment and rage.

Fortunately, my stepdaughter recently married a young man who 11
loves her son as his own, although he is not the father. Together, the three of them are a family who, like many a young family, are struggling to make ends meet. Neither my stepdaughter nor her husband has yet finished high school, but they are not a drain on society as many teenage parents are. She and her husband seem to be honest, hard workers, and I really think they will make it. Their story will have a happy ending.

My stepdaughter says she can't even understand the person she used 12
to be, and I believe her. Unfortunately, the minds of adults are not quite as malleable as those of constantly changing adolescents. My husband and I haven't forgotten — and I'm not sure we've forgiven — either our daughter or ourselves. We're still writing the ending to our own story, and I believe it's time for society to write an ending of its own. If a pregnant teenager's parents are ultimately responsible for the teenager and her baby, then give those parents the right to decide whether or not the teenager keeps her baby. Taking the decision away from the teen mother would eliminate her power over her parents and could give pause to her reckless pursuit of the "in" thing.

Abortion Consent Law Creates Support System

JULIET K. MOYNA

To the Editor:

As a young woman who attends an academic institution famous for its social conscience, I am dismayed after having read Rebecca L. Walkowitz's rambling and misguided defense of abortions for minors (Op-Ed, October 11). I also resent such an opinion's being published in the guise of "Voices of the New Generation." 1

Miss Walkowitz seems to be concerned that the courts, by taking away the "rights" of young women to control their own bodies without consulting parents or the state, are not permitting them to be "individuals with personal choices and political power." What she, as a product of the sexual "revolution," fails to understand, though, is that women are already powerless victims. Such a victimization results not from the moral strictness she protests, but actually from the laxity and open-mindedness of the courts. 2

Women are already conditioned to assume the consequences of such a sexual "revolution." A young woman of the New Generation, egged on by a society dominated by the male libido, has the "power" to choose either the pill, which allows her to gain weight, develop varicose veins, and wonder about cancer, or less effective forms of birth control, which afford her monthly anxiety the likes of which young men have never experienced. Should her birth control fail, she has the power to "choose" to become a mother or to deny herself motherhood. Either way, she must face another choice. If the baby is born, society lets her raise the child alone, or give it up for adoption and wonder all her life about the benevolence of the motives of the adoptive parents. If the baby is aborted, and society pats her reassuringly on the back, she can either succumb to consuming regret or stubbornly bury it each time it resurfaces. 3

Such are the liberating choices young women of the New Generation hold within their power. Unfortunately, the ruling in the Florida Supreme Court to strike down a law requiring minors to obtain parental consent for an abortion (news story, October 6) reaffirms the burdening of women with a responsibility that borders on culpability. From such a culpability, to use Miss Walkowitz's phrase, "young men are exempted, creating a double standard based on gender." 4

Juliet K. Moyna's letter appeared in the *New York Times* on October 30, 1989. The writer is a member of the class of 1991 at Columbia College.

How is a young woman to face all these choices on her own? Were 5
this a society that concerned itself with the well-being of its female constituency, it would possess a court system that ensures that women did not have to make such wrenching decisions alone. A consent law would not implicate young women as incompetent decision makers, as Miss Walkowitz thinks; rather, it would acknowledge the pained torment that accompanies their decision.

A consent law would provide young women with a support system 6
that should exist in their parents or in their state. A consent law would force society to wrestle with the same responsibilities that it has been forcing women to handle alone since the birth of the sexual revolution. What such a law would accomplish for women is far more liberating than the mockery of power and choice they now possess. And until every young woman realizes this, she will remain the voice of the Middle Ages, not the voice of a New Generation.

—Juliet K. Moyna

Parental Consent Could Justify Forced Abortion

ANGELA R. HOLDER

To the Editor:

Poll after poll indicates that the American public is strongly behind 1
statutes that require minors to obtain parental consent for abortions. I wonder how much thought the respondents (and the legislators who enact these statutes) give to the consequences.

Is it generally known that the parents of a teenage mother have no 2
financial or other obligation toward their grandchild? Wisconsin enacted a grandparent-responsibility statute a few years ago; in no other state do the grandparents assume any legal responsibility for a minor daughter's baby. If they can veto their daughter's abortion decision, it seems to me they should be obliged to put their money where their mouths are and assume responsibility for the baby's care and support.

In many states as well, a girl becomes an emancipated minor when 3
she becomes a mother. Her parents are then no longer obligated to support her either. Thus, a statute that allows parental intervention on the

---

Angela R. Holder's letter was printed in the *New York Times* on November 27, 1989. Holder is clinical professor of Pediatrics (Law) at the Yale School of Medicine.

ground that the girl is too immature to decide may well result in the same immature girl and her baby being thrown out of her parents' home.

Also, as adolescents' rights to consent for themselves to other forms of medical care have been recognized by courts and legislatures all over the country since the early 1950s, an accepted corollary has been that a minor too young to consent to some form of treatment is also too young to refuse it when a parent consents. If a parent is empowered to block an abortion on the ground that the girl is too immature to make the decision, it is equally logical that the same parent can decide that it is not in the girl's best interests to be a mother and require her to have an abortion she does not want. 4

All the reported court decisions have been in situations where physicians have refused to perform abortions on unwilling girls at the insistence of their parents, unless the parents obtained a court order. No one knows how many physicians will now perform an abortion without a court order on an objecting teenager if her parents insist. 5

In all reported cases, courts have ruled that a parent may not force a girl to have an abortion against her will because it is her right to choose, but none of these decisions have come from a state with a parental consent statute. Requiring parental decision making in these cases may well lead to increased acceptance of forced abortions, just as parents have the unquestioned authority to force their unwilling adolescent to have an appendectomy or enter a drug treatment facility. 6

Perhaps we should let these young women make their own decisions after all? 7

—Angela R. Holder

A Problem for Couples

ARTHUR B. SHOSTAK

To the Editor:

I agree with John R. Silber that government should not enact laws to restrict abortion (Op-Ed, January 3). Still, Americans on all sides of the issue seek to reduce abortion's toll on the couple and the nation alike. To achieve this, we must revise our perception of abortion, viewing it in terms of the couple involved, not of the woman alone. 1

Arthur B. Shostak is professor of sociology at Drexel University and the principal author of *Men and Abortion* (1984). His letter appeared in the *New York Times* on January 22, 1990.

As a result of the 1973 *Roe v. Wade* decision, too many Americans 2
mistakenly consider abortion solely a woman's problem, a matter of a woman's rights. We would have been better served if the Supreme Court had defined abortion as a couple's problem, a question of the rights and responsibilities of a twosome.

The Supreme Court ruling on *Webster v. Reproductive Health Services* 3
has placed the onus on state legislators. State lawmakers should put away their cliché-ridden arguments and their probably unconstitutional tactics. In their place, we should urge enactment of legislation that is both pro-choice and pro-couple.

For instance, states could require clinics, hospitals, and physician pro- 4
viders to offer males, as well as females, counseling on contraception and postabortion emotional healing. This would benefit the 700,000 males who annually accompany their mates to abortion procedures, only to sit ignored and idle for three hours in the waiting room.

A second pro-couple law could require providers to end their heart- 5
less practice of isolating males from their mates: 70 percent of such men recently told researchers they wanted to provide comfort during the fifteen-minute abortion procedure, and 90 percent wanted to offer support in the hour-long recovery period, provided, of course, that their mate gave prior approval. But few if any providers make these caring options possible.

Clinics should also be required to hire at least one male counselor, 6
who, on being voluntarily provided by a female client with the name of her partner, would offer to help him "process" his feelings (with or without his mate in attendance). Because 25 percent of these males are abortion repeaters, this counseling might go far in lowering that rate.

Construing abortion, as we have since *Roe v. Wade*, as solely the 7
problem of one gender has been a costly mistake. It resembles our foolishness in decades past when we barred men from the delivery room, trivialized their emotional involvement in their imminent parenthood, and limited the loving support they could provide their mates. Today, we perceive childbirth as a couple's challenge and take pride in the presence of four out of five fathers as "coaches" during labor. New fathers are also grateful recipients of counseling in postbirth emotional difficulties and contraceptive options.

Unless we make similar strides toward abortion as well, we will miss 8
an opportunity to diminish its awesome toll.

—Arthur B. Shostak

THINKING AND WRITING ABOUT ABORTION

Questions for Discussion and Writing

1. The Planned Parenthood advertisement lays out nine important reasons in favor of the legality of abortion. Is it possible to tell whether the authors of the ad agree with the proposals in the article by Hiatt and Levinthal? Does the ad address all the issues in the *Commonweal* editorial? How would it respond to the charge in *Commonweal* that abortions are necessary because women have been careless in their responsibilities? What inconsistency does the *Commonweal* editorial find in advocacy of abortion by feminists? Is this argument valid?
2. What arguments in favor of public funding for abortion would pro-choice advocates use to refute Pattullo?
3. Summarize the warrants on each side in the argument between pregnant teenagers who want abortions and their parents who want them to give birth. Make clear the nature of the moral conflicts. Can they be resolved?
4. What are the advantages, according to Shostak, of allowing prospective fathers to participate in abortion decisions? Do you think that there may also be disadvantages?
5. What dangers does Keath see in encouraging blacks to endorse abortion on demand? Why does he feel it necessary to write this warning? Do you think most blacks would agree with him? Why or why not?

Topics for Research

Which restrictions on abortion, if any, should be imposed by the states, and why?

A history of abortion since 1973: Changes brought about by legalization

A review of legislation by the states since the 1989 Supreme Court ruling: Are the changes significant?

An evaluation of arguments by public officials who personally oppose abortion but publicly support the law permitting abortion (e.g., the continuing controversy between Governor Mario Cuomo of New York and Cardinal O'Connor)

The effects of legalized abortion on the lives of teenage girls.

CHAPTER 11

AIDS Testing

AIDS (Acquired Immune Deficiency Syndrome) is a fatal condition that destroys the immune system, leaving the body incapable of defending itself against numerous life-threatening diseases. Estimates of the number of people in the United States infected with the virus have recently been revised downward. Most experts now agree that the number of people with AIDS, some of whom have no symptoms, is between 800,000 and 1.3 million. So far, AIDS has killed 70,313 people, and the Federal Centers for Disease Control estimate that "179,000 to 206,000 new cases will be reported [from January 1990] through the end of 1992."

Approximately 90 percent of people with the disease are either men who have had sex with other men (about 65 percent), intravenous drug users who have shared needles with other people (17 percent), or men who have engaged in both practices (8 percent). The number of heterosexually transmitted cases is still small (at least 4 percent), but this number has begun to rise.

Since the largest group of people with the AIDS virus exhibits few or no symptoms, these carriers can be identified only by a blood test for the antibody to the AIDS virus. Advocates of testing argue that knowledge of positive results will inhibit the spread of the disease by enabling the carriers of the virus not only to begin treatments that may delay the onset of

AIDS but also to inform their sexual partners of possible risks. But proposals for testing have been met with a storm of questions and counterproposals from health officials, advocates of civil liberties, and gay-rights activists. Should the testing be voluntary or mandatory? How wide should the testing be? (Should applicants for marriage licenses be tested?) What uses will be made of the results? If confidentiality is violated, is there a danger that people discovered to be carriers will lose their jobs, housing, and access to public places?

At a federally sponsored meeting on the control of AIDS in 1987, disagreement arose over the definition of terms. One participant pointed out that "mandatory," "routine," "anonymous," "standard," "required," and "confidential" were being used in different ways.

As AIDS claims more victims, public anxiety will mount, and the demand for mandatory testing and controls may grow. State laws written in the 1920s and 1930s to limit the spread of sexually transmitted diseases seem inadequate for protection against AIDS. But it remains unclear whether new laws requiring mandatory testing would produce sufficient health benefits to justify possible violations of civil liberties.

Don't Tell Me on Friday

THOMAS RICHARDS

I am a gay man who discovered last summer that I had antibodies to human T cell lymphotropic virus III. For me there are two central strands to the question of whether or not people should be tested for such antibodies; firstly, will knowing that you are positive help your own health; and secondly, will it make you more or less likely to infect others? 1

Like many people, when I first discovered that I was antibody positive I felt shock and disorientation. I woke up in the mornings shaking, had problems sleeping, and lost my appetite. I wrote a will, drank heavily, and seriously considered suicide. I thought, like others, that I was bound to develop acquired immune deficiency syndrome. [The newspaper] *Capital Gay* recently reported that a Newcastle conference on AIDS had been told of six people who had killed themselves on discovering that they were positive. 2

But, though good counseling from both the doctor at the special clinic and a clinical psychologist, after three to four weeks I got used to being 3

Thomas Richards is the pseudonym of a British actor. His article appeared in the *British Medical Journal* on April 5, 1986.

positive. I was put in touch with a gay self-help group in London called Body Positive. The support, both practical and emotional, that both the psychologist and Body Positive gave were all-important for me. Where I should have been without their help I dare not consider.

Such help should, I believe, be available to everybody immediately 4
that they find out that they have antibodies. This belief explains my title because people should not be given this news if an appointment with a psychologist cannot be arranged until after a weekend — the first seventy-two hours are the worst. Given the restricted counseling facilities that are as yet available, I think it inevitable that doctors are going to have to make full use of voluntary organizations such as Body Positive.

Knowing that you are positive gives you a chance to alter your life- 5
style. It becomes more likely that you will adopt a healthier diet and cut down on alcohol, tobacco, or cannabis. As an actor I decided that stress was my main problem, and I took up yoga for the first time in my life with great success.

The most important question is — will knowingly that you are posi- 6
tive alter your sexual behavior? Gays in this country have up until now followed a free and easy existence. All we risked living in the "fast lane" was, it seemed, the occasional social disease. Clearly we must adopt a more responsible attitude, and it does seem that gay men who are discovered to be positive and who are properly counseled do behave responsibly and change their sexual practices. They follow the "safe sex" guidelines suggested by organizations such as the Terrence Higgins Trust.

While in a perfect world all gay men should for the last two years 7
have adopted safer sexual practices, including the use of condoms, this is not a perfect world and they have not. The reality is that at one o'clock in the morning after four or five pints in a gay pub or club, gay men go home with each other without checking that one of them has condoms.

I do not advocate the compulsory testing of gay men. But so long as 8
we understand the test and its limitations and so long as good counseling is available, I think we should be encouraged to take the test — both for our own good and that of the community, gay and straight. The decision must, however, remain a personal one. My experience — and that of St. Mary's Hospital — is that those who change their behavior most are those who are tested, found positive, and properly counseled.

AIDS: In Plagues, Civil Rights Aren't the Issue

RICHARD RESTAK

Paradoxically, the truly humanitarian position in the face of an AIDS plague is that we not identify with the victims and instead cast our lot with what in earlier times was dubbed the "common good." 1

More than 1 million Americans may have been infected with the AIDS virus. And the 13,000 Americans with confirmed cases of the disease, whose number is doubling every year, should be treated with the care and compassion due to anyone with a disease that is thus far incurable and invariably fatal. This shouldn't be confused, however, with a refusal to make painful, sometimes anguishing but nonetheless necessary distinctions in the interest of diminishing the likelihood that this awful disease will spread further. 2

Plagues are not new. They have been encountered in every age and among every nationality: syphilis among the Spanish, bubonic plague among the French, tuberculosis among the Eskimos, polio in America. 3

What is new are efforts by medically unsophisticated politicians and attorneys to dictate policy in regard to an illness that has the potential for wreaking devastation on a scale that has not been encountered on this planet in hundreds of years. 4

Also different is the response that, in some quarters, is being suggested: Accept the AIDS victim into our schools, place little or no restrictions on employment or housing. The AIDS victims' "rights" in these areas, we are told, should take precedence over the so far incompletely determined potential for these victims to spread this dread illness. 5

But what some are describing as "discrimination" and "segregation" has a long and not inglorious history in medicine. Quarantines have been effective in beating outbreaks of scarlet fever, smallpox, and typhoid in this century. Indeed, by protecting the well from the ill we follow a long-established, sensible, and ultimately compassionate course. Throughout history, true humanitarianism traditionally has involved the compassionate but firm segregation of those afflicted with communicable diseases from the well. By carrying out such a policy, diseases have been contained. 6

Richard Restak is a Washington-based neurologist who has been studying the effects of AIDS on the brain. This essay is from the September 23, 1985 issue of *The Washington Post National Weekly Edition*.

Refusing to Distinguish

Only sentimentalists refuse to distinguish between the victims of a 7
scourge and those not currently afflicted.

Scientists still are unsure why the AIDS virus targets the white blood 8
cells that are the one indispensable element of the body's immune system. But the threat of AIDS demands from us all a discrimination based on our instinct for survival against a peril that, if not somehow controlled, can destroy this society. This is a discrimination that recognizes that caution is in order when knowledge is incomplete, so the public interest can be protected.

This argument is not a counsel against good medical care or proper 9
concern for AIDS victims. Nor is it a suggestion that we curtail any "civil right" which doesn't potentially imperil the lives of others.

It is a suggestion that the humanitarian response to AIDS is exactly 10
the opposite of a humanitarian response to sexism or racism: In the presence of considerable ignorance about the causes and effects of the syndrome, the benefit of the doubt should not be given to the victim of AIDS. This is not a civil-rights issue; this is a medical issue. To take a position that the AIDS virus must be eradicated is not to make judgments on morals or life-styles. It is to say that the AIDS virus has no "civil rights."

At the moment, social and legal solutions to the AIDS problem are 11
proceeding at a pace disproportionate to the knowledge experts possess concerning the illness.

For instance, on August 14, [1985], the Los Angeles City Council 12
unanimously approved an ordinance making it illegal to discriminate against AIDS patients in regard to jobs, housing, and health care.

"We have an opportunity to set an example for the whole nation, to 13
protect those people who suffer from AIDS against insidious discrimination," said the councilman who introduced the measure. Councilman Ernani Bernardi said the ordinance was meant to educate the public to "prevent hysteria."

Preventing hysteria is good, but this ordinance was passed despite 14
doctors' not having yet made up their minds about the degree of contact required for the disease to be spread from one person to another.

Consider, for example, the varied and patently contradictory mea- 15
sures put into effect across the country in response to the recent discovery that the AIDS virus can be isolated from a victim's tears.

Contradictory Measures

At Boston University, when an AIDS patient is examined, "We are 16
not using the applanation tonometer [a device that tests for glaucoma] be-

cause we don't feel we can adequately sterilize it," said the chairman of the department of ophthalmology.

The Massachusetts Eye and Ear Infirmary specialists plan to "review 17
our technique." Translation: We're not sure yet what we're going to do.

At San Francisco General Hospital, the chief of the eye service rou- 18
tinely sterilizes his optic instruments with merthiolate which "as far as I know" kills the AIDS virus.

At this point live AIDS virus has been isolated from blood, semen, se- 19
rum, saliva, urine, and now tears. If the virus exists in these fluids, the better part of wisdom dictates that we assume the possibility that it can also be transmitted by these routes.

It seems reasonable, therefore, that AIDS victims should not donate 20
blood or blood products, should not contribute to semen banks, should not donate tissues or organs to organ banks, should not work as dental or medical technicians, and should probably not be employed as food handlers.

While the Los Angeles ordinance exempts blood banks and sperm 21
banks, it's prepared to exert the full power of the law against nonconformists who exclude AIDS sufferers from employment in restaurants, hotels, barber shops, and dental offices.

According to the new law, then, a person afflicted with AIDS may, if 22
properly trained, work as a dental hygienist. He may clean your teeth. He may even clean your teeth if he has a paper cut on one of his fingers. This despite the fact that the AIDS virus can be transmitted from bloodstream to bloodstream.

AIDS in the Schools

The battle lines forming over the admission of AIDS victims in the 23
schools are similarly disturbing. "This is the test case for the nation," says attorney Charles Vaughn, who represents thirteen-year-old AIDS victim Ryan White, who has been refused admission to his local school in Kokomo, Indiana. "What happens here will set the trends across the country." (In America there are about 180 children, not all of school age, diagnosed as having AIDS.)

To those like Vaughn who see this issue in civil liberties terms, the 24
plight of Ryan White represents simply another instance of discrimination that should be opposed with all the vigor that has marked past efforts against racism and sexism. In support of their position, they point to the recent directive of the Centers for Disease Control that AIDS cases be evaluated on an individual basis to determine whether a child should be admitted to school.

Not Contagious?

Spokesmen from the CDC and other AIDS authorities, including Dr. 25
Arye Rubenstein, who treats the largest group of children with AIDS, may be correct in stating that there is "overwhelming evidence that AIDS is not a highly contagious disease." However, in a combined interview, they gave the following responses to the interviewer's questions:

Q: Suppose my child got into a fight with an AIDS victim and both be- 26
gan to bleed?

A: That kind of fight with a possible exchange of body fluids would 27
arouse some concern about transmission of the virus.

Q: What if my child is in a classroom with an AIDS victim who threw 28
up or had diarrhea?

A: Such events would be a matter of concern. In its guidelines, the 29
CDC said that AIDS victims who cannot control body secretions should be kept out of ordinary classrooms.

Q: Suppose a child with AIDS bit my child? 30

A: Again, a bite would arouse concern. 31

Any grade-school teacher can attest that "body-fluid contamination" 32
in the form of scratching, throwing up, diarrhea, biting, and spitting are everyday fare in a schoolroom. That's why infectious diseases like the flu spread through schools like flash fires.

It is difficult to imagine how the CDC or anyone else is going to make 33
individual determinations under such circumstances.

"I'd rather err on the side of caution," says New York Mayor Edward 34
Koch about admitting AIDS-afflicted children to schools. In this sentiment, he echoes the concerns of parents everywhere: What if future research shows AIDS can be caught in other ways? Isn't it more sensible to forgo premature steps against "discrimination" and await scientific developments?

AIDS Is Not about Civil Rights

AIDS is not about civil rights, political power, or "alternative life- 35
styles." It's a disease, a true plague which, in the words of infectious disease expert Dr. John Seale, writing in the August [1985] issue of Britain's *Journal of the Royal Society of Medicine*, is already capable of producing "a lethal pandemic throughout the crowded cities and villages of the Third World of a magnitude unparalleled in human history." This disease is only partially understood, is currently untreatable, and is invariably fatal. For these reasons alone, caution would seem in order when it comes to exposing the public to those suffering from this illness.

But in addition, the incubation period is sufficiently lengthy to cast doubt on any proclamations, no matter how seemingly authoritative, in regard to the transmissibility of the illness: "The virus may be transmitted from an infected person many years before the onset of clinical manifestations," according to Dr. George D. Lundberg, editor-in-chief of the *Journal of the American Medical Association.* "Latency of many years may occur between transmission, infection, and clinically manifest disease." 36

Indeed, truly authoritative statements regarding AIDS cannot currently be made. "The eventual mortality following infection with a lentivirus such as the AIDS virus cannot be ascertained by direct observation till those recently infected have been followed well into the twenty-first century," according to Dr. Seale. 37

Given these grim realities, lawyers and legislators should ponder long and hard whether or not they wish, by means of legal maneuvering, to inadvertently create stituations — child AIDS victims in the schools, adult AIDS victims working in medical, dental offices, and other health-care facilities — in which those afflicted are in a position to pass this virus on to the general public. 38

Obviously, the most pressing issue at this point is to arrive at an understanding of all of the ways the AIDS virus spreads. But until we do that, political posturing, sloganeering, hollow reassurances, and the inappropriate application of legal remedies to a medical problem can only make matters worse and potentially imperil the health of us all. 39

How Not *to Control the AIDS Epidemic*

MATHILDE KRIM

Historically, nations under military attack have first reacted by expelling undesirables and closing borders. When the enemy was an apparently transmissible disease-causing agent, boundaries were erected between the sick and the well. The sick were physically isolated, often forcibly, and the suffering caused by this approach was justified by 1

Mathilde Krim, a virologist and a geneticist, is cofounder of the American Foundation for AIDS Research. Her article, which appeared in the November/December issue of *The Humanist*, is adapted from her acceptance speech for the 1987 Humanist Distinguished Service Award.

proclamations of its effectiveness and, importantly, by the attribution of imprudent or intemperate behavior to those afflicted. Therefore, the afflicted came to be regarded as undesirables on both health *and* moral grounds, and whatever unease their misery caused in the minds of others could be dismissed on the grounds that the misfortune of the sick was largely self-inflicted.

In more recent times and with a better understanding of the nature of 2
infectious agents and their mode of transmission, more rational measures could be adopted. Improvements in sanitation now prevent epidemics of cholera and typhus. Vaccination against many infectious diseases as well as antibiotics for their treatment have silenced the call for isolation or quarantine. The spectacular success of modern methods for the control of many infectious diseases has spurred great confidence in the biomedical approach.

However, in their newly acquired faith in the fruits of scientific deter- 3
minism, Western societies have overlooked the fact that medicine is still powerless with regard to the prevention of many infections caused by viruses and that no drugs or antibiotics exist, to date, that can cure *any* viral disease. Such a disease, the Acquired Immunodeficiency Syndrome, or AIDS, is now upon us. In addition, Western societies have not yet renounced loathing certain groups of human beings. And so it is that the extraordinary conjunction in our modern societies of a lethal, virally induced, transmissible disease with life-styles that are generally despised — along with those practicing them — is a recipe for social disaster. The powerlessness of medicine in the face of AIDS has elicited atavistic fears. Uninhibited talk of screening for the purpose of isolating the sick is heard once again. . . .

Following the discovery of HIV [Human Immunodeficiency Virus] in 4
1983, a better understanding of the pathogenesis of AIDS could be acquired, and tests diagnostic for HIV infection could be developed. An unanticipated, very large number of apparently healthy "high-risk group" people were found infected in the United States. Their number was estimated to be one million in 1985. In addition, a significant proportion of certain sexually active young adults in the general population (one in two hundred fifty) were also found infected as well as people from what appears to be a "low-risk" population — namely, blood donors (one in two thousand). In 1987, in the United States alone, the total number of infected people may be as high as two million. The longitudinal study of groups of men who became infected as early as 1979 has revealed that, in the very long run — perhaps as long as ten to fifteen years after infection — a large majority, if not all those infected with HIV, will suffer grievous physical harm in the guise of AIDS or ARC [AIDS-Related Complex]. Therefore, the blood tests that detect the presence of antibodies to HIV —

and hence infection with it — are acquiring increasingly serious prognostic significance.

5 When used in combination, these tests — namely, the enzyme linked immunosorbent assay, or ELISA test, and confirmatory tests, such as the Western Blot — are as sensitive and specific and, therefore, as reliable as a great many other tests used in medicine. However, they are obviously *not* diagnostic of AIDS but only of HIV infection, and they provide false-negative results on blood obtained from individuals who have become infected recently. This is so because it takes three to eight weeks to develop detectable levels of circulating antibodies to HIV and because certain individuals never develop such antibodies despite the presence of infectious virus in their blood. More specific, second-generation HIV ELISA tests are now being developed, as well as different tests that will detect the virus itself. But, predictably, the latter will also result in some false negative and some false positive results.

6 The use of *any* medical test for the screening of populations is fraught with technical and other difficulties. In the case of HIV infection, any mass screening is a particularly perilous undertaking for a number of reasons in addition to the unavoidable technical shortcomings mentioned above. To start with, the serious long-term prognosis attached to a positive test result — a diagnosis of HIV infection — constitutes psychologically devastating news. Secondly, the social stigma attached to such a diagnosis can, and often does, result in serious social and economic harm to individuals. Last but not least, awareness of one's infected status cannot lead to useful medical intervention at this time, since none exists.

7 Nevertheless, a desire to respond to the public's fear of AIDS, an urge to "do something," has already compelled some politicians to advocate the use of the HIV-antibody tests for the mandatory mass screening of various population groups. Unfortunately, little thought was given by these politicians to the cost of such an enterprise in dollars and human resources or to what is to be done, and with what resources, with those identified as infected. No provisions were made or resources allocated by these politicians to provide for the intensive, long-term counseling that alone can help individuals identified as infected live with their devastating knowledge, since medicine will certainly *not* be able to help them in any way for some time to come. No legislation has been enacted or even proposed to prevent the emergence, as a result of discrimination against them, of a class of destitute and sick pariahs in our midst.

8 Those of us who have urged caution, further reflection, and careful planning with regard to the uses to be made of the HIV-antibody tests have been told that we are putting the civil liberties of the few ahead of the protection of the public health. Whether or not this is so has been carefully considered by the surgeon general of the United States, by the

scholars participating in the Hastings Center's and other studies, and by hundreds of public health officials. They all concluded, in a remarkable consensus of opinion, that not only is there no contradiction between safeguarding individual liberties and privacy on the one hand and the protection of the public health on the other but that the individual and the public good are inseparable in the AIDS epidemic. This is so for the very simple reason that the protection of the public health does *not* rest on the identification, per se, of the infected *but on their individual willingness to assume and act upon their personal responsibility not to infect others.* Testing must, therefore, be an adjunct to education — for example, the provision of factual information on the biological aspects of AIDS, on the responsibility each infected person has not to infect others, and on the responsibility each uninfected person has not to become infected. Testing cannot be separated from supportive counseling received in an environment in which respect for person is proclaimed to be of paramount value. Therefore, testing can and should be facilitated and encouraged but must remain voluntary, and its results must be protected by strict and, when necessary, legally protected assurances of confidentiality in order to avert possible discrimination or even just the fear of it.

It was heartening that a bioethicist was chosen to deliver the keynote 9
address at the meeting convened by the U.S. Centers for Disease Control in April 1987. The purpose of this meeting was to discuss the possible role of HIV-antibody testing in the prevention of HIV infection. That bioethicist, Dr. Ronald Bayer, clearly set the tone of the crucial debate that followed his presentation. The humanistic approach prevailed, despite the pressure of public anxieties on all those present and despite the fact that "mandatory screening" and "isolation" are concepts inculcated, by tradition, in all public health officials. It was agreed at that meeting that the AIDS epidemic will become gradually controllable through a combination of intensive public education and research. It was also agreed that, whether this is intended or not, any form of compulsory, mandatory mass screening would inevitably carry the threat of forcible isolation for those found to be infected. Such a threat would frighten away from testing and counseling those very people who need such services most and, rather than foster responsible behavior, the fear and resentment that would result would foster irresponsible conduct.

The opinion of all the experts of the U.S. Public Health Service and 10
the Centers for Disease Control, as well as that of the scholars who have given careful thought to various possible approaches to the control of the AIDS epidemic, is now that the protection of the public health from the scourge of AIDS is best served by a diligent protection of individual liberties and privacy. Mandatory testing is, therefore, clearly *not* the way to attempt to control this epidemic.

Let us hope for our sake and the sake of generations to come that the counsel of humanists will continue to be sought in the formulation of public health policies. And let us hope that this counsel will continue to be heard. The battle against AIDS is one humanity cannot afford to lose. 11

HIV Testing: Voluntary, Mandatory, or Routine?

THERESA L. CRENSHAW

The AIDS virus is formidable. For a preventable disease, it continues 1
to spread at an alarming rate. As long as 90 percent of those who are infected — 1.5 million people or more in the United States — don't know it and continue to spread it to others, we have little hope of controlling this epidemic.

Yet, there are many dilemmas and questions that face us as individ- 2
uals and as a society. Isn't it better for a person who is infected not to know? How can one expect an infected person to stop having sex when he or she is already suffering more than a human being can bear? Are condoms sufficient protection? Is testing dependable? How can we protect the civil rights of the ill and the civil rights of the healthy?

There is no simple solution. Testing alone is not enough. We need all 3
of our resources: common sense, sexual integrity, compassion, love, exclusivity, education, discipline, testing, condoms, and spermicides — to name just a few. We also need an emphatic, positive message that promotes *quality* sex rather than *quantity* sex. Multiple partners and casual sex are not in the best interest of health, but within an exclusive relationship quality sex can thrive.

In this context, perhaps we could take an in-depth look at the contro- 4
versial issue of HIV-testing. Widespread voluntary testing, if encouraged by health officials and physicians, will most probably be successful, making widespread mandatory testing unnecessary. The general population will cooperate. However, under certain circumstances, required or routine testing might be considered and could be implemented whenever common sense dictates without the feared repercussions of quarantine and discrimination. Regardless of whether testing is voluntary, required,

---

Dr. Theresa L. Crenshaw was appointed to the Presidential Commission on the Human Immunodeficiency Virus Epidemic in July 1987, and is a widely published author and lecturer. Her article appeared in the January/February 1988 issue of *The Humanist*.

or routine, maintaining confidentiality is critical. It is vitally important to understand that public health officials are trained to maintain confidentiality in all cases; they do not put advertisements in the newspaper or call a person's employer.

Confidentiality is nonetheless a genuine concern. Lists of infected per- 5
sons have been stolen. There is probably no way humanly possible to ensure against any and all breaches of confidentiality throughout the United States and the world. It would be unrealistic to falsely assure individuals that confidentiality would be 100 percent secure. On the other hand, we must do everything within our power to come as close as possible to 100 percent confidentiality and to assure those who are concerned that these efforts are being made. There are many things we can do to improve our recording and to improve confidentiality systems. These aspects are being investigated and will hopefully be implemented by federal, state, and local authorities.

An encouraging point is that in Colorado, where HIV-positive status is 6
reportable and contact tracing is routine, *there has not been one episode of breach of confidentiality*, demonstrating that when extra care is taken there can be great success. Often forgotten is the fact that confidentiality is equally important for voluntary, required, and routine testing. It must be applied to *all* forms of testing, and it must not be used to distinguish between them.

Mandatory testing brings to mind visions of concentration camps and 7
human beings subjected to arbitrary and insensitive public health tactics. In practice, however, nothing could be further from the truth. Urine tests and blood counts are routinely required upon hospital admission. If a patient refuses, he or she will generally not be accepted by the hospital and certainly won't be allowed to undergo surgery. That's mandatory testing, but we take it in stride. And it has no hint of repressiveness; it is simply a reasonable measure for the protection and well-being of both the patient and the hospital.

Likewise, tests for syphilis are mandatory in many states. In many 8
countries, certain tests and inoculations are required before one can travel. In the not-so-distant past, health cards had to be carried by travelers along with their passports, proving that they had had certain immunizations. There is also required testing of schoolchildren for childhood diseases, which includes the tuberculin skin test, and various inoculations, without which they are not permitted to enter school. These are just a few examples of mandatory testing or treatments that are routine in our everyday lives — and that do not compromise our civil rights. However, since the term *mandatory* is emotionally charged, substituting the term *required* might more accurately reflect the intent.

Our society takes in stride sensible, necessary tests and treatments which in many circumstances are required in order to travel abroad or to perform certain jobs. However, strenuous arguments against any form of required testing for AIDS persist. The following are some of the issues most commonly raised by opponents of mandatory testing. I have attempted to analyze each argument. 9

Mandatory testing will drive infected individuals underground. They will hide out and refuse to be tested. 10

Since 90 percent of the 1.5 million or more individuals who are infected within the United States don't even know it, *they are already underground.* While certain numbers of people may use creative methods to avoid testing procedures, we would be able to reduce that percentage of people who do not know their HIV status to 10 percent instead of 90 percent, because most people would cooperate voluntarily. 11

Testing would cause more problems than it solves because huge numbers of people would receive false positive test results. Their lives would be destroyed by such test results. 12

The enzyme linked immunosorbent assay, or ELISA test, does have a high percentage of false positives, just as the tuberculin skin test has a high percentage of false positives. *That does not mean it is without value.* Whenever a test such as this is performed, a physician never stops at screening tests. Follow-up studies are required to confirm a positive test result. For example, with tuberculosis, chest X-rays and sputum cultures are performed until a positive diagnosis of tuberculosis can be made. The tuberculin skin test is used to determine whether there are indications for further studies. The AIDS antibody test is used in the same fashion. If the ELISA is positive, it should be repeated again and the Western Blot test performed. If these are all positive, the likelihood of the result being a false positive approaches zero (per 400,000, according to Dr. James Curran of the Centers for Disease Control). Immune system studies can then be done and, although it is expensive and somewhat logistically difficult, a patient who wants additional proof of infection can request actual viral cultures. Since recent research demonstrates that there can be a year or more during which the virus is present but antibodies have not yet developed — the so-called window in time — the far greater problem with testing is the high number of false negatives that still will be missed. Another study by A. Ranki et al., in the September 12, 1987, issue of *Lancet*, indicates that up to 36 percent of ELISAs are false negatives in those individuals who have had sex with an infected person. As you see, the screening test is not perfect. There will be false negatives that escape detection, so that test should be repeated periodically. All false positives would be followed up with additional tests until a confirmed positive result can be 13 established. In the near future, we will have a test for the virus itself, solving some of the problems we now face, especially the "window in time" between infection and antibody development.

There is no point in having yourself tested because there is no cure. 14

Although there is no cure, and indeed *because* there is no cure, it is 15
even more essential to be tested and to know what your antibody status is, because, if you test positive, you must take every precaution not to infect another person. If this disease were curable, perhaps we could be more cavalier. But since we must protect individuals in society from it, we must motivate those who are already infected not to infect anyone else. To assume that everyone should and will behave as though they were infected is optimistic and unreasonable, although I think many can achieve this end. It is unlikely, however, for an individual to take complete responsibility for his or her actions without definitive knowledge of infection. Even then it is a challenge.

There are other reasons for being tested. Someone who tests positive 16
will live longer if counseled not to become exposed unnecessarily to other infections by visiting sick friends at home or in the hospital or by traveling extensively to countries where foreign organisms can cause unusual infections. Additional health counseling can lead to a healthier life-style, the avoidance of other opportunistic infections or cofactors, improved nutrition, and planning for the future — which includes estate planning, a will, and making other practical arrangements as indicated.

Perhaps the most important reason for being tested early is that 17
many of the treatments becoming available are more effective the earlier they are instituted. If you know you are HIV-positive, you can apply for research projects for experimental protocols or arrange to take AZT (which is now available) or other similar drugs when they become approved for clinical use. In short, the reasons for being tested far outweigh the reasons for not being tested.

Testing is undesirable for many individuals who are unable to cope 18
with the knowledge that they are infected. These people are better off not being tested.

Anyone who is asked whether or not they think they will be able to 19
cope with the news of an HIV-positive test result would ordinarily say no. It is normal not to be able to cope well with a deadly, incurable disease. Most people who are tested receive pretest counseling. Often pretest counseling, advertently or inadvertently, dissuades individuals from being tested. At a recent conference in New York cosponsored by the American Medical Association and the Centers for Disease Control, one physician said that, with just three minutes on the telephone with someone inquiring about being tested, he succeeds in talking 57 percent of potential patients out of being tested. In the anonymous testing centers, we

need only look at the numbers of people who show up for testing compared to those who leave without being tested to assess the effectiveness of some counseling in discouraging testing.

Yet, imagine an analogous situation for a woman needing a breast bi- 20
opsy. If the physician asked, "Are you sure you want this biopsy? Do you realize that the results could show that you have cancer? Are you prepared to live with that? If the biopsy is positive, you'll need to have your breast removed. Do you think you can cope? How do you think your husband will feel about you sexually? What if the cancer is incurable and you're given a short time to live? Do you think you can handle that?" Of course, the answer to most of these questions would be "no," and many women needing breast biopsies would not pursue them. Instead, doctors help a woman confront the need for the biopsy. They support her in helping her to deal with the natural reluctance and fear involved and help her to find the courage and determination to proceed.

We must do the same with AIDS testing. Instead of asking, "Are you 21
sure you want this test?" and "Do you think you can cope?" the physician, psychologist, or therapist must take the same kind of approach they do with other necessary or valuable medical procedures. Assume it is a good idea to be tested. Compliment the person for his or her courage and self-responsibility in pursuing the test. Let each person know that you intend to help him or her get through some of the difficulties and will be there to talk in detail about the issues should that person's test turn out to be positive. Let patients know that you appreciate the courage it takes for them to proceed with the test. Emphasize that the test will be of value to them whether it turns out to be negative or positive. By taking the approach that it is valuable and worthwhile to be tested, counselors can help patients deal with their fear and discomfort rather than contribute to it. Many counseling centers are beginning to change to this approach, but too many still follow the one that effectively discourages testing.

Testing isn't cost-effective except in high-risk populations. Required 22
testing will simply waste a lot of money getting nothing but negative results.

A negative result is exceedingly valuable and can be utilized to main- 23
tain health. Any individual who tests negative should be given written, taped, or individual information on how to remain uninfected so that they are motivated to protect that fortunate status. Some studies have found that an HIV-negative result alone is sometimes not sufficient to motivate a change in sexual behavior. It is exceedingly worthwhile to test negative, especially if it can be combined with some information or counseling so that the individual can be given an opportunity to remain HIV-negative for life.

The cost of testing the entire population and counseling those who are HIV-positive on how not to spread the disease is a fraction of the cost that would be required to care for those who would otherwise become infected. 24

Testing is no good. The day after someone has the test they could become infected. That's why safe-sex cards don't work. 25

It is true that moments after blood has been drawn for an AIDS test the person could have sex and become infected. There is no question that the test is only as good as the behavior that follows it. On the other hand, if a person gets tested fairly regularly (every six months or once a year) and you meet that person five years after their first test and learn that that person has had the discipline and the concern about his or her health to remain negative for that period of time, it tells you something about that person's judgment and health status. One test may not carry a great deal of meaning, except to the individual who knows whether or not his or her behavior has been risky since the last test. On the other hand, a series of tests that are negative makes a statement of great importance. 26

It is also important to emphasize that testing is not enough. I do not support safe-sex cards if they are used in singles clubs with the recommendation that anyone who tests negative and carries a card can have sex with anyone else holding a similar card. Multiple partners multiplies the possible error. On the other hand, I think that one or more tests are very valuable if used as a prerequisite to a monogamous relationship and if condoms and spermicide are also used until at least a year has passed to protect against the window in time mentioned earlier. 27

If you institute mandatory testing, what are you going to do with the individuals who test positive? Isolate them? Quarantine them? 28

Society will do the same thing with individuals who test HIV-positive on mandatory testing that they will do with any individuals who test HIV-positive on widespread voluntary testing. Most people who are fighting mandatory testing are actually fighting quarantine, afraid that one will lead to the other. I would much prefer that they support the valuable and meaningful step of testing and fight the issue of quarantine, rather than fight step two to avoid step three. 29

You should not test because some people will panic when they are told of a positive result and commit suicide. 30

This is one of the most worrisome consequences of testing. It is understandable that someone who tests positive would fleetingly consider taking his or her own life, and some individuals might progress to actually doing so. This is one of the reasons a positive test result should never be given by phone. A patient should be called to see his or her physician or counselor or to the anonymous testing center so that he or she can be counseled extensively at that moment. 31

There are no guarantees that will ensure that someone would not commit suicide, but we must do everything humanly possible to prevent it — short of not testing. The reason for this is simple: If that person were not tested and did not know that he or she were HIV-positive, the odds are good that that person would take someone else's life unknowingly through continued sexual activity. So, even in this case, informing and counseling the individual are preferable to allowing that person to remain ignorant and perhaps infect not one but many others, thereby sentencing them to death. 32

Contact tracing is of no value, requires too much manpower, and violates privacy. 33

Contact tracing is *always* voluntary. A patient must be willing to identify sexual partners for it to be successful. When the public health department performs contact tracing, it contacts the sexual partner without giving him or her the name of the person involved. Instead, health officials say, "It has come to our attention that you have been exposed to the AIDS virus, and it is important that you be tested in order to determine whether you have become infected." It is true that if the individual has had only one sexual partner in his or her entire life he or she will be able to deduce who the person was. Since this is the exception rather than the general rule, and since the incubation period of this disease might go back a decade or more, in most cases it would be very difficult to identify the other individual involved. 34

Under what circumstances could required testing be instituted, and what rationale would justify implementing this system? 35

Hospital admission is an important opportunity for mandatory or required testing. In order to give the best care to a patient who is HIV-positive, a physician must know the patient's antibody status. A physician would treat a postoperative infection or any other infection far more aggressively with antibiotics in a patient that the physician knew to be HIV-positive than in one who did not have the potential for immune system compromise. Anyone admitted with an infection would be watched more closely if HIV-positive and would probably be treated earlier than someone whose immune system was more dependable. 36

Many argue that the doctor should use his or her discretion on whom to test. I argue that that feeds into a discriminatory bias suggesting that one can prejudge who might be suspiciously gay. There are no indicators in the healthy HIV-positive person to cause a physician to suspect which person needs testing. 37

One case history was particularly convincing that physicians need the test to help make a proper diagnosis. A woman called a television program in San Francisco. She said that she had AIDS. Several months before, she had flown to San Diego to donate blood for her mother's elective 38 surgery. Subsequently, she returned to San Francisco, had several additional sexual partners, and eventually was admitted to San Francisco General Hospital for acute respiratory distress. She was treated for allergies and asthma but almost died. During the time that she was in the hospital, she received a letter from the blood bank informing her that her blood had tested HIV-positive. She asked her roommate to open the letter. The doctors then made the diagnosis of Pneumocystis pneumonia, treated her, and she was discharged from the hospital a few days later.

San Francisco General is one of the hospitals that has the most experi- 39
ence in diagnosing and dealing with the AIDS virus. They missed this diagnosis and might not have made it without the aid of the mandatory AIDS test performed by the blood bank. The patient would have died without a change in treatment approach. It seems to me that if such a sophisticated treatment center can miss the diagnosis it would be common in less-experienced hospitals. Physicians need the assistance of this kind of testing to guide them.

This also pertains to mental hospital admissions. AIDS dementia and 40
central nervous system infection are proving to be more common than uncommon. Some researchers believe that over 90 percent of those infected manifest some degree of central nervous system involvement. Most psychologists and psychiatrists would still not suspect organic disease due to AIDS when a patient manifests acute or chronic depression, psychoses, schizophrenia, sociopathy, or aggressive or violent behavior. The virus can infect any part of the brain and, depending upon the location of infection, the resultant behavioral changes can be quite varied.

Should HIV testing be required for any special jobs? 41

Another challenging aspect of HIV infection not yet confronted by 42
our society is the otherwise asymptomatic individual who has extensive central nervous system or brain infection causing impaired judgment and interference with fine motor coordination. Pilots, air traffic controllers, and those in similar professions could be affected. Testing for the AIDS virus under these circumstances is common sense, not discrimination.

Mandatory or routine testing has been suggested for many other situ- 43
ations and occupations. Testing is already common in the military, prisons, and during immigration. Other situations becoming more common opportunities for testing are during prenatal examinations and in substance abuse programs. Other situations being heatedly debated are premarital testing and testing for food handlers, teachers, health-care workers, and business travelers. . . .

Having reviewed the common arguments against mandatory or re- 44
quired testing, we have only to devise methods that will alleviate the concerns of those who oppose mandatory testing. The two greater obstacles are concerns about confidentiality and fear of quarantine. Everything pos-

sible must be done to improve the security of our record-keeping systems. Simultaneously, society must be taught that everyone who is ill deserves our compassion, care, and respect, regardless of the source of infection.

The issue of testing must be separated from the issue of quarantine. We have tested and reported people with AIDS to the public health department for many years, and there has been no hint of quarantining unless violent or aggressive behavior puts others in danger. The issue of quarantining is independent, but related, and should be fought on a different front. 45

Mandatory, or preferably "required," testing under certain circumstances incorporates all the virtues of voluntary testing without the drawbacks. We do not now have widespread compliance with voluntary testing. Many individuals still prefer not to know. If only one person's health were at stake, this privilege could persist. However, the ostrich approach has never demonstrated itself to be of much value. In order to deal with reality, one must face it. Self-responsibility and responsibility to others requires it. 46

There would be widespread voluntary compliance with required testing just as there is for blood counts and tuberculin tests once it becomes widely recognized as a matter of common sense for health — for the benefit of every individual — and not an issue of coercion. 47

Voluntary testing is ideal but unrealistic in many situations. Required testing under certain circumstances is best for all concerned if handled with confidentiality and consideration. Routine testing in other circumstances will naturally evolve out of the preceding two. Should these trends materialize, being tested for AIDS will become a way of life. The challenge then becomes how to preserve the quality of life for everyone — the healthy and the ill. 48

AIDS: What Is to Be Done?

HARPER'S *FORUM*

The following Forum is based on a discussion held at the Princeton Club in New York City. Jonathan Lieberson served as moderator.

Jonathan Lieberson is contributing editor of *New York Review of Books* and an associate at the Population Council, an organization concerned with social scientific and biomedical research on population and development.

This selection is excerpted from the October 1985 issue of *Harper's* magazine.

Mervyn F. Silverman is a consultant to local governments and private organizations on AIDS and other health issues. From 1977 to January 1985 he was director of health for the city and county of San Francisco.

Mathilde Krim is chairperson of the board of trustees of the AIDS Medical Foundation and former head of the interferon laboratory at the Sloan-Kettering Institute for Cancer Research.

Ronald Bayer is an associate for policy studies at the Hastings Center and codirector of the center's Project on AIDS, Public Health, and Civil Liberties.

Gerald Friedland is director of Medical Service 1 at Montefiore Medical Center in New York City and an associate professor of medicine at Albert Einstein College of Medicine. He supervises the care of many AIDS patients and conducts clinical and epidemiological research into how the disease is transmitted.

Gary MacDonald is executive director of the AIDS Action Council of the Federation of AIDS-Related Organizations, a Washington, D.C., lobbying group that represents local organizations providing a wide range of support services.

Ann Giudici Fettner writes about AIDS for the *New York Native*. She was senior health adviser to the government of Kenya from 1977 to 1980. A revised edition of her book *The Truth about AIDS* will be published in October.

Stephen Schultz is deputy commissioner for epidemiologic services at the New York City Health Department and oversees the department's research on AIDS.

Allan M. Brandt is an assistant professor of the history of medicine and science at Harvard Medical School and the author of *No Magic Bullet: A Social History of Venereal Disease in the United States since 1880.*

Matthew J. Shebar was director of legal services for Gay Men's Health Crisis. He is the author of *The Gay Men's Health Crisis Attorneys' Manual.* His forthcoming book, *Lowenstein's Protégé*, describes his experiences representing people with AIDS.

Bayer: It's clear mass quarantine couldn't work, at least not in a way 1
that would benefit public health; but it would have a profound effect on civil liberties. Many less extreme measures have also been discussed, and because they are more plausible, they are even more troubling.

For example, some have proposed mandatory screening for AIDS in 2
schools, in the military, in places of employment. It's not unreasonable to expect that many who are deeply concerned about public health — and not necessarily right-wingers — will begin to discuss this possibility. If nothing else, such a discussion might help us confront the fact that in some sense we have lost the ability to consider "the public" when we de-

Shebar: Behind such cynicism must lie the hope that *everyone* in the gay community will test positive — what a great motivator that would be! Among our clients at the Gay Men's Health Crisis Center who committed suicide, three times as many were suffering from ARC as from AIDS itself. It's the waiting, the checking for symptoms every day, that's so terrible. Every cold seems like a sign of the end. 20

The blood test does not diagnose disease. It does not suggest any treatment. And it is extraordinarily dangerous in its implications for civil rights. Last summer, I got a call from a man who had been given an annual physical by his employer — a Fortune 500 pharmaceutical corporation — and had been tested without his knowledge for the LAV/HTLV-III antibody. His employer — not a physician — called him in, told him he had tested positive for the antibody, and summarily fired him. This man had no idea what the test meant. I helped him get his job back and have the test result deleted from his medical records. 21

Silverman: To prevent such abuses, California just passed a law forbidding use of the test in screening employees or insurance applicants. 22

MacDonald: The implications of mass screening are frightening. When a bureaucracy like the Public Health Service is given a very simple task — and screening blood is a very simple task — it tends to reduce a complex phenomenon to very simple formulas: If someone tests positive, thus and thus is true; if someone tests negative, thus and thus is true. The bureaucracy doesn't pay attention to whether anything is really being accomplished. Look at the Red Cross's policy of sending people with confirmed positive results to their physicians. Their physicians can't *do* anything. 23

Fettner: The Red Cross is also putting the names of those who test positive on a list. 24

Bayer: Blood banks always maintain something called a deferral directory, which lists anyone whose blood has been rejected for medical or other reasons. Its purpose is basically to screen out blood that may not be safe. 25

Of course any kind of list, whatever its purpose, presents a problem. The Red Cross list presents a particular problem for those who believe that individuals should *not* be notified of positive results because they might be terrified by information that is not necessarily accurate. 26

At present, a blood donor is notified only if both the ELISA screen test and the confirmatory Western Blot test are positive. If someone tests positively on the ELISA but negatively on the Western Blot, his blood is not used and his name appears on the deferral list — but he is not notified. This list presents the problem, especially since no computer list can be absolutely confidential. Are health-care professionals ethically bound to tell people their names are on the list, even though it has not been confirmed that they have the antibody? 27

Almost everyone acknowledges that many gay men want to take the 28
test, whether it will mean their names end up on a list or not. That's why people are worried that members of high-risk groups will flock to donate blood in order to get the test results, and thereby risk infecting the blood supply. So now we are in the strange position of spending public money to set up testing centers while acknowledging that the test can't give much useful information.

Shebar: Creating alternative centers has to be done. But gay leaders 29
should be sending out a clear message that people should *not* take the test, both to ensure that high-risk people don't flock to blood banks and to protect their rights.

Discrimination Goes On

ROBERT H. COHEN

To the Editor:

"Dr. Joseph and AIDS Testing" (editorial, November 16) supports the 1
call by Dr. Stephen Joseph, New York City's departing health commissioner, for tracing the sexual contacts of those who test positive for the human immunodeficiency virus, apparently in the belief that discrimination is no longer a problem.

Unfortunately, discrimination against HIV-infected people is real. Be- 2
yond press reports, I know people who have been fired from jobs, evicted from their homes, denied health insurance, or refused medical or dental care once their HIV-positive status became known. Legal protections are often ineffective because of expenses of the legal system; often the complainant dies before a case can be heard.

And while HIV infection is probably lifelong, antidiscrimination ordi- 3
nances may not be: Just this month, after a well-funded and professional campaign by religious zealots, voters in the town of Concord, California, repealed a city ordinance banning HIV-related discrimination. No law can prevent mindless violence; only two years ago, angry townspeople in Arcadia, Florida, firebombed the home of three HIV-infected children.

Without a federal antidiscrimination law for people with HIV, and a 4
commitment to enforcing that law, contact tracing will not be effective and will frighten away those the program is intended to reach. I know

Robert H. Cohen's letter appeared in the *New York Times* on December 20, 1989.

Colorado residents who traveled out of state for anonymous testing elsewhere or deferred testing until too late.

If the solution to this epidemic were as simple as testing and contact 5
tracing, life would be easier for public officials and medical experts. Under a national commitment to bar discrimination, infected people could come forward without fear and receive treatment that could not only prolong their lives but that also shows promise of reducing their infectivity and the risk to others.

—Robert H. Cohen

THINKING AND WRITING ABOUT AIDS TESTING

Questions for Discussion and Writing

1. What are the principal differences between Krim and Crenshaw? Are they in agreement on any important issues?
2. What is Restak's definition of "the truly humanitarian position" in regard to AIDS? What aspect of AIDS testing does Restak emphasize? This article was written in 1985. Do more recent articles in this chapter — or elsewhere — refute some of Restak's data? Be specific. Would new information change Restak's message?
3. What considerations cause Richards to advocate testing of gay men? Why do you think that he does not advocate compulsory testing? Does Cohen agree with Richards about testing?
4. Examine the credentials of the participants in the *Harper's* symposium. How do their messages reflect their professional positions and interests? What are the principal objections to informing people that they carry the AIDS virus? Would it make a difference if the tests could predict the presence of the AIDS virus with complete accuracy?
5. Should doctors and counselors inform people that they carry the AIDS virus, even if there is no cure and no danger to sexual partners? What are the benefits, if any, of disclosure? What are the disadvantages?

Topics for Research

A review of legal decisions to date concerning testing

Comparison of AIDS with plagues of the past

Treatment of communicable diseases in the past

The spread of AIDS to the heterosexual population

Responses of college students to education about AIDS

CHAPTER 12

Animal Rights

Advocates for the rights of animals object to several different kinds of human exploitation of animals — for food, clothing, research, and recreation (as in hunting and bullfighting). In this chapter we confine our discussion to the uses of animals for food and medical research.

Although organized concern for the rights of animals is at least 200 years old in the West, the movement has acquired new momentum, perhaps as a result of human rights movements, which have succeeded in raising people's consciousness about the rights of women, minorities, homosexuals, the handicapped, and others whose interests have often been ignored by those who are more powerful.

Ethical vegetarianism, based on the belief that the lives of animals are as sacred as those of human beings, is very old. Strict Hindus have practiced vegetarianism for 2,000 years. But it is relatively new in the West. Especially in the last quarter of a century, the growth of factory farming of animals has induced numbers of people to stop eating meat.

Experimentation with animals for medical and other scientific research has proliferated dramatically with immeasurable benefits for human beings, above all in medicine — in the conquest of rabies, bacterial infection, sterile surgical techniques, syphilis, and organ transplants. Less-defensible experimentation has been performed by cosmetic companies.

The question is to what extent the welfare of human beings should take precedence over the rights of animals. The answer will rest on religious and philosophical grounds that define the relationship between human beings and their fellow creatures.

Animal Liberation

PETER SINGER

We are familiar with Black Liberation, Gay Liberation, and a variety of other movements. With Women's Liberation some thought we had come to the end of the road. Discrimination on the basis of sex, it has been said, is the last form of discrimination that is universally accepted and practiced without pretense, even in those liberal circles which have long prided themselves on their freedom from racial discrimination. But one should always be wary of talking of "the last remaining form of discrimination." If we have learned anything from the liberation movements, we should have learned how difficult it is to be aware of the ways in which we discriminate until they are forcefully pointed out to us. A liberation movement demands an expansion of our moral horizons, so that practices that were previously regarded as natural and inevitable are now seen as intolerable. 1

Animals, Men and Morals is a manifesto for an Animal Liberation movement. The contributors to the book may not all see the issue this way. They are a varied group. Philosophers, ranging from professors to graduate students, make up the largest contingent. There are five of them, including the three editors, and there is also an extract from the unjustly neglected German philosopher with an English name, Leonard Nelson, who died in 1927. There are essays by two novelist/critics, Brigid Brophy and Maureen Duffy, and another by Muriel the Lady Dowding, widow of Dowding of Battle of Britain fame and the founder of "Beauty Without Cruelty," a movement that campaigns against the use of animals for furs and cosmetics. The other pieces are by a psychologist, a botanist, a sociologist, and Ruth Harrison, who is probably best described as a professional campaigner for animal welfare. 2

Whether or not these people, as individuals, would all agree that they are launching a liberation movement for animals, the book as a whole 3

Peter Singer teaches philosophy at Monash University in Melbourne, Australia. This essay appeared in the April 15, 1973 issue of the *New York Review of Books* as a review of *Animals, Men and Morals,* edited by Stanley and Roslind Godlovitch and John Harris.

amounts to no less. It is a demand for a complete change in our attitudes to nonhumans. It is a demand that we cease to regard the exploitation of other species as natural and inevitable, and that, instead, we see it as a continuing moral outrage. Patrick Corbett, Professor of Philosophy at Sussex University, captures the spirit of the book in his closing words:

> . . . We require now to extend the great principles of liberty, equality and fraternity over the lives of animals. Let animal slavery join human slavery in the graveyard of the past.

The reader is likely to be skeptical. "Animal Liberation" sounds more like a parody of liberation movements than a serious objective. The reader may think: We support the claims of blacks and women for equality because blacks and women really are equal to whites and males — equal in intelligence and in abilities, capacity for leadership, rationality, and so on. Humans and nonhumans obviously are not equal in these respects. Since justice demands only that we treat equals equally, unequal treatment of humans and nonhumans cannot be an injustice. 4

This is a tempting reply, but a dangerous one. It commits the nonracist and nonsexist to a dogmatic belief that blacks and women really are just as intelligent, able, etc., as whites and males — and no more. Quite possibly this happens to be the case. Certainly attempts to prove that racial or sexual differences in these respects have a genetic origin have not been conclusive. But do we really want to stake our demand for equality on the assumption that there are no genetic differences of this kind between the different races or sexes? Surely the appropriate response to those who claim to have found evidence for such genetic differences is not to stick to the belief that there are no differences, whatever the evidence to the contrary; rather one should be clear that the claim to equality does not depend on IQ. Moral equality is distinct from factual equality. Otherwise it would be nonsense to talk of the equality of human beings, since humans, as individuals, obviously differ in intelligence and almost any ability one cares to name. If possessing greater intelligence does not entitle one human to exploit another, why should it entitle humans to exploit nonhumans? 5

Jeremy Bentham expressed the essential basis of equality in his famous formula: "Each to count for one and none for more than one." In other words, the interest of every being that has interests are to be taken into account and treated equally with the like interests of any other being. Other moral philosophers, before and after Bentham, have made the same point in different ways. Our concern for others must not depend on whether they possess certain characteristics, though just what concern involves may, of course, vary according to such characteristics. 6

Bentham, incidentally, was well aware that the logic of the demand for racial equality did not stop at the equality of humans. He wrote: 7

> The day *may* come when the rest of the animal creation may acquire those rights which never could have been withholden from them but by the hand of tyranny. The French have already discovered that the blackness of the skin is no reason why a human being should be abandoned without redress to the caprice of a tormentor. It may one day come to be recognized that the number of the legs, the villosity of the skin, or the termination of the *os sacrum*, are reasons equally insufficient for abandoning a sensitive being to the same fate. What else is it that should trace the insuperable line? Is it the faculty of reason, or perhaps the faculty of discourse? But a full-grown horse or dog is beyond comparison a more rational, as well as a more conversable animal, than an infant of a day, or a week, or even a month, old. But suppose they were otherwise, what would it avail? The question is not, Can they *reason*? nor Can they *talk*? but, Can they *suffer*?[1]

Surely Bentham was right. If a being suffers, there can be no moral justification for refusing to take that suffering into consideration, and, indeed, to count it equally with the like suffering (if rough comparisons can be made) of any other being.

So the only question is: Do animals other than man suffer? Most people agree unhesitatingly that animals like cats and dogs can and do suffer, and this seems also to be assumed by those laws that prohibit wanton cruelty to such animals. Personally, I have no doubt at all about this and find it hard to take seriously the doubts that a few people apparently do have. The editors and contributors of *Animals, Men and Morals* seem to feel the same way, for although the question is raised more than once, doubts are quickly dismissed each time. Nevertheless, because this is such a fundamental point, it is worth asking what grounds we have for attributing suffering to other animals. 8

It is best to begin by asking what grounds any individual human has for supposing that other humans feel pain. Since pain is a state of consciousness, a "mental event," it can never be directly observed. No observations, whether behavioral signs such as writhing or screaming or physiological or neurological recordings, are observations of pain itself. Pain is something one feels, and one can only infer that others are feeling it from various external indications. The fact that only philosophers are ever skeptical about whether other humans feel pain shows that we regard such inference as justifiable in the case of humans. 9

---

[1] *The Principles of Morals and Legislation*, ch. XVII, sec. 1, footnote to paragraph 4.

Is there any reason why the same inference should be unjustifiable for other animals? Nearly all the external signs which lead us to infer pain in other humans can be seen in other species, especially "higher" animals such as mammals and birds. Behavioral signs — writhing, yelping, or other forms of calling, attempts to avoid the source of pain, and many others — are present. We know, too, that these animals are biologically similar in the relevant respects, having nervous systems like ours which can be observed to function as ours do. 10

So the grounds for inferring that these animals can feel pain are nearly as good as the grounds for inferring other humans do. Only nearly, for there is one behavioral sign that humans have but nonhumans, with the exception of one or two specially raised chimpanzees, do not have. This, of course, is a developed language. As the quotation from Bentham indicates, this has long been regarded as an important distinction between man and other animals. Other animals may communicate with each other, but not in the way we do. Following Chomsky, many people now mark this distinction by saying that only humans communicate in a form that is governed by rules of syntax. (For the purposes of this argument, linguists allow those chimpanzees who have learned a syntactic sign language to rank as honorary humans.) Nevertheless, as Bentham pointed out, this distinction is not relevant to the question of how animals ought to be treated, unless it can be linked to the issue of whether animals suffer. 11

This link may be attempted in two ways. First, there is a hazy line of philosophical thought, stemming perhaps from some doctrines associated with Wittgenstein, which maintains that we cannot meaningfully attribute states of consciousness to beings without language. I have not seen this argument made explicit in print, though I have come across it in conversation. The position seems to me very implausible, and I doubt that it would be held at all if it were not thought to be a consequence of a broader view of the significance of language. It may be that the use of a public, rule-governed language is a precondition of conceptual thought. It may even be, although personally I doubt it, that we cannot meaningfully speak of a creature having an intention unless that creature can use a language. But states like pain, surely, are more primitive than either of these, and seem to have nothing to do with language. 12

Indeed, as Jane Goodall points out in her study of chimpanzees, when it comes to the expression of feelings and emotions, humans tend to fall back on nonlinguistic modes of communication which are often found among apes, such as a cheering pat on the back, an exuberant embrace, a clasp of hands, and so on.[2] Michael Peters makes a similar point in his con- 13

---

[2] Jane van Lawick-Goodall, *In the Shadow of Man* (Boston: Houghton Mifflin, 1971), p. 225.

tribution to *Animals, Men and Morals* when he notes that the basic signals we use to convey pain, fear, sexual arousal, and so on are not specific to our species. So there seems to be no reason at all to believe that a creature without language cannot suffer.

The second, and more easily appreciated way of linking language and the existence of pain is to say that the best evidence that we can have that another creature is in pain is when he tells us that he is. This is a distinct line of argument, for it is not being denied that a non-language-user conceivably could suffer, but only that we could know that he is suffering. Still, this line of argument seems to me to fail, and for reasons similar to those just given. "I am in pain" is not the best possible evidence that the speaker is in pain (he might be lying) and it is certainly not the only possible evidence. Behavioral signs and knowledge of the animal's biological similarity to ourselves together provide adequate evidence that animals do suffer. After all, we would not accept linguistic evidence if it contradicted the rest of the evidence. If a man was severely burned, and behaved as if he were in pain, writhing, groaning, being very careful not to let his burned skin touch anything, and so on, but later said he had not been in pain at all, we would be more likely to conclude that he was lying or suffering from amnesia than that he had not been in pain. 14

Even if there were stronger grounds for refusing to attribute pain to those who do not have a language, the consequences of this refusal might lead us to examine these grounds unusually critically. Human infants, as well as some adults, are unable to use language. Are we to deny that a year-old infant can suffer? If not, how can language be crucial? Of course, most parents can understand the responses of even very young infants better than they understand the responses of other animals, and sometimes infant responses can be understood in the light of later development. 15

This, however, is just a fact about the relative knowledge we have of our own species and other species, and most of this knowledge is simply derived from closer contact. Those who have studied the behavior of other animals soon learn to understand their responses at least as well as we understand those of an infant. (I am not referring to Jane Goodall's and other well-known studies of apes. Consider, for example, the degree of understanding achieved by Tinbergen from watching herring gulls.)[3] Just as we can understand infant human behavior in the light of adult human behavior, so we can understand the behavior of other species in the light of our own behavior (and sometimes we can understand our own behavior better in the light of the behavior of other species). 16

[3] N. Tinbergen, *The Herring Gull's World* (New York: Basic Books, 1961).

The grounds we have for believing that other mammals and birds suffer are, then, closely analogous to the grounds we have for believing that other humans suffer. It remains to consider how far down the evolutionary scale this analogy holds. Obviously it becomes poorer when we get further away from man. To be more precise would require a detailed examination of all that we know about other forms of life. With fish, reptiles, and other vertebrates the analogy still seems strong, with molluscs like oysters it is much weaker. Insects are more difficult, and it may be that in our present state of knowledge we must be agnostic about whether they are capable of suffering. 17

If there is no moral justification for ignoring suffering when it occurs, and it does occur in other species, what are we to say of our attitudes toward these other species? Richard Ryder, one of the contributors to *Animals, Men and Morals*, uses the term "speciesism" to describe the belief that we are entitled to treat members of other species in a way in which it would be wrong to treat members of our own species. The term is not euphonious, but it neatly makes the analogy with racism. The nonracist would do well to bear the analogy in mind when he is inclined to defend human behavior toward nonhumans. "Shouldn't we worry about improving the lot of our own species before we concern ourselves with other species?" he may ask. If we substitute "race" for "species" we shall see that the question is better not asked. "Is a vegetarian diet nutritionally adequate?" resembles the slave-owner's claim that he and the whole economy of the South would be ruined without slave labor. There is even a parallel with skeptical doubts about whether animals suffer, for some defenders of slavery professed to doubt whether blacks really suffer in the way whites do. 18

I do not want to give the impression, however, that the case for Animal Liberation is based on the analogy with racism and no more. On the contrary, *Animals, Men and Morals* describes the various ways in which humans exploit nonhumans, and several contributors consider the defenses that have been offered, including the defense of meat-eating mentioned in the last paragraph. Sometimes the rebuttals are scornfully dismissive, rather than carefully designed to convince the detached critic. This may be a fault, but it is a fault that is inevitable, given the kind of book this is. The issue is not one on which one can remain detached. As the editors state in their Introduction: 19

> Once the full force of moral assessment has been made explicit there can be no rational excuse left for killing animals, be they killed for food, science, or sheer personal indulgence. We have not assembled this book to provide the reader with yet another manual on how to make brutalities less brutal. Compromise, in the traditional sense of the term, is simple unthinking weakness

when one considers the actual reasons for our crude relationships with the other animals.

The point is that on this issue there are few critics who are genuinely detached. People who eat pieces of slaughtered nonhumans every day find it hard to believe that they are doing wrong; and they also find it hard to imagine what else they could eat. So for those who do not place nonhumans beyond the pale of morality, there comes a stage when further argument seems pointless, a stage at which one can only accuse one's opponent of hypocrisy and reach for the sort of sociological account of our practices and the way we defend them that is attempted by David Wood in his contribution to this book. On the other hand, to those unconvinced by the arguments, and unable to accept that they are merely rationalizing their dietary preferences and their fear of being thought peculiar, such sociological explanations can only seem insultingly arrogant. 20

The logic of speciesism is most apparent in the practice of experimenting on nonhumans in order to benefit humans. This is because the issue is rarely obscured by allegations that nonhumans are so different from humans that we cannot know anything about whether they suffer. The defender of vivisection cannot use this argument because he needs to stress the similarities between man and other animals in order to justify the usefulness to the former of experiments on the latter. The researcher who makes rats choose between starvation and electric shocks to see if they develop ulcers (they do) does so because he knows that the rat has a nervous system very similar to man's, and presumably feels an electric shock in a similar way. 21

Richard Ryder's restrained account of experiments on animals made me angrier with my fellow men than anything else in this book. Ryder, a clinical psychologist by profession, himself experimented on animals before he came to hold the view he puts forward in his essay. Experimenting on animals is now a large industry, both academic and commercial. In 1969, more than 5 million experiments were performed in Britain, the vast majority without anesthetic (though how many of these involved pain is not known). There are no accurate U.S. figures, since there is no federal law on the subject, and in many cases no state law either. Estimates vary from 20 million to 200 million. Ryder suggests that 80 million may be the best guess. We tend to think that this is all for vital medical research, but of course it is not. Huge numbers of animals are used in university departments from Forestry to Psychology, and even more are used for commercial purposes, to test whether cosmetics can cause skin damage, or shampoos eye damage, or to test food additives or laxatives or sleeping pills or anything else. 22

A standard test for foodstuffs is the "LD50." The object of this test is to find the dosage level at which 50 percent of the test animals will die. This means that nearly all of them will become very sick before finally succumbing or surviving. When the substance is a harmless one, it may be necessary to force huge doses down the animals, until in some cases sheer volume or concentration causes death. 23

Ryder gives a selection of experiments, taken from recent scientific journals. I will quote two, not for the sake of indulging in gory details, but in order to give an idea of what normal researchers think they may legitimately do to other species. The point is not that the individual researchers are cruel men, but that they are behaving in a way that is allowed by our speciesist attitudes. As Ryder points out, even if only 1 percent of the experiments involve severe pain, that is 50,000 experiments in Britain each year, or nearly 150 every day (and about fifteen times as many in the United States, if Ryder's guess is right). Here then are two experiments: 24

> O. S. Ray and R. J. Barrett of Pittsburgh gave electric shocks to the feet of 1,042 mice. They then caused convulsions by giving more intense shocks through cup-shaped electrodes applied to the animals' eyes or through pressure spring clips attached to their ears. Unfortunately some of the mice who "successfully completed Day One training were found sick or dead prior to testing on Day Two." [*Journal of Comparative and Physiological Psychology*, vol. 67, 1969, pp. 110–116]
>
> At the National Institute for Medical Research, Mill Hill, London, W. Feldberg and S. L. Sherwood injected chemicals into the brains of cats — "with a number of widely different substances, recurrent patterns of reaction were obtained. Retching, vomiting, defaecation, increased salivation and greatly accelerated respiration leading to panting were common features." . . .
>
> The injection into the brain of a large dose of Tubocuraine caused the cat to jump "from the table to the floor and then straight into its cage, where it started calling more and more noisily whilst moving about restlessly and jerkily . . . finally the cat fell with legs and neck flexed, jerking in rapid clonic movements, the condition being that of a major [epileptic] convulsion . . . within a few seconds the cat got up, ran for a few yards at high speed and fell in another fit. The whole process was repeated several times within the next ten minutes, during which the cat lost faeces and foamed at the mouth."
>
> The animal finally died thirty-five minutes after the brain injection. [*Journal of Physiology*, vol. 123, 1954, pp. 148–167]

There is nothing secret about these experiments. One has only to open any recent volume of a learned journal, such as the *Journal of Comparative and Physiological Psychology*, to find full descriptions of experiments of this sort, together with the results obtained — results that are frequently trivial and obvious. The experiments are often supported by public funds. 25

It is a significant indication of the level of acceptability of these practices that, although these experiments are taking place at this moment on university campuses throughout the country, there has so far as I know, not been the slightest protest from the student movement. Students have been rightly concerned that their universities should not discriminate on grounds of race or sex, and that they should not serve the purposes of the military or big business. Speciesism continues undisturbed, and many students participate in it. There may be a few qualms at first, but since everyone regards it as normal, and it may even be a required part of a course, the student soon becomes hardened and, dismissing his earlier feelings as "mere sentiment," comes to regard animals as statistics rather than sentient beings with interests that warrant consideration. 26

Argument about vivisection has often missed the point because it has been put in absolutist terms: Would the abolitionist be prepared to let thousands die if they could be saved by experimenting on a single animal? The way to reply to this purely hypothetical question is to pose another: Would the experimenter be prepared to experiment on a human orphan under six months old, if it were the only way to save many lives? (I say "orphan" to avoid the complication of parental feelings, although in doing so I am being overfair to the experimenter, since the nonhuman subjects of experiments are not orphans.) A negative answer to this question indicates that the experimenter's readiness to use nonhumans is simple discrimination, for adult apes, cats, mice, and other mammals are more conscious of what is happening to them, more self-directing, and, so far as we can tell, just as sensitive to pain as a human infant. There is no characteristic that human infants possess that adult mammals do not have to the same or a higher degree. 27

(It might be possible to hold that what makes it wrong to experiment on a human infant is that the infant will in time develop into more than the nonhuman, but one would then, to be consistent, have to oppose abortion, and perhaps contraception, too, for the fetus and the egg and sperm have the same potential as the infant. Moreover, one would still have no reason for experimenting on a nonhuman rather than a human with brain damage severe enough to make it impossible for him to rise above infant level.) 28

The experimenter, then, shows a bias for his own species whenever he carries out an experiment on a nonhuman for a purpose that he would not think justified him in using a human being at an equal or lower level of sentience, awareness, ability to be self-directing, etc. No one familiar with the kind of results yielded by these experiments can have the slightest doubt that if this bias were eliminated the number of experiments performed would be zero or very close to it. 29

If it is vivisection that shows the logic of speciesism most clearly, it is 30
the use of other species for food that is at the heart of our attitudes toward them. Most of *Animals, Men and Morals* is an attack on meat-eating — an attack which is based solely on concern for nonhumans, without reference to arguments derived from considerations of ecology, macrobiotics, health, or religion.

The idea that nonhumans are utilities, means to our ends, pervades 31
our thought. Even conservationists who are concerned about the slaughter of wild fowl but not about the vastly greater slaughter of chickens for our tables are thinking in this way — they are worried about what we would lose if there were less wildlife. Stanley Godlovitch, pursuing the Marxist idea that our thinking is formed by the activities we undertake in satisfying our needs, suggests that man's first classification of his environment was into Edibles and Inedibles. Most animals came into the first category, and there they have remained.

Man may always have killed other species for food, but he has never 32
exploited them so ruthlessly as he does today. Farming has succumbed to business methods, the objective being to get the highest possible ratio of output (meat, eggs, milk) to input (fodder, labor costs, etc.). Ruth Harrison's essay "On Factory Farming" gives an account of some aspects of modern methods, and of the unsuccessful British campaign for effective controls, a campaign which was sparked off by her *Animal Machines* (London: Stuart, 1964).

Her article is in no way a substitute for her earlier book. This is a pity 33
since, as she says, "Farm produce is still associated with mental pictures of animals browsing in the fields . . . of hens having a last forage before going to roost. . . ." Yet neither in her article nor elsewhere in *Animals, Men and Morals* is this false image replaced by a clear idea of the nature and extent of factory farming. We learn of this only indirectly, when we hear of the code of reform proposed by an advisory committee set up by the British government.

Among the proposals, which the government refused to implement 34
on the grounds that they were too idealistic, were *"Any animal should at least have room to turn around freely."*

Factory farm animals need liberation in the most literal sense. Veal 35
calves are kept in stalls five feet by two feet. They are usually slaughtered when about four months old, and have been too big to turn in their stalls for at least a month. Intensive beef herds, kept in stalls only proportionately larger for much longer periods, account for a growing percentage of beef production. Sows are often similarly confined when pregnant, which, because of artificial methods of increasing fertility, can be most of the time. Animals confined in this way do not waste food by exercising, nor do they develop unpalatable muscle.

"A dry bedded area should be provided for all stock." Intensively kept animals usually have to stand and sleep on slatted floors without straw, because this makes cleaning easier. 36

"Palatable roughage must be readily available to all calves after one week of age." In order to produce the pale veal housewives are said to prefer, calves are fed on an all-liquid diet until slaughter, even though they are long past the age at which they would normally eat grass. They develop a craving for roughage, evidenced by attempts to gnaw wood from their stalls. (For the same reason, their diet is deficient in iron.) 37

"Battery cages for poultry should be large enough for a bird to be able to stretch one wing at a time." Under current British practice, a cage for four or five laying hens has a floor area of twenty inches by eighteen inches, scarcely larger than a double page of the *New York Review of Books.* In this space, on a sloping wire floor (sloping so the eggs roll down, wire so the dung drops through) the birds live for a year or eighteen months while artificial lighting and temperature conditions combine with drugs in their food to squeeze the maximum number of eggs out of them. Table birds are also sometimes kept in cages. More often they are reared in sheds, no less crowded. Under these conditions all the birds' natural activities are frustrated, and they develop "vices" such as pecking each other to death. To prevent this, beaks are often cut off, and the sheds kept dark. 38

How many of those who support factory farming by buying its produce know anything about the way it is produced? How many have heard something about it, but are reluctant to check up for fear that it will make them uncomfortable? To nonspeciesists, the typical consumer's mixture of ignorance, reluctance to find out the truth, and vague belief that nothing really bad could be allowed seems analogous to the attitudes of "decent Germans" to the death camps. 39

There are, of course, some defenders of factory farming. Their arguments are considered, though again rather sketchily, by John Harris. Among the most common: "Since they have never known anything else, they don't suffer." This argument will not be put by anyone who knows anything about animal behavior, since he will know that not all behavior has to be learned. Chickens attempt to stretch wings, walk around, scratch, and even dustbathe or build a nest, even though they have never lived under conditions that allowed these activities. Calves can suffer from maternal deprivation no matter at what age they were taken from their mothers. "We need these intensive methods to provide protein for a growing population." As ecologists and famine relief organizations know, we can produce far more protein per acre if we grow the right vegetable crop, soy beans for instance, than if we use the land to grow crops to be converted into protein by animals who use nearly 90 percent of the protein themselves, even when unable to exercise. 40

There will be many readers of this book who will agree that factory 41
farming involves an unjustifiable degree of exploitation of sentient creatures, and yet will want to say that there is nothing wrong with rearing animals for food, provided it is done "humanely." These people are saying, in effect, that although we should not cause animals to suffer, there is nothing wrong with killing them.

There are two possible replies to this view. One is to attempt to show 42
that this combination of attitudes is absurd. Roslind Godlovitch takes this course in her essay, which is an examination of some common attitudes to animals. She argues that from the combination of "animal suffering is to be avoided" and "there is nothing wrong with killing animals" it follows that all animal life ought to be exterminated (since all sentient creatures will suffer to some degree at some point in their lives). Euthanasia is a contentious issue only because we place some value on living. If we did not, the least amount of suffering would justify it. Accordingly, if we deny that we have a duty to exterminate all animal life, we must concede that we are placing some value on animal life.

This argument seems to me valid, although one could still reply that 43
the value of animal life is to be derived from the pleasures that life can have for them, so that, provided their lives have a balance of pleasure over pain, we are justified in rearing them. But this would imply that we ought to produce animals and let them live as pleasantly as possible, without suffering.

At this point, one can make the second of the two possible replies to 44
the view that rearing and killing animals for food is all right so long as it is done humanely. This second reply is that so long as we think that a nonhuman may be killed simply so that a human can satisfy his taste for meat, we are still thinking of nonhumans as means rather than as ends in themselves. The factory farm is nothing more than the application of technology to this concept. Even traditional methods involve castration, the separation of mothers and their young, the breaking up of herds, branding or ear-punching, and of course transportation to the abattoirs and the final moments of terror when the animal smells blood and senses danger. If we were to try rearing animals so that they lived and died without suffering, we should find that to do so on anything like the scale of today's meat industry would be a sheer impossibility. Meat would become the prerogative of the rich.

I have been able to discuss only some of the contributions to this 45
book, saying nothing about, for instance, the essays on killing for furs and for sport. Nor have I considered all the detailed questions that need to be asked once we start thinking about other species in the radically different way presented by this book. What, for instance, are we to do about genuine conflicts of interest like rats biting slum children? I am not sure of the

answer, but the essential point is just that we *do* see this as a conflict of interest, that we recognize that rats have interests too. Then we may begin to think about other ways of resolving the conflict — perhaps by leaving out rat baits that sterilize the rats instead of killing them.

I have not discussed such problems because they are side issues compared with the exploitation of other species for food and for experimental purposes. On these central matters, I hope that I have said enough to show that this book, despite its flaws, is a challenge to every human to recognize his attitudes to nonhumans as a form of prejudice no less objectionable than racism or sexism. It is a challenge that demands not just a change of attitudes, but a change in our way of life, for it requires us to become vegetarians. 46

Can a purely moral demand of this kind succeed? The odds are certainly against it. The book holds out no inducements. It does not tell us that we will become healthier, or enjoy life more, if we cease exploiting animals. Animal Liberation will require greater altruism on the part of mankind than any other liberation movement, since animals are incapable of demanding it for themselves, or of protesting against their exploitation by votes, demonstrations, or bombs. Is man capable of such genuine altruism? Who knows? If this book does have a significant effect, however, it will be a vindication of all those who have believed that man has within himself the potential for more than cruelty and selfishness. 47

Vivisection

C. S. LEWIS

It is the rarest thing in the world to hear a rational discussion of vivisection. Those who disapprove of it are commonly accused of "sentimentality," and very often their arguments justify the accusation. They paint pictures of pretty little dogs on dissecting tables. But the other side lies open to exactly the same charge. They also often defend the practice by drawing pictures of suffering women and children whose pain can be relieved (we are assured) only by the fruits of vivisection. The one appeal, quite as clearly as the other, is addressed to emotion, to the particular emotion we call pity. And neither appeal proves anything. If the thing is 1

Clive Staples Lewis (1898–1963) was a professor of English literature at Oxford and Cambridge universities. His writings on Christianity and his moralistic fantasy tales for children continue to be widely popular. "Vivisection" was first published as a pamphlet in 1947 by the New England Anti-Vivisection Society.

right — and if right at all, it is a duty — then pity for the animal is one of the temptations we must resist in order to perform that duty. If the thing is wrong, then pity for human suffering is precisely the temptation which will most probably lure us into doing that wrong thing. But the real question — *whether* it is right or wrong — remains meanwhile just where it was.

A rational discussion of this subject begins by inquiring whether pain is, or is not, an evil. If it is not, then the case against vivisection falls. But then so does the case for vivisection. If it is not defended on the ground that it reduces human suffering, on what ground can it be defended? And if pain is not an evil, why should human suffering be reduced? We must therefore assume as a basis for the whole discussion that pain is an evil, otherwise there is nothing to be discussed. 2

Now if pain is an evil then the infliction of pain, considered in itself, must clearly be an evil act. But there are such things as necessary evils. Some acts which would be bad, simply in themselves, may be excusable and even laudable when they are necessary means to a greater good. In saying that the infliction of pain, simply in itself, is bad, we are not saying that pain ought never to be inflicted. Most of us think that it can rightly be inflicted for a good purpose — as in dentistry or just and reformatory punishment. The point is that it always requires justification. On the man whom we find inflicting pain rests the burden of showing why an act which in itself would be simply bad is, in those particular circumstances, good. If we find a man giving pleasure it is for us to prove (if we criticize him) that his action is wrong. But if we find a man inflicting pain it is for him to prove that his action is right. If he cannot, he is a wicked man. 3

Now vivisection can only be defended by showing it to be right that one species should suffer in order that another species should be happier. And here we come to the parting of the ways. The Christian defender and the ordinary "scientific" (i.e., naturalistic) defender of vivisection have to take quite different lines. 4

The Christian defender, especially in the Latin countries, is very apt to say that we are entitled to do anything we please to animals because they "have no souls." But what does this mean? If it means that animals have no consciousness, then how is this known? They certainly behave as if they had, or at least the higher animals do. I myself am inclined to think that far fewer animals than is supposed have what we should recognize as consciousness. But that is only an opinion. Unless we know on other grounds that vivisection is right we must not take the moral risk of tormenting them on a mere opinion. On the other hand, the statement that they "have no souls" may mean that they have no moral responsibilities and are not immortal. But the absence of "soul" in that sense makes the infliction of pain upon them not easier but harder to justify. For it means 5 that animals cannot deserve pain, nor profit morally by the discipline of pain, nor be recompensed by happiness in another life for suffering in this. Thus all the factors which render pain more tolerable or make it less totally evil in the case of human beings will be lacking in the beasts. "Soullessness," in so far as it is relevant to the question at all, is an argument against vivisection.

The only rational line for the Christian vivisectionist to take is to say 6
that the superiority of man over beast is a real objective fact, guaranteed by Revelation, and that the propriety of sacrificing beast to man is a logical consequence. We are "worth more than many sparrows,"[1] and in saying this we are not merely expressing a natural preference for our own species simply because it is our own but conforming to a hierarchical order created by God and really present in the universe whether anyone acknowledges it or not. The position may not be satisfactory. We may fail to see how a benevolent Deity could wish us to draw such conclusions from the hierarchical order He has created. We may find it difficult to formulate a human right of tormenting beasts in terms which would not equally imply an angelic right of tormenting men. And we may feel that though objective superiority is rightly claimed for men, yet that very superiority ought partly to *consist in* not behaving like a vivisector: that we ought to prove ouselves better than the beasts precisely by the fact of acknowledging duties to them which they do not acknowledge to us. But on all these questions different opinions can be honestly held. If on grounds of our real, divinely ordained, superiority a Christian pathologist thinks it right to vivisect, and does so with scrupulous care to avoid the least dram or scruple of unnecessary pain, in a trembling awe at the responsiblility which he assumes, and with a vivid sense of the high mode in which human life must be lived if it is to justify the sacrifices made for it, then (whether we agree with him or not) we can respect his point of view.

But of course the vast majority of vivisectors have no such theologi- 7
cal background. They are most of them naturalistic and Darwinian. Now here, surely, we come up against a very alarming fact. The very same people who will most contemptuously brush aside any consideration of animal suffering if it stands in the way of "research" will also, on another context, most vehemently deny that there is any radical difference between man and the other animals. On the naturalistic view the beasts are at bottom just the same *sort* of thing as ourselves. Man is simply the cleverest of the anthropoids. All the grounds on which a Christian might defend vivisection are thus cut from under our feet. We sacrifice other species to our own not because our own has any objective metaphysical

[1] Matthew 10:31.

privilege over others, but simply because it is ours. It may be very natural to have this loyalty to our own species, but let us hear no more from the naturalists about the "sentimentality" of antivivisectionists. If loyalty to our own species, preference for man simply because we are men, is not a sentiment, then, what is? It may be a good sentiment or a bad one. But a sentiment it certainly is. Try to base it on logic and see what happens!

But the most sinister thing about modern vivisection is this. If a mere sentiment justifies cruelty, why stop at a sentiment for the whole human race? There is also a sentiment for the white man against the black, for a *Herrenvolk* against the non-Aryans, for "civilized" or "progressive" peoples against "savages" or "backward" peoples. Finally, for our own country, party, or class against others. Once the old Christian idea of a total difference in kind between man and beast has been abandoned, then no argument for experiments on animals can be found which is not also an argument for experiments on inferior men. If we cut up beasts simply because they cannot prevent us and because we are backing our own side in the struggle for existence, it is only logical to cut up imbeciles, criminals, enemies, or capitalists for the same reasons. Indeed, experiments on men have already begun. We all hear that Nazi scientists have done them. We all suspect that our own scientists may begin to do so, in secret, at any moment. 8

The alarming thing is that the vivisectors have won the first round. In the nineteenth and eighteenth centuries a man was not stamped as a "crank" for protesting against vivisection. Lewis Carroll protested, if I remember his famous letter correctly, on the very same ground which I have just used[2] Dr. Johnson — a man whose mind had as much *iron* in it as any man's — protested in a note on *Cymbeline* which is worth quoting in full. In Act I, scene v, the Queen explains to the Doctor that she wants poisons to experiment on "such creatures as We count not worth the hanging, — but none human."[3] The Doctor replies: 9

Your Highness
Shall from this practice but make hard your heart.[4]

Johnson comments: "The thought would probably have been more amplified, had our author lived to be shocked with such experiments as have been published in later times, by a race of men that have practiced tor-

---

[2] "Vivisection as a Sign of the Times," *The Works of Lewis Carroll,* ed. Roger Lancelyn-Green (London, 1965), pp. 1089–92. See also "Some Popular Fallacies about Vivisection," ibid., pp. 1092–1100.

[3] Shakespeare, *Cymbeline, I,* v, 19–20.

[4] Ibid., 23.

tures without pity, and related them without shame, and are yet suffered to erect their heads among human beings."[5]

The words are his, not mine, and in truth we hardly dare in these days to use such calmly stern language. The reason why we do not dare is that the other side has in fact won. And though cruelty even to beasts is an important matter, their victory is symptomatic of matters more important still. The victory of vivisection marks a great advance in the triumph of ruthless, nonmoral utilitarianism over the old world of ethical law; a triumph in which we, as well as animals, are already the victims, and of which Dachau and Hiroshima mark the more recent achievments. In justifying cruelty to animals we put ourselves also on the animal level. We choose the jungle and must abide by our choice. 10

You will notice I have spent no time in discussing what actually goes on in the laboratories. We shall be told, of course, that there is surprisingly little cruelty. That is a question with which, at present, I have nothing to do. We must first decide what should be allowed: After that it is for the police to discover what is already being done. 11

The Trials of Animals

CLEVELAND AMORY

Ask an experimenter about the animals in his laboratory. Nine times out of ten he will tell you that they are well cared for and that he abides by the Animal Welfare Act passed by Congress in 1966. 1

What he will not say is that both he and his colleagues fought the act and the amendments to it every step of the way; that, under the act, his laboratory is inspected at most (if at all) once a year; that when his animals are under experimentation, the act doesn't apply. Nor will he say that many laboratories ignore the act's most important amendment, passed in 1986, which mandates that at least one member of the public vote on the laboratory's animal-care committee. 2

Your experimenter is not a scoff-law. Having been for so long sole judge and jury of what he does, he believes that he is above the law. A prime example is that of the monkeys in Silver Spring, Maryland. 3

---

[5] *Johnson on Shakespeare: Essays and Notes Selected and Set Forth with an Introduction* by Sir Walter Raleigh (London, 1908), p. 181.

Cleveland Amory is a leading animal-rights activist and the author of *The Cat Who Came for Christmas*. His perspective appeared in the September 17, 1989 issue of the *New Yo*[illegible] *Times*.

The monkeys were used in experiments in which, first, nerves in 4
their limbs were removed and then stimuli — including electrical shocks and flames — were applied to see if they could still use their appendages.

Dr. Edward Taub, who ran the laboratory, was eventually tried and 5
found guilty, not of cruelty to animals but of maintaining a filthy lab. Maryland is one of many states that exempts federally funded experiments from cruelty charges.

Dr. Taub is today a free man. His monkeys, however, are not. They 6
are still in a laboratory under the jurisdiction of the National Institutes of Health, which first funded these cruel experiments. Three hundred members of Congress have asked the NIH to release the monkeys; the NIH says it does not want them; two animal sanctuaries have offered to take them. Why can't they live what remains of their lives receiving the first evidence of human kindness they have ever known?

In the overcrowded field of cat experimentation, researchers at Loui- 7
siana State University, under an eight-year, $2 million Department of Defense contract, put cats in vises, remove part of their skulls, and then shoot them in the head.

More than two hundred doctors and Senator Daniel Inouye, chairman 8
of the Defense Appropriations Subcommittee, have protested this cruelty. The experimenters say that their purpose is to find a way to return brain-wounded soldiers to active duty.

"Basic training for an Army infantryman costs $9,000" one experi- 9
menter argued. "If our research allows only 170 additional men to return to active duty . . . it will have paid for itself." But Dr. Donald Doll of Truman Veterans Hospital in Columbia, Missouri, said of these experiments: "I can find nothing which supports applying any of this data to humans."

At the University of Oregon, under a seventeen-year, $1.5 million 10
grant, psychologists surgically rotated the eyes of kittens, implanted electrodes in their brains, and forced them to jump onto a block in a pan of water to test their equilibrium. These experiments resulted in a famous laboratory break-in in 1986, and the subsequent trial and conviction of one of the animals' liberators.

During the trial, experimenters were unable to cite a single case in 11
which their research had benefited humans. Additional testimony revealed instances of cats being inadequately anesthetized while having their eye muscles cut, untrained and unlicensed personnel performing the surgery, and mother cats suffering such stress that they ate their babies.

The trial judge, Edwin Allen, stated that the testimony was "disturb- 12
ing to me as a citizen of this state and as a graduate of the University of Oregon. It would be highly appropriate to have these facilities opened to the public."

It would, indeed — and a judge is just what is needed. A judge first, then a jury. The experimenters have been both long enough. 13

Vigilant Protocol

THOMAS E. HAMM, JR.

To the Editor:

Cleveland Amory's central point seems to be that researchers using animals may do any procedure they wish and that laboratories are inspected "at most (if at all) once a year." (Op-Ed, September 17). This is not an accurate representation of the elaborate monitoring program that has been in place for many years to assure the humane treatment of research animals. 1

At Stanford University (which is not unique in this respect), before beginning any research using animals, each investigator must submit a rationale that includes the appropriateness of using animals, a justification for the number of animals needed and a description of all procedures. Any pain or distress greater than that caused by a routine injection resulting from these procedures must be minimized. 2

The protocol also requires a complete list of anesthetics and pain-killing drugs to be used, if needed. The University Administrative Panel on Laboratory Animal Care must then review and approve the protocol before any animal may be purchased or used. The current panel, appointed by the president of the university, is composed of twelve voting members. Nine of these individuals are affiliated with Stanford; there are five scientists, the veterinarian who is director of the Division of Laboratory Animal Medicine, a law school professor, the dean of the chapel, and a student selected by the student body. The three others, a scientist and two veterinarians in local practice; have no ties with Stanford except in their role as panel members. 3

If the panel approves a project and the investigator begins work, the Division of Laboratory Animal Medicine assumes responsibility for ensuring that animals are used and treated humanely and in accordance with the approved protocol. The division staff currently includes 4

Thomas E. Hamm, Jr., is the director of the Division of Laboratory Animal Medicine at the Stanford University School of Medicine. His letter appeared in the October 19, 1989 *New York Times*.

six veterinarians, twelve veterinary technicians and twenty animal-care personnel who work for the division, not for the investigators doing the studies. These people are all specially trained to be able to assure humane care of the research animals. We also have a policy that allows any individual to report any suspected abuse of animals and to remain anonymous if so desired.

The administrative panel is currently required by law to inspect all of 5
the animal facilities every six months and to submit a report to the government. In addition, the facilities are subject to unannounced inspections by government veterinarians a minimum of once each year. We are visited, both announced and unannounced, by various other governmental and private organizations.

This extensive regulation of research with animals does not mean 6
that acts of cruelty or abuse will never occur. It does, however, decrease the possibility of such rare events ever happening, and provides for strong sanctions should transgressions be uncovered. Our government has spent a great deal of time and money and has listened to all sides of this argument to set up the current system. Those individuals whose agenda is the total elimination of the use of animals for any human purpose will not be satisfied with any system of regulation, and wish to impose more and more stringent regulations simply to make the process as expensive as possible.

Even if Mr. Amory were correct and none of these procedures were 7
being followed, I hope the vast majority of people would find it hard to believe that scientists devoted to finding ways to treat the diseases of man and animals would participate in "needless cruelty to animals" or "torture in the name of science" as implied by the article. Without any regulations I am confident that genuine examples of animal abuse by scientists would still be extremely rare events. We are proud of our research programs and the care that we give our laboratory animals.

—Thomas E. Hamm, Jr.

Holding Human Health Hostage

MICHAEL E. DEBAKEY

1 As a patient-advocate, both in and out of the operating room, I feel a responsibility to protect the rights of patients to medical advances resulting from animal research. Had the animal legislation now pending in Congress been enacted when I began my career, it would have prevented me from developing a number of lifesaving procedures in my research laboratory. Instead of restoring thousands of patients to a normal life and a return to productive work, my colleagues and I would have been helpless to offer many of our patients any real hope at all. This legislation, known as the Mrazek bill, seeks to ban the use of pound animals for any research supported by the National Institutes of Health, the chief source of funds for biomedical research in this country. Are we now to hold human health hostage to the rights of abandoned animals to be killed in pounds?

2 Even with today's technology, I could not have developed on a computer the roller pump that made open-heart surgery possible or the artificial artery that restored to health previously doomed patients with aneurysms. Nor could we have attempted the first successful coronary artery bypass or implanted the first temporary mechanical heart with which we saved a patient's life two decades ago. Would animal-rights activists have objected to the first kidney, heart, or liver transplant? Would they forgo the protection humanity enjoys today against poliomyelitis, tetanus, diphtheria, and whooping cough or the treatment for strep throat, ear infections, bronchitis, and pneumonia — all the products of animal research? Would they have denied the 11 million diabetics the right to life that insulin has given them — or victims of cancer the help they have received from radiation and chemotherapy? It was in monkeys that the deadly AIDS virus was isolated, and that isolation is the initial step in the ultimate development of a vaccine. Would the animal-rights activists halt that research and allow an epidemic to rage unopposed? The truth is that there are no satisfactory insentient models at present for certain types of biomedical research and testing. A computer is not a living system and would not have produced the dramatic medical advances of the past few decades.

3 Only about 1 percent of abandoned dogs are released for research. If pounds are such a meager source of research animals, you may ask, why am I concerned about losing that source? My reasons are well founded, I

Michael E. DeBakey, M.D., is chancellor, chairman of surgery, and director of the DeBakey Heart Center at Baylor College of Medicine in Houston, Texas. His editorial appeared in the *Journal of Investigative Surgery*, Vol. I, 1988.

believe: Not only are pound animals of particular value in research on heart and kidney disease, brain injury, stroke, blindness, and deafness, but a ban on their use could have grave and far-reaching consequences for human and animal health. In addition, such a ban would impose an extra burden on taxpayers and could price many important research projects out of existence. Each dog and cat bred specifically for research costs hundreds of dollars more than a pound animal. The Mrazek bill makes no accommodation in appropriations for this substantial rise in cost. For many of our most productive researchers, the additional expense would shut down their laboratories. Critical work on inducing tolerance in organ grafts, for example, and on minimizing damage to cardiac muscles after heart attacks has been halted in some research laboratories because of soaring costs of dogs.

Moreover, eliminating the use of pound animals in research would, 4
paradoxically, cause even more animals to die. According to the American Humane Society, 7 million pet dogs are abandoned to pounds or shelters each year, 5 million of which are killed — 600 "trusting pets" killed hourly. Yet some would have you believe that killing animals in a pound is more virtuous than having them help to advance medical knowledge and ultimately benefit human and animal health. I don't like to see life taken from any species unnecessarily, and that would happen if this law is enacted. Every year we would have to breed an additional 138,000 dogs and 50,000 cats for research to replace the pound animals, which would then be put to death anyway because no one wants them. With the current overpopulation of dogs and cats, the logic of such a policy escapes me.

It was humane concerns that led me into medicine. I strongly disap- 5
prove of cruelty to animals as well as humans. Medical scientists are not engaged in cockfighting, bullfighting, bull-dogging, calf-roping, or any other "sport" imposing stress or violence on animals. Rather, they are searching for ways to relieve suffering and preserve life. Unquestionably, every precaution should be taken, and enforced, to ensure that laboratory animals are treated humanely. Responsible scientists observe humane guidelines, not only because their search for new medical knowledge is motivated by compassion for the suffering, but because they know that improper treatment adversely affects the quality of their research. Scientists are also obligated to use insentient models when these are satisfactory, but, again, no responsible scientist would incur the substantial expense and devote the considerable space required for housing and caring for animals when other equally satisfactory models were available.

If scientists abandon cat and dog experiments for other models that 6
are not as suitable or as well understood, many potential medical breakthroughs may be severely crippled or halted. Grave diseases such as AIDS, cancer, heart disease, muscular dystrophy, Alzheimer's disease,

and other serious conditions will, however, continue to plague our families, friends, and fellow citizens, and those patients will properly expect to receive effective treatments and cures.

Remember, too, that pets have also profited from animal research. It is doubtful that animals could be treated today for heart or kidney disease, leukemia, or other serious disorders if animal research had been prohibited previously. If an animal is seriously ill or injured, would the animal-rights activist deny him a form of treatment potentially beneficial but never used before — and therefore experimental? Until one is faced with a life-threatening condition of a loved one — human or animal — it is difficult to answer that question truthfully. 7

We have aggressive advocates of the rights of trees, sharks, bats, whales, seals, and other mammals, but what about the rights of ailing humans? Shrill attacks against speciesism are difficult to defend when one observes pit bulldogs mauling and killing children, wolves killing deer, cats consuming rats and birds, and birds consuming worms. And even vegetarians destroy living plants for consumption. Self-preservation is a primary instinct of all members of the animal kingdom, and patients with that instinct deserve our compassion, protection, and assistance as much as other species. 8

Some animal-rights zealots have been quoted as regarding "the right to human life as a perversion," meat-eating as "primitive, barbaric, and arrogant," and pet ownership as an "absolutely abysmal situation brought about by human manipulation." It is difficult to believe that many animal lovers would embrace such an extreme position. There is a difference, moreover, between animal welfare and antisciencism. Infiltrating laboratories surrepitiously by posing as volunteer workers, destroying research records, vandalizing research facilities, bombing, and threatening scientists are all irrational methods of persuasion. At one research institution, damages amounted to more than a half million dollars when computers were destroyed, blood was poured on files, and liberationist slogans were painted on laboratory walls. Research on infant blindness was halted for eight months while claims of animal abuse were investigated, only to be found baseless. Such harassment, demoralization, and interference divert funds from productive research to security and discourage bright young people from entering research. Once the manpower chain is broken, it will not be easily restored. And where will we then turn for answers to devastating human diseases? Guerrilla tactics, lurid pictures, and sensational headlines may inflame emotions, but they do not lead to rational judgments. More important, should we condone harassment, terrorism, and violence masquerading as concern for animal rights? 9

As a physician, my greatest concern is, of course, for the suffering human beings who will be denied effective treatment because we took action that seems superficially humane but may ultimately render us 10 powerless against certain diseases. What do I tell dying patients who are waiting for the medical advances that these threatened investigations may produce — that there is no hope because we have been prevented from acquiring the new knowledge needed to correct their conditions? As a human being and physician, I cannot conceive of telling parents their sick child is doomed because we cannot use all the tools at our disposal. Surely those who object to animals in research laboratories must be equally distressed at seeing sick children hooked up to tubes. How will those parents feel about a society that legislates the rights of animals above those of humans?

Through research, we have made remarkable advances in medicine, 11
but we still do not have all the answers. If the animal-rights activists could witness the heartbreaking suffering of patients and families that I encounter daily, I doubt that they would deliberately pose a direct threat to human and animal health by demanding that we abandon some of our most fruitful methods of medical investigation. The American public must decide: Shall we tell hundreds of thousands of victims of heart attacks, cancer, AIDS, and numerous other dread diseases that the right of abandoned animals to die in a pound supersedes the patients' rights to relief from suffering and premature death? In making that decision, let us use not anger and hatred but reason and good will.

Alternatives to Animals

THE ECONOMIST

The number of laboratory animals used in America and Britain has 1
halved since its peak in the mid-1970s. Several chemical and drug companies are spending plenty of money on finding ways to cut down. A few, such as Avon and Revlon, have announced the closure of their animal-testing laboratories. However, it seems that the decade-long decline in animal experimentation is bottoming out. Why?

The decline itself was caused by a range of factors. Some are eco- 2
nomic and have to do with a fall in demand. Research establishments closed during the recession of the early 1980s. The number of cosmetics and pharmaceuticals developed each year has dropped. And rising costs — a monkey can cost more than $2,000 to buy and $100 a week to keep — have led to cutbacks.

This unsigned report is from the December 2, 1989 issue of *The Economist*.

Also, now that regulators insist that animals should be treated better, fewer are needed to spot biological effects. Several years ago it took thirty-six monkeys to determine whether there were any contaminants that might wreck the nervous system in polio vaccine. Nowadays a similar job takes only twenty-two. This drop is attributed solely to the monkeys' well-being. 3

There have been a few legislative reforms affecting the use of laboratory animals. After years of review, the European Commission decided to abandon the LD50 test, which requires large numbers of animals to be killed to check whether a chemical is dangerous. Tests with smaller, nonlethal doses will now do. Few other reforms are on the agenda, except for replacing the Draize test (in which chemicals are tested for irritancy by dropping them into rabbits' eyes). This may be superseded by a test in which smaller, less irritating doses are placed at the edge of the eye. 4

What of the alternatives to animals? In theory, plenty of basic biological research (which accounts for 40 percent of animal experiments) can be conducted on cells rather than whole creatures. The explosion of knowledge in molecular biology, and new techniques such as laser fluorimetry (which can measure biological activity in a single cell) have helped improve the quality of data that can be collected from experiments done on cells in test-tubes (*in vitro*). 5

Neuropharmacologists used to study the effect of depressants or tranquilizers in whole animals. Now they study isolated synapses, the junctions between nerve cells, to measure the chemical and electrical signals that pass between them. Although an animal must be killed to extract the synapses, one death provides many of them. 6

More scientists would like to switch to the test tube. They are hampered by the availability and expense of cell cultures to work on. Cells are usually cultured in a cocktail of substances. The most effective of these seems to be fetal calf serum, which is costly, and involves the slaughter of calf embryos. Recently there have been worries about contamination with bovine spongiform encephalopathy, an infectious disease first spotted in British cattle in 1986. There are big technical problems, too. Cultured human cells can quickly lose their characteristics and become "undifferentiated." 7

Over the past decade several "growth factors," which help cells grow in dishes, have been discovered in human serum and other tissues. Synthetic substitutes are also being developed, but progress is slow. Calf serum is a complex mix of ingredients and nobody is sure what all of them are. Scientists think it will be some time before they find a cocktail that supports whole differentiated human cells. 8

Although computers and *in vitro* screening are increasingly used to pick out new drugs, animal alternatives have yet to gain wide acceptance. 9

The alternatives account for perhaps 5 percent of preclinical drug testing. Preclinical tests, which account for 25–30 percent of the animal toll, are those conducted before a drug is tested on people.

Regulators have been slow to recognize *in vitro* tests. Only two have 10
been approved: the Ames test, which uses bacterial cells to determine the cancer-causing potential of a chemical by measuring its ability to cause genetic damage; and the mammalian cell test, which does much the same in Chinese hamster cells. Both have been around for more than a decade and are anyway used only in conjunction with conventional animal tests.

Several new test-tube methods have been developed. Tissue cultures 11
containing the kind of cell found in the skin can screen for drugs that might cause allergies. There are tests which look at dispersed embryonic cells and how they reassociate in the presence of chemicals suspected of causing birth defects. Instead of injecting chemicals into rabbits and taking their temperatures, the potential of a chemical for causing fever can be monitored by looking at how crab's blood coagulates.

None of these tests is foolproof. In a recent international trial, the per- 12
formance of a range of known and unknown carcinogens was measured by the Ames test and compared with data from animals and people. The Ames test agreed with the human and animal standards only 60 percent of the time. And *in vitro* tests for damage to fetuses will not identify trypan blue — a dye used for research on cells — as dangerous because it interferes with the flow of nutrients along the placenta, not with the fetus itself.

Still, several scientific and regulatory hurdles may yet be leaped suc- 13
cessfully. Recent work in genetic engineering is providing new ways to develop alternative tests. More immediately, animal suffering could be reduced if regulators changed their ways. They argue that alternatives must be compared to a "gold standard," and that animals are closer to people than a handful of cells in a dish. But, in general, animal tests yield false negatives (hazardous chemicals are passed) and false positives (safe chemicals get turned down) almost as often as test-tube work. And there are countless examples in which chemicals perform differently in animals and people. Practolol, a heart drug, made people — but not any known test animal — go blind. If animal tests are not perfect, why should regulators insist that the alternatives are?

Animals and Sickness

THE WALL STREET JOURNAL

If it's spring, the "animal rights movement" can't be far behind. It will be on display today at the National Institutes of Health in Washington, demonstrating on behalf of World Laboratory Animal Liberation Week. On Wednesday, two of this country's most renowned doctors will travel to Washington to try to counteract the demonstration with a news conference. Dr. Michael DeBakey of Baylor is the well-known pioneer in heart surgery. Dr. Thomas Starzl of the University of Pittsburgh has become famous in recent years for his work in providing liver transplants for children. Both consider the animal-rights movement to be one of the greatest threats to continued medical research in the United States. 1

Polio, drug addiction, cystic fibroids, most vaccines and antibiotics, pacemakers, cancer, Alzheimer's, surgical technique — it's hard to identify many breakthroughs in medical progress that don't depend on research using higher animal forms. For most of the past decade, the animal-rights movement hasn't merely opposed animal research; it has tried to destroy it. 2

On April 2, in an Animal Liberation Front break-in at the University of Arizona, two buildings were set on fire (causing $100,000 damage) and 1,000 animals including mice infected with a human parasite, were stolen. The list of such incidents in the United States is long: 3

The director of Stanford's animal facility got a bomb threat in December. Intruders stole dogs and records of heart-transplant research at Loma Linda University in August. Indeed, dating back to 1982 there have been break-ins and thefts of animals at medical-research laboratories at Berkeley; Johns Hopkins (rats in Alzheimer's research); the head-injury lab and the veterinary school at Penn (arthritis research, sudden infant-death syndrome); University of California, Davis (an arson attack); New York State Psychiatric Institute (Parkinson's research); University of Oregon; and University of California, Irvine (lung research). Currently, a trial is imminent for a woman who allegedly tried to murder the president of U.S. Surgical Corporation in Connecticut with a remote-control bomb. 4

The animal-rights movement is a textbook example of how many activist groups press their agendas into today's political system. It hardly matters, for instance, that an American Medical Association poll found that 77 percent of adults think that using animals in medical research is necessary. Those people answered the phone and went back to their daily 5

This editorial is from the April 24, 1989 issue of the *Wall Street Journal*.

lives, working at real jobs and raising families. Meanwhile the professional activists — animal rights, anti-nukers, fringe environmentalists, Hollywood actresses — descend on the people who create "issues" in America.

They elicit sympathetic, free publicity from newspapers and maga- 6
zines. They do Donahue and Oprah. And they beat on the politicians and bureaucrats. They create a kind of nonstop Twilight Zone of "issues" and "concerns" that most American voters are barely aware of. They do this because it has succeeded so many times.

As an outgrowth of congressional legislation, the U.S. Agriculture De- 7
partment recently proposed animal-research regulations that would engulf medical scientists in reporting requirements, animal committees, "whistleblower" procedures, and directives to redesign laboratories ("the method of feeding nonhuman primates must be varied daily in order to promote their psychological well-being"). The cost of compliance, in an era of declining funding support for much research, is estimated to be $1.5 billion, and of course this will not satisfy the "movement."

If the United States is forced to work under the constant burden of all 8
these varieties of public-issue nonsense, it can never hope to realize continued gains in either human welfare or its international competitiveness. Happily, evidence is emerging that the scientific community has decided it's time to fight back against all these activist movements.

In what should be the beginning of a countermovement against the 9
animal-rights groups, NIH Director James Wyngaarden, HHS Secretary Louis Sullivan, and drug czar Bill Bennett all issued statements last Friday supporting medical researchers who must work with animals. Dr. David Hubel, of Harvard Medical School and 1981 winner of the Nobel Prize in medicine, has just sent a letter signed by twenty-nine other Nobel laureates, urging U.S. Surgeon General C. Everett Koop to speak out against these groups. Led by a multiple sclerosis victim, there is now a countergroup called Incurably Ill for Animal Research.

And of course, scientists rallied against the National Resources De- 10
fense Council's recent assault on the chemicals used to kill insects that prey on the U.S. food supply. The spectacle of schools protecting students from apples was too much even for the gullible. Now perhaps it's time to see through "animal rights," a clear and present danger to the health of us all.

Breakthroughs Don't Require Torture

STEPHEN ZAWISTOWSKI, SUZANNE E. ROY, STEPHEN KAUFMAN, and MARJORIE CRAMER

Your April 24 editorial "Animals and Sickness" perpetuates the false impression that recognition of animal rights will result in catastropic levels of sickness and disease. Most people who seek protection of animals from abusive treatment would accept a good-faith effort by the biomedical establishment to improve conditions for research animals and increase efforts to develop nonanimal alternatives. 1

Asking the simplistic question, "Your child's health or a rat's life," is an insult to the many intelligent scientists, doctors, and citizens concerned about the medical-research practices. The real question is whether that rat (or mouse or dog or monkey) should be given a larger cage, better food and postoperative medication to alleviate pain; or whether the same information could have been collected using fewer animals, or none at all. 2

Biomedical researchers typically argue that research animals get adequate care as mandated by federal regulations, and that publicized examples of abuse are exceptions. It is difficult to verify such statements when access to animal-care facilities generally is denied to those interested in the well-being of the animals. 3

—Stephen Zawistowski

Brutal head-trauma experiments at two universities — in which the skulls of thousands of cats and primates were crushed — have been halted. Funding for drug-addiction experiments that subjected cats to the horrors of chemical withdrawal was returned by a researcher. In each case physicians and scientists joined animal advocates in criticizing the studies for their scientific irrelevance and cruelty. A military research project at another university involving hundreds of cats who are shot in the head continues, but it has been condemned by neurosurgeons and trauma experts, and as a result, the U.S. General Accounting Office is investigating. 1

These letters appeared in the May 19, 1989 issue of the *Wall Street Journal* in response to the editorial "Animals and Sickness." Stephen Zawistowski is science adviser for the American Society for the Prevention of Cruelty to Animals; Suzanne E. Roy is a member of the Physicians Committee for Responsible Medicine; Stephen Kaufman, M.D., is the vice chairman of the Medical Research Modernization Committee; and Marjorie Cramer, M.D., is a fellow of the American College of Surgeons.

In the worst cases, animal studies do not just hurt animals and waste 2
money, they harm people too. The drugs thalidomide, Zomex, and DES were tested on animals, but had devastating consequences when humans used them. Just this week, the Food and Drug Administration warned doctors against the use of two heart drugs, Tambocor and Enkaid, which were thought to control irregular heartbeats but were found to actually kill human patients.

—Suzanne E. Roy

You grossly exaggerate the value of animal research. Contrary to sci- 1
entists' self-serving interpretation of medical history, historian Brandon Reines has found that nearly every important advance in areas such as heart disease and cancer has come from human clinical investigation. While animal experiments had some value in the management of infectious diseases at the turn of the century, they have made little contribution since.

The development of modern research techniques, such as CAT scans, 2
PET scans, needle biopsies, and tissue cultures, permit safe, ethical study of disease with human patients and tissues. This has rendered many uses of animals obsolete.

—Stephen Kaufman, M.D.

Where, may I ask, are the "breakthroughs" in drug addiction, cancer, 1
and Alzheimer's disease that you attribute to animal research? They have not been presented in medical journals nor in the press. Billions are spent each year on medical and scientific "research," most of which is worthless. Many of the real breakthroughs have been a result of clinical work: observations in human patients.

The animal-rights movement is here to stay and has very wide grass- 2
roots support. The vast majority of the people involved are also working at "real jobs and raising their families" and are not professional activists as you imply.

While a few animal-rights activists have participated in terrorist at- 3
tacks, the vast majority are opposed to such tactics.

—Marjorie Cramer, M.D.

In Defense of the Animals

MEG GREENFIELD

I might as well come right out with it: Contrary to some of my most cherished prejudices, the animal-rights people have begun to get to me. I think that in some part of what they say they are right. 1

I never thought it would come to this. As distinct from the old-style animal rescue, protection, and shelter organizations, the more aggressive newcomers, with their "liberation" of laboratory animals and periodic championship of the claims of animal well-being over human well-being when a choice must be made, have earned a reputation in the world I live in as fanatics and just plain kooks. And even with my own recently (relatively) raised consciousness, there remains a good deal in both their critique and their prescription for the virtuous life that I reject, being not just a practicing carnivore, a wearer of shoe leather, and so forth, but also a supporter of certain indisputably agonizing procedures visited upon innocent animals in the furtherance of human welfare, especially experiments undertaken to improve human health. 2

So, viewed from the pure position, I am probably only marginally better than the worst of my kind, if that: I don't buy the complete "speciesist" analysis or even the fundamental language of animal "rights" and continue to find a large part of what is done in the name of that cause harmful and extreme. But I also think, patronizing as it must sound, that the zealots are required early on in any movement if it is to succeed in altering the sensibility of the leaden masses, such as me. Eventually they get your attention. And eventually you at least feel obliged to weigh their arguments and think about whether there may not be something there. 3

It is true that this end has often been achieved — as in my case — by means of vivid, cringe-inducing photographs, not by an appeal to reason or values so much as by an assault on squeamishness. From the famous 1970s photo of the newly skinned baby seal to the videos of animals being raised in the most dark, miserable, stunting environment as they are readied for their life's sole fulfillment as frozen patties and cutlets, these sights have had their effect. But we live in a world where the animal protein we eat comes discreetly prebutchered and prepacked so the original beast and his slaughtering are remote from our consideration, just as our furs come on coat hangers in salons, not on their original proprietors; and I see nothing wrong with our having to contemplate the often unsettling 4

Meg Greenfield is a regular columnist for *Newsweek*, where this essay appeared on April 17, 1989.

reality of how we came by the animal products we make use of. Then we can choose what we want to do.

The objection to our being confronted with these dramatic, disturbing 5
pictures is first that they tend to provoke a misplaced, uncritical, and highly emotional concern for animal life at the direct expense of a more suitable concern for human suffering. What goes into the animals' account, the reasoning goes, necessarily comes out of ours. But I think it is possible to remain stalwart in your view that the human claim comes first and in your acceptance of the use of animals for human betterment and *still* to believe that there are some human interests that should not take precedence. For we have become far too self-indulgent, hardened, careless, and cruel in the pain we routinely inflict upon these creatures for the most frivolous, unworthy purposes. And I also think that the more justifiable purposes, such as medical research, are shamelessly used as cover for other activities that are wanton.

For instance, not all of the painful and crippling experimentation that 6
is undertaken in the lab is being conducted for the sake of medical knowledge or other purposes related to basic human well-being and health. Much of it is being conducted for the sake of superrefinements in the cosmetic and other frill industries, the noble goal being to contrive yet another fragrance or hair tint or commercially competitive variation on all the daft, fizzy, multicolored "personal care" products for the medicine cabinet and dressing table, a firmer-holding hair spray, that sort of thing. In other words, the conscripted, immobilized rabbits and other terrified creatures, who have been locked in boxes from the neck down, only their heads on view, are being sprayed in the eyes with different burning, stinging substances for the sake of adding to our already obscene store of luxuries and utterly superfluous vanity items.

Phony Kinship

Oddly, we tend to be very sentimental about animals in their ideal- 7
ized, fictional form and largely indifferent to them in realms where our lives actually touch. From time immemorial, humans have romantically attributed to animals their own sensibilities — from Balaam's biblical ass who providently could speak and who got his owner out of harm's way right down to Lassie and the other Hollywood pups who would invariably tip off the good guys that the bad guys were up to something. So we simulate phony cross-species kinship, pretty well drown in the cuteness of it all — Mickey and Minnie and Porky — and ignore, if we don't actually countenance, the brutish things done in the name of Almighty Hair Spray.

This strikes me as decadent. My problem is that it also causes me to 8
reach a position that is, on its face, philosophically vulnerable, if not ab-

surd — the muddled, middling, inconsistent place where finally you are saying it's all right to kill them for some purposes, but not to hurt them gratuitously in doing it or to make them suffer horribly for one's own trivial whims.

I would feel more humiliated to have fetched up on this exposed rock, 9 if I didn't suspect I had so much company. When you see pictures of people laboriously trying to clean the Exxon gunk off of sea otters even knowing that they will only be able to help out a very few, you see this same outlook in action. And I think it *can* be defended. For to me the biggest cop-out is the one that says that if you don't buy the whole absolutist, extreme position it is pointless and even hypocritical to concern yourself with lesser mercies and ameliorations. The pressure of the animal-protection groups has already had some impact in improving the way various creatures are treated by researchers, trainers, and food producers. There is much more in this vein to be done. We are talking about rejecting wanton, pointless cruelty here. The position may be philosophically absurd, but the outcome is the right one.

THINKING AND WRITING ABOUT ANIMAL RIGHTS

Questions for Discussion and Writing

1. What values do the antivivisectionists — Peter Singer and C. S. Lewis — appeal to? Might these same values be held by those on the other side? If so, which side seems to you to have the better right to make such appeals?
2. How do Cleveland Amory and Thomas Hamm disagree? Can you decide which arguer is closer to the truth? If you have decided, explain how you reached your decision.
3. Which issues do you think Dr. DeBakey argues most persuasively? Summarize his attack against animal-rights activists. Does he meet the objections of Cleveland Amory?
4. Are you convinced by the arguments of *The Economist* and Marjorie Cramer that the degree of animal experimentation today is not necessary? Do they respond effectively to DeBakey?
5. Meg Greenfield takes a middle position. Where do you think she would draw the line on killing animals "for some purpose"?
6. Some people believe that experimentation on animals unrelated to us, such as rats and rabbits, is acceptable but that experimentation on primates — rhesus monkeys and chimpanzees — is not. Or to put it in more extreme terms, is there a difference between experimentation on a chimpanzee and on a human being with very low intelligence? Is there some point on the evolutionary scale when it becomes immoral to continue experimentation? Explain your position as fully as possible.

7. If you have ever seen animals slaughtered for food, either on a farm or in a stockyard, describe your reactions and explain whether the experience influenced your attitude toward meat eating.

Topics for Research

The case for (or against) ethical vegetarianism

Federal laws governing use of animals in laboratories

The case for (or against) animal sports — dogfighting, cockfighting, etc.

The case for (or against) hunting

What the Bible tells us about the rights of animals

CHAPTER 13

Collegiate Sports Reform

Although college sports scandals are not new, in the last few years a different and potentially more threatening problem, one that casts doubt on the function of the university, has captured national attention. This problem concerns the recruitment of athletes who bring glory to their teams but fail to receive an education, in some glaring cases graduating or leaving college without even being able to read. These athletes have often received extraordinarily generous scholarships to attend prestigious institutions.

Proposition 48, passed in 1986 by the National Collegiate Athletic Association — the body that governs big-time college sports — was an attempt to redress this situation. It established academic standards for athletes, who must either fulfill them or remain on the bench. Another rule, Proposition 42, passed in 1989, "barred all institutional aid to freshman athletes who failed to achieve minimum scores on standardized college-entrance tests, a 2.0 cumulative grade point average or a 2.0 average in eleven core courses." Growing criticism of the financial hardships inflicted on incoming student-athletes brought about another change. In January 1990 the NCAA voted on a new regulation, Proposition 26, which still barred these freshmen from receiving athletic scholarships and participating in sports for a year but allowed them to receive financial aid and to be counted against the school's scholarship total after they became eligible for practice.

These propositions aroused strong feelings both for and against because they raised fundamental questions about the purpose of higher education and the future of big-time college athletic competitions. Did the terms of Proposition 48 make things either too easy or too hard for college athletes? Would talented high school athletes with weak academic credentials be denied opportunities for higher education? Should the university prepare students for all kinds of vocations, even those which require no academic training? Have sports programs played too important a role in college financing and publicity? As a *New York Times* headline summed up the dilemma, "Can Big-Time College Athletics and Education Co-Exist?"

Should College Athletes Be Paid Salaries?

GEORGE SAGE and JOHN DAVIS

Q: Professor Sage, why do you believe college athletes ought to be paid a salary on top of any scholarships and allowances they receive? 1

A: Because major-college athletics is a form of entertainment. As with other entertainments, talented people perform for audiences who pay to watch. What universities are doing is using the performance for publicity purposes. College athletes should be paid for their part in this. Other people in the collegiate-sport industry — coaches, athletic directors, trainers — are making good livings. Why not the athletes, the actual producers of the event? 2

No other business enterprise treats its largest employee group with such contempt. It's really a serious restraint of trade. Any other industry that tried to limit payments to its employees would be considered an illegal labor-market cartel. 3

Q: How much should collegiate athletes be paid? 4

A: They should get at least a minimum wage, but superstars should receive substantially more than journeymen. After all, that's what the free-enterprise system is all about — salary based on job and merit. 5

George Sage is a professor of physical education and sociology at the University of Northern Colorado. John Davis is the president of the National Collegiate Athletic Association. Their comments appeared in *U.S. News and World Report*, December 23, 1985.

Q: Isn't one attraction of college sports the idea that amateurs are playing for the love of the game — and not for money? 6

A: Amateurism is an ideological instrument to keep athletes from sharing in the wealth they create. It's based on two myths: that being paid for athletic achievement is immoral or unethical and that the ancient Greek athletes didn't receive valuable rewards. If colleges are serious about amateurism, then coaches shouldn't be paid. 7

Q: Wouldn't this only stimulate the bidding by boosters and schools that has become a scandal in college sports? 8

A: No. It wouldn't prevent a jock-worshipping booster from giving an athlete money, but outright payments would reduce the need to engage in illegal activity. 9

Q: And academics would take a back-seat role for athletes — 10

A: Among major-college athletes who go on to become professionals, there's already a low graduation rate: Fewer than 30 percent of the professional athletes who attend college receive degrees. So not many top athletes are serious students at the present time. 11

Q: Wouldn't the payment of salaries to athletes be too costly for many schools? 12

A: The professionals are able to pay their players, and they play to the same size crowds as major-university teams. There are ways intercollegiate athletics could market its product to generate enough income for reasonable payments to athletes. 13

Q: Will this idea ever overcome the opposition it has sparked? 14

A: When I first proposed this ten years ago, it provoked a great deal of horror on the part of people in college athletics. Within the last year, however, a number of coaches have called for the same thing. 15

Q: Mr. Davis, why do you oppose the idea of giving college athletes a salary? 16

A: A student athlete is part of a university family, along with other students, the faculty and so on. Only a handful of students — a maximum of 110 in men's football and basketball — play sports that generate revenue. Shouldn't an institution's resources, regardless of how they are generated, be used to benefit the entire college, considering the needs of all students? 17

I agree that college sports is entertainment to generate revenues, but there is a big difference between operating an educational institution and a professional sports franchise. 18

Q: Couldn't colleges afford to pay athletes? 19

A: To pay athletes in football and basketball — most of whom already receive full tuition and fees, room and board, and books — the institution would need to cut some nonrevenue sports or reassign resources from other academic areas. A 1981 study showed 40 percent of big-school 20 athletic departments operating with a deficit. Among smaller schools, about 70 percent ran deficits. With costs increasing and ticket prices staying about level, I would imagine the situation is even worse in 1985.

Q: Isn't an athlete exploited when his college makes big money off his performance? 21

A: I fail to see the logic of an argument that athletes who receive a full grant for five years and a priceless education are exploited. You aren't exploited simply because you're in programs that make money. How about other athletes, like wrestlers, the volleyball and softball players, swimmers? They must train just as rigorously and may receive only a partial grant or none at all. Nobody says they're exploited. 22

Q: Don't the stories of snap courses and low graduation rates suggest athletes aren't serious students? 23

A: That's untrue. A study by the American College Testing Program showed that the graduation rates within a five-year period ending in 1980 were about 10 percent higher for male athletes than for students in general. The tragic cases of athletes who didn't get a good education aren't many compared with the 225,000 men and women athletes at NCAA institutions. But even one is too many. Effective August 1986, there will be increased academic requirements for initial eligibility. That, I think, will dispel any feeling that student athletes are not students first. 24

Q: Wouldn't paying athletes put an end to cheating scandals in colleges? 25

A: Recently, university presidents and coaches increased the penalties for those who don't want to play by the rules. Instead of caving in to the selfish interests of a few who want to make their own rules, let's hear it for honesty. If we want equity in athletic competition, we need reasonable rules — and honesty in pursuing those rules. 26

What Can Be Done?

TED GUP

1. Colleges should have the same entrance and academic requirements for athletes as for other students, while reaffirming their commitment to admitting minority and disadvantaged students.
2. Athletic dorms should be abolished. They only reinforce the isolation of players from the rest of the university community.

These guidelines appeared in *Time* magazine as part of a report by Washington correspondent Ted Gup on April 3, 1989.

3. Practice time should be reduced.
4. All freshmen should be ineligible to practice or play.
5. Games should be scheduled on weekends only.
6. Coaches should be paid on the same scale as faculty members and made eligible for tenure. As long as their jobs are tied to win-loss records, their self-interest may be pitted against the interests of the students in their charge.
7. A greater portion of revenues from sports should go into the general university coffers rather than remain within the athletic departments.
8. The NCAA should require coaches to come forward when they learn of violations. Penalties should be stiffened for all rule breakers.

College Basketball: Issues and Answers

BILLY PACKER

Proposition 48

When it comes to athletic eligibility, no bylaw has been more controversial than Proposition 48, which established a formula of college board scores and high school grade point averages to determine the minimum standards for scholarship aid in Division I. I think Proposition 48 is working. It has shown that the academic caliber of the athlete can be upgraded even though it creates a hardship on a number of young men and women. 1

Detractors of the rule include such outstanding coaches as John Thompson of Georgetown, who presents an eloquent response to the issue. "I agree with the objective but I don't agree with the method," he said. "There is nothing more unequal than equal treatment for those who are unequal." (Thompson is now protesting a new scholarship limitation, Proposal 42, which was passed by the NCAA last week.) 2

It has been suggested that standardized test scores are biased against both female and minority students. But a recent study of the University of North Carolina's system of fifteen colleges seems to show a significant increase in the academic quality of the athletes since the institution of Proposition 48. Two years ago, 20 percent of their student-athletes scored below 700 on the college board scores. This past year only one student failed to meet those minimum requirements for eligibility. 3

Billy Packer is a college basketball analyst for CBS Sports. This excerpt is from an article that appeared in the *New York Times* on January 15, 1989.

Proposal 42 Closes the Door on the Poor

ACEL MOORE

Until the NCAA amended it last week, Proposition 48 was a good rule. It made athletes who did not meet basic academic guidelines ineligible to play sports in their freshmen years or until they proved that they could handle a college curriculum. During their year of trial, they could remain on scholarship. 1

The rule required students to have a combined score of 700 on the college Scholastic Aptitude Test (SAT) and achieve a 2.0 grade point average in high school in order to compete in sports as freshmen. 2

Given our highly technological economy, any rule that sets academic standards for athletes or other students is a good rule. Any rule that enables a college athlete to get an education and become employable is a good rule. After all, 99 percent of college athletes don't make it to professional sports. 3

In fact any rule that encourages an economically deprived and a scholastically marginal student to stay in school is a good rule. And if that student graduates from college, it is even a better rule. 4

But an amendment to Proposition 48, called Proposal 42, which was approved by college athletic directors attending the NCAA national convention last week in San Francisco, is simply a punitive measure. In the long run it will not foster academic scholarship. 5

It takes away the scholarship money from the student-athlete who is declared ineligible — a move that clearly penalizes economically disadvantaged student-athletes. Most students and their families who come under Proposition 48 cannot afford to pay their tuition. The bottom line is that most of them simply will not be able to go to college under Proposal 42. 6

Those who support the amendment argue that economically disadvantaged students would be eligible for other aid, such as general grants and loans. That sounds good but the facts suggest otherwise. If not, how do those who support the proposal explain the fact that college enrollment for black students and particularly black males has declined sharply. 7

In fact on Tuesday, before I had gotten over my outrage over Proposal 42, an *Inquirer* news story reported on a study conducted by the American Council on Education, a national organization in Washington, 8

Acel Moore is associate editor of the *Philadelphia Inquirer*, where this article appeared on January 18, 1989.

that showed that enrollment by black males in college declined by 34,000 between 1976 and 1986. This was the largest decline by any racial or ethnic group during a period when college enrollment grew by more than a million students.

Educators call the decline "a national crisis." The report said that although some of those not attending college are working, seeking employment, or attending for-profit career vocational schools, the overwhelming majority of those black males are probably unemployed and not seeking work. Many are in prison, the report said. 9

The report listed the major factors in the decline in college enrollment of black males: federal financial aid policy, which has shifted from grants to loans as the primary form of assistance; the lack of aggressive recruiting by colleges; and heightened entry requirements. 10

College education today is the purview of mainly the white affluent. 11

Proposal 42 will worsen the problems outlined in the study. The proposal will come up for a vote again at the next NCAA convention. If Proposal 42 remains in effect, there is no doubt that there will be a further decline in black male enrollment in college. 12

Since its inception three years ago, 1,800 athletes, or an average of 600 students a year, have been disqualified under the academic guidelines of Proposition 48. Of that total, most were poor and 90 percent were black. 13

Given the trend and demographics of who is currently receiving a college education in America today, Proposal 42 smacks of both racism and classism. 14

You do not have to score 700 in your SATs and have a 2.0 average in high school to understand that. 15

The Case in Favor of Proposition 42

FREDERICK P. WHIDDON

In attempting to understand the controversy over Proposition 42, it is necessary to look to the reason behind it. Students who enter college without basic academic skills will not have the opportunity to succeed without assistance in acquiring those skills. 1

Frederick P. Whiddon is founder and president of the University of South Alabama. His article appeared in the *New York Times* on January 22, 1989.

Proposition 42 is designed to protect these students. Students with athletic abilities have been exploited in the past. Proposition 42 is an attempt to halt exploitation. It shows sensitivity to the needs of the educationally disadvantaged because it will prevent inadequately prepared students from participating in an intensive athletic program while attempting to meet the rigorous academic standards of the university. Too often, such student-athletes are abandoned by the institution after eligibility expires. 2

A score of 15 on the American College Test or 700 on the Scholastic Aptitude Test with a 2.0 cumulative grade point average is a useful standard in measuring student achievement in the core academic areas: English, mathematics, the sciences, and the social studies. 3

I personally find the minimal academic requirements set by the National Collegiate Athletic Association reasonable and fair. 4

Proposition 42 does not close the door on students. It does, however, prohibit awarding athletic scholarships to students not yet academically prepared to perform at the university level. 5

In my opinion, this is in the best interest of the student-athlete. The majority of high school graduates are prepared for university-level work. But we must find a way of dealing fairly with those students who require remedial instruction. 6

We must meet the needs of all such students without discrimination against either athletes or nonathletes. Each student with demonstrated financial need should have equal access to funds. These funds should be awarded according to established policies and should be fully reported. 7

Many well-meaning people have reacted to Proposition 42 by claiming that it forever closes the door to disadvantaged students. This is not true. It is probably fair to say that most institutions that voted for Proposition 42 have some concerns about its total implementation. It may well need to be revised once the total impact has been assessed. But it does send a message to those who would use any means possible, ethical or unethical, to build winning athletic programs without concern for the long-term damage to young adults and, ultimately, to society. 8

It is unfortunate that a few people involved in athletics have no qualms about this practice. Many say that this new rule will simply encourage more dishonesty and lead to more devious ways to circumvent the system. Should this prove to be true, then it would illustrate that the very fabric of our society and way of life is being pushed aside with no regard for structure, order and the belief that rules are made for everyone. 9

Coaches establish rigorous physical and mental standards relative to the level of play and achievement required in sports. No coach allows a 10 player with minimal athletic talent to stay on the squad simply because of a 4.0 average. Is the concept that a student is a student first and an athlete second archaic?

The University of South Alabama supports Proposition 42 and will continue to provide educational opportunity to all who meet minimal academic standards. 11

Only Two Ways to Free College Sport

IRA BERKOW

When Dale Brown was asked why he was trying to recruit a 7-foot-4-inch, 285-pound basketball player from Lithuania named Arvidas Sabonis to attend Louisiana State University, the coach said it was for humanitarian reasons. 1

That is, Coach Brown was saving the young man from the clutches of communism. "Lithuanians as a people have always been very much opposed to communism, anyway," he said. And therefore it would be an act of charity to spirit the young fellow to America. 2

A noble and altruistic gesture, to be sure. Of course, if the fellow decided to play basketball for LSU, well, there would be no complaint from Coach Brown. After all, this is a free country. 3

The above was all part of a discussion recently in which Coach Brown came out squarely against Proposition 42, the National Collegiate Athletic Association's new rule that tightens restrictions on financial aid to student-athletes, or athlete-students, as the case may be. 4

Coach Brown contended that young men should not be deprived of an opportunity to attend college, and Prop 42 would surely have that effect. 5

It was mentioned to Coach Brown that he never brought up the Lithuanian basketball player's academic credentials, beyond being 7-4 and weighing 285 pounds. 6

Coach Brown smiled. "Well," he replied, "no one asked me." 7

Was Brown being hypocritical, was he evasive? Both and neither. His answer was characteristic of the tidy package in which big-time 8

Ira Berkow is a sports writer whose books include *Red: A Biography of Red Smith* and *Pitchers Do Get Lonely and Other Short Stories*. His article appeared in the *New York Times* on January 27, 1989.

inter-collegiate athletics — particularly those sports known as revenue-producing — is wrapped, and has been for most of this century.

Forget about the Lithuanian as a student. He would come to America 9
to play basketball. He would come to help entertain the students, the faculty, the regents, and, the university would hope, great masses of television viewers, which would stimulate large network payments to the university. The Lithuanian would be the hoop equivalent of the Bolshoi Ballet or the Moscow Circus.

Everyone understands this game. It's professionalism poorly masked 10
as amateurism. It's entertainment, not education.

The NCAA keeps making more rules to seek an honest and fair level 11
of competition among the colleges; that's because they can't enforce the myriad they already have on the books.

Prop 42 is the latest. It says that, starting in 1990, if a high school sen- 12
ior who hasn't earned a C average or scores below 700 of 1,600 in the Scholastic Aptitude Test or 15 of 36 in the American College Test, he isn't allowed an athletic scholarship in his freshman year.

Coaches like John Thompson and John Chaney and Dale Brown say 13
this causes a hardship on minority groups in particular. They contend that high school students who play basketball and football and who can't meet these standards will lose the chance for an education.

This is nonsense. High school boys gifted in sports can also work to 14
earn money for school, just as those not gifted in sports do. And if they are truly interested in an education, they can go to community colleges or night schools or junior colleges or schools with general standards not as high as the ones offering athletic scholarships.

Only in America have athletes played so prominent a role in colleges 15
and turned the educational priorities topsy-turvy. As an Oklahoma football player was supposed to have said, "We want a college that the football team can be proud of."

The tilt in college sports began in football and basketball because, un- 16
like baseball, there were no professional leagues. So collegiate football and basketball became virtual commercial entities.

While big-time sports brings in considerable funds for many schools, 17
it also debases the integrity of the educational systems.

Helpful suggestions are made by thoughtful people. Fred Hargadon, 18
for example, the admissions director at Princeton, said, "For each athlete graduated in a year, the school can give a corresponding athletic scholarship to a freshman."

With every well-meaning suggestion, however, most big-time schools 19
have historically found ways to circumvent it.

Only two plans are foolproof: 20

a. Drop the big-time sports programs and keep athletics as they were originally intended: purely as recreation for the undergraduates in order, as Juvenal suggested, to seek a sound *mens* in a sound *corpore*; or
b. Drop the sham and place sports in an entertainment department, and let the athlete stay as long as he wants to or until the university dismisses him (as is done with coaches), and pay him accordingly, but also give him the chance to attend classes if he wishes.

The school would return to dealing only with qualified students, while giving a young man the chance to earn an honest buck, and, on occasion, save him from the perils of communism, too. 21

Fair Play for College Athletes: Racism and NCAA Rules

HERBERT I. LONDON

Last year, John Thompson, the basketball coach at Georgetown University, walked out of a game to protest a new National Collegiate Athletic Association (NCAA) rule. After the "Star-Spangled Banner" was played and the starting lineups were announced, Thompson strode off the court to a standing ovation from the fans and the members of his team. 1

Mr. Thompson's dramatic gesture was aimed at the NCAA's Proposition 48 and the recently passed Proposal 42. Proposition 48 bars high school graduates from athletic scholarships if they do not achieve a 2.0 grade point average in eleven academic courses and attain at least a combined score of 700 on the Scholastic Aptitude Test (SAT) or a 15 on the American College Test (ACT). Because the severity of this bylaw generated a good deal of opposition from coaches and some black educators, a compromise was proposed and passed. 2

According to Proposal 42, partial qualifiers, i.e., students who graduate with a 2.0 grade point average but fail to meet the minimum standardized test score, can still receive an athletic scholarship, but are obliged to 3

Herbert I. London is chairman of the National Association of Scholars, dean of the Gallatin Division of New York University, and editor of *Academic Questions*, where this argument appeared in the fall of 1989.

lose a year of athletic eligibility. Coach Thompson declared, however, that even thus modified the new rule represents an iniquitous attempt to stem the flow of black athletes into predominantly white universities. As evidence for this contention, he argued that the SAT and the ACT "have been proven culturally biased."

John Cheney, the basketball coach at Temple University, also didn't 4
mince words. He referred to the NCAA as "that racist organization" and admonished parents not to send their children to any institution that endorsed Proposal 42. Dale Brown, the basketball coach at Louisiana State University concurred, observing that he "smelled" an effort at "disguise"; presumably, a disguise meant to conceal subtle forms of racism.

Clearly these coaches aren't disinterested parties. Big-time college 5
athletic programs demand a steady supply of top quality athletes in order to maintain a competitive edge. The money involved is astronomical. Recent revelations suggest, for example, that North Carolina State University coach Jim Valvano is paid at least five times as much as the university's president. This is hardly unprecedented. Several big-time college coaches have seven-figure incomes.

What Proposition 48 and Proposal 42 are intended to achieve is a 6
modicum of academic respectability for big-time sports programs. And lest John Thompson give a false impression, no one in the NCAA is demanding a knowledge of differential calculus to play college basketball. Keep in mind that a student scores 400 (200 math and 200 verbal) simply by writing his name and address correctly on the SAT, and is assured of an 800 score if he can read and understand a typical newspaper editorial and perform seventh-grade arithmetic problems.

That black students are disproportionately affected by the new rule is 7
probably correct. But the measures were designed to introduce minimal academic standards where none previously existed and to force high school administrations to institute curriculum reforms that teach high school athletes basic study skills. After all, it is as important for a black high school athlete to be able to solve a long-division problem and comprehend a newspaper article as it is for a less athletically inclined student, black *or* white. If anything, the suggestion that black athletes shouldn't have to meet these minimal standards itself smacks of racism.

Behavioral standards are also frequently waived for the sake of the 8
team. When athletes are found guilty of a university infraction such as drug use or fighting, coaches, players, and the administration often protectively close ranks. Thus, when Vernon Maxwell, the University of Florida's all-time leading scorer, reportedly tested positive for drugs three times before his senior season, school administrators failed to enforce their standard policy of a one-year suspension. Justifying the three-game

suspension thought more appropriate, Dr. Richard Sharra, the team physician, said university officials wanted "to help" the star player, who has since gone on to become the starting guard for the San Antonio Spurs of the National Basketball Association.

Similarly, after a university judicial board found that they had "engaged in wrongful behavior in violation of general university regulations," Syracuse basketball star Derrick Coleman and four other student-athletes were reprimanded and given the lightest possible penalty for a fight that they started and for two apartment break-ins. Following this slap on the wrist, Syracuse coach Jim Boeheim commented that Coleman "admitted what he did was wrong and now he's been punished for it. It's over with." Not so quickly dispatched, however, were the criminal charges resulting from the allegedly unprovoked assault by these athletes on a fellow student during an attempt to crash a fraternity-sponsored dance. Had such an altercation been prompted by anyone other than a basketball or football player, the university penalty would certainly have been far more severe. 9

So obsessed with winning teams are John Thompson and many of his colleagues that they have lost all perspective on their roles: They are presumed to be educators first and coaches second, and their recruits should be students first and basketball players second. If this isn't the case — and in many Division I schools it is not — the pretense should be eliminated. 10

Perhaps the problem could best be solved by letting basketball teams become clubs, like track and field associations, which rent space from universities. The players on such teams would then not need a university affiliation. If college kids want to go to their games and root for them, so be it, but unless they could meet undeviating academic standards the players would not be students. 11

However, if the present system is to continue unaltered, we should at least have the courage to acknowledge certain uncomfortable facts, among them that only a small minority of black college athletes actually complete degrees and that even those who graduate often lack minimal communication and computation skills. It's time to reveal the hoax that is being foisted on many black kids. Most won't make the pros; they will merely be coddled through four years and then left to drop out disillusioned and uneducated. This is the real pattern of exploitation and it behooves Thompson, Cheney, Brown, et al., to acknowledge its reality. 12

It is certainly unadorned hypocrisy to argue for an "educational opportunity" that allows a 6-foot-10-inch, 240-pound center to enter the university, but limits his meaningful "educational experience" to the gym and weight room. The coaches crying foul over modestly tightened NCAA standards should look at themselves in the mirror and ask why 13 their humanitarianism doesn't result in higher rates of graduation, or anything but cruel disappointment for the dropout. I suspect that honest answers would lead to broken mirrors.

Prop 48 Makes Athletes Study

CLIFF SJOGREN

It is probably true that the majority of entering freshmen in some colleges and universities in the United States know more than graduating seniors in others. The strength of American higher education is its diversity, which is characterized by widely differing standards and expectations at both the entry and degree-completion levels. Thus any externally applied standard designed to bring conformity to the admission and academic achievement processes will be considered inappropriate or even unfair by some of the participants affected by the standardization. 1

The National Collegiate Athletic Association, a membership organization whose rules are made by those who must comply with them, is charged with establishing a set of minimum freshman eligibility standards that will apply to all of the NCAA's approximately 550 Division I and II colleges and universities. Three years ago, a proposal I drafted while serving as admissions director at the University of Michigan became Proposition 48. Officially NCAA bylaw 14.3 under the new manual, it replaced a freshman eligibility rule that was markedly counterproductive to sound academic principles. 2

The need for such a bylaw was clear to me. Until 1986, recruited freshmen were eligible for athletic grants if they earned a school-computed 2.0 grade point average after either the sixth, seventh, or eighth semester of high school. High school officials merely reported the student-athlete's overall grade point average using whatever plan was applied to all students of the high school. In most schools, both academic and nonacademic courses are used to compute the average. 3

That ill-conceived standard proved to be a simple and efficient way to do the wrong thing. 4

Young student-athletes were sent the message that to become eligible for an athletic scholarship one should attend a weak high school and 5

Cliff Sjogren is the former admissions director of the University of Michigan. His article appeared in the *New York Times* on March 12, 1989.

avoid rigorous courses. It was common practice for high school personnel, often under the guidance of an ambitious college recruiter, to advise promising athletes entering their senior year with borderline qualifications to elect few, if any, academic courses. Why take English, advanced algebra, and chemistry, one might ask, when weight lifting, fun with numbers, and bachelor living will satisfy the eligibility requirement?

High school counselors were caught. Should students be advised to elect a solid academic program as preparation for college work or take the easy path to achieve a satisfactory grade point average for college athletic eligibility? If the student-athlete was very big, very fast, or very accurate, the latter course usually was taken. And the expected happened. While many college staffs were quite creative in keeping students eligible for four years of competition, an embarrassingly high percentage of blue-chip athletes did not graduate from college. 6

Something had to be done. In 1982, as a member of the NCAA Academic Requirements Committee, I drafted a proposal to amend bylaw 5-1-(j) which subsequently became Proposition 48 of the 1983 NCAA Convention. The proposal was based on a simple educational principle: The best predictor of academic success is previous academic behavior. Thus, students who choose, for whatever reason, to go to college should take courses that will prepare them for the college academic experience. 7

A review of numerous public and independent college minimum admission requirements, as well as those mandated by state systems, revealed a pattern of college preparatory subjects that students should have successfully completed. That pattern consisted of at least three years of English and two years each of mathematics (at algebra level, and above) social sciences, and natural/physical science, including a laboratory experience. At least two additional academic credits should be completed. That course distribution plan became the core requirement of Prop 48. 8

As the last few years have shown, the standardized test requirement has become the most controversial aspect of Proposition 48. The test minimum of 700 on the Scholastic Aptitude Test or 15 on the American College Test with at least 2.0 in the core courses was intended as a secondary means of qualifying because it gave students who elected strong high school programs, late bloomers, or students who attended schools with high standards a fair chance to qualify. That provision would, it was thought, encourage students to accept rather than avoid academic challenges. 9

Interestingly, my original draft of the bylaw provided for an exemption from the Scholastic Aptitude Test or the American College Test if the student earned at least a 2.5 grade point average in the core courses. The reason for this was to reduce the impact of a rigid test standard. 10

But the sponsors of the legislation, the President's Council of the NCAA, chose to drop the 2.5 standard with the test exemption because of their fear of grade fixing, or grade inflation that might occur at the high school level. Thus, that part of the proposed rule that required the test became the only standard. 11

While there has been almost universal acceptance of the core course standard, serious criticisms have been made about the test requirement. Although I generally oppose the use of cutoff scores as the single criterion for college admission, scholarship awards and athletic eligibility, the temptation to cheat has probably been somewhat lessened by the requirement of a nationally recognized standardized measurement of basic educational skills. The test thresholds are at a reasonable level: About two-thirds of all college-bound students score higher than those minimum scores. 12

Proposition 48 is working. A major strength of the rule lies in the provision that a student-athlete who does not satisfy the requirement will nevertheless be given the opportunity for an education. Data already being reviewed by conference officials and independent researchers suggest that a substantial number of Prop 48's are achieving well in the classroom. Some credit for that progress, it seems, must be given to the rule that required nonqualifiers to give up athletic competition for a year and concentrate on their studies. 13

And a pleasant byproduct of the rule is emerging. Anecdotal information from middle and high schools indicates that students, their parents, and school officials are making sure that promising young athletes are electing the proper courses and are taking seriously their preparation for college entrance examinations. 14

In the meantime, well-meaning but ill-advised educators are suggesting that to make a good thing even better, those student-athletes who do not qualify under Proposition 48 should be denied athletic grants, thereby greatly discouraging their admission to college. Thus, by a slim margin, Proposal 42 was passed at the January 1989 NCAA Convention. 15

For many convention delegates, Proposal 42 represented higher academic standards, and today nobody wishes to be considered as being against higher standards for athletes. The rule, however, places an exaggerated importance on test scores. 16

While I do not accept the common thought that tests are biased against certain groups (except groups of poorly prepared students), I feel that Proposal 42 is too harsh and infringes unnecessarily upon the responsibility of the college to determine who should enroll and on what terms. 17

Let's allow Proposition 48 and the improved satisfactory progress rules show that, given the chance and some support, young athletes will be successful in the classroom as well as on the field and floor. Proposal 42 is bad legislation and is not needed. 18

The Myth of the Student-Athlete

SHANNON BROWNLEE with NANCY S. LINNON

College sport is being undermined by its own mythology. The entire enterprise is founded on the whimsical notion of the amateur, the scholar-athlete who studies and trains hard and is rewarded for his efforts, not with money but with sporting values and, above all, an education. But this implicit bargain has today become a mockery, and the cause is an overriding need — both psychological and economic — to win. 1

Consider the economics: The teams competing in Pasadena's Rose Bowl this week will each walk away with $6 million. Bowl games alone were worth more than $55 million last season, and basketball powers will rake in a $1 billion bonanza over seven years starting in 1991 for granting CBS the privilege of broadcasting college games. 2

That's big business — a business sustained by the dreams of athletes, a disproportionate number of whom are black. Few of those dreams come true. Fewer than 30 percent of football and basketball players graduate, a rate far lower than for all students, and only a tiny fraction make it to the pros. While a handful of exemplary programs can claim to graduate nearly 100 percent — Notre Dame, Duke, and Penn State, for example — too many follow the lead of Memphis State, which graduated six out of fifty-eight basketball players between 1973 and 1983. 3

These broken bargains can be traced to the peculiar economics of college sports. Despite the enormous sums of money involved, athletics are not a profitable enterprise for most colleges. Only about forty-five athletic departments operate in the black each year. And only a few of those — notably Penn State, Notre Dame, and Miami — do so consistently, because college sports as they're staged today, and football in particular, are very expensive businesses. Says John Slaughter, former chancellor of the University of Maryland, who is now president of Occidental College, "Winning is the thing that ensures the income. Football and basketball have to make money, and they have to win to make money, and that's how the cycle becomes so vicious." 4

The cycle has become vicious indeed. Last year, twenty-one universities were penalized by the National Collegiate Athletic Association (NCAA) for infractions ranging from falsifying entrance exams to wooing recruits with cash to paying players, while an additional twenty-eight were under NCAA investigation. Such ethical lapses belie the myth that 5

Shannon Brownlee is an associate editor and Nancy S. Linnon a reporter-researcher at *U.S. News and World Report*, where this article appeared on January 8, 1990.

college sports provide a moral education, and the effect is clear in the behavior of athletes. Since 1987, more than 250 college athletes have been arrested for violent crimes ranging from fistfights to attempted murder.

Why do universities tolerate a business that is exploitative and vio- 6
lent — and loses money on top of it all? First, and most obviously, a lot of people — from coaches to recruiters to concessionaires — make their living off it. And some make a very good living; college coaches earn as much as $1 million a year in salary and endorsement fees. But more to the point, big-time college sports satisfy a psychological need. As Robert Atwell, president of the American Council on Education, notes, "It's the nature of this highly competitive society of ours that loves winners and hates losers. College sports feed the insatiable appetite of the American male to be a couch potato and watch all this stuff. . . ."

While college athletes are technically amateurs — their scholarships 7
cover tuition, fees, books, room and board — their sweat is the fuel that runs an enormous machine. In 1988, Division I-A football generated $500 million in gate, TV and licensing revenues, and untold amounts from corporate sponsors and boosters. Ironically, this income rarely shows up on university ledgers. At many big-time schools, athletic departments are run as separate corporations — financially shaky corporations. The University of Michigan, for example, one of the largest athletic departments in the country, operates twenty-one sports on a $21.3 million budget. Last year, the Wolverines were $2.6 million in the hole (see table, page 417).

Going to Carnival

The explanation is simple: To make money, a school has to spend it. 8
At the University of Colorado, all of the modest $4.5 million that football earns is churned right back into football, a practice that paid off this season, when the perennially mediocre Buffaloes won a trip to the Orange Bowl with their 11–0 record. Of the $4.1 million CU will take home from its Orange Bowl appearance this week, $3.1 million will be distributed evenly among the eight schools in the Big Eight Conference, including Oklahoma State and Oklahoma, both on NCAA probation. Ten days of carnival in Miami gobbled up the rest (see table, p. 417).

Boosters, athletic directors, presidents, and coaches like to claim that 9
a winning program translates into something they call "the intangibles," prestige and donations for a school. "How many people know we have a Nobel Prize winner this year?" asks Jon Burianek, Colorado's associate athletic director. "Not many compared with the number who know this football team's Cinderella story."

Maybe so, but the fact is a high-profile team benefits the athletic de- 10
partment, not the university. James Frey, a sociologist at the University of

Nevada at Las Vegas, citing twelve different studies conducted over the past fifty years, concludes, "There's no relation between a winning record and donations that come into the university for academic programs."

As critics see it, the most hypocritical justification offered for football's excesses is that the game builds character. The values that truly can be gained from sports — an appreciation for hard work, sportsmanship, the joy of playing — have been distorted by the desperate need to win. Boosterism is the perfect example. As Rick Telander, author of *The Hundred Yard Lie*, points out, "The Bull Gators, the booster club of the University of Florida, is giving money to win — not to build character but to beat the living daylights out of Florida State. That's got nothing to do with education." 11

Farms for the Pros

To be sure, not all athletes object to the system. Some view college as a mere formality standing between them and lucrative professional contracts. Colleges serve as farm teams for the National Football League and National Basketball Association, which have struck a cozy deal with the NCAA by agreeing not to take an athlete before his college eligibility is up. Deion "Neon" Sanders, a defensive back of electrifying physical talents who signed a $4.4-million four-year contract last April with the Atlanta Falcons, graced few classrooms with his presence during his senior year at Florida State. Asked whether he wanted to be in college, Sanders told Telander, "No, but I have to be." 12

But for every athlete who makes it to the big time there are hundreds more who neglect their studies in the mistaken belief that they too can cash in on their physical skills for a shot at a sweeter life. In reality, the road to the pros, where salaries in the NFL average $256,000 and in the NBA $650,000, is long and narrow. More than 17,600 young men play Division I-A basketball and football, and each year only 150 of them will reach the big leagues; even fewer will last more than a year or so. Yet according to a recent NCAA Presidents Commission study of athletes, more than 23 percent of college athletes (and 44 percent of the blacks) believe they are headed for the pros. "There's nothing wrong with having those dreams," says Thomas Tutko, a sports psychologist at San Jose State University. "It's when you sacrifice everything else that the problem occurs." 13

The blame for the dismal state of college athletes must be shared — with the media for worshiping athletes and with the high schools for failing at basic education. "Colleges and universities are receiving products of an inferior educational system," says Richard Lapchick, director of the Center for the Study of Sport in Society at Northeastern University. "They didn't create the attitudes of the players, the high schools did." And 14 increasingly, the sins of the colleges are being visited upon the lower schools. In many parts of the country, high school coaches recruit elementary school students. Last year, high school games began appearing on television.

Arthur Ashe, the only black male tennis player ever to win at 15
Wimbledon, believes that black athletes suffer most acutely from the worship of sports. Only 4 percent of Division I college students are black, yet they represent 56 percent of basketball players and 37 percent of football players — in part, says Ashe, because "the screening of black athletes in black communities starts very early. It is cold-blooded, and by the time a young black boy is thirteen, we know if he's a good athlete or not, and junior-high coaches have already started recruiting him."

Even those who come to college hoping to exchange their physical 16
skills for a degree often discover the promise of an education is an illusion. And no wonder. The NCAA Presidents Commission study found that football and basketball players devote, on average, thirty hours a week to their sport, sixteen more hours than they spend in class. Detroit Lions running back Barry Sanders, last year's Heisman Trophy winner, quit school early to turn pro, saying that college athletes spend so much time on sports they "might as well get paid for it."

Tinkering with Reform

College presidents will have a chance to act on their concerns at the 17
annual NCAA meeting next week, where they will discuss shortening the basketball season and spring football practice. There will also be further debate over Proposition 42, the NCAA's plan to refuse scholarships to students who score below 700 on the standardized college-entrance exams. Critics charge that Prop 42 discriminates against black athletes, while others maintain that such measures will eventually force high schools to prepare their athletes academically. Already, seven states have adopted a "no pass, no play" rule. NCAA members are likely to endorse a plan devised by Senator Bill Bradley (D-N.J.) to make graduation rates public.

All of which amounts to modest tinkering. More effective would be to 18
marry the number of athletic scholarships the NCAA will allow to a school's graduation rate and to divorce monetary incentives from winning by bringing athletic departments back under the president's control. Better yet, require winning teams to share TV and bowl receipts with all Division I schools, an idea not likely to be greeted enthusiastically. "When I brought this up," says the Council on Education's Atwell, "[Georgetown basketball coach] John Thompson blasted me. He said, 'Am I the only capitalist in the room? Georgetown money belongs to Georgetown.'"

Some proponents of reform would go so far as to pay college players, 19 thus ending the hypocrisy of the amateur student-athlete. Certainly, the NFL and NBA ought to be contributing to the training of their future recruits, if not by starting farm teams then by aiding college programs. But more than anything, coaches, athletic directors, college presidents and the NCAA must acknowledge — as polls reveal the general public already has — that college basketball and football are careering out of control. "[Football] has become a business, carried on too often by professionals, bringing in vast gate receipts, demoralizing student ethics, and confusing the ideals of sport, manliness, and decency." These words were delivered at the University of Wisconsin by historian Frederick Jackson Turner. The year was 1906.

A POWERHOUSE LOSES MONEY

The University of Michigan's athletic department consistently makes money on only two of its 21 sports, football and basketball, and it ran a deficit last year of $2.6 million. It receives no funds from the university, nor does it funnel money into academics.

Expenses	
Salaries	$5.6 mil.
Recruiting, travel, equipment	$4.6 mil.
Grant-in-aid programs	$3.6 mil.
Facilities maintenance	$3.0 mil.
Administrative costs	$2.6 mil.
Debt service	$1.7 mil.
Total expenses:	$21.1 mil.
Revenues	
Football receipts	$7.4 mil.
Basketball receipts	$1.8 mil.
Hockey receipts	$200,000
Championships, bowl games	$2.4 mil.
Misc. (royalty fees, camp)	$2.6 mil.
Television and radio	$1.9 mil.
Concessions, souvenirs	$1.5 mil.
Athletic-facility fees	$700,000
Total revenues:	$18.5 mil.

USN&WR—Basic data: University of Michigan athletic department

THAT'S ENTERTAINMENT

The University of Colorado's athletic department spends nearly $1 million to go to the Orange Bowl. It transports and houses more than 600 people, including 16 cheerleaders, 250 band members, 160 members of the president's official party, and 8 caretakers for Ralphie the Buffalo, the team mascot.

The Cost of an Orange Bowl Appearance	
Transportation	$325,000
Hotel accommodations	$300,000
Per diems for players and staff	$50,000
Bonuses for coaches and staff	$50,000
Misc. and unbudgeted expenses	$50,000
University admin. charge	$45,000–$50,000
Equipment	$35,000–$40,000
Gifts for players	$30,000
Telephone, mailings, supplies	$16,500
Complimentary tickets	$15,000
Photos, game films	$10,000–$15,000
Extra personnel	$10,000
Press guide	$7,500–$10,000
Practice facility	$5,000–$10,000
Laundry	$5,000
Insurance	$5,000
Total expenses (approx.)	$981,500

USN&WR—Basic data: University of Colorado athletic department

THINKING AND WRITING ABOUT COLLEGIATE SPORTS REFORM

Questions for Discussion and Writing

1. What is the main point of contention between Whiddon and Moore concerning the effects of Proposition 42? Does either Whiddon or Moore ignore certain issues in order to press his claim? Would Whiddon's arguments be stronger if he offered statistical data to refute Moore?
2. What original changes in Proposition 48 does Sjogren criticize? Why? Why does he oppose Proposition 42?
3. What arguments does Sage use to justify the payment of salaries to athletes? Why does Davis object to such payments? To what extent can their arguments be characterized as moral rather than practical?
4. What are the assumptions on which Berkow bases his proposals for reform? Do his references to specific examples weaken or strengthen his argument? (Compare Berkow to Whiddon, whose argument is framed in general terms.)
5. Do all the proposals by *Time* seem practical? Fair? Discuss the assumptions about education that underlie your answers. Which arguments in this chapter provide support for some of these proposals?
6. How does London refute the accusation of racism in the disputes over Propositions 48 and 42? What values support his argument?
7. Brownlee and Linnon claim that "college basketball and football are careering out of control." How do they attempt to prove this? Which components of the college sports enterprise do the authors attack most directly? What do the tables of athletic expenses and revenues prove?

Topics for Research

The mission of the university: Do collegiate sports contribute?

A case study of an uneducated athlete

How Proposition 48 has worked

How star athletes are wooed and won: Recruitment incentives

Who argues against reform and why?

CHAPTER 14

Environmental Policy

In the last decade the state of the environment has become a matter of global as well as regional concern. Air and water pollution, radon, and acid rain continue to threaten selected areas of the earth, but two new dangers have taken over our headlines and provoked controversy among scientists: depletion of the ozone layer and, above all, global warming (the "greenhouse effect").

The urgency of these problems is obvious. If they exist and worsen, all life on earth will be affected, and policy decisions for limiting the damage will be crucial to our survival. But two questions must be answered before solutions to these problems can be implemented.

One is a question of fact. Does the greenhouse effect — or the depletion of the ozone layer — actually exist? Not many years ago scientists who had observed changes in a global temperature warned of a coming ice age. Today respectable scientists are divided about the dangers of a drop in stratospheric ozone and the possibility that a subsequent global warming might transform conditions on earth. There is also disagreement about the extent to which human activity contributes to these phenomena.

The other question concerns the values that should inform any policy decisions. If serious global warming and ozone depletion can be verified, the causes will probably be found to lie, at least in part, on the use of fossil fuels and chlorofluorocarbons, both significant factors in the technological development and high standards of living in the industrialized world. Should economic growth, then, be reduced? If it is, the poor in all countries will be denied the right to achieve higher standards of living. How should the burden of extreme conservation measures be shared?

Overview of the State of the Environment: Toward the Nineties

WILLIAM K. REILLY

For many of the long-standing environmental issues, there is at least a track record of programmatic successes and failures on which to build. Yet, in virtually every instance, the easy steps have been taken, the obvious solutions applied. The difficulty of making further progress on these issues, as well as on problems more recently recognized, is compounded by a number of factors: 1

The nation's budget situation provides a major source of conflict. Competition among federal activities, including environmental programs, for a share of the U.S. budget is fierce. States and localities are little better off, for they have been asked to pick up many programs that the federal government has pared in efforts to reduce budget deficits. 2

The process by which policies are set and decisions made leaves much to be desired. Better information is a requisite for better decisions. Yet the degree of uncertainty surrounding the data on which environmental decisions are based is often frightening. For example, many of the air quality models used to support regulatory decisions have enormous margins of error. Equally lacking is information about how well programs work; compliance statistics are notoriously incomplete, and monitoring of program implementation is problematic at best. Little evaluation has been done, for example, on the municipal sewage-treatment program to deter- 3

William K. Reilly is president of the board of directors of the Conservation Foundation, a research institute based in Washington, D.C. This excerpt is from a 1987 report from the Conservation Foundation.

mine how much actual improvement in water quality has been brought by the billions of dollars the nation has invested. In addition, decisions are still too often made in the confrontational manner that has polarized environmental decision making in the past.

Many issues cut across the boundaries of traditional programs, thus 4
requiring herculean efforts at integration and cooperation among multiple offices, agencies, and levels of government whose activities, as often as not, are competitive or adversarial. Each of dozens of regulatory programs — for underground storage tanks, old hazardous waste sites, new hazardous waste sites, indoor air pollution, outdoor air pollution, workplace air pollution, and on and on — concentrates only on its narrowly defined mission, generally ignoring often critical ecological interrelationships. Several different permitting systems exist at federal and state levels to regulate activities in wetlands, for example: as part of these programs, agencies use at least one-half dozen different definitions of wetlands, making compliance difficult and helping create interagency confusion and battles.

Some of today's problems are less visible, less tangible, and thus more 5
difficult to mobilize for than those with which the country has been grappling over the past two decades. Public outrage in this country over foul, dirty water or over brown-colored smog — problems people could readily see — helped marshal a constituency for environmental cleanup. The 1972 clean water legislation set a goal of "swimmable and fishable waters," a powerful image capable of capturing public attention and motivating action. People could see results. But no one can see acid rain or carbon dioxide or the ozone layer or indoor air pollutants or groundwater. Though the effects of these recently identified problems may be felt all the same, experts with access to sophisticated equipment and computer programs are increasingly needed to identify environmental problems and convince officials and the public of their scope and consequences.

The sources of many environmental problems are becoming far more 6
diffuse. Basic U.S. pollution control laws have relied on the states for their implementation and are premised on the assumption that damage caused by pollution occurs primarily in the state in which the pollution arises. Two decades ago, consensus for action in a community could develop over nailing a specific culprit — take action, and the problem would go away. Technology could reduce a power plant's emissions. A manufacturing plant could be required to treat its effluents. If pollution sources were numerous, they nonetheless were discernible, and strategies or

controls for correcting the problems were available even if results fell short of expectations.

But it is much harder to target those who are responsible for the environmental problems now being recognized. Few strategies can be easily devised, few controls readily applied. No single culprit is causing the buildup of carbon dioxide and other gases in the atmosphere; countless individuals and economic activities, highly decentralized, are responsible. Similarly, depletion of ozone in the upper atmosphere can be laid at no one's doorstep in particular. Responsibility is shared widely. Tropical forests are falling, endangering wildlife, not only because of ill-conceived development projects but even more because of the activities of countless subsistence farmers eking out their living from the forests. Radon, a health hazard only recently recognized as such in this country, occurs naturally. Human activities are not to blame for the basic problem, though decisions by innumerable local officials over the years unknowingly have allowed homes to be sited in places of high exposure; the drive to create more energy-efficient buildings has exacerbated the situation. 7

Some of the problems now confronting the country are likely to cause environmental and economic damage on a global scale. Among these are climate warming; the threat of depletion of the earth's ozone layer, with its potential for increasing the incidence of skin cancer; the rampant loss of tropical forests and other highly productive ecosystems; and inadequate coordination and control of agricultural, chemical, and other goods traded in international commerce. No one country can solve these problems on its own. Different cultures and languages can turn the simplest transactions into complex undertakings. Above all, the weakness of international institutions, arising from jealously guarded national sovereignty, means that implementation would remain extremely difficult at best, even if nations could agree on cooperative measures. 8

Nature Under Glass

JAMES R. UDALL

Last summer's scorching drought spawned a firestorm of articles analyzing the potential impact of global warming on humankind. But few of these starve-drown-and-swelter pieces paid more than passing attention to how species and ecosystems might fare. If rapid climatic change could cause a disruption equivalent to a nuclear war for *Homo sapiens* — one of the world's most adaptable species and, moreover, the only one that will have been forewarned — what unfathomable decimation might it wreak on the rest of Earth's creatures? 1

Climatologists believe Earth will warm three to nine degrees Fahrenheit by 2050 if current trends in greenhouse-gas emissions continue. Biologists are more than alarmed by these figures — they are spooked by the possibility that global warming, if and when it occurs, may cause a biological apocalypse. Their fears might be hard to understand. Spooked? Why? A warming of a few degrees — won't that just mean less snow, more Coppertone? 2

George Woodwell, a greenhouse expert who is director of the Woods Hole Research Center in Massachusetts, doesn't see it that way. "Rapid change is, almost by definition, the enemy of life," he says. "Great caution seems appropriate before committing the world to irreversible changes of unknown magnitude and effects." 3

According to ecologist Norman Myers, there's a striking correlation in the fossil record between previous mass extinctions and climatic change. Habitat destruction has already put hundreds of thousands of species at death's door, Myers says. Global warming may well open it and shove them through. 4

Michael Oppenheimer, an atmospheric scientist with the Environmental Defense Fund, says that by fundamentally altering the composition of the atmosphere we are venturing into uncharted, risky terrain. "Remember," Oppenheimer cautions, "nobody predicted the ozone hole. This suggests that we ought to be extremely skeptical of our predictive capabilities regarding global warming — and we ought to expect further nasty surprises." 5

So much for the generalities. But how will warming affect polar bears? Turtles? Redwoods? Plankton? Alligators? Oceans? The Arctic National Wildlife Refuge? 6

James R. Udall writes on environmental matters for several publications, including *Sierra* magazine, where this report appeared in the July/August 1989 issue.

Last October, at a conference organized by the World Wildlife Fund, nearly 400 scientists and environmentalists met to compare notes on these and similar questions. Using a West African term for magic, conference organizer and conservation biologist Robert Peters summarized the grim take-home message succinctly: "Lots of bad juju." 7

"If the climate models turn out to be right, the new world will be biologically less rich and less stable," said Dennis Murphy of the Center for Conservation Biology at Stanford University. "As climatic zones move north and south, away from the equator, species will have to move too, in order to survive. Some will fail and become extinct." 8

Peters warned that when it comes time to move, many species will find themselves "man-locked," their escape routes blocked by highways, cities, and "agricultural deserts." According to Peters, types of species and communities particularly at risk include poor dispersers (snails and most trees, for example), peripheral populations (plants and animals now found at the edges of their ranges), geographically localized species (redwoods), genetically impoverished species (any currently endangered), specialized species (the Everglades kite, which is dependent on the apple snail as its single food source), annuals (which would suffer reproductive failure due to droughts and heat waves), montane and alpine communities (butterflies and wildflowers isolated on mountaintops), Arctic communities (where temperatures are predicted to increase most), and coastal ecosystems (which would be devastated by sea-level rises). 9

Of course, not every species would see its range shrink. Environmental disruption would usher in a heyday for plant and animal pests. Tropical insects, parasites, and diseases would migrate to more temperate regions. The range of the African tsetse fly, for example, would shift southward, bringing sleeping sickness with it. Hookworm infestations could become rampant throughout the Northern Hemisphere. 10

Because global warming is projected to be greatest at high latitudes, polar regions would likely show the first signs of ecological damage. The Arctic and Antarctic oceans currently harbor the world's most productive fisheries. At the base of these fertile food chains are plankton — microscopic plants and animals that thrive beneath the ice covering these waters for much of the year. Declines in the extent of sea ice, however, could cause a plankton crash that would topple a huge biomass of fish and seabirds. And if the sea ice vanishes, as some climate models predict, polar bears, seals, walruses, and other animals that depend on it will vanish, too. 11

Research by Margaret Davis, an ecologist at the University of Minnesota, indicates that forests throughout the United States would shrink like cheap T-shirts along their warmer and drier margins, with the Southeast's forests vanishing entirely over a period of decades. By the year 2090, cli- 12 mate zones in the East would have shifted 300 miles to the north — at rates ten times faster than most tree species can migrate. "Trees aren't very good at picking up and walking north," notes Deborah Jensen, an ecologist at the Pacific Institute. "Acorns get carried around by birds and squirrels, so oaks may have a chance to track the changing climate. But many other tree species will be left behind."

Sea-level rises would devastate coastal wetlands. For example, a three-foot rise, possible by 2050, would drown most of Everglades National Park and the already endangered Louisiana coastal wetlands. Attempts to protect buildings and roads with sea walls would only compound the biological loss by directing the full force of storm surges onto adjacent wetlands. 13

Because temperature has ceased to be a major constraint on human activities, it's easy to forget that it governs many aspects of plant and animal reproduction. For example, the gender of some reptile offspring is controlled by the eggs' incubation temperature. Alligator eggs incubated at 93 degrees or above produce males; temperatures below 86 degrees produce females. (In sea turtles, it's just the reverse: Warmer temperatures produce females.) "It's conceivable that we could end up with a total absence of one sex," says biologist Daniel Rubenstein of Princeton University. 14

University of California at Berkeley ecologist John Harte fears that an altered climate will have ripple effects that could be far more damaging than the more obvious direct impacts. For example, a melting of permafrost in Alaska's Arctic National Wildlife refuge would destroy its tundra ecosystem. These windswept plains are the main calving grounds for 180,000 caribou and a critical staging area for snow geese and other birds. As the tundra thawed, the underlying peat would begin to decay. This would release immense quantities of carbon dioxide, leading to even more warming. 15

Oceans are the largest Pandora's box in the global-warming scenario. The greenhouse effect has the potential to change the upwelling patterns that sustain world fisheries as well as the rainfall patterns on which agriculture depends. If oceans warm and rise, coral reefs, which currently harbor two thirds of the fish in tropical waters, may shrivel. Even ocean currents could switch — a nasty surprise whose impacts, says Oppenheimer, "would dwarf those of the ozone hole." If the Gulf Stream stopped carrying warm water from the Caribbean northward, for instance, temperatures in Northern Europe could fall eight to fifteen degrees, ushering in a new ice age. 16

The implications of global warming for conservation policy could not be more profound. The warming is expected to be more rapid than any in human history; yet all preservation efforts to date have assumed a stable 17 climate. If climatic upheaval yanks the habitat "rug" from beneath national parks, forests, rangelands, and wildlife refuges, we can expect a wholesale reshuffling of biotic communities, disruption of predator-prey relationships, and the loss of many species. The conclusion is inescapable: The specter of global warming puts everything conservations thought they had saved at risk once again. We're back to square one.

In a world where rapid climatic change became the norm, conservationists would have to consider not merely how to preserve a species in a place, but also how to preserve it through time. UC Berkeley's Harte thinks we should hedge our bets, by diversifying the number, location, and size of the parks in our portfolio, and by making conservation of biodiversity a higher priority on the 95 percent of the planet not dedicated to parklands. 18

"If we are concerned with maintaining biological diversity — not just to eke out another fifty years or so of species survival but to preserve some remnants of the natural world for the year 2100 and beyond — we must begin now to incorporate information about global warming, as it becomes available, in the planning process," Robert Peters says. 19

This would mean different things in different places. For instance, coastal preserves might be expanded inland to include terrain at a variety of elevations. "That way," says biologist Larry Harris of the University of Florida, "whatever the sea-level rise, you'll have something left." 20

Climatologists believe that we're already committed to one to three degrees of warming due to past greenhouse-gas emissions. Beyond that, however, additional warming is *not* inevitable — the planet's destiny is cradled in human hands. 21

More than a few ecologists think this may be the spookiest thing of all. Placing the challenge in a cultural context, George Woodwell says, "Until now Western civilization has assumed that the world would take care of itself. But Earth is no longer large enough to accommodate the assaults of contemporary civilization. . . . The world is life itself, and we need to provide a new stewardship that we have not yet been willing to provide. That stewardship must bring about a revolution in the world's governments — or we face a crippling, global biotic impoverishment." 22

Getting Warmer?

JANE S. SHAW and RICHARD L. STROUP

Beginning last summer, as a severe drought and record heat dried up fields and streams across the United States, a big story hit the headlines: The earth may be getting dangerously warmer. James E. Hansen, a scientist with the National Aeronautics and Space Administration (NASA), told a congressional hearing that the evidence is "pretty strong" that the greenhouse effect had begun to operate. 1

"Seldom has there been such a strong consensus among scientists on a major environmental issue," intoned Richard A. Houghton and George M. Woodwell, scientists at the Woods Hole Research Center, in *Scientific American* this April. Stephen Schneider of the National Center for Atmospheric Research calculates that human-caused climate change will proceed ten to forty times as fast as any previous natural climate change. 2

Experts speculate on what the world might look like when the greenhouse effect takes hold. They predict rising sea-levels inundating wetlands, beaches, and coastal cities; forests shifting northward; new drought belts; worsening air pollution; and more catastrophes such as fires, plagues, and floods. 3

Self-appointed guardians of the environment are urging immediate steps to reduce emissions of "greenhouse gases" — especially CO_2 [carbon dioxide], but also methane, nitrous oxides, and CFCs (chlorofluorocarbons), which are believed to trap heat radiating from the earth. They urge cutting back on fossil-fuel use by such measures as special taxes on carbon dioxide emissions, increased funding for alternative energy sources, incentives for solar and nuclear power, an end to deforestation, and a doubling of the current fuel-efficiency standards. 4

Cutting back significantly on the use of fossil fuels would require great sacrifices. Is global warming a sufficiently pressing issue to justify such steps? 5

The case for a greenhouse effect is based on the fact that the amount of CO_2 in the atmosphere is indeed increasing. Studying gas trapped in glacial ice, scientists estimate that in the 1850s, at the start of the industrial revolution, the atmosphere had less than 290 parts of CO_2 per million parts of air; that has risen to over 340 ppm, an increase of about 20 percent over some 135 years. 6

Jane S. Shaw and Richard L. Stroup are senior associates of the Political Economy Research Center in Bozeman, Montana. Their article appeared in the July 14, 1989 issue of the *National Review*.

There is also evidence that global temperatures have been going up 7
during the past century. Hansen and his colleagues at NASA believe that the average global temperature has increased by between 0.5° and 0.7° C [degrees Celsius] since 1860. And the six warmest years globally during the past century appear to have been in the 1980s, with 1988 the warmest.

But whether there is a connection between the two factors is highly 8
debatable. Scientists aren't even sure the warming has occurred. Andrew R. Solow, a statistician at Woods Hole, points out that measured global temperatures are "not really global at all." Monitoring stations tend to be located on land rather than on oceans, where trends may be quite different, and more are in the Northern Hemisphere than in the Southern Hemisphere. Furthermore, some regions, including the contiguous United States, have not shown any observable warming during the past century. The Northern Hemisphere actually experienced a cooling period between the 1940s and the 1970s, which led to predictions in the 1970s that we might be headed for a new Ice Age. Some scientists are convinced that the recent warm years can be explained by a periodic weather perturbation known as El Niño.

Assuming, however, that the global warming trend is real, could CO_2 9
be the cause? If so, says Solow, we should be seeing much warmer temperatures than we have seen so far. "For example, for the planet to warm by 2°C in the next hundred years, the average rate of warming would have to be four times greater than that in the historic record." Greenhouse warming is expected to be greatest at high latitudes and more rapid in the north than in the south, but this pattern hasn't appeared either, he says.

Hugh W. Elsaesser of Lawrence Livermore National Laboratory ques- 10
tions the computer models that predict the greenhouse effect, because of "the gross differences I see between how the atmosphere works and how it is modeled to work." But if carbon dioxide and other greenhouse gases didn't cause the warming that has apparently occurred, what did? Solow and Ellsaesser both think it is natural and that it simply reflects the aftermath of a period of unusual cooling, the so-called "Little Ice Age" that ended during the nineteenth century.

But suppose that a correlation could be made between increased 11
greenhouse gases and warming. Even that doesn't mean that the warming will simply continue. Much remains to be learned about the carbon cycle, the process by which carbon is taken up by plants and released into the atmosphere. Biological factors could enter in. For example, Trevor Platt of the Bedford Institute of Oceanography in Nova Scotia has been studying the role of phytoplankton, marine plants that consume enormous amounts of CO_2. He believes that the phytoplankon increase in

number as atmospheric CO_2 builds up, creating a new "steady state" that will interfere with the greenhouse effect. Scientists also point to the importance of volcanic eruptions, which are largely unpredictable. Volcanic fallout tends to cool the earth because the particles help reflect sunlight back into space.

And Reid Bryson, director of the Institute of Environmental Studies at the University of Wisconsin at Madison, believes dust and smoke are the primary culprits in climate change, rather than carbon dioxide. He and a colleague, Gerald Dittberner, contend that atmospheric dust is responsible for about 90 percent of the Northern Hemisphere's temperature variation in this century. Kenneth E. F. Watt, professor of environmental studies at the University of California at Davis, anticipates a long-term cooling. Increased carbon dioxide will heat tropical ocean surfaces, he explains, leading to additional evaporation and to denser clouds, which will decrease the penetration of sunlight. Watt suspects that the elevated level of the Great Salt Lake is a sign of cooling, not warming. 12

Even so, most people probably believe the greenhouse effect has arrived. In January, the *New York Times* airily dismissed a recent report that there was no warming in the United States during the last century. Any sign of the trend would be "hard to spot," explained the *Times*, and the uncertainty should not stand in the way of immediate action. ("The Greenhouse Effect Is for Real," read the editorial's headline.) In the United States and other Western democracies, public perceptions are critical to political outcomes. These perceptions are strongly influenced by the media, and they frequently differ from those of experts. The process has been substantiated by Stanley Rothman and S. Robert Lichter in a study published in *American Political Science Review*. They found that journalists are far more opposed to nuclear power than scientists who actually study nuclear issues, and that journalists more often quote the smaller group of scientists who are opposed to nuclear power. So, as *Science* editor Daniel Koshland put it, the government is "tilted to overreaction." 13

Thus the stage is set for very strong measures to reduce emissions of greenhouse gases. These measures would give governments greater power, would force people to make large sacrifices, and would probably limit innovation. Yet such measures will be introduced as moderate, even conservative, steps — in the words of the *New York Times*, as "cheap insurance against risks of such magnitude." 14

Yet any measures to remove CO_2 and other gases from the atmosphere will divert resources — land, labor, and capital — from other productive uses. The unintended consequences of mandatory action can be severe. 15

Take the *Times*'s recommendation to force Detroit to double the fuel efficiency of its cars. Such a requirement would result in many deaths. A study by Robert W. Crandall of the Brookings Institution and John D. Graham of the Harvard School of Public Health indicates that current fuel-efficiency standards are already causing deaths because automakers have had to lighten their cars, giving less protection in crashes. Crandall and Graham estimated that the congressionally established standards for 1989 models would have caused between 2,200 and 3,900 deaths. (The executive branch softened the standards a bit, so not quite that many people are dying.) 16

By the same token, some years ago the City of Los Angeles encouraged owners to tear down buildings that weren't earthquake-proof. The result, according to one study, was that 17,000 low-income people were deprived of housing, and replacement housing was not built. Even the best precautions typically have high costs. 17

Then there was the multibillion-dollar Synthetic Fuels Corporation that the U.S. government set up in response to the energy crisis of the late 1970s to spur production from new energy sources such as gasified coal. With no assistance from the corporation, the oil shortage turned into a worldwide glut; the Synfuels effort was simply wasted. 18

In general, government policies in the environmental arena shift with the political winds and nurture special interests. For example, after World War II the federal government wished to encourage nuclear power; the Price-Anderson Act was passed, limiting owners' liability for nuclear accidents, which reduced the incentives for effective safety measures. Then, in the sixties, antinuclear groups became politically powerful. This led to extensive regulation of nuclear utilities; costs became prohibitive and safety regulations became so complex that some analysts contend that they actually reduce safety. 19

Environmental policy often becomes a political tool of regional interests. The 1977 amendments to the Clean Air Act required that all electric utilities use scrubbers to eliminate sulphur dioxide emissions — even if they could reduce emissions more effectively by just using low-sulphur coal. As Bruce Ackerman and W. T. Hassler show in *Clean Coal, Dirty Air*, the scrubber requirement saved the Appalachian coal-mine owners and unions from serious competition from low-sulphur western coal. 20

If things are this bad on a national scale, what can we expect on a global scale? Negotiations over the past decade to establish a Law of the Sea Treaty illustrate the problem. Nations couldn't agree on how to develop seabed minerals; Third World governments demanded that an international authority be formed to collect fees that would be distributed to Third World nations. The United States opposed this demand and refused to sign the treaty. Similar conflicts are emerging with the effort to control 21

CFCs. China has indicated it plans to increase its use of CFCs tenfold by the year 2000.

Even modest familiarity with history adds to one's skepticism about taking immediate and drastic action to combat global warming. Over the centuries, competent, highly respected people have predicted timber shortages, worldwide famines, permanent energy crises, and critical mineral depletion. None of these predictions has materialized. 22

In 1865, the noted British economist William Jevons argued that industrial growth could not be continued for long because the world was running out of coal. He concluded that it was "inevitable that our present happy progressive condition is a thing of limited duration." 23

At the turn of the century, President Teddy Roosevelt and his first chief of the Forest Service, Gifford Pinchot, thought the country was running out of timber. Indeed, a *New York Times* headline, "Hickory Disappearing, Supply of Wood Nears End — Much Wasted and There's No Substitute," was typical, as Sherry Olson relates in her book *The Depletion Myth.* 24

In 1968 Paul Ehrlich wrote: "In the 1970s the world will undergo famines — hundreds of millions of people are going to starve to death." Fortunately, this did not prove correct, and increasing privatization of agriculture in the Third World has significantly increased food production. 25

Finally, what confidence can we have in the global-warming predictions when we note that less than fifteen years ago the idea that another Ice Age was pending was popular enough for a book, *The Cooling*, to be written and to receive respectful scientific comment? 26

Nevertheless, the doomsayers could be right. The good news is that we probably have time to find out. Scientists are constantly accumulating information that brings them closer to understanding climatic sensitivity to greenhouse gases. As this knowledge emerges, a true consensus may develop that something should be done about the greenhouse effect. 27

But, since massive government solutions tend to be counterproductive, what should we do? As we learn more about the potential for global warming (or cooling), individuals will adapt their plans to defend their property, and to take advantage of the new conditions. If they are allowed to do this each in his own way, the results will be illuminating — whereas if individuals believe instead that the government will prevent the problem, then less will be tried and less will be learned. If the governments actually try and fail, then more serious dangers are likely. 28

The most effective thing that we can do to cope with global warming is to allow progress to continue. This is just the opposite of what Lester Brown, president of Worldwatch Institute, would like. He and two 29 colleagues, Christopher Flavin and Sandra Postel, recently wrote that climate change "calls the whole notion of human progress into question" and urge that we take action "before it is too late." Yet Brown is flat wrong. Human progress is exactly what enabled people to cope with catastrophes in the past and it can continue to do so.

What countries can best handle the epidemic of AIDS? Clearly, countries that have sophisticated medicine, extensive hospital facilities, and a population in generally good health will cope better than countries lacking even basic sanitation for much of their population. Similarly, political scientist Aaron Wildavsky points out that an earthquake in California in 1971 caused sixty-two deaths. The next year a slightly less powerful earthquake in Nicaragua killed tens of thousands. Why the difference? The wealthier country had better-built houses, better transportation and communication, better health facilities. Shouldn't we encourage such progress, rather than stop it in its tracks? 30

In sum, mandatory steps to avert this potential disaster are the wrong way to go — especially in the near future, while scientific knowledge about global warming is seriously incomplete. As scientific understanding of the global atmosphere improves, our ability to make well-informed policy decisions should improve, too. Let's hope that those decisions take into account the resilience that comes from freedom and material progress. 31

Rethinking the Greenhouse

THE ECONOMIST

There is nothing like a good apocalypse, particularly in the closing years of a millennium. Obliteration by nuclear weapons once fitted the bill, but that threat has seemed less pressing in the past few years. Luckily the hot summer of 1988 raised a new mega-threat: a twenty-first century parched by "greenhouse" warming. For the world's worriers, that did the job nicely. But for how long? A fickle public might soon lose interest after a few cooler years (of which, overall, 1989 was one). And there are already signs of a greenhouse backlash from some scientists and politicians. 1

The skeptics do not say there is no greenhouse effect. They know that without it the earth would be as coldly inhospitable as Mars. The fact that gases and moisture in the atmosphere trap heat that would otherwise be 2

This essay appeared without a by-line in the December 16, 1989 issue of *The Economist.*

radiated into space — acting like the roof of a hothouse — has been known since 1895. The dispute is over how much that effect will be intensified by man's additions to the atmosphere — mainly carbon dioxide produced by burning fossil fuels. The skeptics think it is too early to tell whether man is overheating the world, and so too early to try expensive remedies.

The skeptics' case is set out in a paper from the George C. Marshall 3
Institute in Washington, D.C. Its authors are eminent, including a past president of America's National Academy of Sciences. Their paper went down well at the White House and probably influenced America's recent refusal to commit itself to a reduction in carbon dioxide emissions. On several counts, their case looks reasonable.

The authors show that the past century's slight warming does not fit 4
the pattern of increased emission of carbon dioxide. A better match might be the pattern of solar activity, which they think may have caused the warming. (Other skeptics doubt whether the warming happened at all, arguing that, only recently, cooling was a fashionable scare.) More speculatively, they think that solar trends since A.D. 1000 (which can be measured by a form of radioactivity) suggest that the next century will bring less solar activity, and so a slight cooling that will offset some of the greenhouse effect.

Debunkers of greenhouse fears are on firmer ground when stressing 5
two of the big uncertainties which dog attempts to predict global warming. Computer models are highly sensitive to assumptions about clouds and other even more complicated imponderables. Debunkers stress the uncertainties that might mitigate any dangerously fast warming; believers stress the ones that might make it worse. The believers point out that most of the skeptics, although knowledgeable scientists, are not specialists on the greenhouse effect. But those who are paid to study glass houses should be careful not to throw stones. They are more likely to exaggerate the importance of their own subject.

Keep Cool about the Heat

Despite these disagreements, the balance of probabilities still lies with 6
the believers — just. Their predictions are, for now, based on more thorough work, which is all that politicians have to rely on. There will anyway be no certainties about global warming until it has all but started — by which time any remedies would be ruinously costly. And, conveniently, most of what would need to be done to fight a greenhouse catastrophe needs doing anyway, for other reasons.

Some 15–20 percent of any man-made greenhouse could be caused 7
by chlorofluorocarbons (CFCs). These are also known to be attacking the

earth's ozone layer, risking other damage. A smaller but still significant boost to the greenhouse effect comes out of cars' exhaust pipes. The same pollutants cause smog and acid rain, which is one reason why the development of alternative fuels (such as hydrogen) and better fuel efficiency have more than the greenhouse effect to recommend them. Conservationists have their own reasons for wanting to slow down the burning of tropical forest, which has a doubly bad effect on warming. Forests swallow carbon dioxide when they expand and give it off when they burn. And nitrous oxide from nitrogen fertilizers is a greenhouse gas; the same fertilizers pollute water and contribute to the rich world's hugely expensive agricultural policies.

At the top of the greenhouse agenda are power stations burning fossil 8
fuels. Conservation-conscious consumers might want to avoid those in any case. But one problem is that if the utilities expect weaker demand, the first thing they will do is cut back on the cleaner power stations, such as nuclear ones, which produce electricity that is usually more expensive. Still, many politicians think it prudent to develop diverse and renewable sources of energy, such as solar — and perhaps nuclear — power.

So even if the earth is not likely to warm up, there are good environ- 9
mental and economic reasons to adopt policies whose by-product will be a curb on greenhouse gases. Even a small chance of global warming means that governments should see a small extra argument for such policies. Scientific uncertainty about the links between greenhouse gases and global warming will never be resolved, but it may be reduced. Meanwhile, wise governments will take the cheapest, most cost-effective steps first, especially those that have other benefits. Just as apocalyptic visions in science are usually followed by a skeptical backlash, so the backlash is followed by calmer calculation. While waiting for better clues about warming, complacency would be distinctly uncool.

Hot Air in the Greenhouse Debate

GLENN T. WILSON

Global warming is much less of a problem than painted by the extremists. 1

(1) Even if the extreme forecasts were correct, we would condemn billions of people to poverty and starvation if we tried to reverse the Industrial Revolution. (2) Warming is not all bad. The Sahara desert would be hotter, but Canada and Siberia would have a better climate. (3) The warming is partly counteracted by the cooling effect of fine particles sent high into the atmosphere by the smokestacks. (4) The sea holds several times as much dissolved carbon dioxide as the air. Hence, most of the CO_2 [carbon dioxide] will end up in the ocean, after allowing decades for mixing. (5) The remaining greenhouse warming will be partly counteracted by increased clouds, which reflect sunlight. (The same feedback would occur if the sun's radiation increased.) (6) Increased carbon dioxide will allow green plants to flourish better, both on land and sea. Part of the CO_2 will go right back into increased biomass of crops, forests, grass, and seaweed. 2

— Glenn T. Wilson

Staggering Cost Is Foreseen to Curb Warming of Earth

PETER PASSELL

World political leaders may be rushing to broad accord on the urgent need to halt global warming. But since the mid-1980s, economists have been worrying about the bill. Their misgivings have been deepened by recent estimates of the cost of limiting emissions of carbon dioxide, which is the primary cause of the problem. 1

Economic analysts do not speak with one voice on the issue. But all recent studies, including those carried out by environmentalists, implicitly 2

Wilson's letter appeared in the December 4, 1989 *Wall Street Journal*. The writer is from the School of Business, Middle Tennessee State University.

Peter Passell reports on economics for the *New York Times*, where this article appeared on November 19, 1989.

share one conclusion: Unless it proves remarkably easy to adapt technologies that drastically cut the need for oil, natural gas, and coal, the price of correcting the carbon dioxide problem will run to trillions of dollars through the next century.

By one pessimistic but not implausible estimate, the United States' annual cost of holding the line on carbon dioxide production could rival the current level of military spending. 3

Economists also agree that the benefits of reducing carbon dioxide are sure to vary greatly from place to place. That will make it difficult for countries to develop a consensus for a collective response to the problem. 4

Carbon dioxide and other pollutants trap infrared radiation from the sun in the earth's atmosphere, in much the same way a greenhouse works. 5

Some effort to curb carbon dioxide may eventually prove to be a cost-effective means of coping with the greenhouse effect. But in the near term, most economists conclude, a major effort to limit carbon effluent makes little economic sense unless it can be justified on grounds of energy security or tax revenue. 6

Overwhelmed Natural Processes

Scientists have long understood that certain trace gases in the atmosphere efficiently trap solar energy and heat the planet. Some are naturally produced. But many, notably carbon dioxide, methane, and chlorofluorocarbons, are also by-products of modern civilization, and are being spewed out faster than the biosphere can neutralize their effects. It is now generally if not universally believed that a resulting warming effect is overwhelming natural processes that tend to cool the atmosphere. 7

How fast the greenhouse gases are heating the air is not known. Neither the heating effect nor the accumulation of carbon dioxide in the air is thought to have direct effects on human health. But there is at least a chance that another century or perhaps less of unchecked accumulation would melt polar ice and alter weather patterns, leading to coastal flooding and radical changes in land fertility patterns. 8

For many environmental advocates, those who believe in the ethical obligation to pass on the biosphere intact to future generations, the policy message is clear and simple: Move quickly to reduce the production of carbon dioxide, which accounts for about half the greenhouse effect. 9

Using Fear to Get Action

The cause has drawn support from diverse interests who share what David Harrison of the National Economic Research Associates consulting 10 firm, calls "the Christmas tree view." These groups hope to use greenhouse worries as a lever for everything from promoting nuclear power to tightening automobile mileage regulations.

This month, all sixty-eight nations taking part in a high-level confer- 11
ence in the Netherlands agreed that carbon dioxide emissions would have to be stabilized.

Only objections from the United States, the Soviet Union, 12
and Japan prevented the conference from endorsing a goal of cutting emissions to 1988 levels by the year 2000. But William Nitze, a State Department official coordinating Bush administration policy, acknowledges there is now heavy diplomatic pressure for an accord next year.

Simulations by Computer

Greenhouse politics have yet to be influenced by sober economic 13
analysis, however. And while environmental groups would generally be inclined to draw different lessons from a new utility-financed simulation by Alan Manne of Stanford University and Richard Richels of the Electric Power Research Institute, almost everyone agrees that the computer model does illustrate the potential cost dimensions of carbon dioxide containment.

The Manne-Richels model compares a hypothetical future of uncon- 14
strained carbon dioxide output with one in which carbon emissions are limited to the 1990 rate through 2000 and then gradually cut by 20 percent.

Even if no technological adapatation to break the link between en- 15
ergy production and fossil fuels proved possible, consumers could muddle through for a while by switching to natural gas, which delivers 70 percent more energy per pound of carbon effluent. But the carbon limit begins to bite deeply around the year 2010.

With cheap supplies of gas exhausted, the model estimates that a 16
twentyfold increase in the price of coal would be needed to force sufficient changes toward energy conservation. Annual losses in output would reach about 5 percent of national income, or about $500 billion, in the year 2030.

Optimists, including the economist Irving Mintzer of the World Re- 17
sources Institute, argue that technological innovations might sharply cut these costs. And the computer model bears him out. Some reasonably priced way of trapping smokestack carbon would reduce the economic impact by one-tenth.

A low-cost source of electricity from noncarbon fuels, providing solar, 18
nuclear, or geothermal energy, would trim it further. Technical change

that increased the efficiency of energy use for the entire economy by 1 percent each year at low cost would do yet more.

Drop in American Incomes

But even the happy circumstance of technological victories on every 19
front would still permanently reduce American incomes by about 1 percent, according to the Manne-Richels model. And 1 percent in a $5 trillion economy is a whooping $50 billion a year.

Other studies suggest that this most optimistic Manne-Richels sce- 20
nario is too optimistic. William Nordhaus, an economist at Yale University, pegs the cost of containing carbon emissions to 1990 levels at 1 percent to 2 percent of national income by the middle of the next century. A study in progress by the Congressional Budget Office is reportedly yielding numbers in the same range.

High cost alone need not rule out action, of course, if the alternative 21
is catastrophe. The mere possibility that the greenhouse effect could lead to greater climatic changes in the next one hundred years than those experienced in the previous 10,000 might be expected to give even the most detached bean-counters cause to lose sleep.

But according to Thomas Schelling, an economist at the Kennedy 22
School of Government at Harvard, such projections can be misleading. While climate has not changed rapidly in the last century, both the will and technological ability to adapt to radically different weather obviously has. In 1960, he says, 2 percent of Americans lived outside temperate or subtropical zones. By 1980, the percentage had increased to 22 percent.

Adjusting to Climate Changes

While changes in rainfall, temperature, and sea level could be dra- 23
matic, there is yet no reason to believe that the process would be completed too quickly to allow evolutionary responses — expanding irrigation, for example, or building dikes. The cost of growing food might conceivably rise by 20 percent, Mr. Schelling speculates. But this loss, he argues, is almost certain to be overwhelmed by a century's worth of improvements in seed strains and growing techniques.

By the same logic, Mr. Schelling says, the appealing idea of bequeath- 24
ing the biosphere intact seems arbitrary. The quality of life in one hundred years, he suspects, will depend as much or more on the endowment of technology and capital as on the percentage of carbon dioxide in the air. And if money to contain carbon emissions comes out of other investment, future civilizations could be the losers.

25 This hardly means that the greenhouse effect can be safely ignored. But it does imply that it should be viewed as a problem in balancing costs against benefits. And here, crude initial estimates suggest that for the next half-century or more it may be cheapest to deal with the effects of global warming rather than the causes.

26 For example, according to the Environmental Protection Agency, the cost of protecting America's coastal cities against a three-foot rise in sea level would be $73 billion to $111 billion, a lot of money but not so much compared with the likely cost of prevention.

27 A doubling of atmospheric carbon dioxide, likely to occur by the middle of the next century if output is not constrained, would dramatically reduce yields for some crops in some regions. But according to a 1989 study by three Agriculture Department economists, the net losses would be less than one-tenth of 1 percent of income in industrial countries. Argentina and Australia would actually be economic winners, since the likely fall in yields would be smaller than the increases in world prices.

Nations Most at Risk

28 This illustrates a looming problem in prevention strategies. The benefits from controlling greenhouse gases would be far greater in some countries than in others. Bangladesh, India, and the Netherlands are at great risk from coastal flooding. But many countries would be able to expand farming into regions that are now too cold or too dry to support it. And a few, like Saudi Arabia, would lose much of their national income in a successful attempt to curb the use of fossil fuels.

29 The costs of carbon conservation would vary enormously. China, for example, is counting on its rich supplies of coal to develop with limited dependence on imported energy and capital.

30 Yet without a broad, enforceable agreement on containing carbon, expenditures by individual countries would not pay off. Lester Lave, an economist at Carnegie-Mellon University, argues that an early commitment by the United States to tough carbon standards could lead to the worst of both worlds. "We pay attention to treaties," he says. But big carbon emitters like China and the Soviet Union might ignore their obligations, undermining the whole logic of collective action."

31 Such considerations lead many economists, including Mr. Lave, to counsel waiting until more is known before trying to devise preventative measures. Dan Dudek, an economist for the Environmental Defense Fund, draws a different conclusion. He wants to buy a modest amount of insurance against the small possibility of a true greenhouse-effect disaster, some as yet undiscovered ecological effect that is impossible to reverse.

32 This is the time, he argues, to experiment with flexible "emissions-trading" systems that "improve the menu of options" for slowing global warming at minimum cost. Electric utilities might, for example, buy the right to emit carbon from existing emitters, or plant a sufficient number of trees to absorb an equivalent amount of carbon effluent.

33 Mr. Nordhaus offers a different rationale for action soon. The potential damage from the greenhouse effect has not been pinned down yet, he concludes; but some damage is almost certainly being done. And any sensible approach to balancing costs and benefits in the future will almost certainly involve a limited attempt to control greenhouse gas emissions, along with parallel efforts to sequester carbon and mitigate the effects of global warming.

A Financial Incentive

34 A modest tax on greenhouse gases, one targeted at heavily damaging chlorofluorcarbons as well as carbon dioxide, would thus be very likely to increase economic efficiency; it would also give emitters a financial incentive to search for alternative carbon-free technologies. And it could provide billions in taxes to offset the federal deficit.

35 Virtually all economists seem to agree on the need to get beyond what Mr. Lave calls the "Earth Day come back" syndrome. The symbol of greenhouse effect, they argue, cannot be allowed to obscure the dimensions of the perplexing, high-stakes problem that lies beneath.

Bottom-Line Thinking Won't Save Our Climate

PETER H. GLEICK

To the Editor:

1 Your Economic Watch article on the costs of limiting the emissions of carbon dioxide (front page, November 19) raises troublesome issues. The extent to which society chooses to spend money slowing greenhouse gas emissions or adapting to inevitable climatic impacts does depend partly on the costs and benefits of the different actions. But traditional cost-

---

Peter H. Gleick directs the global environment program of the Pacific Institute for Studies in Development, Environment, and Security. His letter appeared in the November 30, 1989 *New York Times*.

benefit studies, such as the ones you cite, are an unsatisfactory basis for guiding such decisions.

The true costs to society of global climatic changes are unknown, and they are unlikely ever to be accurately determined. We are not likely to know the full range of global consequences until climatic changes are upon us because of the difficulties of accurately modeling the climate. More important, many of the probable effects, such as the extinction of species, the loss of natural ecosystems, and long-term human-health effects, simply cannot be put into classic economic terms. Even calculating the costs to society of the more obvious effects, such as a rise in sea level, is fraught with computational pitfalls, methodological complications, and controversial assumptions. Economic analysis simply ignores these issues, leading to the fallacy that what can be most easily counted is what really counts. 2

Equally disturbing, however, the costs of climatic impacts and the costs of reducing emissions will be unequally distributed. Many of the worst impacts of climatic change are likely to fall on poorer, developing countries without the resources to adapt to the changes. But the costs of prevention will fall on the industrialized countries responsible for the vast majority of the emissions. Thus the richer countries responsible for the problem may prefer to delay action on limiting emissions, while poor countries that cannot build sea walls or develop irrigation systems to save their agricultural production will be forced to suffer the consequences. 3

Finally, many studies suggest that some actions to slow the rate of climate change are economical and could be taken today, such as improving our energy efficiency to the level of Japan's, or eliminating chlorofluorocarbons that contribute to the destruction of the ozone layer and to the greenhouse effect. Such actions should be considered prudent and inexpensive, preferable to taking no action and suffering the consequences. Waiting until imperfect traditional cost-benefit studies are done means waiting until climatic changes are upon us. 4

— Peter H. Gleick

THINKING AND WRITING ABOUT ENVIRONMENTAL POLICY

Questions for Discussion and Writing

1. What are the main obstacles to the establishment of policies that can stop or reverse global warming and other threats to the environment? Do some writers in this chapter express optimism about the future? If so, what is the basis of their optimism?
2. What are the principal points of disagreement between Udall and Shaw/

Stroup? Are there also points of agreement? Why do Shaw and Stroup advocate action by individuals rather than by government?

3. *The Economist* presents both sides of the debate but comes down on one side. What is the basis for its choice? How does this article respond to Wilson's skepticism about the greenhouse effect?
4. Can you make up your mind about the severity of the greenhouse effect from reading these articles? Is there other information that you would want to have? Is there any evidence that experts might be influenced by political doctrines or ideology?
5. What competing interests does Passell summarize in his report? What possible advantages of the greenhouse effect are cited? Can the views of Passell and Gleick be reconciled? Does Gleick prove his point that we cannot afford to wait? What moral issues does he raise?

Topics for Research

The relationship between national security and global environmental threats

Evidence that the greenhouse effect is not a serious threat

Views of developing countries toward conservation measures

A worst-case scenario

Population growth: Its impact on global warming

CHAPTER 15

Euthanasia

Euthanasia means "good death" or "mercy killing," that is, causing the death of one who is so ill or disabled that continued existence will produce intolerable suffering. Euthanasia may be active or passive; in the first case, death is deliberately inflicted, sometimes by a relative; in the second case, life-support systems are withdrawn and the patient dies naturally.

Controversy surrounding the morality of euthanasia has been heightened enormously in recent years because of advances in medical technology that make it possible for human beings, both newborn and old, to be kept alive almost indefinitely, even when severely impaired. As our life span lengthens, more and more people will reach an age when illness and disability create the possibility for euthanasia.

In those cases in which the patient cannot make a rational choice, decisions to prolong or terminate life must be left to families, doctors, and, not infrequently, the courts. Even the definition of *life* is at issue. A person may be declared "brain dead" while vital functions persist. Other problems of definition have become increasingly important. Where a patient has signed a living will, a physician may nevertheless refuse to remove the feeding tube, arguing that continuing to provide nourishment does not constitute "medication, artificial means, or heroic measures." In June 1990 the Supreme Court ruled that a state may pass laws allowing patients to refuse unwanted life-sustaining treatment, provided that the patient has previously expressed "clear and convincing evidence" of such a desire.

On one side are those who regard the problems posed by euthanasia as essentially religious: Life is sacred, no matter how severely disabled the patient may be, and no human being can arrogate to him- or herself a decision reserved for God. On the other side are those who insist that it is the quality of life that should influence the decision and that death may be preferable to a severely impaired life. Euthanasia thus becomes an act of charity.

One final problem confronts us in all the discussions about euthanasia. Will increasingly widespread acceptance of such deaths lead to a more relaxed attitude toward the taking of life in general and toward taking the lives of those in need of constant and lifelong attention in particular? One writer asks if the same principle of withholding food and water from a woman in a coma should be extended "to the thousands of others who fall into a coma every year, and to the many more mentally retarded or deranged, and sufferers of Alzheimer's disease who are a 'burden' on their families."

Death by Choice: Who Should Decide?

DANIEL C. MAGUIRE

Who would dare arrogate to himself the decision to impose death on 1
a child or unconscious person who is not in a position to assent or dissent to the action? What right does any person have to make decisions about life and death in any way that assumes absolute and ultimate authority over another human being? Could a doctor make such a decision? It would seem that he could not. His medical skills are one thing, the moral decision to end a life is another. How would a family feel who learned that a doctor had reached an independent decision to terminate their father's life?

Could the family make such a decision? It would seem not, for several 2
good reasons. There might be a conflict of interest arising from avarice, spite, or impatience with the illness of the patient. And even if these things were not present, the family might be emotionally traumatized when their pain of loss is complicated by the recollection of their decision.

Daniel Maguire is a professor of ethics at Marquette University and a former Roman Catholic priest. This excerpt is from his book, *Death by Choice* (1974).

Also, the family might constitute a split and therefore a hung jury. Then what?

Could a court-appointed committee of impartial persons make the decision? No, it would seem not. They would not only be impartial but also uninformed about the personal realities of the patient. The decision to terminate life requires a full and intimate knowledge of all the reality-constituting circumstances of the case. Strangers would not have this. 3

The conclusion, therefore, would seem inescapable that there is no moral way in which death could be imposed on a person who is incapable of consent because of youth or irreversible loss of consciousness. 4

This objection contains so much truth that my reply to it will contain much agreement as well as disagreement. To begin with, it should be noted that we are discussing not the legality but the morality of terminating life without the consent of the patient. Terminating life by a deliberate act of commission in the kinds of cases here discussed is illegal in this country. By an ongoing fiction of American law it would be classified as murder in the first degree. Terminating by calculated omission is murky at best and perilous at worst under current law. Therefore, it can be presumed that any conclusion we reach here will probably be illegal. This is a morally relevant fact; it is not to be presumed morally decisive, however, since there may be good moral grounds to assume the risk of illegality. As we have stated, morality and legality are not identical. 5

With this said, then, let us face up to the objection. There are two parts to my response. First, holding the question of *who should decide* in abeyance for the moment, I would suggest that there are cases where, if that difficult question could be satisfactorily answered, it would seem to be a morally good option (among other morally good options) to terminate a life. In other words, there are cases where the termination of a life could be defended as a moral good if the proper authority for making the decision could be located. Of course, if the objections raised against all those who could decide are decisive, then this otherwise morally desirable act would be immoral by reason of improper agency. 6

There are cases where it would appear to be arguably moral to take the necessary action (or to make the necessary omission) to end a life. Dr. Ruth Russell tells this story: 7

> I used to annually take a class of senior students in abnormal psychology to visit the hospital ward in a training school for medical defectives. There was a little boy about four years old the first time we visited him in the hospital. He was a hydrocephalic with a head so immensely large that he had never been able to raise it off the pillow and he never would. He had a tiny little body with this huge head and it is very difficult to keep him from developing sores. The students asked, "Why do we keep a child like that alive?"
>
> The next year we went back with another class. This year the child's hands had been padded to keep him from hitting his head. Again the students

> asked, "Why do we do this?" The third year we went back and visited the same child. Now the nurses explained that he had been hitting his head so hard that in spite of the padding he was injuring it severely and they had tied his arms down to the sides of his crib.[1]

What are the defensible moral options in this kind of case? One might be to keep the child alive in the way that was being done. This might show a great reverence for life and re-enforce society's commitment to weak and defective human life. It may indeed be the hallmark of advancing civilization that continuing care would be taken of this child. Termination of this child's life by omission or commission might set us on the slippery slope that has led other societies to the mass murder of physically and mentally defective persons. 8

All of this is possibly true but it is by no means self-evidently true to the point that other alternatives are apodictically excluded. This case is a singularly drastic one. Given its special qualities, action to end life here is not necessarily going to precipitate the killing of persons in distinguishably different circumstances. 9

Furthermore, keeping this child alive might exemplify the materialistic error of interpreting the sanctity of life in merely physical terms. This interpretation, of course, is a stark oversimplification. It is just as wrong as the other side of the simplistic coin, which would say that life has no value until it attains a capacity for distinctively personal acts such as intellectual knowledge, love, and imagination. A fetus, while not yet capable of intellectual and other distinctively personal activity, is on a trajectory towards personhood and already shares in the sanctity of human life. (This does not mean that it may never be terminated when other sacred values outweigh its claim to life in a conflict situation.) 10

The sanctity of life is a generic notion that does not yield a precisely spelled-out code of ethics. Deciding what the sanctity of life requires in conflict situations, such as the case of the hydrocephalic child described by Dr. Russell, may lead persons to contradictory judgments. To say that the sanctity of life requires keeping that child alive regardless of his condition, and that all other alternatives impeach the perception of life as sacred, is both arrogant and epistemologically unsound. In this case, maintaining this child in this condition might be incompatible with its sacred human dignity. It might not meet the minimal needs of human physical existence. In different terms, the sanctity of death might here take precedence over a physicalist interpretation of the sanctity of life. There is a 11

---

[1] See *Dilemmas of Euthanasia*, a pamphlet containing excerpts, papers, and discussions from the Fourth Euthanasia Conference, held in New York on December 4, 1971; this is a publication of the Euthanasia Educational Council, Inc., [now called Concern for Dying], New York, p. 35.

time when human death befits human life, when nothing is more germane to the person's current needs. This conclusion appears defensible in the case of the hydrocephalic boy.

Also, to keep this child alive to manifest and maintain society's respect for life appears to be an unacceptable reduction of this child to the status of means. Society should be able to admit the value of death in this case and still maintain its respect for life. Our reverence for life should not be dependent on this sort of martyrdom. 12

The decision, therefore, that it is morally desirable to bring on this boy's death is a defensible conclusion from the facts and prognosis of this case. (We are still holding in abeyance the question of who should make that decision.) There are two courses of action that could flow from that decision. The decision could be made to stop all special medication and treatment and limit care to nourishment, or the decision could be made in the light of all circumstances to take more direct action to induce death. 13

There is another case, a famous one . . . , where the life of a radically deformed child was ended. This is the tragic case of Corinne van de Put, who was a victim of thalidomide, a drug that interfered with the limb buds between the sixth and eighth weeks of pregnancy. Corinne was born on May 22, 1962, with no arms or shoulder structure and with deformed feet. It would not even be possible to fit the child with artificial limbs since there was no shoulder structure, but only cartilage. Some experts said the chances for survival were one in ten and a Dr. Hoet, a professor of pathological embryology at the Catholic University of Louvain, was of the opinion that the child had only a year or two to live. Eight days after the baby was born, the mother, Madame Suzanne van de Put, mixed barbiturates with water and honey in the baby's bottle and thus killed her daughter. 14

During the trial, Madame van de Put was asked why she had not followed the gynecologist's advice to put the child in a home. "I did not want it," she replied. "Absolutely not. For me, as an egoist, I could have been rid of her. But it wouldn't have given her back her arms." The president of the court pointed out that the child appeared to be mentally normal. "That was only worse," said Madame van de Put. "If she had grown up to realize the state she was in, she would never have forgiven me for letting her live."[2] 15

Is Madame van de Put's decision to be seen as one of the several morally defensible options available in this case? I think that it is. Again, this does not say that other solutions have no moral probability. As Norman St. John-Stevas points out in his discussion of this case, there are 16

---

[2] For an account of this case and a negative judgment on Madame van de Put's action, see Norman St. John-Stevas, *The Right to Life* (New York, Chicago, San Francisco: Holt, Rinehart & Winston, 1964), pp. 3–24.

individuals who, though terribly disadvantaged, live fruitful and apparently happy lives. He speaks of Arthur Kavanagh, who was born in 1831 without limbs. No mechanical mechanism could be devised to help him. According to St. John-Stevas, however, Kavanagh managed to achieve some mystifying successes.

> Yet throughout his life he rode and drove, traveled widely, shot and fished. From 1868 until 1880 he sat as Member for Carlow and spoke in the Commons. In addition, he was a magistrate, a grand juror, a poor-law guardian, and he organized a body to defend the rights of landlords.[3]

St. John-Stevas, however, does admit that "Not everyone can be an 17
Arthur Kavanagh. . . ." Neither could everyone be a Helen Keller. The problem is that no one knows this when these decisions are made. The option to let the person live and find out is not necessarily safe. The person may not have the resources of a Kavanagh or a Keller and may rue both the day of birth and the decision to let him live. As Madame van de Put said, Corinne may "never have forgiven me for letting her live." The decision to let live is not inherently safe. It may be a decision for a personal disaster. There are persons living who have found their lives a horror, who do not think they have the moral freedom to end their lives, and who ardently wish someone had ended life for them before they reached consciousness. It is little consolation to these people to be told that they were let live on the chance that they might have been a Beethoven. The presumption that the decision to let live will have a happy moral ending is gratuitous and is not a pat solution to the moral quandary presented by such cases.

Interestingly, in the van de Put case, the defense counsel told the jury 18
that he did not think Madame van de Put's solution was the only one, but that it was not possible to condemn her for having chosen it.[4] It could have been moral also to muster all possible resources of imagination and affection and give Corinne the ability to transcend her considerable impairments and achieve fullness of life. In this very unclear situation, this could have been a defensible option. It was not, however, one without risks. It could have proved itself wrong.

The decision to end Corinne's life was also arguably moral, though, 19
again, not without risks. It could not be called immoral on the grounds that it is better to live than not to live regardless of the meaning of that life. This is again a physicalist interpretation of the sanctity of life. It also could not be called immoral on the grounds that this kind of killing is

---

[3] Ibid., p. 16.

[4] Ibid., pp. 7–8.

likely to spill over and be used against unwanted children, etc., since this case has its own distinguishing characteristics which make it quite exceptional. It could not be called immoral because it is direct killing since . . . the issue is not directness or indirectness, but whether there is proportionate reason.

In this case, then, as in the case of the hydrocephalic boy, we have a 20
situation where the imposition of death could seem a moral good, prescinding still from the question of who should decide. There could be other cases, too, where death could be seen as a good. Suppose someone suffers severe cerebral damage in an accident but due to continuing brainstem activity can be kept alive almost indefinitely through tubal nourishing and other supportive measures. Would it not seem a clear good if a decision could be made to withdraw support and allow death to have its final say? The spectacle of living with the breathing but depersonalized remains of a loved one could make death seem a needed blessing. In conclusion, then, there are cases where the imposition of death would seem a good. It was logically indicated to state that conclusion before going to the main thrust of the objection, the question of who could decide when the person in question can give no consent.

In Defense of Voluntary Euthanasia

SIDNEY HOOK

A few short years ago, I lay at the point of death. A congestive heart 1
failure was treated for diagnostic purposes by an angiogram that triggered a stroke. Violent and painful hiccups, uninterrupted for several days and nights, prevented the ingestion of food. My left side and one of my vocal cords became paralyzed. Some form of pleurisy set in, and I felt I was drowning in a sea of slime. At one point, my heart stopped beating; just as I lost consciousness, it was thumped back into action again. In one of my lucid intervals during those days of agony, I asked my physician to discontinue all life-supporting services or show me how to do it. He refused and predicted that someday I would appreciate the unwisdom of my request.

This essay by Sidney Hook (1902–1989), former professor of philosophy at New York University and senior research fellow at the Hoover Institution on War, Revolution, and Peace, was published in the *New York Times* on March 1, 1987.

A month later, I was discharged from the hospital. In six months, I re- 2
gained the use of my limbs, and although my voice still lacks its old resonance and carrying power I no longer croak like a frog. There remain some minor disabilities and I am restricted to a rigorous, low-sodium diet. I have resumed my writing and research.

My experience can be and has been cited as an argument against 3
honoring requests of stricken patients to be gently eased out of their pain and life. I cannot agree. There are two main reasons. As an octogenarian, there is a reasonable likelihood that I may suffer another "cardiovascular accident" or worse. I may not even be in a position to ask for the surcease of pain. It seems to me that I have already paid my dues to death — indeed, although time has softened my memories they are vivid enough to justify my saying that I suffered enough to warrant dying several times over. Why run the risk of more?

Secondly, I dread imposing on my family and friends another grim 4
round of misery similar to the one my first attack occasioned.

My wife and children endured enough for one lifetime. I know that 5
for them the long days and nights of waiting, the disruption of their professional duties and their own familial responsibilities counted for nothing in their anxiety for me. In their joy at my recovery they have been forgotten. Nonetheless, to visit another prolonged spell of helpless suffering on them as my life ebbs away, or even worse, if I linger on into a comatose senility, seems altogether gratuitous.

But what, it may be asked, of the joy and satisfaction of living, of 6
basking in the sunshine, listening to music, watching one's grandchildren growing into adolescence, following the news about the fate of freedom in a troubled world, playing with ideas, writing one's testament of wisdom and folly for posterity? Is not all that one endured, together with the risk of its recurrence, an acceptable price for the multiple satisfactions that are still open even to a person of advanced years?

Apparently those who cling to life no matter what think so. I do not. 7

The zest and intensity of these experiences are no longer what they 8
used to be. I am not vain enough to delude myself that I can in the few remaining years make an important discovery useful for mankind or can lead a social movement or do anything that will be historically eventful, no less event-making. My autobiography, which describes a record of intellectual and political experiences of some historical value, already much too long, could be posthumously published. I have had my fill of joys and sorrows and am not greedy for more life. I have always thought that a test of whether one had found happiness in one's life is whether one would be willing to relive it — whether, if it were possible, one would accept the opportunity to be born again.

Having lived a full and relatively happy life, I would cheerfully accept 9
the chance to be reborn, but certainly not to be reborn again as an infirm octogenarian. To some extent, my views reflect what I have seen happen to the aged and stricken who have been so unfortunate as to survive crippling paralysis. They suffer, and impose suffering on others, unable even to make a request that their torment be ended.

I am mindful too of the burdens placed upon the community, with its 10
rapidly diminishing resources, to provide the adequate and costly services necessary to sustain the lives of those whose days and nights are spent on mattress graves of pain. A better use could be made of these resources to increase the opportunities and qualities of life for the young. I am not denying the moral obligation the community has to look after its disabled and aged. There are times, however, when an individual may find it pointless to insist on the fulfillment of a legal and moral right.

What is required is no great revolution in morals but an enlargement 11
of imagination and an intelligent evaluation of alternative uses of community resources.

Long ago, Seneca observed that "the wise man will live as long as he 12
ought, not as long as he can." One can envisage hypothetical circumstances in which one has a duty to prolong one's life despite its costs for the sake of others, but such circumstances are far removed from the ordinary prospects we are considering. If wisdom is rooted in knowledge of the alternatives of choice, it must be reliably informed of the state one is in and its likely outcome. Scientific medicine is not infallible, but it is the best we have. Should a rational person be willing to endure acute suffering merely on the chance that a miraculous cure might presently be at hand? Each one should be permitted to make his own choice — especially when no one else is harmed by it.

The responsibility for the decision, whether deemed wise or foolish, 13
must be with the chooser.

Euthanasia Is Not the Answer

MATTHEW E. CONOLLY

From the moment of our conception, each of us is engaged in a personal battle that we must fight alone, a battle whose final outcome is never in any doubt, for, naked, and all too often alone, sooner or later we *all* must die. 1

We do not all make life's pilgrimage on equal terms. For some the path is strewn with roses, and after a long and healthy life, death comes swiftly and easily, for others it is not so. The bed of roses is supplanted by a bed of nails, with poverty, rejection, deformity, and humiliation the only lasting companions they ever know. 2

I know that many people here today carry this problem of pain in a personal way, or else it has been the lot of someone close to you. Otherwise you would not be here. So let me say right at the outset, that those of us who have not had to carry such a burden dare not criticize those who have, if they should plead with us for an early end to their dismal sojourn in this world. 3

Hard Cases Make Bad Laws

Society in general, and the medical profession in particular, cannot just turn away. We must do *something*; the question is — what? 4

The "what" we are being asked to consider today, of course, is voluntary euthanasia. So that there be no confusion, let me make it quite clear that to be opposed to the active taking of life, one does not have to be determined to keep the heart beating at all costs. 5

I believe I speak for all responsible physicians when I say that there clearly comes a time when death can no longer be held at bay, and when we must sue for peace on the enemy's terms. At such a time, attending to the patient's comfort in body, mind, and soul becomes paramount. There is no obligation, indeed no justification, for pressing on at such a time with so-called life-sustaining measures, be they respirators, intravenous fluids, CPR, or whatever. I believe that there is no obligation to continue a treatment once it has been started, if it becomes apparent that it is doing no good. Also, withholding useless treatment and letting nature take its course is *not* equivalent to active euthanasia. Some people have attempted to blur this distinction by creating the term "passive euthanasia." 6

Matthew E. Conolly is a professor of medicine and pharmacology at UCLA. This excerpt is from a speech he delivered at the Hemlock Society's Second National Voluntary Euthanasia Conference on February 9, 1985.

The least unkind thing that can be said about this term is that it is very confusing.

Today's discussion really boils down to the question — do hard and tragic cases warrant legalization of euthanasia? There can be no doubt that hard and tragic cases do occur. However, the very natural tendency to want to alleviate human tragedy by legislative change is fraught with hazard, and I firmly believe that every would-be lawmaker should have tattooed on his or her face, where it can be seen in the mirror each morning, the adage that HARD CASES MAKE BAD LAWS. 7

If we take the superficially humane step of tailoring the law to the supposed wishes of an Elizabeth Bouvia (who, incidentally, later changed her mind), we will not only bring a hornet's nest of woes about our own ears, but, at a stroke, we will deny many relatives much good that we could have salvaged from a sad situation, while at the same time giving many *more* grief and guilt to contend with. Even worse, we will have denied our patients the best that could have been offered. Worst of all, that soaring of the human spirit to heights of inspiration and courage which only adversity makes possible will be denied, and we will all, from that, grow weaker, and less able to deal with the crisis of tomorrow. 8

Unleashing Euthanasia

Let's look at these problems one by one. The first problem is that once we unleash euthanasia, once we take to ourselves the right actively to terminate a human life, we will have no means of controlling it. Adolf Hitler showed with startling clarity that once the dam is breached, the principle somewhere compromised, death in the end comes to be administered equally to all — to the unwanted fetus, to the deformed, the mentally defective, the old and the unproductive, and thence to the politically inconvenient, and finally to the ethnically unacceptable. There is no logical place to stop. 9

The founders of Hemlock no doubt mean euthanasia only for those who feel they can take no more, but if it is available for one it must be available for all. Then what about those precious people who even to the end put others before themselves? They will now have laid upon them the new and horrible thought that perhaps they ought to do away with themselves to spare their relatives more trouble or expense. What will they feel as they see their 210 days of Medicare hospice payments run out, and still they are alive. Not long ago, Governor Lamm of Colorado suggested that the old and incurable have a *duty* to get out of the way of the next generation. And can you not see where these pressures will be the greatest? It will be amongst the poor and dispossessed. Watts will have sunk 10 in a sea of euthanasia long before the first ripple laps the shore of Brentwood. Is that what we mean to happen? Is that what we want? Is there nobility of purpose there?

It matters to me that my patients trust me. If they do so, it is because they believe that I will always act in their best interests. How could such trust survive if they could never be sure each time I approached the bed that I had not come to administer some coup de grace when they were not in a state to define their own wishes? 11

Those whose relatives have committed more conventional forms of suicide are often afterwards assailed by feelings of guilt and remorse. It would be unwise to think that euthanasia would bring any less in its wake. 12

A Better Way

Speaking as a physician, I assert that unrelieved suffering need never occur, and I want to turn to this important area. Proponents of euthanasia make much of the pain and anguish so often linked in people's minds with cancer. I would not dare to pretend that the care we offer is not sometimes abysmal, whether because of the inappropriate use of aggressive technological medicine, the niggardly use of analgesics, some irrational fear of addiction in a dying patient, or a lack of compassion. 13

However, for many, the process of dying is more a case of gradually loosing life's moorings and slipping away. Oftentimes the anguish of dying is felt not by the patient but by the relatives: just as real, just as much in need of compassionate support, but hardly a reason for killing the patient! 14

But let us consider the patients who do have severe pain, turmoil, and distress, who find their helplessness or incontinence humiliating, for it is these who most engage our sympathies. It is wrong to assert that they must make a stark choice between suicide or suffering. 15

There is another way. 16

Experience with hospice care in England and the United States has shown repeatedly that in *every* case, pain and suffering can be overwhelmingly reduced. In many cases it can be abolished altogether. This care, which may (and for financial reasons perhaps must) include home care, is not easy. It demands infinite love and compassion. It must include the latest scientific knowledge of analgesic drugs, nerve blocks, anti-nausea medication, and so on. But it can be done, it can be done, it can be done! 17

Life Is Special

Time and again our patients have shown us that life, even a deformed, curtailed, and, to us, who are whole, an unimaginable life, can be 18 made noble and worth living. Look at Joni Earickson — paraplegic from the age of seventeen — now a most positive, vibrant and inspirational person who has become world famous for her triumph over adversity. Time and time again, once symptoms are relieved, patients and relatives share quality time together, when forgiveness can be sought and given — for many a time of great healing.

Man, made in the image of his Creator, is *different* from all other ani- 19
mals. For this reason, his life is special and may not be taken at will.

We do not know why suffering is allowed, but Old and New Testa- 20
ment alike are full of reassurances that we have not been, and will not ever be, abandoned by our God. "Yea, though I walk through the valley of the shadow of death, I will fear no evil *for thou art with me*."

Call to Change Direction

Our modern tragedy is that man has turned his back on God, who 21
alone can help, and has set himself up as the measure of all things. Gone then is the absolute importance of man, gone the sanctity of his life, and the meaning of it. Gone too the motivation for loving care which is our responsible duty to the sick and dying. Goodbye love. Hello indifference.

With our finite minds, we cannot know fully the meaning of life, but 22
though at times the storms of doubt may rage, I stake my life on the belief that to God we are special, that with Him, murder is unacceptable, and suicide (whatever you call it) becomes unnecessary.

Abandon God, and yes, you can have euthanasia. But a *good* death it 23
can never be, and no subterfuge of law like that before us today can ever make it so.

My plea to the Hemlock Society is: Give up your goal of self-destruc- 24
tion. Instead, lend your energy, your anger, your indignation, your influence and creativity to work with us in the building of such a system of hospice care that death, however it come, need no longer be feared. Is not this a nobler cause? Is not this a better way?

Consequences of Imposing the Quality of Life Ethic

EILEEN DOYLE

Under the American Constitution, all who belong to the human species *are persons* and are guaranteed the protection of their inalienable right to life (and other inalienable rights). 1

(The only exceptions are living human beings before birth who have unjustly been denied their right to life by the 1973 Supreme Court abortion decisions, *Roe v. Wade* and *Doe v. Bolton.)* 2

The Constitution adheres to the sanctity of life ethic and the theory of natural rights which state that human beings by their very nature are of intrinsic value — they do not have to earn their value; it belongs to them simply because they are human. 3

Therefore they are endowed with inalienable rights to life and other rights. The state cannot bestow or take away these inalienable rights because they do not belong to the state to dispose of, but rather to each individual human being. The state exists to protect these rights. 4

The problem for euthanasia proponents is that under our Constitution, euthanasia (killing human beings who are innocent of unjust aggression on others' lives) cannot be legalized. It is obvious that the American people would not permit them to tear up the Constitution and write a new one to fit their purposes, so they have devised a clever strategy to make it appear that we would be abiding by the Constitution even while violating it. 5

First they attack the sanctity of life ethic as a religious doctrine because it is based on the religious belief that human beings are created by God in His Image. They fail to realize that whatever the religious beliefs upon which it was founded, its principles embodied in our Constitution are right now held dear by the vast majority of American people. 6

They propose to replace this sanctity of life ethic with a new one which we call the quality of life ethic. But underlying this new ethic is another religious belief of secular humanism which believes that human life is the result of random evolution and denies or questions the existence of God or at least God's involvement in human affairs — a remote God. 7

The Supreme Court has declared that secular humanism as a world view is a religion in the First Amendment sense (*Torasco v. Watkins, United States v. Seeger, Welsh v. United States*). 8

Eileen Doyle, R.N., is a member of New York State Nurses for Life. This selection is from *A Pro-Life Primer on Euthanasia* (1985).

Redefining Some People

This quality of life ethic proposes that some human beings have a 9
quality of life so poor that they ought not be classified as legal persons with inalienable rights. To be declared a person with human rights, a human being must be able to pass certain tests. The tests vary according to who is proposing them but in general, it requires that to be declared a person (with inalienable rights) a human being must be able to: think and reason; give or receive love; be useful in some way; be capable of meaningful life, i.e., able to enjoy or appreciate life.

Those who fail the test would lose legal personhood and have no in- 10
alienable rights. Therefore, these human beings could be killed without violating anyone's inalienable rights.

This is precisely what the Court did in the abortion decisions in de- 11
claring the unborn as not persons, thus allowing them to be killed. The whole idea is pure legal fiction, a subterfuge to quiet the consciences of the American people who have a horror of killing innocent people.

Killing a "nonperson" demoted to a less-than-human status by legal 12
fiat seems then to be more like killing a dog or a cat to put it out of its misery. Then all can pretend that no evil, unjust deed has been done.

This quality of life ethic also holds that even among those who pass 13
the tests of personhood, there may be many who have a quality of life so poor because of grave illness or birth defects that life itself is no longer a value to be preserved for these people. So to take these lives would not be an injustice but a benefit for them.

And finally (as discussed last month), this quality of life ethic allows 14
that there is a compelling state interest sufficient to deny the inalienable right to life to a class of citizens: permanently dependent, institutionalized people who put an inordinate burden on the state to provide public funds and medical resources for their care.

The Awesome Result

If the proponents of this quality of life ethic succeed in having it re- 15
place the sanctity of life ethic, what would be the consequences?

1. It would destroy the underlying principles embodied in our Consti- 16
tution, reducing it to a worthless, ineffective, hypocritical document. A new constitution would have to be written to replace it.

2. It would be an injustice to the vast majority of the Americans who 17
adhere to the principles of the Constitution and who treasure our Constitution to have those principles overridden and the Constitution destroyed by a small elite who wish to impose their own set of principles, not accepted by most people.

3. Large numbers of people whose inalienable right to life is now pro- 18
tected by the law of homicide would be killed without their consent because somebody else had decided they are not persons. These could include newborn infants with birth defects, autistic children, psychotic people, senile aged, comatose people, those with severe drug or alcohol addiction, and so on. All these could easily fail the tests of personhood.

Then there are the huge numbers of people who by somebody's 19
definition other than their own have lives not worth living, who could be disposed of.

And finally there are those millions of dependent, institutionalized 20
people on the public dole eating up the valuable resources of the powerful, so-called nondependent taxpayers. To dispose of them — the dependents — would become a "patriotic duty."

Equal protection of the law would become a mockery. 21

4. The psychological and spiritual damage to those who do the killing 22
and to those who permit it would corrupt our entire nation. All would be a party to killing and to the lying to ourselves that we are doing good rather than admitting the crimes.

5. Inordinate power, tyrannical power, would be vested in the Su- 23
preme Court. For it would be the Court that would ultimately decide who is and who is not a legal person; who has and who has not a sufficient quality of life to give it value worth preserving; and at what point there is a compelling state interest sufficient to override the inalienable right to life of dependent citizens.

As with the concept of a constitutional right to die, the concept of a 24
quality of life ethic becomes absurd as well, when analyzed to its logical conclusions. For we would literally be handing over our priceless freedom and all inalienable rights to an oligarchy of nine Justices on the Supreme Court.

And for what? To give power to an elite few to create their idea of a 25
"brave new world" — for themselves, who in turn might become their own victims should misfortune make them dependent and powerless.

Active and Passive Euthanasia

JAMES RACHELS

The distinction between active and passive euthanasia is thought to be crucial for medical ethics. The idea is that it is permissible, at least in some cases, to withhold treatment and allow a patient to die, but it is never permissible to take any direct action designed to kill the patient. This doctrine seems to be accepted by most doctors, and it is endorsed in a statement adopted by the House of Delegates of the American Medical Association on December 4, 1973: 1

> The intentional termination of the life of one human being by another — mercy killing — is contrary to that for which the medical profession stands and is contrary to the policy of the American Medical Association.
>
> The cessation of the employment of extraordinary means to prolong the life of the body when there is irrefutable evidence that biological death is imminent is the decision of the patient and/or his immediate family. The advice and judgment of the physician should be freely available to the patient and/or his immediate family.

However, a strong case can be made against this doctrine. In what follows I will set out some of the relevant arguments, and urge doctors to reconsider their views on this matter.

To begin with a familiar type of situation, a patient who is dying of incurable cancer of the throat is in terrible pain, which can no longer be satisfactorily alleviated. He is certain to die within a few days, even if present treatment is continued, but he does not want to go on living for those days since the pain is unbearable. So he asks the doctor for an end to it, and his family joins in the request. 2

Suppose the doctor agrees to withhold treatment, as the conventional doctrine says he may. The justification for his doing so is that the patient is in terrible agony, and since he is going to die anyway, it would be wrong to prolong his suffering needlessly. But now notice this. If one simply withholds treatment, it may take the patient longer to die, and so he may suffer more than he would if more direct action were taken and a lethal injection given. This fact provides strong reason for thinking that, once the initial decision not to prolong his agony has been made, active euthanasia is actually preferable to passive euthanasia, rather than the reverse. To say otherwise is to endorse the option that leads to more suffering 3

James Rachels, a professor at the University of Miami, is editor of *Moral Problems*, a reader on the ethical aspects of contemporary social issues. "Active and Passive Euthanasia" was published in the *New England Journal of Medicine*, Vol. 292, in 1975.

rather than less, and is contrary to the humanitarian impulse that prompts the decision not to prolong his life in the first place.

Part of my point is that the process of being "allowed to die" can be 4
relatively slow and painful, whereas being given a lethal injection is relatively quick and painless. Let me give a different sort of example. In the United States about one in 600 babies is born with Down's syndrome. Most of these babies are otherwise healthy — that is, with only the usual pediatric care, they will proceed to an otherwise normal infancy. Some, however, are born with congenital defects such as intestinal obstructions that require operations if they are to live. Sometimes, the parents and the doctor will decide not to operate, and let the infant die. Anthony Shaw describes what happens then:

> . . . When surgery is denied [the doctor] must try to keep the infant from suffering while natural forces sap the baby's life away. As a surgeon whose natural inclination is to use the scalpel to fight off death, standing by and watching a salvageable baby die is the most emotionally exhausting experience I know. It is easy at a conference, in a theoretical discussion, to decide that such infants should be allowed to die. It is altogether different to stand by in the nursery and watch as dehydration and infection wither a tiny being over hours and days. This is a terrible ordeal for me and the hospital staff — much more so than for the parents who never set foot in the nursery.[1]

I can understand why some people are opposed to all euthanasia, and insist that such infants must be allowed to live. I think I can also understand why other people favor destroying these babies quickly and painlessly. But why should anyone favor letting "dehydration and infection wither a tiny being over hours and days"? The doctrine that says that a baby may be allowed to dehydrate and wither, but may not be given an injection that would end its life without suffering, seems so patently cruel as to require no further refutation. The strong language is not intended to offend, but only to put the point in the clearest possible way.

My second argument is that the conventional doctrine leads to deci- 5
sions concerning life and death made on irrelevant grounds.

Consider again the case of the infants with Down's syndrome who 6
need operations for congenital defects unrelated to the syndrome to live. Sometimes there is no operation, and the baby dies, but when there is no such defect, the baby lives on. Now, an operation such as that to remove an intestinal obstruction is not prohibitively difficult. The reason why such operations are not performed in these cases is, clearly, that the child has Down's syndrome and the parents and doctor judge that because of that fact it is better for the child to die.

---

[1]A Shaw, "Doctor, Do We Have a Choice?" *New York Times Magazine*, January 30, 1972, p. 54.

But notice that this situation is absurd, no matter what view one takes of the lives and potential of such babies. If the life of such an infant is worth preserving, what does it matter if it needs a simple operation? Or, if one thinks it better that such a baby should not live on, what difference does it make that it happens to have an unobstructed intestinal tract? In either case, the matter of life and death is being decided on irrelevant grounds. It is the Down's syndrome, and not the intestines, that is the issue. The matter should be decided, if at all, on that basis, and not be allowed to depend on the essentially irrelevant question of whether the intestinal tract is blocked. 7

What makes this situation possible, of course, is the idea that when there is an intestinal blockage, one can "let the baby die," but when there is no such defect there is nothing that can be done, for one must not "kill" it. The fact that this idea leads to such results as deciding life or death on irrelevant grounds is another good reason why the doctrine should be rejected. 8

One reason why so many people think that there is an important moral difference between active and passive euthanasia is that they think killing someone is morally worse than letting someone die. But is it? Is killing, in itself, worse than letting die? To investigate this issue, two cases may be considered that are exactly alike except that one involves killing whereas the other involves letting someone die. Then, it can be asked whether this difference makes any difference to the moral assessments. It is important that the cases be exactly alike, except for this one difference, since otherwise one cannot be confident that it is this difference and not some other that accounts for any variation in the assessments of the two cases. So, let us consider this pair of cases: 9

In the first, Smith stands to gain a large inheritance if anything should happen to his six-year-old cousin. One evening while the child is taking his bath, Smith sneaks into the bathroom and drowns the child, and then arranges things so that it will look like an accident. 10

In the second, Jones also stands to gain if anything should happen to his six-year-old cousin. Like Smith, Jones sneaks in planning to drown the child in his bath. However, just as he enters the bathroom Jones sees the child slip and hit his head, and fall face down in the water. Jones is delighted; he stands by, ready to push the child's head back under if it is necessary, but it is not necessary. With only a little thrashing about, the child drowns all by himself, "accidentally," as Jones watches and does nothing. 11

Now Smith killed the child, whereas Jones "merely" let the child die. That is the only difference between them. Did either man behave better, from a moral point of view? If the difference between killing and letting die were in itself a morally important matter, one should say that Jones's behavior was less reprehensible than Smith's. But does one really want to 12 say that? I think not. In the first place, both men acted from the same motive, personal gain, and both had exactly the same end in view when they acted. It may be inferred from Smith's conduct that he is a bad man, although that judgment may be withdrawn or modified if certain further facts are learned about him — for example, that he is mentally deranged. But would not the very same thing be inferred about Jones from his conduct? And would not the same further considerations also be relevant to any modification of this judgment? Moreover, suppose Jones pleaded, in his own defense, "After all, I didn't do anything except just stand there and watch the child drown. I didn't kill him; I only let him die." Again, if letting die were in itself less bad than killing, this defense should have at least some weight. But it does not. Such a "defense" can only be regarded as a grotesque perversion of moral reasoning. Morally speaking, it is no defense at all.

Now, it may be pointed out, quite properly, that the cases of euthana- 13
sia with which doctors are concerned are not like this at all. They do not involve personal gain or the destruction of normal, healthy children. Doctors are concerned only with cases in which the patient's life is of no further use to him, or in which the patient's life has become or will soon become a terrible burden. However, the point is the same in these cases: The bare difference between killing and letting die does not, in itself, make a moral difference. If a doctor lets a patient die, for humane reasons, he is in the same moral position as if he had given the patient a lethal injection for humane reasons. If his decision was wrong — if, for example, the patient's illness was in fact curable — the decision would be equally regrettable no matter which method was used to carry it out. And if the doctor's decision was the right one, the method used is not in itself important.

The AMA policy statement isolates the crucial issue very well; the 14
crucial issue is "the intentional termination of the life of one human being by another." But after identifying this issue, and forbidding "mercy killing," the statement goes on to deny that the cessation of treatment is the intentional termination of a life. This is where the mistake comes in, for what is the cessation of treatment, in these circumstances, if it is not "the intentional termination of the life of one human being by another"? Of course it is exactly that, and if it were not, there would be no point to it.

Many people will find this judgment hard to accept. One reason, I 15
think, is that it is very easy to conflate the question of whether killing is, in itself, worse than letting die, with the very different question of whether most actual cases of killing are more reprehensible than most actual cases of letting die. Most actual cases of killing are clearly terrible (think, for example, of all the murders reported in the newspapers), and one hears of such cases every day. On the other hand, one hardly ever hears of a case

of letting die, except for the actions of doctors who are motivated by humanitarian reasons. So one learns to think of killing in a much worse light than of letting die, for it is not the bare difference between killing and letting die that makes the difference in these cases. Rather, the other factors — the murderer's motive of personal gain, for example, contrasted with the doctor's humanitarian motivation — account for different reactions to the different cases.

I have argued that killing is not in itself any worse than letting die; if 16
my contention is right, it follows that active euthanasia is not any worse than passive euthanasia. What arguments can be given on the other side? The most common, I believe, is the following:

"The important difference between active and passive euthanasia is 17
that, in passive euthanasia, the doctor does not do anything to bring about the patient's death. The doctor does nothing, and the patient dies of whatever ills already afflict him. In active euthanasia, however, the doctor does something to bring about the patient's death: He kills him. The doctor who gives the patient with cancer a lethal injection has himself caused his patient's death; whereas if he merely ceases treatment, the cancer is the cause of the death."

A number of points need to be made here. The first is that it is not ex- 18
actly correct to say that in passive euthanasia the doctor does nothing, for he does do one thing that is very important: He lets the patient die. "Letting someone die" is certainly different in some respects, from other types of action — mainly in that it is a kind of action that one may perform by way of not performing certain other actions. For example, one may let a patient die by way of not giving medication, just as one may insult someone by way of not shaking his hand. But for any purpose of moral assessment, it is a type of action nonetheless. The decision to let a patient die is subject to moral appraisal in the same way that a decision to kill him would be subject to moral appraisal: It may be assessed as wise or unwise, compassionate or sadistic, right or wrong. If a doctor deliberately let a patient die who was suffering from a routinely curable illness, the doctor would certainly be to blame for what he had done, just as he would be to blame if he had needlessly killed the patient. Charges against him would then be appropriate. If so, it would be no defense at all for him to insist that he didn't "do anything." He would have done something very serious indeed, for he let his patient die.

Fixing the cause of death may be very important from a legal point of 19
view, for it may determine whether criminal charges are brought against the doctor. But I do not think that this notion can be used to show a moral difference between active and passive euthanasia. The reason why it is considered bad to be the cause of someone's death is that death is regarded as a great evil — and so it is. However, if it had been decided that

euthanasia — even passive euthanasia — is desirable in a given case, it has also been decided that in this instance death is no greater an evil than the patient's continued existence. And if this is true, the usual reason for not wanting to be the cause of someone's death simply does not apply.

Finally, doctors may think that all of this is only of academic interest 20
— the sort of thing that philosophers may worry about but that has no practical bearing on their own work. After all, doctors must be concerned about the legal consequences of what they do, and active euthanasia is clearly forbidden by the law. But even so, doctors should also be concerned with the fact that the law is forcing upon them a moral doctrine that may well be indefensible and has a considerable effect on their practices. Of course, most doctors are not now in the position of being coerced in this matter, for they do not regard themselves as merely going along with what the law requires. Rather, in statements such as the AMA policy statement that I have quoted, they are endorsing this doctrine as a central point of medical ethics. In that statement, active euthanasia is condemned not merely as illegal but as "contrary to that for which the medical profession stands," whereas passive euthanasia is approved. However, the preceding considerations suggest that there is really no moral difference between the two, considered in themselves (there may be important moral differences in some cases in their *consequences*, but, as I pointed out, these differences may make active euthanasia, and not passive euthanasia, the morally preferable option). So, whereas doctors may have to discriminate between active and passive euthanasia to satisfy the law, they should not do any more than that. In particular, they should not give the distinction any added authority and weight by writing it into official statements of medical ethics.

That Right Belongs Only to the State

MORTIMER OSTOW

To the Editor:

Nine members of the Kennedy Institute for the Study of Human Re- 1
production and Bioethics commented on May 18 on your May 2 editorial "Who Shall Make the Ultimate Decision?" Their assertion that it is im-

Dr. Ostow's letter appeared in the *New York Times* on June 1, 1971.

portant to establish precise criteria to guide the judgment of reasonable people cannot be faulted.

I believe comment is called for, however, on your argument that vital decisions respecting life and death belong to the patient or, when he is incompetent to make them, to those who are presumed to have his best interests at heart. The members of the Kennedy Institute concur. 2

It is a basic assumption of our society that individual members possess no right to determine matters of life and death respecting other individuals, or even themselves. That right belongs only to the state. The prohibition of murder, suicide and, until recently, abortion, has rested on this assumption. The right to determine whether life-preserving efforts are to be continued or discontinued therefore belongs neither to the physician nor to the patient or his guardian, but to the state. 3

In practical terms, when such a decision is called for, the decision is to be made only by some agency or agent of the state, and it is to be made only by due process. To cede the right to the individuals involved is to license murder. 4

Aside from the philosophic argument, which not everyone will find cogent, there are two practical reasons for requiring due process in such instances. In discussion of matters of continuing or withholding life-support systems and euthanasia, the arguments usually offered relate to the best interests of the patient or to the economic cost to society. Abortion, too, is discussed in these terms. A far more important consideration, it seems to me, is what making life-and-death decisions does to the individuals who decide. 5

While most of us will doubt that having made a decision to terminate life support to a suffering relative will then incline one to commit murder, still, making such a decision does condition the unconditional respect for life, and does weaken the concept of the distinction between what is permitted and what is forbidden. 6

One can see a tendency to pass from withdrawing life support from the moribund to facilitating the death of the suffering, and from there to the neglect or even abandonment of the profoundly defective, and from there to the degradation or liquidation of any whom society might consider undesirable. The undisciplined making of life-and-death decisions tends to corrupt the individual who makes them, and corrupted individuals tend to corrupt society. 7

Second, it is not necessarily true that the individual himself has his own interests at heart. Afflicted with a painful and long-drawn-out illness, many individuals will wish for death, even when objectively there is a reasonable possibility of recovery. Permitting the patient to make the decision to die may amount to encouraging his suicide. Anyone familiar with the ambivalence which prevails in family relationships will not take it for 8 granted that family members will necessarily represent the patient's best interests.

It is important for the morale and morality of our society that "the ul- 9
timate decision" be made only by a disinterested agent or agency of our society, and only by due process.

— Mortimer Ostow, M.D.

A Living Will

CONCERN FOR DYING

To Make Best Use of Your Living Will

[Concern for Dying suggests that] You may wish to add specific statements to the Living Will *in the space provided for that purpose above your signature.* Possible additional provisions are: (1) "Measures of artificial life-support in the face of impending death that I specifically refuse are: (a) Electrical or mechanical resuscitation of my heart when it has stopped beating. (b) Nasogastric tube feeding when I am paralyzed or unable to take nourishment by mouth. (c) Mechanical respiration when I am no longer able to sustain my own breathing. (d) ______." (2) "I would like to live out my last days at home rather than in a hospital if it does not jeopardize the chance of my recovery to a meaningful and sentient life or does not impose an undue burden on my family." (3) "If any of my tissues are sound and would be of value as transplants to other people, I freely give my permission for such donation."

The optional Durable Power of Attorney feature allows you to name someone else to serve as your proxy in case you are unable to communicate your wishes. Should you choose to fill in this portion of the document, you must have your signature notarized.

If you choose more than one proxy for decision making on your behalf, please give order of priority (1, 2, 3, etc.).

Space is provided at the bottom of the Living Will for notarization should you choose to have your Living Will witnessed by a Notary Public.

The Living Will was first developed by Concern for Dying, an educational council, in 1968. In most states the Living Will is legally binding under certain circumstances.

My Living Will
To My Family, My Physician, My Lawyer and All Others Whom It May Concern

Death is as much a reality as birth, growth, maturity and old age—it is the one certainty of life. If the time comes when I can no longer take part in decisions for my own future, let this statement stand as an expression of my wishes and directions, while I am still of sound mind.

If at such a time the situation should arise in which there is no reasonable expectation of my recovery from extreme physical or mental disability, I direct that I be allowed to die and not be kept alive by medications, artificial means or "heroic measures". I do, however, ask that medication be mercifully administered to me to alleviate suffering even though this may shorten my remaining life.

This statement is made after careful consideration and is in accordance with my strong convictions and beliefs. I want the wishes and directions here expressed carried out to the extent permitted by law. Insofar as they are not legally enforceable, I hope that those to whom this Will is addressed will regard themselves as morally bound by these provisions.

(Optional specific provisions to be made in this space – see other side)

DURABLE POWER OF ATTORNEY (optional)

I hereby designate ________________ to serve as my attorney-in-fact for the purpose of making medical treatment decisions. This power of attorney shall remain effective in the event that I become incompetent or otherwise unable to make such decisions for myself.

Optional Notarization:

"Sworn and subscribed to

before me this ________ day

of ________, 19______."

____
Notary Public
(seal)

Signed________________

Date ________________

Witness ________________

____
Address

Witness ________________

____
Address

Copies of this request have been given to ________________

________________ ________________

(Optional) My Living Will is registered with Concern for Dying (No. ________)

Distributed by Concern for Dying, 250 West 57th Street, New York, NY 10107 (212) 246-6962

Not Everybody Wants to Sign a Living Will

FELICIA ACKERMAN

To the Editor:

As a potential terminally ill person (who isn't?), I object to Jane E. Brody's one-sided discussion of living wills (Personal Health column, September 21). What it overlooks is that many people have excellent reasons for choosing *not* to sign one. 1

Living wills are useful for people who would rather bow out quickly and gracefully than fight for their lives as long as possible. But it is naive to suppose this is everyone's preference and cruel to suggest it ought to be. The case of Carrie A. Coons, a Rensselaer, New York, octogenerian who regained consciousness after a diagnosis of "irreversible vegetative state" (news story, April 13) is bound to make people who value their lives wonder about the reliability of such diagnoses. The article does not mention this case. 2

Perhaps the most alarming thing about the column is its repeated emphasis on the family's undue emotional suffering when a patient lingers on life supports. The view that hopelessly ill people ought to sacrifice their lives in order to make things pleasanter for their healthy families is becoming increasingly popular nowadays. But it is a brutal view that has no place in a decent society. 3

—Felicia Ackerman

Felicia Ackerman is an associate professor of philosophy at Brown University. Her letter appeared in the October 13, 1989 *New York Times*.

A Time to Die

THE ECONOMIST

Once upon a time there was a court physician — the eponymous Makropoulos of Janacek's opera — who discovered the elixir of life. His daughter drank it and regretted it for 600 years. A stretched-out existence had made her cold and sated; she stopped taking the elixir and gratefully died. Tithonous, another mythological figure, did even worse. When his lover asked Jupiter to give him immortality she forgot to ask for youth to go with it, so Tithonous inherited an eternity of senescence (and ended up as a grasshopper). Today's court physicians, and playthings of the medical gods, should ponder the morals that these old stories hold for them. 1

Modern medicine is nowhere near to providing immortality, and there are millions of lives prematurely lost every year for the physicians still to save. Yet the inhabitants of rich countries, with their recently elongated lifespans and their hospitals that make once-quick deaths take what seems like an eternity, are too often seduced by an idea as dangerous as Makropoulos's elixir. They sometimes seem, like Woody Allen, to want to achieve immortality not through their work but through not dying. 2

Tithonous is alive, reasonably well, and wearing jogging shorts. It is his dream of death as something indefinitely postponable that is distorting the medical priorities of rich countries, especially America. Medicine has increased the quantity of life far beyond its capacity to preserve the quality of it, and a greater proportion of old age is now spent in chronic illness and misery. The average life expectancy of an American man has risen remarkably, from just under 60 in the late 1920s to 76 in 1984. That is a big blessing for some, but only a mixed one for many others. Just as an extension of credit is no guarantee of the ability to pay, so an extension of life is no guarantee of the ability to enjoy it. Hospitals are full of people who are tragically overdrawn. For such people, the last weeks, days, and hours are often the worst. As ever more intrusive and desperate machinery is wheeled in to keep Tithonous hanging on for a little longer, the dignity and sense of his life trickles out of him. 3

Cost is not the problem. True enough, the statistics of the Tithonous generation are the sort that give demographers a thrill of self-importance: In 1900 there were seven elderly Americans for every one hundred workers, while now there are nineteen; in 2050 (when one person in twenty will be over 85) there may be thirty-eight. In 1980 some 29 percent of personal health-care spending in America went on the over-60s; in 2040, so 4

This unsigned essay appeared in the pages of *The Economist*, August 5, 1989.

the health economists say, nearly half of it will be. But it is the pain and misery, not the numbers, that are the worst of it. Not only have the old acute killers merely been swapped for the wasting chronic diseases — cancer, heart disease, and strokes — but the great misery-makers of arthritis, dementia, and others go from horrible strength to strength. No calculating utilitarian, applying Bentham's cold arithmetic of pleasure versus pain, can demand that the old be killed or starved to save money for the young. It is the old themselves who, for their own dignity and out of concern for their successors, must learn to demand less of the court physicians.

For Better or for Worse

Consider first what a better life and death would look like, then how 5
to get there. There are five main types of misery that make old age worse than it need be, and win less attention from researchers than the big killers. Alzheimer's disease and other brain disorders can slowly rob life of all meaning by disintegrating the mind. Osteoarthritis can mean almost permanent pain. Osteoporosis — thinning of the bones — makes stumbling a serious danger and so makes the old less active because of their fear. Deafness is deeply isolating in another way. Incontinence is a humiliating reminder of the loss of control. Research into the killers obviously needs to continue — for one thing, cancer is the second-biggest killer of children in rich countries. But the misery-makers need more attention too. And the use of new medical techniques and devices should be guided by a simple principle: Do not extend life at the cost of worsening it.

The shape of medicine is, one way or another, determined in consid- 6
erable part by popular demand. Demand is dominated by the fear of death. Ask people in rich countries what they most want to see cured and they quickly say "cancer, AIDS, and heart disease." It is not until it is too late that they begin to see that other things matter too. Given this obsession with death, it is understandable that doctors all too often struggle to extend life through its last moments at practically any cost. But there is another, nobler challenge that they can take on. They should use their role as advisers and confidants, from a patient's earliest days, to teach the importance of the quality as well as the length of life. Their hope should be that patients will eventually make wiser demands of them. Those who channel money, both public and private, to medical research need the courage to see that they will earn gratitude by gunning for misery as well as for the headline-making killers.

If the length of life is not all-important, when should life end? There is 7
room for plenty of theories about what makes life worth living, but none of them can include longevity as an end in itself. The enjoyment of food,

for example, cannot reside entirely in the fact that it reminds one of yet more food to come. Think of a person's life in biographical rather than biological terms — in terms of achievements, experiences, responsibilities discharged, and so on, not in terms of blips on a hospital scanner. It then becomes easier to see when somebody's life has been completed. When a person (or his relatives) can see that a biography is finished, it is not for doctors to try to write a painful extra chapter. Ask Tithonous.

THINKING AND WRITING ABOUT EUTHANASIA

Questions for Discussion and Writing

1. Ostow argues that only the state should be allowed to make a decision concerning the lives of the terminally ill. What reasons, including analogies, does Ostow offer in support of his argument? Do you agree with his conclusion? Why or why not? What other writers in this chapter might disagree?
2. Does Rachels prove that there is no moral difference between active and passive euthanasia? Is his attempt to meet the arguments of the opposition a convincing tactic? Which of his arguments do you find most persuasive? Why?
3. What is Hook's principal reason for regretting that his request to discontinue the life support was denied? What qualities in the author are reflected in this article? Does the fact that this article is written by the patient himself make the argument more or less powerful? Can Hook's argument for voluntary euthanasia be used to answer Doyle's and Conolly's arguments?
4. Define the "quality of life ethic," as Eileen Doyle sees it. According to the author, how does the Constitution of the United States prevent the legalization of euthanasia? What consequences does the author foresee if euthanasia is permitted by law, as abortion is? Do you think her predictions are soundly based?
5. What does it mean to argue, as Conolly does, that hard cases make bad laws? How does Conolly answer those who assert that euthanasia is sometimes justifiable to relieve suffering?

Topics for Research

Changing views of suicide

The hospice solution

Handicapped newborns: the government role

The changing definition of death

Noteworthy cases involving the right to die

CHAPTER 16

Freedom of Speech

The First Amendment to the Constitution of the United States reads, "Congress shall make no laws respecting an establishment of religion, or prohibiting the free expression thereof; or abridging the freedom of speech, or of the press; or the right of the people peaceably to assemble, and to petition the Government for a redress of grievances." (The first ten amendments were ratified on December 15, 1791, and form what is known as the "Bill of Rights.") The arguments in this section will consider primarily the issue of "abridging the freedom of speech, or of the press."

The limits of free speech in the United States are constantly being adjusted as social values change and new cases testing those limits emerge. Two highly controversial issues are emphasized in the following selection of essays and letters.

One is the flag-burning case, which arose when Gregory Johnson, a Texan, was convicted in 1984 for burning an American flag during the Republican National Convention. The Supreme Court later overturned that decision, ruling that Mr. Johnson's act was an expression of political dissent and therefore protected by the First Amendment. This decision prompted the President and some members of Congress to call for an amendment to the Constitution that would make flag-burning a crime under any circumstances. Some critics of the Supreme Court decision have argued that freedom of *speech* and freedom of *expression* are not synonymous. "But surely it is possible," said one, "to distinguish between an idea and the manner in which it is expressed." In response to the Supreme Court decision, Congress passed the Flag Protection Act in 1989, outlawing desecration of the flag. In June 1990 the Supreme Court ruled that the law was unconstitutional.

A second issue of much wider significance concerns the right to use abusive language about others, especially language commonly defined as "racist, sexist, or homophobic." Some of the most troublesome cases have arisen on college campuses where administration officials have introduced rules banning such language and subjecting violators to serious penalties, including expulsion. But civil libertarians have challenged these rules, arguing that they dangerously infringe free speech.

Freedom of speech is also a central issue in the argument over the dissemination of pornographic materials. (See the articles by Brownmiller and Jacoby in the section on pornography.) Some critics find pornography in the lyrics of popular rock music and are proposing a ratings system that would give parents a measure of control over the purchase of record albums, tapes, and compact discs by their children. Opponents argue that such rating systems constitute censorship.

In Praise of Censure

GARRY WILLS

Rarely have the denouncers of censorship been so eager to start practicing it. When a sense of moral disorientation overcomes a society, people from the least expected quarters begin to ask, "Is nothing sacred?" Feminists join reactionaries to denounce pornography as demeaning to women. Rock musician Frank Zappa declares that when Tipper Gore, the wife of Senator Albert Gore from Tennessee, asked music companies to label sexually explicit material, she launched an illegal "conspiracy to extort." A *Penthouse* editorialist says that housewife Terry Rakolta, who asked sponsors to withdraw support from a sitcom called *Married . . . with Children*, is "yelling fire in a crowded theater," a formula that says her speech is not protected by the First Amendment. 1

But the most interesting movement to limit speech is directed at defamatory utterances against blacks, homosexuals, Jews, women, or other 2

Garry Wills is the author of many books on politics including *Nixon Agonistes* and *Reagan's America*. His essay appeared in *Time* on July 31, 1989.

stigmatizable groups. It took no Terry Rakolta of the left to bring about the instant firing of Jimmy the Greek and Al Campanis from sports jobs when they made racially denigrating comments. Social pressure worked far more quickly on them than on *Married . . . with Children*, which is still on the air.

The rules being considered on college campuses to punish students for making racist and other defamatory remarks go beyond social and commercial pressure to actual legal muzzling. The right-wing *Dartmouth Review* and its imitators have understandably infuriated liberals, who are beginning to take action against them and the racist expressions they have encouraged. The American Civil Liberties Union considered this movement important enough to make it the principal topic at its biennial meeting last month in Madison, Wisconsin. Ironically, the regents of the University of Wisconsin had passed their own rules against defamation just before the ACLU members convened on the university's campus. Nadine Strossen, of New York University School of Law, who was defending the ACLU's traditional position on free speech, said of Wisconsin's new rules, "You can tell how bad they are by the fact that the regents had to make an amendment at the last minute exempting classroom discussion! What is surprising is that Donna Shalala [chancellor of the university] went along with it." So did constitutional lawyers on the faculty. 3

If a similar code were drawn up with right-wing imperatives in mind — one banning unpatriotic, irreligious, or sexually explicit expressions on campus — the people framing Wisconsin-type rules would revert to their libertarian pasts. In this competition to suppress, is regard for freedom of expression just a matter of whose ox is getting gored at the moment? Does the left just get nervous about the Christian cross when Klansmen burn it, while the right will react only when Madonna flirts crucifixes between her thighs? 4

The cries of "un-American" are as genuine and as frequent on either side. Everyone is protecting the country. Zappa accuses Gore of undermining the moral fiber of America with the "sexual neuroses of these vigilant ladies." He argues that she threatens our freedoms with "connubial insider trading" because her husband is a senator. Apparently her marital status should deprive her of speaking privileges in public — an argument Westbrook Pegler used to make against Eleanor Roosevelt. *Penthouse* says Rakolta is taking us down the path toward fascism. It attacks her for living in a rich suburb — the old "radical chic" argument that rich people cannot support moral causes. 5

There is a basic distinction that cuts through this free-for-all over freedom. It is the distinction, too often neglected, between censorship and censure (the free expression of moral disapproval). What the campuses 6 are trying to do (at least those with state money) is use the force of government to contain freedom of speech. What Donald Wildmon, the freelance moralist from Tupelo, Mississippi, does when he gets Pepsi to cancel its Madonna ad is censure the ad by calling for a boycott. Advocating boycotts is a form of speech protected by the First Amendment. As Nat Hentoff, journalistic custodian of the First Amendment, says, "I would hate to see boycotts outlawed. Think what that would do to Cesar Chavez." Or, for that matter, to Ralph Nader. If one disapproves of a social practice, whether it is racist speech or unjust hiring in lettuce fields, one is free to denounce that and to call on others to express their disapproval. Otherwise there would be no form of persuasive speech except passing a law. This would make the law coterminous with morality.

Equating morality with legality is in effect what people do when they claim that anything tolerated by law must, in the name of freedom, be approved by citizens in all their dealings with one another. As Zappa says, "Masturbation is not illegal. If it is not illegal to do it, why should it be illegal to sing about it?" He thinks this proves that Gore, who is not trying to make raunch in rock illegal, cannot even ask distributors to label it. Anything goes, as long as it's legal. The odd consequence of this argument would be a drastic narrowing of the freedom of speech. One could not call into question anything that was not against the law — including, for instance, racist speech. 7

A false ideal of tolerance has not only outlawed censorship but discouraged censoriousness (another word for censure). Most civilizations have expressed their moral values by mobilization of social opprobrium. That, rather than specific legislation, is what changed the treatment of minorities in films and TV over recent years. One can now draw opprobrious attention by gay bashing, as the Beastie Boys rock group found when their distributor told them to cut out remarks about "fags" for business reasons. Or by anti-Semitism, as the just disbanded rap group Public Enemy has discovered. 8

It is said that only the narrow-minded are intolerant or opprobrious. Most of those who limited the distribution of Martin Scorsese's movie *The Last Temptation of Christ* had not even seen the movie. So do we guarantee freedom of speech only for the broad-minded or the better educated? Can one speak only after studying whatever one has reason, from one's beliefs, to denounce? Then most of us would be doing a great deal less speaking than we do. If one has never seen any snuff movies, is that a bar to criticizing them? 9

Others argue that asking people not to buy lettuce is different from asking them not to buy a rocker's artistic expression. Ideas (carefully disguised) lurk somewhere in the lyrics. All the more reason to keep 10 criticism of them free. If ideas are too important to suppress, they are also too important to ignore. The whole point of free speech is not to make ideas exempt from criticism but to expose them to it.

One of the great mistakes of liberals in recent decades has been the ceding of moral concern to right-wingers. Just because one opposes censorship, one need not be seen as agreeing with pornographers. Why should liberals, of all people, oppose Gore when she asks that labels be put on products meant for the young, to inform those entrusted by law with the care of the young? Liberals were the first to promote "healthy" television shows like *Sesame Street* and *The Electric Company*. In the 1950s and 1960s they were the leading critics of television, of its mindless violence, of the way it ravaged the attention span needed for reading. Who was keeping kids away from TV sets then? How did promoters of Big Bird let themselves be cast as champions of the Beastie Boys — not just of their *right* to perform but of their performance itself? Why should it be left to Gore to express moral disapproval of a group calling itself Dead Kennedys (sample lyric: "I kill children, I love to see them die")? 11

For that matter, who has been more insistent that parents should "interfere" in what their children are doing. Tipper Gore or Jesse Jackson? All through the 1970s, Jackson was traveling the high schools, telling parents to turn off TVs, make the kids finish their homework, check with teachers on their performance, get to know what the children are doing. This kind of "interference" used to be called education. 12

Belief in the First Amendment does not preempt other beliefs, making one a eunuch to the interplay of opinions. It is a distortion to turn "You can express any views" into the proposition "I don't care what views you express." If liberals keep equating equality with approval, they will be repeatedly forced into weak positions. 13

A case in point is the Corcoran Gallery's sudden cancellation of an exhibit of Robert Mapplethorpe's photographs. The whole matter was needlessly confused when the director, Christina Owr-Chall, claimed she was canceling the show to *protect* it from censorship. She meant that there might be pressure to remove certain pictures — the sadomasochistic ones or those verging on kiddie porn — if the show had gone on. But she had in mind, as well, the hope of future grants from the National Endowment for the Arts, which is under criticism for the Mapplethorpe show and for another show that contained Andres Serrano's *Piss Christ*, the photograph of a crucifix in what the title says is urine. Owr-Chall is said to be yielding to censorship, when she is clearly yielding to political and financial pressure, as Pepsi yielded to commercial pressure over the Madonna ad. 14

What is at issue here is not government suppression but government subsidy. Mapplethorpe's work is not banned, but showing it might have endangered federal grants to needy artists. The idea that what the gov- 15 ernment does not support it represses is nonsensical, as one can see by reversing the statement to read: "No one is allowed to create anything without the government's subvention." What pussycats our supposedly radical artists are. They not only want the government's permission to create their artifacts, they want federal authorities to supply the materials as well. Otherwise they feel "gagged." If they are not given government approval (and money), they want to remain an avant-garde while being bankrolled by the Old Guard.

What is easily forgotten in this argument is the right of citizen taxpayers. They send representatives to Washington who are answerable for the expenditure of funds exacted from them. In general these voters want to favor their own values if government is going to get into the culture-subsidizing area at all (a proposition many find objectionable in itself). Politicians, insofar as they support the arts, will tend to favor conventional art (certainly not masochistic art). Anybody who doubts that has no understanding of a politician's legitimate concern for his or her constituents' approval. Besides, it is quaint for those familiar with the politics of the art world to discover, with a shock, that there is politics in politics. 16

Luckily, cancellation of the Mapplethorpe show forced some artists back to the flair and cheekiness of unsubsidized art. Other results of pressure do not turn out as well. Unfortunately, people in certain regions were deprived of the chance to see *The Last Temptation of Christ* in the theater. Some, no doubt, considered it a loss that they could not buy lettuce or grapes during a Chavez boycott. Perhaps there was even a buyer perverse enough to miss driving the unsafe cars Nader helped pressure off the market. On the other hand, we do not get sports analysis made by racists. These mobilizations of social opprobrium are not examples of repression but of freedom of expression by committed people who censured without censoring, who expressed the kinds of belief the First Amendment guarantees. I do not, as a result, get whatever I approve of subsidized, either by Pepsi or the government. But neither does the law come in to silence Tipper Gore or Frank Zappa or even that filthy rag, the *Dartmouth Review*. 17

Interim Policy on Discrimination and Discriminatory Conduct by Students in the University Environment

THE UNIVERSITY OF MICHIGAN

Preamble

Discrimination, as defined in Regental Bylaw 14.06 and the Presidential Policy Statement issued in March, 1984, is unacceptable on the University of Michigan campus. Such behavior threatens to destroy the environment of tolerance and mutual respect which must prevail if a university is to fulfill its purpose. 1

Of equal importance on the University of Michigan campus is a strong commitment to the principle of freedom of speech guaranteed by the First Amendment to the United States Constitution, as stated in the University's Policy on Freedom of Speech, Section 601.1 in the Standard Practice Guide. The University is dedicated to allowing students vigorous and open academic discourse and intellectual inquiry, including speech that espouses controversial or even offensive ideas. 2

In the University context, a commitment to not interfere with free speech may lead to sheltering speech by students that is repugnant or morally offensive. Because of our respect for individual freedom and dignity, the sheltering of such speech is allowed in order to arrive at truth, to promote clearer reasoning by necessitating argument against opposing views, and in recognition of the fallibility of any one individual or institution in discerning the one, correct idea. Perhaps most important is that it reinforces our society's commitment to tolerance as a value. 3

It is clear, however, that under existing free-speech jurisprudence all speech is not protected. The United States Supreme Court in *Cohen v. California* (1971) recognized that the First Amendment would not protect speech when "substantial privacy interests are . . . invaded in an essentially intolerable manner." In the secondary school context, the Court said speech can be prohibited that "would materially and substantially interfere with the requirement of appropriate discipline in the operation of the 4

This policy went into effect at the University of Michigan on April 14, 1988. Subsequently, it was contested by a graduate student in biopsychology who argued that it would perniciously inhibit the free expression of ideas in the classroom. The policy was rescinded on September 22, 1989.

school" (*Tinker v. Des Moines Community School District*; 1969). "Fighting words" also do not enjoy First Amendment protection (*Chaplinsky v. New Hampshire*, 315 US 568; 1942). The language of these decisions shows that the Supreme Court is struggling to articulate the boundaries of protected speech.

After a thorough review of the issue, the University of Michigan has 5
determined that it needs to intervene in speech when a student intentionally uses racial, ethnocentric, or sexual invectives, epithets, slurs, or utterances directly to attack or injure another individual rather than express or discuss an idea, ideology, or philosophy. Such attacks go beyond the boundaries of protected free speech. In those instances, the University must protect the educational environment of the University.

Because there is tension between freedom of speech, the right of indi- 6
viduals to be free from injury caused by discrimination, and the University's duty to protect the educational process, the enforcement procedures assume that it is necessary to have varying standards depending upon the locus of the regulated conduct. Thus a distinction is drawn among public forums, educational and academic centers, and housing units.

Prohibited Discrimination and Discriminatory Conduct

A. Discrimination and discriminatory conduct in public forums. 7
Places such as the Diag, Regents' Plaza, the Fishbowl, and the area around Burton Tower are dedicated public forums which lend themselves to facilitating the free exchange of ideas within the University community. In many respects they resemble the public park or street corner. Similarly, the *Michigan Review*, the *Michigan Daily*, and other mass media enhance the discussion and debate of important ideas and issues. The broadest range of speech and expression will be tolerated in these areas and by these publications. Nevertheless, malicious and intentional verbal threats of physical violence, directed towards an individual, sexual harassment, physical violence, and destruction of property in public forums which is the result of discriminatory behavior as defined in paragraph B below are misconduct and subject to discipline.

*B. Discrimination and discriminatory conduct and harassment in edu- 8
cational and academic centers.* Educational and academic centers, such as classroom buildings, libraries, research laboratories, recreation and study centers, etc., are the locus of the University's educational mission. Accordingly the University has a compelling interest in assuring an environment in which learning may thrive. Such an environment requires

free and unfettered discussion of the widest possible nature, encouraging expression of all points of view. The University acknowledges that the frank and open discussion of social, cultural, artistic, religious, scientific, and political issues may be disturbing and even hurtful for some individuals. In such instances, the principle of free exchange and inquiry takes precedence as it is so fundamental to the educational enterprise.

Discrimination and discriminatory harassment have no place in this 9
educational enterprise. Physical acts or threats or verbal slurs, invectives or epithets, referring to an individual's race, ethnicity, religion, sex, sexual orientation, creed, national origin, ancestry, age, or handicap, made with the purpose of injuring the person to whom the words or actions are directed and that are not made as a part of a discussion or exchange of an idea, ideology, or philosophy, are prohibited.

In order to illustrate the types of conduct which this subsection is de- 10
signed to cover, the following examples are set forth. These examples do not illustrate the only situations or types of conduct intended to be covered.

1. A student states in a physiology class the theory that the average size of the craniums of each race is related to the average intelligence of that race. A student in the class finds the remarks personally demeaning and files a complaint. There is no violation of the Policy because, although the remarks refer to race, they were not slurs, invectives, epithets, or utterances directed with intent to injure any individual student and were made as part of a classroom discussion.
2. In a classroom before an exam a white student uses a racial epithet to a black student and tells her to go home and stop using a white person's space. The black student files a complaint. There is a violation of the Policy because the remark is a slur referring to race made with the purpose of affecting a particular student's performance on the exam and is not part of an exchange or discussion of ideas.
3. A student during a political science class discussion of the Holocaust states that it was a good thing because it destroyed members of an inferior religion. A Jewish student in the class files a complaint. Even though the remark may have been intended to upset Jewish members of the class, it is protected under the Policy because it was made during a discussion of ideas.
4. A student tells a joke during class which slurs members of an ethnic group. The joke is extraneous to the class discussion at that time. A member of the ethnic group files a complaint. There is no violation of the Policy. Although the joke is not part of an exchange or discussion of ideas, it is not directed towards any individual with the purpose of injuring that person.

Students may not use race, ethnicity, religion, sex, sexual orientation, creed, national origin, ancestry, age, marital status, handicap, or Vietnam-era veteran status to affect the terms, conditions, privileges, or benefits of an individual's education, employment, housing, or participation in a University activity. 11

Students may also not use threats, whether explicit or implicit, concerning the terms or conditions of an individual's education, employment, housing, or participation in a University activity as a way to gain sex and sexual favors. Unwelcome sexual advances, requests for sexual favors, and other conduct of a sexual nature that interferes with an individual's academic efforts, employment, or participation in University-sponsored activities are also prohibited. . . . 12

D. Interpretive Guide. Shortly after the promulgation of the policy in the fall of 1988, the University Office of Affirmative Action issued an interpretive guide (Guide) entitled *What Students Should Know about Discrimination and Discriminatory Harassment by Students in the University Environment.* The Guide purported to be an authoritative interpretation of the Policy and provided examples of sanctionable conduct. These included: 13

A flier containing racist threats distributed in a residence hall.

Racist graffiti written on the door of an Asian student's study carrel.

A male student makes remarks in class like "Women just aren't as good in this field as men," thus creating a hostile learning atmosphere for female classmates.

Students in a residence hall have a floor party and invite everyone on their floor except one person because they think she might be a lesbian.

A black student is confronted and racially insulted by two white students in a cafeteria.

Male students leave pornographic pictures and jokes on the desk of a female graduate student.

Two men demand that their roommate in the residence hall move out and be tested for AIDS.

In addition, the Guide contained a separate section entitled "YOU are a harasser when . . . " which contains the following examples of discriminatory conduct: 14

You exclude someone from a study group because that person is of a different race, sex, or ethnic origin than you are.

You tell jokes about gay men and lesbians.

Your student organization sponsors entertainment that includes a comedian who slurs Hispanics.

You display a Confederate flag on the door of your room in the residence hall.

You laugh at a joke about someone in your class who stutters.

You make obscene telephone calls or send racist notes or computer messages.

You comment in a derogatory way about a particular person or group's physical appearance or sexual orientation, or their cultural origins, or religious beliefs. . . .

15 According to the University, the Guide was withdrawn at an unknown date in the winter of 1989, because "the information in it was not accurate."

The Debate over Placing Limits on Racist Speech Must Not Ignore the Damage It Does to Its Victims

CHARLES R. LAWRENCE III

1 I have spent the better part of my life as a dissenter. As a high school student, I was threatened with suspension for my refusal to participate in a civil-defense drill, and I have been a conspicuous consumer of my First Amendment liberties ever since. There are very strong reasons for protecting even racist speech. Perhaps the most important of these is that such protection reinforces our society's commitment to tolerance as a value, and that by protecting bad speech from government regulation, we will be forced to combat it as a community.

2 But I also have a deeply felt apprehension about the resurgence of racial violence and the corresponding rise in the incidence of verbal and symbolic assault and harassment to which blacks and other traditionally subjugated and excluded groups are subjected. I am troubled by the way

---

Charles R. Lawrence III is a professor of law at Stanford University. His article, which appeared in the October 25, 1989 *Chronicle of Higher Education*, is adapted from a speech to a conference of the American Civil Liberties Union.

the debate has been framed in response to the recent surge of racist incidents on college and university campuses and in response to some universities' attempts to regulate harassing speech. The problem has been framed as one in which the liberty of free speech is in conflict with the elimination of racism. I believe this has placed the bigot on the moral high ground and fanned the rising flames of racism.

Above all, I am troubled that we have not listened to the real victims, that we have shown so little understanding of their injury, and that we have abandoned those whose race, gender, or sexual preference continues to make them second-class citizens. It seems to me a very sad irony that the first instinct of civil libertarians has been to challenge even the smallest, most narrowly framed efforts by universities to provide black and other minority students with the protection the Constitution guarantees them. 3

The landmark case of *Brown v. Board of Education* is not a case that we normally think of as a case about speech. But *Brown* can be broadly read as articulating the principle of equal citizenship. *Brown* held that segregated schools were inherently unequal because of the *message* that segregation conveyed — that black children were an untouchable caste, unfit to go to school with white children. If we understand the necessity of eliminating the system of signs and symbols that signal the inferiority of blacks, then we should hesitate before proclaiming that all racist speech that stops short of physical violence must be defended. 4

University officials who have formulated policies to respond to incidents of racial harassment have been characterized in the press as "thought police," but such policies generally do nothing more than impose sanctions against intentional face-to-face insults. When racist speech takes the form of face-to-face insults, catcalls, or other assaultive speech aimed at an individual or small group of persons, it falls directly within the "fighting words" exception to First Amendment protection. The Supreme Court has held that words which "by their very utterance inflict injury or tend to incite an immediate breach of the peace" are not protected by the First Amendment. 5

If the purpose of the First Amendment is to foster the greatest amount of speech, racial insults disserve that purpose. Assaultive racist speech functions as a preemptive strike. The invective is experienced as a blow, not as a proffered idea, and once the blow is struck, it is unlikely that a dialogue will follow. Racial insults are particularly undeserving of First Amendment protection because the perpetuator's intention is not to discover truth or initiate dialogue but to injure the victim. In most situations, members of minority groups realize that they are likely to lose if they respond to epithets by fighting and are forced to remain silent and submissive. 6

Courts have held that offensive speech may not be regulated in public forums such as streets where the listener may avoid the speech by moving on, but the regulation of otherwise protected speech has been permitted when the speech invades the privacy of the unwilling listener's home or when the unwilling listener cannot avoid the speech. Racist posters, fliers, and graffiti in dormitories, bathrooms, and other common living spaces would seem to clearly fall within the reasoning of these cases. Minority students should not be required to remain in their rooms in order to avoid racial assault. Minimally, they should find a safe haven in their dorms and in all other common rooms that are a part of their daily routine. 7

I would also argue that the university's responsibility for ensuring that these students receive an equal educational opportunity provides a compelling justification for regulations that ensure them safe passage in all common areas. A minority student should not have to risk becoming the target of racially assaulting speech every time he or she chooses to walk across campus. Regulating vilifying speech that cannot be anticipated or avoided would not preclude announced speeches and rallies — situations that would give minority-group members and their allies the chance to organize counterdemonstrations or avoid the speech altogether. 8

The most commonly advanced argument against the regulation of racist speech proceeds something like this: We recognize that minority groups suffer pain and injury as the result of racist speech, but we must allow this hate mongering for the benefit of society as a whole. Freedom of speech is the lifeblood of our democratic system. It is especially important for minorities because often it is their only vehicle for rallying support for the redress of their grievances. It will be impossible to formulate a prohibition so precise that it will prevent the racist speech you want to suppress without catching in the same net all kinds of speech that it would be unconscionable for a democratic society to suppress. 9

Whenever we make such arguments, we are striking a balance on the one hand between our concern for the continued free flow of ideas and the democratic process dependent on that flow, and, on the other, our desire to further the cause of equality. There can be no meaningful discussion of how we should reconcile our commitment to equality and our commitment to free speech until it is acknowledged that there is real harm inflicted by racist speech and that this harm is far from trivial. 10

To engage in a debate about the First Amendment and racist speech without a full understanding of the nature and extent of that harm is to risk making the First Amendment an instrument of domination rather than a vehicle of liberation. We have not all known the experience of victimization by racist, misogynist, and homophobic speech, nor do we 11 equally share the burden of the societal harm it inflicts. We are often quick to say that we have heard the cry of the victims when we have not.

The *Brown* case is again instructive because it speaks directly to the psychic injury inflicted by racist speech by noting that the symbolic message of segregation affected "the hearts and minds" of negro children "in a way unlikely ever to be undone." Racial epithets and harassment often cause deep emotional scarring and feelings of anxiety and fear that pervade every aspect of a victim's life. 12

Brown also recognized that black children did not have an equal opportunity to learn and participate in the school community if they bore the additional burden of being subjected to the humiliation and psychic assault contained in the message of segregation. University students bear an analogous burden when they are forced to live and work in an environment where at any moment they may be subjected to denigrating verbal harassment and assault. The same injury was addressed by the Supreme Court when it held that sexual harassment that creates a hostile or abusive work environment violates the ban on sex discrimination in employment of Title VII of the Civil Rights Act of 1964. 13

Carefully drafted university regulations would bar the use of words as assault weapons and leave unregulated even the most heinous of ideas when those ideas are presented at times and places and in manners that provide an opportunity for reasoned rebuttal or escape from immediate injury. The history of the development of the right to free speech has been one of carefully evaluating the importance of free expression and its effects on other important societal interests. We have drawn the line between protected and unprotected speech before without dire results. (Courts have, for example, exempted from the protection of the First Amendment obscene speech and speech that disseminates official secrets, that defames or libels another person, or that is used to form a conspiracy or monopoly.) 14

Blacks and other people of color are skeptical about the argument that even the most injurious speech must remain unregulated because, in an unregulated marketplace of ideas, the best ones will rise to the top and gain acceptance. Our experience tells us quite the opposite. We have seen too many demagogues elected by appealing to America's racism. We have seen too many good liberal politicians shy away from the issues that might brand them as being too closely allied with us. 15

Whenever we decide that racist speech must be tolerated because of the importance of maintaining societal tolerance for all unpopular speech, we are asking blacks and other subordinated groups to bear the burden for the good of all. We must be careful that the ease with which we strike the balance against the regulation of racist speech is in no way influenced by the fact that the cost will be borne by others. We must be certain that 16 those who will pay that price are fairly represented in our deliberations and that they are heard.

At the core of the argument that we should resist all government regulation of speech is the ideal that the best cure for bad speech is good, that ideas that affirm equality and the worth of all individuals will ultimately prevail. This is an empty ideal unless those of us who would fight racism are vigilant and unequivocal in that fight. We must look for ways to offer assistance and support to students whose speech and political participation are chilled in a climate of racial harassment. 17

Civil-rights lawyers might consider suing on behalf of blacks whose right to an equal education is denied by a university's failure to ensure a nondiscriminatory educational climate or conditions of employment. We must embark upon the development of a First Amendment jurisprudence grounded in the reality of our history and our contemporary experience. We must think hard about how best to launch legal attacks against the most indefensible forms of hate speech. Good lawyers can create exceptions and narrow interpretations that limit the harm of hate speech without opening the floodgates of censorship. 18

Everyone concerned with these issues must find ways to engage actively in actions that resist and counter the racist ideas that we would have the First Amendment protect. If we fail in this, the victims of hate speech must rightly assume that we are on the oppressors' side. 19

How to Handle Hate on Campus

THE NEW YORK TIMES

How do America's colleges and universities — devoted to free inquiry and expression — cope with racist, sexist, or homophobic speech? A recent Connecticut case illustrates the special complexities of the issue for public institutions. 1

Private colleges and universities have some freedom to regulate behavior; their students attend under an agreement to abide by rules. If a student wished to put up a sign that, for instance, women found offensive, such an institution might condone it on the inside of his door but forbid it on the outside. 2

This editorial is from the December 13, 1989 issue of the *New York Times*.

Public institutions are different. They exercise governmental power and must abide more strictly by the Constitution, including First Amendment guarantees of free speech. 3

The public University of Connecticut is the latest to learn that. After incidents involving racial and sexual slurs and harassment, the university issued rules banning written or spoken "slurs or epithets based on race, sex, ethnic origin, disability, religion, or sexual orientation." 4

Acting under those rules, the university this spring expelled Nina Wu, a student at the Storrs campus, for hanging a handmade poster on the outside of her door listing "homos," among others, as unwelcome. She sued, claiming infringement of her free speech rights. She denied using the offensive term, but the school ruled against her and she conceded the point for purposes of her suit. 5

The university is now settling with her, admitting she has a legal point. It is changing its rules to outlaw only the most incendiary speech "inherently likely to provoke an immediate violent reaction" in a direct personal confrontation. 6

One need not condone hateful speech to conclude that the settlement was prudent and that the changes are appropriate. The previous rules and the expulsion cast a dismaying chill. Some students feared the rules would apply to them even for voicing strong opinions in class. The rules as amended still forbid disruptive conduct. 7

That leaves a lot of emotional hurt unredressed — but colleges can respond to that in other ways. They can condemn hateful intolerance. They can undertake special lectures and teaching. They can offer mediation services and moral support for students who feel abused. 8

It may be hard to maintain respect simultaneously for personal dignity and for free speech, but it can be done within the law. 9

Free Speech on the Campus

NAT HENTOFF

A flier distributed at the University of Michigan some months ago proclaimed that blacks "don't belong in classrooms, they belong hanging from trees." 1

At other campuses around the country, manifestations of racism are becoming commonplace. At Yale, a swastika and the words WHITE POWER! 2

Nat Hentoff is the author of *The First Freedom* and is an editor for the *Village Voice*. This article appeared in the May 1989 issue of the *Progressive*.

were painted on the building housing the University's Afro-American Cultural Center. At Temple University, a White Students Union has been formed with some 130 members.

Swastikas are not directed only at black students. The Nazi symbol has been spray-painted on the Jewish Student Union at Memphis State University. And on a number of campuses, women have been singled out as targets of wounding and sometimes frightening speech. At the law school of the State University of New York at Buffalo, several women students have received anonymous letters characterized by one professor as venomously sexist. 3

These and many more such signs of the resurgence of bigotry and know-nothingism throughout the society — as well as on campus — have to do solely with speech, including symbolic speech. There have also been physical assaults on black students and on black, white, and Asian women students, but the way to deal with physical attacks is clear: Call the police and file a criminal complaint. What is to be done, however, about speech alone — however disgusting, inflammatory, and rawly divisive that speech may be? 4

At more and more colleges, administrators — with the enthusiastic support of black students, women students, and liberal students — have been answering that question by preventing or punishing speech. In public universities, this is a clear violation of the First Amendment. In private colleges and universities, suppression of speech mocks the secular religion of academic freedom and free inquiry. 5

The Student Press Law Center in Washington, D.C. — a vital source of legal support for student editors around the country — reports, for example, that at the University of Kansas, the student host and producer of a radio news program was forbidden by school officials from interviewing a leader of the Ku Klux Klan. So much for free inquiry on that campus. 6

In Madison, Wisconsin, *The Capital Times* ran a story in January about Chancellor Sheila Kaplan of the University of Wisconsin branch at Parkside, who ordered her campus to be scoured of "some anonymously placed white-supremacist hate literature." Sounding like the legendary Mayor Frank ("I am the law") Hague of Jersey City, who booted "bad speech" out of town, Chancellor Kaplan said, "This institution is not a lamppost standing on the street corner. It doesn't belong to everyone." 7

Who decides what speech can be heard or read by everyone? Why, the chancellor, of course. That's what George III used to say, too. 8

University of Wisconsin political science professor Carol Tebben thinks otherwise. She believes university administrators "are getting confused when they are acting as censors and trying to protect students from bad ideas. I don't think students need to be protected from bad ideas. I think they can determine for themselves what ideas are bad." 9

After all, if students are to be "protected" from bad ideas, how are 10
they going to learn to identify and cope with them? Sending such ideas underground simply makes them stronger and more dangerous.

Professor Tebben's conviction that free speech means just that has 11
become a decidedly minority view on many campuses. At the University of Buffalo Law School, the faculty unanimously adopted a "Statement Regarding Intellectual Freedom, Tolerance, and Political Harassment." Its title implies support of intellectual freedom, but the statement warned students that once they enter "this legal community," their right to free speech must become tempered "by the responsibility to promote equality and justice."

Accordingly, swift condemnation will befall anyone who engages in 12
"remarks directed at another's race, sex, religion, national origin, age, or sex preference." Also forbidden are "other remarks based on prejudice and group stereotype."

This ukase is so broad that enforcement has to be alarmingly subjec- 13
tive. Yet the University of Buffalo Law School provides no due-process procedures for a student booked for making any of these prohibited remarks. Conceivably, a student caught playing a Lenny Bruce, Richard Pryor, or Sam Kinison album in his room could be tried for aggravated insensitivity by association.

When I looked into this wholesale cleansing of bad speech at Buffalo, 14
I found it had encountered scant opposition. One protester was David Gerald Jay, a graduate of the law school and a cooperating attorney for the New York Civil Liberties Union. Said the appalled graduate: "Content-based prohibitions constitute prior restraint and should not be tolerated."

You would think that the law professors and administration at this 15
public university might have known that. But hardly any professors dissented, and among the students only members of the conservative Federalist Society spoke up for free speech. The fifty-strong chapter of the National Lawyers Guild was on the other side. After all, it was more important to go on record as vigorously opposing racism and sexism than to expose oneself to charges of insensitivity to these malignancies.

The pressures to have the "right" attitude — as proved by having the 16
"right" language in and out of class — can be stifling. A student who opposes affirmative action, for instance, can be branded a racist.

At the University of California at Los Angeles, the student newspaper 17
ran an editorial cartoon satirizing affirmative action. (A student stops a rooster on campus and asks how the rooster got into UCLA. "Affirmative action," is the answer.) After outraged complaints from various minority groups, the editor was suspended for violating a publications policy against running "articles that perpetuate derogatory or cultural stereotypes." The art director was also suspended.

When the opinion editor of the student newspaper at California State University at Northridge wrote an article asserting that the sanctions against the editor and art director at UCLA amounted to censorship, he was suspended too. 18

At New York University Law School, a student was so disturbed by the pall of orthodoxy at that prestigious institution that he wrote to the school newspaper even though, as he said, he expected his letter to make him a pariah among his fellow students. 19

Barry Endick described the atmosphere at NYU created by "a host of watchdog committees and a generally hostile classroom reception regarding any student comment right of center." This "can be arguably viewed as symptomatic of a prevailing spirit of academic and social intolerance of . . . any idea which is not 'politically correct.'" 20

He went on to say something that might well be posted on campus bulletin boards around the country, though it would probably be torn down at many of them: 21

> We ought to examine why students, so anxious to wield the Fourteenth Amendment, give short shrift to the First. Yes, Virginia, there are racist assholes. And you know what, the Constitution protects them, too.

Not when they engage in violence or vandalism. But when they speak or write, racist assholes fall right into this Oliver Wendell Holmes definition — highly unpopular among bigots, liberals, radicals, feminists, sexists, and college administrators: 22

> If there is any principle of the Constitution that more imperatively calls for attachment than any other, it is the principle of free thought — not free only for those who agree with us, but freedom for the thought we hate.

The language sounds like a pietistic Sunday sermon, but if it ever falls wholly into disuse, neither this publication nor any other journal of opinion — Right or Left — will survive. 23

Sometimes, college presidents and administrators sound as if they fully understand what Holmes was saying. Last year, for example, when *The Daily Pennsylvanian* — speaking for many at the University of Pennsylvania — urged that a speaking invitation to Louis Farrakhan be withdrawn, University President Sheldon Hackney disagreed. 24

"Open expression," said Hackney, "is the fundamental principle of a university." Yet consider what the same Sheldon Hackney did to the free-speech rights of a teacher at his own university. If any story distills the essence of the current decline of free speech on college campuses, it is the Ballad of Murray Dolfman. 25

For twenty-two years, Dolfman, a practicing lawyer in Philadelphia, had been a part-time lecturer in the Legal Studies Department of the Uni- 26 versity of Pennsylvania's Wharton School. For twenty-two years, no complaint had ever been made against him; indeed, his student course-evaluations had been outstanding. Each year students competed to get into his class.

On a November afternoon in 1984, Dolfman was lecturing about personal-service contracts. His style somewhat resembles that of Professor Charles Kingsfield in *The Paper Chase.* Dolfman insists that students he calls on be prepared — or suffer the consequences. He treats all students this way — regardless of race, creed, or sex. 27

This day, Dolfman was pointing out that no one can be forced to work against his or her will — even if a contract has been signed. A court may prevent the resister from working for someone else so long as the contract is in effect but, Dolfman said, there can "be nothing that smacks of involuntary servitude." 28

Where does this concept come from? Dolfman looked around the room. Finally, a cautious hand was raised: "The Constitution?" 29

"Where in the Constitution?" No hands. "The Thirteenth Amendment," said the teacher. So, what does *it* say? The students were looking everywhere but at Dolfman. 30

"We will lose our liberties," Dolfman often told his classes, "if we don't know what they are." 31

On this occasion, he told them that he and other Jews, as ex-slaves, spoke at Passover of the time when they were slaves under the Pharaohs so that they would remember every year what it was like not to be free. 32

"We have ex-slaves here." Dolfman continued, "who should know about the Thirteenth Amendment." He asked black students in the class if they could tell him what was in that amendment. 33

"I wanted them to really think about it," Dolfman told me recently, "and know its history. You're better equipped to fight racism if you know all about those post–Civil War amendments and civil-rights laws." 34

The Thirteenth Amendment provides that "neither slavery nor involuntary servitude . . . shall exist within the United States." 35

The black students in his class did not know what was in that amendment, and Dolfman had them read it aloud. Later, they complained to university officials that they had been hurt and humiliated by having been referred to as ex-slaves. Moreover, they said, they had no reason to be grateful for a constitutional amendment which gave them rights which should never have been denied them — and gave them precious little else. They had not made these points in class, although Dolfman — unlike Professor Kingsfield — encourages rebuttal. 36

Informed of the complaint, Dolfman told the black students he had intended no offense, and he apologized if they had been offended. 37

That would not do — either for the black students or for the administration. Furthermore, there were mounting black-Jewish tensions on 38 campus, and someone had to be sacrificed. Who better than a part-time Jewish teacher with no contract and no union? He was sentenced by — George Orwell would have loved this — the Committee on Academic Freedom and Responsibility.

On his way to the stocks, Dolfman told President Sheldon Hackney that if a part-time instructor "can be punished on this kind of charge, a tenured professor can eventually be booted out, then a dean, and then a president." 39

Hackney was unmoved. Dolfman was banished from the campus for what came to be a year. But first he was forced to make a public apology to the entire university and then he was compelled to attend a "sensitivity and racial awareness" session. Sort of like a Vietnamese reeducation camp. 40

A few conservative professors objected to the stigmatization of Murray Dolfman. I know of no student dissent. Indeed, those students most concerned with making the campus more "sensitive" to diversity exulted in Dolfman's humiliation. So did most liberals on the faculty. 41

If my children were still of college age and wanted to attend the University of Pennsylvania, I would tell them this story. But where else could I encourage them to go? 42

Flag-Saving

MELVIN L. WULF

That President George Bush and members of Congress would denounce the Supreme Court for deciding that flag-burning is a protected exercise of the right to free speech (in *Texas v. Johnson*) was predictable. Less predictable were attempts by otherwise liberal constitutional scholars to appease the superpatriots by offering solutions that would seriously dilute accepted First Amendment principles. 1

A salient fact about this case — and one that most of the press seems to have missed — is that the Supreme Court's ruling simply affirmed a decision of the Texas Court of Criminal Appeals. The Texas court does not include any card-carrying members of the American Civil Liberties Union, which makes even more impressive its opinion recognizing "that the right to differ is the centerpiece of our First Amendment freedoms." (Per- 2

Melvin L. Wulf practices law in New York City and was the legal director of the American Civil Liberties Union from 1962 to 1977. His article appeared in the *Nation* on September 4–11, 1989.

haps we would have been saved all the melodrama if the press had pointed out that the Supreme Court opinion came down in favor of states' rights.)

Despite the example set by the Texas court's language, both Profes- 3
sor Laurence Tribe of Harvard Law School and Professor Burt Neuborne of New York University School of Law (who is also a former legal director of the ACLU) have on this issue departed from strict civil libertarian principles, Tribe more than Neuborne. Tribe's solution to the outcry against the opinion would be to make it a crime to burn the flag under any circumstance. Though this might get around First Amendment objections to a statute that prohibits destruction of the flag only when done for political purposes, it also proscribes one form of effective political expression.

If one is politically engaged, one wants to be able to make political 4
statements with the most powerful tools available. The flag is such a tool, and protesters should be able to express disagreement with the policies it represents by burning or otherwise destroying it, as well as by voting, marching, speaking, and writing. Totemization of the flag is inconsistent with the concept of the First Amendment. There is no good constitutional justification for excluding the flag from the available arsenal of political speech, as Professor Tribe proposes.

Neuborne does not go nearly as far, but he takes a position that is at 5
odds with good First Amendment doctrine. After first assuring readers of his letter to the *New York Times* that no goldarn flag-burner would ever dine at his table, he proposed that flag-burning in a political context should be made criminal when it threatens to provoke violence against the protester. The *Times* endorsed that position in an editorial the day it published Neuborne's letter. But that too is a misguided position.

If expressive conduct is protected by the First Amendment, the state 6
has an absolute duty to protect protesters from any illegal conduct directed against them that might be provoked by their protests. To allow opponents to convert otherwise protected activity into a crime inverts the accepted constitutional principle, which is that speech can be punished when it threatens to incite an audience to take immediate illegal action advocated by the speaker. That is an entirely different kettle of fish from an audience being incited to attack a speaker because it disagrees with his or her speech. As Justice Oliver Wendell Holmes once said, "Every idea is an incitement." If voicing an idea, by actual or symbolic speech, can be made illegal because someone in response threatens to harm the speaker, then no idea will be safe. Everything makes someone angry. Salman Rushdie's novel *The Satanic Verses* made Ayatollah Ruhollah Khomeini *very* angry. The idea that speech that might provoke an illegal response should be punished is a dangerous dilution of the First Amendment, as the Rushdie affair teaches us all too dramatically.

Another strong argument in favor of the flag-burning opinion is that Justices Antonin Scalia and Anthony Kennedy — both ultraconservative Reagan appointees — were two of the five justices in the majority. That these two should join the Court's liberals in upholding the decision shows the power of the idea of the First Amendment. Justice Kennedy, in a short apologia, said, "Sometimes we must make decisions we do not like. We make them because they are right, right in the sense that the law and the Constitution, as we see them, compel the result." It is disappointing that liberals like Tribe and Neuborne would take any position other than absolute support of the majority in the flag-burning case. If burning the flag is done to make a political statement, as it was in the Texas case, it must be protected without qualification. 7

The Dynamics of Flag-Burning

JAMES M. WALL

In its 5–4 decision to extend First Amendment freedoms to cover flag-burning, the U.S. Supreme Court confused signs with symbols. The court majority determined that a law under which a Texas man was convicted for burning a flag during the 1984 Republican National Convention was in violation of that man's right to freedom of expression. Said Justice William J. Brennan in his majority opinion, "If there is a bedrock principle underlying the First Amendment, it is that the government may not prohibit the expression of an idea simply because society finds the idea itself offensive or disagreeable." And certainly one of the more repugnant expressions a citizen can make is to convey disdain for this nation by burning its flag. 1

The decision appears, however, to blur the careful distinction between signs and symbols that theologian Paul Tillich makes in discussing "the meaning of symbol" in *Dynamics of Faith*. Signs, Tillich argues, involve elements of communication which "point beyond themselves to something else." Words are signs in that they connote a meaning common to all those who understand the language being used. But signs, Tillich writes, "do not participate in the reality of that to which they point." Symbols do. 2

Signs can be changed by common agreement. But symbols are not so susceptible to change; symbols are born and they may die, but they can- 3

This argument appeared in the July 5–12, 1989 issue of the *Christian Century*, a journal of which James M. Wall is an editor.

not be changed by popular fiat. Symbols "grow out of the individual or collective unconscious dimension of our being," and they touch a level of reality that cannot, Tillich insists, "be reached in any other way." Thus, visual art, poetry, and other artistic expressions use symbols that have the capacity to touch us in ways that cannot be done otherwise."

Although he did not make Tillich's distinction between sign and symbol in his dissenting opinion, Chief Justice William H. Rehnquist did touch upon some artistic expressions that reveal the symbolic power of our flag. For example, in his "Concord Hymn," Ralph Waldo Emerson describes the first skirmishes of the Revolutionary War with these lines: 4

> By the rude bridge that arched the flood,
> Their flag to April's breeze unfurled,
> Here once the embattled farmers stood.

Rehnquist also cited John Greenleaf Whittier's Civil War poem "Barbara Frietchie," which includes these familiar lines: "Shoot, if you must, this old gray head, / But spare your country's flag, she said." 5

Undoubtedly there will be too much July Fourth rhetoric this year focusing on the Supreme Court ruling. But even if the arguments are self-serving and politically motivated, the flag remains a potent symbol for this nation. As Tillich reminds us, a symbol "participates in that to which it points; the flag participates in the power and dignity of the nation for which it stands." As a symbol, then, the flag is more than a device for communicating. And it is not the flag that took us into unpopular wars, or prompted leaders to lie or deceive, or designed policies to exploit the poor. Burn the flag and you do more than express a dissenting opinion; you attack the nation itself. As a symbol which participates in the "power and dignity of the nation for which it stands," the flag is not a sign representing opinions and actions that may generate opposition. It is, in its fluttering presence on a flagpole, the nation itself. 6

In his dissent, Chief Justice Rehnquist pointed to the flag's connection to "thousands of our countrymen [who] died on foreign soil fighting for the American cause." It is appropriate to make that connection between the flag and making the supreme sacrifice for one's country. This nation is more than its wars, more than the violent defense of freedom. And the flag is not just a sign pointing to the nation's history; it is the symbol of the nation in perpetuity. (Flags can die, of course, Tillich reminds us — if a historic catastrophe "changes the reality of the nation which it symbolizes." Tillich was no doubt thinking of the Nazi symbol that once constituted the flag of Germany, a flag no longer in use because of a change in reality.) 7

When one visits a United States embassy in a foreign nation and sees the flag displayed over that small parcel of land, one experiences more than a "sign" saying "United States." Rather, one senses the presence not 8 of something ultimate but of the land to which one is committed. The flag does not fly as a sign pointing to policies or leaders; it flies as a symbol of the nation itself.

In their majority decision the justices carefully limited the protection 9
of flag-burning to an expression of dissent, and specifically excluded protection in those instances in which vandalism is involved or in which the flag's desecration incites violence. The opinion, however, did not represent an ideological consensus. Justice Anthony M. Kennedy, the most recent appointee to the court, had been expected to side with the conservatives, but in this case he joined fellow conservative Justice Antonin Scalia and liberal Justices Brennan, Harry A. Blackmun, and Thurgood Marshall. In his separate concurring opinion, Justice Kennedy adhered to his strict constructionist view of the Constitution, insisting that the Texas law against flag-burning had to be "judged against a pure command of the Constitution." He admitted, further, that "the hard fact is that sometimes we must make decisions we do not like. We make them because they are right, right in the sense that the law and the Constitution, as we see them, compel the result." He also acknowledged that so great is his respect for the process of court actions that only in a rare case would it be appropriate to "express distaste for the result, perhaps for fear of undermining a valued principle that dictates the decision. This is one of those rare cases."

Had Kennedy considered Tillich's distinction between sign and sym- 10
bol, he might not have come down on the side he finds "distasteful." He appears to confuse the two when he argues that "though symbols often are what we ourselves make of them, the flag is constant in expressing beliefs Americans share, beliefs in law and peace and that freedom which sustains the human spirit." As a sign, the flag would indeed express beliefs; but as a symbol, the flag is more than an expression, more than a means of conveying the importance of law and peace and freedom. The flag is a symbol that participates in the reality of the nation itself, and, in Tillich's phrase, "an attack on the flag is felt as an attack on the majesty of the group in which it is acknowledged."

The First Amendment's "free-speech" clause guarantees unpopular 11
expressions of opinion against the nation, but the Constitution does not protect direct attacks on the nation itself. As Justice Brennan states, the court has long recognized that the protection of free speech "does not end at the spoken or written word." In its decision to overturn the law in Texas (and forty-seven other states) forbidding the burning of the flag, the court determined that, in Justice Kennedy's phrase, "the flag protects those who hold it in contempt." But Chief Justice Rehnquist insisted that Gregory L. Johnson, the defendant in the Texas case, had "every conceivable form of verbal expression to express his deep disapproval of national policy."

In making this ruling, it could be argued that the justices in the majority failed to distinguish between sign and symbol. If we understand the flag as that unique symbol which participates in the "power and dignity of the nation for which it stands," then we do not violate the Constitution when we protect that symbol from desecration. Justice Kennedy should have followed his instincts and stayed on the conservative side on this one. 12

Legislating the Imagination

JON PARELES

In South Korea and East Germany until recently, the government had to approve every song, book, film, or play. In Singapore, the Undesirable Publications Act forbids song lyrics that make references to drugs or have obscene connotations. And if legislators in about a dozen states have their way, the United States will join such havens of enlightenment in allowing the power of the government to regulate the arts. What they're up to, in effect, is an attempt to regulate the imagination. 1

The Pennsylvania House of Representatives recently passed legislation that prohibits the sale — to anyone — of recordings with lyrics on a number of rude topics unless their packages are labeled as follows: "WARNING: May contain explicit lyrics descriptive of or advocating one or more of the following: suicide, incest, bestiality, sadomasochism, sexual activity in a violent context, murder, morbid violence, illegal use of drugs or alcohol. PARENTAL ADVISORY." (See p. 501.) 2

The labels are to be fluorescent yellow and not readily removable. While the Pennsylvania Senate considers the bill, similar measures are pending in Virginia, Arizona, Iowa, New Mexico, Illinois, Oklahoma, Delaware, and Kansas. A Missouri version adds "sodomy" to the possible offenses, while one in Florida, which adds "sexual activity" to the list, would prohibit selling stickered albums to minors. Unlike movie ratings, which are voluntarily applied by film companies, the state laws would carry the threat of fines and jail terms for sellers of recordings. 3

It's not a free-speech issue, advocates say, just a label that provides consumer information. That it also makes recordings look like radioactive waste barrels isn't their concern. 4

Jon Pareles is a music critic for the *New York Times*, where this article appeared on February 11, 1990.

5 Whether or not they survive constitutional tests, the bills are the latest fruit of the uproar raised over rock lyrics by the Parents' Music Resource Center, the Arlington, Virginia–based group that pressured recording companies into voluntarily placing "Explicit Lyrics — Parental Advisory" stickers on many potentially offensive albums — a few dozen of the nearly 3,000 albums released every year.

6 The group has always asserted that it does not advocate legislation and quietly gave up its initial idea about citing lyrics for specific offenses, admitting the difficulties of interpretation. (In the group's newsletter, *The Record*, songs are categorized, targeted albums are still listed without explanations, and readers are urged to write their legislators about material they don't like.)

7 But the group's tactics — selective and often misleading excerpts from lyrics, exaggeration of both the virulence and quantity of offensive material — are now being replayed in state legislatures, as legislatures strive to equate some recordings with pornography. In an election year, an antismut crusade is always boffo.

8 Labeling is certainly a clever tactic. To be obscene, under Supreme Court guidelines, a publication has to be pornographic through and through, without any "redeeming social value" — not one song of a dozen or some four-letter words. It also has to impress a reasonable adult — not just the "most susceptible" audience — as being geared exclusively to prurient interest. (Scare groups often posit a susceptible adolescent, on the brink of violence or suicide, as the typical rock listener. But beyond anecdotal cases, no research has established causal links between entertainment choices and actions.)

9 Labeling trickily sidesteps such stringent tests. Slap on a sticker because somebody, sometime, might complain, and a whole album is categorized by its nastiest moment, no discussion necessary. Where criticism explains, examines, and sometimes condemns the meaning gleaned from lyrics — free speech at work — lists like those published by the Parents' Music Resource Center and the stickers proposed by legislators are blanket condemnations: The album is evil.

10 Hardly any albums — perhaps 2 Live Crew's "As Nasty as They Wanna Be," which is so raunchy that the group released an alternate (and poorly selling) version, "As Clean as They Gotta Be" — would fail the legal obscenity tests. But labeling would be more pervasive. The center's newsletter lists (without explanation) current albums by Aerosmith and Love and Rockets; neither performers nor manufacturers thought they needed labels.

11 Grouping categories together is ingenious. In all of rock, there are probably fewer songs about bestiality than about molecular biology, un-

less Clifton Chenier's bayou classic, "I'm a Hog for You, Baby" counts. But a label doesn't distinguish between bestiality and adultery, a not infrequent topic in any narrative form; better slap a sticker on the Bible. Meanwhile, why worry about interpretation? "Descriptive of or advocating" covers a lot of ground; antisuicide or antidrug songs would be targets along with their opposites. And somebody's going to have to explain to me the difference between morbid violence and other kinds.

Those yellow stickers would be scary in themselves. They'd be a lot more prominent than package warnings on, for instance, cigarettes, which actually kill people. And since every country album — what's country music without booze or adultery? — along with nearly every opera (adultery, morbid violence, sadomasochism) or collection of patriotic songs (violence) will have a sticker, record stores will look awfully forbidding. That, in the end, seems to be the plan. Any leftover stickers could always be used on books. 12

Music, like the other arts, shares dreams, conjectures, and fantasies in ways that aren't usually as simple as indoctrination. Art is fictive and ambiguous, and it's a way to explore both the ordinary and the forbidden in a symbolic realm where nobody gets hurt; the popular-culture marketplace strives to deliver a fabrication to fit every daydream. But music's amorphous playfulness makes some people nervous. They seem to assume that listeners can't distinguish between fantasy and reality — or, going even further, that fantasy overwhelms reality. 13

But is it that easy? William Bennett, the United States drug policy director, recently asserted that purposeful, forthright drug education programs don't "inoculate children against drug abuse." Record labelers, by contrast, insist that a line or two about drugs, pro or con, garbled over a loud beat, can send an impressionable child down the road to perdition. 14

Initiatives like the Pennsylvania bill and the Helms amendment that would have prohibited federal financing of "obscene or indecent" art are attempts to rein in the public's fantasy life — to put certain areas of the imagination off limits, to equate a fleeting adulterous longing with violent murder or bestiality, to close down the mental playground where creativity flourishes alongside sinful daydreams. 15

George Clinton, mastermind of Parliament-Funkadelic, often leads his audiences in a chant: "Think! It ain't illegal yet!" Not at the moment, but legislators are working on it. 16

Not Just a Few Prudes . . .

DAVID J. MELTZ

To the Editor:

Jon Pareles's column against labeling recordings with parental advisories ["Legislating the Imagination," February 11] is disturbing at several levels. First, he is correct in stating that it is unfair to equate murder, illegal drug and alcohol use, and bestiality in a blanket sticker. He also points out the difficulty in determining what is obscenity and the fact that an album would have to be categorized by its "nastiest moment," leading to misleading labeling. He could have mentioned that the proposed labels make no mention of sexism, racism, or homophobic gay bashing. He could have added the chilling effect such labels would have on creativity, pitting artists against businessmen at record companies. 1

He then weakens his position by raising nonsensical arguments about the yellow color of the stickers ("scary in themselves") and the look they would give to the records ("like radioactive waste barrels") and the record stores ("awfully forbidding"). And Mr. Pareles is, I believe, a bit disingenuous when he denies understanding the difference between morbid violence and other kinds. 2

Ultimately, however, my main objection to his column is the fact that it never once addresses the concerns of the parents and legislators who support these bills — and it is precisely because industry representatives are guilty of that disregard that such bills may become law. Choosing to portray the labeling movement as intended to "regulate imagination" rather than providing parents with information as to their children's exposure to things that *many*, not just a few prudes or crazies, find offensive, is both dishonest and a tactical error. Such remarks as "Any leftover stickers could be used on books" are not helpful and merely demagogic. 3

As a lifelong liberal I oppose censorship, but I have not found movie rating to be onerous or unfair, even though far from perfect. Moreover, Mr. Pareles intentionally blurs the line between general censorship and that directed at children. Again, very few liberals find it inappropriate to keep certain magazines and videotapes out of the reach of children while opposing a blanket ban on their sale. The issue is not one of lyrics sending an "impressionable child down the road to perdition" but of responsible parents' concern about what their children are listening to when the lyrics are not available without buying the product. 4

This response to Jon Pareles's "Legislating the Imagination" appeared in the March 4, 1990 *New York Times*.

WARNING:

Contains lyrics or matter which describes or advocates one or more of the following:
- suicide
- explicit sexual acts
  including but not
  limited to rape,
  sodomy,
  incest,
  bestiality, and
  sadomasochism;
- murder
- morbid violence, or
- the use of illegal drugs

WARNING:

This product contains backmasking that makes a verbal statement when this program is played backward

WARNING:

May contain explicit lyrics descriptive of or advocating one or more of the following:
- suicide
- incest
- bestiality
- sadomasochism
- sexual activity in a violent context
- murder
- morbid violence
- illegal use of drugs or alcohol

PARENTAL ADVISORY

Labels proposed for album, compact disc, and cassette covers in Missouri (above left), Rhode Island (top right) and Pennsylvania (right).

As with so many difficult issues today, the extremists should recognize that their positions alienate moderates and give aid and comfort to their opponents. I do not like the proposed labels, but as a parent I find them preferable to the total lack of self-regulation offered by Mr. Pareles and the pop music industry. Labeling contents is not censorship, no matter how you make it try to fit that Procrustean bed, and the industry would do itself and everyone else a service by taking the lead in this issue, while it still has the chance to do so. 5

— David J. Meltz, M.D.

THINKING AND WRITING ABOUT FREEDOM OF SPEECH

Questions for Discussion and Writing

1. According to Garry Wills, why is "censure" superior to censorship? (Look up or ask about the specific references in his essay if you aren't familiar with them.) Would he agree with Pareles that labeling rock music albums is a form of censorship?
2. After reading the University of Michigan policy and the article by Lawrence, can you decide on the specific kinds of speech, if any, that should be prohibited on campus? Does the place in which the speech is expressed make a difference? What principles guided you in your decision?
3. Hentoff argues for exposure of students to bad ideas as well as good ones. (See page 6 for a quotation from *Aeropagitica*, in which John Milton makes the same point.) What bad ideas does Hentoff have in mind? Spell out the educational advantages of such exposure.

   Hentoff uses examples freely to argue his case. Do you think that all his examples support the points he wants to make? What is his main criticism of university officials? Is it justified?
4. Summarize Wall's detailed rebuttal to the Supreme Court decision on flag-burning. Is the flag, as Wall argues, a symbol which must not be abused? Or is it, as Wulf claims, an object that can be used to express dissent? What arguments does Wulf use to defend the Supreme Court decision?
5. What values are in conflict in the debate over the offensive lyrics in rock music? One writer has pointed out that while commentator Andy Rooney was suspended by CBS in 1990 for allegedly making racist and homophobic remarks, a rap group was nominated in the same year for a Grammy award despite racist, sexist, and anti-Semitic language in its songs. Does the different treatment accorded Rooney show inconsistency on the part of the media? If not, what is the justification for it?

Topics for Research

Recent extensions of freedom of speech by the courts (e.g., the right to beg on the street, the right to abuse people verbally)

The Andy Rooney case: A violation of free speech?

Lyrics in rock music: How dangerous are they?

Public funds for offensive art (see the cases of Robert Mapplethorpe and Andres Serrano, whose works scandalized some members of Congress in the summer and fall of 1989). Is withdrawal of public funds a "regulation of the imagination"?

CHAPTER 17

Legalizing Drugs

Almost every public opinion poll shows that Americans regard the widespread use of drugs as our number one problem. This concern is based on fears of the consequences of current drug use — crime, social degradation, disease — which in some places have reached epidemic proportions.

For most of the nineteenth century, however, Americans consumed large quantities of heroin and cocaine, which were available without a prescription and at low cost from drug stores, grocery stores, and through the mail. But, as one commentator points out, "drugs were not considered a menace to society." In 1914 the Harrison Narcotic Act made drugs illegal. Historians attribute the passage of this law to "missionary convictions and sympathies" as well as prejudice against Chinese-Americans, with whom opium use was associated.

The difficulty of solving the drug problem today — that is, vastly reducing drug use throughout the population — is compounded by opposing views concerning the best solution. One approach calls for vigorous law enforcement against producers, sellers, and buyers. Another approach emphasizes education about the dangers of drugs and treatment for addiction. At present both of these strategies are at work, but the results so far have been unimpressive. Finally, legalization of drugs, a solution that

Americans have long rejected — a poll in 1988 showed that 90 percent favor keeping drugs illegal — has resurfaced as a serious alternative to criminal prosecution and imprisonment for drug dealers and users. Advocates of legalization consider prosecution and punishment to be a misuse of resources and a violation of individual rights.

Limited legalization exists in some European countries, but the opponents of legalization in this country insist that even positive results, however defined, in countries like Switzerland and the Netherlands would not be relevant to the United States.

The big questions in the debate are both practical and moral. Would legalization lead to increased use? If so, would there be undesirable social consequences? Are the political and financial costs of prohibition too high? Perhaps the basic question is whether government should deny people the right to use harmful substances.

Drugs

GORE VIDAL

It is possible to stop most drug addiction in the United States within a very short time. Simply make all drugs available and sell them at cost. Label each drug with a precise description of what effect — good and bad — the drug will have on the taker. This will require heroic honesty. Don't say that marijuana is addictive or dangerous when it is neither, as millions of people know — unlike "speed," which kills most unpleasantly, or heroin, which is addictive and difficult to kick. 1

For the record, I have tried — once — almost every drug and liked none, disproving the popular Fu Manchu theory that a single whiff of opium will enslave the mind. Nevertheless many drugs are bad for certain people to take and they should be told why in a sensible way. 2

Along with exhortation and warning, it might be good for our citizens to recall (or learn for the first time) that the United States was the creation of men who believed that each man has the right to do what he wants with his own life as long as he does not interfere with his neighbor's pursuit of happiness (that his neighbor's idea of happiness is persecuting others does confuse matters a bit). 3

This is a startling notion to the current generation of Americans. They reflect a system of public education which has made the Bill of 4

Novelist and man of letters Gore Vidal has twice been a candidate for Congress. This essay first appeared in the *New York Times Magazine* on September 26, 1970.

Rights, literally, unacceptable to a majority of high school graduates (see the annual Purdue reports) who now form the "silent majority" — a phrase which that underestimated wit Richard Nixon took from Homer who used it to describe the dead.

5 Now one can hear the warning rumble begin: If everyone is allowed to take drugs everyone will and the GNP will decrease, the Commies will stop us from making everyone free, and we shall end up a race of zombies, passively murmuring "groovy" to one another. Alarming thought. Yet it seems most unlikely that any reasonably sane person will become a drug addict if he knows in advance what addiction is going to be like.

6 Is everyone reasonably sane? Some people will always become drug addicts just as some people will always become alcoholics, and it is just too bad. Every man, however, has the power (and should have the legal right) to kill himself if he chooses. But since most men don't, they won't be mainliners either. Nevertheless, forbidding people things they like or think they might enjoy only makes them want those things all the more. This psychological insight is, for some mysterious reason, perennially denied our governors.

7 It is a lucky thing for the American moralist that our country has always existed in a kind of time-vacuum: We have no public memory of anything that happened before last Tuesday. No one in Washington today recalls what happened during the years alcohol was forbidden to the people by a Congress that thought it had a divine mission to stamp out Demon Rum — launching, in the process, the greatest crime wave in the country's history, causing thousands of deaths from bad alcohol, and creating a general (and persisting) contempt among the citizenry for the laws of the United States.

8 The same thing is happening today. But the government has learned nothing from past attempts at prohibition, not to mention repression.

9 Last year when the supply of Mexican marijuana was slightly curtailed by the Feds, the pushers got the kids hooked on heroin and deaths increased dramatically, particularly in New York. Whose fault? Evil men like the Mafiosi? Permissive Dr. Spock? Wild-eyed Dr. Leary? No.

10 The government of the United States was responsible for those deaths. The bureaucratic machine has a vested interest in playing cops and robbers. Both the Bureau of Narcotics and the Mafia want strong laws against the sale and use of drugs because if drugs are sold at cost there would be no money in it for anyone.

11 If there was no money in it for the Mafia, there would be no friendly playground pushers, and addicts would not commit crimes to pay for the next fix. Finally, if there was no money in it, the Bureau of Narcotics would wither away, something they are not about to do without a struggle.

Will anything sensible be done? Of course not. The American people are as devoted to the idea of sin and its punishment as they are to making money — and fighting drugs is nearly as big a business as pushing them. Since the combination of sin and money is irresistible (particularly to the professional politician), the situation will only grow worse. 12

Should Drugs Be Legalized?

WILLIAM J. BENNETT

Since I took command of the war on drugs, I have learned from former secretary of state George Shultz that our concept of fighting drugs is "flawed." The only thing to do, he says, is to "make it possible for addicts to buy drugs at some regulated place." Conservative commentator William F. Buckley, Jr., suggests I should be "fatalistic" about the flood of cocaine from South America and simply "let it in." Syndicated columnist Mike Royko contends it would be easier to sweep junkies out of the gutters "than to fight a hopeless war" against the narcotics that send them there. Labeling our efforts "bankrupt," federal judge Robert W. Sweet opts for legalization, saying, "If our society can learn to stop using butter, it should be able to cut down on cocaine." 1

Flawed, fatalistic, hopeless, bankrupt! I never realized surrender was so fashionable until I assumed this post. 2

Though most Americans are overwhelmingly determined to go toe-to-toe with the foreign drug lords and neighborhood pushers, a small minority believe that enforcing drug laws imposes greater costs on society than do drugs themselves. Like addicts seeking immediate euphoria, the legalizers want peace at any price, even though it means the inevitable proliferation of a practice that degrades, impoverishes, and kills. 3

I am acutely aware of the burdens drug enforcement places upon us. It consumes economic resources we would like to use elsewhere. It is sometimes frustrating, thankless, and often dangerous. But the consequences of *not* enforcing drug laws would be far more costly. Those consequences involve the intrinsically destructive nature of drugs and the toll they exact from our society in hundreds of thousands of lost and broken lives . . . human potential never realized . . . time stolen from families and jobs . . . precious spiritual and economic resources squandered. 4

William J. Bennett is the director of National Drug Control Policy in Washington, D.C. This article is from the March 1990 issue of *Reader's Digest.*

That is precisely why virtually every civilized society has found it 5 necessary to exert some form of control over mind-altering substances and why this war is so important. Americans feel up to their hips in drugs now. They would be up to their necks under legalization.

Even limited experiments in drug legalization have shown that when 6 drugs are more widely available, addiction skyrockets. In 1975 Italy liberalized its drug law and now has one of the highest heroin-related death rates in Western Europe. In Alaska, where marijuana was decriminalized in 1975, the easy atmosphere has increased usage of the drug, particularly among children. Nor does it stop there. Some Alaskan schoolchildren now tout "coco puffs," marijuana cigarettes laced with cocaine.

Many legalizers concede that drug legalization might increase use, 7 but they shrug off the matter. "It may well be that there would be more addicts, and I would regret that result," says Nobel laureate economist Milton Friedman. The late Harvard Medical School psychiatry professor Norman Zinberg, a longtime proponent of "responsible" drug use, admitted that "use of now-illicit drugs would certainly increase. Also casualties probably would increase."

In fact, Dr. Herbert D. Kleber of Yale University, my deputy in charge 8 of demand reduction, predicts legalization might cause a "five-to-sixfold increase" in cocaine use. But legalizers regard this as a necessary price for the "benefits" of legalization. What benefits?

1. Legalization will take the profit out of drugs. The result supposedly 9 will be the end of criminal drug pushers and the big foreign drug wholesalers, who will turn to other enterprises because nobody will need to make furtive and dangerous trips to his local pusher.

But what, exactly, would the brave new world of legalized drugs look 10 like? Buckley stresses that "adults get to buy the stuff at carefully regulated stores." (Would you want one in *your* neighborhood?) Others, like Friedman, suggest we sell the drugs at "ordinary retail outlets."

Former City University of New York sociologist Georgette Bennett as- 11 sures us that "brand-name competition will be prohibited" and that strict quality control and proper labeling will be overseen by the Food and Drug Administration. In a touching egalitarian note, she adds that "free drugs will be provided at government clinics" for addicts too poor to buy them.

Almost all legalizers point out that the price of drugs will fall, even 12 though the drugs will be heavily taxed. Buckley, for example, argues that somehow federal drugstores will keep the price "low enough to discourage a black market but high enough to accumulate a surplus to be used for drug education."

Supposedly, drug sales will generate huge amounts of revenue, which 13
will then be used to tell the public not to use drugs and to treat those who don't listen.

In reality, this tax would only allow government to *share* the drug 14
profits now garnered by criminals. Legalizers would have to tax drugs heavily in order to pay for drug education and treatment programs. Criminals could undercut the official price and still make huge profits. What alternative would the government have? Cut the price until it was within the lunch-money budget of the average sixth-grade student?

2. Legalization will eliminate the black market. Wrong. And not just 15
because the regulated prices could be undercut. Many legalizers admit that drugs such as crack or PCP are simply too dangerous to allow the shelter of the law. Thus criminals will provide what the government will not. "As long as drugs that people very much want remain illegal, a black market will exist," says legalization advocate David Boaz of the libertarian Cato Institute.

Look at crack. In powdered form, cocaine was an expensive indul- 16
gence. But street chemists found that a better and far less expensive — and far more dangerous — high could be achieved by mixing cocaine with baking soda and heating it. Crack was born, and "cheap" coke invaded low-income communities with furious speed.

An ounce of powdered cocaine might sell on the street for $1200. 17
That same ounce can produce 370 vials of crack at $10 each. Ten bucks seems like a cheap hit, but crack's intense ten- to fifteen-minute high is followed by an unbearable depression. The user wants more crack, thus starting a rapid and costly descent into addiction.

If government drugstores do not stock crack, addicts will find it in the 18
clandestine market or simply bake it themselves from their legally purchased cocaine.

Currently crack is being laced with insecticides and animal tranquiliz- 19
ers to heighten its effect. Emergency rooms are now warned to expect victims of "sandwiches" and "moon rocks," life-threatening smokable mixtures of heroin and crack. Unless the government is prepared to sell these deadly variations of dangerous drugs, it will perpetuate a criminal black market by default.

And what about children and teenagers? They would obviously be 20
barred from drug purchases, just as they are prohibited from buying beer and liquor. But pushers will continue to cater to these young customers with the old, favorite come-ons — a couple of free fixes to get them hooked. And what good will antidrug education be when these youngsters observe their older brothers and sisters, parents, and friends lighting up and shooting up with government permission?

Legalization will give us the worst of both worlds: millions of *new* drug users *and* a thriving criminal black market. 21

3. Legalization will dramatically reduce crime. "It is the high price of drugs that leads addicts to robbery, murder, and other crimes," says Ira Glasser, executive director of the American Civil Liberties Union. A study by the Cato Institute concludes: "Most, if not all 'drug-related murders' are the result of drug prohibition." 22

But researchers tell us that many drug-related felonies are committed by people involved in crime *before* they started taking drugs. The drugs, so routinely available in criminal circles, make the criminals more violent and unpredictable. 23

Certainly there are some kill-for-a-fix crimes, but does any rational person believe that a cut-rate price for drugs at a government outlet will stop such psychopathic behavior? The fact is that under the influence of drugs, normal people do not act normally, and abnormal people behave in chilling and horrible ways. DEA agents told me about a teenage addict in Manhattan who was smoking crack when he sexually abused and caused permanent internal injuries to his one-month-old daughter. 24

Children are among the most frequent victims of violent, drug-related crimes that have nothing to do with the cost of acquiring the drugs. In Philadelphia in 1987 more than half the child-abuse fatalities involved at least one parent who was a heavy drug user. Seventy-three percent of the child-abuse deaths in New York City in 1987 involved parental drug use. 25

In my travels to the ramparts of the drug war, I have seen nothing to support the legalizers' argument that lower drug prices would reduce crime. Virtually everywhere I have gone, police and DEA agents have told me that crime rates are highest where crack is cheapest. 26

4. Drug use should be legal since users only harm themselves. Those who believe this should stand beside the medical examiner as he counts the thirty-six bullet wounds in the shattered corpse of a three-year-old who happened to get in the way of his mother's drug-crazed boyfriend. They should visit the babies abandoned by cocaine-addicted mothers — infants who already carry the ravages of addiction in their own tiny bodies. They should console the devastated relatives of the nun who worked in a homeless shelter and was stabbed to death by a crack addict enraged that she would not stake him to a fix. 27

Do drug addicts only harm themselves) Here is a former cocaine addict describing the compulsion that quickly draws even the most "responsible" user into irresponsible behavior: "Everything is about getting high, and any means necessary to get there becomes rational. If it means stealing something from somebody close to you, lying to your family, 28 borrowing money from people you know you can't pay back, writing checks you know you can't cover, you do all those things — things that are totally against everything you have ever believed in."

Society pays for this behavior, and not just in bigger insurance premiums, losses from accidents, and poor job performance. We pay in the loss of a priceless social currency as families are destroyed, trust between friends is betrayed, and promising careers are never fulfilled. I cannot imagine sanctioning behavior that would increase that toll. 29

I find no merit in the legalizers' case. The simple fact is that drug use is wrong. And the moral argument, in the end, is the most compelling argument. A citizen in a drug-induced haze, whether on his backyard deck or on a mattress in a ghetto crack house, is not what the founding fathers meant by the "pursuit of happiness." Despite the legalizers' argument that drug use is a matter of "personal freedom," our nation's notion of liberty is rooted in the ideal of a self-reliant citizenry. Helpless wrecks in treatment centers, men chained by their noses to cocaine — these people are slaves. 30

Imagine if, in the darkest days of 1940, Winston Churchill had rallied the West by saying, "This war looks hopeless, and besides, it will cost too much. Hitler can't be *that* bad. Let's surrender and see what happens." That is essentially what we hear from the legalizers. 31

This war *can* be won. I am heartened by indications that education and public revulsion are having an effect on drug use. The National Institute on Drug Abuse's latest survey of current users shows a 37-percent *decrease* in drug consumption since 1985. Cocaine is down 50 percent; marijuana use among young people is at its lowest rate since 1972. In my travels I've been encouraged by signs that Americans are fighting back. 32

I am under no illusion that such developments, however hopeful, mean the war is over. We need to involve more citizens in the fight, increase pressure on drug criminals, and build on antidrug programs that have proved to work. This will not be easy. But the moral and social costs of surrender are simply too great to contemplate. 33

Thinking about Drug Legalization

JAMES OSTROWSKI

Defining the Issue

Much of the confusion surrounding drug policy discussions could be alleviated by asking the right question initially. The question that must be addressed in determining whether to legalize drugs is this: Do drug laws do more harm than good? 1

The focus here is not how dangerous drugs are or how much damage drug users inflict upon themselves. If these factors were decisive, then surely alcohol and tobacco would be banned. Rather, the proper focus is how effective drug laws are in preventing damage from drugs, compared with the amount of injury the laws themselves cause. 2

With this emphasis in mind, the respective burdens of proof resting upon the parties to the debate can now be specified. Supporters of prohibition must demonstrate *all* of the following: 3

1. that drug use would increase substantially after legalization;
2. that the harm caused by any increased use would not be offset by the increased safety of legal drug use;
3. that the harm caused by any increased use would not be offset by a reduction in the use of dangerous drugs that are already legal (e.g., alcohol and tobacco); and
4. that the harm caused by any increased drug use not offset by (2) or (3) would exceed the harm now caused by the side effects of prohibition (e.g., crime and corruption).

In the absence of data supporting these propositions, neither the theoretical danger of illegal drugs nor their actual harmful effects can be sufficient basis for prohibition. Neither can the bare fact, if proven, that illegal drug use would rise under legalization.

Prohibitionists face a daunting task — one that no one has yet accomplished or, apparently, even attempted. It might be noted, parenthetically, that a 1984 study by the Research Triangle Institute on the economic costs of drug abuse has been erroneously cited in support of drug prohibition. This report, which estimates the cost of drug abuse at 4

James Ostrowski, an attorney, was vice chairman of the New York County Lawyers Association Committee on Law Reform. His article appeared in the *Cato Institute Policy Analysis* on May 25, 1989.

$60 billion for 1983, is not, and was not intended to be, an evaluation of the efficacy of prohibition or the wisdon of legalization. It does not mention the terms "legalization" and "decriminalization" and makes no attempt to separate the costs attributable to drug use per se from the costs attributable to the illegality of drug use. In fact, the study seems to include some costs of *legal* drugs in its estimates. Many of the costs cited are clearly the result of prohibition, for example, interdiction costs ($677 million). Furthermore, the report considers only costs that prohibition has failed to prevent, making no attempt to measure the costs prevented — or caused — by prohibition. In its present form, the study is therefore almost entirely irrelevant to the issue of legalizing drugs.

The case for legalization is sustained if *any* of the following proposi- 5
tions is true:

1. prohibition has no substantial impact on the level of illegal drug use;
2. prohibition increases illegal drug use;
3. prohibition merely redistributes drug use from illegal drugs to harmful legal drugs; or
4. even though prohibition might decrease the use of illegal drugs, the negative effects of prohibition outweigh the beneficial effects of reduced illegal drug use.

This paper relies primarily upon point (4) and secondarily upon points 6
(1) and (3). The paper does not rely upon point (2), but Edward Brecher presented much historical evidence for that point in his masterly work *Licit and Illicit Drugs*, coauthored by the editors of *Consumer Reports*.

Street Crime by Drug Users

Drug laws greatly increase the price of illegal drugs, often forcing 7
users to steal to get the money to obtain them. Although difficult to estimate, the black market prices of heroin and cocaine appear to be about 100 times greater than their pharmaceutical prices. For example, a hospital-dispensed dose of morphine (a drug from which heroin is relatively easily derived) costs only pennies; legal cocaine costs about $20 per ounce. It is frequently estimated that at least 40 percent of all property crime in the United States is committed by drug users so that they can maintain their habits. That amounts to about to about 4 million crimes per year and $7.5 billion in stolen property.

Supporters of prohibition have traditionally used drug-related crime 8
as a simplistic argument for enforcement: Stop drug use to stop drug-related crime. They have even exaggerated the amount of such crime in the hopes of demonstrating a need for larger budgets and greater powers. But in recent years, the more astute prohibitionists have noticed that drug-related crime is in fact drug-*law*-related. Thus, in many cases they

have begun to argue that even if drugs were legal and thus relatively inexpensive, drug users would still commit crimes simply because they are criminals at heart.

The fact is, while some researchers have questioned the causal con- 9
nection between illegal drugs and street crime, many studies over a long period have confirmed what every inner-city dweller already knows: Drug users steal to get the money to buy expensive illegal drugs. These studies were reviewed in 1985 in an article entitled "Narcotics and Crime: An Analysis of Existing Evidence for a Causal Relationship." The authors conclude:

> Heroin addiction can be shown to dramatically increase property crime levels. . . . A high proportion of addicts' preaddiction criminality consists of minor and drug offenses, while postaddiction criminality is characterized much more by property crime.

Moreover, prohibition also stimulates crime by

- criminalizing users of illegal drugs, creating disrespect for the law;
- forcing users into daily contact with professional criminals, which often leads to arrest and prison records that make legitimate employment difficult to obtain;
- discouraging legitimate employment because of the need to "hustle" for drug money;
- encouraging young people to become criminals by creating an extremely lucrative black market in drugs;
- destroying, through drug crime, the economic viability of low-income neighborhoods, leaving young people fewer alternatives to working in the black market; and
- removing the settling of drug-related disputes from the legal process, creating a context of violence for the buying and selling of drugs.

Every property crime committed by a drug user is potentially a vio- 10
lent crime. Many victims are beaten and severely injured, and 1,600 are murdered each year. Last year, a sixteen-year-old boy murdered thirty-nine-year-old Eli Wald of Brooklyn, father of a baby girl, taking $200 to buy crack. Another New York City crack user murdered five people in an eight-day period to get the money to buy crack. The user survived the crack, but his victims did not survive the user.

Black Market Violence

Prohibition also causes what the media and police misname "drug- 11
related violence." This *prohibition*-related violence includes all the random shootings and murders associated with black market drug trans-

actions: ripoffs, eliminating the competition, killing informers, and killing suspected informers.

Those who doubt that prohibition is responsible for this violence need only note the absence of violence in the legal drug market. For example, there is no violence associated with the production, distribution, and sale of alcohol. Such violence was ended by the repeal of Prohibition. 12

The President's Commission on Organized Crime estimates a total of about seventy drug-market murders yearly in Miami alone. Based on that figure and FBI data, a reasonable nationwide estimate would be at least 750 such murders each year. Recent estimates from New York and Washington would suggest an even higher figure. 13

Since the black market in illegal drugs is the source of most drug-related problems, that market must be eliminated to the greatest extent possible. The most efficient means of doing so is legalization. 14

Hope for the Future

It is clear that most of the serious problems the public associates with illegal drug use are, in reality, caused directly or indirectly by drug prohibition. 15

Let's assume the war on drugs was given up as the misguided enterprise that it is. What would happen? The day after legalization went into effect, the streets of America would be safer. The drug dealers would be gone. The shootouts between drug dealers would end. Innocent bystanders would not be murdered anymore. Hundreds of thousands of drug "addicts" would no longer roam the streets, shoplifting, mugging, breaking into homes in the middle of the night to steal, and dealing violently with those who happened to wake up. One year after prohibition was repealed, 1,600 innocent people who would otherwise have been dead at the hands of drug criminals would be alive. 16

Within days of prohibition repeal, thousands of judges, prosecutors, and police would be freed up to catch, try, and imprison violent career criminals — criminals who commit fifty to one hundred serious crimes per year when on the loose, including robbery, rape, and murder. For the first time in years, our overcrowded prisons would have room for them. Ultimately, repeal of prohibition would open up *75,000* jail cells. 17

The day after repeal, organized crime would get a big pay cut — $80 billion a year. 18

How about those slick young drug dealers who are the new role models for the youth of the inner cities, with their designer clothes and Mercedes convertibles, always wearing a broad, smug smile that says crime pays? They snicker at the honest kids going to school or to work at the minimum wage. The day after repeal, the honest kids will have the last laugh. The dealers will be out of a job, unemployed. 19

The day after repeal, real drug education can begin and, for the first 20
time in history, it can be honest. No more need to prop up the failed war on drugs.

The year before repeal, 500,000 Americans would have died from ill- 21
nesses related to overeating and lack of exercise; 390,000, from smoking; and 150,000, from drinking alcohol. About 3,000 would have died from cocaine, heroin, and marijuana combined, with many of these deaths the result of the lack of quality control in the black market. The day after repeal, cocaine, heroin, and marijuana would, by and large, do no harm to those who chose not to consume them. In contrast, the day before prohibition repeal, all Americans, whether or not they chose to use illegal drugs, were forced to endure the violence, street crime, erosion of civil liberties, corruption, and social and economic decay caused by the war on drugs.

That is why, at this point in the argument, drug legalization unavoid- 22
ably becomes a moral issue. The war on drugs is immoral as well as impractical. It imposes enormous costs, including the ultimate cost of death, on large numbers of non-drug-abusing citizens in the failed attempt to save a relatively small group of hard-core drug abusers from themselves. It is immoral and absurd to *force* some people to bear costs so that others might be prevented from *choosing* to do harm to themselves. This crude utilitarian sacrifice — so at odds with traditional American values — has never been, and can never be, justified. That is why the war on drugs must end and why it *will* be ended once the public comes to understand the truth about this destructive policy.

We're Losing the Drug War because Prohibition Never Works

HODDING CARTER III

There is clearly no point in beating a dead horse, whether you are a politician or a columnist, but sometimes you have to do it just the same, if only for the record. So, for the record, here's another attempt to argue that a majority of the American people and their elected representatives can be and are wrong about the way they have chosen to wage the "war against drugs." Prohibition can't work, won't work, and has never worked, but it can and does have monumentally costly effects on the criminal justice system and on the integrity of government at every level. 1

Experience should be the best teacher, and my experience with prohibition is a little more recent than most Americans for whom the "noble experiment" ended with repeal in 1933. In my home state of Mississippi, it lasted for an additional thirty-three years, and for all those years it was a truism that the drinkers had their liquor, the preachers had their prohibition, and the sheriffs made the money. Al Capone would have been proud of the latitude that bootleggers were able to buy with their payoffs of constables, deputies, police chiefs, and sheriffs across the state. 2

But as a first-rate series in the *New York Times* made clear early last year, Mississippi's Prohibition-era corruption (and Chicago's before that) was penny ante stuff compared with what is happening in the United States today. From Brooklyn police precincts to Miami's police stations to rural Georgia courthouses, big drug money is purchasing major breakdowns in law enforcement. Sheriffs, other policemen, and now judges are being bought up by the gross. But that money, with the net profits for the drug traffickers estimated at anywhere from $40 billion to $100 billion a year, is also buying up banks, legitimate businesses and, to the south of us, entire governments. The latter becomes an increasingly likely outcome in a number of cities and states in this country as well. Cicero, Illinois, during Prohibition is an instructive case in point. 3

The money to be made from an illegal product that has about 23 million current users in this country also explains why its sale is so attractive on the mean streets of America's big cities. A street salesman can gross about $2,500 a day in Washington, which puts him in the pay category of 4

Hodding Carter III is a political commentator who heads a television production firm. His article appeared in the July 13, 1989 *Wall Street Journal*.

a local television anchor, and this in a neighborhood of dead-end job chances.

5 Since the courts and jails are already swamped beyond capacity by the arrests that are routinely made (44,000 drug dealers and users over a two-year period in Washington alone, for instance), and since those arrests barely skim the top of the pond, arguing that stricter enforcement is the answer begs a larger question: Who is going to pay the billions of dollars required to build the prisons, hire the judges, train the policemen, and employ the prosecutors needed for the load already on hand, let alone the huge one yet to come if we ever get serious about arresting dealers and users?

6 Much is made of the cost of drug addiction, and it should be, but the current breakdown in the criminal justice system is not one of them. That breakdown is the result of prohibition, not addiction. Drug addiction, after all, does not come close to the far vaster problems of alcohol and tobacco addiction (as former Surgeon General Koop correctly noted, tobacco is at least as addictive as heroin). Hard drugs are estimated to kill 4,000 people a year directly and several tens of thousands a year indirectly. Alcohol kills at least 100,000 a year, addicts millions more and costs the marketplace billions of dollars. Tobacco kills over 300,000 a year, addicts tens of millions, and fouls the atmosphere as well. But neither alcohol nor tobacco threaten to subvert our system of law and order, because they are treated as personal and societal problems rather than as criminal ones.

7 Indeed, every argument that is made for prohibiting the use of currently illegal drugs can be made even more convincingly about tobacco and alcohol. The effects on the unborn? Staggeringly direct. The effects on adolescents? Alcoholism is the addiction of choice for young Americans on a ratio of about one hundred to one. Lethal effect? Tobacco's murderous results are not a matter of debate anywhere outside the Tobacco Institute.

8 Which leaves the lingering and legitimate fear that legalization might produce a surge in use. It probably would, although not nearly as dramatic a one as opponents usually estimate. The fact is that personal use of marijuana, whatever the local laws may say, has been virtually decriminalized for some time now, but there has been a stabilization or slight decline in use, rather than an increase, for several years. Heroin addiction has held steady at about 500,000 people for some time, though the street price of heroin is far lower now than it used to be. Use of cocaine in its old form also seems to have stopped climbing and begun to drop off among young and old alike, though there is an abundantly available supply.

9 That leaves crack cocaine, stalker of the inner city and terror of the suburbs. Instant and addictive in effect, easy to use and relatively cheap to buy, it is a personality-destroying substance that is a clear menace to its

users. But it is hard to imagine it being any more accessible under legalization than it is in most cities today under prohibition, while the financial incentives for promoting its use would virtually disappear with legalization.

10 Proponents of legalization should not try to fuzz the issue, nonetheless. Addiction levels might increase, at least temporarily, if legal sanctions were removed. That happened after the repeal of Prohibition, or so at least some studies have suggested. But while that would be a personal disaster for the addicts and their families, and would involve larger costs to society as a whole, those costs would be miniscule compared with the costs of continued prohibition.

11 The young Capones of today own the inner cities, and the wholesalers behind these young retailers are rapidly buying up the larger system which is supposed to control them. Prohibition gave us the Mafia and organized crime on a scale that has been with us ever since. The new prohibition is writing a new chapter on that old text. Hell-bent on learning nothing from history, we are witnessing its repetition, predictably enough, as tragedy.

War on Drugs Falls through the Crack

GUY PIAZZA

1 Mr. Carter's comparison of street drugs and alcohol is ludicrous. If my surgeon has wine with lunch he can operate on me that afternoon, but if he wanted to smoke some crack I think I'd get a second opinion. Whereas 9 percent of alcohol users have a problem and a dependency, 90 percent of cocaine users are enslaved by their drug use. Hard street drugs are fast-acting, incredibly potent, and extremely hazardous to your health and your neighbor's health. Legalization can only broaden the market and hurt greater numbers of people.

2 Where will legalization stop and how will children be protected from it? Will heroin be available? How about needles? Will PCP and other hallucinogens come under legalization?

3 If the state tries to regulate the market it will need billions in enforcement as it does now, but it also will face an army of state-sanctioned junk-

---

This criticism of Hodding Carter's anti-drug-war argument appeared in the July 24, 1989 *Wall Street Journal*.

ies ripping the nation to shreds. The lacuna in the legalization argument is that if certain drugs are kept from the marketplace, those will be the drugs that people will want and the enforcement imbroglio will begin again.

—Guy Piazza

Legalize Drugs? Not on Your Life

CHARLES B. RANGEL

The escalating drug crisis is beginning to take its toll on many Americans. And now growing numbers of well-intentioned officials and other opinion leaders are saying that the best way to fight drugs is to legalize them. But what they're really admitting is that they're willing to abandon a war that we have not even begun to fight. 1

For example, the newly elected and promising mayor of Baltimore, Kurt Schmoke, at a meeting of the United States Conference of Mayors, called for a full-scale study of the feasibility of legalization. His comments could not have come at a worse time, for we are in the throes of the worst drug epidemic in our history. 2

Here we are talking about legalization, and we have yet to come up with any formal national strategy or any commitment from the Administration on fighting drugs beyond mere words. We have never fought the war on drugs like we have fought other legitimate wars — with all the forces at our command. 3

Just the thought of legalization brings up more problems and concerns than already exist. 4

Advocates of legalization should be reminded, for example, that it's not as simple as opening up a chain of friendly neighborhood pharmacies. Press them about some of the issues and questions surrounding this proposed legalization, and they never seem to have any answers. At least not any logical, well-thought-out ones. 5

Those who tout legalization remind me of fans sitting in the cheap seats at the ballpark. They may have played the game, and they may think they know all the rules, but from where they're sitting they can't judge the action. 6

Charles B. Rangel, Democrat of New York, is chairman of the House Senate Committee of Narcotics Abuse and Control. This argument appeared in the May 17, 1988 *New York Times*.

Has anybody ever considered which narcotic and psychotropic drugs 7
would be legalized?

Would we allow all drugs to become legally sold and used, or would 8
we select the most abused few, such as cocaine, heroin, and marijuana?

Who would administer the dosages — the state or the individual? 9

What quantity of drugs would each individual be allowed to get? 10

What about addicts: Would we not have to give them more in order 11
to satisfy their craving, or would we give them enough to just whet their appetites?

What do we do about those who are experimenting? Do we sell them 12
the drugs, too, and encourage them to pick up the habit?

Furthermore, will the Government establish tax-supported facilities 13
to sell these drugs?

Would we get the supply from the same foreign countries that sup- 14
port our habit now, or would we create our own internal sources and "dope factories," paying people the minimum wage to churn out mounds of cocaine and bales of marijuana?

Would there be an age limit on who can purchase drugs, as exists 15
with alcohol? What would the market price be and who would set it? Would private industry be allowed to have a stake in any of this?

What are we going to do about underage youngsters — the age group 16
hardest hit by the crack crisis? Are we going to give them identification cards? How can we prevent adults from purchasing drugs for them?

How many people are projected to become addicts as a result of the 17
introduction of cheaper, more available drugs sanctioned by government?

Since marijuana remains in a person's system for weeks, what would 18
we do about pilots, railroad engineers, surgeons, police, cross-country truckers, and nuclear plant employees who want to use it during off-duty hours? And what would be the effect on the health-insurance industry?

Many of the problems associated with drug abuse will not go away 19
just because of legalization. For too long we have ignored the root cause, failing to see the connection between drugs and hopelessness, helplessness, and despair.

We often hear that legalization would bring an end to the bloodshed 20
and violence that has often been associated with the illegal narcotics trade. The profit will be taken out of it, so to speak, as will be the urge to commit crime to get money to buy drugs. But what gives anybody the impression that legalization would deter many jobless and economically deprived people from resorting to crime to pay for their habits?

Even in a decriminalized atmosphere, money would still be needed 21
to support habits. Because drugs would be cheaper and more available, people would want more and would commit more crime. Does anybody

really think the black market would disappear? There would always be opportunities for those who saw profit in peddling larger quantities, or improved versions, of products that are forbidden or restricted.

Legalization would completely undermine any educational effort we undertake to persuade kids about the harmful effects of drugs. Today's kids have not yet been totally lost to the drug menace, but if we legalize these substances they'll surely get the message that drugs are O.K. 22

Not only would our young people realize that the threat of jail and punishment no longer exists. They would pick up the far more damaging message that the use of illegal narcotics does not pose a significant enough health threat for the Government to ban its use. 23

If we really want to do something about drug abuse, let's end this nonsensical talk about legalization right now. 24

Let's put the pressure on our leaders to first make the drug problem a priority issue on the national agenda, then let's see if we can get a coordinated national battle plan that would include the deployment of military personnel and equipment to wipe out this foreign-based national security threat. Votes by the House and more recently the Senate to involve the armed forces in the war on drugs are steps in the right direction. 25

Finally, let's take this legalization issue and put it where it belongs — amid idle chit-chat as cocktail glasses knock together at social events. 26

We Already Know the Folly of Decriminalized Drugs

ELIZABETH GESSNER

To the Editor:

It seems to me that the spate of pro-legalization articles that have appeared recently in the *Times* are founded on a misconception, namely that drug use has not already been decriminalized. Drug use underwent a de facto decriminalization in America some twenty years ago. From the Hollywood celebrity publicly snorting coke at a party to the teenager smoking marijuana in front of his high school, Americans have ceased to worry about criminal penalties for drug use. It is the failure of decriminalization that we are living with now. 1

This letter appeared in the October 20, 1989 *New York Times*.

Prohibitions against drug use are not founded in some abstract and hypocritical morality, as is often implied. Advocates of legalization seem curiously unable to distinguish gradations in human behavior. The argument that it is impermissible to outlaw drugs because people are legally "addicted" to coffee or aspirin is the ludicrous extension of a feeble train of thought. Teenagers are not prostituting themselves in Times Square to buy another bottle of aspirin, nor are men and women destroying their families for the sake of another cup of coffee. It is not merely the sale and distribution of drugs that is destroying lives. It is the effects of the drugs themselves and the things that people do under their influence that are the real hazards to the lives and happiness of millions of our citizens. 2

I suggest we try actually enforcing penalties for drug use and see if that has any effect before we give up and turn our society into a drug bazaar. Or possibly we should simply admit what A. M. Rosenthal perceptively argued in his column of September 26, that the lives currently being destroyed by drugs are not lives most Americans consider important. Mr. Rosenthal's analogy of drug use to slavery was a particularly apt one. Slavery was defended by many citizens as being an economic necessity, while abolitionists were ridiculed as moralizing meddlers or naive idealists. 3

However, even if charity and morality do not compel us to abolish this new form of slavery, prudence should, for we must remember that throughout history the well-off have never succeeded in finding a refuge remote enough to protect them from the results of the injustices they have inflicted upon the poor. Our society is creating a class of slaves who have been stripped by drugs of pity, hope, love, kindness, and even fear, and I think that their retribution will eventually fall on all of us. 4

—Elizabeth Gessner

We Can Control Drugs, but We Can't Ban Them

IRA GLASSER

To the Editor:

In "Crack Brained" (editorial, November 6), you suggest that ending criminal prohibitions against marijuana and heroin "deserves discussion." That judgment is welcome and long overdue. 1

Americans have been led to believe that prohibition is required to prevent drugs from destroying our society. This belief is encouraged by creating the image of a devil drug — a substance so dangerous that using it would cause violent behavior in otherwise law-abiding people and so powerful that a single exposure might lead an otherwise normal American to hopeless addiction. 2

Thus we have been subjected at various times to powerful images of "demon rum," "reefer madness," and "heroin dope fiends." All these images turned out to be politically manipulative, but scientifically false. They were used to promote policies of prohibition, rather than policies to control drug use and limit its harms. It is happening again with cocaine and smokable cocaine (crack). 3

Examples from your editorial: 4

- You suggest that the violence associated with crack use is caused by the chemical effects of the drug. A recent study of crack and homicide in New York showed that three-quarters of "drug-related" homicides were caused by territorial disputes and other incidents relating to the criminal trafficking system. Only 7.5 percent of the homicides were related to the effects of the drug itself, and two-thirds of those involved alcohol, not crack.
- You suggest that if prohibition were ended, crack use would spread rapidly. There is no scientific evidence to support that assertion, and some evidence to rebut it. Studies of cocaine users indicate that the barrier created by prohibition is relatively unimportant, that the market is relatively inelastic, and that the fear that use would expand significantly if prohibition were ended is exaggerated.
- You also assert that crack is so powerful that, unlike alcohol and tobacco, a high proportion of people who use it will "carry their habits

This letter appeared in the November 20, 1989 *New York Times*. Ira Glasser is executive director of the American Civil Liberties Union.

to the point of serious health damage." There's little evidence to support that assertion, a good deal to rebut it.

Studies here and abroad show that controlled use of cocaine is pos- 5
sible and that no more than 20 percent of users ever carried their habits to the point of adverse effects, and most of those returned to lower levels of use. Such research must be considered if we mean to assess the effect of ending prohibition. Generalizing about the effects of cocaine and crack by looking only at pathological users is like trying to infer the effects of alcohol at a cocktail party by looking only at skid-row alcoholics.

Yes, proposals to end criminal prohibition of marijuana and heroin 6
deserve discussion. But so do proposals to end criminal prohibition of cocaine. The goal of being drug free must be abandoned. Abstinence makes as little practical sense in this context as in combating acquired immune deficiency syndrome. We need policies to control drug use and reduce the harms associated with it. Most of those harms are now the result of prohibition, not drugs.

—Ira Glasser

THINKING AND WRITING ABOUT LEGALIZING DRUGS

Questions for Discussion and Writing

1. Vidal predicted in 1970 that if drugs were legalized, most people would not abuse them. But two decades later, even though drugs remain illegal and presumably harder to get, we have not escaped a drug epidemic. Does this fact weaken the argument for legalization? What views of human nature underlie Vidal's belief about the moderate use of drugs?
2. Both Vidal and Ostrowski offer moral reasons for legalizing drugs. How many different issues do they raise? Are some more important than others?
3. Bennett's argument uses the device of negation; that is, he lists the arguments of those in favor of legalization and proceeds to refute them. How successful is his refutation? What is Bennett's main argument against legalization? Do Bennett and Rangel agree on the reasons for pursuing the war against drugs? Do they emphasize different issues?
4. Some of the arguers in this chapter cite the history of use and enforcement of drug laws to support their claims. How would you evaluate the lessons gained from history? How relevant are they to the present drug problem?
5. Arguments both for and against legalization rely heavily on analogies with other drug experiences. (See Glasser, for example.) What are these analogies? How effective are they in supporting the claims? Are some more convincing than others?

Topics for Research

Use of drugs before the Harrison Narcotic Act of 1914

The effectiveness of education against drugs

The case for legalizing some drugs, banning others

The effects on society of widespread drug use

The effectiveness of law enforcement so far in the war against drugs

CHAPTER 18

Pornography

The debate over pornography opposes two views of the rights of citizens. On the one hand, advocates of legal access to pornography argue that adults should be free to read or see whatever they wish. On the other hand, those who are opposed argue that widespread distribution of pornographic material degrades society and especially women, who are often seen as its victims.

In any debate about pornography the first problem to emerge is that of definition. One dictionary defines *pornography* as "the depiction of erotic behavior (as in pictures or writing) intended to cause sexual excitement." But as numerous court cases have demonstrated, this definition does not make a clear distinction between pornography and art. In 1987 the Supreme Court ruled that material was *obscene* (the legal term for pornographic) if a "reasonable person" found it offensive without "serious literary, artistic, political, or scientific value." But this definition did no more than previous ones to settle the controversy. The dissenters on the Court pointed out that the "reasonable person" test was too vague.

Nevertheless, despite these difficulties of interpretation, any definition of pornography must rest on the values of the community. As these values change, so do our attitudes toward offensive material. The Puritan and Victorian standards of sexual morality that prevailed earlier in our history dictated restraint in the portrayal of sexual behavior. The novel *Ulysses* by James Joyce, now considered one of the masterpieces of twentieth-century literature, was banned in Britain and America in 1922. The United States Post Office Department charged the novel with obscenity; not until 1933 was the ban lifted. Censorship also affected the reception of *Lady Chatterley's Lover* (1928) by D. H. Lawrence, which was available for many years only in expurgated form.

Today our tolerance for "obscenity" makes the descriptions in these books seem tame, even commonplace. Laws based on the First Amendment that protect freedom of speech for the most flagrant depictions of sexual activity reflect our more permissive attitudes.

In recent years, however, the demands for censorship have been strongly revived. At least two social phenomena are propelling them. One is the growth of evangelical religion, whose practitioners adopt a conservative position on explicit displays of erotic behavior. The other is the growth of the women's liberation movement, which regards pornography not only as degrading to women but also as threatening their physical safety.

At one time pornography was largely confined to books, magazines, and movies. Now some critics find it in the lyrics of popular rock music and are proposing a ratings system that would give parents a measure of control over the purchase of record albums and tapes by their children. Whether such ratings systems constitute censorship is another issue under growing public discussion. (See the arguments by Jon Pareles and David J. Meltz in the chapter on freedom of speech.)

Notes from a Free-Speech Junkie

SUSAN JACOBY

It is no news that many women are defecting from the ranks of civil libertarians on the issue of obscenity. The conviction of Larry Flynt, publisher of *Hustler* magazine — before his metamorphosis into a born-again Christian — was greeted with unabashed feminist approval. Harry Reems, the unknown actor who was convicted by a Memphis jury for conspiring 1

Susan Jacoby is a journalist and essayist who writes frequently on feminist concerns. "Notes from a Free-Speech Junkie" appeared in the "Hers" column in the *New York Times* on January 26, 1978.

to distribute the movie *Deep Throat*, has carried on his legal battles with almost no support from women who ordinarily regard themselves as supporters of the First Amendment. Feminist writers and scholars have even discussed the possibility of making common cause against pornography with adversaries of the women's movement — including opponents of the equal rights amendment and "right to life" forces.

2 All of this is deeply disturbing to a woman writer who believes, as I always have and still do, in an absolute interpretation of the First Amendment. Nothing in Larry Flynt's garbage convinces me that the late Justice Hugo L. Black was wrong in his opinion that "the federal government is without any power whatsoever under the Constitution to put any type of burden on free speech and expression of ideas of any kind (as distinguished from conduct)." Many women I like and respect tell me I am wrong; I cannot remember having become involved in so many heated discussions of a public issue since the end of the Vietnam War. A feminist writer described my views as those of a "First Amendment junkie."

3 Many feminist arguments for controls on pornography carry the implicit conviction that porn books, magazines, and movies pose a greater threat to women than similarly repulsive exercises of free speech pose to other offended groups. This conviction has, of course, been shared by everyone — regardless of race, creed, or sex — who has ever argued in favor of abridging the First Amendment. It is the argument used by some Jews who have withdrawn their support from the American Civil Liberties Union because it has defended the right of American Nazis to march through a community inhabited by survivors of Hitler's concentration camps.

4 If feminists want to argue that the protection of the Constitution should not be extended to *any* particularly odious or threatening form of speech, they have a reasonable argument (although I don't agree with it). But it is ridiculous to suggest that the porn shops on 42nd Street are more disgusting to women than a march of neo-Nazis is to survivors of the extermination camps.

5 The arguments over pornography also blur the vital distinction between expression of ideas and conduct. When I say I believe unreservedly in the First Amendment, someone always comes back at me with the issue of "kiddie porn." But kiddie porn is not a First Amendment issue. It is an issue of the abuse of power — the power adults have over children — and not of obscenity. Parents and promoters have no more right to use their children to make porn movies than they do to send them to work in coal mines. The responsible adults should be prosecuted, just as adults who use children for back-breaking farm labor should be prosecuted.

6 Susan Brownmiller, in *Against Our Will: Men, Women and Rape*, has described pornography as "the undiluted essence of anti-female propa-

ganda." I think this is a fair description of some types of pornography, especially of the brutish subspecies that equates sex with death and portrays women primarily as objects of violence.

The equation of sex and violence, personified by some glossy rock record album covers as well as by *Hustler*, has fed the illusion that censorship of pornography can be conducted on a more rational basis than other types of censorship. Are all pictures of naked women obscene? Clearly not, says a friend. A Renoir nude is art, she says, and *Hustler* is trash. "Any reasonable person" knows that. 7

But what about something between art and trash — something, say, along the lines of *Playboy* or *Penthouse* magazines? I asked five women for their reactions to one picture in *Penthouse* and got responses that ranged from "lovely" and "sensuous" to "revolting" and "demeaning." Feminists, like everyone else, seldom have rational reasons for their preferences in erotica. Like members of juries, they tend to disagree when confronted with something that falls short of 100 percent vulgarity. 8

In any case, feminists will not be the arbiters of good taste if it becomes easier to harass, prosecute, and convict people on obscenity charges. Most of the people who want to censor girlie magazines are equally opposed to open discussion of issues that are of vital concern to women: rape, abortion, menstruation, contraception, lesbianism — in fact, the entire range of sexual experience from a woman's viewpoint. 9

Feminist writers and editors and filmmakers have limited financial resources: Confronted by a determined prosecutor, Hugh Hefner will fare better than Susan Brownmiller. Would the Memphis jurors who convicted Harry Reems for his role in *Deep Throat* be inclined to take a more positive view of paintings of the female genitalia done by sensitive feminist artists? *Ms.* magazine has printed color reproductions of some of those art works; *Ms.* is already banned from a number of high school libraries because someone considers it threatening and/or obscene. 10

Feminists who want to censor what they regard as harmful pornography have essentially the same motivation as other would-be censors: They want to use the power of the state to accomplish what they have been unable to achieve in the marketplace of ideas and images. The impulse to censor places no faith in the possibilities of democratic persuasion. 11

It isn't easy to persuade certain men that they have better uses for $1.95 each month than to spend it on a copy of *Hustler*? Well, then, give the men no choice in the matter. 12

I believe there is also a connection between the impulse toward censorship on the part of people who used to consider themselves civil libertarians and a more general desire to shift responsibility from individuals 13 to institutions. When I saw the movie *Looking for Mr. Goodbar*, I was stunned by its series of visual images equating sex and violence, coupled with what seems to me the mindless message (a distortion of the fine Judith Rossner novel) that casual sex equals death. When I came out of the movie, I was even more shocked to see parents standing in line with children between the ages of ten and fourteen.

I simply don't know why a parent would take a child to see such a 14
movie, any more than I understand why people feel they can't turn off a television set their child is watching. Whenever I say that, my friends tell me I don't know how it is because I don't have children. True, but I do have parents. When I was a child, they did turn off the TV. They didn't expect the Federal Communications Commission to do their job for them.

I am a First Amendment junkie. You can't OD on the First Amend- 15
ment, because free speech is its own best antidote.

Pornography: Anti-Female Propaganda

SUSAN BROWNMILLER

Pornography has been so thickly glossed over with the patina of chic 1
these days in the name of verbal freedom and sophistication that important distinctions between freedom of political expression (a democratic necessity), honest sex education for children (a societal good) and ugly smut (the deliberate devaluation of the role of women through obscene, distorted depictions) have been hopelessly confused. Part of the problem is that those who traditionally have been the most vigorous opponents of porn are often those same people who shudder at the explicit mention of any sexual subject. Under their watchful, vigilante eyes, frank and free dissemination of educational materials relating to abortion, contraception, the act of birth, and female biology in general is also dangerous, subversive, and dirty. (I am not unmindful that a frank and free discussion of rape, "the unspeakable crime," might well give these righteous vigilantes further cause to shudder.) Because the battle lines were falsely drawn a long time ago, before there was a vocal women's movement, the anti-pornography forces appear to be, for the most part, religious, Southern,

---

Susan Brownmiller, a journalist, is cofounder of Radical Feminists and an organizer of Women Against Pornography. Her books include *Femininity* (1984) and *Against Our Will: Men, Women and Rape* (1975), from which this excerpt is taken.

conservative, and right-wing, while the pro-porn forces are identified as Eastern, atheistic, and liberal.

But a woman's perspective demands a totally new alignment, or at least a fresh appraisal. The majority report of the President's Commission on Obscenity and Pornography (1970), a report that argued strongly for the removal of all legal restrictions on pornography, soft and hard, made plain that 90 percent of all pornographic material is geared to the male heterosexual market (the other 10 percent is geared to the male homosexual taste), that buyers of porn are "predominantly white, middle-class, middle-aged married males" and that the graphic depictions, the meat and potatoes of porn, are of the naked female body and of the multiplicity of acts done to that body. 2

Discussing the content of stag films, "a familiar and firmly established part of the American scene," the commission report dutifully, if foggily, explained, "Because pornography historically has been thought to be primarily a masculine interest, the emphasis in stag films seems to represent the preferences of the middle-class American male. Thus male homosexuality and bestiality are relatively rare while lesbianism is rather common." 3

The commissioners in this instance had merely verified what purveyors of porn have always known: Hard-core pornography is not a celebration of sexual freedom; it is a cynical exploitation of female sexual activity through the device of making all such activity, and consequently all females, "dirty." Heterosexual male consumers of pornography are frankly turned on by watching lesbians in action (although never in the final scenes, but always as a curtain raiser); they are turned off with the sudden swiftness of a water faucet by watching naked men act upon each other. One study quoted in the commission report came to the unastounding conclusion that "seeing a stag film in the presence of male peers bolsters masculine esteem." Indeed. The men in groups who watch the films, it is important to note, are *not* naked. 4

When male response to pornography is compared to female response, a pronounced difference in attitude emerges. According to the commission, "Males report being more highly aroused by depictions of nude females, and show more interest in depictions of nude females than [do] females." Quoting the figures of Alfred Kinsey, the commission noted that a majority of males (77 percent) were "aroused" by visual depictions of explicit sex while a majority of females (68 percent) were not aroused. Further, "females more often than males reported 'disgust' and 'offense.' " 5

From whence comes this female disgust and offense? Are females sexually backward or more conservative by nature? The gut distaste that a majority of women feel when we look at pornography, a distaste that, incredibly, it is no longer fashionable to admit, comes, I think, from the 6 gut knowledge that we and our bodies are being stripped, exposed, and contorted for the purpose of ridicule to bolster that "masculine esteem" which gets its kick and sense of power from viewing females as anonymous, panting playthings, adult toys, dehumanized objects to be used, abused, broken, and discarded.

This, of course, is also the philosophy of rape. It is no accident (for what else could be its purpose?) that females in the pornography genre are depicted in two cleanly delineated roles: as virgins who are caught and "banged" or as nymphomaniacs who are never sated. The most popular and prevalent pornographic fantasy combines the two: An innocent, untutored female is raped and "subjected to unnatural practices" that turn her into a raving, slobbering nymphomaniac, a dependent sexual slave who can never get enough of the big, male cock. 7

There can be no "equality" in porn, no female equivalent, no turning of the tables in the name of bawdy fun. Pornography, like rape, is a male invention, designed to dehumanize women, to reduce the female to an object of sexual access, not to free sensuality from moralistic or parental inhibition. The staple of porn will always be the naked female body, breasts and genitals exposed, because as man devised it, her naked body is the female's "shame," her private parts the private property of man, while his are the ancient, holy, universal, patriarchal instrument of his power, his rule by force over *her*. 8

Pornography is the undiluted essence of anti-female propaganda. Yet the very same liberals who were so quick to understand the method and purpose behind the mighty propaganda machine of Hitler's Third Reich, the consciously spewed-out anti-Semitic caricatures and obscenities that gave an ideological base to the Holocaust and the Final Solution, the very same liberals who, enlightened by blacks, searched their own conscience and came to understand that their tolerance of "nigger" jokes and portrayals of shuffling, rolling-eyed servants in movies perpetuated the degrading myths of black inferiority and gave an ideological base to the continuation of black oppression — these very same liberals now fervidly maintain that the hatred and contempt for women that find expression in four-letter words used as expletives and in what are quaintly called "adult" or "erotic" books and movies are a valid extension of freedom of speech that must be preserved as a Constitutional right. 9

To defend the right of a lone, crazed American Nazi to grind out propaganda calling for the extermination of all Jews, as the ACLU has done in the name of free speech, is, after all, a self-righteous and not particularly courageous stand, for American Jewry is not currently threatened by storm troopers, concentration camps, and imminent extermination, but I wonder if the ACLU's position might change if, come tomorrow morning, the bookstores and movie theatres lining Forty-second Street in 10

New York City were devoted not to the humiliation of women by rape and torture, as they currently are, but to a systematized, commercially successful propaganda machine depicting the sadistic pleasures of gassing Jews or lynching blacks?

Is this analogy extreme? Not if you are a woman who is conscious of the ever-present threat of rape and the proliferation of a cultural ideology that makes it sound like "liberated" fun. The majority report of the President's Commission on Obscenity and Pornography tried to pooh-pooh the opinion of law enforcement agencies around the country that claimed their own concrete experience with offenders who were caught with the stuff led them to conclude that pornographic material is a causative factor in crimes of sexual violence. The commission maintained that it was not possible at this time to scientifically prove or disprove such a connection. 11

But does one need scientific methodology in order to conclude that the anti-female propaganda that permeates our nation's cultural output promotes a climate in which the acts of sexual hostility directed against women are not only tolerated but ideologically encouraged? A similar debate has raged for many years over whether or not the extensive glorification of violence (the gangster as hero; the loving treatment accorded bloody shoot-'em-ups in movies, books, and on TV) has a causal effect, a direct relationship to the rising rate of crime, particularly among youth. Interestingly enough, in this area — nonsexual and not specifically related to abuses against women — public opinion seems to be swinging to the position that explicit violence in the entertainment media does have a deleterious effect; it makes violence commonplace, numbingly routine, and no longer morally shocking. 12

More to the point, those who call for a curtailment of scenes of violence in movies and on television in the name of sensitivity, good taste, and what's best for our children are not accused of being pro-censorship or against freedom of speech. Similarly, minority group organizations, black, Hispanic, Japanese, Italian, Jewish, or American Indian, that campaign against ethnic slurs and demeaning portrayals in movies, on television shows, and in commercials are perceived as waging a just political fight, for if a minority group claims to be offended by a specific portrayal, be it Little Black Sambo or the Frito Bandido, and relates it to a history of ridicule and oppression, few liberals would dare to trot out a constitutional argument in theoretical opposition, not if they wish to maintain their liberal credentials. Yet when it comes to the treatment of women, the liberal consciousness remains fiercely obdurate, refusing to be budged, for the sin of appearing square or prissy in the age of so-called sexual revolution has become the worst offense of all. 13

Sexual McCarthyism

HUGH HEFNER

> I have in my possession the names of 57 Communists who are in the State Department at present.
>
> Senator Joseph McCarthy, February 11, 1950

It wasn't true, but it touched off hysterics that would last half a decade. For the next five years, just being accused of Communist leanings could get you fired or blacklisted. It is a measure of the witches' brew McCarthy stirred up that in 1954, just months before the Senate finally worked up the courage to condemn him, a Gallup poll showed that 50 percent of America supported him. But when the weird spectacle of the Army-McCarthy hearings appeared on TV, the nation saw that its esrtwhile hero was a fraud and a demagogue. In December 1954, he was censured by the Senate. His name entered the dictionary (McCarthyism: The use of indiscriminate, often unfounded, accusations, sensationalism, inquisitorial investigative methods); the man died, disgraced, three years later. 1

One of the minor McCarthy-era players was one Ronald Reagan, B-movie actor, president of the Screen Actors Guild, FBI informant on members of his own union. In Hollywood in 1947, Reagan had appeared with like-minded movie folks (Gary Cooper, Adolphe Menjou) as a friendly witness before the Red-hunting House Un-American Activities Committee. Almost forty years later, President Reagan would set up a little hunt of his own. 2

Early last year, Reagan's Attorney General, Edwin Meese, launched a seek-and-destroy mission called The Attorney General's Commission on Pornography. There had been a President's Commission on Obscenity and Pornography under Nixon eighteen years earlier. It concluded that there was no connection between pornography and antisocial behavior. That wasn't good enough for Reagan and Meese. "Reexamination of the issue of pornography is long overdue," Meese told reporters last year. "No longer must one go out of the way to find pornographic materials. With the advent of cable television and video recorders, pornography now is available at home to almost anyone." 3

The Meese commission's ostensible goal is to study the effects of sexually explicit materials, but it will hear some viewpoints more sympathetically than others. At the hearings, law-enforcement officers and pornogra- 4

Hugh Hefner is the editor in chief of *Playboy* magazine, where this column appeared in January 1986.

phy "victims" — often hidden behind screens, like spies on *60 Minutes* — relate sexual horror stories. Civil-liberties types get to speak, too, but the ringside seats are packed for the commission's slide shows of explicit pornography. The witnesses who draw headlines are the ones willing to blame their sad lives on "the evils of pornography."

How are the witnesses selected? 5

The Meese commission uses five investigators to screen potential witnesses. You'd think the investigators would be interested in all sides of what even the commission admits is a complicated issue, but it seems you'd be wrong. 6

Dr. Lois Lee is director of Children of the Night, a prominent Los Angeles organization that helps street kids, most of them young prostitutes, get off the streets. On August 5 of last year, Dr. Lee was contacted by Ed Chapman, a Virginia law-enforcement officer working for the Meese commission. He said he wanted her to line up some of her teenagers to testify. Chapman then told Lee what he wanted the witnesses to say — that pornography had been used as a tool when their parents molested them and that this experience had led them into prostitution. 7

"Wait a minute," Lee said. She told Chapman that that was not the way it happened. Chapman replied that the investigators had talked with a lot of people about pornography being used by child molesters and that they knew this was generally the case. 8

"I said it *wasn't* the case," Lee told *Playboy*, "and he said, 'I don't think we're going to want your kids.' The conversation was over." 9

The commission's investigators, it was clear, wanted witnesses to support a cause-and-effect relationship between porn use and antisocial behavior. They wanted witnesses like the one who was willing to testify that her father had molested her after looking at a Playmate Calendar. What was the connection? It was, as Meese-commission investigator Joe Haggerty told Lee with some enthusiasm, the fact that the witness had testified that she believed her father molested her because she was closer to the ages of the Playmates on the calendar and looked more like them than her mother. Lee found this cause-and-effect notion preposterous. 10

> The professional Communist-hunters of the time were able to summon a stream of professional witnesses who seemed always ready, willing, and able to testify that they had known so-and-so at Communist meetings in the past. Their testimony was as suspect as their claims that although they might have once been fooled by the Communist doctrines, they had suddenly seen the light and were now blessed with total recall.
>
> From *Days of Shame*, by Senator Charles E. Potter,
> a Member of the 1954 McCarthy Committee

The witness whose father had had the Playmate Calendar was — probably not coincidentally — a born-again Christian. It is an article of 11 faith with born-agains that the more impressive one's list of early sins, the more glorious one's salvation. A long list of sins recanted helps assure redemption. (See *The Self-Crucifixion of Cathleen Crowell Webb,* by Elizabeth and Edwin Black, *Playboy*, October 1985.)

Much of the testimony belongs in revivalist meetings. Born-again Brenda MacKillop, another Meese-commission witness, almost speaks in tongues. 12

> I am a former Playboy Bunny. . . . I was extremely suicidal and sought psychiatric help for the eight years I lived in a sexually promiscuous fashion. There was no help for me until I changed my life-style to be a follower of Jesus Christ and obeyed the Biblical truths, including no premarital sex. . . . I implore the Attorney General's commission to see the connection between sexual promiscuity, venereal disease, abortion, divorce, homosexuality, sexual abuse of children, suicide, drug abuse, rape, and prostitution to pornography. . . . Come back to God, America, before it's too late.

For witness MacKillop, everything from divorce to acid indigestion can be chalked up to pornography. MacKillop described for the commission the episodes of her formerly promiscuous personal life. In each instance, she attempted to blame *Playboy* — the magazine, the Clubs, and the philosophy — for her sexual downfall. 13

The Meese commission had trundled out a parade of born-again basket cases, antisex feminists, and fun-hating fundamentalists. More than anything else, the testimony of these witnesses struck us as sad, misdirected — even pathetic. It was also inflammatory, misinformed scapegoating. 14

In a court of law, such witnesses would be dismissed for lack of credibility. Trial by headline — unsupported by evidence, unchallenged by cross-examination or witnesses for the defense — is not due process. But it is the method of the Meese commission, as it was for McCarthy. 15

The Meese commission has the trappings of an inquiry but not the substance. The Government is putting on a circus show of misinformation. It is using the power of its position to prove that pornography is harmful rather than to research the facts. On another front, Dr. C. Everett Koop, the surgeon general, who should have more respect for science, released a statement warning that "pornography may be dangerous to your health." He told the nation, "Pornography is a destructive phenomenon. . . . It does not contribute anything to society but, rather, takes away from and diminishes what we regard as socially good." He then listed, without supporting evidence, some of its dangers: Pornography "intervenes in normal sexual relationships and alters them." 16

What, if any, scientific evidence exists to support such claims? Professor Joseph E. Scott of Ohio State University analyzed all the research available on what we have learned in the more than fifteen years since 17 the commission's 1970 report about the relationship among violence, pornography, and antisocial behavior. In a report to the American Association for the Advancement of Science, Professor Scott took on some of the common myths about pornography.

Myth one: Porn is more violent today than fifteen years ago. *Wrong!* 18
This is the addiction theory of porn, asserting that consumers become jaded and desensitized. Fundamentalists believe that one taste of sexually explicit material gets you hooked on the hard stuff. Porn has not become more violent. The porn slide shows mentioned earlier may be frightening and certainly are offensive to some, but they contain selected images. They do not reflect the marketplace. Scott says that when *Time* magazine runs an article claiming that S-M is the latest trend in porn, it misinterprets the available research. How violent is porn? Scott found that X-rated movies had less violence that G-, PG-, or R-rated movies. The average number of violent acts per movies was 20.3 for the R-rated, 16.2 for the G-rated, 15.3 for the PG movies, and 4.4 for the X-rated movies.

Myth two: Exposure to porn leads to violence. *Wrong!* There is no 19
scientific evidence that reading or viewing sexually explicit material causes antisocial behavior. (In fact, several studies have shown that exposure to gentle erotica actually lessens aggression.) However, there are two endlessly quoted researchers who say they've proved that exposure to violent sexual depiction increases the likelihood of certain males "condoning or expressing willingness to act aggressively against females." We're not sure what that means in real life. Scott reports that the only long-term study of violent porn disproved that myth: "Researchers examined married couples over a three-month period. They found that exposure to violent themes produced no significant changes in the participants' behavior." The most frequently quoted research has been that done by UCLA professor Neil Malamuth, the "professor of porn," using college undergraduates in lab situations. No one believes that the artificial effects created by watching pornographic films in a lab carry over to real life. Has anyone ever participated in the experiments, then raped a coed? If viewing X-rated films leads automatically to violence against women, then Malamuth, who has been showing these films for years, would have been arrested for rape a long time ago.

Is there a way to gauge the effect of erotic material on the general pop- 20
ulation? One study compared sex-magazine-readership rates with rape rates by state. The researchers found a moderately strong relationship between rape rates and the consumption of adult magazines. Taken by itself, this would be cause for concern. However, a correlation is not the same as cause and effect. Subsequent studies have shown how tenuous that relation is. Consider *Field & Stream* or *Guns & Ammo*. Researchers found that the circulation of outdoor magazines has a higher correlation with rape than the number of adult bookstores in each state. One would

assume that rape rates might be higher in those states with the most adult theaters. No relationship has been found. To further confuse the issue, researchers have found rape rates to be higher in urban areas, in poor areas, in areas with high proportions of nonwhites, and in areas of high alcohol consumption. Each of these variables showed a stronger relationship to rape than the number of adult theaters and bookstores.

Perhaps the best way to confront the myths about porn violence is to look at the Danish experience. Denmark legalized pornography in the late sixties. Last year, a conference was held to review the effects of porn on social and criminal behavior. Berl Kutchinsky, a criminologist from the University of Copenhagen, summarized fifteen years of research: 21

> The conclusion is very clear that pornography is not a danger — neither to persons, neither to society, neither to children nor to adults. It doesn't lead to sex offenses; it doesn't lead to sexual deviations. . . . The only thing about pornography is that it makes people masturbate. . . . People's attitude toward sexuality and, therefore, toward pornography is almost 100 percent determined by their religious convictions. And those are not altered by facts.

The Meese commission, with its fundamentalist foundation, is not likely to be swayed by facts. In effect, Kutchinsky was voicing the 1970 findings of the President's Commission on Obscenity and Pornography: 22

> The commission believes that much of the "problem" regarding materials which depict explicit sexual activity stems from the inability or reluctance of people in our society to be open and direct in dealing with sexual matters. . . . The commission believes that there is no warrant for continued interference with the full freedom of adults to read, obtain, or view whatever such materials they wish.

The Meese commission has written its own warrant for interference with our freedom. It despises fact. This sexual McCarthyism is as rooted in deception, innuendo, and outright lies as the original version. 23

We think women *and* men have a right to sexual knowledge. We think that, as free adults, they have a right to choose what they will and will not see. But then, we thought the smell of McCarthyism had dissipated thirty years ago. Until it departs again, those who believe in free minds must take every effort to oppose the new wave of sexual McCarthyism. 24

The Bitter Harvest of Pornography

HAVEN BRADFORD GOW

To the Editor:

Christie Hefner, president of Playboy Enterprises, maintains pornography does not contribute to antisocial behavior (April 15, Washington Talk page), but some alarming evidence suggests otherwise. 1

The Los Angeles Police Department points out that in the more than forty child-sex-abuse cases it investigated between October 1976 and March 1977, pornographic photos were found to be present in every case.

According to Charles Keating, founder of the Phoenix-based Citizens for Decency Through Law, "Police vice squads report that 77 percent of child molesters of boys and 87 percent of child molesters of girls admitted trying out the sexual behavior modeled by pornography."

William Marshall, studying Canadian rapists in prison, reports, "various forms of pornographic fantasies may lead to crime." Ten of eighteen rapists confessed that pornography influenced them to force females to have sex.

Thirty-six serial murderers interviewed by FBI agents confessed that pornography influenced their thinking and conduct.

Adult and child pornography is used by pedophiles to seduce children into sex. In one case, a six-year-old girl testified that her father used pornography to entice her into sex.

Law enforcement people throughout the United States have found in thousands of cases that most child molesters collected or produced child pornography.

Detective Darrell Pope, Michigan State Police, found that of 38,000 sexual-assault cases on file in Michigan, 41 percent involved use of pornography before or during the assault.

Clearly, pornography helps create a moral and social climate that is conducive to sexual abuse and exploitation. 2

— Haven Bradford Gow

Haven Bradford Gow, of Arlington Heights, Illinois, is associate editor of *Police Times*, published by the American Federation of Police. This letter appeared in the April 23, 1986 edition of the *New York Times*.

Feminists Are Wrong about Pornography

AL GOLDSTEIN

As a maker of pornography, and as a champion of the rights of free expression, I've been called on again and again to defend sexually explicit material. Over the years, the censors, the bluenoses, the antisex forces have been presented in various guises: as Christians, as protectors of youth, and lately, more and more, as feminists. But these distinctions don't interest me very much. The difference between the fundamentalist and the feminist arguments against porn is verbiage; the underpinnings are the same. Sexual repressiveness is rooted in self-hate, self-loathing, in a Puritanical inability to enjoy the full sensuality of the body. . . . 1

With one exception, I take the First Amendment to be absolute, plenary. That exception concerns the sexualization of children; . . . I think constitutional guarantees must be abrogated to that extent in order to protect our children. . . . 2

Porn and Violence Are Not Synonymous

The argument against violent porn has been very well refuted. . . . 3

There have been studies which show that representations of rape desensitize people to violence against women, but there have been no studies which show that nonviolent pornography causes anything like a similar reaction. Time and again, studies either have shown that porn does *not* cause antisocial behavior or have failed to show that it does. Yet I am still seeing signs in antiporn "Take Back the Night" parades: "Porn Is Violence Against Women." These people don't care about the truth; they care about their tenuously constructed, house-of-cards logic. 4

Let me reiterate: Pornography and violence against women are not coterminous, no matter how much feminist theorists say they are or wish they were. Edward Donnerstein, out of the University of Wisconsin, used sado-masochistic pornography in a study of its effect on men. And it turned out that it did desensitize his subjects to violence to some extent. Yet the Donnerstein study is trundled out repeatedly to indict *all* porn, including that with no S-M content. Donnerstein himself said if there are studies showing that nonviolent porn causes desensitivity to abuse of women, he'd like to see them. 5

Al Goldstein publishes and edits *Screw*, a sexually explicit magazine. This excerpt is from the December 1984 issue of *Film Comment*.

The feminists' argument against porn feeds off such hazy distinctions as the blurring of the line between S-M and nonviolent porn. The rhetorical weight of the argument depends on that line being ignored. But it is on such distinctions that rational discourse and social decision making ought to be based; otherwise we live in an Orwellian "Truth-is-lies" society. . . . 6

Why are the feminists so hysterical about pornography? One could see it as a single issue of the women's movement, maybe even a major, but *the* issue? I believe women who object so stridently to representations of explicit sexuality are reacting not on a political basis but on a moral basis. Women have been indoctrinated for centuries to hate sex, to fear it, above all to remain ignorant about it. That this is an element of male control over them may be true. But the result is that feminists just cannot throw off the yoke of centuries in a generation, that when they see a picture of female genitals they just cannot stop themselves from saying "dirty" — afterward modified to "politically incorrect." 7

I was astonished that, in the controversy surrounding Vanessa Williams [1984's Miss America, deposed for modeling in a sex magazine photo feature], it was always assumed she did something wrong by posing nude. She did nothing wrong. She celebrated her body by doing so. Yet the starting point in discussions about her is "How could she do something so bad?" Puritanism is rampant in this society, and Puritanism has always been just as large an element in feminism as it has been in fundamentalism. . . . 8

It is the repression of sexuality which leads to rape, violence against women, and a host of other social ills. By agitating for censorship, for repressing that sexuality which porn represents [a flawed representation, to be sure], feminists and fundamentalists are prolonging an already too-long struggle for sexual freedom. Instead of calling for an end to porn, we should be seeking ways in which to make it better. 9

Pornography on the March

BETTY WEIN

These days there is no escaping hard-core pornography. It assaults us from magazine racks in convenience markets and drugstores; from shelves in video-rental stores; from card displays in neighborhood shops tucked in comfortably with the "Happy Birthday" and "Get Well" greetings. It screams its triple-X message from movie marquees. It entices those with juvenile fantasies into porno bookstores, ironically called "adult." It sneaks into family-oriented computer magazines as "innocent" ads for dirty home-computer video texts. And it finds it way into mailboxes — unsolicited, unwanted, unsparing. 1

Even our homes are not safe. Pornography slithers through telephone wires as "dial-a-porn" and through public-access porn channels that are part and parcel of some cable-TV packages. 2

Sexual Madness

Manipulating the First Amendment, pornographers have claimed their so-called right to open up cesspools of sexual slime — and in so doing have taken priority over the rights and welfare of an entire generation of children. When shell-shocked parents complain about cable porn accidentally reaching their children, they're told, "Buy a lockout box for your TV set." 3

But what's really being locked out is plain, ordinary decency and the inalienable right to protect children from psychic damage and the chilling effects of pornography. 4

The smut assaulting our sensibilities today capitalizes on violently explicit depictions of sexual acts — heterosexual, homosexual, bisexual. It includes portrayals of orgies, incest, bestiality, sadomasochism, bondage, necrophilia, sodomy, even blueprints for raping women with everything from loaded guns to cucumbers and beer bottles. 5

If these descriptions shock you as an adult, then imagine the effects upon the emotional development of children. 6

What's even more shocking is that this potentially traumatizing hard-core pornography is reaching American children for one reason only — obscenity laws are not being enforced. *Obscenity is illegal.* The federal 7

Betty Wein is a senior editor at Morality in Media. This argument originally appeared in the Winter 1986 *World Media Report* and was reprinted in the November 1987 *Reader's Digest.*

government has strict laws against the mailing, interstate transporting, and importing of obscene materials. There is also a federal broadcasting law prohibiting obscene programming. Furthermore, almost every state has its own obscenity law.

But obscenity laws are so rarely enforced that most citizens don't even realize pornography is illegal. When I asked twenty-four people if they thought the hard-core pornographic magazines on display at their newsstands are legal, the unanimous response was: "They must be; otherwise they wouldn't be there." 8

Lame Excuse

Why aren't state and federal obscenity laws being enforced? I asked 9 that question in a 1975 interview with Manhattan District Attorney Robert Morgenthau, who was, and still is, responsible for the investigation and prosecution in Manhattan of violations against New York State's obscenity law, one of the strongest in the nation.

Morgenthau's excuse was "limited financial resources," with priority 10 given to the prosecution of murderers, rapists, and burglars. Little has changed since then. Hardly a penny has been found in all those years to enforce New York's law against "adult" pornography, in which organized crime is heavily involved. With few exceptions, this lame "no priority, limited resources" excuse prevails among local prosecutors throughout the country.

But what about the federal laws? What's Uncle Sam's excuse? In 11 1986, for instance, the U.S. Postal Inspection Service investigated only nine cases of "prohibitive mailing" of "adult" pornography, resulting in only four convictions — an appalling record considering the tons of filth going through the mails daily.

Videocassettes that depict sexual aberrations — openly advertised in 12 homosexual tabloids — are the latest hot items using the U.S. mails. All a customer has to do is charge these hard-core videos to a major credit card and a mailman delivers them right to the door.

In 1985, I purchased three hard-core pornographic magazines openly 13 displayed in a Vermont country store. Since two were published in Cleveland and one in New York City, there was no question that the federal law prohibiting the interstate transportation of obscene materials had been violated.

When I telephoned the FBI and asked for an appointment to place in 14 their hands evidence of illegal smut, two agents politely rejected my request with the explanation that only child porn was being investigated because of limited resources. "The investigation of obscenity is in a holding pattern until the courts give us a better definition," one agent told me.

Plenty of Proof

The present test for obscenity asks (among other criteria) whether 15
the average person, applying contemporary community standards, would find that the work, taken as a whole, appeals to prurient interest. Those two key words — community standards — seem to be paralyzing the FBI and our nation's prosecutors. Yet past generations, not stripped of common sense, had no trouble at all in defining obscenity. It was simply "dirty books" and "dirty pictures," to be kept away from children.

Today, however, scientific "proof" is required that obscenity is harm- 16
ful. We need research grants and commissions and studies. We need to expose young men to violent pornography in isolation booths, hook up their genitals to electrodes, their chests to bellows and then pick their brains in order to reach a conclusion that my grandparents could have told them in a minute — that continued exposure to smut darkens the deepest recesses of men's minds.

Well, if it's studies that are needed, there are studies galore: 17

- In 1970 a research project financed by the Presidential Commission on Obscenity and Pornography (the Goldstein study) found that 55 percent of the males studied — rapists included — admitted being "excited to sex relations by pornography."
- Edward Donnerstein, a psychologist at the University of California at Santa Barbara, and Neil M. Malamuth, a psychologist at UCLA, have done separate studies on the effects of sexually violent material on men. Their findings indicate a desensitization of attitude toward violence against women, particularly with regard to rape.
- Research by Dolf Zillmann of Indiana University on *nonviolent* pornography shows that continued exposure to pornography featuring sex only, without physical violence, can result in callousness toward women and trivialization of rape.

If studies aren't enough, examples abound of how children's lives are 18
devastated by exposure to hard-core pornography. Yet law-enforcement officials simply aren't making the connection. Perhaps they haven't considered the tragic number of males, estimated at 250 a year, who have accidentally hanged themselves while following instructions in pornographic magazines for a bizarre autoerotic practice in which orgasm is supposedly intensified by momentary diminution of oxygen to the brain. Maybe they've overlooked the psychological rape of a nine-year-old, traumatized by her first exposure to sex — an orgy that included lesbian scenes, accidentally spilling over onto her TV screen from a subscription service. Perhaps they haven't heard about the fourteen-year-old boy who

had been reading porno magazines since the age of nine and became so totally out of control that several times weekly he'd rape his sister and two brothers (ages seven, six, and three when the sexual abuse began).

Sadistic Fantasies

How many bad seeds have been brought to fruition by a constant bombardment of depraved porn messages? Do we just put down the newspaper with a sigh and the proceed to forget cases such as the one involving David Eugene Pyles? The twenty-nine-year-old Pyles collected pornography and wrote stories about violent attacks on women. On October 14, 1985, he decided to act out his fantasies on a seventeen-year-old girl who was taking a walk at 1 P.M. in Joyce, Washington. He struck her with his car, then he drove to a wooded area where he sexually assaulted her and repeatedly cut her with a knife before she managed to escape. 19

Meanwhile, the American Civil Liberties Union continues to defend the free flow of pornography by arguing that a book never harmed anyone. In the next breath, however, ACLU officials assert that the best weapons against bad ideas are good ideas. Can they really believe that good books with good ideas are so powerful that pornography will just melt away in their presence? Or that bad books with bad ideas — such as *How to Have Sex With Kids* — have no more potential for harm than reading the phone book? They oppose the obscenity laws as having a "chilling effect" on the First Amendment, even though obscenity is not a First Amendment right any more than yelling "Fire!" in a crowded theater is. 20

Keep Shouting

From tiny hamlets to major cities, Americans are saying: ENOUGH! The court of public opinion — the most powerful force we have — wants hard-core pornography out of circulation. 21

How? Through vigorous enforcement of the obscenity laws; by enacting "harmful to minors" display laws that require soft-core porn be kept out of sight; by placing porn cable TV under the same legal strictures as conventional TV, with the full realization that what's inhaled in the privacy of the home is exhaled in the community. 22

Finally, let me share with you an old tale as I heard it told by Holocaust survivor and Nobel Peace Prize winner Elie Wiesel on the critical role of the individual: 23

A just man comes to Sodom hoping to save the city. He pickets. What else can he do? He goes from street to street, from marketplace to marketplace, shouting, "Men and women, repent. What you are doing is 24 wrong. It will kill you; it will destroy you." They laugh, but he goes on shouting, until one day a child stops him. "Poor stranger, don't you see it's useless?" "Yes," the just man replies. "Then why do you go on?" the child asks. "In the beginning," he says, "I was convinced that I would change them. Now I go on shouting because I don't want them to change me."

The message is profound. Let us not put away our pickets against por- 25
nography — ubiquitous, dehumanizing, desensitizing, brutal. Let us keep on shouting.

Pornography's Many Forms: Not All Bad

BARRY W. LYNN

The Justice Department has announced the creation of a new com- 1
mission to study "the serious national problem of pornography." Although many Americans might agree with this assessment, this judgmental mandate starts the inquiry too far along the course.

Is More Worse?

There is unquestionably more pornography available today than 2
fifteen years ago. However, is it legitimate to assume that more is worse? Pornography is speech, words, and pictures about sexuality. No one would consider an increase in the level of speech about religion or politics to be a completely negative development. What makes speech about sexuality different?

The examples used lately by antipornography advocates to charac- 3
terize the phenomenon, such as "women hung on meat-hooks," do tend to skew the debate. We are led to believe that billions of dollars are spent each year primarily to purchase chronicles of bestiality and mutilation. Focusing on these conceals many other kinds of explicit material.

In truth, pornography comes in many forms, but its general themes 4
are still consensual sex in a variety of places, couplings, and positions. Pornography both reflects and encourages sexual fantasies, possibly the most intimate form of human expression. It offers messages that are understood by viewers in distinctive ways.

Barry W. Lynn is a legislative counsel for the American Civil Liberties Union. His column appeared in the *Los Angeles Times,* May 23, 1985.

Female Subordination or "People Making It"?

Its critics accurately charge some of it with advocating the "subordination" of women, the very kind of repugnant message for which First Amendment protections are necessary. But does every centerfold really urge "subordination," or can it conceivably be an apolitical, aesthetic expression? A photo that theoretically fits the Women Against Pornography definition of acceptable erotica (depicting "mutual, respectful, affectionate, humorous, and power-balanced" sexuality) may still just be a picture of "naked people making it" to a seventeen-year-old with a copy under his bedcovers. 5

Like it or not, the eye and mind of the sexual beholder remain highly individual. 6

Taken as a whole, pornography advocates sexual experimentation. It asserts the pleasure of human sexuality even if unaccompanied by affection, permanent relationships, privacy, intent to procreate, or responsibility. There is certain to be heated and lengthy debate about the morality and aesthetics of such conduct. 7

The First Amendment does not only protect speech that is socially useful; the American Civil Liberties Union takes no institutional stand on the "quality" of speech, pornographic or otherwise. However, the increased availability of sexually explicit speech might make some beneficial contribution to society, even if it resists elevation to the status of high art. 8

Positive Uses of Pornography

The failure to examine some of its uses could be dangerous. Pornography certainly plays a cathartic role at times. Does the masturbation that it assists for adolescents serve as a substitute for sexual activity that could be far more detrimental, particularly for young women who risk pregnancy? 9

Similarly, Johns Hopkins therapist John Money notes, "Patients who request treatment in a sex-offender clinic commonly disclose that pornography helps them contain their abnormal sexuality within imagination, as a fantasy, instead of having to act it out in real life with an unconsenting, resentful partner, or by force." If it is legitimate to try to understand why pornography might trigger a rare individual to commit a crime of sexual violence, it is equally appropriate to try to understand how the material might prevent one. 10

For others the material has a claimed sex-education function, teaching couples about the varieties of sexual response and stimulating mutual interest. The increasingly graphic nature of the material is itself a 11 repudiation of the idea that only certain body parts of one gender are attractive. Sexual expression is no longer limited to fascination with large breasts and aversion to male genitalia. This, too, may be seen as a healthy development, particularly since the 1970 commission found that pornography was so controversial because of the "inability or reluctance of people in our society to be open and direct in dealing with sexual matters."

Our society also breeds an unequal distribution of sexual experience. 12
The myriad sexual opportunities open to those culturally defined as "beautiful" or "handsome" are denied to some who are shy, unattractive, or physically disabled. The role of pornography in the lives of such lonely persons, for whom visual images must substitute for sexual experiences with partners, is also worth consideration.

A defensible inquiry by a new commission should take fully into ac- 13
count all the competing claims about the meanings, effects, and significance of pornography, instead of proceeding doggedly on a moral crusade against fantasies.

The Place of Pornography

JEAN BETHKE ELSHTAIN

What is the place of pornography today? Pornography's place 1
changes as a society transforms itself politically, economically, morally, and aesthetically. Pornography has been heavily commercialized and is now readily available to all classes of society, as Al Goldstein pointed out. Porn has become a growth industry — a $7-billion-a-year business, by most estimates — and a very public vice, available as it once was not on Main Street, on videotapes sold in the corner drugstore. That pornography's place is now anywhere it can gain a toehold points to complex social transformations: Social fragmentation has increased over the past decade in our society; there are no longer any widely shared moral rules; the traditional ties of community that once served to guide people in living moral lives have broken down. This fragmentation has allowed a very ancient theme to emerge in a blatantly public way — the theme of absolutely unbridled erotic freedom.

Pornography has obviously been affected by changes in technology 2
— pornographers now use modern equipment such as videotape. Finally,

Jean Bethke Elshtain is a professor of political science at Vanderbilt University. Her remarks are from a forum moderated by Lewis Lapham that appeared in the November 1984 issue of *Harper's* magazine.

pornography may be encouraged by challenges to the traditional patriarchal prerogative in our society — challenges to male dominance. As Steven Marcus suggested in his book *The Other Victorians*, there is an inverse relationship between the growing number of dominating and sadistic images of masculine sexuality in pornography and the decline of male dominance in everyday life. In a sense, this is the reverse side of Susan Brownmiller's argument.

What is pornography's function? There are several. First, and most blatantly, porn has a commercial function — it's a big moneymaker. Todd Gitlin observed in his essay "The Left and Porno" that "porn occupies the shadow of legitimate culture and extends the boundaries of it. The marginal moral enterprise, like all crime in capitalist society, becomes big business." Second, if pornography is the marketing of fantasies, then we can assume, following Freud, that these fantasies provide something that is missing from real life — perhaps a sense of robust eroticism and joy in the body, perhaps a feeling of possessing crude power to compel others to do one's bidding. Third, as I mentioned, pornography helps reassure those frightened by the waning male prerogatives in our culture. 3

Why is there so much pornography? Perhaps because our need to celebrate ourselves and to express our dominance is so great. By "our" I mean a collective masculine we: men in a society that remains male dominated, men who live and work according to an intensely competitive performance principle and who evaluate themselves according to that principle. To attempt to eliminate these fantasies of dominance by censoring pornography — and here I agree with Erica Jong — is futile; such efforts only cover up the deeper truths that the fantasies themselves express. 4

Pornography Here and Abroad

ARYEH NEIER

For a good many years, I confronted the issue of pornography as a civil libertarian, defending the right of anyone to express himself in any way he chose as long as he did not directly infringe on the rights of others. Since I left the American Civil Liberties Union six years ago I've worked for organizations that are concerned with human rights in various repressive countries. In these countries, whether they are in Central 1

Aryeh Neier, of the Human Rights Watch, is former national executive director of the American Civil Liberties Union. His remarks were part of the *Harper's* magazine forum, November 1984.

America or Africa or Eastern Europe or wherever, there is virtually no pornography; but there is a great deal of the same hostility toward women and the same violence against women that one finds in the United States. In fact, in many of these countries sexual violence — mass rape or sexual torture or sexual humiliation — is one of the main forms political repression takes. I conclude from the astounding level of sexual violence in these countries and the absence of pornography that pornography is really not very important, that it is no more or less important than the great variety of images that dominates the media in the United States and other Western countries: images of sex and violence and melodrama and ugliness and beauty.

I suppose there is so much pornography because, like the nightly 2
melodramas on television, pornography is not very satisfying stuff; one seeks satisfaction by exposing oneself to more and more and more of it. Obviously, improvements in the technology involved in producing and distributing pornography contribute to the growing quantity of it. But more important is the fact that no particular pornographic image in Mr. Goldstein's magazine, or 100 or 1,000 other magazines, or 1,000 movies or live shows or whatever, means a great deal to the viewer. Thus he needs more and more images. In much the same way, one exposes oneself to a vast number of violent images or a vast number of melodramatic plots because none of them amounts to a great deal. What is really important about the surfeit of pornographic images is that it reflects one side of a society that is spoiled by too much of everything, including violent images of all sorts.

THINKING AND WRITING ABOUT PORNOGRAPHY

Questions for Discussion and Writing

1. The debate in this section revolves around several crucial distinctions. One such distinction is outlined by Goldstein, that between violent porn and non-violent porn. Is this distinction valid? In another confrontation Brownmiller asserts that pornography degrades women, but Goldstein argues that the real objection is derived from the Puritan and feminist hatred and fear of sex. How can one establish the validity of either of these claims?
2. Both Hefner and Lynn argue that pornography can have beneficial consequences. Are they responsive to Brownmiller's objections to pornography? How do you think Brownmiller would answer Hefner and Lynn in a debate?
3. Do the data provided by Gow refute the claims made by Hefner and Lynn that pornography does not promote violence? Explain why or why not. If not, what further evidence would be convincing? What bearing, if any, do such data have on the civil-rights position advocated by Jacoby?

4. How does Neier answer the charge that pornography causes rape? Does he prove his point? If you are not convinced, what would you say in rebuttal?
5. Does Elshtain satisfactorily explain the reasons for pornography? Can you think of others?
6. Is Wein's appeal for restraint equivalent to censorship? Does her evidence of the spread of pornography — beyond X-rated films and books — increase the strength of her argument? How does the language of her article affect her message?

Topics for Research

Pornography in rock music lyrics and/or comic books

Reasons for the growth of pornography (e.g., in rock music, comic books, dial-a-porn, computer messages)

The case for (or against) showing pornographic films on campus

Pornography causes (or does not cause) violent behavior

"A Renoir nude is art . . . and *Hustler* is trash." Are art and pornography distinguishable?

PART FOUR

CLASSIC ARGUMENTS

From Crito

PLATO

Plato, who died in 347 B.C., was one of the greatest Greek philosophers. He was a student of the Greek philosopher Socrates, whose teachings he recorded in the form of dialogues between Socrates and his pupils. In the dialogue below, Crito visits Socrates in prison — condemned to death for corrupting the youth of Athens — and tries to persuade him to escape. Socrates, however, refuses, basing his decision on his definition of justice and virtue.

Socrates: . . . Ought a man to do what he admits to be right, or ought he to betray the right? 1

Crito: He ought to do what he thinks right. 2

Socrates: But if this is true, what is the application? In leaving the prison against the will of the Athenians, do I wrong any? Or rather do I not wrong those whom I ought least to wrong? Do I not desert the principles which are acknowledged by us to be just — what do you say? 3

Crito: I cannot tell, Socrates; for I do not know. 4

Socrates: Then consider the matter in this way: — Imagine that I am about to play truant (you may call the proceeding by any name which you like), and the laws of the government come and interrogate me: "Tell us, Socrates," they say: "what are you about? Are you not going by an act of yours to overturn us — the laws, and the whole state, as far as in you lies? Do you imagine that a state can subsist and not be overthrown, in which the decisions of law have no power, but are set aside and trampled upon by individuals?" What will be our answer, Crito, to these and the like words? Any one, and especially a rhetorician, will have a good deal to say on behalf of the law which requires a sentence to be carried out. He will argue that this law should not be set aside; and shall we reply, "Yes, but the state has injured us and given an unjust sentence." Suppose I say that? 5

Crito: Very good, Socrates. 6

Socrates: "And was that our agreement with you?" the law would answer; "or were you to abide by the sentence of the state?" And if I were to express my astonishment at their words, the law would probably add: "Answer, Socrates, instead of opening your eyes — you are in the habit of asking and answering questions. Tell us, — What complaint have you to make against us which justifies you in attempting to destroy us and the state? In the first place did we not bring you into existence? Your father 7

From Plato's *Crito*, translated by Benjamin Jowett (3rd edition, 1982).

married your mother by our aid and begat you. Say whether you have any objection to urge against those of us who regulate marriage?" None, I should reply. "Or against those of us who after birth regulate the nurture and education of children, in which you also were trained? Were not the laws, which have the charge of education, right in commanding your father to train you in music and gymnastics?" Right, I should reply. "Well then, since you were brought into the world and nurtured and educated by us, can you deny in the first place that you are our child and slave, as your fathers were before you? And if this is true you are not on equal terms with us; nor can you think that you have a right to do to us what we are doing to you. Would you have any right to strike or revile or do any other evil to your father or your master, if you had one, because you have been struck or reviled by him, or received some other evil at his hands? — you would not say this? And because we think right to destroy you, do you think that you have any right to destroy us in return, and your country as far as in you lies? Will you, O professor of true virtue, pretend that you are justified in this? Has a philosopher like you failed to discover that our country is more to be valued and higher and holier far than mother or father or any ancestor, and more to be regarded in the eyes of the gods and of men of understanding? Also to be soothed, and gently and reverently entreated when angry, even more than a father, and either to be persuaded, or if not persuaded, to be obeyed? And when we are punished by her, whether with imprisonment or stripes, the punishment is to be endured in silence, and if she leads us to wounds or death in battle, thither we follow as is right; neither may any one yield or retreat or leave his rank, but whether in battle or in a court of law, or in any other place, he must do what his city and his country order him; or he must change their view of what is just: and if he may do no violence to his father or mother, much less may he do violence to his country." What answer shall we make to this, Crito? Do the laws speak truly, or do they not?

Crito: I think that they do. 8

Socrates: Then the laws will say, "Consider, Socrates, if we are speaking truly that in your present attempt you are going to do us an injury. For, having brought you into the world, and nurtured and educated you, and given you and every other citizen a share in every good which we had to give, we further proclaim to any Athenian by the liberty which we allow him, that if he does not like us when he has become of age and has seen the ways of the city, and made our acquaintance, he may go where he pleases and take his goods with him. None of us laws will forbid him or interfere with him. Any one who does not like us and the city, and who wants to emigrate to a colony or to any other city, may go where he likes, retaining his property. But he who has experience of the manner in which we order justice and administer the state, and still remains, has entered 9 into an implied contract that he will do as we command him. And he who disobeys us is, as we maintain, thrice wrong; first, because in disobeying us he is disobeying his parents; secondly, because we are the authors of his education; thirdly, because he has made an agreement with us that he will duly obey our commands; and he neither obeys them nor convinces us that our commands are unjust; and we do not rudely impose them, but give him the alternative of obeying or convincing us; — that is what we offer, and he does neither.

"These are the sort of accusations to which, as we were saying, you, 10
Socrates, will be exposed if you accomplish your intentions; you, above all other Athenians." Suppose now I ask, why I rather than anybody else? They will justly retort upon me that I above all other men have acknowledged the agreement. "There is clear proof," they will say, "Socrates, that we and the city were not displeasing to you. Of all Athenians you have been the most constant resident in the city, which, as you never leave, you may be supposed to love. For you never went out of the city either to see the games, except once when you went to the Isthmus, or to any other place unless when you were on military service; nor did you travel as other men do. Nor had you any curiosity to know other states or their laws: your affections did not go beyond us and our state; we were your special favourites, and you acquiesced in our government of you; and here in this city you begat your children, which is a proof of your satisfaction. Moreover, you might in the course of the trial, if you had liked, have fixed the penalty at banishment; the state which refuses to let you go now would have let you go then. But you pretended that you preferred death to exile, and that you were not unwilling to die. And now you have forgotten these fine sentiments, and pay no respect to us the laws, of whom you are the destroyer; and are doing what only a miserable slave would do, running away and turning your back upon the compacts and agreements which you made as a citizen. And first of all answer this very question: Are we right in saying that you agreed to be governed according to us in deed, and not in word only? Is that true or not?" How shall we answer, Crito? Must we not assent?

Crito: We cannot help it, Socrates. 11

Socrates: Then will they not say: "You, Socrates, are breaking the 12
covenants and agreements which you made with us at your leisure, not in any haste or under any compulsion or deception, but after you have had seventy years to think of them, during which time you were at liberty to leave the city, if we were not to your mind, or if our covenants appeared to you to be unfair. You had your choice, and might have gone either to Lacedaemon or Crete, both which states are often praised by you for their good government, or to some other Hellenic or foreign state. Whereas you, above all other Athenians, seemed to be so fond of the state, or, in

other words, of us her laws (and who would care about a state which has no laws?), that you never stirred out of her; the halt, the blind, the maimed were not more stationary in her than you were. And now you run away and forsake your agreements. Not so, Socrates, if you will take our advice; do not make yourself ridiculous by escaping out of the city.

"For just consider, if you transgress and err in this sort of way, what 13
good will you do either to yourself or to your friends? That your friends will be driven into exile and deprived of citizenship, or will lose their property, is tolerably certain; and you yourself, if you fly to one of the neighboring cities, as, for example, Thebes or Megara, both of which are well governed, will come to them as an enemy, Socrates, and their government will be against you, and all patriotic citizens will cast an evil eye upon you as a subverter of the laws, and you will confirm in the minds of the judges the justice of their own condemnation of you. For he who is a corrupter of the laws is more than likely to be a corrupter of the young and foolish portion of mankind. Will you then flee from well-ordered citizens and virtuous men? and is existence worth having on these terms? Or will you go to them without shame, and talk to them, Socrates? And what will you say to them? What you say here about virtue and justice and institutions and laws being the best things among men? Would that be decent of you? Surely not. But if you go away from well-governed states to Crito's friends in Thessaly, where there is a great disorder and licence, they will be charmed to hear the tale of your escape from prison, set off with ludicrous particulars of the manner in which you were wrapped in a goatskin or some other disguise, and metamorphosed as the manner is of runaways; but will there be no one to remind you that in your old age you were not ashamed to violate the most sacred laws from a miserable desire of a little more life? Perhaps not, if you keep them in a good temper; but if they are out of temper you will hear many degrading things; you will live, but how? — as the flatterer of all men, and the servant of all men; and doing what? — eating and drinking in Thessaly, having gone abroad in order that you may get a dinner. And where will be your fine sentiments about justice and virtue? Say that you wish to live for the sake of your children — you want to bring them up and educate them — will you take them into Thessaly and deprive them of Athenian citizenship? Is this the benefit which you will confer upon them? Or are you under the impression that they will be better cared for and educated here if you are still alive, although absent from them; for your friends will take care of them? Do you fancy that if you are an inhabitant of Thessaly they will take care of them, and if you are an inhabitant of the other world that they will not take of them? Nay: but if they who call themselves friends are good for anything, they will — to be sure they will.

"Listen, then, Socrates, to us who have brought you up. Think not of life and children first, and of justice afterwards, but of justice first, that you may be justified before the princes of the world below. For neither will you nor any that belong to you be happier or holier or juster in this life, or happier in another, if you do as Crito bids. Now you depart in innocence, a sufferer and not a doer of evil; a victim, not of the laws of men. But if you go forth, returning evil for evil, and injury for injury, breaking the covenants and agreements which you have made with us, and wronging those whom you ought least of all to wrong, that is to say, yourself, your friends, your country, and us, we shall be angry with you while you live, and our brethren, the laws in the world below, will receive you as an enemy; for they will know that you have done your best to destroy us. Listen, then, to us and not to Crito." 14

This, dear Crito, is the voice which I seem to hear murmuring in my ears, like the sound of the flute in the ears of the mystic; that voice, I say, is humming in my ears, and prevents me from hearing any other. And I know that anything more which you may say will be vain. Yet speak, if you have anything to say. 15

Crito: I have nothing to say, Socrates. 16

Socrates: Leave me then, Crito, to fulfill the will of God, and to follow whither he leads. 17

Discussion Questions

1. What debt to the law and his country does Socrates acknowledge? Mention the specific reasons for which he owes obedience. Is the analogy of the country to parents a plausible one? Why or why not?
2. Explain the nature of the "implied contract" that exists between Socrates and the state. According to the state, how has Socrates forfeited his right to object to punishment?
3. What appeal does the state make to Socrates' sense of justice and virtue?

Writing Suggestions

1. Socrates bases his refusal to escape the death penalty on his definition of justice and virtue. Basing your own argument on other criteria, make a claim for the right of Socrates to try to escape his punishment. Would some good be served by his escape?
2. The analogy between one's country and one's parents is illustrated at great length in Socrates' argument. In the light of modern ideas about the relationship between the state and the individual in a democracy, write a refutation of the analogy. Perhaps you can think of a different and more fitting one.

A Modest Proposal

JONATHAN SWIFT

*This essay is acknowledged by almost all critics to be the most powerful example of irony in the English language. (*Irony *means saying one thing but meaning another.) In 1729 Jonathan Swift, prolific satirist and dean of St. Patrick's Cathedral in Dublin, was moved to write in protest against the terrible poverty in which the Irish were forced to live under British rule. Notice that the essay is organized according to one of the patterns outlined in Part Two of this book (see "Presenting the Stock Issues," p. 261). First, Swift establishes the need for a change, then he offers his proposal, and finally, he lists its advantages.*

It is a melancholy object to those who walk through this great town[1] or travel in the country, when they see the streets, the roads, and cabin doors, crowded with beggars of the female sex, followed by three, four, or six children, all in rags and importuning every passenger for an alms. These mothers, instead of being able to work for their honest livelihood, are forced to employ all their time in strolling to beg sustenance for their helpless infants, who, as they grow up, either turn thieves for want of work, or leave their dear native country to fight for the Pretender in Spain, or sell themselves to the Barbados.[2] 1

I think it is agreed by all parties that this prodigious number of children in the arms, or on the backs, or at the heels of their mothers, and frequently of their fathers, is in the present deplorable state of the kingdom a very great additional grievance; and therefore whoever could find out a fair, cheap, and easy method of making these children sound, useful members of the commonwealth would deserve so well of the public as to have his statue set up for a preserver of the nation. 2

But my intention is very far from being confined to provide only for the children of professed beggars; it is of a much greater extent, and shall take in the whole number of infants at a certain age who are born of parents in effect as little able to support them as those who demand our charity in the streets. 3

From *A Tale of a Tub and Other Stories*, edited by Kathleen Williams (1975).

[1]Dublin. — Ed.

[2] The Pretender was James Stuart, who was exiled to Spain. Many Irishmen had joined an army attempting to return him to the English throne in 1715. Others had become indentured servants, agreeing to work for a set number of years in Barbados or other British colonies in exchange for their transportation out of Ireland. — Ed.

As to my own part, having turned my thoughts for many years upon this important subject, and maturely weighed the several schemes of other projectors,[3] I have always found them grossly mistaken in their computation. It is true, a child just dropped from its dam may be supported by her milk for a solar year, with little other nourishment; at most not above the value of two shillings, which the mother may certainly get, or the value in scraps, by her lawful occupation of begging; and it is exactly at one year that I propose to provide for them in such a manner as instead of being a charge upon their parents or the parish, or wanting food and raiment for the rest of their lives, they shall on the contrary contribute to the feeding, and partly to the clothing, of many thousands. 4

There is likewise another great advantage in my scheme, that it will prevent those voluntary abortions, and that horrid practice of women murdering their bastard children, alas, too frequent among us, sacrificing the poor innocent babes, I doubt, more to avoid the expense than the shame, which would move tears and pity in the most savage and inhuman breast. 5

The number of souls in this kingdom being usually reckoned one million and a half, of these I calculate there may be about two hundred thousand couples whose wives are breeders; from which number I subtract thirty thousand couples who are able to maintain their own children, although I apprehend there cannot be so many under the present distress of the kingdom; but this being granted, there will remain an hundred and seventy thousand breeders. I again subtract fifty thousand for those women who miscarry, or whose children die by accident or disease within the year. There only remain an hundred and twenty thousand children of poor parents annually born. The question therefore is, how this number shall be reared and provided for, which, as I have already said, under the present situation of affairs, is utterly impossible by all the methods hitherto proposed. For we can neither employ them in handicraft or agriculture; we neither build houses (I mean in the country) nor cultivate land. They can very seldom pick up a livelihood by stealing till they arrive at six years old, except where they are of towardly parts;[4] although I confess they learn the rudiments much earlier, during which time they can however be looked upon only as probationers, as I have been informed by a principal gentleman in the county of Cavan, who protested to me that he never knew above one or two instances under the age of six, even in a part of the kingdom so renowned for the quickest proficiency in that art. 6

---

[3] Planners. — Ed.

[4] Innate talents. — Ed.

I am assured by our merchants that a boy or a girl before twelve years old is no salable commodity; and even when they come to this age they will not yield above three pounds, or three pounds and a half a crown at most on the Exchange; which cannot turn to account either to the parents or the kingdom, the charge of nutriment and rags having been at least four times that value. 7

I shall now therefore humbly propose my own thoughts, which I hope will not be liable to the least objection. 8

I have been assured by a very knowing American of my acquaintance in London, that a young healthy child well nursed is at a year old a most delicious, nourishing, and wholesome food, whether stewed, roasted, baked, or boiled; and I make no doubt that it will equally serve in a fricassee or a ragout.[5] 9

I do therefore humbly offer it to public consideration that of the hundred and twenty thousand children, already computed, twenty thousand may be reserved for breed, whereof only one fourth part to be males, which is more than we allow to sheep, black cattle, or swine; and my reason is that these children are seldom the fruits of marriage, a circumstance not much regarded by our savages, therefore one male will be sufficient to serve four females. That the remaining hundred thousand may at a year old be offered in sale to the persons of quality and fortune through the kingdom, always advising the mother to let them suck plentifully in the last month, so as to render them plump and fat for a good table. A child will make two dishes at an entertainment for friends; and when the family dines alone, the fore or hind quarter will make a reasonable dish, and seasoned with a little pepper or salt will be very good boiled on the fourth day, especially in winter. 10

I have reckoned upon a medium that a child just born will weigh twelve pounds, and in a solar year if tolerably nursed increaseth to twenty-eight pounds. 11

I grant this food will be somewhat dear, and therefore very proper for landlords, who, as they have already devoured most of the parents, seem to have the best title to the children. 12

Infant's flesh will be in season throughout the year, but more plentiful in March, and a little before and after. For we are told by a grave author, an eminent French physician,[6] that fish being a prolific diet, there are more children born in Roman Catholic countries about nine months after Lent than at any other season; therefore, reckoning a year after Lent, the markets will be more glutted than usual, because the number 13

---

[5] Stew. — Ed.

[6] A reference to Swift's favorite French writer, François Rabelais (1494?–1553), who was actually a broad satirist known for his coarse humor. — Ed.

of popish infants is at least three to one in this kingdom; and therefore it will have one other collateral advantage, by lessening the number of Papists among us.

I have already computed the charge of nursing a beggar's child (in 14
which list I reckon all cottagers, laborers, and four-fifths of the farmers) to be about two shillings per annum, rags included; and I believe no gentleman would repine to give ten shillings for the carcass of a good fat child, which, as I have said, will make four dishes of excellent nutritive meat, when he hath only some particular friend or his own family to dine with him. Thus the squire will learn to be a good landlord, and grow popular among the tenants; the mother will have eight shillings net profit, and be fit for work till she produces another child.

Those who are more thrifty (as I must confess the times require) may 15
flay the carcass; the skin of which artificially[7] dressed will make admirable gloves for ladies, and summer boots for fine gentlemen.

As to our city of Dublin, shambles[8] may be appointed for this purpose 16
in the most convenient parts of it, and butchers we may be assured will not be wanting; although I rather recommend buying the children alive, and dressing them hot from the knife as we do roasting pigs.

A very worthy person, a true lover of his country, and whose virtues I 17
highly esteem, was lately pleased in discoursing on this matter to offer a refinement upon my scheme. He said that many gentlemen of his kingdom, having of late destroyed their deer, he conceived that the want of venison might be well supplied by the bodies of young lads and maidens, not exceeding fourteen years of age nor under twelve, so great a number of both sexes in every county being now ready to starve for want of work and service; and these to be disposed of by their parents, if alive, or otherwise by their nearest relations. But with due deference to so excellent a friend and so deserving a patriot, I cannot be altogether in his sentiments; for as to the males, my American acquaintance assured me from frequent experience that their flesh was generally tough and lean, like that of our schoolboys, by continual exercise, and their taste disagreeable; and to fatten them would not answer the charge. Then as to the females, it would, I think with humble submission, be a loss to the public, because they soon would become breeders themselves; and besides, it is not improbable that some scrupulous people might be apt to censure such a practice (although indeed very unjustly) as a little bordering upon cruelty; which, I confess, hath always been with me the strongest objection against any project, how well soever intended.

---

[7] With art or craft. — Ed.

[8] Butcher shops or slaughterhouses. — Ed.

But in order to justify my friend, he confessed that this expedient was put into his head by the famous Psalmanazar,[9] a native of the island Formosa, who came from thence to London above twenty years ago, and in conversation told my friend that in his country when any young person happened to be put to death, the executioner sold the carcass to persons of quality as a prime dainty; and that in his time the body of a plump girl of fifteen, who was crucified for an attempt to poison the emperor, was sold to his Imperial Majesty's prime minister of state, and other great mandarins of the court, in joints from the gibbet, at four hundred crowns. Neither indeed can I deny that if the same use were made of several plump young girls in this town, who without one single groat to their fortunes cannot stir abroad without a chair, and appear at the playhouse and assemblies in foreign fineries which they never will pay for, the kingdom would not be the worse. 18

Some persons of a desponding spirit are in great concern about that vast number of poor people who are aged, diseased, or maimed, and I have been desired to employ my thoughts what course may be taken to ease the nation of so grievous an encumbrance. But I am not in the least pain upon that matter, because it is very well known that they are every day dying and rotting by cold and famine, and filth and vermin, as fast as can be reasonably expected. And as to the younger laborers, they are now in almost as hopeful a condition. They cannot get work, and consequently pine away for want of nourishment to a degree that if any time they are accidentally hired to common labor, they have not strength to perform it; and thus the country and themselves are happily delivered from the evils to come. 19

I have too long digressed, and therefore shall return to my subject. I think the advantages by the proposal which I have made are obvious and many, as well as of the highest importance. 20

For first, as I have already observed, it would greatly lessen the number of Papists, with whom we are yearly overrun, being the principal breeders of the nation as well as our most dangerous enemies; and who stay at home on purpose to deliver the kingdom to the Pretender, hoping to take their advantage by the absence of so many good Protestants, who have chosen rather to leave their country than to stay at home and pay tithes against their conscience to an Episcopal curate. 21

Secondly, the poorer tenants will have something valuable of their own, which by law may be made liable to distress,[10] and help to pay their 22

[9] Georges Psalmanazar was a Frenchman who pretended to be Japanese and wrote an entirely imaginary *Description of the Isle Formosa*. He had become well known in gullible London society. — Ed.

[10] Subject to possession by lenders. — Ed.

landlord's rent, their corn and cattle being already seized and money a thing unknown.

23 Thirdly, whereas the maintenance of an hundred thousand children, from two years old and upwards, cannot be computed at less than ten shillings a piece per annum, the nation's stock will be thereby increased fifty thousand pounds per annum, besides the profit of a new dish introduced to the tables of all gentlemen of fortune in the kingdom who have any refinement in taste. And the money will circulate among ourselves, the goods being entirely of our own growth and manufacture.

24 Fourthly, the constant breeders, besides the gain of eight shillings sterling per annum by the sale of their children, will be rid of the charge of maintaining them after the first year.

25 Fifthly, this food would likewise bring great custom to taverns, where the vintners will certainly be so prudent as to procure the best receipts for dressing it to perfection, and consequently have their houses frequented by all the fine gentlemen, who justly value themselves upon their knowledge in good eating; and a skillful cook, who understands how to oblige his guests, will contrive to make it as expensive as they please.

26 Sixthly, this would be a great inducement to marriage, which all wise nations have either encouraged by rewards or enforced by laws and penalties. It would increase the care and tenderness of mothers toward their children, when they were sure of a settlement for life to the poor babes, provided in some sort by the public, to their annual profit instead of expense. We should see an honest emulation among the married women, which of them could bring the fattest child to the market. Men would become as fond of their wives during the time of their pregnancy as they are now of their mares in foal, their cows in calf, or sows when they are ready to farrow; nor offer to beat or kick them (as is too frequent a practice) for fear of a miscarriage.

27 Many other advantages might be enumerated. For instance, the addition of some thousand carcasses in our exportation of barreled beef, the propagation of swine's flesh, and improvements in the art of making good bacon, so much wanted among us by the great destruction of pigs, too frequent at our tables, which are no way comparable in taste or magnificence to a well-grown, fat, yearling child, which roasted whole will make a considerable figure at a lord mayor's feast or any other public entertainment. But this and many others I omit, being studious of brevity.

28 Supposing that one thousand families in this city would be constant customers for infants' flesh, besides others who might have it at merry meetings, particularly weddings and christenings, I compute that Dublin would take off annually about twenty thousand carcasses, and the rest of the kingdom (where probably they will be sold somewhat cheaper) the remaining eighty thousand.

I can think of no one objection that will possibly be raised against this proposal, unless it should be urged that the number of people will be thereby much lessened in the kingdom. This I freely own, and it was indeed one principal design in offering it to the world. I desire the reader will observe, that I calculate my remedy for this one individual kingdom of Ireland and for no other that ever was, is, or I think ever can be upon earth. Therefore let no man talk to me of other expedients: of taxing our absentees at five shillings a pound: of using neither clothes nor household furniture except what is of our own growth and manufacture: of utterly rejecting the materials and instruments that promote foreign luxury: of curing the expensiveness of pride, vanity, idleness, and gaming in our women: of introducing a vein of parsimony, prudence, and temperance: of learning to love our country, in the want of which we differ even from Laplanders and the inhabitants of Topinamboo:[11] of quitting our animosities and factions, nor acting any longer like the Jews, who were murdering one another at the very moment their city was taken:[12] of being a little cautious not to sell our country and conscience for nothing: of teaching landlords to have at least one degree of mercy toward their tenants: lastly, of putting a spirit of honesty, industry, and skill into our shopkeepers; who, if a resolution could now be taken to buy only our native goods, would immediately unite to cheat and exact upon us in the price, the measure, and the goodness, nor could ever yet be brought to make one fair proposal of just dealing, though often and earnestly invited to it. 29

Therefore I repeat, let no man talk to me of these and the like expedients, till he hath at least some glimpse of hope that there will ever be some hearty and sincere attempt to put them in practice. 30

But as to myself, having been wearied out for many years with offering vain, idle, visionary thoughts, and at length utterly despairing of success, I fortunately fell upon this proposal, which, as it is wholly new, so it hath something solid and real, of no expense and little trouble, full in our own power, and whereby we can incur no danger in disobliging England. For this kind of commodity will not bear exportation, the flesh being of too tender a consistence to admit a long continuance in salt, although perhaps I could name a country which would be glad to eat up our whole nation without it. 31

After all, I am not so violently bent upon my own opinion as to reject any offer proposed by wise men, which shall be found equally innocent, cheap, easy, and effectual. But before something of that kind shall be advanced in contradiction to my scheme, and offering a better, I desire the 32

---

[11] District of Brazil inhabited by primitive natives. — Ed.

[12] During the Roman siege of Jerusalem (A.D. 70), prominent Jews were charged with collaborating with the enemy and put to death. — Ed.

author or authors will be pleased maturely to consider two points. First, as things now stand, how they will be able to find food and raiment for an hundred thousand useless mouths and backs. And secondly, there being a round million of creatures in human figure throughout this kingdom, whose sole subsistence put into a common stock would leave them in debt two millions of pounds sterling, adding those who are beggars by profession to the bulk of farmers, cottagers, and laborers, with their wives and children who are beggars in effect; I desire those politicians who dislike my overture, and may perhaps be so bold to attempt an answer, that they will first ask the parents of these mortals whether they would not at this day think it a great happiness to have been sold for food at a year old in this manner I prescribe, and thereby have avoided such a perpetual scene of misfortunes as they have since gone through by the oppression of landlords, the impossibility of paying rent without money or trade, the want of common sustenance, with neither house nor clothes to cover them from the inclemencies of the weather, and the most inevitable prospect of entailing the like or greater miseries upon their breed forever.

I profess, in the sincerity of my heart, that I have not the least per- 33
sonal interest in endeavoring to promote this necessary work, having no other motive than the public good of my country, by advancing our trade, providing for infants, relieving the poor, and giving some pleasure to the rich. I have no children by which I can propose to get a single penny; the youngest being nine years old, and my wife past childbearing.

Discussion Questions

1. What implicit assumption about the treatment of the Irish underlies Swift's proposal? Do expressions such as "just dropped from its dam" and "whose wives are breeders" give the reader a clue?
2. In this essay Swift assumes a persona; that is, for the purposes of the proposal he makes, he pretends to be a different person. Describe the characteristics of that person. Point out the places in the essay that reveal them.
3. In several places, however, Swift reveals himself as the outraged witness of English cruelty and indifference. Note the language that seems to reflect his own feelings.
4. Throughout the essay Swift recites lists of facts, many of them in the form of statistics. How do these facts contribute to the persuasiveness of his argument? How do they affect the reader?
5. What social practices and attitudes of both the Irish and the English does Swift condemn?
6. Does Swift offer any solutions for the problems he attacks? How do you know?
7. When this essay first appeared in 1729, some readers took it seriously and

accused Swift of monstrous cruelty. Can you think of reasons why these readers failed to recognize the ironic intent?

Writing Suggestions

1. Try an ironical essay of your own. Choose a subject that clearly lends itself to such treatment. As Swift did, use logic and restraint in your language.
2. Choose a problem for which you think you have a solution. Defend your solution by using the stock issues as your pattern of organization.

Civil Disobedience

HENRY DAVID THOREAU

Henry David Thoreau (1817–1862), philosopher and writer, is best known for Walden, *an account of his solitary retreat to Walden Pond, near Concord, Massachusetts. Here he remained for more than two years in an effort to "live deliberately, to front only the essential facts of life." "Civil Disobedience" was first given as a lecture in 1848 and published in 1849. It was widely read and influenced both Mahatma Gandhi in the passive-resistance campaign he led against the British in India and Martin Luther King, Jr., in the civil-rights movement.*

I heartily accept the motto, — "That government is best which governs least"; and I should like to see it acted up to more rapidly and systematically. Carried out, it finally amounts to this, which I also believe, — "That government is best which governs not at all"; and when men are prepared for it, that will be the kind of government which they will have. Government is at best but an expedient; but most governments are usually, and all governments are sometimes, inexpedient. The objections which have been brought against a standing army, and they are many and weighty, and deserve to prevail, may also at last be brought against a standing government. The standing army is only an arm of the standing government. The government itself, which is only the mode which the people have chosen to execute their will, is equally liable to be abused and perverted before the people can act through it. Witness the present Mexican war, the work of comparatively a few individuals using the standing government as their tool; for, in the outset, the people would not have consented to this measure. 1

This American government, — what is it but a tradition, though a recent one, endeavoring to transmit itself unimpaired to posterity, but each instant losing some of its integrity? It has not the vitality and force of a single living man; for a single man can bend it to his will. It is a sort of wooden gun to the people themselves. But it is not the less necessary for this; for the people must have some complicated machinery or other, and hear its din, to satisfy that idea of government which they have. Governments show thus how successfully men can be imposed on, even impose on themselves, for their own advantage. It is excellent, we must all allow. Yet this government never of itself furthered any enterprise, but by the alacrity with which it got out of its way. *It* does not keep the country free. *It* does not settle the West. *It* does not educate. The character inherent in the American people has done all that has been accomplished; and it would have done somewhat more, if the government had not sometimes 2 got in its way. For government is an expedient by which men would fain succeed in letting one another alone; and, as has been said, when it is most expedient, the governed are most let alone by it. Trade and commerce, if they were not made of India-rubber, would never manage to bounce over the obstacles which legislators are continually putting in their way; and, if one were to judge these men wholly by the effects of their actions and not partly by their intentions, they would deserve to be classed and punished with those mischievous persons who put obstructions on railroads.

But, to speak practically and as a citizen, unlike those who call them- 3
selves no-government men, I ask for, not at once no government, but *at once* a better government. Let every man make known what kind of government would command his respect, and that will be one step toward obtaining it.

After all, the practical reason why, when the power is once in the 4
hands of the people, a majority are permitted, and for a long period continue, to rule, is not because they are most likely to be in the right, nor because this seems fairest to the minority, but because they are physically the strongest. But a government in which the majority rule in all cases cannot be based on justice, even as far as men understand it. Can there not be a government in which majorities do not virtually decide right and wrong, but conscience? — in which majorities decide only those questions to which the rule of expediency is applicable? Must the citizen ever for a moment, or in the least degree, resign his conscience to the legislator? Why has every man a conscience, then? I think that we should be men first, and subjects afterward. It is not desirable to cultivate a respect for the law, so much as for the right. The only obligation which I have the right to assume, is to do at any time what I think right. It is truly enough said, that a corporation has no conscience; but a corporation of conscientious men is a corporation *with* a conscience. Law never made men a whit more just; and, by means of their respect for it, even the well-disposed are daily made the agents of injustice. A common and natural result of an undue respect for law is, that you may see a file of soldiers, colonel, captain, corporal, privates, powder-monkeys, and all, marching in admirable order over hill and dale to the wars, against their wills, ay, against their common sense and consciences, which makes it very steep marching indeed, and produces a palpitation of the heart. They have no doubt that it is a damnable business in which they are concerned; they are all peaceably inclined. Now, what are they? Men at all? or small movable forts and magazines, at the service of some unscrupulous man in power? Visit the Navy-Yard, and behold a marine, such a man as an American government can make, or such as it can make a man with its black arts, — a mere shadow and reminiscence of humanity, a man laid out alive and

standing, and already, as one may say, buried under arms with funeral accompaniments, though it may be, —

> Not a drum was heard, not a funeral note,
> As his corse to the rampart we hurried;
> Not a soldier discharged his farewell shot
> O'er the grave where our hero we buried.

The mass of men serve the state thus, not as men mainly, but as machines, with their bodies. They are the standing army, and the militia, jailers, constables, posse comitatus, &c. In most cases there is no free exercise whatever of the judgment or of the moral sense; but they put themselves on a level with wood and earth and stones; and wooden men can perhaps be manufactured that will serve the purpose as well. Such command no more respect than men of straw or a lump of dirt. They have the same sort of worth only as horses and dogs. Yet such as these even are commonly esteemed good citizens. Others, — as most legislators, politicians, lawyers, ministers, and office-holders, — serve the state chiefly with their heads; and, as they rarely make any moral distinctions, they are as likely to serve the Devil, without *intending* it, as God. A very few, as heroes, patriots, martyrs, reformers in the great sense, and *men*, serve the state with their consciences also, and so necessarily resist it for the most part; and they are commonly treated as enemies by it. A wise man will only be useful as a man, and will not submit to be "clay," and "stop a hole to keep the wind away," but leave that office to his dust at least: — 5

> I am too high-born to be propertied,
> To be a secondary at control,
> Or useful serving-man and instrument
> To any sovereign state throughout the world.

He who gives himself entirely to his fellow-men appears to them useless and selfish; but he who gives himself partially to them is pronounced a benefactor and philanthropist. 6

How does it become a man to behave toward this American government today? I answer, that he cannot without disgrace be associated with it. I cannot for an instant recognize that political organization as *my* government which is the *slave's* government also. 7

All men recognize the right of revolution; that is, the right to refuse allegiance to, and to resist, the government, when its tyranny or its inefficiency are great and unendurable. But almost all say that such is not the case now. But such was the case, they think, in the Revolution of '75. If one were to tell me that this was a bad government because it taxed certain foreign commodities brought to its ports, it is most probable that I 8 should not make an ado about it, for I can do without them. All machines have their friction; and possibly this does enough good to counterbalance the evil. At any rate, it is a great evil to make a stir about it. But when the friction comes to have its machine, and oppression and robbery are organized, I say, let us not have such a machine any longer. In other words, when a sixth of the population of a nation which has undertaken to be the refuge of liberty are slaves, and a whole country is unjustly overrun and conquered by a foreign army, and subjected to military law, I think that it is not too soon for honest men to rebel and revolutionize. What makes this duty the more urgent is the fact, that the country so overrun is not our own, but ours is the invading army.

Paley, a common authority with many on moral questions, in his chapter on the "Duty of Submission to Civil Government," resolves all civil obligation into expediency; and he proceeds to say, "that so long as the interest of the whole society requires it, that is, so long as the established government cannot be resisted or changed without public inconveniency, it is the will of God that the established government be obeyed, and no longer. . . . . This principle being admitted, the justice of every particular case of resistance is reduced to a computation of the quantity of the danger and grievance on the one side, and of the probability and expense of redressing it on the other. Of this, he says, every man shall judge for himself. But Paley appears never to have contemplated those cases to which the rule of expediency does not apply, in which a people, as well as an individual, must do justice, cost what it may. If I have unjustly wrested a plank from a drowning man, I must restore it to him though I drown myself. This, according to Paley, would be inconvenient. But he that would save his life, in such a case, shall lose it. This people must cease to hold slaves, and to make war on Mexico, though it cost them their existence as a people. 9

In their practice, nations agree with Paley; but does any one think that Massachusetts does exactly what is right at the present crisis? 10

> A drab of state, a cloth-'o-silver slut,
> To have her train borne up, and her soul trail in the dirt.

Practically speaking, the opponents to a reform in Massachusetts are not a hundred thousand politicians at the South, but a hundred thousand merchants and farmers here, who are more interested in commerce and agriculture than they are in humanity, and are not prepared to do justice to the slave and to Mexico, *cost what it may*. I quarrel not with far-off foes, but with those who, near at home, cooperate with, and do the bidding of, those far away, and without whom the latter would be harmless. We are accustomed to say, that the mass of men are unprepared; but improvement is slow, because the few are not materially wiser or better than the many. It is not so important that many should be as good as you, as that there be some absolute goodness somewhere; for that will leaven the whole lump. There are thousands who are *in opinion* opposed to slavery and to the war, who yet in effect do nothing to put an end to them; who, esteeming themselves children of Washington and Franklin, sit down with their hands in their pockets, and say that they know not what to do, and do nothing; who even postpone the question of freedom to the question of free-trade, and quietly read the prices-current along with the latest advices from Mexico, after dinner, and, it may be, fall asleep over them both. What is the price-current of an honest man and a patriot today? They hesitate, and they regret, and sometimes they petition; but they do nothing in earnest and with effect. They will wait, well disposed, for others to remedy the evil, that they may no longer have it to regret. At most, they give only a cheap vote, and a feeble countenance and God-speed, to the right, as it goes by them. There are nine hundred and ninety-nine patrons of virtue to one virtuous man. But it is easier to deal with the real possessor of a thing than with the temporary guardian of it.

All voting is a sort of gaming, like checkers or backgammon, with a 11
slight moral tinge to it, a playing with right and wrong, with moral questions; and betting naturally accompanies it. The character of the voters is not staked. I cast my vote, perchance, as I think right; but I am not vitally concerned that that right should prevail. I am willing to leave it to the majority. Its obligation, therefore, never exceeds that of expediency. Even voting *for the right* is *doing* nothing for it. It is only expressing to men feebly your desire that it should prevail. A wise man will not leave the right to the mercy of chance, nor wish it to prevail through the power of the majority. There is but little virtue in the action of masses of men. When the majority shall at length vote for the abolition of slavery, it will be because they are indifferent to slavery, or because there is but little slavery left to be abolished by their vote. *They* will then be the only slaves. Only *his* vote can hasten the abolition of slavery who asserts his own freedom by his vote.

I hear of a convention to be held at Baltimore, or elsewhere, for the 12
selection of a candidate for the Presidency, made up chiefly of editors, and men who are politicians by profession; but I think, what is it to any independent, intelligent, and respectable man what decision they may come to? Shall we not have the advantage of his wisdom and honesty, nevertheless? Can we not count upon some independent votes? Are there not many individuals in the country who do not attend conventions? But no: I find that the respectable man, so called, has immediately drifted from his position, and despairs of his country, when his country has more reason to despair of him. He forthwith adopts one of the candidates thus selected as the only *available* one, thus proving that he is himself *avail-*

able for any purposes of the demagogue. His vote is of no more worth than that of any unprincipled foreigner or hireling native, who may have been bought. O for a man who is *a man*, and, as my neighbor says, has a bone in his back which you cannot pass your hand through! Our statistics are at fault: The population has been returned too large. How many *men* are there to a square thousand miles in this country? Hardly one. Does not America offer any inducement for men to settle here? The American has dwindled into an Odd Fellow, — one who may be known by the development of his organ of gregariousness, and a manifest lack of intellect and cheerful self-reliance; whose first and chief concern, on coming into the world, is to see that the Almshouses are in good repair; and, before yet he has lawfully donned the virile garb, to collect a fund for the support of the widows and orphans that may be; who, in short, ventures to live only by the aid of the Mutual Insurance company, which has promised to bury him decently.

It is not a man's duty, as a matter of course, to devote himself to the eradication of any, even the most enormous wrong; he may still properly have other concerns to engage him; but it is his duty, at least, to wash his hands of it, and, if he gives it no thought longer, not to give it practically his support. If I devote myself to other pursuits and contemplations, I must first see, at least, that I do not pursue them sitting upon another man's shoulders. I must get off him first, that he may pursue his contemplations too. See what gross inconsistency is tolerated. I have heard some of my townsmen say, "I should like to have them order me out to help put down an insurrection of the slaves, or to march to Mexico; — see if I would go"; and yet these very men have each, directly by their allegiance, and so indirectly, at least, by their money, furnished a substitute. The soldier is applauded who refuses to serve in an unjust war by those who do not refuse to sustain the unjust government which makes the war; is applauded by those whose own act and authority he disregards and sets at naught; as if the State were penitent to that degree that it hired one to scourge it while it sinned, but not to that degree that it left off sinning for a moment. Thus, under the name of Order and Civil Government, we are all made at last to pay homage to and support our own meanness. After the first blush of sin comes its indifference; and from immoral it becomes, as it were, *un*moral, and not quite unnecessary to that life which we have made. 13

The broadest and most prevalent error requires the most disinterested virtue to sustain it. The slight reproach to which the virtue of patriotism is commonly liable, the noble are most likely to incur. Those who, while they disapprove of the character and measures of a government, yield to it their allegiance and support, are undoubtedly its most conscientious supporters, and so frequently the most serious obstacles to reform. Some are petitioning the State to dissolve the Union, to disregard the req- 14 uisitions of the President. Why do they not dissolve it themselves, — the union between themselves and the State, — and refuse to pay their quota into its treasury? Do not they stand in the same relation to the State, that the State does to the Union? And have not the same reasons prevented the State from resisting the Union, which have prevented them from resisting the State?

How can a man be satisfied to entertain an opinion merely, and enjoy 15
it? Is there any enjoyment in it, if his opinion is that he is aggrieved? If you are cheated out of a single dollar by your neighbor, you do not rest satisfied with knowing that you are cheated, or with saying that you are cheated, or even with petitioning him to pay you your due; but you take effectual steps at once to obtain the full amount, and see that you are never cheated again. Action from principle, the perception and the performance of right, changes things and relations; it is essentially revolutionary, and does not consist wholly with anything which was. It not only divides states and churches, it divides families; ay, it divides the *individual*, separating the diabolical in him from the divine.

Unjust laws exist: Shall we be content to obey them, or shall we en- 16
deavor to amend them, and obey them until we have succeeded, or shall we transgress them at once? Men generally, under such a government as this, think that they ought to wait until they have persuaded the majority to alter them. They think that, if they should resist, the remedy would be worse than the evil. But it is the fault of the government itself that the remedy *is* worse than the evil. *It* makes it worse. Why is it not more apt to anticipate and provide for reform? Why does it not cherish its wise minority? Why does it cry and resist before it is hurt? Why does it not encourage its citizens to be on the alert to point out its faults, and *do* better than it would have them? Why does it always crucify Christ, and excommunicate Copernicus and Luther, and pronounce Washington and Franklin rebels?

One would think, that a deliberate and practical denial of its authority 17
was the only offence never contemplated by government; else, why has it not assigned its definite, its suitable and proportionate penalty? If a man who has no property refuses but once to earn nine shillings for the State, he is put in prison for a period unlimited by any law that I know, and determined only by the discretion of those who placed him there; but if he should steal ninety times nine shillings from the State, he is soon permitted to go at large again.

If the injustice is part of the necessary friction of the machine of gov- 18
ernment, let it go, let it go: Perchance it will wear smooth, — certainly the machine will wear out. If the injustice has a spring, or a pulley, or a rope, or a crank, exclusively for itself, then perhaps you may consider whether the remedy will not be worse than the evil; but if it is of such a nature that it requires you to be the agent of injustice to another, then, I say, break

the law. Let your life be a counter friction to stop the machine. What I have to do is to see, at any rate, that I do not lend myself to the wrong which I condemn.

As for adopting the ways which the State has provided for remedying the evil, I know not of such ways. They take too much time, and a man's life will be gone. I have other affairs to attend to. I came into this world, not chiefly to make this a good place to live in, but to live in it, be it good or bad. A man has not everything to do, but something; and because he cannot do *everything*, it is not necessary that he should do *something* wrong. It is not my business to be petitioning the Governor or the Legislature any more than it is theirs to petition me; and, if they should not hear my petition, what should I do then? But in this case the State has provided no way: Its very Constitution is the evil. This may seem to be harsh and stubborn and unconciliatory; but it is to treat with the utmost kindness and consideration the only spirit that can appreciate or deserves it. So is all change for the better, like birth and death, which convulse the body. 19

I do not hesitate to say, that those who call themselves Abolitionists should at once effectually withdraw their support, both in person and property, from the government of Massachusetts, and not wait till they constitute a majority of one, before they suffer the right to prevail through them. I think that it is enough if they have God on their side, without waiting for that other one. Moreover, any man more right than his neighbors constitutes a majority of one already. 20

I meet this American government, or its representative, the State government, directly, and face to face, once a year — no more — in the person of its tax-gatherer; this is the only mode in which a man situated as I am necessarily meets it; and it then says distinctly, Recognize me; and the simplest, the most effectual, and, in the present posture of affairs, the indispensablest mode of treating with it on this head, of expressing your little satisfaction with and love for it, is to deny it then. My civil neighbor, the tax-gatherer, is the very man I have to deal with, — for it is, after all, with men and not with parchment that I quarrel, — and he has voluntarily chosen to be an agent of the government. How shall he ever know well what he is and does as an officer of the government, or as a man, until he is obliged to consider whether he shall treat me, his neighbor, for whom he has respect, as a neighbor and well-disposed man, or as a maniac and disturber of the peace, and see if he can get over this obstruction to his neighborliness without a ruder and more impetuous thought or speech corresponding with his action. I know this well, that if one thousand, if one hundred, if ten men whom I could name, — if ten *honest* men only, — ay, if *one* HONEST man, in this State of Massachusetts, *ceasing to hold slaves*, were actually to withdraw from this copartnership, and be locked up in the county jail therefor, it would be the abolition of slavery in Amer- 21 ica. For it matters not how small the beginning may seem to be: What is once well done is done forever. But we love better to talk about it; That we say is our mission. Reform keeps many scores of newspapers in its service, but not one man. If my esteemed neighbor, the State's ambassador, who will devote his days to the settlement of the question of human rights in the Council Chamber, instead of being threatened with the prisons of Carolina, were to sit down the prisoner of Massachusetts, that State which is so anxious to foist the sin of slavery upon her sister, — though at present she can discover only an act of inhospitality to be the ground of a quarrel with her, — the Legislature would not wholly waive the subject the following winter.

Under a government which imprisons any unjustly, the true place for a just man is also a prison. The proper place today, the only place which Massachusetts has provided for her freer and less desponding spirits, is in her prisons, to be put out and locked out of the State by her own act, as they have already put themselves out by their principles. It is there that the fugitive slave, and the Mexican prisoner on parole, and the Indian come to plead the wrongs of his race, should find them; on that separate, but more free and honorable ground, where the State places those who are not *with* her, but *against* her, — the only house in a slave State in which a free man can abide with honor. If any think that their influence would be lost there, and their voices no longer afflict the ear of the State, that they would not be as an enemy within its walls, they do not know by how much truth is stronger than error, nor how much more eloquently and effectively he can combat injustice who has experienced a little in his own person. Cast your whole vote, not a strip of paper merely, but your whole influence. A minority is powerless while it conforms to the majority; it is not even a minority then; but it is irresistible when it clogs by its whole weight. If the alternative is to keep all just men in prison, or give up war and slavery, the State will not hesitate which to choose. If a thousand men were not to pay their tax-bills this year, that would not be a violent and bloody measure, as it would be to pay them, and enable the State to commit violence and shed innocent blood. This is, in fact, the definition of a peaceable revolution, if any such is possible. If the tax-gatherer, or any other public officer, asks me, as one has done, "But what shall I do?" my answer is, "If you really wish to do anything, resign your office." When the subject has refused allegiance, and the officer has resigned his office, then the revolution is accomplished. But even suppose blood should flow. Is there not a sort of blood shed when the conscience is wounded? Through this wound a man's real manhood and immortality flow out, and he bleeds to an everlasting death. I see this blood flowing now. 22

I have contemplated the imprisonment of the offender, rather than the seizure of his goods, — though both will serve the same purpose, — 23 because they who assert the purest right, and consequently are most dangerous to a corrupt State, commonly have not spent much time in accumulating property. To such the State renders comparatively small service, and a slight tax is wont to appear exorbitant, particularly if they are obliged to earn it by special labor with their hands. If there were one who lived wholly without the use of money, the State itself would hesitate to demand it of him. But the rich man, — not to make any invidious comparison, — is always sold to the institution which makes him rich. Absolutely speaking, the more money, the less virtue; for money comes between a man and his objects, and obtains them for him; and it was certainly no great virtue to obtain it. It puts to rest many questions which he would otherwise be taxed to answer; while the only new question which it puts is the hard but superfluous one, how to spend it. Thus his moral ground is taken from under his feet. The opportunities of living are diminished in proportion as what are called the "means" are increased. The best thing a man can do for his culture when he is rich is to endeavor to carry out those schemes which he entertained when he was poor. Christ answered the Herodians according to their condition. "Show me the tribute-money," said he; — and one took a penny out of his pocket; — if you use money which has the image of Cæsar on it, and which he has made current and valuable, that is, *if you are men of the State*, and gladly enjoy the advantages of Cæsar's government, then pay him back some of his own when he demands it; "Render therefore to Cæsar that which is Cæsar's, and to God those things which are God's," — leaving them no wiser than before as to which was which; for they did not wish to know.

When I converse with the freest of my neighbors, I perceive that, 24
whatever they may say about the magnitude and seriousness of the question, and their regard for the public tranquility, the long and the short of the matter is, that they cannot spare the protection of the existing government, and they dread the consequences to their property and families of disobedience to it. For my own part, I should not like to think that I ever rely on the protection of the State. But, if I deny the authority of the State when it presents its tax-bill, it will soon take and waste all my property, and so harass me and my children without end. This is hard. This makes it impossible for a man to live honestly, and at the same time comfortably, in outward respects. It will not be worth the while to accumulate property; that would be sure to go again. You must hire or squat somewhere, and raise but a small crop, and eat that soon. You must live within yourself, and depend upon yourself always tucked up and ready for a start, and not have many affairs. A man may grow rich in Turkey even, if he will be in all respects a good subject of the Turkish government. Confucius said: "If a state is governed by the principles of reason, poverty and misery are subjects of shame; if a state is not governed by the principles of

reason, riches and honors are the subjects of shame." No: Until I want the protection of Massachusetts to be extended to me in some distant Southern port, where my liberty is endangered, or until I am bent solely on building up an estate at home by peaceful enterprise, I can afford to refuse allegiance to Massachusetts, and her right to my property and life. It costs me less in every sense to incur the penalty of disobedience to the State, than it would to obey. I should feel as if I were worth less in that case.

Some years ago, the State met me in behalf of the Church, and com- 25
manded me to pay a certain sum toward the support of a clergyman whose preaching my father attended, but never I myself, "Pay," it said, "or be locked up in the jail." I declined to pay. But, unfortunately, another man saw fit to pay it. I did not see why the schoolmaster should be taxed to support the priest, and not the priest the schoolmaster; for I was not the State's schoolmaster, but I supported myself by voluntary subscription. I did not see why the lyceum should not present its tax-bill, and have the State to back its demand, as well as the Church. However, at the request of the selectmen, I condescended to make some such statement as this in writing: — "Know all men by these presents, that I, Henry Thoreau, do not wish to be regarded as a member of any incorporated society which I have not joined." This I gave to the town clerk; and he has it. The State, having thus learned that I did not wish to be regarded as a member of that church, has never made a like demand on me since; though it said that it must adhere to its original presumption that time. If I had known how to name them, I should then have signed off in detail from all the societies which I never signed on to; but I did not know where to find a complete list.

I have paid no poll-tax for six years. I was put into a jail once on this 26
account, for one night; and, as I stood considering the walls of solid stone, two or three feet thick, the door of wood and iron, a foot thick, and the iron grating which strained the light, I could not help being struck with the foolishness of that institution which treated me as if I were mere flesh and blood and bones, to be locked up. I wondered that it should have concluded at length that this was the best use it could put me to, and had never thought to avail itself of my services in some way. I saw that, if there was a wall of stone between me and my townsmen, there was a still more difficult one to climb or break through, before they could get to be as free as I was. I did not for a moment feel confined, and the walls seemed a great waste of stone and mortar. I felt as if I alone of all my townsmen had paid my tax. They plainly did not know how to treat me, but behaved like persons who are underbred. In every threat and in every compliment there was a blunder; for they thought that my chief desire was to stand the other side of that stone wall. I could not but smile to see how industriously they locked the door on my meditations, which

followed them out again without let or hindrance, and *they* were really all that was dangerous. As they could not reach me, they had resolved to punish my body; just as boys, if they cannot come at some person against whom they have a spite, will abuse his dog. I saw that the State was half-witted, that it was timid as a lone woman with her silver spoons, and that it did not know its friends from its foes, and I lost all my remaining respect for it, and pitied it.

Thus the State never intentionally confronts a man's sense, intellectual or moral, but only his body, his senses. It is not armed with superior wit or honesty, but with superior physical strength. I was not born to be forced. I will breathe after my own fashion. Let us see who is the strongest. What force has a multitude? They only can force me who obey a higher law than I. They force me to become like themselves. I do not hear of *men* being *forced* to live this way or that by masses of men. What sort of life were that to live? When I meet a government which says to me, "Your money or your life," why should I be in haste to give it my money? It may be in a great strait, and not know what to do: I cannot help that. It must help itself; do as I do. It is not worth the while to snivel about it. I am not responsible for the successful working of the machinery of society. I am not the son of the engineer. I perceive that, when an acorn and a chestnut fall side by side, the one does not remain inert to make way for the other, but both obey their own laws, and spring and grow and flourish as best they can, till one, perchance, overshadows and destroys the other. If a plant cannot live according to its nature, it dies; and so a man. 27

The night in prison was novel and interesting enough. The prisoners in their shirt-sleeves were enjoying a chat and the evening air in the doorway, when I entered. But the jailer said, "Come, boys, it is time to lock up"; and so they dispersed, and I heard the sound of their steps returning into the hollow apartments. My roommate was introduced to me by the jailer, as "a first-rate fellow and a clever man." When the door was locked, he showed me where to hang my hat, and how he managed matters there. The rooms were white-washed once a month; and this one, at least, was the whitest, most simply furnished, and probably the neatest apartment in the town. He naturally wanted to know where I came from, and what brought me there; and, when I had told him, I asked him in my turn how he came there, presuming him to be an honest man, of course; and, as the world goes, I believe he was. "Why," said he, "they accuse me of burning a barn; but I never did it." As near as I could discover, he had probably gone to bed in a barn when drunk, and smoked his pipe there; and so a barn was burnt. He had the reputation of being a clever man, had been there some three months waiting for his trial to come on, and would have to wait as much longer; but he was quite domesticated and 28 contented, since he got his board for nothing, and thought that he was well-treated.

He occupied one window, and I the other; and I saw, that, if one stayed there long, his principal business would be to look out the window. I had soon read all the tracts that were left there, and examined where former prisoners had broken out, and where a grate had been sawed off, and heard the history of the various occupants of that room; for I found that even here there was a history and a gossip which never circulated beyond the walls of the jail. Probably this is the only house in the town where verses are composed, which are afterward printed in a circular form, but not published. I was shown quite a long list of verses which were composed by some young men who had been detected in an attempt to escape, who avenged themselves by singing them. 29

I pumped my fellow-prisoner as dry as I could, for fear I should never see him again; but at length he showed me which was my bed, and left me to blow out the lamp. 30

It was like travelling into a far country, such as I had never expected to behold, to lie there for one night. It seemed to me that I never had heard the town-clock strike before, nor the evening sounds of the village; for we slept with the windows open, which were inside the grating. It was to see my native village in the light of the Middle Ages, and our Concord was turned into a Rhine stream, and visions of knights and castles passed before me. They were the voices of old burghers that I heard in the streets. I was an involuntary spectator and auditor of whatever was done and said in the kitchen of the adjacent village-inn, — a wholly new and rare experience to me. It was a closer view of my native town. I was fairly inside of it. I never had seen its institutions before. This is one of its peculiar institutions; for it is a shire town. I began to comprehend what its inhabitants were about. 31

In the morning, our breakfasts were put through the hole in the door, in small oblong-square tin pans, made to fit, and holding a pint of chocolate, with brown bread, and an iron spoon. When they called for the vessels again, I was green enough to return what bread I had left; but my comrade seized it, and said that I should lay that up for lunch or dinner. Soon after he was let out to work at haying in a neighboring field, whither he went every day, and would not be back till noon; so he bade me good-day, saying that he doubted if he should see me again. 32

When I came out of prison, — for some one interfered, and paid that tax, — I did not perceive that great changes had taken place on the common, such as he observed who went in a youth, and emerged a tottering and gray-headed man; and yet a change had to my eyes come over the scene, — the town, and State, and country, — greater than any mere time could effect. I saw yet more distinctly the State in which I lived. I saw to 33 what extent the people among whom I lived could be trusted as good neighbors and friends; that their friendship was for summer weather only; that they did not greatly propose to do right; that they were a distinct race from me by their prejudices and superstitions, as the Chinamen and Malays are; that, in their sacrifices to humanity, they ran no risks, not even to their property; that, after all, they were not so noble but they treated the thief as he had treated them, and hoped, by a certain outward observance and a few prayers, and by walking in a particular straight though useless path from time to time, to save their souls. This may be to judge my neighbors harshly; for I believe that many of them are not aware that they have such an institution as the jail in their village.

It was formerly the custom in our village, when a poor debtor came out of jail, for his acquaintances to salute him, looking through their fingers, which were crossed to represent the grating of a jail window, "How do ye do?" My neighbors did not thus salute me, but first looked at me, and then at one another, as if I had returned from a long journey. I was put into jail as I was going to the shoemaker's to get a shoe which was mended. When I was let out the next morning, I proceeded to finish my errand, and having put on my mended shoe, joined a huckleberry party, who were impatient to put themselves under my conduct; and in half an hour, — for the horse was soon tackled, — was in the midst of a huckleberry field, on one of our highest hills, two miles off, and then the State was nowhere to be seen. 34

This is the whole history of "My Prisons." 35

I have never declined paying the highway tax, because I am as desirous of being a good neighbor as I am of being a bad subject; and, as for supporting schools, I am doing my part to educate my fellow-countrymen now. It is for no particular item in the tax-bill that I refuse to pay it. I simply wish to refuse allegiance to the State, to withdraw and stand aloof from it effectually. I do not care to trace the course of my dollar, if I could, till it buys a man or a musket to shoot one with, — the dollar is innocent, — but I am concerned to trace the effects of my allegiance. In fact, I quietly declare war with the State, after my fashion, though I will still make what use and get what advantage of her I can, as is usual in such cases. 36

If others pay the tax which is demanded of me, from a sympathy with the State, they do but what they have already done in their own case, or rather they abet injustice to a greater extent than the State requires. If they pay the tax from a mistaken interest in the individual taxed, to save his property, or prevent his going to jail, it is because they have not considered wisely how far they let their private feelings interfere with the public good. 37

This, then, is my position at present. But one cannot be too much on his guard in such a case, lest his action be biased by obstinacy, or an un- 38 due regard for the opinions of men. Let him see that he does only what belongs to himself and to the hour.

I think sometimes, Why, this people mean well; they are only igno- 39
rant; they would do better if they knew how: why give your neighbors this pain to treat you as they are not inclined to? But I think again, this is no reason why I should do as they do, or permit others to suffer much greater pain of a different kind. Again, I sometimes say to myself, When many millions of men, without heat, without ill will, without personal feeling of any kind, demand of you a few shillings only, without the possibility, such is their constitution, of retracing or altering their present demand, and without the possibility, on your side, of appeal to any other millions, why expose yourself to this overwhelming brute force? You do not resist cold and hunger, the winds and the waves, thus obstinately; you quietly submit to a thousand similar necessities. You do not put your head into the fire. But just in proportion as I regard this as not wholly a brute force, partly a human force, and consider that I have relations to those millions as to so many millions of men, and not of mere brute or inanimate things, I see that appeal is possible, first and instantaneously, from them to the Maker of them, and, secondly, from them to themselves. But, if I put my head deliberately into the fire, there is no appeal to fire or to the Maker of fire, and I have only myself to blame. If I could convince myself that I have any right to be satisfied with men as they are, and to treat them according, and not according, in some respects, to my requisitions and expectations of what they and I ought to be, then, like a good Mussulman and fatalist, I should endeavor to be satisfied with things as they are, and say it is the will of God. And, above all, there is this difference between resisting this and a purely brute or natural force, that I can resist this with some effect; but I cannot expect, like Orpheus, to change the nature of the rocks and trees and beasts.

I do not wish to quarrel with any man or nation. I do not wish to split 40
hairs, to make fine distinctions, or set myself up as better than my neighbors. I seek rather, I may say, even an excuse for conforming to the laws of the land. I am but too ready to conform to them. Indeed, I have reason to suspect myself on this head; and each year, as the tax-gatherer comes round, I find myself disposed to review the acts and position of the general and State governments, and the spirit of the people, to discover a pretext for conformity.

> We must affect our country as our parents;
> And if at any time we alienate
> Our love or industry from doing it honor,
> We must respect effects and teach the soul
> Matter of conscience and religion,
> And not desire of rule or benefit.

I believe that the State will soon be able to take all my work of this sort out of my hands, and then I shall be no better a patriot than my fellow-countrymen. Seen from a lower point of view, the Constitution, with all its faults, is very good; the law and the courts are very respectable; even this State and this American government are, in many respects, very admirable and rare things, to be thankful for, such as a great many have described them; but seen from a point of view a little higher, they are what I have described them; seen from a higher still, and the highest, who shall say what they are, or that they are worth looking at or thinking of at all?

However, the government does not concern me much, and I shall be- 41
stow the fewest possible thoughts on it. It is not many moments that I live under a government, even in this world. If a man is thought-free, fancy-free, imagination-free, that which *is not* never for a long time appearing *to be* to him, unwise rulers or reformers cannot fatally interrupt him.

I know that most men think differently from myself; but those whose 42
lives are by profession devoted to the study of these or kindred subjects, content me as little as any. Statesmen and legislators, standing so completely within the institution, never distinctly and nakedly behold it. They speak of moving society, but have no resting-place without it. They may be men of a certain experience and discrimination, and have no doubt invented ingenious and even useful systems, for which we sincerely thank them; but all their wit and usefulness lie within certain not very wide limits. They are wont to forget that the world is not governed by policy and expediency. Webster never goes behind government, and so cannot speak with authority about it. His words are wisdom to those legislators who contemplate no essential reform in the existing government; but for thinkers, and those who legislate for all time, he never once glances at the subject. I know of those whose serene and wise speculations on this theme would soon reveal the limits of his mind's range and hospitality. Yet, compared with the cheap professions of most reformers, and the still cheaper wisdom and eloquence of politicians in general, his are almost the only sensible and valuable words, and we thank Heaven for him. Comparatively, he is always strong, original, and, above all, practical. Still his quality is not wisdom, but prudence. The lawyer's truth is not Truth, but consistency, or a consistent expediency. Truth is always in harmony with herself, and is not concerned chiefly to reveal the justice that may consist with wrong-doing. He well deserves to be called, as he has been called, the Defender of the Constitution. There are really no blows to be given by him but defensive ones. He is not a leader, but a follower. His leaders are the men of '87. "I have never made an effort," he says, "and never propose to make an effort; I have never countenanced an effort, and never mean to countenance an effort, to disturb the arrangement as originally made, by which the various States came into the Union." Still

thinking of the sanction which the Constitution gives to slavery, he says, "Because it was a part of the original compact, — let it stand." Notwithstanding his special acuteness and ability, he is unable to take a fact out of its merely political relations, and behold it as it lies absolutely to be disposed of by the intellect, — what, for instance, it behooves a man to do here in America today with regard to slavery, but ventures, or is driven, to make some such desperate answer as the following, while professing to speak absolutely, and as a private man, — from which what new and singular code of social duties might be inferred? "The manner," says he, "in which the governments of those States where slavery exists are to regulate it, is for their own consideration, under their responsibility to their constituents, to the general laws of propriety, humanity, and justice, and to God. Associations formed elsewhere, springing from a feeling of humanity, or any other cause, have nothing whatever to do with it. They have never received any encouragement from me, and they never will."[1]

They who know of no purer sources of truth, who have traced up its stream no higher, stand, and wisely stand, by the Bible and the Constitution, and drink at it there with reverence and humility; but they who behold where it comes trickling into this lake or that pool, gird up their loins once more, and continue their pilgrimage toward its fountain-head. 43

No man with a genius for legislation has appeared in America. They are rare in the history of the world. There are orators, politicians, and eloquent men, by the thousand; but the speaker has not yet opened his mouth to speak, who is capable of settling the much-vexed questions of the day. We love eloquence for its own sake, and not for any truth which it may utter, or any heroism it may inspire. Our legislators have not yet learned the comparative value of free-trade and of freedom, of union, and of rectitude, to a nation. They have no genius or talent for comparatively humble questions of taxation and finance, commerce and manufactures and agriculture. If we were left solely to the wordy wit of legislators in Congress for our guidance, uncorrected by the seasonable experience and the effectual complaints of the people, America would not long retain her rank among the nations. For eighteen hundred years, though perchance I have no right to say it, the New Testament has been written; yet where is the legislator who has wisdom and practical talent enough to avail himself of the light which it sheds on the science of legislation? 44

The authority of government, even such as I am willing to submit to, — for I will cheerfully obey those who know and can do better than I, and in many things even those who neither know nor can do so well, — is still an impure one: To be strictly just, it must have the sanction and consent 45

[1]These extracts have been inserted since the Lecture was read.

of the governed. It can have no pure right over my person and property but what I concede to it. The progress from an absolute to a limited monarchy, from a limited monarchy to a democracy, is a progress toward a true respect for the individual. Even the Chinese philosopher was wise enough to regard the individual as the basis of the empire. Is a democracy, such as we know it, the last improvement possible in government? Is it not possible to take a step further towards recognizing and organizing the rights of man? There will never be a really free and enlightened State, until the State comes to recognize the individual as a higher and independent power, from which all its own power and authority are derived, and treats him accordingly. I please myself with imagining a State at last which can afford to be just to all men, and to treat the individual with respect as a neighbor; which even would not think it inconsistent with its own repose, if a few were to live aloof from it, not meddling with it, nor embraced by it, who fulfilled all the duties of neighbors and fellowmen. A State which bore this kind of fruit, and suffered it to drop off as fast as it ripened, would prepare the way for a still more perfect and glorious State, which also I have imagined, but not yet anywhere seen.

Discussion Questions

1. Summarize briefly Thoreau's reasons for arguing that civil disobedience is sometimes a *duty*.
2. Thoreau, like Martin Luther King, Jr., in "Letter from Birmingham Jail" (p. 611), speaks of "unjust laws." Do they agree on the positions that citizens should take in response to these laws? Are Thoreau and King guided by the same principles? In Plato's "Crito" (p. 555), what does Socrates say about obedience to unjust laws?
3. What examples of government policy and action does Thoreau use to prove that civil disobedience is a duty? Explain why they are — or are not — effective.
4. Why do you think Thoreau provides such a detailed account of his one day in prison? (Notice that King does not give a description of his confinement.) What observation about the community struck Thoreau when he emerged from jail?

Writing Suggestions

1. Choose a government policy or law with which you are familiar, and argue that civil disobedience to it is justified. (Examples might include the Vietnam War, the draft, dangers to the environment, a university regulation.) Be specific about the injustice of the law or policy and the values that underlie the resistance.

2. Under what circumstances might civil disobedience prove to be dangerous and immoral? Can you think of cases of disobediences when *conscience*, as Thoreau uses the term, did not appear to be the guiding principle? Try to identify what you think is the true motivation for the resistance.

Declaration of Sentiments and Resolutions, Seneca Falls

ELIZABETH CADY STANTON

Elizabeth Cady Stanton (1815–1902) was an early activist in the movement for women's rights, including the right to vote and the freedom to enroll in college and to enter professions that were closed to women. She was also active in the campaign to abolish slavery. In 1848 the first women's rights convention was held in her home in Seneca Falls, New York, where the "Declaration of Sentiments and Resolutions" was issued.

When, in the course of human events, it becomes necessary for one portion of the family of man to assume among the people of the earth a position different from that which they have hitherto occupied, but one to which the laws of nature and of nature's God entitle them, a decent respect to the opinions of mankind requires that they should declare the causes that impel them to such a course. 1

We hold these truths to be self-evident: that all men and women are created equal; that they are endowed by their Creator with certain inalienable rights; that among these are life, liberty, and the pursuit of happiness; that to secure these rights governments are instituted, deriving their just powers from the consent of the governed. Whenever any form of government becomes destructive of these ends, it is the right of those who suffer from it to refuse allegiance to it, and to insist upon the institution of a new government, laying its foundation on such principles, and organizing its powers in such form, as to them shall seem most likely to effect their safety and happiness. Prudence, indeed, will dictate that governments long established should not be changed for light and transient causes; and accordingly all experience hath shown that mankind are more disposed to suffer, while evils are sufferable, then to right themselves by abolishing the forms to which they were accustomed. But when a long train of abuses and usurpations, pursuing invariably the same object evinces a design to reduce them under absolute despotism, it is their duty to throw off such government, and to provide new guards for their future security. Such has been the patient sufferance of the women under this government, and such is now the necessity which constrains them to demand the equal station to which they are entitled. 2

The history of mankind is a history of repeated injuries and usurpations on the part of man toward woman, having in direct object the estab- 3

From *Feminism: The Essential Historical Writings*, edited by Miriam Schneir (1972).

lishment of an absolute tyranny over her. To prove this, let facts be submitted to a candid world.

He has never permitted her to exercise her inalienable right to the 4
elective franchise.

He has compelled her to submit to laws, in the formation of which she 5
had no voice.

He has withheld from her rights which are given to the most ignorant 6
and degraded men — both natives and foreigners.

Having deprived her of this first right of a citizen, the elective fran- 7
chise, thereby leaving her without representation in the halls of legislation, he has oppressed her on all sides.

He has made her, if married, in the eye of the law, civilly dead. 8

He has taken from her all right in property, even to the wages she 9
earns.

He has made her, morally, an irresponsible being, as she can commit 10
many crimes with impunity, provided they be done in the presence of her husband. In the covenant of marriage, she is compelled to promise obedience to her husband, he becoming, to all intents and purposes, her master — the law giving him power to deprive her of her liberty, and to administer chastisement.

He has so framed the laws of divorce, as to what shall be the proper 11
causes, and in case of separation, to whom the guardianship of the children shall be given, as to be wholly regardless of the happiness of women — the law, in all cases, going upon a false supposition of the supremacy of man, and giving all power into his hands.

After depriving her of all rights as a married woman, if single, and the 12
owner of property, he has taxed her to support a government which recognizes her only when her property can be made profitable to it.

He has monopolized nearly all the profitable employments, and from 13
those she is permitted to follow, she receives but a scanty remuneration. He closes against her all the avenues to wealth and distinction which he considers most honorable to himself. As a teacher of theology, medicine, or law, she is not known.

He has denied her the facilities for obtaining a thorough education, all 14
colleges being closed against her.

He allows her in Church, as well as State, but a subordinate position, 15
claiming Apostolic authority for her exclusion from the ministry, and, with some exceptions, from any public participation in the affairs of the Church.

He has created a false public sentiment by giving to the world a 16
different code of morals for men and women, by which moral delinquencies which exclude women from society, are not only tolerated, but deemed of little account in man.

He has usurped the prerogative of Jehovah himself, claiming it as his right to assign for her a sphere of action, when that belongs to her conscience and to her God. 17

He has endeavored, in every way that he could, to destroy her confidence in her own powers, to lessen her self-respect, and to make her willing to lead a dependent and abject life. 18

Now, in view of this entire disfranchisement of one-half the people of this country, their social and religious degradation—in view of the unjust laws above mentioned, and because women do feel themselves aggrieved, oppressed, and fraudulently deprived of their most sacred rights, we insist that they have immediate admission to all the rights and privileges which belong to them as citizens of the United States. 19

In entering upon the great work before us, we anticipate no small amount of misconception, misrepresentation, and ridicule; but we shall use every instrumentality within our power to effect our object. We shall employ agents, circulate tracts, petition the State and National legislatures, and endeavor to enlist the pulpit and the press in our behalf. We hope this Convention will be followed by a series of Conventions embracing every part of the country. 20

Resolutions

WHEREAS, The great precept of nature is conceded to be, that "man shall pursue his own true and substantial happiness." Blackstone in his Commentaries remarks, that this law of Nature being coeval with mankind, and dictated by God himself, is of course superior in obligation to any other. It is binding over all the globe, in all countries and at all times; no human laws are of any validity if contrary to this, and such of them as are valid, derive all their force, and all their validity, and all their authority, mediately and immediately, from this original; therefore, 21

Resolved, That such laws as conflict, in any way, with the true and substantial happiness of woman, are contrary to the great precept of nature and of no validity, for this is "superior in obligation to any other." 22

Resolved, That all laws which prevent woman from occupying such a station in society as her conscience shall dictate, or which place her in a position inferior to that of man, are contrary to the great precept of nature, and therefore of no force or authority. 23

Resolved, That woman is man's equal—was intended to be so by the Creator, and the highest good of the race demands that she should be recognized as such. 24

Resolved, That the women of this country ought to be enlightened in regard to the laws under which they live, that they may no longer publish their degradation by declaring themselves satisfied with their present po- 25 sition, nor their ignorance, by asserting that they have all the rights they want.

Resolved, That inasmuch as man, while claiming for himself intellectual superiority, does accord to woman moral superiority, it is preeminently his duty to encourage her to speak and teach, as she has an opportunity, in all religious assemblies. 26

Resolved, That the same amount of virtue, delicacy, and refinement of behavior that is required of woman in the social state, should also be required of man, and the same transgressions should be visited with equal severity on both man and woman. 27

Resolved, That the objection of indelicacy and impropriety, which is so often brought against woman when she addresses a public audience, comes with a very ill-grace from those who encourage, by their attendance, her appearance on the stage, in the concert, or in feats of the circus. 28

Resolved, That woman has too long rested satisfied in the circumscribed limits which corrupt customs and a perverted application of the Scriptures have marked out for her, and that it is time she should move in the enlarged sphere which her great Creator has assigned her. 29

Resolved, That it is the duty of the women of this country to secure to themselves their sacred right to the elective franchise. 30

Resolved, That the equality of human rights results necessarily from the fact of the identity of the race in capabilities and responsibilities. 31

Resolved, therefore, That, being invested by the Creator with the same capabilities, and the same consciousness of responsibility for their exercise, it is demonstrably the right and duty of woman, equally with man, to promote every righteous cause by every righteous means; and especially in regard to the great subjects of morals and religion, it is self-evidently her right to participate with her brother in teaching them, both in private and in public, by writing and by speaking, by any instrumentalities proper to be used, and in any assemblies proper to be held; and this being a self-evident truth growing out of the divinely implanted principles of human nature, any custom or authority adverse to it, whether modern or wearing the hoary sanction of antiquity, is to be regarded as a self-evident falsehood, and at war with mankind. 32

[At the last session Lucretia Mott offered and spoke to the following resolution:]

Resolved, That the speedy success of our cause depends upon the zealous and untiring efforts of both men and women, for the overthrow of the monopoly of the pulpit, and for the securing to woman an equal participation with men in the various trades, professions, and commerce. 33

Discussion Questions

1. Are all the grievances listed in the document of equal importance? If not, which seem the most important? Why?
2. What is the great precept of nature on which the resolutions are based? How does this compare to the motivating principle of the Declaration of Independence?
3. What characteristics of male thinking and behavior are attacked in the Declaration at Seneca Falls?
4. Does the Declaration at Seneca Falls anywhere suggest that women have gifts superior to those of men? Does it suggest that equal rights for women bestow benefits on others as well?

Writing Suggestions

1. Is it necessary today to call attention to some of the old grievances or to suggest new ones? Pick out one or two old issues and offer examples to show that such a need no longer exists. Or argue that women are still being deprived of their right to their own "true and substantial happiness."
2. Most newspapers and journals treated the Declaration at Seneca Falls with contempt and ridicule. What attitudes and convictions in the midnineteenth century could have caused such a reaction?

Professions for Women

VIRGINIA WOOLF

Virginia Woolf (1882–1941) was a novelist and essayist and a leading member of the Bloomsbury group, a celebrated circle of writers, artists, and intellectuals that flourished in London in the early part of the century. Her novels, among them Mrs. Dalloway, To the Lighthouse, *and* The Waves, *were brilliant technical experiments. Her essays and literary criticism were highly original, distinguished by wit and spontaneity. All her life she suffered from nervous depression, and in 1941 she committed suicide. "Professions for Women" was a paper read to the Women's Service League in London in 1931.*

When your secretary invited me to come here, she told me that your 1
Society is concerned with the employment of women and she suggested that I might tell you something about my own professional experiences. It is true I am a woman; it is true I am employed; but what professional experiences have I had? It is difficult to say. My profession is literature; and in that profession there are fewer experiences for women than in any other, with the exception of the stage — fewer, I mean, that are peculiar to women. For the road was cut many years ago — by Fanny Burney, by Aphra Behn, by Harriet Martineau, by Jane Austen, by George Eliot — many famous women, and many more unknown and forgotten, have been before me, making the path smooth, and regulating my steps. Thus, when I came to write, there were very few material obstacles in my way. Writing was a reputable and harmless occupation. The family peace was not broken by the scratching of a pen. No demand was made upon the family purse. For ten and sixpence one can buy paper enough to write all the plays of Shakespeare — if one has a mind that way. Pianos and models, Paris, Vienna and Berlin, masters and mistresses, are not needed by a writer. The cheapness of writing paper is, of course, the reason why women have succeeded as writers before they have succeeded in the other professions.

But to tell you my story — it is a simple one. You have only got to 2
figure to yourselves a girl in a bedroom with a pen in her hand. She had only to move that pen from left to right — from ten o'clock to one. Then it occurred to her to do what is simple and cheap enough after all — to slip a few of those pages into an envelope, fix a penny stamp in the corner, and drop the envelope into the red box at the corner. It was thus that I

From *The Death of the Moth and Other Essays* (1942).

became a journalist; and my effort was rewarded on the first day of the following month — a very glorious day it was for me — by a letter from an editor containing a check for one pound ten shillings and sixpence. But to show you how little I deserve to be called a professional woman, how little I know of the struggles and difficulties of such lives, I have to admit that instead of spending that sum upon bread and butter, rent, shoes, and stockings, or butcher's bills, I went out and bought a cat — a beautiful cat, a Persian cat, which very soon involved me in bitter disputes with my neighbors.

What could be easier than to write articles and to buy Persian cats 3
with the profits? But wait a moment. Articles have to be about something. Mine, I seem to remember, was about a novel by a famous man. And while I was writing this review, I discovered that if I were going to review books I should need to do battle with a certain phantom. And the phantom was a woman, and when I came to know her better I called her after the heroine of a famous poem, the Angel in the House. It was she who used to come between me and my paper when I was writing reviews. It was she who bothered me and wasted my time and so tormented me that at last I killed her. You who come of a younger and happier generation may not have heard of her — you may not know what I mean by the Angel in the House. I will describe her as shortly as I can. She was intensely sympathetic. She was immensely charming. She was utterly unselfish. She excelled in the difficult arts of family life. She sacrificed herself daily. If there was a chicken, she took the leg; if there was a draft she sat in it — in short she was so constituted that she never had a mind or a wish of her own, but preferred to sympathize always with the minds and wishes of others. Above all — I need not say it — she was pure. Her purity was supposed to be her chief beauty — her blushes, her great grace. In those days — the last of Queen Victoria — every house had its Angel. And when I came to write I encountered her with the very first words. The shadow of her wings fell on my page; I heard the rustling of her skirts in the room. Directly, that is to say, I took my pen in my hand to review that novel by a famous man, she slipped behind me and whispered: "My dear, you are a young woman. You are writing about a book that has been written by a man. Be sympathetic; be tender; flatter; deceive; use all the arts and wiles of our sex. Never let anybody guess that you have a mind of your own. Above all, be pure." And she made as if to guide my pen. I now record the one act for which I take some credit to myself, though the credit rightly belongs to some excellent ancestors of mine who left me a certain sum of money — shall we say five hundred pounds a year? — so that it was not necessary for me to depend solely on charm for my living. I turned upon her and caught her by the throat. I did my best to kill her. My excuse, if I were to be had up in a court of law, would be that I acted in self-defense.

Had I not killed her she would have killed me. She would have plucked the heart out of my writing. For, as I found, directly I put pen to paper, you cannot review even a novel without having a mind of your own, without expressing what you think to be the truth about human relations, morality, sex. And all these questions, according to the Angel of the House, cannot be dealt with freely and openly by women; they must charm, they must conciliate, they must — to put it bluntly — tell lies if they are to succeed. Thus, whenever I felt the shadow of her wing or the radiance of her halo upon my page, I took up the inkpot and flung it at her. She died hard. Her fictitious nature was of great assistance to her. It is far harder to kill a phantom than a reality. She was always creeping back when I thought I had dispatched her. Though I flatter myself that I killed her in the end, the struggle was severe; it took much time that had better have been spent upon learning Greek grammar; or in roaming the world in search of adventures. But it was a real experience; it was an experience that was found to befall all women writers at that time. Killing the Angel in the House was part of the occupation of a woman writer.

But to continue my story. The Angel was dead; what then remained? 4
You may say that what remained was a simple and common object — a young woman in a bedroom with an inkpot. In other words, now that she had rid herself of falsehood, that young woman had only to be herself. Ah, but what is "herself"? I mean, what is a woman? I assure you, I do not know. I do not believe that you know. I do not believe that anybody can know until she has expressed herself in all the arts and professions open to human skill. That indeed is one of the reasons why I have come here — out of respect for you, who are in process of showing us by your experiments what a woman is, who are in process of providing us, by your failures and successes, with that extremely important piece of information.

But to continue the story of my professional experiences, I made one 5
pound ten and six by my first review; and I bought a Persian cat with the proceeds. Then I grew ambitious. A Persian cat is all very well, I said; but a Persian cat is not enough. I must have a motor car. And it was thus that I became a novelist — for it is a very strange thing that people will give you a motor car if you will tell them a story. It is a still stranger thing that there is nothing so delightful in the world as telling stories. It is far pleasanter than writing reviews of famous novels. And yet, if I am to obey your secretary and tell you my professional experiences as a novelist, I must tell you about a very strange experience that befell me as a novelist. And to understand it you must try first to imagine a novelist's state of mind. I hope I am not giving away professional secrets if I say that a novelist's chief desire is to be as unconscious as possible. He has to induce in himself a state of perpetual lethargy. He wants life to proceed with the utmost quiet and regularity. He wants to see the same faces, to read the

same books, to do the same things day after day, month after month, while he is writing, so that nothing may break the illusion in which he is living — so that nothing may disturb or disquiet the mysterious nosings about, feelings round, darts, dashes, and sudden discoveries of that very shy and illusive spirit, the imagination. I suspect that this state is the same both for men and women. Be that as it may, I want you to imagine me writing a novel in a state of trance. I want you to figure to yourselves a girl sitting with a pen in her hand, which for minutes, and indeed for hours, she never dips into the inkpot. The image that comes to my mind when I think of this girl is the image of a fisherman lying sunk in dreams on the verge of a deep lake with a rod held out over the water. She was letting her imagination sweep unchecked round every rock and cranny of the world that lies submerged in the depths of our unconscious being. Now came the experience, the experience that I believe to be far commoner with women writers than with men. The line raced through the girl's fingers. Her imagination had rushed away. It had sought the pools, the depths, the dark places where the largest fish slumber. And then there was a smash. There was an explosion. There was foam and confusion. The imagination had dashed itself against something hard. The girl was roused from her dream. She was indeed in a state of the most acute and difficult distress. To speak without figure she had thought of something, something about the body, about the passions which it was unfitting for her as a woman to say. Men, her reason told her, would be shocked. The consciousness of what men will say of a woman who speaks the truth about her passions had roused her from her artist's state of unconsciousness. She could write no more. The trance was over. Her imagination could work no longer. This I believe to be a very common experience with women writers — they are impeded by the extreme conventionality of the other sex. For though men sensibly allow themselves great freedom in these respects, I doubt that they realize or can control the extreme severity with which they condemn such freedom in women.

These then were two very genuine experiences of my own. These 6
were two of the adventures of my professional life. The first — killing the Angel in the House — I think I solved. She died. But the second, telling the truth about my own experiences as a body, I do not think I solved. I doubt that any woman has solved it yet. The obstacles against her are still immensely powerful — and yet they are very difficult to define. Outwardly, what is simpler than to write books? Outwardly, what obstacles are there for a woman rather than for a man? Inwardly, I think, the case is very different; she has still many ghosts to fight, many prejudices to overcome. Indeed it will be a long time still, I think, before a woman can sit down to write a book without finding a phantom to be slain, a rock to be dashed against. And if this is so in literature, the freest of all professions for

women, how is it in the new professions which you are now for the first time entering?

Those are the questions that I should like, had I time, to ask you. And indeed, if I have laid stress upon these professional experiences of mine, it is because I believe that they are, though in different forms, yours also. Even when the path is nominally open — when there is nothing to prevent a woman from being a doctor, a lawyer, a civil servant — there are many phantoms and obstacles, as I believe, looming in her way. To discuss and define them is I think of great value and importance; for thus only can the labor be shared, the difficulties be solved. But besides this, it is necessary also to discuss the ends and the aims for which we are fighting, for which we are doing battle with these formidable obstacles. Those aims cannot be taken for granted; they must be perpetually questioned and examined. The whole position, as I see it — here in this hall surrounded by women practicing for the first time in history I know not how many different professions — is one of extraordinary interest and importance. You have won rooms of your own in the house hitherto exclusively owned by men. You are able, though not without great labor and effort, to pay the rent. You are earning your five hundred pounds a year. But this freedom is only a beginning; the room is your own, but it is still bare. It has to be furnished; it has to be decorated; it has to be shared. How are you going to furnish it, how are you going to decorate it? With whom are you going to share it, and upon what terms? These, I think are questions of the utmost importance and interest. For the first time in history you are able to ask them; for the first time you are able to decide for yourselves what the answers should be. Willingly would I stay and discuss those questions and answers — but not tonight. My time is up; and I must cease. 7

Discussion Questions

1. How does Woolf explain the attraction of writing as a profession for women in the eighteenth and nineteenth centuries?
2. Who is the Angel in the House? What advice did she give to Woolf? Why did Woolf think it necessary to kill her?
3. What other experience constituted an adventure in her professional life? Is such an experience relevant for women writers today?
4. What questions does Woolf pose at the end to her audience of professional women? Why does she leave them vague and undefined?

Writing Suggestions

1. Woolf says, "Even when the path is nominally open — when there is nothing to prevent a woman from being a doctor, a lawyer, a civil servant — there are many phantoms and obstacles . . . looming in her way." Choose a specific

profession, describe it, and try to explain the "many phantoms and obstacles" in it for women. Or make a case for an opposing view — that women no longer experience the problems described by Woolf in 1931.

2. Some critics argue that men entering professions generally practiced only by women suffer the same "phantoms and obstacles." Choose one or more vocations and spell out the prejudices that such men might encounter. Or, if you disagree with the critics, argue that these men do not experience difficulties.

Politics and the English Language

GEORGE ORWELL

This essay, written after World War II, develops George Orwell's claim that careless and dishonest use of language contributes to careless and dishonest thought and political corruption. Political language, he argues, is "largely the defense of the indefensible." But Orwell, novelist, critic, and political satirist — best known for his book 1984 *— believes that bad language habits can be reversed, and he lists rules for getting rid of some of the most offensive.*

Most people who bother with the matter at all would admit that the English language is in a bad way, but it is generally assumed that we cannot by conscious action do anything about it. Our civilization is decadent and our language — so the argument runs — must inevitably share in the general collapse. It follows that any struggle against the abuse of language is a sentimental archaism, like preferring candles to electric light or hansom cabs to aeroplanes. Underneath this lies the half-conscious belief that language is a natural growth and not an instrument which we shape for our own purposes. 1

Now, it is clear that the decline of a language must ultimately have political and economic causes: It is not due simply to the bad influence of this or that individual writer. But an effect can become a cause, reinforcing the original cause and producing the same effect in an intensified form, and so on indefinitely. A man may take to drink because he feels himself to be a failure, and then fail all the more completely because he drinks. It is rather the same thing that is happening to the English language. It becomes ugly and inaccurate because our thoughts are foolish, but the slovenliness of our language makes it easier for us to have foolish thoughts. The point is that the process is reversible. Modern English, especially written English, is full of bad habits which spread by imitation and which can be avoided if one is willing to take the necessary trouble. If one gets rid of these habits one can think more clearly, and to think clearly is a necessary first step towards political regeneration: so that the fight against bad English is not frivolous and is not the exclusive concern of professional writers. I will come back to this presently, and I hope that by that time the meaning of what I have said here will have become clearer. 2

From *Horizon*, April 1946.

Meanwhile, here are five specimens of the English language as it is now habitually written.

3 These five passages have not been picked out because they are especially bad — I could have quoted far worse if I had chosen — but because they illustrate various of the mental vices from which we now suffer. They are a little below the average, but are fairly representative samples. I number them so that I can refer back to them when necessary:

> (1) I am not, indeed, sure whether it is not true to say that the Milton who once seemed not unlike a seventeenth-century Shelley had not become out of an experience ever more bitter in each year, more alien [*sic*] to the founder of that Jesuit sect which nothing could induce him to tolerate.
>
> Professor Harold Laski (Essay in *Freedom of Expression*).

> (2) Above all, we cannot play ducks and drakes with a native battery of idioms which prescribes such egregious collocations of vocables as the Basic *put up with* for *tolerate* or *put at a loss* for *bewilder*.
>
> Professor Lancelot Hogben (*Interglossa*).

> (3) On the one side we have the free personality: By definition it is not neurotic, for it has neither conflict nor dream. Its desires, such as they are, are transparent, for they are just what institutional approval keeps in the forefront of consciousness; another institutional pattern would alter their number and intensity; there is little in them that is natural, irreducible, or culturally dangerous. But *on the other side*, the social bond itself is nothing but the mutual reflection of these self-secure integrities. Recall the definition of love. Is not this the very picture of a small academic? Where is there a place in this hall of mirrors for either personality or fraternity?
>
> Essay on psychology in *Politics* (New York).

> (4) All the "best people" from the gentlemen's clubs, and all the frantic fascist captains, united in common hatred of Socialism and bestial horror of the rising tide of the mass revolutionary movement, have turned to acts of provocation, to foul incendiarism, to medieval legends of poisoned wells, to legalize their own destruction of proletarian organizations, and rouse the agitated petty-bourgeoisie to chauvinistic fervor on behalf of the fight against the revolutionary way out of the crisis.
>
> Communist pamphlet.

> (5) If a new spirit *is* to be infused into this old country, there is one thorny and contentious reform which must be tackled, and that is the humanization and galvanization of the BBC. Timidity here will bespeak cancer and atrophy of the soul. The heart of Britain may be sound and of strong beat, for instance, but the British lion's roar at present is like that of Bottom in Shakespeare's *Midsummer Night's Dream* — as gentle as any sucking dove. A virile new Britain cannot continue indefinitely to be traduced in the eyes or rather ears, of the world by the effete languors of Langham Place, brazenly masquerading as "standard English." When the Voice of Britain is heard at nine o'clock, better far and infinitely less ludicrous to hear aitches honestly

dropped than the present priggish, inflated, inhibited, school-ma'amish arch braying of blameless bashful mewing maidens!

Letter in *Tribune.*

Each of these passages has faults of its own, but, quite apart from avoidable ugliness, two qualities are common to all of them. The first is staleness of imagery: The other is lack of precision. The writer either has a meaning and cannot express it, or he inadvertently says something else, or he is almost indifferent as to whether his words mean anything or not. The mixture of vagueness and sheer incompetence is the most marked characteristic of modern English prose, and especially of any kind of political writing. As soon as certain topics are raised, the concrete melts into the abstract and no one seems to think of turns of speech that are not hackneyed: Prose consists less and less of *words* chosen for the sake of their meaning, and more and more of *phrases* tacked together like the sections of a prefabricated hen-house. I list below, with notes and examples, various of the tricks by means of which the work of prose-construction is habitually dodged: 4

Dying Metaphors. A newly invented metaphor assists thought by evoking a visual image, while on the other hand a metaphor which is technically "dead" (e.g., *iron resolution*) has in effect reverted to being an ordinary word and can generally be used without loss of vividness. But in between these two classes there is a huge dump of worn-out metaphors which have lost all evocative power and are merely used because they save people the trouble of inventing phrases for themselves. Examples are: *ring the changes on, take up the cudgels for, toe the line, ride roughshod over, stand shoulder to shoulder with, play into the hands of, no axe to grind, grist to the mill, fishing in troubled waters, rift within the lute, on the order of the day, Achilles' heel, swan song, hotbed.* Many of these are used without knowledge of their meaning (what is a "rift," for instance?), and incompatible metaphors are frequently mixed, a sure sign that the writer is not interested in what he is saying. Some metaphors now current have been twisted out of their original meaning without those who use them even being aware of the fact. For example, *toe the line* is sometimes written *tow the line.* Another example is *the hammer and the anvil,* now always used with the implication that the anvil gets the worst of it. In real life it is always the anvil that breaks the hammer, never the other way about: A writer who stopped to think what he was saying would be aware of this, and would avoid perverting the original phrase. 5

Operators or Verbal False Limbs. These save the trouble of picking out appropriate verbs and nouns, and at the same time pad each sentence 6 with extra syllables which give it an appearance of symmetry. Characteristic phrases are: *render inoperative, militate against, make contact with, be subjected to, give rise to, give grounds for, have the effect of, play a leading part (role) in, make itself felt, take effect, exhibit a tendency to, serve the purpose of*, etc., etc. The keynote is the elimination of simple verbs. Instead of being a single word, such as *break, stop, spoil, mend, kill*, a verb becomes a *phrase*, made up of a noun or adjective tacked on to some general-purpose verb such as *prove, serve, form, play, render*. In addition, the passive voice is wherever possible used in preference to the active, and noun constructions are used instead of gerunds (*by examination of* instead of *by examining*). The range of verbs is further cut down by means of the *-ize* and *de-* formation, and the banal statements are given an appearance of profundity by means of the *not un-* formation. Simple conjunctions and prepositions are replaced by such phrases as *with respect to, having regard to, the fact that, by dint of, in view of, in the interests of, on the hypothesis that*; and the ends of sentences are saved from anticlimax by such resounding commonplaces as *greatly to be desired, cannot be left out of account, a development to be expected in the near future, deserving of serious consideration, brought to a satisfactory conclusion*, and so on and so forth.

Pretentious Diction. Words like *phenomenon, element, individual* (as noun), *objective, categorical, effective, virtual, basic, primary, promote, constitute, exhibit, exploit, utilize, eliminate, liquidate*, are used to dress up simple statements and give an air of scientific impartiality to biased judgments. Adjectives like *epoch-making, epic, historic, unforgettable, triumphant, age-old, inevitable, inexorable, veritable*, are used to dignify the sordid processes of international politics, while writing that aims at glorifying war usually takes on an archaic color, its characteristic words being: *realm, throne, chariot, mailed fist, trident, sword, shield, buckler, banner, jackboot, clarion*. Foreign words and expressions such as *cul de sac, ancien régime, deus ex machina, mutatis mutandis, status quo, gleichshaltung, weltanschauung*, are used to give an air of culture and elegance. Except for the useful abbreviations *i.e., e.g.*, and *etc.*, there is no real need for any of the hundreds of foreign phrases now current in English. Bad writers, and especially scientific, political, and sociological writers, are nearly always haunted by the notion that Latin or Greek words are grander than Saxon ones, and unnecessary words like *expedite, ameliorate, predict, extraneous, deracinated, clandestine, subaqueous*, and hundreds of others constantly gain ground from their Anglo-Saxon opposite numbers.[1] The jargon peculiar to Marxist writing (*hyena, hangman,* 7

[1]An interesting illustration of this is the way in which the English flower names which were in use till very recently are being ousted by Greek ones, *snapdragon* becoming *antir-*

cannibal, petty bourgeois, these gentry, lackey, flunkey, mad dog, White Guard, etc.) consists largely of words and phrases translated from Russian, German, or French; but the normal way of coining a new word is to use a Latin or Greek root with the appropriate affix and, where necessary, the *-ize* formation. It is often easier to make up words of this kind (*deregionalize, impermissible, extramarital, nonfragmentatory*, and so forth) than to think up the English words that will cover one's meaning. The result, in general, is an increase in slovenliness and vagueness.

Meaningless Words. In certain kinds of writing, particularly in art criticism and literary criticism, it is normal to come across long passages which are almost completely lacking in meaning.[2] Words like *romantic, plastic, values, human, dead, sentimental, natural, vitality*, as used in art criticism, are strictly meaningless in the sense that they not only do not point to any discoverable object, but are hardly ever expected to do so by the reader. When one critic writes, "The outstanding feature of Mr. X's work is its living quality," while another writes, "The immediately striking thing about Mr. X's work is its peculiar deadness," the reader accepts this as a simple difference of opinion. If words like *black* and *white* were involved, instead of the jargon words *dead* and *living*, he would see at once that language was being used in an improper way. Many political words are similarly abused. The word *fascism* has now no meaning except in so far as it signifies "something not desirable." The words *democracy, socialism, freedom, patriotic, realistic, justice*, have each of them several different meanings which cannot be reconciled with one another. In the case of a word like *democracy*, not only is there no agreed definition, but the attempt to make one is resisted from all sides. It is almost universally felt that when we call a country democratic we are praising it: Consequently the defenders of every kind of regime claim that it is a democracy, and fear that they might have to stop using the word if it were tied down to any one meaning. Words of this kind are often used in a consciously dishonest way. That is, the person who uses them has his own private definition, but allows his hearer to think he means something quite different. Statements like *Marshal Pétain was a true patriot, The* 8

---

rhinum, forget-me-not becoming *myosotis*, etc. It is hard to see any practical reason for this change of fashion: It is probably due to an instinctive turning-away from the more homely word and a vague feeling that the Greek word is scientific.

[2]Example: "Comfort's catholicity of perception and image, strangely Whitmanesque in range, almost the exact opposite in aesthetic compulsion, continues to evoke that trembling atmospheric accumulative hinting at a cruel, an inexorably serene timelessness . . . Wrey Gardiner scores by aiming at simple bull's-eyes with precision. Only they are not so simple, and through this contended sadness runs more than the surface bitter-sweet of resignation." *(Poetry Quarterly.)*

Soviet Press is the freest in the world, The Catholic Church is opposed to persecution, are almost always made with intent to deceive. Other words used in variable meanings, in most cases more or less dishonestly, are: *class, totalitarian, science, progressive, reactionary, bourgeois, equality*.

Now that I have made this catalog of swindles and perversions, let me give another example of the kind of writing that they lead to. This time it must of its nature be an imaginary one. I am going to translate a passage of good English into modern English of the worst sort. Here is a well-known verse from *Ecclesiastes:* 9

> I returned and saw under the sun, that the race is not to the swift, nor the battle to the strong, neither yet bread to the wise, nor yet riches to men of understanding, nor yet favor to men of skill; but time and chance happeneth to them all.

Here it is in modern English:

> Objective consideration of contemporary phenomena compels the conclusion that success or failure in competitive activities exhibits no tendency to be commensurate with innate capacity, but that a considerable element of the unpredictable must invariably be taken into account.

This is a parody, but not a very gross one. Exhibit (3), above, for instance, contains several patches of the same kind of English. It will be seen that I have not made a full translation. The beginning and ending of the sentence follow the original meaning fairly closely, but in the middle the concrete illustrations — race, battle, bread — dissolve into the vague phrase "success or failure in competitive activities." This had to be so, because no modern writer of the kind I am discussing — no one capable of using phrases like "objective consideration of contemporary phenomena" — would ever tabulate his thoughts in that precise and detailed way. The whole tendency of modern prose is away from concreteness. Now analyze these two sentences a little more closely. The first contains forty-nine words but only sixty syllables, and all its words are those of everyday life. The second contains thirty-eight words of ninety syllables: Eighteen of its words are from Latin roots, and one from Greek. The first sentence contains six vivid images, and only one phrase ("time and chance") that could be called vague. The second contains not a single fresh, arresting phrase, and in spite of its ninety syllables it gives only a shortened version of the meaning contained in the first. Yet without a doubt it is the second kind of sentence that is gaining ground in modern English. I do not want to exaggerate. This kind of writing is not yet universal, and outcrops of simplicity will occur here and there in the worst-written page. Still, if you or I were told to write a few lines on the uncertainty of human fortunes, we should 10 probably come much nearer to my imaginary sentence than to the one from *Ecclesiastes.*

As I have tried to show, modern writing at its worst does not consist in picking out words for the sake of their meaning and inventing images in order to make the meaning clearer. It consists in gumming together long strips of words which have already been set in order by someone else, and making the results presentable by sheer humbug. The attraction of this way of writing is that it is easy. It is easier — even quicker once you have the habit — to say *In my opinion it is a not unjustifiable assumption that* than to say *I think*. If you use ready-made phrases, you not only don't have to hunt about for words; you also don't have to bother with the rhythms of your sentences, since these phrases are generally so arranged as to be more or less euphonious. When you are composing in a hurry — when you are dictating to a stenographer, for instance, or making a public speech — it is natural to fall into a pretentious, Latinized style. Tags like a *consideration which we should do well to bear in mind* or *a conclusion to which all of us would readily assent* will save many a sentence from coming down with a bump. By using stale metaphors, similes, and idioms, you save much mental effort, at the cost of leaving your meaning vague, not only for your reader but for yourself. This is the significance of mixed metaphors. The sole aim of a metaphor is to call up a visual image. When these images clash — as in *The Fascist octopus has sung its swan song, the jackboot is thrown into the melting pot* — it can be taken as certain that the writer is not seeing a mental image of the objects he is naming; in other words he is not really thinking. Look again at the examples I gave at the beginning of this essay. Professor Laski (1) uses five negatives in fifty-three words. One of these is superfluous, making nonsense of the whole passage, and in addition there is the slip *alien* for akin, making further nonsense, and several avoidable pieces of clumsiness which increase the general vagueness. Professor Hogben (2) plays ducks and drakes with a battery which is able to write prescriptions, and, while disapproving of the everyday phrase *put up with*, is unwilling to look *egregious* up in the dictionary and see what it means. (3), if one takes an uncharitable attitude towards it, is simply meaningless: Probably one could work out its intended meaning by reading the whole of the article in which it occurs. In (4), the writer knows more or less what he wants to say, but an accumulation of stale phrases chokes him like tea leaves blocking a sink. In (5), words and meaning have almost parted company. People who write in this manner usually have a general emotional meaning — they dislike one thing and want to express solidarity with another — but they are not interested in the detail of what they are saying. A scrupulous writer, in every sentence that he writes, will ask himself at least four questions, thus: What am I trying to say? What words will express it? What image or idiom will make it clearer? Is this image fresh enough to have an effect? And he will probably ask himself two more: Could I put it more shortly? Have I said anything that is avoidably ugly? But you are not obliged to go to all this trouble. You can shirk it by simply throwing your mind open and letting the ready-made phrases come crowding in. They will construct your sentences for you — even think your thoughts for you, to a certain extent — and at need they will perform the important service of partially concealing your meaning even from yourself. It is at this point that the special connection between politics and the debasement of language becomes clear.

In our time it is broadly true that political writing is bad writing. 12
Where it is not true, it will generally be found that the writer is some kind of rebel, expressing his private opinions and not a "party line." Orthodoxy, of whatever color, seems to demand a lifeless, imitative style. The political dialects to be found in pamphlets, leading articles, manifestos, White Papers, and the speeches of undersecretaries do, of course, vary from party to party, but they are all alike in that one almost never finds in them a fresh, vivid, home-made turn of speech. When one watches some tired hack on the platform mechanically repeating the familiar phrases — *bestial atrocities, iron heel, bloodstained tyranny, free peoples of the world, stand shoulder to shoulder* — one often has a curious feeling that one is not watching a live human being but some kind of dummy; a feeling which suddenly becomes stronger at moments when the light catches the speaker's spectacles and turns them into blank discs which seem to have no eyes behind them. And this is not altogether fanciful. A speaker who uses that kind of phraseology has gone some distance towards turning himself into a machine. The appropriate noises are coming out of his larynx, but his brain is not involved as it would be if he were choosing his words for himself. If the speech he is making is one that he is accustomed to make over and over again, he may be almost unconscious of what he is saying, as one is when one utters the responses in church. And this reduced state of consciousness, if not indispensable, is at any rate favorable to political conformity.

In our time, political speech and writing are largely the defense of the 13
indefensible. Things like the continuance of British rule in India, the Russian purges and deportations, the dropping of the atom bombs on Japan, can indeed be defended, but only by arguments which are too brutal for most people to face, and which do not square with the professed aims of political parties. Thus political language has to consist largely of euphemism, question-begging, and sheer cloudy vagueness. Defenseless villages are bombarded from the air, the inhabitants driven out into the countryside, the cattle machine-gunned, the huts set on fire with incendiary bullets: This is called *pacification*. Millions of peasants are robbed of

their farms and sent trudging along the roads with no more than they can carry; this is called *transfer of population* or *rectification of frontiers.* People are imprisoned for years without trial, or shot in the back of the neck, or sent to die of scurvy in Arctic lumber camps: This is called *elimination of unreliable elements.* Such phraseology is needed if one wants to name things without calling up mental pictures of them. Consider for instance some comfortable English professor defending Russian totalitarianism. He cannot say outright, "I believe in killing off your opponents when you can get good results by doing so." Probably, therefore, he will say something like this:

> While freely conceding that the Soviet régime exhibits certain features which the humanitarian may be inclined to deplore, we must, I think, agree that a certain curtailment of the right to political opposition is an unavoidable concomitant of transitional periods, and that the rigors which the Russian people have been called upon to undergo have been amply justified in the sphere of concrete achievement.

The inflated style is itself a kind of euphemism. A mass of Latin words fall upon the facts like soft snow, blurring the outlines and covering up all the details. The great enemy of clear language is insincerity. When there is a gap between one's real and one's declared aims, one turns as it were instinctively to long words and exhausted idioms, like a cuttlefish squirting out ink. In our age there is no such thing as "keeping out of politics." All issues are political issues, and politics itself is a mass of lies, evasions, folly, hatred, and schizophrenia. When the general atmosphere is bad, language must suffer. I should expect to find — this is a guess which I have not sufficient knowledge to verify — that the German, Russian, and Italian languages have all deteriorated in the last ten or fifteen years, as a result of dictatorship. 14

But if thought corrupts language, language can also corrupt thought. A bad usage can spread by tradition and imitation, even among people who should and do know better. The debased language that I have been discussing is in some ways very convenient. Phrases like *a not unjustifiable assumption, leaves much to be desired, would serve no good purpose, a consideration which we should do well to bear in mind,* are a continuous temptation, a packet of aspirins always at one's elbow. Look back through this essay, and for certain you will find that I have again and again committed the very faults I am protesting against. By this morning's post I have received a pamphlet dealing with conditions in Germany. The author tells me that he "felt impelled" to write it. I open it at random, and here is almost the first sentence that I see: "(The Allies) have an opportunity not only of achieving a radical transformation of Germany's social and political structure in such a way as to avoid a nationalistic reaction in 15

Germany itself, but at the same time of laying the foundations of a co-operative and unified Europe." You see, he "feels impelled" to write — feels, presumably, that he has something new to say — and yet his words, like cavalry horses answering the bugle, group themselves automatically into the familiar dreary pattern. This invasion of one's mind by ready-made phrases (*lay the foundations, achieve a radical transformation*) can only be prevented if one is constantly on guard against them, and every such phrase anesthetizes a portion of one's brain.

I said earlier that the decadence of our language is probably curable. 16
Those who deny this would argue, if they produced an argument at all, that language merely reflects existing social conditions, and that we cannot influence its development by any direct tinkering with words and constructions. So far as the general tone or spirit of a language goes, this may be true, but it is not true in detail. Silly words and expressions have often disappeared, not through any evolutionary process but owing to the conscious action of a minority. Two recent examples were *explore every avenue* and *leave no stone unturned*, which were killed by the jeers of a few journalists. There is a long list of flyblown metaphors which could similarly be got rid of if enough people would interest themselves in the job; and it should also be possible to laugh the *not un-* formation out of existence,[3] to reduce the amount of Latin and Greek in the average sentence, to drive out foreign phrases and strayed scientific words, and, in general, to make pretentiousness unfashionable. But all these are minor points. The defense of the English language implies more than this, and perhaps it is best to start by saying what it does *not* imply.

To begin with it has nothing to do with archaism, with the salvaging 17
of obsolete words and turns of speech, or with the setting up of a "standard English" which must never be departed from. On the contrary, it is especially concerned with the scrapping of every word or idiom which has outworn its usefulness. It has nothing to do with correct grammar and syntax, which are of no importance so long as one makes one's meaning clear, or with the avoidance of Americanisms, or with having what is called a "good prose style." On the other hand it is not concerned with fake simplicity and the attempt to make written English colloquial. Nor does it even imply in every case preferring the Saxon word to the Latin one, though it does imply using the fewest and shortest words that will cover one's meaning. What is above all needed is to let the meaning choose the word, and not the other way about. In prose, the worst thing one can do with words is to surrender to them. When you think of a con-

---

[3]One can cure oneself of the *not un-* formation by memorizing this sentence: *A not unblack dog was chasing a not unsmall rabbit across a not ungreen field.*

crete object, you think wordlessly, and then, if you want to describe the thing you have been visualizing you probably hunt about till you find the exact words that seem to fit. When you think of something abstract you are more inclined to use words from the start, and unless you make a conscious effort to prevent it, the existing dialect will come rushing in and do the job for you, at the expense of blurring or even changing your meaning. Probably it is better to put off using words as long as possible and get one's meaning as clear as one can through pictures or sensations. Afterwards one can choose — not simply *accept* — the phrases that will best cover the meaning, and then switch round and decide what impression one's words are likely to make on another person. This last effort of the mind cuts out all stale or mixed images, all prefabricated phrases, needless repetitions, and humbug and vagueness generally. But one can often be in doubt about the effect of a word or a phrase, and one needs rules that one can rely on when instinct fails. I think the following rules will cover most cases:

(i) Never use a metaphor, simile, or other figure of speech which you are used to seeing in print.
(ii) Never use a long word where a short one will do.
(iii) If it is possible to cut a word out, always cut it out.
(iv) Never use the passive where you can use the active.
(v) Never use a foreign phrase, a scientific word, or a jargon word if you can think of an everyday English equivalent.
(vi) Break any of these rules sooner than say anything outright barbarous.

These rules sound elementary, and so they are, but they demand a deep change in attitude in anyone who has grown used to writing in the style now fashionable. One could keep all of them and still write bad English, but one could not write the kind of stuff that I quoted in those five specimens at the beginning of this article.

I have not here been considering the literary use of language, but 18
merely language as an instrument for expressing and not for concealing or preventing thought. Stuart Chase and others have come near to claiming that all abstract words are meaningless, and have used this as a pretext for advocating a kind of political quietism. Since you don't know what Fascism is, how can you struggle against Fascism? One need not swallow such absurdities as this, but one ought to recognize that the present political chaos is connected with the decay of language, and that one can probably bring about some improvement by starting at the verbal end. If you simplify your English, you are freed from the worst follies of orthodoxy. You cannot speak any of the necessary dialects, and when you make a stupid remark its stupidity will be obvious, even to yourself.

Political language — and with variations this is true of all political parties, from Conservatives to Anarchists — is designed to make lies sound truthful and murder respectable, and to give an appearance of solidity to pure wind. One cannot change this all in a moment, but one can at least change one's own habits, and from time to time one can even, if one jeers loudly enough, send some worn-out and useless phrase — some *jackboot, Achilles' heel, hotbed, melting pot, acid test, veritable inferno*, or other lump of verbal refuse — into the dustbin where it belongs.

Discussion Questions

1. Orwell disagrees with a common assumption about language. What is it? Where in the essay does he attack this assumption directly?
2. What faults do his five samples of bad language have in common? Select examples of these faults in each passage.
3. What "tricks" for avoiding good prose does Orwell list? Do you think that some are more dangerous or misleading than others? Explain the reasons for your answer.
4. What different reasons does Orwell suggest for the slovenliness of much political writing and speaking? What examples does he give to support these reasons? Are they persuasive?
5. How does Orwell propose that we get rid of our bad language habits? Do you think his recommendations are realistic? Can the teaching of writing in school assist in the remedy?
6. Why does Orwell urge the reader to "look back through this essay" to find "the very faults I am protesting against"? Can you, in fact, find any?

Writing Suggestions

1. Choose a speech or an editorial whose meaning seems to be obscured by pretentious diction, meaningless words, euphemism, or "sheer cloudy vagueness." Point out the real meaning of the piece. If you think that its purpose is deceptive, expose the unpleasant truth that the author is concealing. Use Orwell's device, giving concrete meaning to any abstractions. (One source of speeches is a publication called *Vital Speeches of the Day*. Another is the *New York Times*, which often prints in full or excerpts major portions of speeches by leading figures in public life.)
2. Orwell's essay appeared before the widespread use of television. Do you think that TV makes it harder for politicians to be dishonest? Choose a particular public event — a war, a street riot, a terrorist activity, a campaign stop — and argue either for or against the claim that televised coverage makes it harder for a politician to engage in "sheer cloudy vagueness." Or does it make no difference at all? Be specific in your use of evidence.

Letter from Birmingham Jail

MARTIN LUTHER KING, JR.

Martin Luther King, Jr., (1929–1968) was a clergyman, author, distinguished civil-rights leader, and winner of the Nobel Peace Prize in 1964 for his contributions to racial harmony and his advocacy of nonviolent response to aggression. He was assassinated in 1968. In the following selections we meet King in two of his various roles. In "Letter from Birmingham Jail," he appears as historian and philosopher. He wrote the letter from a jail cell on April 16, 1963, after his arrest for participation in a demonstration for civil rights for blacks. The letter was a reply to eight Alabama clergymen who, in a public statement, had condemned demonstrations in the streets.

My dear Fellow Clergymen,

While confined here in the Birmingham city jail, I came across your 1
recent statement calling our present activities "unwise and untimely." Seldom, if ever, do I pause to answer criticism of my work and ideas. If I sought to answer all of the criticisms that cross my desk, my secretaries would be engaged in little else in the course of the day, and I would have no time for constructive work. But since I feel that you are men of genuine good will and your criticisms are sincerely set forth, I would like to answer your statement in what I hope will be patient and reasonable terms.

I think I should give the reason for my being in Birmingham, since 2
you have been influenced by the argument of "outsiders coming in." I have the honor of serving as president of the Southern Christian Leadership Conference, an organization operating in every southern state, with headquarters in Atlanta, Georgia. We have some eighty-five affiliate organizations all across the South — one being the Alabama Christian Movement for Human Rights. Whenever necessary and possible we share staff, educational, and financial resources with our affiliates. Several months ago our local affiliate here in Birmingham invited us to be on call to engage in a nonviolent direct-action program if such were deemed necessary. We readily consented and when the hour came we lived up to our promises. So I am here, along with several members of my staff, because we were invited here. I am here because I have basic organizational ties here.

Beyond this, I am in Birmingham because injustice is here. Just as the 3
eighth-century prophets left their little villages and carried their "thus

From *A Testament of Hope* (1986).

saith the Lord" far beyond the boundaries of their hometowns; and just as the Apostle Paul left his little village of Tarsus and carried the gospel of Jesus Christ to practically every hamlet and city of the Graeco-Roman world, I too am compelled to carry the gospel of freedom beyond my particular hometown. Like Paul, I must constantly respond to the Macedonian call for aid.

Moreover, I am cognizant of the interrelatedness of all communities and states. I cannot sit idly by in Atlanta and not be concerned about what happens in Birmingham. Injustice anywhere is a threat to justice everywhere. We are caught in an inescapable network of mutuality, tied in a single garment of destiny. Whatever affects one directly affects all indirectly. Never again can we afford to live with the narrow, provincial "outside agitator" idea. Anyone who lives in the United States can never be considered an outsider anywhere in this country. 4

You deplore the demonstrations that are presently taking place in Birmingham. But I am sorry that your statement did not express a similar concern for the conditions that brought the demonstrations into being. I am sure that each of you would want to go beyond the superficial social analyst who looks merely at effects, and does not grapple with underlying causes. I would not hesitate to say that it is unfortunate that so-called demonstrations are taking place in Birmingham at this time, but I would say in more emphatic terms that it is even more unfortunate that the white power structure of this city left the Negro community with no other alternative. 5

In any nonviolent campaign there are four basic steps: (1) collection of the facts to determine whether injustices are alive, (2) negotiation, (3) self-purification, and (4) direct action. We have gone through all of these steps in Birmingham. There can be no gainsaying of the fact that racial injustice engulfs this community. 6

Birmingham is probably the most thoroughly segregated city in the United States. Its ugly record of police brutality is known in every section of this country. Its unjust treatment of Negroes in the courts is a notorious reality. There have been more unsolved bombings of Negro homes and churches in Birmingham than any city in this nation. These are the hard, brutal, and unbelievable facts. On the basis of these conditions Negro leaders sought to negotiate with the city fathers. But the political leaders consistently refused to engage in good faith negotiation. 7

Then came the opportunity last September to talk with some of the leaders of the economic community. In these negotiating sessions certain promises were made by the merchants — such as the promise to remove the humiliating racial signs from the stores. On the basis of these promises Rev. Shuttlesworth and the leaders of the Alabama Christian Movement for Human Rights agreed to call a moratorium on any type of demonstra- 8 tions. As the weeks and months unfolded we realized that we were the victims of a broken promise. The signs remained. Like so many experiences of the past we were confronted with blasted hopes, and the dark shadow of a deep disappointment settled upon us. So we had no alternative except that of preparing for direct action, whereby we would present our very bodies as a means of laying our case before the conscience of the local and national community. We were not unmindful of the difficulties involved. So we decided to go through a process of self-purification. We started having workshops on nonviolence and repeatedly asked ourselves the questions, "Are you able to accept blows without retaliating?" "Are you able to endure the ordeals of jail?" We decided to set our direct-action program around the Easter season, realizing that with the exception of Christmas, this was the largest shopping period of the year. Knowing that a strong economic withdrawal program would be the by-product of direct action, we felt that this was the best time to bring pressure on the merchants for the needed changes. Then it occurred to us that the March election was ahead and so we speedily decided to postpone action until after election day. When we discovered that Mr. Connor was in the run-off, we decided again to postpone action so that the demonstrations could not be used to cloud the issues. At this time we agreed to begin our nonviolent witness the day after the run-off.

9 This reveals that we did not move irresponsibly into direct action. We too wanted to see Mr. Connor defeated; so we went through postponement after postponement to aid in this community need. After this we felt that direct action could be delayed no longer.

10 You may well ask, "Why direct action? Why sit-ins, marches, etc? Isn't negotiation a better path?" You are exactly right in your call for negotiation. Indeed, this is the purpose of direct action. Nonviolent direct action seeks to create such a crisis and establish such creative tension that a community that has constantly refused to negotiate is forced to confront the issue. It seeks so to dramatize the issue that it can no longer be ignored. I just referred to the creation of tension as a part of the work of the nonviolent resister. This may sound rather shocking. But I must confess that I am not afraid of the word tension. I have earnestly worked and preached against violent tension, but there is a type of constructive nonviolent tension that is necessary for growth. Just as Socrates felt that it was necessary to create a tension in the mind so that individuals could rise from the bondage of myths and half-truths to the unfettered realm of creative analysis and objective appraisal, we must see the need of having nonviolent gadflies to create the kind of tension in society that will help men to rise from the dark depths of prejudice and racism to the majestic heights of understanding and brotherhood. So the purpose of the direct action is to create a situation so crisis-packed that it will inevitably open

the door to negotiation. We, therefore, concur with you in your call for negotiation. Too long has our beloved Southland been bogged down in the tragic attempt to live in monologue rather than dialogue.

One of the basic points in your statement is that our acts are untimely. Some have asked, "Why didn't you give the new administration time to act?" The only answer that I can give to this inquiry is that the new administration must be prodded about as much as the outgoing one before it acts. We will be sadly mistaken if we feel that the election of Mr. Boutwell will bring the millennium to Birmingham. While Mr. Boutwell is much more articulate and gentle than Mr. Connor, they are both segregationists, dedicated to the task of maintaining the status quo. The hope I see in Mr. Boutwell is that he will be reasonable enough to see the futility of massive resistance to desegregation. But he will not see this without pressure from the devotees of civil rights. My friends, I must say to you that we have not made a single gain in civil rights without determined legal and nonviolent pressure. History is the long and tragic story of the fact that privileged groups seldom give up their privileges voluntarily. Individuals may see the moral light and voluntarily give up their unjust posture; but as Reinhold Niebuhr has reminded us, groups are more immoral than individuals. 11

We know through painful experience that freedom is never voluntarily given by the oppressor; it must be demanded by the oppressed. Frankly, I have never yet engaged in a direct action movement that was "well-timed," according to the timetable of those who have not suffered unduly from the disease of segregation. For years now I have heard the words "Wait!" It rings in the ear of every Negro with a piercing familarity. This "Wait" has almost always meant "Never." It has been a tranquilizing thalidomide, relieving the emotional stress for a moment, only to give birth to an ill-formed infant of frustration. We must come to see with the distinguished jurist of yesterday that "justice too long delayed is justice denied." We have waited for more than 340 years for our constitutional and God-given rights. The nations of Asia and Africa are moving with jetlike speed toward the goal of political independence, and we still creep at horse and buggy pace toward the gaining of a cup of coffee at a lunch counter. I guess it is easy for those who have never felt the stinging darts of segregation to say, "Wait." But when you have seen vicious mobs lynch your mothers and fathers at will and drown your sisters and brothers at whim; when you seen hate-filled policemen curse, kick, brutalize, and even kill your black brothers and sisters with impunity; when you see the vast majority of your twenty million Negro brothers smothering in an airtight cage of poverty in the midst of an affluent society; when you suddenly find your tongue twisted and your speech stammering as you seek to explain to your six-year-old daughter why she can't go to the public 12 amusement park that has just been advertised on television, and see tears welling up in her little eyes when she is told that Funtown is closed to colored children, and see the depressing clouds of inferiority begin to form in her little mental sky, and see her begin to distort her little personality by unconsciously developing a bitterness toward white people; when you have to concoct an answer for a five-year-old son asking in agonizing pathos: "Daddy, why do white people treat colored people so mean?"; when you take a cross-country drive and find it necessary to sleep night after night in the uncomfortable corners of your automobile because no motel will accept you; when you are humiliated day in and day out by nagging signs reading "white" and "colored"; when your first name becomes "nigger" and your middle name becomes "boy" (however old you are) and your last name becomes "John," and when your wife and mother are never given the respected title "Mrs."; when you are harried by day and haunted by night by the fact that you are a Negro, living constantly at tiptoe stance never quite knowing what to expect next, and plagued with inner fears and outer resentments; when you are forever fighting a degenerating sense of "nobodiness"; then you will understand why we find it difficult to wait. There comes a time when the cup of endurance runs over, and men are no longer willing to be plunged into an abyss of injustice where they experience the blackness of corroding despair. I hope, sirs, you can understand our legitimate and unavoidable impatience.

You express a great deal of anxiety over our willingness to break 13
laws. This is certainly a legitimate concern. Since we so diligently urge people to obey the Supreme Court's decision of 1954 outlawing segregation in the public schools, it is rather strange and paradoxical to find us consciously breaking laws. One may well ask, "How can you advocate breaking some laws and obeying others?" The answer is found in the fact that there are two types of laws: There are *just* and there are *unjust* laws. I would agree with Saint Augustine that "An unjust law is no law at all."

Now what is the difference between the two? How does one deter- 14
mine when a law is just or unjust? A just law is a man-made code that squares with the moral law or the law of God. An unjust law is a code that is out of harmony with the moral law. To put it in the terms of Saint Thomas Aquinas, an unjust law is a human law that is not rooted in eternal and natural law. Any law that uplifts human personality is just. Any law that degrades human personality is unjust. All segregation statutes are unjust because segregation distorts the soul and damages the personality. It gives the segregator a false sense of superiority, and the segregated a false sense of inferiority. To use the words of Martin Buber, the great Jewish philosopher, segregation substitutes an "I-it" relationship for the "I-thou" relationship, and ends up relegating persons to the status of things. So segregation is not only politically, economically, and sociologi-

cally unsound, but it is morally wrong and sinful. Paul Tillich has said that sin is separation. Isn't segregation an existential expression of man's tragic separation, an expression of his awful estrangement, his terrible sinfulness? So I can urge men to disobey segregation ordinances because they are morally wrong.

Let us turn to a more concrete example of just and unjust laws. An unjust law is a code that a majority inflicts on a minority that is not binding on itself. This is difference made legal. On the other hand a just law is a code that a majority compels a minority to follow that it is willing to follow itself. This is sameness made legal. 15

Let me give another explanation. An unjust law is a code inflicted upon a minority which that minority had no part in enacting or creating because they did not have the unhampered right to vote. Who can say that the legislature of Alabama which set up the segregation laws was democratically elected? Throughout the state of Alabama all types of conniving methods are used to prevent Negroes from becoming registered voters, and there are some counties without a single Negro registered to vote despite the fact that the Negro constitutes a majority of the population. Can any law set up in such a state be considered democratically structured? 16

These are just a few examples of unjust and just laws. There are some instances when a law is just on its face and unjust in its application. For instance, I was arrested Friday on a charge of parading without a permit. Now there is nothing wrong with an ordinance which requires a permit for a parade, but when the ordinance is used to preserve segregation and to deny citizens the First Amendment privilege of peaceful assembly and peaceful protest, then it becomes unjust. 17

I hope you can see the distinction I am trying to point out. In no sense do I advocate evading or defying the law as the rabid segregationist would do. This would lead to anarchy. One who breaks an unjust law must do it *openly, lovingly* (not hatefully as the white mothers did in New Orleans when they were seen on television screaming, "nigger, nigger, nigger"), and with a willingness to accept the penalty. I submit that an individual who breaks a law that conscience tells him is unjust, and willingly accepts the penalty by staying in jail to arouse the conscience of the community over its injustice, is in reality expressing the very highest respect for law. 18

Of course, there is nothing new about this kind of civil disobedience. It was seen sublimely in the refusal of Shadrach, Meshach, and Abednego to obey the laws of Nebuchadnezzar because a higher moral law was involved. It was practiced superbly by the early Christians who were willing to face hungry lions and the excruciating pain of chopping blocks, before submitting to certain unjust laws of the Roman Empire. To a degree aca- 19 demic freedom is a reality today because Socrates practiced civil disobedience.

We can never forget that everything Hitler did in Germany was "legal" and everything the Hungarian freedom fighters did in Hungary was "illegal." It was "illegal" to aid and comfort a Jew in Hitler's Germany. But I am sure that if I had lived in Germany during that time I would have aided and comforted my Jewish brothers even though it was illegal. If I lived in a Communist country today where certain principles dear to the Christian faith are suppressed, I believe I would openly advocate disobeying these antireligious laws. I must make two honest confessions to you, my Christian and Jewish brothers. First, I must confess that over the last few years I have been gravely disappointed with the white moderate. I have almost reached the regrettable conclusion that the Negro's great stumbling block in the stride toward freedom is not the White Citizen's Counciler or the Ku Klux Klanner, but the white moderate who is more devoted to "order" than to justice; who prefers a negative peace which is the absence of tension to a positive peace which is the presence of justice; who constantly says, "I agree with you in the goal you seek, but I can't agree with your methods of direct action"; who paternalistically feels that he can set the timetable for another man's freedom; who lives by the myth of time and who constantly advises the Negro to wait until a "more convenient season." Shallow understanding from people of good will is more frustrating than absolute misunderstanding from people of ill will. Lukewarm acceptance is much more bewildering than outright rejection. 20

I had hoped that the white moderate would understand that law and order exist for the purpose of establishing justice, and that when they fail to do this they become dangerously structured dams that block the flow of social progress. I had hoped that the white moderate would understand that the present tension of the South is merely a necessary phase of the transition from an obnoxious negative peace, where the Negro passively accepted his unjust plight, to a substance-filled positive peace, where all men will respect the dignity and worth of human personality. Actually, we who engage in nonviolent direct action are not the creators of tension. We merely bring to the surface the hidden tension that is already alive. We bring it out in the open where it can be seen and dealt with. Like a boil that can never be cured as long as it is covered up but must be opened with all its pus-flowing ugliness to the natural medicines of air and light, injustice must likewise be exposed, with all of the tension its exposing creates, to the light of human conscience and the air of national opinion before it can be cured. 21

In your statement you asserted that our actions, even though peaceful, must be condemned because they precipitate violence. But can this assertion be logically made? Isn't this like condemning the robbed man 22 because his possession of money precipitated the evil act of robbery? Isn't this like condemning Socrates because his unswerving commitment to truth and his philosophical delvings precipitated the misguided popular mind to make him drink the hemlock? Isn't this like condemning Jesus because His unique God-consciousness and never-ceasing devotion to his will precipitated the evil act of crucifixion? We must come to see, as federal courts have consistently affirmed, that it is immoral to urge an individual to withdraw his efforts to gain his basic constitutional rights because the quest precipitates violence. Society must protect the robbed and punish the robber.

I had also hoped that the white moderate would reject the myth of time. I received a letter this morning from a white brother in Texas which said: "All Christians know that the colored people will receive equal rights eventually, but it is possible that you are in too great of a religious hurry. It has taken Christianity almost two thousand years to accomplish what it has. The teachings of Christ take time to come to earth." All that is said here grows out of a tragic misconception of time. It is the strangely irrational notion that there is something in the very flow of time that will inevitably cure all ills. Actually time is neutral. It can be used either destructively or constructively. I am coming to feel that the people of ill will have used time much more effectively than the people of good will. We will have to repent in this generation not merely for the vitriolic words and actions of the bad people, but for the appalling silence of the good people. We must come to see that human progress never rolls in on wheels of inevitability. It comes through the tireless efforts and persistent work of men willing to be coworkers with God, and without this hard work time itself becomes an ally of the forces of social stagnation. We must use time creatively, and forever realize that the time is always ripe to do right. Now is the time to make real the promise of democracy, and transform our pending national elegy into a creative psalm of brotherhood. Now is the time to lift our national policy from the quicksand of racial injustice to the solid rock of human dignity. 23

You spoke of our activity in Birmingham as extreme. At first I was rather disappointed that fellow clergymen would see my nonviolent efforts as those of the extremist. I started thinking about the fact that I stand in the middle of two opposing forces in the Negro community. One is a force of complacency made up of Negroes who, as a result of long years of oppression, have been so completely drained of self-respect and a sense of "somebodiness" that they have adjusted to segregation, and of a few Negroes in the middle class who, because of a degree of academic and economic security, and because at points they profit by segregation, have unconsciously become insensitive to the problems of the masses. The other force is one of bitterness and hatred, and comes perilously 24 close to advocating violence. It is expressed in the various black nationalist groups that are springing up over the nation, the largest and best known being Elijah Muhammad's Muslim movement. This movement is nourished by the contemporary frustration over the continued existence of racial discrimination. It is made up of people who have lost faith in America, who have absolutely repudiated Christianity, and who have concluded that the white man is an incurable "devil." I have tried to stand between these two forces, saying that we need not follow the "do-nothingism" of the complacent or the hatred and despair of the black nationalist. There is the more excellent way of love and nonviolent protest. I'm grateful to God that, through the Negro church, the dimension of nonviolence entered our struggle. If this philosophy had not emerged, I am convinced that by now many streets of the South would be flowing with floods of blood. And I am further convinced that if our white brothers dismiss us as "rabble-rousers" and "outside agitators" those of us who are working through the channels of nonviolent direct action and refuse to support our nonviolent efforts, millions of Negroes, out of frustration and despair, will seek solace and security in black nationalist ideologies, a development that will lead inevitably to a frightening racial nightmare.

Oppressed people cannot remain oppressed forever. The urge for 25
freedom will eventually come. This is what happened to the American Negro. Something within has reminded him of his birthright of freedom; something without has reminded him that he can gain it. Consciously and unconsciously, he has been swept in by what the Germans call the *Zeitgeist*, and with his black brothers of Africa, and his brown and yellow brothers of Asia, South America, and the Caribbean, he is moving with a sense of cosmic urgency toward the promised land of racial justice. Recognizing this vital urge that has engulfed the Negro community, one should readily understand public demonstrations. The Negro has many pent-up resentments and latent frustrations. He has to get them out. So let him march sometime; let him have his prayer pilgrimages to the city hall; understand why he must have sit-ins and freedom rides. If his repressed emotions do not come out in these nonviolent ways, they will come out in ominous expressions of violence. This is not a threat; it is fact of history. So I have not said to my people "get rid of your discontent." But I have tried to say that this normal and healthy discontent can be channelized through the creative outlet of nonviolent direct action. Now this approach is being dismissed as extremist. I must admit that I was initially disappointed in being so categorized.

But as I continued to think about the matter I gradually gained a bit of 26
satisfaction from being considered an extremist. Was not Jesus an extremist in love — "Love your enemies, bless them that curse you, pray for them that despitefully use you." Was not Amos an extremist for justice —

"Let justice roll down like waters and righteousness like a mighty stream." Was not Paul an extremist for the gospel of Jesus Christ — "I bear in my body the marks of the Lord Jesus." Was not Martin Luther an extremist — "Here I stand; I can do none other so help me God." Was not John Bunyan an extremist — "I will stay in jail to the end of my days before I make a butchery of my conscience." Was not Abraham Lincoln an extremist — "This nation cannot survive half slave and half free." Was not Thomas Jefferson an extremist — "We hold these truths to be self-evident, that all men are created equal." So the question is not whether we will be extremist but what kind of extremist will we be. Will we be extremists for hate or will we be extremists for love? Will we be extremists for the preservation of injustice — or will we be extremists for the cause of justice? In that dramatic scene on Calvary's hill, three men were crucified. We must not forget that all three were crucified for the same crime — the crime of extremism. Two were extremists for immorality, and thusly fell below their environment. The other, Jesus Christ, was an extremist for love, truth, and goodness, and thereby rose above his environment. So, after all, maybe the South, the nation, and the world are in dire need of creative extremists.

I had hoped that the white moderate would see this. Maybe I was too optimistic. Maybe I expected too much. I guess I should have realized that few members of a race that has oppressed another race can understand or appreciate the deep groans and passionate yearnings of those that have been oppressed and still fewer have the vision to see that injustice must be rooted out by strong, persistent and determined action. I am thankful, however, that some of our white brothers have grasped the meaning of this social revolution and committed themselves to it. They are still all too small in quantity, but they are big in quality. Some like Ralph McGill, Lillian Smith, Harry Golden, and James Dabbs have written about our struggle in eloquent, prophetic, and understanding terms. Others have marched with us down nameless streets of the South. They have languished in filthy roach-infested jails, suffering the abuse and brutality of angry policemen who see them as "dirty nigger-lovers." They, unlike so many of their moderate brothers and sisters, have recognized the urgency of the moment and sensed the need for powerful "action" antidotes to combat the disease of segregation. 27

Let me rush on to mention my other disappointment. I have been so greatly disappointed with the white church and its leadership. Of course, there are some notable exceptions. I am not unmindful of the fact that each of you has taken some significant stands on this issue. I commend you, Rev. Stallings, for your Christian stance on this past Sunday, in welcoming Negroes to your worship service on a nonsegregated basis. I commend the Catholic leaders of this state for integrating Springhill College several years ago. 28

But despite these notable exceptions I must honestly reiterate that I have been disappointed with the church. I do not say that as one of the negative critics who can always find something wrong with the church. I say it as a minister of the gospel, who loves the church; who was nurtured in its bosom; who has been sustained by its spiritual blessings, and who will remain true to it as long as the cord of life shall lengthen. 29

I had the strange feeling when I was suddenly catapulted into the leadership of the bus protest in Montgomery several years ago that we would have the support of the white church. I felt that the white ministers, priests, and rabbis of the South would be some of our strongest allies. Instead, some have been outright opponents, refusing to understand the freedom movement and misrepresenting its leaders; all too many others have been more cautious than courageous and have remained silent behind the anesthetizing security of the stained-glass windows. 30

In spite of my shattered dreams of the past, I came to Birmingham with the hope that the white religious leadership of this community would see the justice of our cause, and with deep moral concern, serve as the channel through which our just grievances would get to the power structure. I had hoped that each of you would understand. But again I have been disappointed. I have heard numerous religious leaders of the South call upon their worshipers to comply with a desegregation decision because it is the *law*, but I have longed to hear white ministers say, "Follow this decree because integration is morally *right* and the Negro is your brother." In the midst of blatant injustices inflicted upon the Negro, I have watched white churches stand on the sideline and merely mouth pious irrelevancies and sanctimonious trivialities. In the midst of a mighty struggle to rid our nation of racial and economic injustice, I have heard so many ministers say, "Those are social issues with which the gospel has no real concern," and I have watched so many churches commit themselves to a completely otherworldly religion which made a strange distinction between body and soul, the sacred and the secular. 31

So here we are moving toward the exit of the twentieth century with a religious community largely adjusted to the status quo, standing as a taillight behind other community agencies rather than a headlight leading men to higher levels of justice. 32

I have traveled the length and breadth of Alabama, Mississippi, and all the other southern states. On sweltering summer days and crisp autumn mornings I have looked at her beautiful churches with their lofty spires pointing heavenward. I have beheld the impressive outlay of her massive religious education buildings. Over and over again I have found myself asking: "What kind of people worship here? Who is their God? Where were their voices when the lips of Governor Barnett dripped with words of interposition and nullification? Where were they when Governor Wallace gave the clarion call for defiance and hatred? Where were their 33 voices of support when tired, bruised and weary Negro men and women decided to rise from the dark dungeons of complacency to the bright hills of creative protest?"

Yes, these questions are still in my mind. In deep disappointment, I have wept over the laxity of the church. But be assured that my tears have been tears of love. There can be no deep disappointment where there is not deep love. Yes, I love the church; I love her sacred walls. How could I do otherwise? I am in the rather unique position of being the son, the grandson, and the great-grandson of preachers. Yes, I see the church as the body of Christ. But, oh! How we have blemished and scarred that body through social neglect and fear of being nonconformists. 34

There was a time when the church was very powerful. It was during that period when the early Christians rejoiced when they were deemed worthy to suffer for what they believed. In those days the church was not merely a thermometer that recorded the ideas and principles of popular opinion; it was a thermostat that transformed the mores of society. Wherever the early Christians entered a town the power structure got disturbed and immediately sought to convict them for being "disturbers of the peace" and "outside agitators." But they went on with the conviction that they were "a colony of heaven," and had to obey God rather than man. They were small in number but big in commitment. They were too God-intoxicated to be "astronomically intimidated." They brought an end to such ancient evils as infanticide and gladiatorial contest. 35

Things are different now. The contemporary church is often a weak, ineffectual voice with an uncertain sound. It is so often the arch-supporter of the status quo. Far from being disturbed by the presence of the church, the power structure of the average community is consoled by the church's silent and often vocal sanction of things as they are. 36

But the judgment of God is upon the church as never before. If the church of today does not recapture the sacrificial spirit of the early church, it will lose its authentic ring, forfeit the loyalty of millions, and be dismissed as an irrelevant social club with no meaning for the twentieth century. I am meeting young people every day whose disappointment with the church has risen to outright disgust. 37

Maybe again, I have been too optimistic. Is organized religion too inextricably bound to the status quo to save our nation and the world? Maybe I must turn my faith to the inner spiritual church, the church within the church, as the true *ecclesia* and the hope of the world. But again I am thankful to God that some noble souls from the ranks of organized religion have broken loose from the paralyzing chains of conformity and joined us as active partners in the struggle for freedom. They have left their secure congregations and walked the streets of Albany, Georgia, with us. They have gone through the highways of the South on tortuous 38 rides for freedom. Yes, they have gone to jail with us. Some have been kicked out of their churches, and lost support of their bishops and fellow ministers. But they have gone with the faith that right defeated is stronger than evil triumphant. These men have been the leaven in the lump of the race. Their witness has been the spiritual salt that has preserved the true meaning of the gospel in these troubled times. They have carved a tunnel of hope through the dark mountain of disappointment.

I hope the church as a whole will meet the challenge of this decisive 39
hour. But even if the church does not come to the aid of justice, I have no despair about the future. I have no fear about the outcome of our struggle in Birmingham, even if our motives are presently misunderstood. We will reach the goal of freedom in Birmingham and all over the nation, because the goal of America is freedom. Abused and scorned though we may be, our destiny is tied up with the destiny of America. Before the Pilgrims landed at Plymouth we were here. Before the pen of Jefferson etched across the pages of history the majestic words of the Declaration of Independence, we were here. For more than two centuries our foreparents labored in this country without wages; they made cotton king; and they built the homes of their masters in the midst of brutal injustice and shameful humiliation — and yet out of a bottomless vitality they continued to thrive and develop. If the inexpressible cruelties of slavery could not stop us, the opposition we now face will surely fail. We will win our freedom because the sacred heritage of our nation and the eternal will of God are embodied in our echoing demands.

I must close now. But before closing I am impelled to mention one 40
other point in your statement that troubled me profoundly. You warmly commended the Birmingham police force for keeping "order" and "preventing violence." I don't believe you would have so warmly commended the police force if you had seen its angry violent dogs literally biting six unarmed, nonviolent Negroes. I don't believe you would so quickly commend the policemen if you would observe their ugly and inhuman treatment of Negroes here in the city jail; if you would watch them push and curse old Negro women and young Negro girls; if you would see them slap and kick old Negro men and young boys; if you will observe them, as they did on two occasions, refuse to give us food because we wanted to sing our grace together. I'm sorry that I can't join you in your praise for the police department.

It is true that they have been rather disciplined in their public han- 41
dling of the demonstrators. In this sense they have been rather publicly "nonviolent." But for what purpose? To preserve the evil system of segregation. Over the last few years I have consistently preached that nonviolence demands that the means we use must be as pure as the ends we seek. So I have tried to make it clear that it is wrong to use immoral

means to attain moral ends. But now I must affirm that it is just as wrong, or even more so, to use moral means to preserve immoral ends. Maybe Mr. Connor and his policemen have been rather publicly nonviolent, as Chief Pritchett was in Albany, Georgia, but they have used the moral means of nonviolence to maintain the immoral end of flagrant racial injustice. T. S. Eliot has said that there is no greater treason than to do the right deed for the wrong reason.

I wish you had commended the Negro sit-inners and demonstrators of 42
Birmingham for their sublime courage, their willingness to suffer, and their amazing discipline in the midst of the most inhuman provocation. One day the South will recognize its real heroes. They will be the James Merediths, courageously and with a majestic sense of purpose facing jeering and hostile mobs and the agonizing loneliness that characterizes the life of the pioneer. They will be old, oppressed, battered Negro women, symbolized in a seventy-two-year-old woman of Montgomery, Alabama, who rose up with a sense of dignity and with her people decided not to ride the segregated buses, and responded to one who inquired about her tiredness with ungrammatical profundity: "My feet is tired, but my soul is rested." They will be the young high school and college students, young ministers of the gospel, and a host of their elders courageously and nonviolently sitting-in at lunch counters and willingly going to jail for conscience's sake. One day the South will know that when these disinherited children of God sat down at lunch counters they were in reality standing up for the best in the American dream and the most sacred values in our Judeo-Christian heritage, and thusly, carrying our whole nation back to those great wells of democracy which were dug deep by the Founding Fathers in the formulation of the Constitution and the Declaration of Independence.

Never before have I written a letter this long (or should I say a book?). 43
I'm afraid that it is much too long to take your precious time. I can assure you that it would have been much shorter if I had been writing from a comfortable desk, but what else is there to do when you are alone for days in the dull monotony of a narrow jail cell other than write long letters, think strange thoughts, and pray long prayers?

If I have said anything in this letter that is an overstatement of the 44
truth and is indicative of an unreasonable impatience, I beg you to forgive me. If I have said anything in this letter that is an understatement of the truth and is indicative of my having a patience that makes me patient with anything less than brotherhood, I beg God to forgive me.

I hope this letter finds you strong in the faith. I also hope that circum- 45
stances will soon make it possible for me to meet each of you, not as an integrationist or a civil rights leader, but as a fellow clergyman and a Christian brother. Let us all hope that the dark clouds of racial prejudice

will soon pass away and the deep fog of misunderstanding will be lifted from our fear-drenched communities and in some not too distant tomorrow the radiant stars of love and brotherhood will shine over our great nation with all of their scintillating beauty.

Yours for the cause of Peace and Brotherhood,
Martin Luther King, Jr.

Discussion Questions

1. As in "I Have a Dream" (p. 626), King uses figurative language in his letter. Find some particularly vivid passages and evaluate their effect in the context of this letter.
2. Explain King's distinction between just and unjust laws. Are there dangers in attempting to make such a distinction?
3. What characteristics of mind and behavior does King exhibit in the letter? Select the specific passages that provide proof.
4. Why does King say that "the white moderate" is a greater threat to Negro progress than the outspoken racist? Is his explanation convincing?
5. How does King justify his philosophy of nonviolence in the face of continued aggression against the Negro?

Writing Suggestions

1. Can you think of a law against which defiance would be justified? Explain why the law is unjust and why refusal to obey is morally defensible.
2. In paragraph 12 King lists the grievances of Negroes in this country. King's catalog is similar to the lists in the Declaration of Independence and the Declaration at Seneca Falls. Can you think of any other group who might compile a list of grievances? If so, choose a group and draw up such a list, making sure that your list is as clear and specific as those you have read.

I Have a Dream

MARTIN LUTHER KING, JR.

In the widely reprinted "I Have a Dream" speech, Martin Luther King, Jr., appears as the charismatic leader of the civil-rights movement. This inspirational address was delivered on August 28, 1963, in Washington, D.C., at a demonstration by two hundred thousand people for civil rights for blacks.

Five score years ago, a great American, in whose symbolic shadow we stand, signed the Emancipation Proclamation. This momentous decree came as a great beacon light of hope to millions of Negro slaves who had been seared in the flames of withering injustice. It came as a joyous daybreak to end the long night of captivity. 1

But one hundred years later, we must face the tragic fact that the Negro is still not free. One hundred years later, the life of the Negro is still sadly crippled by the manacles of segregation and the chains of discrimination. One hundred years later, the Negro lives on a lonely island of poverty in the midst of a vast ocean of material prosperity. One hundred years later, the Negro is still languishing in the corners of American society and finds himself an exile in his own land. So we have come here today to dramatize an appalling condition. 2

In a sense we have come to our nation's capital to cash a check. When the architects of our republic wrote the magnificent words of the Constitution and the Declaration of Independence, they were signing a promissory note to which every American was to fall heir. This note was a promise that all men would be guaranteed the unalienable rights of life, liberty, and the pursuit of happiness. 3

It is obvious today that America has defaulted on this promissory note insofar as her citizens of color are concerned. Instead of honoring this sacred obligation, America has given the Negro people a bad check; a check which has come back marked "insufficient funds." But we refuse to believe that the bank of justice is bankrupt. We refuse to believe that there are insufficient funds in the great vaults of opportunity of this nation. So we have come to cash this check — a check that will give us upon demand the riches of freedom and the security of justice. We have also come to this hallowed spot to remind America of the fierce urgency of *now*. This is no time to engage in the luxury of cooling off or to take the tranquilizing drugs of gradualism. *Now* is the time to make real the prom- 4

From *A Testment of Hope* (1986).

ises of Democracy. *Now* is the time to rise from the dark and desolate valley of segregation to the sunlit path of racial justice. *Now* is the time to open the doors of opportunity to all of God's children. *Now* is the time to lift our nation from the quicksands of racial injustice to the solid rock of brotherhood.

It would be fatal for the nation to overlook the urgency of the mo- 5
ment and to underestimate the determination of the Negro. This sweltering summer of the Negro's legitimate discontent will not pass until there is an invigorating autumn of freedom and equality. 1963 is not an end, but a beginning. Those who hope that the Negro needed to blow off steam and will now be content will have a rude awakening if the nation returns to business as usual. There will be neither rest nor tranquillity in America until the Negro is granted his citizenship rights. The whirlwinds of revolt will continue to shake the foundations of our nation until the bright day of justice emerges.

But there is something that I must say to my people who stand on the 6
warm threshold which leads into the palace of justice. In the process of gaining our rightful place we must not be guilty of wrongful deeds. Let us not seek to satisfy our thirst for freedom by drinking from the cup of bitterness and hatred. We must forever conduct our struggle on the high plane of dignity and discipline. We must not allow our creative protest to degenerate into physical violence. Again and again we must rise to the majestic heights of meeting physical force with soul force. The marvelous new militancy which has engulfed the Negro community must not lead us to a distrust of all white people, for many of our white brothers, as evidenced by their presence here today, have come to realize that their destiny is tied up with our destiny and their freedom is inextricably bound to our freedom. We cannot walk alone.

And as we walk, we must make the pledge that we shall march 7
ahead. We cannot turn back. There are those who are asking the devotees of civil rights, "When will you be satisfied?" We can never be satisfied as long as the Negro is the victim of the unspeakable horrors of police brutality. We can never be satisfied as long as our bodies, heavy with the fatigue of travel, cannot gain lodging in the motels of the highways and the hotels of the cities. We cannot be satisfied as long as the Negro's basic mobility is from a smaller ghetto to a larger one. We can never be satisfied as long as a Negro in Mississippi cannot vote and a Negro in New York believes he has nothing for which to vote. No, no, we are not satisfied, and we will not be satisfied until justice rolls down like waters and righteousness like a mighty stream.

I am not unmindful that some of you have come here out of great tri- 8
als and tribulations. Some of you have come fresh from narrow jail cells. Some of you have come from areas where your quest for freedom left you

battered by the storms of persecution and staggered by the winds of police brutality. You have been the veterans of creative suffering. Continue to work with the faith that unearned suffering is redemptive.

Go back to Mississippi, go back to Alabama, go back to South Carolina, go back to Georgia, go back to Louisiana, go back to the slums and ghettos of our northern cities, knowing that somehow this situation can and will be changed. Let us not wallow in the valley of despair. 9

I say to you today, my friends, that in spite of the difficulties and frustrations of the moment I still have a dream. It is a dream deeply rooted in the American dream. 10

I have a dream that one day this nation will rise up and live out the true meaning of its creed: "We hold these truths to be self-evident; that all men are created equal." 11

I have a dream that one day on the red hills of Georgia the sons of former slaves and the sons of former slaveowners will be able to sit down together at the table of brotherhood. 12

I have a dream that one day even the state of Mississippi, a desert state sweltering with the heat of injustice and oppression, will be transformed into an oasis of freedom and justice. 13

I have a dream that my four little children will one day live in a nation where they will not be judged by the color of their skin but by the content of their character. 14

I have a dream today. 15

I have a dream that one day the state of Alabama, whose governor's lips are presently dripping with the words of interposition and nullification, will be transformed into a situation where little black boys and black girls will be able to join hands with little white boys and white girls and walk together as sisters and brothers. 16

I have a dream today. 17

I have a dream that one day every valley shall be exalted, every hill and mountain shall be made low, the rough places will be made plain, and the crooked places will be made straight, and the glory of the Lord shall be revealed, and all flesh shall see it together. 18

This is our hope. This is the faith with which I return to the South. With this faith we will be able to hew out of the mountain of despair a stone of hope. With this faith we will be able to transform the jangling discords of our nation into a beautiful symphony of brotherhood. With this faith we will be able to work together, to pray together, to struggle together, to go to jail together, to stand up for freedom together, knowing that we will be free one day. 19

This will be the day when all of God's children will be able to sing with new meaning 20

My country, 'tis of thee,
Sweet land of liberty,

Of thee I sing:
Land where my fathers died,
Land of the pilgrims' pride,
From every mountain-side
Let freedom ring.

And if America is to be a great nation this must become true. So let freedom ring from the prodigious hilltops of New Hampshire. Let freedom ring from the mighty mountains of New York. Let freedom ring from the heightening Alleghenies of Pennsylvania! 21

Let freedom ring from the snowcapped Rockies of Colorado! 22

Let freedom ring from the curvaceous peaks of California! 23

But not only that; let freedom ring from Stone Mountain of Georgia! 24

Let freedom ring from Lookout Mountain of Tennessee! 25

Let freedom ring from every hill and molehill of Mississippi. From every mountainside, let freedom ring. 26

When we let freedom ring, when we let it ring from every village and every hamlet, from every state and every city, we will be able to speed up that day when all of God's children, black men and white men, Jews and Gentiles, Protestants and Catholics, will be able to join hands and sing in the words of the old Negro spiritual, "Free at last! free at last! thank God almighty, we are free at last!" 27

Discussion Questions

1. King's style alternates between the abstract and the concrete, between the grandiloquent and the simple, with abundant use of metaphors. Find examples of these qualities. Are all the stylistic strategies equally effective? Explain your answer.
2. What specific injustices suffered by black people does King mention? Why does he interrupt his series of "Let freedom ring" imperatives at the end with the statement, "But not only that"?
3. What values does the speech stress? Would these values be equally appealing to both blacks and whites? Why or why not?
4. More than twenty years later, how much of King's indictment of conditions remains true? Mention specific changes or lack of changes. If conditions have improved, does that make his speech less meaningful today?

Writing Suggestions

1. Using the same material as the original, rewrite this speech for an audience that is not impressed with the inspirational style. Think carefully about the changes in language you would make to convince this audience that, despite your dispassionate treatment, injustices exist and should be rectified.
2. Choose another highly emotional subject — for example, women's rights,

child pornography, nuclear power — and write an inspirational speech or advertisement urging your audience to change their views. Be passionate, but try to avoid sentimentality or corniness. (You may want to look at other examples of the inspirational or hortatory style in a collection of speeches, among them speeches made in favor of the abolition of slavery and women's suffrage, declarations of war, and inaugural addresses.)

ACKNOWLEDGMENTS (continued from p. iv)

American Forest Institute advertisement, "The great American forest is closer than you think." Reprinted by permission of the American Forest Institute.

Cleveland Amory, "The Trials of Animals." Copyright © 1989 by The New York Times Company. Reprinted by permission.

William J. Bennett, "Should Drugs Be Legalized?" Reprinted with permission from the March 1990 *Reader's Digest*. Copyright © 1990 by The Reader's Digest Assn., Inc.

Ira Berkow, "Only Two Ways to Free College Sport." Copyright © 1989 by The New York Times Company. Reprinted by permission.

Shannon Brownlee and Nancy S. Linnon, "The Myth of the Student-Athlete." Copyright, January 8, 1990, *U.S. News & World Report*. Reprinted by permission of *U.S. News & World Report.*

Susan Brownmiller, "Pornography: Anti-Female Propaganda." From *Against Our Will: Men, Women and Rape* by Susan Brownmiller. Copyright © 1975 by Susan Brownmiller. Reprinted by permission of Simon & Schuster, Inc.

Warren E. Burger, "The Right to Bear Arms." From *Parade*, January 14, 1990. Reprinted with permission from *Parade*, copyright © 1990, and the author.

Hodding Carter III, "We're Losing the Drug War because Prohibition Never Works." From the *Wall Street Journal*, July 13, 1989. Reprinted with permission of the *Wall Street Journal*. © 1990 Dow Jones & Company, Inc. All rights reserved.

Robert H. Cohen, "Discrimination Goes On." From the *New York Times*, December 20, 1989. Copyright © 1989 by The New York Times Company. Reprinted by permission.

Commonweal, "Too Many Abortions." Editorial from *Commonweal*, August 11, 1989. Reprinted by permission.

Concern for Dying, "A Living Will." Reprinted with permission of Concern for Dying, 250 West 57th Street, New York, NY 10107.

Matthew E. Conolly, "Euthanasia Is Not the Answer." Reprinted by permission of the author.

Louis L. Cregler and Herbert Mark, "Cocaine Is Even Deadlier Than We Thought." From the *New York Times*, July 30, 1986. Copyright © 1986 by The New York Times Company. Reprinted by permission.

Theresa L. Crenshaw, "HIV Testing: Voluntary, Mandatory, or Routine?" Reprinted from the January/February 1988 issue of *The Humanist*. Copyright 1988 by *The Humanist*. Reprinted by permission.

The d-Con Company advertisement, "A trap can catch more than a mouse." © 1989 The d-Con Company, Inc.

Michael E. DeBakey, "Holding Human Health Hostage." Reprinted by permission of the author.

Eileen Doyle, "Consequences of Imposing the Quality of Life Ethic." From *A Pro-Life Primer on Euthanasia* by the American Life Lobby, 1985. Reprinted by permission of the American Life Lobby.

The Economist, "Alternatives to Animals." From *The Economist*, December 2, 1989. © 1989 The Economist Newspaper Ltd. All rights reserved. Reprinted by permission of *The Economist.* "Rethinking the Greenhouse." From *The Economist*, December 16, 1989. © 1989 The Economist Newspaper Ltd. All rights reserved. Reprinted by permission of *The Economist*. "A Time to Die." From *The Economist*, August 5, 1989. © 1989 The Economist Newspaper Ltd. All rights reserved. Reprinted by permission of *The Economist.*

Barbara Ehrenreich, "The Silenced Majority." From the *Utne Reader*, January/February 1990, excerpted from *Zeta*, September 1989. Reprinted by permission of *Zeta*.

Jean Bethke Elshtain, "The Place of Pornography." From *Harper's* Forum. Copyright © 1984 by *Harper's* Magazine. All rights reserved. Reprinted from the November issue by special permission.

57 Restaurant advertisement, "Everything a good restaurant ought to be." Reprinted by permission of the 57 Restaurant.

General Electric advertisement, "General Electric: The initials of a friend." Reprinted by permission of General Electric.

Elizabeth Gessner, "We Already Know the Folly of Decriminalized Drugs." From the *New York Times*, October 20, 1989. Copyright © 1989 by The New York Times Company. Reprinted by permission.

Ira Glasser, "We Can Control Drugs, but We Can't Ban Them." From the *New York Times*, November 20, 1989. Copyright © 1989 by The New York Times Company. Reprinted by permission.

Peter H. Gleick, "Bottom-Line Thinking Won't Save Our Climate." From the *New York Times*, November 30, 1989. Copyright © 1989 by The New York Times Company. Reprinted by permission.

Al Goldstein, "Feminists Are Wrong about Pornography." From the December 1984 issue of *Film Comment*. Reprinted by permission of the author.

Paul Goodman, "A Proposal to Abolish Grading." Reprinted from *Compulsory Miseducation* by Paul Goodman. Copyright 1964, by permission of the publisher, Horizon Press, New York.

Haven Bradford Gow, "The Bitter Harvest of Pornography." From the *New York Times*, March 4, 1986. Copyright © 1986 by The New York Times Company. Reprinted by permission.

Meg Greenfield, "In Defense of the Animals." From *Newsweek*, April 17, 1989. © 1989, Newsweek, Inc. All rights reserved. Reprinted by permission.

Ronnie Gunnerson, "Parents Also Have Rights." From *Newsweek*, March 2, 1987. Reprinted by permission.

Ted Gup, "What Can Be Done?" From *Time*, April 3, 1989. Copyright 1989 The Time Inc. Magazine Company. Reprinted by permission.

Thomas E. Hamm, Jr., "Vigilant Protocol." From the *New York Times*, October 19, 1989. Copyright © 1989 by The New York Times Company. Reprinted by permission.

Harper's Forum, "AIDS: What Is to Be Done?" From *Harper's* Magazine. Copyright © 1985 by *Harper's* Magazine. All rights reserved. Reprinted from the October issue by special permission.

Hugh Hefner, "Sexual McCarthyism." Reproduced by special permission of *Playboy* Magazine. Copyright © 1985 by *Playboy*.

Nat Hentoff, "Free Speech on the Campus." From *The Progressive*, May 1989. Copyright 1989 by Nat Hentoff. Reprinted by permission of the author.

Howard H. Hiatt and Cyrus Levinthal, "Is Abortion Ever Equal to Murder?" Copyright © 1989 by The New York Times Company. Reprinted by permission.

Adolf Hitler, "On Nation and Race." From *Mein Kampf* by Adolf Hitler, translated by Ralph Manheim. Copyright 1943 and copyright © renewed 1971 by Houghton Mifflin Company. Reprinted by permission of Houghton Mifflin Company and the Random Century Group.

Angela R. Holder, Clinical Professor of Pediatrics (Law), Yale University School of Medicine, "Parental Consent Could Justify Forced Abortion." From the *New York Times*, November 27, 1989. Copyright © 1989 by The New York Times Company. Reprinted by permission.

H. P. Hood advertisement, "Good taste comes naturally to women all over New England." Ketchum Advertising. Reprinted by permission of H. P. Hood.

Sidney Hook, "In Defense of Voluntary Euthanasia." Copyright © 1987 by The New York Times Company. Reprinted by permission.

Inter-Continental Hotels Corp. advertisement, "Success has its own rewards." Reprinted by permission of Inter-Continental Hotels Corp., Lintas–New York, and Michel Granger.

Susan Jacoby, "Notes from a Free-Speech Junkie." Reprinted by permission of Susan Jacoby. Copyright © 1978 by Susan Jacoby.

Greg Keath, "Abortion Is Not a Civil Right." From the *Wall Street Journal*, September 27, 1989. Reprinted with permission of the *Wall Street Journal*. © 1990 Dow Jones & Company, Inc. All rights reserved.

Patricia Keegan, "Playing Favorites." Copyright © 1989 by The New York Times Company. Reprinted by permission.

Martin Luther King, Jr., "I Have a Dream." Reprinted by permission of Joan Daves. Copyright © 1963 by Martin Luther King, Jr. "Letter from Birmingham Jail." From *Why We Can't Wait* by Martin Luther King, Jr. Copyright © 1963, 1964 by Martin Luther King, Jr. Reprinted by permission of Harper & Row, Publishers, Inc.

William Severini Kowinski, "Kids in the Mall: Growing Up Controlled." From *The Malling of America: An Inside Look at the Great Consumer Paradise* by William Severini Kowinski. Copyright © 1985 by the author. By permission of William Morrow & Co.

Mathilde Krim, "How *Not* to Control the AIDS Epidemic." Reprinted from the November/December 1987 issue of *The Humanist*. Copyright 1987 by *The Humanist*. Reprinted by permission.

Charles R. Lawrence III, "The Debate over Placing Limits on Racist Speech Must Not Ingore the Damage It Does to Its Victims." From *The Chronicle of Higher Education*, October 25, 1989. Reprinted by permission of the author.

Michael Levin, "The Case for Torture." Reprinted by permission of the author.

C. S. Lewis, "Vivisection." From *Undeceptions*, edited by Walter Hooper. Copyright © 1971 by William Collins Sons & Company, Ltd. Reprinted by permission of Collins Publishers.

Herbert I. London, "Fair Play for College Athletes: Racism and NCAA Rules." From *Academic Questions*, Fall 1989. Herbert I. London, Dean Gallatin Division, New York University; Chairman, National Association of Scholars. Reprinted by permission.

Barry W. Lynn, "Pornography's Many Forms: Not All Bad." Reprinted by permission of the author.

Daniel C. Maguire, "Death by Choice: Who Should Decide?" Excerpt from *Death by Choice* by Daniel C. Maguire, copyright © 1973, 1974 by Daniel Maguire. Used by permission of Doubleday, a division of Bantam, Doubleday, Dell Publishing Group, Inc.

David J. Meltz, "Not Just a Few Prudes. . . ." From the *New York Times*, March 4, 1990. Copyright © 1990 by The New York Times Company. Reprinted by permission.

Metropolitan Energy Council advertisement, "Gas heat makes me nervous." Reprinted by permission of the Metropolitan Energy Council.

Richard Mitchell, "Nox Quondam, Nox Futura!" From *The Leaning Tower of Babel and Other Affronts from the Underground Grammarian*, by Richard Mitchell. Copyright © 1984 by Richard Mitchell. By permission of Little, Brown and Company.

Acel Moore, "Proposal 42 Closes the Door on the Poor." From the *Philadelphia Inquirer*, January 18, 1989. Used with permission.

Stephen Moore, "Economic and Social Impact of Immigrants." From *Backgrounder*, November 6, 1989. Reprinted by permission of The Heritage Foundation, Washington, D.C.

Juliet K. Moyna, "Abortion Consent Law Creates Support System." From the *New York Times*, October 30, 1989. Copyright © 1989 by The New York Times Company. Reprinted by permission.

Aryeh Neier, "Pornography Here and Abroad." From *Harper's* Forum. Copyright © 1984 by

Harper's Magazine. All rights reserved. Reprinted from the November issue by special permission.

Jacob Neusner, "The Speech the Graduates Didn't Hear." Copyright © 1983 by Jacob Neusner. Reprinted from the *Daily Herald*, June 12, 1983. Used by permission of the author.

New York Times editorial, "How to Handle Hate on Campus." Copyright © 1989 by The New York Times Company. Reprinted by permission.

Susan Orlean, "Saturday Night." From *Saturday Night in America* by Susan Orlean. Copyright © 1990 by Susan Orlean; copyright © 1990 by The New York Times Company. Reprinted by permission of The New York Times Company and Alfred A. Knopf, Inc.

George Orwell, "Politics and the English Language." Copyright 1946 by Sonia Brownell Orwell, renewed 1974 by Sonia Orwell. Reprinted from *Shooting an Elephant and Other Essays* by permission of Harcourt Brace Jovanovich, Inc., the estate of the late Sonia Brownell Orwell, and Secker & Warburg.

Mortimer Ostow, "That Right Belongs Only to the State." Reprinted by permission of the author.

James Ostrowski, "Thinking about Drug Legalization." From *Cato Institute Policy Analysis*, May 25, 1989. Reprinted by permission of the Cato Institute.

Billy Packer, "College Basketball: Issues and Answers." Copyright © 1989 by The New York Times Company. Reprinted by permission.

Jon Pareles, "Legislating the Imagination" and art "Record Companies to Put Warnings." Copyright © 1990 by The New York Times Company. Reprinted by permission.

J. A. Parker, "Capital Punishment — An Idea Whose Time Has Come Again." From *Lincoln Review*, Summer 1986. Reprinted by permission.

Tony Parker and Robert Allerton, "A Criminal Justifies Himself." From *The Courage of His Convictions* by Tony Parker and Robert Allerton. Reprinted by permission of Random Century Group.

Peter Passell, "Lotto Is Financed by the Poor and Won by the States." Copyright © 1989 by The New York Times Company. Reprinted by permission. "Staggering Cost Is Foreseen to Curb Warming of Earth." Copyright © 1989 by The New York Times Company. Reprinted by permission.

E. L. Pattullo, "Public Shouldn't Pay." From the *New York Times*, November 27, 1989. Copyright © 1989 by The New York Times Company. Reprinted by permission.

Guy Piazza, "War on Drugs Falls through the Crack." From the *Wall Street Journal*, July 24, 1989. Reprinted with permission of the *Wall Street Journal*. © 1990 Dow Jones & Company, Inc. All rights reserved.

Planned Parenthood advertisement, "Nine Reasons Why Abortions Are Legal." Copyright revised version Planned Parenthood Federation of America, Inc., March 1989. Copyright PPFA 1985. All rights reserved. Reprinted by permission of Planned Parenthood® Federation of America, Inc.

Anna Quindlen, "Death Penalty's False Promise: An Eye for an Eye." Copyright © 1986 by The New York Times Company. Reprinted by permission.

James Rachels, M.D., "Active and Passive Euthanasia." From the *New England Journal of Medicine*, Vol. 292, pp. 78–80, 1975. Reprinted by permission.

Charles B. Rangel, "Legalize Drugs? Not on Your Life." Copyright © 1988 by The New York Times Company. Reprinted by permission.

William K. Reilly, "Overview of the State of the Environment: Toward the Nineties." From *State of the Environment: A View Toward the Nineties*, The Conservation Foundation, 1987, pp. xlv–xlvii. Reprinted by permission.

Richard M. Restak, M.D., "AIDS: In Plagues, Civil Rights Aren't the Issue." Reprinted by permission of the author.

Thomas Richards, "Don't Tell Me on Friday." From the *British Medical Journal*, April 5, 1986. Permission by Branden Publishing Boston.

Peter H. Rossi, "Homelessness in Colonial and Early America." From *Down and Out in America: The Origins of Homelessness* by Peter H. Rossi. Copyright © 1989 The University of Chicago Press. Reprinted by permission of The University of Chicago Press.

Victoria A. Sackett, "Discriminating Tastes: The Prejudice of Personal Preferences." From *Public Opinion*, July/August 1987. Reprinted with the permission of the American Enterprise Institute, Washington, D.C.

George Sage and John Davis, "Should College Athletes Be Paid Salaries?" Copyright, December 23, 1985, *U.S. News & World Report*. Reprinted from *U.S. News & World Report*.

Helen E. and R. Lynn Sauls, "Erasing the 'R' Words." From *Liberty*, May/June 1989. Copyright 1989 by *Liberty* Magazine. Reprinted by permission of the authors.

Jane S. Shaw and Richard L. Stroup, "Getting Warmer?" From *National Review*, July 14, 1989. © by National Review Inc., 150 East 35th Street, New York, NY 10016. Reprinted by permission.

Arthur B. Shostak, "A Problem for Couples." From the *New York Times*, January 22, 1990. Copyright © 1990 by The New York Times Company. Reprinted by permission.

Peter Singer, "Animal Liberation." Reprinted from the April 15, 1973 issue of *The New York Review of Books* by permission of the author. Copyright © 1973 by Peter Singer.

Roger Sipher, "So That Nobody Has to Go to School If They Don't Want To." Copyright © 1977 by The New York Times Company. Reprinted by permission.

Cliff Sjogren, "Prop 48 Makes Athletes Study." Copyright © 1989 by The New York Times Company. Reprinted by permission.

Andrew Sullivan, "Here Comes the Groom." From *The New Republic*, August 28, 1989. Reprinted by permission of *The New Republic*, © 1989 The New Republic, Inc.

Barbara Tuchman, "The Missing Element: Moral Courage." Reprinted by permission of Russell & Volkening as agents for the author. Copyright © 1978 by Barbara Tuchman.

James R. Udall, "Nature Under Glass." From *Sierra*, July/August 1989. Reprinted by permission of the author.

University of Michigan, "Interim Policy on Discrimination and Discriminatory Conduct by Students in the University Environment." Printed with the permission of the Regents of the University of Michigan, the author of the policy.

U.S. Council for Energy Awareness advertisement, "Nuclear energy can help America find a way out of our dangerous dependence on foreign oil." © 1988 USCEA. Advertisement provided courtesy of the U.S. Council for Energy Awareness, Washington, D.C.

U.S. English, "In Support of Our Common Language. . . ." From brochure by U.S. English. Reprinted by permission.

Gore Vidal, "Drugs." Copyright © 1970 by Gore Vidal. Reprinted from *Homage to Daniel Shays: Collected Essays 1952–1972* by Gore Vidal, by permission of Random House, Inc.

James M. Wall, "The Dynamics of Flag-Burning." Copyright 1989, The Christian Century Foundation. Reprinted by permission from the July 5–12, 1989 issue of *The Christian Century*.

The *Wall Street Journal*, "Animals and Sickness." From the *Wall Street Journal*, April 24, 1989. Reprinted with permission of the *Wall Street Journal*. © 1990 Dow Jones & Company, Inc. All rights reserved.

"Want to Bet?" bar graph. Copyright © 1989 by The New York Times Company. Reprinted by permission.

Betty Wein, "Pornography on the March." Reprinted with permission from the November 1987 *Reader's Digest*. This article was written for the World Media Association and is reprinted with permission.

Ruth Westheimer, "Women Know How to Fight." Copyright © 1990 by The New York Times Company. Reprinted by permission.

Frederick P. Whiddon, "The Case in Favor of Proposition 42." Copyright © 1989 by The New York Times Company. Reprinted by permission.

Garry Wills, "In Praise of Censure." From *Time*, July 31, 1989. Copyright 1989 The Time Inc. Magazine Company. Reprinted by permission.

Glenn T. Wilson, "Hot Air in the Greenhouse Debate." From the *Wall Street Journal*, December 4, 1989. Reprinted with permission of the *Wall Street Journal*. © 1990 Dow Jones & Company, Inc. All rights reserved.

Virginia Woolf, "Professions for Women." From *The Death of the Moth and Other Essays* by Virginia Woolf. Copyright 1942 by Harcourt Brace Jovanovich, Inc. and renewed 1970 by Marjorie T. Parsons, Executrix. Reprinted by permission of the publisher, Executors of the Virginia Woolf Estate, and the Hogarth Press.

Melvin L. Wulf, "Flag-Saving." *The Nation* Magazine/The Nation Company, Inc. Copyright © 1989. Reprinted by permission.

Stephen Zawistowski, Suzanne E. Roy, Stephen Kaufman, and Marjorie Cramer, "Breakthroughs Don't Require Torture." From the *Wall Street Journal*, May 19, 1989. Reprinted with permission of the *Wall Street Journal*. © 1990 Dow Jones & Company, Inc. All rights reserved.

Glossary and Index of Terms

Abstract language: language expressing a quality apart from a specific object or event; opposite of *concrete language* *184–188*

Ad hominem: "against the man"; attacking the arguer rather than the *argument* or issue *227*

Ad populum: "to the people"; playing on the prejudices of the *audience* *231*

Analogy: a *comparison* in which a thing is inferred to be similar to another thing in a certain way because it is similar to the thing in other ways *153–155*

Appeal to tradition: a proposal that something should continue because it has traditionally existed or been done that way *231–232*

Argument: a process of reasoning and advancing proof about issues on which conflicting views may be held; also, a statement or statements providing *support* for a *claim* *3–22*

Audience: those who will hear an *argument*; more generally, those to whom a communication is addressed *13–17*

Authoritative warrant: a *warrant* based on the credibility or trustworthiness of the source *148–149*

Authority: a respectable, reliable source of *evidence* *27, 116–120, 148–149*

Backing: the assurances upon which a *warrant* or assumption is based *144*

Begging the question: making a statement that assumes that the issue being argued has already been decided *229*

Cause and effect: reasoning that assumes one event or condition can bring about another *151–152*

Claim: the conclusion of an argument; what the arguer is trying to prove *10–11, 24–45*

Claim of fact: a *claim* that asserts something exists, has existed, or will exist, based on data that the *audience* will accept as objectively verifiable *10, 24–29*

Claim of policy: a *claim* asserting that specific courses of action should be instituted as solutions to problems *11, 39–45*

Claim of value: a *claim* that asserts some things are more or less desirable than others *10, 31–39*

Cliché: a worn-out expression or idea, no longer capable of producing a visual image or provoking thought about a subject *188–191*

Comparison warrant: a *warrant* based on shared characteristics and circumstances of two or more things or events; an *analogy* is a type of comparison, but the things or events being compared in an analogy are not of the same class *152–153*

Concrete language: language that describes specific, generally observable, persons, places, or things; in contrast to *abstract language* *184–188*

Connotation: the overtones that adhere to a word through long usage *177–179*

Credibility: the audience's belief in the arguer's trustworthiness; see also *ethos* *14–17, 116–119*

Data: see *evidence*

Deduction: reasoning by which we establish that a conclusion must be true because the statements on which it is based are true; see also *syllogism* *214–218*

Definition: an explanation of the meaning of a term, concept, or experience; may be used for clarification, especially of a *claim*, or as a means of developing an *argument* *13, 72–91*

Definition by negation: defining a thing by saying what it is not *79*

Enthymeme: a *syllogism* in which one of the premises is implicit *217*

Ethos: the qualities of character, intelligence, and goodwill in an arguer that contribute to an *audience's* acceptance of the *claim* *14*

Euphemism: a pleasant or flattering expression used in place of one that is less agreeable but possibly more accurate *177–178*

Evidence: *facts* or opinions that support an issue or *claim*; may consist of *statistics*, reports of personal experience, or views of experts *11, 106–120*

Extended definition: a *definition* that uses several different methods of development *80–81*

Fact: something that is believed to have objective reality; a piece of information regarded as verifiable *10, 24–29, 106–108, 113–116*

Factual evidence: *support* consisting of *data* that is considered objectively verifiable by the audience *106–108, 113–114*

Fallacy: an error of reasoning based on faulty use of *evidence* or incorrect *inference* *208–209, 223–233*

False Analogy: assuming without sufficient proof that if objects or processes are similar in some ways, then they are similar in other ways as well; see *analogy* *226*

False Dilemma: simplifying a complex problem into an either/or dichotomy *227–228*

Faulty emotional appeals: basing an argument on feelings, especially pity or fear — often to draw attention away from the real issues or conceal another purpose *232–233*

Faulty use of authority: failing to acknowledge disagreement among experts or otherwise misrepresenting the trustworthiness of sources *224*

Generalization: a statement of general principle derived inferentially from a series of examples *150*

Hasty generalization: drawing conclusions from insufficient evidence *224–226*

Induction: reasoning by which a general statement is reached on the basis of particular examples *209–213*

Inference: an interpretation of the *facts* *27–29*

Major premise: see *syllogism*

Minor premise: see *syllogism*

Motivational appeal: an attempt to reach an *audience* by recognizing their *needs* and *values* and how these contribute to their decision making *11, 120–127*

Motivational warrant: a type of *warrant* based on the *needs* and *values* of an *audience* *148–149*

Need: in the hierarchy of Abraham Maslow, whatever is required, whether psychological or physiological, for the survival and welfare of a human being *122–124*

Non sequitur: "it does not follow"; using irrelevant proof to buttress a *claim* *231*

Picturesque language: words that produce images in the minds of the *audience* *182–184*

Policy: a course of action recommended or taken to solve a problem or guide decisions *11, 39–45*

Post hoc: mistakenly inferring that because one event follows another they have a causal relation; from *post hoc ergo propter hoc* ("after this, therefore because of this"); also called "doubtful cause" *224–226*

Proposition: see *claim*

Qualifier: a restriction placed on the *claim* to state that it may not always be true as stated *26, 145*

Refutation: an attack on an opposing view in order to weaken it, invalidate it, or make it less credible *260–261*

Reservation: a restriction placed on the *warrant* to indicate that unless certain conditions are met, the warrant may not establish a connection between the *support* and the *claim* *145*

Sign warrant: a *warrant* that offers an observable datum as an indicator of a condition *150–151*

Slanting: selecting *facts* or words with *connotations* that favor the arguer's bias and discredit alternatives *179–182*

Slippery slope: predicting without justification that one step in a process will lead unavoidably to a second, generally undesirable step *228–229*

Slogan: an attention-getting expression used largely in politics or advertising to promote support of a cause or product *191–195*

Statistics: information expressed in numerical form *107–108, 114–116*

Stipulative definition: a *definition* that makes clear that it will explore a particular area of meaning of a term or issue *78–79*

Straw man: disputing a view similar to, but not the same as, that of the arguer's opponent *229–230*

Style: choices in words and sentence structure that make a writer's language distinctive *263–264, 267–268*

Substantive warrant: a *warrant* based on beliefs about the reliability of *factual evidence* *148*

Support: any material that serves to prove an issue or *claim*; in addition to *evidence*, it includes appeals to the *needs* and *values* of the *audience* *11, 104–141*

Syllogism: a formula of deductive *argument* consisting of three propositions: a major premise, a minor premise, and a conclusion *214–223*

Thesis: the main idea of an essay *254–256*

Toulmin model: a conceptual system of argument devised by the philosopher Stephen Toulmin; the terms *claim, support, warrant, backing, qualifier*, and *reservation* are adapted from this system *142, 221–223*

Two wrongs make a right: diverting attention from the issue by introducing a new point, e.g., by responding to an accusation with a counter-accusation that makes no attempt to refute the first accusation *230–231*

Values: conceptions or ideas that act as standards for judging what is right or wrong, worthwhile or worthless, beautiful or ugly, good or bad *10, 31–35, 124–127*

Warrant: a general principle or assumption that establishes a connection between the *support* and the *claim* *11–12, 142–174*

Index of Authors and Titles

Abortion Consent Law Creates Support System (Moyna) 331
Abortion Is Not a Civil Right (Keath) 318
Ackerman, Felicia, *Not Everybody Wants to Sign a Living Will* 468
Active and Passive Euthanasia (Rachels) 459
AIDS: In Plagues, Civil Rights Aren't the Issue (Restak) 339
AIDS: What Is to Be Done? (*Harper's* Forum) 355
Allerton, Robert. *See* Parker, Tony
Allport, Gordon, *The Nature of Prejudice* 92
Alternatives to Animals, (The Economist) 386
Amory, Cleveland, *The Trials of Animals* 379
Animal Liberation (Singer) 363
Animals and Sickness (The *Wall Street Journal*) 389

Bennett, William J., *Should Drugs Be Legalized?* 506
Berkow, Ira, *Only Two Ways to Free College Sport* 405
Bitter Harvest of Pornography, The (Gow) 539
Bottom-Line Thinking Won't Save Our Climate (Gleick) 440
Boyd, Cleo, *The New Drinking Laws: A Sour Taste* 273
Breakthroughs Don't Require Torture (Zawistowski, Roy, Kaufman, and Cramer) 391
Brownlee, Shannon, and Nancy S. Linnon, *The Myth of the Student-Athlete* 413
Brownmiller, Susan, *Pornography: Anti-Female Propaganda* 530
Burger, Warren E., *The Right to Bear Arms* 64

Capital Punishment — An Idea Whose Time Has Come Again (Parker) 57
Carter, Hodding, III, *We're Losing the Drug War because Prohibition Never Works* 516
Case for Torture, The (Levin) 157
Case in Favor of Proposition 42, The (Whiddon) 403
Civil Disobedience (Thoreau) 569

Cocaine Is Even Deadlier Than We Thought (Cregler and Mark) 30
Cohen, Robert H., *Discrimination Goes On* 360
College Basketball: Issues and Answers (Packer) 401
Commonweal, Too Many Abortions 325
Concern for Dying, *A Living Will* 466
Conolly, Matthew E., *Euthanasia Is Not the Answer* 452
Consequences of Imposing the Quality of Life Ethic (Doyle) 456
Cramer, Marjorie. *See* Zawistowski, Stephen
Cregler, Louis L., and Herbert Mark, *Cocaine Is Even Deadlier Than We Thought* 30
Crenshaw, Theresa L., *HIV Testing: Voluntary, Mandatory, or Routine?* 347
Criminal Justifies Himself, A (Parker and Allerton) 239
Crito, *From* (Plato) 555

Davis, John. *See* Sage, George
Death by Choice: Who Should Decide? (Maguire) 444
Death Penalty's False Promise: An Eye for an Eye (Quindlen) 169
DeBakey, Michael E., *Holding Human Health Hostage* 383
Debate over Placing Limits on Racist Speech Must Not Ignore the Damage It Does to Its Victims, The (Lawrence) 483
Declaration of Independence, The (Jefferson) 18
Declaration of Sentiments and Resolutions, Seneca Falls (Stanton) 588
Discriminating Tastes: The Prejudice of Personal Preferences (Sackett) 50
Discrimination Goes On (Cohen) 360
Don't Tell Me on Friday (Richards) 337
Doyle, Eileen, *Consequences of Imposing the Quality of Life Ethic* 456
Drugs (Vidal) 504
Dynamics of Flag-Burning, The (Wall) 494

Economic and Social Impact of Immigrants (Moore) 131
Economist, The, Alternatives to Animals 386; *Rethinking the Greenhouse* 432; *A Time to Die* 469
Ehrenreich, Barbara, *The Silenced Majority* 211
Elshtain, Jean Bethke, *The Place of Pornography* 548
Erasing the "R" Words (Sauls and Sauls) 202
Euthanasia Is Not the Answer (Conolly) 452
Everything a good restaurant ought to be [advertisement] 102

Fair Play for College Athletes: Racism and NCAA Rules (London) 407
Feminists Are Wrong about Pornography (Goldstein) 540
Flag-Saving (Wulf) 492
Free Speech on the Campus (Hentoff) 487

Gas heat makes me nervous [advertisement] 140
GE: The initials of a friend [advertisement] 69
Gessner, Elizabeth, *We Already Know the Folly of Decriminalized Drugs* 521
Getting Warmer? (Shaw and Stroup) 427
Glasser, Ira, *We Can Control Drugs, but We Can't Ban Them* 523
Gleick, Peter H., *Bottom-Line Thinking Won't Save Our Climate* 440

Goldstein, Al, *Feminists Are Wrong about Pornography* 540

Good taste comes naturally to women all over New England [advertisement] 206

Goodman, Paul, *A Proposal to Abolish Grading* 161

Gow, Haven Bradford, *The Bitter Harvest of Pornography* 539

Great American forest is closer than you think, The [advertisement] 68

Greenfield, Meg, *In Defense of the Animals* 393

Gunnerson, Ronnie, *Parents Also Have Rights* 328

Gup, Ted, *What Can Be Done?* 400

Hamm, Thomas E., Jr., *Vigilant Protocol* 381

Harper's Forum, *AIDS: What Is to Be Done?* 355

Hefner, Hugh, *Sexual McCarthyism* 534

Hentoff, Nat, *Free Speech on the Campus* 487

Here Comes the Groom (Sullivan) 164

Hiatt, Howard H., and Cyrus Levinthal, *Is Abortion Ever Equal to Murder?* 316

Hitler, Adolf, *On Nation and Race* 233

HIV Testing: Voluntary, Mandatory, or Routine? (Crenshaw) 347

Holder, Angela R., *Parental Consent Could Justify Forced Abortion* 332

Holding Human Health Hostage (DeBakey) 383

Homelessness in Colonial and Early America (Rossi) 45

Hook, Sidney, *In Defense of Voluntary Euthanasia* 449

Hot Air in the Greenhouse Debate (Wilson) 435

How Not *to Control the AIDS Epidemic* (Krim) 343

How to Handle Hate on Campus (*The New York Times*) 486

I Have a Dream (King) 626

In Defense of the Animals (Greenfield) 393

In Defense of Voluntary Euthanasia (Hook) 449

In Praise of Censure (Wills) 473

In Support of Our Common Language . . . (U.S. English) 54

Interim Policy on Discrimination and Discriminatory Conduct by Students in the University Environment (The University of Michigan) 478

Is Abortion Ever Equal to Murder? (Hiatt and Levinthal) 316

Jacoby, Susan, *Notes from a Free-Speech Junkie* 527

Jefferson, Thomas, *The Declaration of Independence* 18

Kaufman, Stephen. *See* Zawistowski, Stephen

Keath, Greg, *Abortion Is Not a Civil Right* 318

Keegan, Patricia, *Playing Favorites* 135

Kids in the Mall: Growing Up Controlled (Kowinski) 35

King, Martin Luther, Jr., *I Have a Dream* 626; *Letter from Birmingham Jail* 611

Kowinski, William Severini, *Kids in the Mall: Growing Up Controlled* 35

Krim, Mathilde, *How* Not *to Control the AIDS Epidemic* 343

Lawrence, Charles R., III, *The Debate over Placing Limits on Racist Speech Must Not Ignore the Damage It Does to Its Victims* 482

Legalize Drugs? Not on Your Life (Rangel) 519

Legislating the Imagination (Pareles) 497
Letter from Birmingham Jail (King) 611
Levin, Michael, *The Case for Torture* 157
Levinthal, Cyrus. *See* Hiatt, Howard H.
Lewis, C. S., *Vivisection* 375
Linnon, Nancy S. *See* Brownlee, Shannon
A Living Will (Concern for Dying) 466
London, Herbert I., *Fair Play for College Athletes: Racism and NCAA Rules* 407
Lotto Is Financed by the Poor and Won by the States (Passell) 127
Lynn, Barry W., *Pornography's Many Forms: Not All Bad* 546

Maguire, Daniel C., *Death by Choice: Who Should Decide?* 444
Mark, Herbert. *See* Cregler, Louis L.
Meltz, David J., *Not Just a Few Prudes . . .* 500
Missing Element, The: Moral Courage, (Tuchman) 84
Mitchell, Richard, *Nox Quondam, Nox Futura!* 196
Modest Proposal, A (Swift) 560
Moore, Acel, *Proposal 42 Closes the Door on the Poor* 402
Moore, Stephen, *Economic and Social Impact of Immigrants* 131
Moyna, Juliet K., *Abortion Consent Law Creates Support System* 331
Myth of the Student-Athlete, The (Brownlee and Linnon) 413

Nature of Prejudice, The (Allport) 92
Nature Under Glass (Udall) 423
Neier, Aryeh, *Pornography Here and Abroad* 549
Neusner, Jacob, *The Speech the Graduates Didn't Hear* 200
New Drinking Laws, The: A Sour Taste (Boyd) 273
New York Times, The, *How to Handle Hate on Campus* 486
Nine Reasons Why Abortions Are Legal (Planned Parenthood) 320
Not Everybody Wants to Sign a Living Will (Ackerman) 468
Not Just a Few Prudes . . . (Meltz) 500
Notes from a Free-Speech Junkie (Jacoby) 527
Nox Quondam, Nox Futura! (Mitchell) 196
Nuclear energy can help America find a way out of our dangerous dependence on foreign oil [advertisement] 70

On Nation and Race (Hitler) 233
Only Two Ways to Free College Sport (Berkow) 405
Orlean, Susan, *Saturday Night* 94
Orwell, George, *Politics and the English Language* 599
Ostow, Mortimer, *That Right Belongs Only to the State* 464
Ostrowski, James, *Thinking about Drug Legalization* 511
Overview of the State of the Environment: Toward the Nineties (Reilly) 420

Packer, Billy, *College Basketball: Issues and Answers* 401
Pareles, Jon, *Legislating the Imagination* 497
Parental Consent Could Justify Forced Abortion (Holder) 332
Parents Also Have Rights (Gunnerson) 328
Parker, J. A., *Capital Punishment — An Idea Whose Time Has Come Again* 57
Parker, Tony, *A Criminal Justifies Himself* 239
Passell, Peter, *Lotto is Financed by the Poor and Won by the*

States 127; *Staggering Cost Is Foreseen to Curb Warming of Earth* 435
Pattullo, E. L., *Public Shouldn't Pay* 325
Piazza, Guy, *War on Drugs Falls through the Crack* 518
Place of Pornography, The (Elshtain) 548
Planned Parenthood, *Nine Reasons Why Abortions Are Legal* 320
Plato, *From* Crito 555
Playing Favorites (Keegan) 135
Politics and the English Language (Orwell) 599
Pornography: Anti-Female Propaganda (Brownmiller) 530
Pornography Here and Abroad (Neier) 549
Pornography on the March (Wein) 542
Pornography's Many Forms: Not All Bad (Lynn) 546
Problem for Couples, A (Shostak) 333
Professions for Women (Woolf) 593
Prop 48 Makes Athletes Study (Sjogren) 410
Proposal 42 Closes the Door on the Poor (Moore) 402
Proposal to Abolish Grading, A (Goodman) 161
Public Shouldn't Pay (Pattullo) 325

Quindlen, Anna, *Death Penalty's False Promise: An Eye for an Eye* 169

Rachels, James, *Active and Passive Euthanasia* 459
Rangel, Charles B., *Legalize Drugs? Not on Your Life* 519
Reilly, William K., *Overview of the State of the Environment: Toward the Nineties* 420
Repp, Amanda, *Why We Don't Need Zoos* 301
Restak, Richard, *AIDS: In Plagues, Civil Rights Aren't the Issue* 339
Rethinking the Greenhouse (The Economist) 432
Richards, Thomas, *Don't Tell Me on Friday* 337
Right to Bear Arms, The (Burger) 64
Rossi, Peter H., *Homelessness in Colonial and Early America* 45
Roy, Suzanne E. *See* Zawistowski, Stephen

Sackett, Victoria A., *Discriminating Tastes: The Prejudice of Personal Preferences* 50
Sage, George, and John Davis, *Should College Athletes Be Paid Salaries?* 398
Saturday Night (Orlean) 94
Sauls, Helen E., and R. Lynn Sauls, *Erasing the "R" Words* 202
Sexual McCarthyism (Hefner) 534
Shaw, Jane S., and Richard L. Stroup, *Getting Warmer?* 427
Shostak, Arthur B., *A Problem for Couples* 333
Should College Athletes Be Paid Salaries? (Sage and Davis) 398
Should Drugs Be Legalized? (Bennett) 506
Silenced Majority, The (Ehrenreich) 211
Singer, Peter, *Animal Liberation* 363
Sipher, Roger, *So That Nobody Has to Go to School If They Don't Want To* 42
Sjogren, Cliff, *Prop 48 Makes Athletes Study* 410
So That Nobody Has to Go to School If They Don't Want To (Sipher) 42
Speech the Graduates Didn't Hear, The (Neusner) 200
Staggering Cost Is Foreseen to Curb Warming of Earth (Passell) 435

Stanton, Elizabeth Cady, *Declaration of Sentiments and Resolutions, Seneca Falls* 588
Stroup, Richard L. *See* Shaw, Jane S.
Success has its own rewards [advertisement] 172
Sullivan, Andrew, *Here Comes the Groom* 164
Swift, Jonathan, *A Modest Proposal* 560

That Right Belongs Only to the State (Ostow) 464
Thinking about Drug Legalization (Ostrowski) 511
Thoreau, Henry David, *Civil Disobedience* 569
Time to Die, A (The Economist) 469
Too Many Abortions (Commonweal) 325
Trap can catch more than a mouse, A [advertisement] 248
Trials of Animals, The (Amory) 379
Tuchman, Barbara, *The Missing Element: Moral Courage* 84

Udall, James R., *Nature Under Glass* 423
U.S. English, *In Support of Our Common Language . . .* 54
University of Michigan, The, *Interim Policy on Discrimination and Discriminatory Conduct by Students in the University Environment* 478

Vidal, Gore, *Drugs* 504
Vigilant Protocol (Hamm) 381
Vivisection (Lewis) 375

Wall, James M., *The Dynamics of Flag-Burning* 494
Wall Street Journal, The, *Animals and Sickness* 389
War on Drugs Falls through the Crack (Piazza) 518
We Already Know the Folly of Decriminalized Drugs (Gessner) 521
We Can Control Drugs, but We Can't Ban Them (Glasser) 523
Wein, Betty, *Pornography on the March* 542
We're Losing the Drug War because Prohibition Never Works (Carter) 516
Westheimer, Ruth, *Women Know How to Fight* 219
What Can Be Done? (Gup) 400
Whiddon, Frederick P., *The Case in Favor of Proposition 42* 403
Why We Don't Need Zoos (Repp) 301
Wills, Garry, *In Praise of Censure* 473
Wilson, Glenn T., *Hot Air in the Greenhouse Debate* 435
Women Know How to Fight (Westheimer) 219
Woolf, Virginia, *Professions for Women* 593
Wulf, Melvin L., *Flag-Saving* 492

Zawistowski, Stephen, Suzanne E. Roy, Stephen Kaufman, and Marjorie Cramer, *Breakthroughs Don't Require Torture* 391

To the Student

We regularly revise the books we publish in order to make them better. To do this well we need to know what instructors and students think of the previous edition. At some point your instructor will be asked to comment on *Elements of Argument*, Third Edition; now we would like to hear from you.

Please take a few minutes to rate the selections and complete this questionnaire. Send it to Bedford Books *of* St. Martin's Press, 29 Winchester Street, Boston, Massachusetts 02116. We promise to listen to what you have to say. Thanks.

School ______________________________

School location (city, state) ______________________________

Course title ______________________________

Instructor's name ______________________________

	Liked a lot	Okay	Didn't like	Didn't read
1. Jefferson	___	___	___	___
2. Cregler and Mark	___	___	___	___
Kowinski	___	___	___	___
Sipher	___	___	___	___
Rossi	___	___	___	___
Sackett	___	___	___	___
U.S. English	___	___	___	___
Parker	___	___	___	___
Burger	___	___	___	___
3. Tuchman	___	___	___	___
Allport	___	___	___	___
Orlean	___	___	___	___
4. Passell	___	___	___	___
S. Moore	___	___	___	___
Keegan	___	___	___	___
5. Levin	___	___	___	___
Goodman	___	___	___	___
Sullivan	___	___	___	___
Quindlen	___	___	___	___
6. Mitchell	___	___	___	___
Neusner	___	___	___	___
Sauls and Sauls	___	___	___	___
Miller	___	___	___	___
7. Ehrenreich	___	___	___	___
Westheimer	___	___	___	___
Hitler	___	___	___	___
Parker and Allerton	___	___	___	___
8. Boyd	___	___	___	___
9. Repp	___	___	___	___
10. Hiatt and Levinthal	___	___	___	___
Keath	___	___	___	___
Planned Parenthood	___	___	___	___
Pattullo	___	___	___	___
Commonweal	___	___	___	___
Gunnerson	___	___	___	___
Moyna	___	___	___	___

		Liked a lot	Okay	Didn't like	Didn't read
	Holder	____	____	____	____
	Shostak	____	____	____	____
11.	Richards	____	____	____	____
	Restak	____	____	____	____
	Krim	____	____	____	____
	Crenshaw	____	____	____	____
	Harper's Forum	____	____	____	____
	Cohen	____	____	____	____
12.	Singer	____	____	____	____
	C. S. Lewis	____	____	____	____
	Amory	____	____	____	____
	Hamm	____	____	____	____
	DeBakey	____	____	____	____
	The Economist	____	____	____	____
	The *Wall Street Journal*	____	____	____	____
	Zawistowski et al	____	____	____	____
	Greenfield	____	____	____	____
13.	Sage and Davis	____	____	____	____
	Gup	____	____	____	____
	Packer	____	____	____	____
	A. Moore	____	____	____	____
	Whiddon	____	____	____	____
	Berkow	____	____	____	____
	London	____	____	____	____
	Sjogren	____	____	____	____
	Brownlee and Linnon	____	____	____	____
14.	Reilly	____	____	____	____
	Udall	____	____	____	____
	Shaw and Stroup	____	____	____	____
	The Economist	____	____	____	____
	Wilson	____	____	____	____
	Passell	____	____	____	____
	Gleick	____	____	____	____
15.	Maguire	____	____	____	____
	Hook	____	____	____	____
	Conolly	____	____	____	____
	Doyle	____	____	____	____
	Rachels	____	____	____	____
	Ostow	____	____	____	____
	Concern for Dying	____	____	____	____
	Ackerman	____	____	____	____
	The Economist	____	____	____	____
16.	Wills	____	____	____	____
	University of Michigan	____	____	____	____
	The *New York Times*	____	____	____	____
	Hentoff	____	____	____	____
	Wulf	____	____	____	____
	Wall	____	____	____	____
	Pareles	____	____	____	____
	Meltz	____	____	____	____

	Liked a lot	Okay	Didn't like	Didn't read
17. Vidal	____	____	____	____
Bennett	____	____	____	____
Ostrowski	____	____	____	____
Carter	____	____	____	____
Piazza	____	____	____	____
Rangel	____	____	____	____
Gessner	____	____	____	____
Glasser	____	____	____	____
18. Jacoby	____	____	____	____
Brownmiller	____	____	____	____
Hefner	____	____	____	____
Gow	____	____	____	____
Goldstein	____	____	____	____
Wein	____	____	____	____
Lynn	____	____	____	____
Elshtain	____	____	____	____
Neier	____	____	____	____
Classic Arguments				
Plato	____	____	____	____
Swift	____	____	____	____
Thoreau	____	____	____	____
Stanton	____	____	____	____
Woolf	____	____	____	____
Orwell	____	____	____	____
King (Letter)	____	____	____	____
King (Dream)	____	____	____	____

Name ________________________________ **Date** ______________________

Address ____

EDITOR'S NOTES TO ACCOMPANY

ELEMENTS OF ARGUMENT

A Text and Reader

ANNETTE T. ROTTENBERG

THIRD EDITION

With an essay by GAIL STYGALL

Miami University

Editor's Notes

PREPARED BY

Annette T. Rottenberg

UNIVERSITY OF MASSACHUSETTS AT AMHERST

With an essay by

Gail Stygall

Miami University

[This material appears only in the Instructor's Edition.]

Manufactured in the United States of America.

5 4 3 2 1 0
f e d c b a

For information, write: St. Martin's Press, Inc.
175 Fifth Avenue, New York, NY 10010

Editorial Offices: Bedford Books *of* St. Martin's Press
29 Winchester Street, Boston, MA 02116

ISBN 0-312-04913-7

Preface

In these notes I have assembled some of the assignments and classroom activities that have proved successful over the years in illuminating the elements of argument and eliciting thoughtful student response. Every teacher will have a collection of favorite devices, and I claim no superiority for mine. If some of the materials are not suitable, they may, however, suggest other kinds that are. Together with the writing suggestions in the text and the "Classic Arguments" they should provide an ample repertory of things to do for every day of the course. Clearly there will be more material than any single class can profitably use. But I keep in mind what a wise supervising teacher long ago gave me as one of her secrets for confidence in the classroom: "Always be overprepared."

The text is flexible. Students usually need or want more practice in some areas than others. If the use of support, for example, is one element in which the majority of students are weak, you may want to spend more time on the material in Chapter 4 and omit an extended discussion of language and fallacies. The heart of the text is, of course, Chapters 2, 3, 4, and 5. Remaining Chapters 6 and 7 can be handled less intensively.

"Opposing Viewpoints" lends itself to formal and informal classroom debate and longer papers that incorporate research. A short unit on debate is included in the *Editor's Notes.* This chapter-by-chapter section can also be used throughout the course as a reference guide for papers that fulfill different kinds of writing assignments, especially those that call for in-depth analysis of opposing arguments. "Classic Arguments" is another source of material for study and reference.

The most ambitious use of "Opposing Viewpoints" is as a source of information and opinion for the research paper. An enlarged section on research and use of the library and a documented research paper appear in Chapter 9. Suggestions for research paper subjects appear at the end of each section in "Opposing Viewpoints." For shorter papers students can limit their reading to material in the text. For longer papers they can look for additional material in the library.

The linear organization of the course should pose no problems. It is true that from the first assignment students will be writing arguments — before they have completed the study of the elements of argument. This practice, however, is the same as that of any other composition course where the process is one of deepening, widening, and enriching a first draft or a series of undeveloped generalizations. Many teachers of composition, myself among them, believe that students should begin to write whole essays from the beginning of the course. Attention to the components of argument follows when students attempt to make their essays stronger by concentrating on the particular areas that need development and revision.

Finally, the essay at the beginning of the *Editor's Notes* provides an overview of some of the special concerns and problems instructors should anticipate when teaching a course in argument, as well as practical general suggestions that might be useful in dealing with these concerns and problems.

Contents

Preface iii

Strategies for Teaching Argumentative Writing: An Overview by Gail Stygall 1

Introduction 1
Students' Experience with Argument 1
Setting the Tone for the Classroom 2
Maintaining the Forum: Debates on Paper 2
Using Peer Responses 3
Providing Background Information to Aid Critical Reading 3
Teaching Warrants and Assumptions 4
Different Wordings of Claims and Warrants 5
Teaching Fallacies: The Editorial Journal 5
Distinguishing between Induction and Deduction: Research Assignments 6
Conclusion 6

Bibliography on the Toulmin Model 7

PART ONE
The Structure of Argument 9

1. Introduction to Argument 9

2. Claims 10

Claims of Fact 10
Claims of Value 12
Claims of Policy 13

3. Definition 14

4. Support 15

Facts and Inferences 15
Evidence 17
Statistics 18
Appeals to Needs and Values 18

5. ***Warrants*** **19**

6. ***Language and Thought*** **21**

7. ***Induction, Deduction, and Logical Fallacies*** **23**

Exercise for Review: Answers **24**

PART TWO
Writing and Researching Arguments **27**

Introduction **27**

8. ***Writing an Argumentative Paper*** **28**

Assignments **28**
Composition: Style, Organization, and Development **29**
Avoiding Plagiarism **30**
Evaluation and Grading **31**
Peer Evaluation **32**
Conferences **32**

9. ***Researching an Argumentative Paper*** **34**

Use of the Library **36**

PART THREE
Opposing Viewpoints **37**

Introduction **37**
Debate **38**

10. ***Abortion*** **39**

11. ***AIDS Testing*** **40**

12. ***Animal Rights*** **42**

13. ***Collegiate Sports Reform*** **44**

14. ***Environmental Policy*** **45**

15. ***Euthanasia*** **47**

16. ***Freedom of Speech*** **48**

17. ***Legalizing Drugs*** **50**

18. ***Pornography*** **52**

PART FOUR
Classic Arguments 54

PLATO
From *Crito* 54

JONATHAN SWIFT
A Modest Proposal 55

HENRY DAVID THOREAU
Civil Disobedience 56

ELIZABETH CADY STANTON
Declaration of Sentiments and Resolutions, Seneca Falls 57

VIRGINIA WOOLF
Professions for Women 59

GEORGE ORWELL
Politics and the English Language 60

MARTIN LUTHER KING, JR.
Letter from Birmingham Jail 61

MARTIN LUTHER KING, JR.
I Have a Dream 64

Strategies for Teaching Argumentative Writing: An Overview by Gail Stygall

INTRODUCTION

One of the joys we experience in teaching argumentative writing is seeing our students take a step into the real rhetorical world. Instructors who have taught many semesters of introductory freshman composition without including argument notice an immediate difference in the papers they read and evaluate when they do opt for a semester of argumentation. After a semester in the argumentative writing classroom, students often find the now have a means for articulating the opinions, views, and knowledge that they feel belong in the public discussion. Moreover, the informal logic model, once understood, may be taken into other classrooms as a means for analyzing readings and writing. With the flexibility of *Elements of Argument* and with the dialogue of argument in the classroom, students have access to a practical, everyday logic, so often missing in our public discussions of issues.

Although teaching argument is different from teaching the purely expository freshman writing course, it is, in many ways, easier for the instructor. Many freshman composition instructors have struggled to create a real purpose for students when the students have to produce brief explanatory or illustrative essays. Not yet knowledgeable enough to join the essayists who populate their readers, students may not see the point of practicing consistency within forms. Even in the studio classroom, with a peer audience available, students in the expository course may reason that writing is just another form of exercise, not something they might ever need to do in the real world. Argument, on the other hand, diminishes the instructor's struggle to create a real audience. Students may participate immediately, whether the forum is the classroom, campuswide issues, or national elections, and they can see that their writing can make a difference with a real audience.

If you are new to teaching argumentative writing, this shift into active argument need not mean you have to reject what you already know. Many of us now teaching English were ourselves taught composition by the modes approach. The various ways in which we articulate arguments make use of those very same patternings — process, cause and effect, classification, comparison, definition. What changes is that we teach our students how to use those structures to serve as support for their arguments.

STUDENTS' EXPERIENCE WITH ARGUMENT

Students arriving in the freshman composition classroom that is focused on argument have rarely been asked to take a stand before in writing contexts. Our nation's comparatively unimpressive performance in the persuasive essay category for seventeen-year-olds participating in the International Education Association writing project indicates how little our students may know about argument and persuasion when they begin college (Purves and Takala). Although many aspects of a process writing curriculum have been developed in the elementary and high schools, we still may not take it for granted that our students have had prior practice in argument. A related problem is that students doubt that we really want their opinions; in high school, they probably experienced institutional constraints on their views. Even if they had offered their opinions, they may have had those opinions rejected and may now hesitate to trust us. Moreover, prior to college they have often been in settings in which their basic belief systems have gone relatively unchallenged. They may offer what appears to them to be the wisdom of a community, but they have not yet had to maintain that wisdom in the face of a decidedly different community, such as the college classroom.

SETTING THE TONE FOR THE CLASSROOM

Because students have often had so little practice in oral or written argument, we must try to maintain a classroom in which open discussion and debate are the standard procedure. Many argumentative writing instructors use intercollegiate debate as a model to set the necessary atmosphere. Instructors may tape sessions of *Firing Line* or *Meet the Press* for classroom discussion. Other instructors arrange for their classes to hear a full intercollegiate debate.

Setting the tone, however, goes beyond having students observe impersonal or distanced third-person demonstrations of debate and argumentation. Students need to hear one another assert and defend arguments, and they must have the opportunity to respond to one another face to face. Planning for discussion time is a useful strategy, following selected reading assignments. Students may be asked to come to class with brief responses to a particular essay, responses that include the students' own arguments about the topic at issue. Arranging for these reaction discussions places tolerance at a premium in the argumentative writing classroom, and the instructor often becomes the immediate arbiter of conflicting views and opinions. You should expect students to ask for your opinion on the various topics, as they invariably will, and prepare your own reactions and responses accordingly.

MAINTAINING THE FORUM: DEBATES ON PAPER

Many instructors continue the open forum by shifting their focus to actual writing assignments, arranging assignments so that one student is graded for responding directly to another student's paper. Argument becomes quite real when a student sees that his or her reasoning does not convince a classmate. Even a skilled argumentative writer learns from this assignment that a good argument acknowledges alternative views. Students who quote out of context, don't order their arguments well, or use logical fallacies without understanding what they represent often see during the refutation process what effect these practices have on the audience. Some instructors extend the dialogue even further by requiring a rebuttal paper in response to the refutation paper. For instructors who have been using a process approach to writing, this paper exchange is a means of helping students recognize the value of audience. In a direct exchange of papers, students cannot help being reminded of the dialogic nature of argumentative writing.

USING PEER RESPONSES

Process approaches can be further adapted for the argumentative writing classroom through the use of the audience questionnaire, as suggested by Professor Rottenberg in Chapter 1 of *Editor's Notes*. Instructors, instead of distributing generic peer-response forms, may ask students to evaluate one another's work in terms of the results of class opinions, requiring students to write briefly about which segments of the class a particular essay will convince, harden, or fail to move. These same peer responders can explore in writing why they think the paper will succeed or fail by pointing to specific parts of the argument and evaluating the strategies informing its delivery. Peer responders may also list and develop counterarguments and offer counterevidence, keeping the focus on the dialogue between writer and reader.

Peer response exercises can also be used effectively with Part One of *Elements of Argument*. In conjunction with specific chapters, instructors can design peer-response forms for assigned student essays that direct the student responders to the important aspects of argument covered in those chapters. Instructors need to know that students who are inexperienced at focused response may need support in the form of a guided response sheet. Early in the semester, an instructor might ask both the student writer and the peer responder to answer the following questions about the student's essay:

What is the claim being made here? Write several sentences explaining your answer. You may want to quote from the text of the essay.

Is this an argument? Use evidence from Chapter 1 of your text to support your answer.

What type of claim is being made? Explain your answer based on what is said about claims in Chapter 2.

As writer, describe the purpose or effect you believe your claim will have on the reader.

As reader, describe the actual effect of the claim. Do you agree? Did you agree before you started reading? Did your opinion change? Why or why not?

Describe the representative person whom you believe would be convinced by this essay. Include several characteristics such as age, sex, education, and family background.

Later in the semester, instructors can include further questions that ask students to evaluate the writer's use of definitions or to provide counterdefinitions in response to inadequately developed definitions. Chapter 4 on support and Chapter 5 on warrants also provide opportunities for students to integrate the material of the text with what they are attempting in their own writing.

PROVIDING BACKGROUND INFORMATION TO AID CRITICAL READING

Although peer response exercises, discussion, and debate can promote critical reading, instructors should expect students to lack knowledge about the issues presented in the readings in the text. Instructors should anticipate that some or all of the students will know little about the issues involved. This cannot be attributed, in my view, to cultural "illiteracy," but rather to reasons of age or development. For example, the first time many people consider euthanasia (one of the topics in the "Opposing Viewpoints" section) is either when they become parents or when they find themselves caring for aged or infirm parents. This issue may simply be one that we do not seek out until it affects us. That is not to say, however, that in an argumentation class we exempt our students from that issue because of their lack of experience. Instead, we simply need to be prepared to support their reading. It might help a student to know Daniel Maguire's stand on abortion or to know that the thalidomide tragedies were the genesis for our current concerns over what medications a pregnant woman takes; or students may need contextual information to understand James Rachels's discussion of a baby born with Down's syndrome.

If you have chosen to make "Opposing Viewpoints" a core part of your course, you may find it useful before you begin assigning the sections to survey your students on the knowledge they have about the particular issue. Often gaps in knowledge revealed by the survey can be filled with very little discussion. But without the knowledge necessary to evaluate fully the arguments in question, students can have more difficulty than is necessary in discerning even the structure or main points of the essays.

TEACHING WARRANTS AND ASSUMPTIONS

At least partly because our students have had so little practice in argument, they may have problems understanding what we mean by warrants and assumptions. Conflating the term *assumption* into *warrant* for the purposes of an introductory class, I have often chosen to illustrate the terms by beginning with an exercise such as "Who Should Survive?" suggested by Professor Rottenberg in Chapter 5 of the *Editor's Notes*. A further step in that exercise would be to ask students to rank survivors in order of their correspondence with students' value systems. Invariably, students are unable to reach a consensus, revealing underlying assumptions that they hold about human behavior.

Instructors can also begin teaching warrants by asking students to complete statements beginning with the following leads: all lawyers . . .; all English teachers . . .; all students. . . . These types of statements often allow students to begin to see the kinds of assumptions they use implicitly on a daily basis. What they say in a discussion about what all lawyers do often reveals what they believe about the criminal justice system or about the civil recovery system. The beliefs about English teachers are interesting, and sometimes disheartening. I have had students say that they speak more carefully in front of an off-duty English teacher, reveal less about whether they read "popular" fiction, think we value grammar above everything, or believe we are the classic otherworldly type of teacher. Inevitably, students begin to recognize warrants and assumptions. Students realize that they have operating warrants about English teachers: that English teachers are always and on every occasion English teachers; that English teachers read only canonical literature; that grammar is all that counts in an English class; and that English classes have little to do with "real" life.

These discussions, however time-consuming, are a necessary part of introducing warrants to students. While the terminology may be foreign to students, the process of using warrants is not, and with very little practice students can learn the appropriate questions to ask themselves as they try to discern warrants in their own work and the work of others.

Students can also practice adding a series of "because" clauses to the main points of their papers as a way of clarifying their assumptions. For example, a student writing a paper about how television viewing negatively affects children noted passivity, exposure to violence, and fear as her main points. When in an in-class exercise she was asked to identify her warrants with a "because" clause for each, she wrote "because interaction, not passivity, is a better learning experience" in response to her first point and "because violence and fear are poor standards for society" to the second and third. Not only did the student gain valuable experience in identifying the warrants behind her claims, she also learned a powerful revision strategy. As her peers pointed out to her, she had grouped two of the points together, with the third being entirely separate. In revising her paper, she concentrated on the last two points, eliminated the first, and turned in a more coherent paper, which included a now-explicit discussion of her warrant.

DIFFERENT WORDINGS OF CLAIMS AND WARRANTS

Students will often propose several versions of claim and warrant for the same essay. Often one group of students will select as claim a very narrow assertion, while another group will select a generalization, perhaps an inference from the text. Let me use the Brownmiller essay from Chapter 18 to illustrate. One group of students will point to the beginning of the second paragraph and say that the claim is that women must develop a new perspective on pornography. This claim is a rather mild generalization. Another group will point to the ninth paragraph and assert more forcefully that Brownmiller's real claim is that "[p]ornography is the undiluted essence of antifemale propaganda." Likewise, students will show variation in their wording of warrants. As long as students do not go beyond what claims and warrants a feminist author such as Brownmiller might make, some variation in wording not only is acceptable, but also is helpful to students working in an argumentative setting. They will learn that the rhetorical effect of different wording is intrinsic to assessing and addressing their audience.

TEACHING FALLACIES: THE EDITORIAL JOURNAL

Another tool for generating material for argument is the editorial journal. Instructors can require students to maintain a weekly folder containing several examples of what they think are successful and unsuccessful editorials and letters from local or campus newspapers and to record their responses to those editorials and letters in an editorial journal. Students assigned this exercise soon develop a standard against which they judge effective and ineffective arguments. It is then often useful to have students use their developing standard in combination with logical fallacies from Chapter 7. Students can submit for group discussion the most effective and least effective examples they've culled from editorial pages. Asking students to respond to the most troubling and fallacious letters and editorials often bridges the gap between classroom writing and the "real world" of discourse. Many students take the additional step of sending their responses to the local or campus newspaper and sometimes experience the delight of seeing their names in print in those pages.

A variation on this same exercise is an in-class letter-writing task in which students select the most troubling problem on campus and attempt to persuade the appropriate administrator to respond. The instructor may ask different groups to vary their approaches by assigning, for example, one group to argue a claim of fact, another a claim of value. Groups may assess the effectiveness of the arguments of other groups, with the entire class selecting the best letter for the particular audience.

DISTINGUISHING BETWEEN INDUCTION AND DEDUCTION: RESEARCH ASSIGNMENTS

One other aspect of teaching an informal logic model in the writing classroom bears discussion. Many traditional argumentative writing courses have assigned induction and deduction separately. In teaching with an informal Toulmin model, the differences between the traditional and informal approaches often become blurred. Students who have become adept in using the informal model complain vigorously that there is no such thing as a truly inductive paper. Arguing that the Toulmin model requires that warrants be acknowledged, whether the paper is inductive or deductive, students assert that the differences are minimal. For the standard school-sponsored paper, in which a thesis appears early in the essay, students are indeed correct, and the distinction is difficult to make. A so-called inductive paper with a thesis indicates that the writer has already drawn a conclusion, thus making it less than purely inductive in nature.

If the course you are teaching requires separate inductive and deductive papers, consider making the distinction on the basis of the style of research supporting the paper. For example, I have assigned one essay that focuses on an inductive style of research as a primary research project. These projects, chosen in collaborative groups, have included student-designed surveys of their classmates, observations of behavior on campus, in parking lots, and in shopping malls, and interviews. I have received essays that developed from student observations of people's behavior while standing in line, from student interviews with hard-core video game players, and from student surveys addressing the necessity of improving the food available in campus vending machines. Because inferencing and the "inductive leap" are highlighted with this approach, students can more easily see the differences between induction and deduction. For a deductive paper, on the other hand, I have stressed a secondary research approach, having students begin from basic assumptions about a subject and then examine a particular instance.

Many philosophers and historians of science have made the same point: that observations are always guided by a particular framework. The informal Toulmin model makes this point quite clear to students. What counts as a fact or as an observation is already warranted before the search for facts and observations begin.

CONCLUSION

I hope I have suggested some of the ways in which you might plan for a forum on issues in your writing classroom. It is probable that many of your students will have only the composition classroom in which to engage in written debates on public policy issues. Becoming engaged in the consideration, analysis, and argument of various positions, students truly prepare to take their place in civic discussions. As English teachers, that is, instructors in written argument, we hold a unique position by virtue of our providing the forum in which this process takes place. Few students leave the argumentative writing classroom without a change of some kind having occurred, and few teachers can resist that kind of opportunity. By providing a model of analysis of argument useful both inside and outside the classroom and by providing the forum for an exchange of views, we can emphasize the uses of writing in unexpectedly productive ways.

Works Cited

Purves, Alan C., and Sauli Takala, eds. *An International Perspective on the Evaluation of Written Composition.* Oxford: Pergamon Press, 1982.

Bibliography on the Toulmin Model

Listed below are articles by teachers of composition, rhetoric, speech, and debate that explain and apply the Toulmin model for use in the classroom.

Brockriede, Wayne, and Douglas Ehninger. "Toulmin on Argument: An Interpretation and Application." *The Quarterly Journal of Speech,* 46 (1960), 44–53. The authors interpret the Toulmin model as presented in Toulmin's *The Uses of Argument.* They clearly define each element of the model and explain its advantages over traditional systems of logic.

Christenson, Thomas, and Paul R. Nelson. "The Toulmin Model: Asset and Millstone." In David A. Thomas (Ed.), *Advanced Debate: Readings in Theory, Practice and Teaching.* Skokie, IL: National Textbook, 1975, 228–234. The authors provide a clear summary of Toulmin, distinguishing between the "basic" model — claim, data, and warrant — and the "expanded" model, which introduces the other elements of backing, reservation, and qualifier.

Kaufer, David S., and Christine M. Neuwirth. "Integrating Formal Logic and the New Rhetoric: A Four-Stage Heuristic." *College English,* 45 (1983), 380–389. The authors argue that formal logic can be used to supplement insights from the new rhetoric (as put forth by Toulmin and others), believing that an argument should be tested for its deductive certainty as well as for the plausibility of its premises. They provide a four-stage model for teaching students how to integrate logical and probabilistic reasoning in arguments.

Kneupper, Charles W. "Teaching Argument: An Introduction to the Toulmin Model." *College Composition and Communication,* 29 (1978), 237–241. Kneupper begins with an attack on the use of logic and fallacies as a means of teaching argumentative composition. He offers a brief summary of Toulmin's model as a superior method, then applies the model to the first paragraph of Thoreau's *Civil Disobedience,* diagramming the argument in simplified form. He emphasizes that for students "how they are arguing will be clearer," and they will be able to see relationships between parts of the argument.

Stratman, James F. "Teaching Written Argument: The Significance of Toulmin's Layout for Sentence-Combining." *College English,* 48 (1982), 718–733. The author believes that in using Toulmin's "layout" for argument in sentence-combining, students can learn new syntactic patterns. They can learn "skills appropriate to argument — estimating the relevance of acts, assessing validity, and planning refutations based on premises shared with an opponent." For example, one way of helping students to learn the function and importance of warrants is to have them adapt such warrants explicitly in a sentence-combining exercise. "Toulmin's layout can reveal how syntactic transformations strengthen or weaken the structure implicit in argumentative exercises by revealing changes in the underlying relations between 'claim' and 'evidence' that these transformations may entail." A complicated analysis but thought-provoking.

Trent, Jimmie D. "Toulmin's Model of an Argument: An Examination and Extension." *The Quarterly Journal of Speech,* 54 (1968), 252–259. Trent views Toulmin's model as a supplement to syllogistic reasoning. He nevertheless argues that Toulmin presents arguments more clearly and accurately than the classical syllogism.

Several textbooks on writing, speech, and debate explain and apply the Toulmin model. A few are listed below.

Ehninger, Douglas. *Influence, Belief, and Argument: An Introduction to Responsible Persuasion.* Glenview, IL: Scott, Foresman, 1974. This book explains the Toulmin model and includes suggestions after each chapter for additional reading.

Ehninger, Douglas, and Wayne Brockriede. *Decision by Debate.* 2d ed. New York: Harper & Row, 1978. This text includes a comprehensive summary of the Toulmin model along with suggestions after each chapter for further reading.

Makay, John J. *Speaking with an Audience: Communicating Ideas and Attitudes.* New York: Harper & Row, 1977.

McCroskey, James C. *An Introduction to Rhetorical Communication.* 4th ed. Englewood Cliffs, NJ: Prentice-Hall, 1982.

Rieke, Richard D., and Malcolm O. Sillars. *Argumentation and the Decision-Making Process.* New York: Wiley, 1975.

Sproule, J. Michael. *Argument: Language and Its influence.* New York: McGraw-Hill, 1980. This book includes a list of references on argument.

Toulmin, Steven, Richard Rieke, and Allan Janik. *An Introduction to Reasoning.* 2d ed. New York: Macmillan, 1984.

Zacharis, John C., and Coleman C. Bender. *Speech Communications: A Rational Approach.* New York: Wiley, 1976. This book includes additional readings after each chapter.

PART ONE
THE STRUCTURE OF ARGUMENT

CHAPTER 1
Introduction to Argument

1. For years, ever since I began to teach argumentation, I have collected articles from every available source on the subjects that we are likely to discuss in class or use as assignment topics. I invite students and colleagues to contribute to the collection, which now numbers about forty different subjects. The materials in these files also serve as a backup resource for students who are unable to find articles in the library on popular subjects such as abortion, euthanasia, gun control, etc., because the materials have been removed by overzealous researchers.

   I also use the clippings to introduce a unit, displaying articles that point to problems connected with definitions or hidden assumptions or fallacious reasonings. Students always show a good deal of interest in the clippings, which represent "real life" and report recent research findings of which they may be unaware.

2. After discussion of the exercises at the end of the chapter, assign a brief search through newspapers and magazines (beginning perhaps with the school newspaper) for arguments about current affairs. Such a search enables students to arrive at several important conclusions.

   a. The most obvious one is that arguments of the kind they will be reading and writing in class are to be found everywhere and that they are the foundation of the democratic process. Students will also discover that a good deal of the factual reporting about political events is reporting of controversies or arguments.

   b. Without much familiarity with formal arguments, students may at first regard them all as vehicles of reasoned analysis. As they reflect on their examples, they will recognize that passion and ideology are formidable — sometimes the only — components of many arguments.

   c. Many, perhaps most, freshman students believe that hard-core problems in our society remain unsolved because at best we lack the will to solve them, or at worst evil people conspire to frustrate attempts at solution. One other explanation of our failures may not readily occur to them: lack of knowledge. We may ask: What kind of knowledge — that is, data and interpretation of data — do we need in order to solve apparently intractable problems of poverty, war, prejudice, crime, mental illness? When we introduce this question, we may find that some students think that these problems are new and peculiar to American society. Much of the information needed will turn out to be psychological, the kind most difficult to discover or verify. I use this discussion to encourage a reflective caution when evaluating and advocating solutions.

d. Not all arguments have two equally valid sides. Some have multiple sides. Others may be said to have only one morally acceptable side. Ask students to suggest subjects that exemplify these conclusions.

3. Students may be asked to keep informal journals that list argumentative subjects appearing in newspapers and magazines, on TV and radio, on the campus and in town. For each subject they may set down some of the important facts, values, and general principles underlying the claims. The journal entries can then serve as a source of subjects for assignments or discussion in class and in conferences with the instructor. A worthwhile dividend of such journal keeping is an increase in the practice of reading and listening, of becoming familiar with the sources and subjects of public controversies.

4. I would leave discussion and analysis of the three major elements of argument — claim, support, and warrant — to the subsequent chapters. At this point I would require only that students show understanding of the definitions.

5. In speech classes students sometimes analyze their audience, i.e., their classmates, before making a proposal that might be unpopular. They distribute questionnaires that they themselves have constructed in an effort to discover the social and political preferences of their classmates. The results of the questionnaire help them to choose an argumentative strategy that will persuade this audience to look more favorably on the proposition being argued.

   An application of this procedure for a writing class might work as follows: At the beginning of the semester, after having read about audience, a small group of students, perhaps four or five, makes up an informal questionnaire that is filled out by the members of the class. The results of the questionnaire are tabulated and distributed to the class. Later in the semester, for selected papers (for example, arguments of policy) the writers are encouraged to examine the results and add a note describing how and why they have adapted their arguments to the values of this particular audience.

CHAPTER 2
Claims

CLAIMS OF FACT

1. Students have little difficulty understanding claims of fact. But before giving an assignment, I offer a dozen or more examples of such claims to make clear what kinds of arguments they produce. These are in addition to examples in the book.

2. If students have already elected a major or are about to do so, they can find subjects in their areas of specialization. At this point library research need

not be emphasized. Students are often able to find sufficient factual data in their memories or their notes. (Wherever possible, they should, of course, give credit to their sources, even to a lecturer in an academic course.)

I point out that the reports they may be asked to make on the job are often claims of fact, in which the students provide proof that a condition exists or that something has been found to be true as a result of research. The claims, or thesis statements of their essays, correspond to the conclusions of their reports, which, like the claims, may appear first. *Example* (in an article about food colorants): "The development of organic chemistry produced a series of compounds that are well suited to coloring food. Today most of the food colorants are chemicals produced by synthesis from simple basic materials." (*A Progress Report,* Massachusetts Agricultural Station, July–August 1974.)

Such straightforward factual reports are not likely to be models of creativity, but they emphasize other important qualities of good writing: adequate support, a direct, unadorned style, and clear transitions between ideas. They offer practice in the kind of clear exposition that all writers are well advised to master before they go further.

3. More challenging are factual claims that are clearly controversial. Some will require only reflection on personal observation as support; others will need objective data. *Examples:* "The students on this campus are increasingly conservative." "Teaching writing on the word processor will not produce better writers." "Children are now judged to be reliable witnesses in child-abuse cases." "Attractive people are regarded by others as more intelligent and sensitive than unattractive people."

   Encourage students to stick to the facts and avoid direct expression of value judgments (although, of course, these may be implicit).

4. Another source of assignments may be the materials in "Opposing Viewpoints." Ask students to choose one of the subjects and, after reading all or most of the selections, derive a limited factual claim. *Examples:* "Animal experimentation has provided enormous medical benefits for human beings." "In analyzing pornography, women and men seem to have different concerns."

   The supporting materials will not be original. This assignment tests the writer's ability to extract relevant data in support of a thesis, express the facts in his or her own language, and organize them logically.

5. In this edition we have introduced advertisements that represent all the elements of argument. In our culture ads are the most prominent examples of abbreviated arguments that often conceal as much as they reveal, and students enjoy uncovering the missing elements. One caution: Although students may have studied ads in high school and can analyze them with some sophistication, they are disposed to treat all advertisement as untruthful. Ads that conceal or distort are usually the most interesting to examine, but I try to get students to make careful distinctions between the ads that support their claims, or seem to, and those that don't.

Classic Arguments

The selections in "Classic Arguments" provide more examples of the elements of argument. For comments on the use of these essays, please see the discussions under "Classic Arguments" in these notes.

CLAIMS OF VALUE

1. As they begin to write, students will discover that the line between claims of fact and claims of value is often blurred, but in real-life arguments outside the classroom, these distinctions are not crucial. We make them in the classroom largely because they allow us to examine the elements more closely.

2. Claims of value are more demanding than claims of fact. Facts remain important, but now students must express an attitude toward them. Despite the fact that values are a part of almost every argument — even in claims of fact they may be implicit in the choices of subjects and data — students are sometimes unclear about how to uncover and express them. These approaches may be helpful:

   a. *Ask personal questions.* What do you want out of life? Do you dislike anything about yourself? Do you have religious beliefs? If so, how do they influence your behavior? What are the good things about your family? What are the most valuable things you own? What kind of country do you want the United States to be? And so on. (Of course, for purposes of the exercise the answers need not be true, and it should be clear to students that they are under no obligation to bare their souls. On the other hand, most students, like the rest of us, enjoy talking about themselves.)

      The answers that emerge can be written on the board, listed as positive and negative values. You will probably have to change the language, finding more precise terms than the ones that the students offer. This exercise defines values and value systems in a readily understandable way. Values as a form of support will be discussed more fully in Chapter 4, but this discussion should assist students to find the values that can be defended in their value claims.

   b. *Analyze one or two essays in the text to discover the values of the author.* Look at "From *Crito,*" in which Socrates argues against his right to avoid punishment. What character traits does Socrates reveal about himself, both explicitly and implicitly? What traits in the citizen does Socrates admire? What traits does he condemn? How would you define his value system?

      I ask students to answer such questions in short, in-class assignments — fifteen minutes — for which they must produce a well-organized paragraph: clear topic sentence and sufficient supporting material. Because they stress economy and directness, such assignments are useful for teaching some elements of style.

3. As with claims of fact, students can draw on campus experience for subjects that lend themselves to class discussion, outlining, and reinforcing the ways in which claims of value differ from claims of fact. *Example:* "Student evaluations of teachers are worthless." "Funds for Gay Awareness Week are unjustified."

4. In this unit, too, I point out that claims of value are often required on the job in the form of personnel reports or reports that evaluate marketing strategies and campaigns. If students are interested, topics for such papers can be obtained from books on technical writing or from the business departments of the school.

CLAIMS OF POLICY

1. Since claims of policy assert that something should or should not be done, they presuppose the existence of a problem needing solution. I emphasize that both facts and values are indispensable to defense of a policy claim, because in many arguments students will first have to establish that a problem exists, then underscore how the desired values will be served by adoption of the proposed solution.

2. As an introduction to this unit, short problems, either real or hypothetical, can test the ability of students to find solutions — that is, to defend claims of policy. The facts are clearly laid out in the summary of the problem. In order to justify the solution, students will need to expose the values that underlie their claims. *Example of a real problem:*

   The Plagiarism Problem

   John Jones, a senior at U__ M___, was enrolled in a second-semester writing course, *Writing about Film.* A few weeks before the end of the semester he suffered a crisis in his love life. The woman who had been his inseparable companion suddenly informed him that she was no longer interested in continuing their friendship. John lost control of himself for a few weeks; he stayed in his room brooding, drank heavily every night, and stopped going to classes. Three days before the end of the semester, he found out that in order to pass the film course and then to graduate, he had to fulfill a final assignment — attend a film and write a review of it. Frantic, John went to the library, copied out a review of a film by a professional critic, and submitted it to the instructor. The instructor recognized the plagiarism and failed John for the course. The failure meant that John could not graduate despite the fact that he had a job waiting for him in Seattle. He argued with the instructor to no avail. The instructor said that he had made it very clear from the beginning of the semester that any plagiarism would result in a failure for the course. John appealed to the provost, who had the authority to grant a Pass for the course.

   Question: Should the provost rule that John need not do anything more to fulfill the writing course and allow him to graduate?

3. I have called attention to this problem in the text, but perhaps it bears repeating. In defending claims of policy, students must guard against offering solutions for enormous problems that have defied solution for decades or even centuries. Their ambitions may be laudable, but nevertheless they should be urged to confine themselves to solutions that can be defended in 750 words.

4. "Opposing Viewpoints" is a collection of problems in search of solutions. Assign readings in any of the subjects and ask students to propose solutions based on their evaluations of the arguments.

In defending their claims of policy students should try to use the pattern of organization we call *defending the stock issues* — need, plan, and advantage (see "Writing an Argumentative Paper"). This pattern permits them to be exhaustive without becoming confused by a multitude of details and a variety of possible approaches.

5. Policy claims are, of course, inherent in any business or professional activity. Ask students who have job experience to write out short summaries of specific problems they remember having encountered on the job, either their own or someone else's. The problems should be substantive, and the facts should be clearly stated. Then ask other students to suggest solutions. Students may also ask for examples of problems from the business departments of the school.

   These short writing exercises emphasize clarity, accuracy, and a sensitivity to the audience — the employer, supervisor, or other employees — who will act on the decision.

   If the solutions differ, students may discuss the differences and try to uncover the reasons for them. Do the differences derive from lack of sufficient data or from conflicting values? Can the differences be reconciled?

6. After reading "The Right to Bear Arms," students may be interested in pursuing the antigun-control arguments based on the Second Amendment to the Constitution. If there is time they can write to The Second Amendment Foundation, 1601 114th S.E., Suite 157, Bellevue, WA, 98004 for material. This foundation, which "defends our constitutional heritage to privately own and possess firearms," has published a series of monographs with such titles as *The Great American Gun War* and *Of Arms and the Law.*

7. In his article, "Second Thoughts about Gun Control," James D. Wright, a professor of sociology at Tulane University, reaches a pessimistic conclusion about gun-control laws. Years of research have convinced him that "a compelling case for 'stricter gun control' *cannot be made,* at least not on empirical grounds." (The article appeared in *Public Interest,* Spring 1988, 23–39.) Students who read it may want to explain why it has or has not provoked second thoughts about Burger's argument. It also offers an interesting account of the way in which a careful analysis of evidence can bring about a change of opinion.

CHAPTER 3
Definition

1. I often begin this unit by dividing the class into four or five groups and assigning to each group the definition of a common object — book, bed, chair, cup, shoe. The definitions that emerge from the group are then compared to those in the dictionary. (The definitions by students are often remarkably close.)

   After this exercise I ask students to describe the process of definition they have just engaged in. As the discussion proceeds, students discover, first of all, that in matters of definition we know more than we can tell. (See

Michael Polany's fascinating examination of this in *The Tacit Dimension.*) Apart from this philosophical dilemma, the attempt to define these familiar objects gives practice in distinguishing the properties that separate similar objects or objects belonging to the same genres. Equally important, students must think of examples if they are to make useful distinctions — between a shoe and a boot, between a chair and a stool, between a book and a magazine. The same necessity to resort to examples will become even clearer when they define abstract terms.

2. You may assign a single vague or ambiguous term, on which there is sure to be disagreement, for an extended discussion by each member of the class: success; the good life; normal sexuality; maturity; heroism; necessities, comforts, and luxuries.

   Some or all of the completed papers may be duplicated and distributed to the whole class. Through a discussion or written assignment the class may examine the criteria governing the different definitions. Can we reach a consensus? Why or why not? What are the implications of success or failure in reaching consensus about these particular terms?

3. I ask students to tackle the definitions of words that have acquired several, sometimes contradictory, meanings. *Example:* discrimination. For most students, this word carries a negative connotation. I sometimes offer the following example:

   > A young woman who knows nothing about the mechanics of a car finds herself stranded in a parking lot because the engine of her car will not start. Passing near her are two people — a young man and a young woman. The car owner ignores the young woman and turns to the young man, asking him if he can identify and perhaps solve the problem of the stalled car.

   Does this action represent "discrimination" in the negative sense? Students must explain their answers in such a way as to make clear how they define the term.

   They might also be directed to examine the use of the word in aesthetic criticism. Why has the word taken on negative connotations in other areas of discourse?

4. Students can find examples of implicit definitions even in their popular songs. *Example:* Pink Floyd in "The Wall": "We don't need no education. We don't need no thought control. . . . Teachers, leave us kids alone." How is education defined in this song?

CHAPTER 4
Support

FACTS AND INFERENCES

1. Ask students to create a set of facts, then request that their classmates derive inferences about the actions or people involved. *Examples:* the contents of a grocery cart in the checkout line; an accident; a crime.

2. Assign reading of the following passage. Ask students to write either a short or a long essay that summarizes some of the inferences we draw from observing what people wear. Since the subject is so large (this excerpt is part of a book about clothing), this exercise gives students practice in narrowing the subject of discussion and choosing a thesis statement or paragraph that can be adequately developed in the number of words assigned.

    > For thousands of years human beings have communicated with one another first in the language of dress. Long before I am near enough to talk to you on the street, in a meeting, or at a party, you announce your sex, age, and class to me through what you are wearing — and possibly give me important information (or disinformation) as to your occupation, origin, personality, opinions, tastes, sexual desires and current mood. I may not be able to put what I observe into words, but I register the information unconsciously, and you simultaneously do the same for me.
    >
    > By the time we meet and converse we have already spoken to each other in an older and more universal tongue.
    >
    > —Alison Lurie
    > *The Language of Clothing*

3. On March 10, 1974 (p. 54), the *New York Times* published a long news account entitled "Death of a Black in a White Bar: Two Versions." This report of the death of a black man by a white off-duty policeman offers students, like the members of a jury, an outstanding opportunity to evaluate the conflicting data surrounding the killing as well as external evidence about the characters and history of the principals.

    A written assignment on this story calls for a clear thesis statement or paragraph, extraction of the most important data, and arrangement of materials, in an orderly and emphatic way. Above all, it calls for an acknowledgment of the distinctions between facts and inferences in the testimony reported in the article and in the students' interpretations of the testimony. Not least, the students find this assignment interesting and provocative.

4. Ask students to look up information by advocates on both sides of the controversies surrounding one of the popular natural mysteries: the Loch Ness monster, the Bermuda Triangle, Findhorn, Bigfoot, or Sasquatch, etc. Then assign a paper, short or long, that reviews the data on both sides and tries to come to a conclusion regarding the validity of the respective claims. Have students justify their conclusions by defending the evidence. If students find that they cannot make up their minds, this is also a conclusion, but they should be prepared to say why the evidence on both sides proved equally strong or equally weak.

5. An assignment with the same objectives but requiring no research can be based on the materials in another article from the *New York Times* (November 1, 1973, p. 45). "Yeti-Like Monster Gives Staid Town in Illinois a Fright." Here students must evaluate factual evidence and consider carefully the reasons that such observations as those described in the article may not be trustworthy.

EVIDENCE

1. From the first paper students have been required to use evidence. Having now read the more elaborate explanations of both factual and opinion evidence in Chapter 4, students can return to their claims of fact, value, and policy and reevaluate the facts and opinions in their essays. would more data strengthen their claim? If so, what kind? Where can it be found? Would additional expert opinion make their arguments more convincing? If so, whose opinions? Where can they be found?

   If the students show some interest in revising their papers to include more data, encourage them to do so.

2. A popular exercise calls on students to look up the *New York Times* edition that appears on their birthdays and write a paper that emphasizes straightforward presentation of data to support their claims. Students must find a thesis around which the information can be organized — about the kinds of films being shown, the nature of women's fashion, advertisements for jobs, scientific discoveries of the day, crimes, etc.

3. Advertisements again. This time students choose ads that offer information about the products. They then evaluate the data. In some cases, of course, they will be unequipped to decide whether the data are accurate or sufficient, but if the ads are directed to a lay audience, readers have a right to ask questions about the sufficiency, relevance, and recency of the data. In other words, if readers think that evidence for the virtues of the product is inadequate, what else would they want to know?

4. Students sometimes approach the subject of information in ads with the preconception that ads do not offer information — only slogans. Students may therefore be asked to contrast two or more ads that offer different amounts and qualities of information. Is information more important in some kinds of ads than others — for example, in car ads, which are often dense with facts?

5. If there is time for lengthier papers, ask students to examine the evidence in the following cases (or any others that remain controversial):

   a. the assassination of President John F. Kennedy, 1963
   b. the kidnapping of Patty Hearst, 1974
   c. the kidnapping and murder of the Lindbergh baby, 1932
   d. the Sacco–Vanzetti case, 1927
   e. the Bernhard Goetz case, 1987

6. In leading students to examine the credentials of experts, ask them to consider the authors in the text and the "Opposing Viewpoints" as "experts." It will be easy enough to identify such writers as Gordon Allport and Peter Rossi — both respected social scientists — as authorities in their fields. Even in more problematic disciplines, such as education, we recognize the authority of Paul Goodman, for example, who spent a lifetime studying and writing about the meaning of education and whose opinions are regarded by other experts as authoritative.

   But what are we to say of writers who reflect on their personal experience or expound their philosophies? Why do we think Barbara Ehrenreich's views worth reading? After all, she is probably no more an "expert" on the silenced majority than many of her readers. It might come as a small revelation to students, and pertinent to their participation in a writing course, to recognize that the credibility of Ehrenreich and other nonprofessional "experts" is based largely on their excellence as writers. They can discover interesting propositions, and organize, develop, and express them in spirited and highly readable prose. They are intelligent, of course, but also curious about most subjects and well informed about many. Students might speculate on the kinds of social phenomena that such writers as Meg Greenfield, C. S. Lewis, Anna Quindlen, and Gore Vidal have examined and become knowledgeable about in order to write the particular essays that appear in the text and "Opposing Viewpoints."

STATISTICS

1. Students usually need practice in reporting statistics — extracting them from news stories and arranging them in interesting and readable form. Students can research the following subjects and report the information as data that might support a claim. They should, of course, limit the time period for the data. Have them submit their prose summaries to their classmates. Are the data clear and accessible to these readers?

   a. world population growth
   b. teenage pregnancies
   c. women in the labor market
   d. growth of ethnic populations in the United States
   e. American marriage patterns
   f. dimensions of poverty
   g. voting patterns in the 1988 elections

2. The two books mentioned below are entertaining and informative references for both teachers and students. They are full of useful examples that should help students avoid some of the common pitfalls in interpreting and reporting statistical evidence.

   Stephen K. Campbell, *Flaws and Fallacies in Statistical Thinking* (Englewood Cliffs, NJ: Prentice-Hall, 1974).

   Darrell Huff, *How to Lie with Statistics* (New York: W. W. Norton, 1954).

3. Some students may be interested in and sufficiently informed about polling techniques to evaluate some of the famous polling gaffes: the *Literary Digest* poll of 1936 that predicted that Alfred Landon would defeat Franklin D. Roosevelt or the 1948 Gallup poll that predicted Dewey would defeat Truman. Students might want to infer the reasons that such mistakes probably will not recur.

APPEALS TO NEEDS AND VALUES

1. A lively and immediate source of appeals to needs and values is found in speeches — students may be directed to *Vital Speeches of the Day,* which publishes speeches from a variety of speechmakers.

   In the "Classic Arguments" section of this book, the speech of Martin Luther King, Jr., "I Have a Dream," is an outstanding example of spoken discourse that makes a profoundly emotional appeal. Other famous speeches for the purposes of this unit include:

a. Clarence Darrow's "Address to the Prisoners of Cook County Jail" in 1902
b. Vice President Richard Nixon's "Checkers" speech in 1952
c. President John F. Kennedy's Inaugural Address in 1961
d. Senator Edward Kennedy's TV address explaining to the people of Massachusetts his behavior during and after the accident at Chappaquiddick in 1969

For example, Darrow's speech is remarkable for the inconsistency of his argument and its numerous fallacies, both of which have been overlooked by textbooks that reprint the address. Edward Kennedy's speech makes a personal appeal, arousing sympathy for his suffering and inducing guilt in the listener for having accused him unjustly.

In the 1980, 1984, and 1988 presidential election campaigns, the *New York Times* published a series of "Basic Speeches," which had been delivered by the major candidates. All the speeches contained specific references to the values held by the candidates: compassion, justice, trust, integrity, competence, etc. George Bush's speech containing the now-famous statement, "When I talk about a kinder and gentler nation, I mean it," was printed on October 24, 1988 (B5).

2. Advertisements by large corporations (Mobil, United Technologies, Exxon) appearing frequently in newspapers and magazines comment on political and social issues rather than the merits of their products. As short essays they can be useful for examination of values based on what is perceived to be common consent.

   a. What values do the advertisers assume that we share?
   b. What evidence (examples, facts, statistics) do they offer to convince the reader that their proposals will support our values?
   c. What is the tone of the essay (reasonable, generous, angry, sarcastic, humorous)?

3. Also useful are the ads that promise power, riches, great beauty, etc. Many of the most outrageous ones appear in *The National Enquirer* and other gossip sheets.

   a. Can you infer to what audience they make a strong appeal?
   b. What fears, needs, desires, do they appeal to?
   c. What attempts are made to provide credibility?

CHAPTER 5
Warrants

1. Although the definition of the warrant in Toulmin's *The Uses of Argument* is more complicated than we have made it appear, for the purposes of a freshman composition course, those of us who have used the Toulmin model with some success believe that the model works best if we define the warrant as synonymous with assumption, a belief we take for granted, or a general principle underlying other beliefs and attitudes. If students raise questions, we can always widen the definition.

For obvious reasons the concept of the warrant is more difficult for students to assimilate than that of support, in part because they have seldom been required to make their assumptions explicit. Fortunately for teaching purposes, the examples that we can use are so numerous and so varied that we may call attention to the warrant repeatedly without losing student interest.

2. Advertisements offer a rich and accessible source of material. Students may choose their own ads for analysis and write or speak about them to the class. The exercise should emphasize discussion of a controversial warrant. For an oral presentation, an ad that contains more than a paragraph of text can be duplicated for distribution, and the whole class can participate in a discussion of the validity of the warrant.

3. Subjects for examination of warrants appear almost every day in school newspapers. Sometimes the subjects are about education or other matters relevant to the function and management of the school; sometimes they respond to the world outside. Below are some current issues on my own campus:

   a. A proposal to introduce a core requirement for cultivating knowledge and awareness of Third World cultures. (What assumptions about education have prompted this proposal?)
   b. A demand by some students that the university disinvest in South African businesses. (What assumptions are indicated about the social functions of the university?)
   c. Beauty pageants. (What assumptions about sex and beauty cause feminists to attack them?)
   d. An appearance on campus by Paul Cameron, a religious fundamentalist who advocates denial of rights to and punishment of homosexuals. (What assumptions about the rights of free speech should we consider if the message is offensive and even dangerous to particular groups?)

4. Other sources of analysis of warrants:

   a. *Etiquette books.* An interesting assignment would compare etiquette books of a generation or more ago with contemporary ones. (Judith Martin's books are valuable and amusing sources of comment about present-day manners.) Have there been large changes? Small changes? In what areas? On what assumptions about social relationships and freedom have these changes been based?
   b. *Advice columns in newspapers and magazines.* What assumptions about marriage, sexual problems, child rearing, religion, etc. underlie the advice of the columnists?
   c. *Magazines for teenagers.* Have they changed in the last fifteen or twenty years? On what assumptions about the lives and values of teenagers have the publishers based their changes?

5. Go back to the earlier papers of definition and defense of value and policy claims and examine the warrants, expressed or unexpressed. *Example:* In defending his decision never to marry, a student writes that he values his freedom. What does he assume about marriage, love, individuality, commitment, etc.?

6. Students enjoy the familiar game in which a disaster has left a small number of people alive, and the players must choose an even smaller number to

survive. The choices of the players reflect their assumptions about an ideal world. Whenever classes engage in this exercise, they discover how difficult it is for even a class of twenty fairly similar students to arrive at a consensus. Of course, the players must defend their selection of particular people and the order in which they rank them.

Who Should Survive?
Task: Choose seven people to survive. List them in the order in which you would choose them and indicate the reasons for our selection, i.e., why you chose these particular persons and why you placed them in this particular order.

People:

1. Dr. Dane — thirty-seven, white, no religious affiliation, Ph.D. in history, college professor, in good health (jogs daily), hobby is botany, enjoys politics, married with one child (Bobby).
2. Mrs. Dane — thirty-eight, white, Jewish, rather obese, diabetic, M.A. in psychology, counselor in a mental health clinic, married to Dr. Dane, has one child.
3. Bobby Dane — ten, white, Jewish, mentally retarded with IQ of 70, healthy and strong for his age.
4. Mrs. Garcia — twenty-three, Spanish-American, Catholic, ninth-grade education, cocktail waitress, worked as a prostitute, married at age sixteen, divorced at age eighteen.
5. Jean Garcia — three months old, Spanish-American, healthy.
6. Mary Evans — eighteen, black, Protestant, trade school education, wears glasses, artistic.
7. Mr. Newton — twenty-five, black power advocate, starting last year of medical school, suspected homosexual activity, music as a hobby, physical fitness nut.
8. Mrs. Clark — twenty-eight, black, Protestant, daughter of a minister, college graduate, electronics engineer, single now after a brief marriage, member of Zero Population.
9. Mr. Blake — fifty-one, white, Mormon, B.S. in mechanics, married with four children, enjoys outdoors, much experience in construction, quite handy, sympathizes with antiblack views.
10. Father Frans — thirty-seven, white, Catholic, priest, active in civil rights, former college athlete, farming background, often criticized for liberal views.
11. Dr. Gonzales — sixty-six, Spanish-American, Catholic, doctor in general practice, two heart attacks in the past five years, loves literature and quotes extensively.

CHAPTER 6
Language and Thought

1. Again we turn to advertisements for their use of slogans, clichés, and emotive language. Advertising claims in airline ads, we are told by a national advertising group, "promise great buys and then dissolve into airline jargon filled with restrictions." Ask students to examine some airline ads for jargon and code words that are meaningless or slippery.

A paperback entitled *I Can Sell You Anything* by Carl P. Wrighter (Ballantine, 1972) offers a popular attack on techniques of advertising. Wrighter supports his claims by offering dozens of examples of "weasel words" in specific commercial advertisements. The claims of each ad are clearly stated. Often the argument is exaggerated, and some of the ads will no longer be familiar to students, but they can use Wrighter's formulas as a model, choosing their own ads and substituting their own weasel words.

2. Have students collect literature from various politically active groups on campus. Assign a study of the language based on some of the categories in the text: connotations, euphemisms, clichés, slogans, slanted language, picturesque language.

   a. Is the message persuasive? How much of the persuasive effect is due to the way that language is used?
   b. Identify terms that you consider effective and tell why.
   c. Identify terms that you consider ineffective and tell why.

3. Students can find slogans everywhere. The slogans will, of course, differ from year to year and from place to place, depending on the emergence of new issues. In 1988, an election year, some slogans were generated, though not so many as we might have expected. Ask students to compose their own political slogans and defend them. To whom does the slogan appeal? What short cuts have been taken; that is, what questions about your abbreviated argument might be asked by an unfriendly reader?

4. Although slogans were scarce in 1988, there were plenty of clichés — statements of obvious ideas. Students can examine the "Basic Speeches" referred to in assignments for Chapter 4. They might consider answers to the following questions: Can the use of clichés be justified? What would be the effect of substituting unusual ideas, even a surprising and perhaps unpleasant truth?

5. Have students examine some of the classic speeches of the past: Patrick Henry's *Speech Before the Virginia Convention of 1775,* Lincoln's *Gettysburg Address,* Winston Churchill's address to the Congress of the United States of America on December 26, 1941. Students will notice that all of these speeches contain memorable phrases. Ask whether they think that the language in these speeches differs in any significant way from the language of the "Basic Speeches" of 1988. Have them explain any differences and describe how they contribute to the success or failure of particular speeches.

6. Students might try writing their own high school commencement addresses, avoiding both the congratulatory clichés of most graduation addresses and the bitter invective of Jacob Neusner.

7. I have used an excerpt describing the actions of Henry VIII to demonstrate the use of partisan language by a Catholic historian. Below is a passage from a Protestant historian, G. M. Trevelyan, about the same events of the English Reformation, but exhibiting, through the use of selective language, an entirely different point of view. Students may be asked to pick out the words and phrases that indicate slanting.

   > It is often falsely asserted that the [Protestant] Reformation was a plunder of the poor; that it dispossessed them of their heritage in favor of a squirearchy [landed proprietor class]. The fact is that the medieval Church, on its financial side, was a squirearchy richer and more jealous

of its possessions than any which had existed since the Reformation. What the revolution did was to transfer enormous wealth from one squirearchy to another; from a squirearchy which, in its very nature, was intensely conservative and seldom let go of anything in its possessions, to another which lived far more among the people, and whose extravagances often led to the division of the land, so that there grew up in Elizabethan and Jacobean times a whole class of small yeoman farmers.

The medieval Church was, no doubt, more friendly to the poor than any State Institution of those days would have been. But it was far from that Christian fraternity and generous beneficence which is often claimed for it, and which the earliest Christianity had actually displaced. It was deeply feudalized; it was no longer a really democratic institution in any strict sense of the word. Popes were the most absolute sovereigns of their day, and sometimes the most luxurious and most directly responsible for those wars which were chronic in Christendom.

I have tried to encourage students to uncover other examples in their own texts, but they find this difficult to do. The exercise above will at least induce a healthy caution about the objectivity of textbook writers, even distinguished historians.

CHAPTER 7
Induction, Deduction, and Logical Fallacies

1. I have expressed elsewhere my reluctance to use exercises in induction and deduction. Because they have only a tenuous connection with the actual process of composing an argument, we may spend our limited time more profitably in attention to the other elements of argument.

2. The teaching of fallacies poses special, though not insuperable, problems. Some fallacious statements by public figures are obvious, like those in the list of exercises in the text. But arguments by professional writers often contain concealed fallacies or fallacies that uninformed students are unable to identify. I have remarked on what I consider to be faulty reasoning in speeches and articles by Clarence Darrow — in fact, I am surprised at the generosity accorded by editors to some clearly deficient arguments. One example that comes immediately to mind is Ashley Montagu's "Man, the Ignoble Savage?" (from *The Nature of Human Aggression*). This essay, reprinted in several readers, purports to be an attack on the use of examples by others, but Montagu offers only one example in rebuttal, and this example is a scarcely credible rumor that remains unsubstantiated. (An interesting assignment would ask students to look for more convincing research to support Montagu's claim.)

The rule for all of us, I think — teachers and students alike — is to cultivate fearlessness in our criticism of articles by putative experts. Since freshman students are naturally disinclined to be critical of their mentors (publicly, at least), we may risk overzealousness in uncovering faulty arguments in textbooks, newspapers, and magazines. Advertisers are not the only arguers guilty of concealment or distorted reasoning.

3. I ask students to be on the alert for dubious arguments in what they read and hear and to bring them in for examination by the class. If they are keeping journals, they may record these fallacies or what they interpret as fallacies in their journals. The nomenclature is not important. Some of their entries will turn out to be examples of sound reasoning after all, but no matter. The objective of the exercise is increased alertness. Sensitive discrimination will, we hope, come later.

   In some cases, students will be lucky to find explicit references to fallacies, as in the beginning of this letter (*Wall Street Journal,* November 15, 1983): "Your editorial is an illustration of the slippery slope argument." Less explicitly, the writer will say (*Wall Street Journal,* December 7, 1983): "Your editorial was critical of Surgeon General C. Everett Koop for 'citing particularly egregious magazine articles and medical cases as proof that the United States could easily slip into some Nazi-like approval of general euthanasia.' I, for one, would not dismiss Dr. Koop's concern quite so readily."

4. In my experience at half a dozen campuses, I have found that school newspapers are rife with weak and fallacious arguments in the editorials and letters to the editor. As a source of fallacies, they have two advantages: They are easily available, and students probably feel fewer inhibitions in attacking their peers.

EXERCISES FOR REVIEW: ANSWERS

In compiling this list of fallacies, I faced a dilemma. Some of the examples, which I didn't want to omit, did not fit neatly into the categories I had chosen to discuss in the chapter. Nevertheless, in order to avoid confusion, I decided to limit the discussion of specific fallacies, of which there are several dozens, and retain the examples. As it turned out, students had no difficulty recognizing and explaining these fallacies even when they could no find the names for them.

1. *Begging the question.* The judge is assuming the answer to the very question that a trial is supposed to answer.
2. Non sequitur. It doesn't follow that because something is good for us the government should enforce compliance.
3. Post hoc *fallacy.* There is no proof that watching these particular TV shows is the cause of high or low school grades. It's more reasonable to suppose that children who do well or poorly in school select one show or the other because of its appeal to their level of intelligence and achievement.
4. *Hasty generalization or small sample.* A faulty prediction for one month is not enough for an accusation of unreliability.
5. *Two wrongs don't make a right.* The writer thinks that death and danger are unacceptable for men in combat, but that subjecting women to death and danger doesn't make these "wrongs" more acceptable.
6. *Faulty use of authority.* Taste is a matter of individual preference. It would be hard to prove that Bruce Willis, however gifted an actor, is superior to anybody else in his preference for a wine cooler. (Of course, we also know that he is only posing for a paid advertisement.)

7. *Two wrongs don't make a right.* The arguer seems to infer that gambling is wrong, but legalizing it won't make it morally right. (This is what Norman Cousins calls "cop-out realism," or "If you can't beat 'em, join 'em.")

8. *Unknown fact or faulty comparison.* What was money spent for in the past? Have conditions changed that may make the expenditure of more money appropriate now?

9. Non sequitur. It doesn't follow that campus newspapers select the best or even good writers. They usually have to settle for those who make themselves available.

10. *Begging the question.* The arguer assumes that standard English is necessary only for certain kinds of employment, but that remains to be proved. Standard English has other uses unrelated to employment.

11. *Faulty definition.* In this case discrimination means making judicious choices. It should not be considered pejorative. To perform their duties, which may involve physical exertion, police officers should be required to fulfill certain physical standards.

12. *Faulty comparison or begging the question.* Qualified doctors and medical students are different. By definition a medical student is still being tested, and access to information in books during the testing process may defeat the purposes of testing.

13. *Faulty definition.* Chemicals are the building blocks of nature. Some may be unsafe, but they are not all synonymous with poisons by any means.

14. *Begging the question.* The arguer assumes that the only relevant criterion for choosing courses is payment of tuition. But a student enters into an implicit contract when he or she enrolls in the college or university and accepts the criteria laid down by the institution for the granting of a diploma.

15. *False dilemma.* The writer assumes that there are only two alternatives available to those who want to marry. But there is at least one more — marriages freely chosen that are not based on romantic love. Besides, we have no way of knowing how well arranged marriages worked. Staying married when divorce is difficult or unavailable doesn't prove the success of the marriage.

16. *Hasty generalization or small sample.* Three examples are not sufficient to support a generalization about a population of hundreds of thousands or millions.

17. *Hasty generalization or small sample.* One example of a highly intelligent athlete is not enough to prove the intelligence of a large population.

18. *Unknown fact.* There is insufficient evidence in this quotation to prove the reasons for Sasway's failure to register, which may or may not be based on moral principles.

19. Post hoc *fallacy.* We have no way of knowing if the exercise salons are the cause of Jane Fonda's great shape.

20. *Faulty analogy.* Harris is making an analogy between inanimate objects — buildings, cars, ham — and animate objects or students. Students, after all, have choices and some control over their education.

21. Post hoc *fallacy.* There is no evidence here that doctrines of feminism have caused women to turn to crime. Anyway, crime is usually the result of many factors that are difficult to separate.

22. Non sequitur. It doesn't follow that just because an activity is healthful the university should require it. (There are numbers of things that are good for us that a center of academic learning does not choose to introduce into its curriculum.)

23. Ad hominem. Meany is attacking the habits of the younger generation, not their views, which remain unknown.

24. Non sequitur. It doesn't follow that early poverty makes a candidate sympathetic to the problems of the poor. In fact, the opposite may be true.

25. *Faulty comparison.* In the European cases troops were engaged in crushing freedom; in the Little Rock case they were engaged in extending it.

26. Post hoc *fallacy.* There is no evidence that the election of Governor Jones is the cause of the corruption. His election and government corruption may be coincidental.

27. *False dilemma.* These may not be the only alternatives for the voters. There may be ways to improve education without a pay increase.

28. Post hoc *fallacy.* It would be hard to prove a cause-effect relationship.

29. *Faulty comparison.* The dissimilarities between the two states are probably much greater than the similarities.

30. Post hoc *fallacy.* Self-explanatory.

31. *Faulty use of authority.* Even Galileo should have asked for stricter evidence than the great Aristotle could provide on the subject of natural science.

32. *Slippery slope fallacy.* The progression projected by Brustein — from Congress curtailing grants to artists whose work is controversial to Congress ordering the execution of artists whose work is deemed blasphemous — is hardly inevitable.

PART TWO

WRITING AND RESEARCHING ARGUMENTS

INTRODUCTION

Although it follows Part One, Part Two is meant to accompany all writing assignments throughout the semester, from Part One through Parts Three and Four. It is one thing for students to grasp the concept of a claim of fact, for example, but writing an essay in which they demonstrate their ability to communicate that understanding is quite another. Chapter 8, then, instructs students in the process of preparing a paper from the very beginning: finding a topic, defining the issues, organizing the material, considering the audience, revising, and preparing the manuscript. The discussion of each step is illuminated with examples from good writers. In addition, we have included a student essay on a subject dear to student hearts — "The New Drinking Laws" — not a model essay which students may find difficult to attribute to a classmate but one which exhibits both strengths *and* weakness of a familiar kind.

In introducing a new textbook, especially a handbook or a composition text, I always review its contents with the students before we begin to use it. This strategy is based on the sound premise that students don't read instruction manuals without judicious coaxing. With all books open to Chapter 8, I go through the material, turning the pages and pointing out the discussions that students ought to find helpful in the process of writing a paper. Most students will recognize the problems this chapter is designed to solve. The purpose of the exercise is, of course, to encourage students to use the material themselves as a reference if they are not sure how to proceed at some point in an essay.

Chapter 9 presents the research paper as a culmination of a course in argumentative writing. Although students in all their papers so far have been demonstrating their mastery of the elements of argument and the process of composition, the research paper will put their skills to a more demanding test. In this chapter we discuss the purposes of the research paper and the procedures for helping students to produce interesting and authoritative documents: preparing a schedule, conferring with the instructor, using the library, taking notes, organizing the paper, using a style sheet. In this chapter, too, we've provided a student research paper, "Why We Don't Need Zoos," which has been annotated to show students exactly how the author proceeds in defending a claim of policy.

CHAPTER 8
Writing an Argumentative Paper

Success in teaching composition, like success in parenting, has its mysteries. Good writers and good children emerge from all kinds of environments — authoritarian, permissive, and unlikely combinations of the two. The suggestions that follow have been tested in a wide variety of programs — from some in which an activity and an assignment were designated for each day of the semester to others in which no structure was provided and floundering was a rite of passage.

When I supervise new teaching assistants, I always advise them to teach from their strengths, which might not be the same as mine, and if necessary to adapt any suggestions for assignments and classroom management to ones with which they felt more secure. New teachers who read these ideas will, I hope, be able to make similar adjustments.

ASSIGNMENTS

Three things deserve comment: choosing a topic, preparing students for the assignment, and above all making sure that students understand the *purpose* of the assignment.

1. In helping students to choose a subject, I try to mediate between structure and flexibility. Students are constrained by the objectives of the assignment, but they have plenty of choices: the suggestions in the text, new topics I might want to add to those in the text, and still others that the students themselves have chosen, based on their own interests or events that are taking place around them. It's no small dividend for us teachers that papers on many different subjects can make reading them a pleasure rather than a chore.

2. Both as teacher and as grievance officer of a large program, I have learned that a surprising number of the writing problems students wrestle with are a result of teacher failure to prepare them for the assignment. I don't assume that reading the material is the same as mastering it. I always spend at least fifteen minutes discussing the purposes of the assignment and reviewing the strategies for fulfilling them. For a definition paper, let us say, I review with students the suggestions at the end of Chapter 3, making sure that they understand the distinctions between controversial terms, asking for examples of soap operas, science fiction films, and slang terms that have recently gained popularity. Sometimes I distribute for critical discussion a faulty definition essay from a previous semester. Then we go over the guidelines for writing an essay of definition. I encourage questions, solicit examples, and otherwise try to ensure that the material has been assimilated.

   At the risk of boring this captive audience, I continue to emphasize the objectives of the assignment — the importance of clarifying words and ideas which people don't understand or about which they may disagree. I want students to feel motivated to write not only because they have found something they want to say but because they recognize that in fulfilling the assignment, they are also fulfilling an intellectual function that serves *their* purposes as learners.

3. Early in the semester, students should be introduced to the library. See the discussion on the use of the library on page 36 in these notes.

COMPOSITION: STYLE, ORGANIZATION, AND DEVELOPMENT

Not surprisingly, these are the three elements of composition where student arguments are most likely to falter. Weaknesses here can, of course, cripple the most promising ideas. The bad news is that in one semester we can do little to produce polished stylists. The good news, however, is that we *can* teach organization and development.

1. Precision and grace in writing almost always depend on a good ear, long familiarity with good writing, and association with family and friends who know how to use language — conditions over which teachers of college freshmen have little control. We have tried and sometimes seen an improvement in style as a result of sentence-combining exercises, imitation of accessible prose stylists like Orwell, and rewriting of clumsy passages by the instructor. Our goals should be modest — clarity would be enough — but our successes will also be modest.

   One of the obstacles of some students on the way to clear and straightforward expression is their adoption of an artificial written style which has little resemblance to their own voices. The style is inflated and slightly pompous, but it seems to these writers that a language closer to colloquial speech would be inappropriate and even frivolous. I encourage these students to look closely at the prose of writers who often use one-syllable words and short sentences with strong rhetorical effect. I want to convince students that simple prose is not merely an instructor's idiosyncratic preference.

   A limited vocabulary, needless to say, is a serious impediment to the reading and writing of arguments. I teach use of a full-size desk dictionary; many college students have never consulted anything but a small paperback dictionary and are at a loss to interpret the symbols in a larger one. I ask questions about the words in the assigned essays and insist that students look them up. I emphasize words that student writers can usefully introduce into their own essays. And I've been surprised and pleased to notice how often students will use these new words in subsequent essays.

2. Organization for argumentative papers can be taught by formula, to both freshman writers and upper classmen alike, and we need not apologize for a lack of invention. Invention resides in the choice of topic and the modes of development. Unlike the arrangement of ideas in description, which may be spatial, or in narration, which may be chronological, the arrangement of ideas in argument is logical, and has, therefore, wide application. I try to make clear to students that the modes of organization outlined in the text are exactly the same as those they will be expected to use in their writing in the workplace or in any activities which call for reports, evaluations, and recommendations.

   If students have trouble arranging the materials of an argument, I ask them first to establish the nature of their claims, then to examine essays in the book that exemplify the appropriate organization (defending the main idea: Tuchman, Rossi, Keegan; refuting the opposing view: Levin, Moore, Parker, Burger; presenting the stock issues: Sipher, Sullivan, Swift). Often the first paragraph of an essay serves as an introduction to the kind of organization. Most beginning writers are glad to learn that these forms exist and are ready for use in any argument. As they gain power in using these conventional forms, they will be free to modify them — for example, withholding the main idea until the end, as Allport does.

3. As for development and support, I stress this throughout the semester in every piece students read and write, pointing out varied strategies that good writers use to convince readers of the soundness of their claims.

   In introducing or summarizing the concepts of organization and development, I often use the blackboard. I write down the claim or thesis statement for an argument suggested by a student — for example, "Schools should remove vending machines of unhealthful snack food" — then ask students to suggest topic sentences for three paragraphs and the means of supporting the ideas summarized in the topic sentences. I can use this device for the three ways of organizing a claim, and I can make ample reference to the forms of support that are treated in Chapter 4.

   From time to time I duplicate good student papers, sometimes from a previous semester, for distribution to the class, and we discuss the successful use of the different ways of organizing and supporting a particular argument. Duplication of less successful papers — without names — can also work if the problems are not severe and the instructor can call attention to some strengths as well.

AVOIDING PLAGIARISM

There is no foolproof way of preventing plagiarism. But a few precautions can reduce the number of incidents.

1. Make sure that students understand the nature of the offense. Many students are genuinely ignorant of the necessity for crediting sources. Review the examples in the text. Some instructors warn students at the beginning of the semester that a finding of plagiarism will result in an F for the course. Urge students to ask questions about citation if they are in doubt.

2. Keep an impromptu paper, one written on the first or second day of class, as a sample of the student's style and thinking. (I assign a short essay in class on a subject that allows students to develop a simple argument.) This paper serves primarily as a test of the skills — or lack of skills — that students bring with them. However, if a subsequent paper exhibits a radical departure in vocabulary, syntax, and development of ideas, the instructor should inquire about the differences. A few judicious questions, starting perhaps with vocabulary, will lead to an acknowledgment of help. This works best, of course, when the source is a professional writer with clearly superior skills.

3. Avoid "free" assignments. Whatever their merits, they may tempt students who have difficulty finding subjects to "borrow" papers from friends or the library.

4. Vary assignments from year to year. It's time-consuming to think of variations on previous assignments, but it should go without saying that if the same assignment is peddled year after year, some student papers will also make the rounds.

5. If your program calls for reviewing several drafts of a paper, you should be able to notice any abrupt changes in the final draft. But be prepared to find that some ambitious plagiarists aren't daunted and will manufacture drafts of another student's essay.

EVALUATION AND GRADING

1. Before assigning the first paper, I discuss with students the criteria for grading. As an introduction, I sometimes ask them to list in order of importance the elements of composition which ought to enter into an evaluation. In some classes half of the students will head their lists with spelling, punctuation, or grammar. What is probably already obvious to them but what they are afraid to say, knowing how perverse English teachers can be, usually comes as a relief — that nobody reads an essay merely for spelling or punctuation. I suggest that the criteria ought to be (1) an interesting and important idea; (2) clarity of expression; (3) adequate development; (4) clear organization; (5) correct spelling and punctuation. In class discussion I try to elicit the reasons for this list and the order in which the items appear. Students need to see how these criteria are justified by their claims on the reader. (If the reader of an essay can't understand what the writer is trying to say, a good outline and lots of data will be powerless to save the argument.)

2. I put a letter grade on each paper to be returned. I make no distinction between evaluation and grading. I've discovered that if we omit letter grades from a paper — in a vain attempt to make students less grade-conscious — they will supply the grades themselves. And grading each paper makes it easier to explain, and defend, the unavoidable final grade. I must add that I never put the letter F on a paper, and sometimes I even withhold the D. If the paper really lacks any redeeming strength, I speak to the writer in conference.

3. Although the emphasis in evaluation rests on the elements of argument, I don't ignore grammar and mechanics in considering the grade. For many students, accuracy will be a hallmark of their professions. In a class of mechanical engineers to whom I taught writing, students were told by the engineer who directed the course that sloppy letters of application were routinely discarded by most companies. Employers would infer that an engineer who was careless about spelling and punctuation might also be careless about specifications for a machine. In a real sense, then, matters of spelling, grammar, and punctuation are an integral part of the argument, and not only for engineers.

4. What students do read with high interest is the paragraph or two that instructors write in summing up their evaluation of the whole paper. Comments and questions in the margin are helpful but no substitute for this final evaluation, which for students represents part of the ongoing dialogue initiated by their arguments.

The student essay on page 273 is above average in style, freedom from mechanical errors, organization, and attention to development. But it is weakened by flaws that are typical of many good student arguments.

My written evaluation would say:

> I think this is a hard claim to defend, but you've handled several things very well. The organization is tight, and you make excellent transitions between ideas. I liked the introduction; it's a lively, well-told personal anecdote, and your reference to it at the end makes clear that it was an integral part of your argument. Even more important, in the body of your argument you offer other kinds of support: an appeal to fairness and data about drinking and driving.

But some changes and additions might have made your argument even stronger. (1) You are probably right that the laws alone have not been responsible for the big drop in alcohol-related deaths — among fifteen- to nineteen-year-olds they have plunged from a peak of 6,281 in 1982 to 2,170 in 1988 — but most experts agree that the laws are at least partly responsible. So you would have to argue that the death rate won't rise if the drinking age is lowered. Can you find data and expert opinion to support that view? You say you are a responsible driver — good point — but are you typical? (2) The analogy with other rights granted to eighteen-year-olds is somewhat shaky. Couldn't someone argue that granting those rights to teenagers was a mistake and that we should raise the ages for all the activities you cite? There's nothing special about age eighteen that guarantees maturity. After all, most eighteen-year-olds don't vote, most marriages at eighteen aren't notably successful, and as soldiers in the army, eighteen-year-olds are under strict supervision. (3) Finally, I wonder who your audience is. Are you writing for adults who might be persuaded to change the laws? I'm not sure that your attempts to evade the law would convince them that you are mature and responsible, or that pleading for the "pleasure of intoxication" — at a time when drinking by young people is declining, for good reasons — will be very persuasive. If you like, we can talk more about this in conference, and I can show you the sources of my data.

B

PEER EVALUATION

Peer review is less useful in argumentation courses than in courses that emphasize other modes of discourse. That is because the student reviewer often lacks sufficient knowledge of the subject of the argument to make informed comment. An example: A student writing about prisons had taken all his data from a *Time* magazine article of about fifteen years ago. The paper was well written, but the student reading it had no way of knowing that the data had changed so greatly that the claims were no longer valid. If instructors want to give students practice in evaluating arguments of classmates — a potentially valuable exercise — they are well advised, I think, to limit the areas on which the critic is asked to comment.

It's true, of course, that instructors can also be ignorant of areas of knowledge investigated by a student writer. But most of us have sufficient experience as laborers in various fields of scholarship to know which questions to ask.

CONFERENCES

Some programs mandate a specific number of conferences during the semester. Some even prescribe the amount of time to be spent. One guide for teachers calls for an initial conference of two minutes! Other syllabi leave the number of conferences to the instructor. But why conferences at all?

1. One teacher of composition in a prestigious university says frankly that his function in a conference is to rewrite the student's paper, explaining the point of his revision as he goes. In fact, such an extreme strategy may work in some cases — if the student is alive to nuances of vocabulary and tone and can understand and accept the changes, if he or she learns by imitation,

and if he or she has sufficient confidence to take issue with some of the teacher's revisions. Most of us, however, see the conference at its best as a dialogue or a conversation which either the teacher or the student may initiate.

Arguments, we have told our students, are implicit dialogues, and a conference represents not only our opportunity to respond at greater length to the student's argument but the student's opportunity to respond to *us* — to the written comments, for example — and to talk about the process of composition. As the student articulates his thesis, answering our questions and explaining what he tried to do and why he chose to do it this way, some things may become clear that remained opaque when he was engaged in a monologue. Conferences can also function as mini-workshops for two, three, or four students who share a composition problem or have argued the same subject with varying degrees of success.

2. I schedule a mandatory conference during the second week of classes, and at this meeting we discuss both the strengths and the weaknesses of the diagnostic essay, which is not graded. It is gratifying to be able to tell students who have never been confident about their writing that in fact their in-class papers show promise. I am specific about the things they have done well and encourage them to build on these strengths. Other students need to know that their papers reveal problems to be worked on throughout the semester. At this point I concentrate on the big things, organization and development, and touch only lightly on style, grammar, and punctuation. (I should add that impromptu papers, although written under imperfect conditions, can nevertheless predict real and continuing weaknesses.)

3. In part, conferences also function as a kinder, gentler substitute for written comments. One instructor wrote, "Think More!" across the top of a student paper. Am I wrong in suspecting that it might be harder to give such peremptory and humiliating advice in person?

   Poor writers, although they may come reluctantly to conference, may profit most from these sessions. They may be unwilling to pay the necessary attention to largely negative written comments, but in conference they must confront them, and the comments can be prefaced, softened, and modified to accommodate a vulnerable human presence. These students may also be more articulate in speech than in writing and better able to assist the instructor by giving a clearer sense of what they really wanted to argue.

4. Some programs require meetings for review of a mid-process paper. I require only a final paper. I will gladly look over any number of drafts and encourage students to come to me with problems they are having difficulty solving, but I don't insist on submission of papers in progress. The difference between a draft or a final paper is not so clear to me. Even a final draft — or one that the writer takes to be final — can and sometimes should be revised, and my preference is to allow as many revisions and as many conferences as a student thinks necessary or desirable. In practice, students seldom make more than one major revision of their "final" paper, and they understand that for administrative reasons, deadlines, however, arbitrary, must be met. But the freedom to go on writing and conferring is available.

5. Finally, conferences allow student and teacher to look at mechanical errors and their corrections in a different way. Corrections on the student essay of spelling, grammar, and punctuation errors don't always produce improvement; many students won't — or can't — read them. And a multitude of

correction results in a trail of red ink that signifies a disaster. A conference has the virtue of allowing you to ask questions, listen to answers, offer explanations, and, most of all, point out with pencil and finger the things that need change. For such problems a small physical demonstration has an impact that the written correction does not.

CHAPTER 9
Researching an Argumentative Paper

The objectives of the freshman research paper should be limited. The paper should be relatively short (no more than eight pages or 2,000 words), it should constitute only one-fifth or less of the final grade, and the preparation for it should not consume more than a week of class time. Conferences with the students can take care of individual problems that arise during the research and the writing.

Unlike many courses in the upper classes, in which the only writing may be an examination and a research paper, our course requires papers from the very first week of class, and students practice research skills at some level throughout the semester. The research paper serves not to introduce but to bring together in a more ambitious exercise the principal elements of argument. But it is only one among many papers.

The purposes of the research paper are twofold: (1) mastering a long paper — perhaps three times longer than any of the weekly papers students have done so far — with its special and more demanding problems of organization; (2) learning how to substantiate more extensive claims of fact, value, and policy that require the data and authoritative opinion the writer cannot supply—in other words, more practice in organization and development.

I don't make the accuracy of footnoting and bibliography a major issue. Students seldom see the necessity for it, and, in fact, they are right to regard the forms as arbitrary and time-consuming. And they do change. The time for rigorous adherence to the style sheets will come when students write research papers in their major disciplines, many of which specify guidelines that professional writers in the field *must* follow. I direct students to copy the appropriate forms provided in the chapter on research, but I don't exact big penalties for the inevitable lapses.

New teachers who are introducing the research paper for the first time may find suggestions in the following outline that can be adapted to their particular programs.

1. Assign a fast reading of Chapter 9. Take ten or fifteen minutes to turn pages with students, pointing out what they will find and which parts deserve a slightly longer glance. For example, they should read the sample paper with care; for this reading, however, they can skip the MLA and APA style sheets.

   At the next class go over the important parts of the chapter. Concentrate on the tasks that must be accomplished first. Encourage questions.

Reassure students that the assignment is not so daunting as they think it is. It might even be fun, and you are ready to help.

2. In class discuss finding a topic. The commonly quoted advice to graduate students about to embark on a dissertation still holds good: Choose something that really interests you, because you'll have to live with it for a while.

   The first and most obvious source of subjects will be in "Opposing Viewpoints." At least five topics are suggested for each chapter, but students may think of others that interest them more. Other subjects may be found in personal experience, at home and at school, and in the neighborhood, in town or on campus.

3. Work out a schedule for the project. Freshman students need help in managing time, and they are grateful for a structure that defines their responsibilities. I favor making the time available for the research paper no longer than a month. (I've found that allowing more time for research and writing doesn't produce better papers.) Set deadlines for specific stages of the project:

   a. the choice of topic
   b. a briefly annotated list of five sources examined in the first week or ten days. Two of the items may be taken from "Opposing Viewpoints," the other three from other sources. (All of these may not appear in the final bibliography, but they represent a start.)
   c. the final paper

4. Announce the availability of conferences with the instructor at any point during the research and writing. Early in the project I schedule one conference with each student. Later conferences can be based on individual need. Some students will have trouble refining and narrowing the topic. Others will need help finding sources. (If I'm familiar with the subject, I offer suggestions. Students also have access to my files with thousands of clippings.) And still others will encounter problems in organizing and in using the sources appropriately. (See No. 6.)

5. While students work on their research papers outside of class, I ask for short papers, sometimes in class, which introduce an idea or present a piece of evidence that is part of the longer paper. Some papers will suggest the need for conference. If not, papers should be returned promptly with comments relevant to the research paper. Needless to say, attention to the ongoing process of the paper should also make plagiarism more difficult.

6. Most of us are prepared for evidence of a scanty research effort. But we should also be prepared for evidence of another kind of failure. Drunk with their newly acquired knowledge of the research tool, some students produce a series of quotations, sometimes as many as twenty in a six-page paper, tightly strung together like a well-made necklace, with nothing visible between the pearls. This is *not* a research paper. We need to make clear to students that *they* are the authors and that the materials derived from other sources must be used *only* to support their claims. We should emphasize that too much research material can be as fatal as too little. "Why We Don't Need Zoos" gives students a model for the intelligent use of quotations.

USE OF THE LIBRARY

At schools with large libraries it's not uncommon to discover that even by the end of the first semester, freshman students will not have visited the library unless assigned to do so. Big libraries can be intimidating, but a guided tour can reinforce the idea that the library is a friend, not an enemy. *The library tour should take place early in the semester, not at research paper time.* In this course students should begin to use the resources of the library at once, as they tackle the very first paper on defending a claim of fact.

Librarians are usually more than willing to cooperate in helping students to become familiar with library resources, and they can offer helpful experience to new instructors. I would turn to the librarians first and try to accommodate their recommendations to the purposes of the course. I make a few suggestions here based on trial and error with my own classes.

1. A tour in which twenty students follow the librarian as he or she points out library services seldom works. The students in the back can't hear, and they lose interest. Even those near the speaker will not remember a couple of weeks later exactly what they learned. At most the librarian or the instructor can walk the students through some of the areas where they are likely to be busiest — the card catalog, the indexes, the major reference works, the microfiche collection.
2. Prepare students for the visit. Go over the material in the book, offering additional information about the sources. Anecdotes about your own experience with research can enliven an apparently lifeless subject.
3. Students will remember much more about the library if they arrive with specific questions. One way to produce questions that will lead to a wide range of answers is to divide the class into three sections: humanities, social sciences, and natural and physical sciences. Each section meets and arrives at a research paper topic in its field; each student in that section then prepares a specific question on the topic. (Some of the questions will be weak, but the librarian can often ask the right questions of the student and elicit a nice rephrasing.) The students assemble with the librarian in a room with a blackboard — an overhead projector is also a useful tool — where he or she can answer students' questions by writing down the names of the materials and their locations.
4. Use student resources. Some students in the class will be more proficient than others in unraveling the mysteries of the library, and they are often pleased and proud to be asked to accompany the others and point out how and where to look.

PART THREE

OPPOSING VIEWPOINTS

INTRODUCTION

1. The debates, articles, and letters in this section represent the argumentative process in its clearest and most understandable form. If throughout the semester we have emphasized that arguments are dialogues, the selections given here will show students how the dialogues work, that is, how people on opposing sides actually respond to each other, whether well or poorly. Where it is clear that the response is not direct, that there is no clash, the debates can be equally instructive.

2. "Opposing Viewpoints" may be used as a discrete unit or as a source of materials for assignments in the text.

   a. If it is used as a self-contained unit, the introduction and the questions that precede it suggest a number of ways of examining the material and writing about it. The debate instructions that follow give, I hope, sufficient details for the organization of a classroom debate, oral or written.

   b. "Opposing Viewpoints" also lends itself as a source of data, expert opinion, motivational appeals, warrants, and ethical and unethical use of language. In fulfilling assignments that call for supporting materials students may find material here, either as a substitute for or in addition to library research. In several places in these notes I have suggested assignments that give students the opportunity to look for support for their claims among the selections in "Opposing Viewpoints."

   c. In addition, as we have pointed out earlier, "Opposing Viewpoints" can furnish the material for a research paper. Longer papers may require supplementary library research, but there is probably sufficient material in each section for a paper of six to seven pages.

3. Some of these subjects will be more effective than others for a given group of students, depending on their experience and knowledge of an involvement with the subject. "Collegiate Sports Reform" for example, may be more interesting for students in schools with highly competitive sports programs and generous athletic scholarships. "Euthanasia" may strike a chord in a place where the fate of a handicapped infant is being publicly debated.

   When time does not permit using all the subjects, I choose the most provocative ones, those that will produce, as far as I can tell, the liveliest feelings, both for and against.

4. Given the timeliness of these subjects, new data will be indispensable to any evaluation. This means research to discover whether the facts have changed since the articles and letters in the text were written. What has happened to the proposals, rejected in spring 1987, for mandatory testing for the AIDS virus? Has Proposition 42 effected any significant changes in

college athletic programs? What legal steps are being taken that will affect experimentation with animals? Once new data have been uncovered, students may want to argue about the effects, predicting whether conditions will be better or worse as a result of changes.

5. An enormously productive unit may be organized around formal classroom debate. Although debate is almost always an oral exercise, there is plenty of opportunity in a writing class for students to commit their outlines to paper, develop major points that cannot be adequately treated in the five minutes allotted to oral presentation, and make extended critiques of the debates of their classmates.

   Each debate usually requires four people, two on the affirmative side, two on the negative, although the Lincoln–Douglas format — one debater on each side — is also possible. If time does not permit a round of formal debates, the class may choose four or five debate subjects, with each team producing an argument that will be duplicated or read aloud for consideration by the whole class. This organization reduces the arguments to one on each side and eliminates rebuttal time. After reading or hearing the arguments, the class may write evaluations based on answers to the questions on the debate sheet.

   For supporting materials students should confine themselves to the data in this section. Their efforts will involve extracting the relevant issues and organizing them in a succinct and understandable way. They may also, of course, need to do further research for more recent data.

DEBATE

Debate may be considered an extension of the problem-solving analysis. The debaters are considering the merits of a solution to some problem, for example, a plan to restrict government agencies in their investigations of private citizens.

The debate proposition is always a two-sided question; it can be answered yes or no.

The proposition is worded so that the affirmative (yes) side will be arguing for a change in policy, or, in the case of value questions, a new idea. (The argument that violence is justified in civil rights cases is an example of the latter.) Because the affirmative is arguing for a change, they are said to have the *burden of proof,* while the negative has only to defend the *status quo.*

The affirmative argument usually centers around three *stock issues* that grow out of the problem-solving analysis. The affirmative will argue:

1. that there is a need for a change;
2. that their proposal will meet the need;
3. that their proposal is the text solution to the problem. These stock issues are referred to as need, plan, and advantages.

The negative may answer the affirmative case in a number of ways.

1. They may debate every issue. "There is no problem, and even if there were your plan is expensive, inefficient, and undesirable."
2. They may *waive* an issue. "Yes, indeed, we agree there is a serious problem, but your proposed solution is useless."

3. They may propose a *counterplan*. "Things are bad all right, but I have a better idea for improving them than yours." Tournament debaters do not do this too often for strategic reasons: It means the negative must assume part of the burden of proof.

Following are some questions you might consider as you listen to a debate:

1. How important is definition of terms? Does it become an issue in the debate?
2. Does the negative attack the affirmative argument on every point, or does the debate narrow to one or two issues?
3. Do the speakers base their arguments on any generally accepted principles or values, such as justice, individual freedom, constitutional guarantees?
4. Do you find examples of causal argument, argument from example, or argument from analogy?
5. How important is evidence in the debate? Do the speakers question the credibility of each other's sources? To what extent, if any, does the argument center around evidence?
6. What comments would you make on the speakers' oral presentation (delivery)?
7. Which side do you think won, and why?

CHAPTER 10
Abortion

1. The central issue — whether or not life begins at conception — is one that still resists definition and compromise. Three selections speak to the question of the "personhood" of the fetus: the Planned Parenthood ad, "Is Abortion Ever Equal to Murder?", and "Too Many Abortions." They offer three different definitions. "Too Many Abortions" addresses the issue from the Catholic point of view. Students are sometimes surprised to find that the anti-abortion movement is by no means exclusively Catholic. An interesting assignment asks for some students to present the views of other Christian denominations and other faiths, such as Judaism and Islam.

2. However, a productive debate is probably best directed toward other issues. Constituencies with special interests, some of whom have been underrepresented in the public debate, have their point of view represented in several selections: blacks, prospective fathers, teenagers and their parents. These are groups with whom many students can identify and for whom they can honestly speak.

   a. Greg Keath argues that blacks must resist "the forces that drive blacks to seek abortion." The history he covers is disturbing — especially the role of Margaret Sanger, one that most students will not be familiar with. Students may want to look at the arguments of black writers who take issue with Keath. They should try to infer the goals and values of each side in the controversy. How does abortion contribute or fail to contribute to achievement of the goals each side pursues?

b. Enter the prospective father. Arthur Shostak thinks that abortion is a couple's problem, "a question of the rights and responsibilities of a twosome." Other writers go further, arguing that the prospective father should be allowed to veto the woman's decision on abortion. What conditions, if any, should determine the contribution of the male partner? Both male and female students should have plenty to say about this. (See the cover story in *U. S. News and World Report,* October 3, 1988.)

c. The issue most likely to arouse controversy in our classes is mandatory parental consent for abortions. As Holder points out, a parental consent law might *compel* as well as *deny* an abortion for a teenager. What are the implications for the teenager and for the family — indeed, for the whole society — of laws that protect the rights of young women to make the decision? Ronnie Gunnerson, a mother, is clearly very angry, and the depth of her anger tells us a good deal about the problem. One teenager, Juliet Moyna, expresses her opinion, but she *favors* a consent law. Some of our students will certainly disagree with her. This issue seems to ignore ideological boundaries. Neither liberals nor conservatives are positioned where we might expect to find them on this question.

2. "Too Many Abortions" from *Commonweal* makes a provocative accusation: All abortions represent a failure of sexual responsibility by both men and women, but especially women. Can women — and men — defend themselves against this charge? And how shall the problem of unwanted pregnancies be solved? The editorial offers two solutions; women are responsible for both of them. Ask students if these solutions seem feasible.

3. Finally, there is the question of public funding for what the letter-writer calls "a private matter." This question of public funding for activities and programs to which some taxpayers are morally opposed goes far beyond abortion. In fact, it can emerge on campuses where some groups have protested the use of money collected from compulsory fees to fund activities they don't support or approve. Students can often discuss with real sophistication the principles underlying the competing claims.

CHAPTER 11
AIDS Testing

1. New information about the course of the AIDS epidemic may generate new perspectives on testing. For example, the availability of new drugs that prolong the life and alleviate the suffering of AIDS victims has made early testing and diagnosis more desirable. But at present the basic question remains the conflict between the right of those who are infected to privacy and the right of potential drug and sex partners to know of their risk of exposure.

   Students should try to infer the reasons that AIDS has been treated differently from other infectious diseases whose victims have been the objects of reporting, contact tracing, and even quarantine. (In New York City people with syphilis are asked to identify their sexual partners, who will then be warned. There is no public outcry over this practice.) Does Robert Cohen fully explain the reasons?

The *New York Times,* May 13, 1990, page 22, reports on "a growing number of states" that "have begun recording the names of people who test positive for infection with the AIDS virus and warning their drug and sex partners." This article, which gives a student researcher partial but up-to-date information about new laws, is, in fact, a debate between several public health officials and the opponents of laws requiring notice to sex and drug partners.

A series of interesting questions "that keep coming up" is listed:

a. Should the names of people who test positive for AIDS virus infection be recorded by government health officials?
b. Should their sex and drug partners be sought by the health agency and warned that they may be infected?
c. Should someone who knowingly spreads the virus to unsuspecting people be isolated or quarantined?
d. Are keeping track of infected people and tracing their contacts counterproductive, driving away people who are likely to need testing and treatment?

2. New information may also enable students to determine whether Restak's statements, published in 1985, are still true. If they are not, how would this fact affect medical opinion on the value of testing?

3. Students have earlier been asked — in the questions in the text — to look for indications that the professional positions and interests of the participants in the *Harper's* symposium may have influenced their arguments. But students may also want to ask if their own views of the testing issue have been influenced by what they know about the arguers and how they themselves feel about AIDS victims.

4. Crenshaw says that she has attempted to analyze each argument of those who oppose mandatory testing. Whether or not she has succeeded, students can nevertheless study the organization of her essay as another model of argument by refutation.

   In studying Crenshaw's arguments, students may also recognize that some arguments are stronger than others. Not surprisingly, the strongest are those based on her knowledge and experience as a physician. What does this tell students about their own roles as arguers?

5. Any discussion of testing among high-risk groups will move inevitably to more immediate areas of concern that include means of controlling spread of the disease. These subjects will reflect some of the same conflicts of rights and values that surround the whole testing issue. For example, should a child with AIDS be permitted to attend school, even if his or her identity is concealed? Students may be familiar with several highly publicized cases. I make clear that we are confining the discussion to elementary school children.

   Students should notice that Restak would probably argue against it, although other physicians would disagree.

6. Students find it rewarding to interview physicians or health-care workers about their views on testing. Sometimes new insights emerge when students have the opportunity to engage in a face-to-face meeting with an expert.

7. Here is a test case for students to consider:

   Take the case of the New York City physician approached by a woman demanding to know whether her husband had AIDS. She had recently discovered she was pregnant and did not want to give birth to a baby with a deadly disease. If her husband had the virus, she would have an abortion.

   Not long before, the husband had been in the clinic because of a painful rash on his back. While he was there, his doctor, who knew the patient used heroin and other intravenous drugs, recommended a test for the AIDS virus. The test came back positive, and the doctor urged the man to tell his wife. "No way, Doc," was the answer. The patient claimed he always used a condom, so his wife was protected. And if he told her, she would leave him. The doctor, who had been working for some time in city clinics, was profoundly frustrated — with the patient, the situation, and, ultimately, the limited ability he had as a physician to combat either of the two diseases: drug addiction or AIDS.

   Now the doctor must confront the patient's wife, knowing that her health and the fate of the two-month-old fetus were jeopardized. Must he protect his patient's confidentiality? Or should he disclose what he knows?[1]

CHAPTER 12
Animal Rights

1. This debate continues to widen, from raids on medical research facilities and state referendums on factory farming to attacks on fur coats and tuna fishing nets that trap dolphins. The central question is how we justify the right to cause suffering to other species. Students should be asked to defend or attack what Peter Singer would characterize as selfish decisions. Can an action taken to ensure our own survival at the expense of helpless animals be defined as *moral?*

   Peter Singer's powerful essay introduces the concept of moral equality: All creatures, regardless of the level of intelligence, should enjoy the right to freedom from exploitation. Singer's position is extreme but eloquently argued and difficult to refute. One strength, to which students should give their attention, is his use of analogy and example. These are the same devices used so effectively in Levin's "The Case for Torture." In both arguments readers are forced to confront their own positions in hypothetical cases. For example, what moral consideration prevents us from experimenting on infants, who are less sentient and less intelligent than adult apes? Singer insists that if we support the exploitation of animals, we should acknowledge that we are guilty of "speciesism."

   Students might ask if Singer would choose to die of an illness rather than benefit from a cure derived from animal experimentation. He doesn't

[1]Michael Wilkes, M.D., and Miriam Shuchman, M.D., "Holy Secrets," *New York Times Magazine,* October 2, 1988.

answer the question directly, but perhaps an answer can be inferred from his argument.

2. C. S. Lewis extends Singer's argument by challenging Christian vivisectionists to justify their actions on theological grounds. Although he does not use the term, Lewis, writing thirty years before Singer, also attacks the concept of "speciesism" — "this loyalty to our own species." He, too, uses analogy. (See paras. 6, 8, and 10.) And he infers a consequence of vivisection of which some writers (Timothy Noah, for example, "Monkey Business," *The New Republic,* June 2, 1982) would deride as a slippery slope fallacy: Cruelty to animals will lead to cruelty to "backward" races different from "civilized" ones like our own. This is, of course, an argument also used by opponents of abortion and euthanasia.

3. Michael DeBakey sets out, probably as clearly as it is possible to do so, the case for sacrificing animals to the cause of human health and survival. He even makes the claim that animal research benefits other animals. His appeal is personal — I am humane, I want to relieve suffering, I disapprove of cruelty to animals — and deeply emotional. His justification for choosing human over animal life is "self-preservation" as a "primary instinct of all members of the animal kingdom." Whether this is a moral defense is something that students should be prepared to discuss. DeBakey's article is a superb example of the judicious use of support — examples, statistics, details, expert opinion (his own), and strong appeals to emotion.

4. Meg Greenfield takes a somewhat shaky stand in the middle — favoring animal research for serious purposes, like saving human lives, but not for frivolous ones, like finding a better hairspray. In a short piece she cannot raise all the important issues, but she takes it for granted that her readers will agree that benefits to human beings must take precedence over other considerations. Here, too, students should be prepared to defend or attack this warrant.

5. In the essays we have mentioned so far, the writers assume that animal experimentation will continue. "Alternatives to Animals" introduces an array of facts about techniques that may some day significantly affect the use of animals in the laboratory. Since most of the articles in this section have been written by partisans of one side or another, this article seems refreshingly moderate in tone and reasonably objective. There may be someone on campus who can contribute up-to-date information on the innovations described in this article.

   Singer asks why students have been so indifferent to discrimination against animals in campus laboratories. If such laboratories exist on your campus, ask a student or students to interview workers responsible for the experiments and to write an evaluative report that explains the nature of these experiments and the justification for them.

6. The adoption of vegetarianism, at least partly for ethical reasons, is growing on our campus and therefore, I suspect, on others as well. Students in the class who are ethical vegetarians can examine their own practice and defend it against arguments of meat eaters.

7. The research paper in Chapter 9 argues that zoos are both cruel and lacking in educational value. Students may want to argue the opposite view — that animals in captivity, in zoos or other kinds of parks, offer a desirable alternative to life in the wild, for both the animals and their spectators.

CHAPTER 13
Collegiate Sports Reform

1. The question of college sports reform should appeal not only to those who love sports and are active boosters of their college teams (mostly men, it seems) but also to those who may have little interest in sports but are concerned about the relationship between the function of a college or university and the support for intermural athletic contests. Definition as a mode of development in assignments on this issue is clearly important.

   Can we define the role of the university in ways that include intercollegiate sports?

2. The number of propositions approved by the NCAA in the last three years suggests a growing desperation over the failure of colleges and universities to achieve "academic respectability for big-time sports programs" (Herbert I. London). The big question for discussion is: How strong is the argument for giving academically underprepared high school athletes an opportunity to attend college when many of them receive an inferior education and fail to graduate? Acel Moore argues the case against Proposition 42 and in favor of funding black athletes. Frederick Whiddon argues the case for Proposition 42 and against favored treatment for athletes "not yet academically prepared to perform at the university level." London agrees with Whiddon. Is the fact that both Whiddon and London are academics relevant to their arguments?

3. Would educational purposes be better served if college sports consisted of intermural contests between teams composed of students from the regular school population? Students might find it enlightening to read how Robert M. Hutchins, president of the University of Chicago from 1929–1951, justified the abolition of intercollegiate football at the university.

4. Berkow as well as Sage and Davis suggest that big-time college sports should be treated as entertainment. Some students feel that the definition of college sports as a form of show business would be offensive, an insult to both coach and players. In order to argue against a redefinition, students must find ways of relating college sports to the conventional function of the university.

5. "The Myth of the Student-Athlete" provides some striking figures for athletic expenses. Students at schools where intermural sports are important ought to be able to uncover similar statistics for their own schools. They will, of course, find it much harder to decide whether a disparity exists between resources for athletics and resources for academic enterprises and if so, whether it is justified.

   The cover story in the issue of *U.S. News and World Report* (January 8, 1990) in which "The Myth of the Student-Athlete" appears is "The Price of Victory: College Sports vs. Education." An interesting feature of this lengthy article is that it includes short biographies of twelve outstanding college athletes, nine of whom did not graduate.

6. The enthusiasm for college sports, represented in part by the sums of money invested in stadiums, salaries for coaches, scholarships, and other costs of funding winning teams, seems to be uniquely American. Why? How did college sports become a huge business with continuing appeal for a public that has no connection with the colleges?

(One reason: College sports became popular at a time when no professional teams existed.)

7. Discussions of class and race are also bound to emerge, since athletic scholarships are often awarded to members of minority groups who have traditionally received an inferior education and so may not be prepared for the academic standards of college. Objections are sometimes voiced, quietly for the most part, to the special treatment — in tutoring and remedial classes — that athletes enjoy in order to make them eligible to play. Why should athletes be the principal beneficiaries of costly remediation?

CHAPTER 14
Environmental Policy

1. Everyone in this debate agrees that the earth must be saved, but both the facts and the policies concerning its survival are controversial. Unfortunately for those who want to know the truth, no other topic has been more subject to media "hype" and repeated prophecies of doom, from scientists, politicians, gonzo journalists, and, of course, rock stars. It is precisely these warnings, broadcast to millions, that make the subject exciting, like a preview of a science fiction film whose ending remains in doubt. But apocalyptic visions should not lead students into the two most obvious traps: (1) that the truth about environmental dangers will be easy to discover and (2) that "simple remedies make a world of difference," as one writer in the *Boston Globe* argued.

2. What can we say about the facts? Above all, it will be difficult for students to keep abreast of the latest information. On December 13, 1989, the *New York Times* ran a front-page story entitled, "Skeptics Are Challenging Dire 'Greenhouse' Effects." On March 3, 1990, another headline read, "No Global Warming Signs Spotted." The data for this report were collected from weather satellites and showed "no long-term warming or cooling trend" from 1979 to 1988. But on May 26, 1990, another article reported that an international panel of scientists working on behalf of the United Nations had warned that unless carbon dioxide and other emissions were immediately cut by more than 60 percent, "global temperatures would rise sharply over the next century, with unforeseeable consequences for humanity."

   According to one estimate, fewer than 300 scientists (in this country — climatologists, meteorologists, geophysicists, and people in related fields — are engaged in serious climatic research, and perhaps the majority have not taken a "firm position in the debate."

   The editorial from *The Economist,* however, claims that the predictions of those who believe in the greenhouse effect are "based on more thorough work." Students might try to determine whether the conclusion of *The Economist* is justified. They can begin by examining the expert opinions in this chapter. Udall quotes ten authorities who are "believers"; Shaw and Stroup quote at least seven who are not. Other experts weigh in with their analyses in letters to the *New York Times.* If students read further, they will even encounter a few experts who welcome global warming. Evaluation of both the experts and their opinions can be based on the criteria set out in

Chapter 4 (pages 104–141). We shouldn't, of course, be surprised if such an evaluation proves to be beyond the problem-solving abilities of freshman students (as it is of many scientists), but the exercise can be instructive.

Having examined the expert opinions in this chapter, students, especially those who are writing longer papers, can go on to look for other opinions in newspapers, magazines, and books. The *Readers' Guide to Periodical Literature* alone will probably list more material than they can handle. On the other hand, as with most highly publicized problems, students will find a good deal of repetition, and they will be learning how to group the reports of many experts under a limited number of headings.

Students might do worse than keep in mind some lessons articulated by Nicholas Wade, an editorial writer for the *New York Times:* (1) Beware scientists grinding axes. (2) Don't expect instant answers. (3) Don't dismiss iconoclasts. (4) Remember the limits of computer models.

As Mark Twain once remarked, "There is something fascinating about science. One gets such wholesale returns of conjecture out of such a trifling investment of facts."

3. As for policies, most participants in the environmental debate call for some form of government action, including aid to poor countries to help them find alternatives to the polluting chemicals they now use. Shaw and Stroup represent those who believe that the free market can solve most problems more efficiently than government. They also claim that journalists' perceptions "frequently differ from those of the experts" but that it is the former who influence public policy. Does evidence exist to prove this claim?

   The articles by Passell and The Conservation Foundation make clear how difficult the formulation of environmental policy will be.

4. Udall, writing in a magazine devoted to discussions of wild life, concentrates on possible dangers to animal and plant life on earth as a result of global warming. He says little about the consequences for human beings, although students who know something about the biosphere can make the connections. In fact, those students who are better informed than their classmates about these issues might act as sources — giving talks, leading discussions, suggesting bibliographies.

5. *The Harvard University Divinity Bulletin,* Fall 1989, reprinted several papers that emerged from a seminar on "Theology for a Small Planet." (They are available for $1 from the Editor, *Harvard Divinity Bulletin,* 45 Francis Avenue, Cambridge, MA 02138.) The religious dimensions of environmental policy may interest some students, especially those who are familiar with the book of Genesis.

   Even the television producer Norman Lear, a longtime advocate of secular humanism, said recently that he did not think "human beings could address major environmental problems facing the planet without a fresh examination of what we regard as sacred in the universe."

6. Some students may be familiar with a computer game, Balance of the Planet ($49.95, published by Accolade, 550 South Winchester Boulevard, Suite 200, San Jose, CA 95128). If so, they can explain to the class how it simulates real-life environmental problems. Some scientists have questioned the accuracy of the computer simulation as a predictor of conditions in the real world.

The game is advertised as a game "for adults, not kids"; one reviewer warns, "This is not a program for someone who doesn't like to read. . . . There is a lot of text." But more to our purposes, he goes on, "The selections you make determine improvements or degradations in a host of categories in ways that are difficult to predict. . . . There are no easy decisions, as there are none in real life." In other words, any solution will represent a trade-off.

7. The following list is a short bibliography of recently published books:

Block, Walter. *Economics and the Environment: A Reconciliation.* Vancouver: Fraser Institute, 1990.

Commoner, Barry. *Making Peace with the Planet.* New York: Pantheon Books, 1990.

Fisher, David E. *Fire and Ice: The Greenhouse Effect, Ozone Depletion, and Nuclear Winter.* New York: Harper & Row, 1990.

Oppenheimer, Michael, and Robert Boyle. *Dead Heat: The Race Against the Greenhouse Effect.* New York: Basic Books/New Republic, 1990.

Sagoff, Mark. *The Economy of the Earth: Philosophy, Law, and the Environment.* Cambridge: Cambridge University Press, 1988.

Schneider, Stephen H. *Global Warming: Are We Entering the Greenhouse Century?* San Francisco: Sierra Books, 1989.

Weimer, Jonathan. *The Next One Hundred Years: Shaping the Fate of Our Living Earth.* New York: Bantam Books, 1990.

CHAPTER 15
Euthanasia

1. James Rachels's "Active and Passive Euthanasia" is a brilliant and provocative example of a definition essay. Among its other virtues two stand out as models for students: (1) clear organization, with signposts for readers such as "In what follows I will set out . . ." (Students are sometimes advised to avoid summarizing introductions — I cannot imagine why), "To begin with," "My second argument is . . .," "I have argued," and "Finally,"; and (2) vivid and compelling examples that lead students toward "real" decisions.

2. Some students may be more interested in the subject of euthanasia for newborn infants. It seems that severely disabled infants are not infrequently the victims of "passive" euthanasia in the hospital, but their cases seldom become public unless doctors and parents disagree and a decision is referred to the courts. Daniel Maguire's riveting account of the trial of Madame van de Put can trigger a lively debate. Discussion can then move to Eileen Doyle's emotionally charged attack on euthanasia that is based on "quality of life" criteria. These criteria were, of course, the heart of Madame van de Put's defense.

   At the end of her article Eileen Doyle employs a risky rhetorical device: predicting the consequences of a "quality of life" ethic. This article appeared in 1985. Students can try to decide whether any of Doyle's predictions have been or are likely to be realized. Or are they examples of slippery slope fallacies? And if so, do they invalidate her argument?

3. Hardly a week passes that the media do not report a case in which death for a terminally ill or severely disabled person is being debated by the family, the physicians, or the state. Students are sometimes able to contribute experiences about such patients in their own families. As assignment requires them to select a recent case, one still undecided, and come to a decision about the proper treatment, basing their argument on some of the assumptions raised by the writers in this section.

4. Sidney Hook provides an eloquent introduction to the subject of suicide for the elderly. In asking that his life-support system be removed, he is invoking passive euthanasia. His case can be viewed as a validation of Rachels' assumption that "euthanasia — even passive euthanasia — is desirable in a given case."

   Hook's essay is also worth examining as an example of the use of personal experience in an argument. Does this account of his suffering make the argument for passive euthanasia more persuasive? We caution students not to assume that one or even several personal experiences can be offered as sound proof of a claim. Students will see that Hook qualifies the evidence. "Apparently those who cling to life no matter what, think so [that life is worth living even for an 'infirm octogenarian']. I do not." His essay makes clear that personal experience as evidence works best (1) when it is enriched by details and explanations, and (2) when the claim is limited. ("Each one must be permitted to make his own choice.")

5. As the population ages, new organizations arise that provide information to those who are interested in the right to die. One is *Society for the Right to Die,* 250 West 57th Street, New York, NY 10107. The organization distributes free a copy of a living will and offers about twenty-five books and pamphlets, free or at low cost, on the legal and medical issues in choosing one's death. For a research paper, students may be interested in learning about "natural death" laws in the United States from material printed by the society.

6. Hospitals around the country are beginning to establish ethics committees to deal with the problems raised by the new medical technologies. Medical schools also have introduced training in the ethics of decision making for terminally ill patients.

   If a hospital, medical school, or philosophy department in your school — or another easily accessible facility — has established an ethics committee or a course that revolves around problems of euthanasia, students may interview one or more of the people connected with the committee or course and analyze the issues that emerge.

CHAPTER 16

Freedom of Speech

1. Freedom of speech on campus may be the most immediately relevant and interesting issue for students, especially if there have been incidents of abusive language at their own schools. The University of Michigan docu-

ment is a starting point. Its examples of unacceptable speech offer a provocative introduction to a debate between competing values.

Students ought to examine any policy statements on their own campuses that define "racism," "sexism," "homophobia," and other discriminatory attitudes and threaten punishment for their expression. If examples like those in the University of Michigan policy statement don't exist, students might be encouraged to supply them. As they do so, they should keep in mind that the University of Michigan was forced to modify its guidelines after a Michigan court ruled that they violated the right to free speech.

Arguers may find themselves walking a narrow line between truth and offense. Students should consider this question: If the truth is offensive to some groups, should it nevertheless be expressed? The issue is complicated by the very nature of the academic purpose, which is usually defined as freedom in the search for truth. And there is another question: Do people have a right to express their feelings, even if the expression is morally repugnant? Nat Hentoff's article, defending the right even of "racist assholes," provides a rich catalog of examples from schools around the country, many of which will test student opinion on this subject. Charles Lawrence III's argument may be treated as a direct reply to Hentoff. But the two essays are also very different in style, tone, and degree of generality. If students find one article more convincing, ask them to explain why.

Lawrence has the hard task of offering solutions for an intolerable condition. He suggests legal remedies against racial harassment, but the specific forms that these remedies will take are left to civil rights lawyers to determine. So far the remedies imposed by college administrations have not been demonstrably successful. Bans on obnoxious speech sometimes work to reduce incivility and tension; more often they do not. The president of the College of William and Mary, explaining why his school overwhelmingly rejected regulation of speech on campus, wrote, "It is almost impossible to define precisely the types of speech that quality for regulation as discriminatory harassment." In the meantime the incidence of abusive speech — to say nothing of behavior — continues to rise. Perhaps students have ideas on the subject of remedies, based on their own experiences in the residence halls and the classroom. Courses in other cultures? Courses in human relations? Severe penalties for those guilty of offensive speech? Can students prove that any of these proposed solutions would work?

2. Is freedom of speech on campus different from freedom of speech on the street? The president of Emory University argues that free speech doesn't protect "vicious epithets," because universities are places where "the habits and manners of our civil society" are passed on to the next generation. But on the street there may be different rules. In New York state the highest court ruled that abusive speech was protected under federal and state constitutional guarantees of free speech. The case, currently under review, arose when a woman and her son, both mentally retarded, were verbally harassed by a neighbor.

3. Compared to the issue of offensive speech on campus, the flag-burning issue may seem relatively straightforward. The conflict begins with *definition.* What *is* the flag? James Wall says it is a symbol that represents the nation, and an attack on the flag is therefore an attack on the nation itself. To Wall the nation represents "beliefs in law and peace and that freedom which sustains the human spirit." To Gregory Johnson, however, the flag is a

symbol of something else — "gross inequality, injustice, and hypocrisy," according to one defender — and therefore merits attack. (Critics have noted the irony that the country whose injustice he despises protects his right to express that hatred.)

But even if the flag is only a sign — more easily changed than a symbol, says Wall — is burning it an act of *speech* protected by the First Amendment? Freedom of expression is not mentioned in the First Amendment, but some judges have interpreted "speech" to include other forms of expression. In a much-publicized case one judge in New York City recently ruled that begging in the subways was a form of free speech calling attention to the plight of the homeless and was therefore protected by the First Amendment. This ruling was later overturned.

In all these cases concerning free speech, students must weigh the costs of suppressing speech that injures or degrades. Writing about the flag-burning case, a senior at Rutgers University said, "The answer to the question, 'Which should we protect, freedom or the flag?' is that we should protect freedom above all else." Nat Hentoff and Susan Jacoby would agree; Lawrence and the president of Emory University would not.

Many of your students may have strong feelings for or against flag-burning. Can they find ways of translating these sometimes inarticulate emotions into appeals to values shared by a wide audience?

4. The reference to lyrics in rock music should also be of special interest to students. Some of the same issues will appear in the discussion of pornography in Chapter 18, but while not all students will be personally familiar with pornographic films and magazines, they will almost certainly know some of the offensive lyrics that have provoked their parents. Is labeling of albums a denial of free speech, a form of censorship, as Pareles suggests? In his article, Garry Wills makes an important distinction between censure and censorship, a distinction often ignored in the debate over offensive works of art.

   The cover story of *Time* magazine, May 7, 1990, is "Dirty Words: America's Foul-Mouthed Pop Culture." Following the report, an essay by Charles P. Alexander, "A Parent's View of Pop Sex and Violence," argues for protests against the language but not censorship.

CHAPTER 17
Legalizing Drugs

1. The literature on this subject is enormous and growing daily. Students should have no difficulty in finding new data, new cases, and new theories to supplement the material in this chapter. But despite the abundance of material, they will find themselves, like the rest of us, hampered in the debate for lack of information. We really don't know whether legalization would increase drug use nor, if it did, to what extent and among which groups of users. We don't know if an increase in legal drug use would be offset by some benefits, such as a reduction in crime. Students will be able

to see that without clear information about consequences, making policy is difficult and risky.

We also don't know exactly why adolescents are attracted to drugs. As one writer says, " . . . we know very little about adolescence, and much of what we think we know is false, incomplete, or out of date." We can ask our students to respond to a prediction (by John Kaplan in "Taking Drugs Seriously," *Public Interest,* Summer 1988) that education "will not do much to reduce illegal drug usage" because "young people often take pleasure in things that adults tell them are bad." Is this always true? In fact, evidence exists that information about the dangers of cigarettes and cocaine has caused a decline in their use in high school students.

Students might analyze the effectiveness of this commencement address at St. Thomas University, Miami, Florida, May 14, 1989 by William J. Byron, president of The Catholic University of America: "A Walk on the Demand Side: The Drug Train." (*Vital Speeches of the Day,* August 1, 1989, pp. 6-7.)

There are other subjects about which we don't know much and which students might be encouraged to investigate. One is the pattern of addiction, including the compulsion to engage in harmful behavior. In a fascinating article, "Patterns of Addiction" (*The New York Times Magazine,* April 10, 1988) William Ira Bennett, editor of *The Harvard Medical School Health Letter,* points out:

> Recognizing, for example, that a schedule of experiences may be as important as the drug itself might help one reevaluate the role of adolescent experimentation in establishing addiction. As scientists gain greater knowledge of the way addictive schedules work, they may provide us with insight into methods of ending dependency. Or, at least, we might be able to move beyond the myth of pleasure and punishment that has helped to make drug policy so ineffective in this country.

2. Both Switzerland and the Netherlands set aside sections of major cities as "reserves" of drug users, in effect removing them from the rest of the population. Students may have seen an extraordinary *60 Minutes* segment on the park in Zurich where young people, mostly middle class, go to buy and inject drugs without interference from the police. Do students believe that a similar policy might work in our big cities? Why or why not?

3. Two selections are examples of rebuttal, excellent models for one kind of argumentative essay. Both Bennett and Glasser select opposition arguments, then rebut them one by one. Students should be aware that this strategy works best when the rebuttal offers authoritative information that speaks directly to the opponent's point.

4. Two selections capture the extreme positions in the debate — Ostrowski in favor of legalization, Bennett against it. Although they come to very different conclusions, both invoke a moral standard as the ultimate criterion. Ostrowski: "It is immoral and absurd to *force* some people to bear costs so that others might be prevented from *choosing* to do harm to themselves." Bennett: ". . . the moral argument, in the end, is the most compelling argument." Although the arguments on both sides are wide-ranging Ostrowski ultimately champions the moral value of individual rights, while Bennett emphasizes the value of relieving suffering. Students should examine both arguments carefully. It may be impossible to decide whether one argument

is more powerful than the other, but both illustrate that the moral issue lies at the heart of the debate.

CHAPTER 18
Pornography

1. The discussion of pornography in any detail can pose problems for some classes. Teachers are often surprised to discover that many students, usually women, have never seen a pornographic film or read a pornographic novel. And secondhand media reports are not generally very informative. In all the stories about artist Robert Mapplethorpe's controversial photographs, very rarely has any newspaper or magazine done more than describe the offending photographs as "homoerotic." It was, in fact, impossible for readers not already familiar with the photographs to know exactly what the fuss was about.

   Nevertheless, despite their relative ignorance of specific material, students can engage in worthwhile debates based on the *implicit* definitions in the articles in this chapter, especially those by Brownmiller, Goldstein, and Lynn. In any discussion the definitions will probably remain unfocused; we know how difficult it has been, even for the Supreme Court, to formulate a clear, explicit definition of pornography.

2. In Betty Wein's angry complaint about the proliferation of pornographic materials, students should recognize a different voice, not that of a social scientist but that of a "plain, ordinary citizen." Wein bravely confronts the intricacies of definition. Obscenity is simply "dirty books" and "dirty pictures." Do students understand her definition? Has she settled the problem? Students may also want to examine the evidence that pornography is harmful. Gow says it is; Hefner, Goldstein, and Lynn say it isn't. *Society* July/August 1987, offers a long section, "Commentaries: Pornography and Its Discontents," in which several psychologists argue that many of the "allegations of harm are baseless." One of the articles also discusses pornography in comic books, which have come a long way since *my* childhood.

3. The movie rating system is under attack again. Some critics are pressing for an A (Adult) rating. This designation would be awarded to films that fall between R and X. How do students feel about the desirability of creating greater access to erotic films? Can they find support for their views in any of the articles in this chapter?

4. On many campuses the debate between free access to pornographic materials and the dangers it may pose to some members of the community has broken out over specific issues. In our school two battles have been fought in recent years — over the right of a group to show X-rated films on campus and over the right of the campus store to sell *Penthouse, Playgirl,* and *Hustler*.

   Whether such specific conflicts have emerged on your campus, hypothetical examples will work equally well to provoke discussion on both sides of the issues. Students will discover that the larger issues of freedom and civil rights are difficult if not impossible to understand unless they are brought down to actual cases.

5. I have found it fruitful to ask advocates of opposing positions, usually members of partisan groups on campus, to address the class. For example, members of a feminist group may be asked to present their views against pornographic films and books. The class then evaluates the arguments, using a set of criteria on which we have agreed beforehand.

   On another day those opposed, who may also be feminists, like Susan Jacoby, offer their arguments. Perhaps the debate club on campus can provide teams that will engage in a formal debate on the subject, which the class can also evaluate.

6. Although some students may be unfamiliar with so-called pornographic films and books, virtually all of them will recognize references to the lyrics in popular music to which parents' groups take exception. Teachers may already have introduced this subject in Chapter 16, "Freedom of Speech." (See the debate between Jon Pareles and David Meltz.) In that chapter students examined the choice between censure and censorship, as defined by Garry Wills in his essay. That problem is equally relevant in this chapter, but the discussion here can be confined to the clearly sexual nature of the lyrics and the harm they produce, if any, leaving aside the issue of language that attacks particular ethnic groups or advocates violence or suicide. Students may be reluctant to repeat these lyrics in class discussion, but they will put them down on paper and write about them with surprising tact.

PART FOUR

CLASSIC ARGUMENTS

INTRODUCTION

"Reading requires more than words." This observation serves as a partial text for the comments that follow on the use of the "Classic Arguments" section. To understand and enjoy the selections in this section, students will need not only the ability to decode the linguistic symbols but also *information* — about historical events and figure.

There are two sources for the background information and the interpretation of that information: the library and the instructor. Use of the library needs no recommendation from me, but I should like to put in a word for the instructor as a resource. Notwithstanding the prevailing distaste for lecturing in composition courses, it seems to me perfectly legitimate for instructors to give students the information they need in a short summary *before* they proceed, and even to interpret the data if necessary, whenever such an introduction saves valuable time, enlivens the information, and arouses student interest as library research often does not.

Since each selection in "Classic Arguments" is followed by questions and writing suggestions, I have offered here only occasional questions and suggestions for classroom activities. Instead I have written about these essays largely as I myself have responded to them — sometimes in full agreement, sometimes in partial acquiescence — and as I have discussed them with students, who have often disagreed with me.

From *Crito* (p. 555)
PLATO

1. This is one of the three selections in "Classic Arguments" that deal with civil disobedience. Both King and Thoreau argue that civil disobedience can be justified by recourse to moral laws that supersede the laws of government. This is an argument that students will understand and recognize as integral to the development of American democracy. Socrates, however, under threat of a death sentence by the state of Athens, refuses to escape, because escape would be a violation of the loyalty the state has a right to expect. Having lived under and been protected by the laws of Athens, he asks how he can now refuse to obey them.

   In history classes ancient Greece is identified as the cradle of Western democracy. Students therefore believe erroneously that the Greek philosophy of government exalted the individual. Socrates' conviction for introducing new deities and corrupting the youth of Athens and his acquiescence in his punishment remind students of the excesses of totalitarianism. But in

Crito Socrates interprets his willingness to die as the decision of a good citizen and a just man who is obedient to the laws that the citizens of the state, including himself, have enacted. Justice is of all things most dear to him, and he prefers to be remembered as a victim rather than a doer of evil.

(The truth is that what Socrates believed is known almost entirely through the dialogues of Plato, who was inclined to express his own views as if they were those of his master. Plato rejected the democratic state and described the perfect society in *The Republic,* which bears little resemblance to a modern democracy.)

2. It's doubtful that one student in a thousand will agree that Socrates should make no attempt to save his own life, especially in view of the questionable nature of his crime. On the other hand, if students were to think of Socrates as one who died for his faith, would they continue to regard his acceptance of death as an act of foolishness?

3. This selection will enable students to become familiar with the celebrated Socratic dialogue, a teaching strategy in which Socrates arrives at the truth through skillful questioning and prolific use of definitions and examples.

4. Character as well as intellect plays a role in Socrates' decision, and the reader of the defense can find evidence of his dignity, his moderation, his serenity, and his regard for parents, children, and friends.

5. Once it is extracted, the argument of this dialogue is clear, and the language of the translation should pose no problem. Any obstacles will probably emerge in the attempt to master or even confront the long paragraphs. Since this is a dialogue, a piece of dramatic prose, it's appropriate and helpful for parts of it to be read aloud by good readers.

   I would ask students to summarize in one or two sentences the meaning of each long paragraph before asking for a précis of the whole dialogue.

6. Socrates and Thoreau stand on opposite sides of the debate over the relationship between the individual and the state. One or two students may want to play devil's advocate and defend Socrates' submission against Thoreau's lofty individualism.

A Modest Proposal (p. 560)
JONATHAN SWIFT

1. If students are reading this essay for the first time without preparation or warning, some of them will take Swift's proposal literally. But, then, so did some seventeenth-century readers with perhaps less justification. Some teachers think that the multiple horrors of organized cruelty and genocide in the twentieth century have made Swift's proposal at least marginally credible. We hope not.

2. Students should be able to describe the person ostensibly making the modest proposal, since the proposer himself calls attention to his characteristics: compassionate but disinterested, thoughtful, reasonable, temperate, well informed. The question is whether such a person — one who is compassionate and reasonable — could make a proposal to breed human infants for food. If students agree that he could not, then why has he done so? If his reasons are not those that he alleges them to be, what can they be?

There are several ways of deciding on the answers. One is to examine the language. Does the voice of the proposer — formal, detached, heavy with statistical data — suggest one who is passionately distressed by the suffering of the Irish? Why does the proposer refer to the Irish in terms descriptive of animals rather than human beings? Is there any place in which the voice and language of the author seem to change, where he offers solutions entirely different in kind from the breeding of children for food? How are we to interpret the difference in these two voices? In the next-to-last paragraph even the voice of the proposer begins to change; to urge that Irish adults would have been fortunate to die within the first year of life is a judgment that can be offered only in bitter irony.

3. It is not just the language or the disparity between the voices that can give away the ironic stance. There are also the external criteria, including the subject itself. Are there people in Swift's audience, no matter how indifferent to the fate of the Irish, who would enjoy the prospect of eating human infants? Would an Anglican dean be likely to make such a suggestion in the expectation that reasonable people would find it acceptable? Why would an essay outlining a serious proposal to breed children for food survive for more than two hundred years not as a curiosity but as a model of expository prose for readers throughout the English-speaking world? Consideration of these questions ought to lead to a suspicion, even in the most undiscerning reader, that some other interpretation than the literal one must exist.

Civil Disobedience (p. 569)
HENRY DAVID THOREAU

Thoreau's classic defense of civil disobedience is the antithesis of Socrates' defense of the rights of the state. Thoreau believes that that government is best which governs least or not at all. He denies the authority of government to command the allegiance of an individual who does not wish to concede it. Civil disobedience is justified when conscience dictates that a greater harm will result from compliance with the law than from refusal to obey.

1. Students will need information about the Mexican War of 1846–48, to which Thoreau makes a number of references. We may assume that students know something about slavery (although a recent study by the National Endowment for the Humanities revealed that 80 percent of college seniors were ignorant of what the Emancipation Proclamation did). They will also need to know that Massachusetts was not a slave state, that Thoreau was objecting to an *implicit* sanction of slavery for economic reasons.

2. Thoreau uses the term "unjust laws," but unlike King he fails to define it. Throughout the essay he speaks of "right" and "wrong," "conscience," "a higher law." In the next-to-last paragraph he mentioned the New Testament. Students can profitably wrestle with a summary of Thoreau's criteria for judgment. They can uncover clues in his opinions of slavery, the constitution of the United States, the majority in a democracy, voting, soldiers, imprisonment, Daniel Webster.

3. Discussing the relevance of Thoreau's ideas and actions to present-day issues — civil rights, racism, U.S. foreign policy, taxation — can test and sharpen student understanding of civil disobedience. What kind of protest would Thoreau engage in today? (His own protest ended after one day in jail

when an aunt bailed him out.) What specific issues would be likely to arouse him? If he were a college student today, would he resort to protests against some college rules and activities? Many student protesters who engage in unlawful activities insist on amnesty as a condition of their surrender to the authorities. What would the participants in this civil disobedience symposium — Socrates, Thoreau, and King — have said about the refusal to accept punishment?

What would Thoreau say about the growth of government since his day? Students might speculate on the state of individual rights 150 years after Thoreau. What examples can they offer of restrictions on individual rights? Can these restrictions be justified by taking into account population growth and the increasing complexity of life?

Can the acts of civil disobedience by Thoreau and King be compared or contrasted? Students should take into consideration the causes for which each was jailed and the principles on which each based his defense.

4. This essay is like a rich cake, studded with unexpected treats. Students may find it indigestible at first, but they can be helped to enjoy it. The claim will be perfectly comprehensible to anyone who is familiar with protests against unjust laws or an unjust government. It is Thoreau's discursive organization and sonorous prose that prevent average or slow readers from appreciating the force of his ideas. Since there is hardly time in one semester to read and discuss a long essay like this one with the thoroughness it deserves, we shall have to settle for an understanding of its major ideas. Fortunately, Thoreau includes homely examples of his most abstract utterances in almost every paragraph. These examples provide the key to decoding the generalizations students may find difficult.

   The essay suggests opportunities for short, in-class exercises to increase student comprehension. (1) Paraphrase an important idea. (2) Offer examples for one of Thoreau's generalizations.

Declaration of Sentiments and Resolutions, Seneca Falls (p. 588)
ELIZABETH CADY STANTON

1. Like "The Declaration of Independence" (reprinted in Chapter 1), this is a classic example of the use of fact, value, and policy in an argument. The argument for women's rights is based on an unambiguous warrant: "Both men *and women* are endowed by the Creator with the right to 'life, liberty, and the pursuit of happiness.'" Both documents make an appeal to a universal audience. The greatest difference between them lies in the policies they espouse. While "The Declaration of Independence" calls for a separation from Great Britain and the institution of a new and independent government, "The Declaration of Sentiments and Resolutions" calls for strenuous efforts by both men and women toward "immediate admission to all the rights and privileges which belong to [women] as citizens of the United States."

   The language of that call to action reminds us that both women's rights activists of the mid–nineteenth century and abolitionists often shared the same goals. Stanton and others supported the antislavery movement, and

Frederick Douglass, the celebrated black writer and orator, attended the Seneca Falls convention and argued for the elective franchise for women.

2. Does the close imitation of "The Declaration of Independence" weaken or enhance the impact of the Seneca Falls declaration? That is, does it suggest a parody or a failure of originality? Or is the imitation based on strong rhetorical principles?

   How do students feel about the grievances outlined by Stanton? Are they all equally compelling? Are they as important as those in "The Declaration of Independence"? (Some critics have argued that they are *more* important.)

3. Some grievances will need explanation, not only of the language but of the ideas and their history.

   a. "He has never permitted her to exercise her inalienable right to the elective franchise" (para. 4).

      (Students may not know that the Nineteenth Amendment to the Constitution, which granted women the right to vote in federal and state elections, was not ratified until 1921.)

   b. "He has created a false public sentiment by giving to the world a different code of morals for men and women, by which moral delinquencies which exclude women from society, are not only tolerated, but deemed of little account in man" (para. 16).

      (Students should recognize a statement of the "double standard," but examples can make it clear for those who are not sure.)

   c. "He allows her in Church, as well as State, but a subordinate position, claiming Apostolic authority for her exclusion from the ministry, and, with some exceptions, from any public participation in the affairs of the Church" (para. 15).

      (Students who know about the current conflicts in some churches over ordination of women can initiate a discussion of this grievance.)

4. In both this selection and the one by Virginia Woolf, students should try to name and evaluate the changes that have occurred in women's lives (and therefore in men's lives, too) since 1848 and 1942 respectively. Most of the changes will be clear; a few will be debatable. A discussion of the changes or lack of them seems especially relevant today, when influential feminists are engaged in assessing the gains and losses brought about by the women's movement. Do students think that the gains offset the losses? (There is an unexpected irony in a recent claim by Joan Ganz Cooney, chair of the Children's Television Workshop, that a majority of working mothers of young children say they would prefer to stay at home but cannot afford to do so. Women, says Cooney, had more choices forty years ago.)

   Stanton's call for reform is broader than Woolf's. "The Declaration" speaks for all women, not merely professionals, and it demands far-reaching legal and political changes. Woolf seems to address a narrower range of problems, as her title indicates, but her demands, though less specific and less directly expressed, encompass changes in deep-rooted cultural attitudes that may be even harder to reshape than laws.

5. Needless to say, male students should be brought into any discussion of women's rights, and they should feel free to express sentiments with which the female students may not agree. The instructor may have to make quick

judgments about what is acceptable in a civil discussion, but I'd be inclined to err on the side of freedom to make a rude noise.

Postscript. Here's a mystery that someone reading this may be able to solve. One of the grievances in Stanton's list reads:

> He has made her, morally, an irresponsible being, as she can commit many crimes with impunity, provided they be done in the presence of her husband.

In an effort to find out what crimes Stanton referred to, I called the Stanton-Anthony Project at the University of Massachusetts, as well as three law professors and three history professors at several well-known universities. None of them could give me the answer. But Michael Grossberg, professor of history at Case Western Reserve University, suggested a promising clue: Joel Prentiss Bishop (1814–1901), *Commentaries on the Laws of Marriage and Divorce* (Boston: Little, Brown & Co. 6th edition, 1881). Unfortunately, this volume is not readily available (although I'm told it probably resides in a good law school library), and these notes must go to press. My thanks to anyone who can identify the crimes that can be committed with impunity.

Professions for Women (p. 593)
VIRGINIA WOOLF

1. Woolf's essay is highly personal and specific; it is her own experiences as a writer that inform her conclusions. Unfortunately, most students will not be familiar with her essays and novels.

   Students may remember how Sidney Hook uses his experience as a dying patient in "In Defense of Voluntary Euthanasia." For both Woolf and Hook personal experience is a crucial element in the support for their arguments.

   In urging students to write about what they know (a sometimes stifling injunction) we have told them often enough to use personal experience as evidence. It bears repeating, however, that personal experience is used most effectively by *student writers* in support of qualified claims. Student writers are often unwilling to confine themselves to the lessons taught by their limited experience. We see that Woolf ventures tentatively outside her own field to speculate about other professions and to suggest that her experiences are relevant to those of other professional women. But it is surely not only for lack of time that she does not pursue these larger questions, which will continue to tease her audience; and her short piece is clearly more effective for its concentration on a narrower theme.

   A writer's use of personal experience also brings the reader close to his or her character and personality. (Perhaps it would be nearer the truth to say "close to the character and personality that the writer wishes us to see"; in her private journals Woolf often shows a very different face.) In "Professions for Women" students should find her frank, modest, engaging, and witty.

2. Despite the fact that Woolf is writing almost one hundred years after Stanton in readable modern prose about recognizable modern problems, many students may find her thesis more exclusive than Stanton's. Woolf is, how-

ever, an excellent introduction to issues which engage students today. Is a woman still enjoined to be "pure," to "be tender, to flatter, to deceive," never to "let anybody guess that you have a mind of your own"? Is it still unfitting for a woman to speak about her passions? Hardly. Ask students to give examples — perhaps from film and television — that support their answers. (But we can also tell them about a recent case in which a woman accountant, the most successful among eighty employees, was denied a partnership in a prestigious accounting firm because she was "too macho" and "in need of a course at charm school.")

We should encourage male students to speculate about the Angels in *their* houses. If one exists, does it, like Woolf's, caution them to behave in ways that seem dishonest and unnatural? Surely the answer is yes.

3. Woolf's style is worth reviewing. Her novelistic use of description and narrative action should appeal to students and suggest ways of animating their own arguments. And students can be helped to see that simple, straightforward vocabulary, uncluttered syntax, and a conversational tone in no way prevent development of a major theme. I'd call attention to Woolf's introduction to her thesis. In the third paragraph, after describing her early success as a writer, she interrupts to say, "But wait a moment." This clear signal to the reader of a change in direction is an *oral* clue. There is no reason students should not be permitted to use oral locutions in written essays. Such expressions can give color and intimacy to bland written discourse.

   Woolf, however, makes things more difficult for many students by her use of metaphors — the Angel in the house and the fisherman lying sunk in dreams. Beautiful and appropriate as they are, these images may baffle students unused to interpreting figures of speech. Such students will need to be led through the meanings and the ways in which they define the stereotypical Victorian woman and illuminate the attitudes of her society toward her.

   The long third paragraph is full of interesting stylistic devices: repetition of sentence structure for emphasis, a succession of four or five very short sentences, and alternation of short and long sentences.

Politics and the English Language (p. 599) GEORGE ORWELL

1. I find that Orwell's great essay grows more and more difficult to teach as our students become less and less sensitive to language and style. In the chapter on language, I have included some examples of inflated language that confirm Orwell's criticism. The deficiencies of these professional writers are not, however, those of which freshmen students are guilty in their own writing. Rather, the examples represent the kinds of obscure and pretentious language that students should be alert to in the arguments that they *read.*

   In order to read Orwell intelligently, students must not only understand his terms — "dying metaphors," "verbal false limbs," "pretentious diction" — but also be able to appreciate the awkwardness and unintelligibility in his examples. If I discover that students are not responsive to these problems, I move on.

2. The organization of the essay, fortunately, lends itself to a study of discrete parts without a loss of sense or purpose. As teachers of argument, we should give our greatest attention to those parts that have a direct relevance to the way in which bad language can distort an argument. Under "Meaningless Words," for example, Orwell uses selections from politics. But the heart of the essay may fairly be said to begin with paragraph 13. I would therefore concentrate on an understanding of Orwell's claim about the relation between politics and language. For this more examples are crucial (Orwell offers only phrases). There are brief selections in the chapter on language to which students may refer. The best long examples will usually be found in the writing and speeches of partisans on the far right and the far left of the political spectrum. You may have to begin by bringing in examples you have found that show what is meant by distortion and deception in political language. Freshman students may not know enough about the history and circumstances surrounding a particular argument to detect its misuse of language. Perhaps some egregious outburst in the school paper will serve.

Letter from Birmingham Jail (p. 611)
MARTIN LUTHER KING, JR.

1. An introduction to the circumstances surrounding King's imprisonment will probably be necessary. Students will have to know something about the segregation laws in the 1960s and the civil-rights demonstrations against them led by King and the Southern Christian Leadership Conference. King's use of "Negro" and "colored" in the sixties should also be explained. King uses the word "black" only in reference to nationalist groups, whose tactics he rejects. I've used his terms in the questions in the text because I thought it would be presumptuous to change them.
2. King's letter, which was clearly addressed to a much wider audience than the white Protestant ministers in Birmingham, is a superb example of a long exposition in which students can find skillful use of all the elements of argument. King's use of support deserves special attention.

Support

a. He recounts the indignities suffered by Negroes (para. 12). This constitutes a list of grievances like the lists in "The Declaration of Independence" and "The Declaration of Sentiments and Resolutions." The grievances are expressed as personal experiences. (Notice the use of the second person and the reference to his five-year-old son.) Some readers will respond to personal experience when abstractions about law and justice fail to move them.
b. He summarizes the history of attempts to gain civil rights to prove that Negroes have been patient. This is an answer to the accusation that his activities were "untimely."
c. He invokes authorities from ancient Greece, the Bible, Christian and Judaic scholarship, American statesmen. These authorities support the validity of his protest and his "extremist" approach (para. 26).
d. He refers to the struggles of other oppressed people, struggles with which the white Protestant ministers and his larger audience will sym-

pathize and which they will recognize as analogous to the protests of Negroes.

e. Equally important are his appeals to the values of his two audiences, small and large: a sense of justice, compassion for the oppressed, a love of freedom, admiration and respect for brave, peaceful — and worthy — resistance, and the willingness of the resisters to suffer severe consequences in the service of a noble cause.

Definition

a. Like any classic, King's letter continues to reverberate. However sketchy their knowledge of specific events, students surely know that millions of people throughout the world are actively opposing "unjust" laws, often for the first time in decades and at great risk, and that King's definition of such laws is still highly relevant.

   King's definition rests primarily on religious foundations (para. 14). Both "The Declaration of Independence" and "The Declaration of Sentiments and Resolutions" also invoke the Creator as the source of justice and morality. Students can study King's language and try to decide if his definition of just and unjust laws can survive without reference to "the law of God." Some readers may feel that King's definition is too broad, too vague. Is there a danger that we may define any laws that we want to support as the laws of God? (In fact, the laws of slavery were so defined by their supporters.)

b. The student essay on drinking laws (p. 273) will ring King's definition into a contemporary issue about which students have strong feelings. The author decries as unjust the new drinking law that prevents her and other eighteen- to twenty-year-olds from enjoying "the pleasure of intoxication." Can their right to purchase alcohol be protected by what King would define as a "just" law? The student author insists that eighteen- to twenty-year-old drinkers are being treated differently from eighteen- to twenty-year-olds who vote, marry, and serve in the armed services. Is King's distinction between "difference" and "sameness" made legal (para. 15) relevant here?

   Restrictive gun laws, regarded by their opponents as "unfair" to law-abiding citizens, offer another subject for discussion of just and unjust laws.

Warrant

a. The warrant in "Letter" — oppressed people have the right to protest their oppression — recalls the warrant in "The Declaration of Independence." This is one of several similarities between the two documents.

b. The white ministers in Birmingham argued that they disagreed with the *tactics* of the demonstrators. Does King's lengthy response suggest that he believes the ministers might also have disapproved of the *right* to protest?

Tone

a. King's tone reflects dignity, humility, and generosity to the opposition. Throughout the letter he skillfully negotiates a narrow line between criticism of his accusers and the belief that "as men of goodwill" they will understand and accept his argument. This conciliatory tone is very different from the tone adopted by more militant black leaders. Students might find it instructive to compare the two voices.

b. In college newspapers and elsewhere the tone adopted by angry writers is often abusive and self-righteous. Ask students to look for examples and comment on the effect such attitudes have on a neutral or unfriendly reader. If there are differences in the responses, how can we account for them?

Language

King's style is lofty, grave, sermonic. Several of the literary strategies he favors emphasize his role as preacher.

a. King uses rhetorical questions throughout (for example, para. 22 and 26). What effect might such questions have on a neutral or unfriendly audience?

b. King also uses structural repetition for emphasis (para. 44). "I Have a Dream" is an even more ambitious example of this literary technique, which King employed frequently in all his writing. Some students may recognize parallels to the language of the King James version of the Bible.

Some readers have found King's long, rhythmic sentences and figurative language pretentious and overblown. (See para. 42.) Is this elevated style appropriate in the context? Or would a less decorative style have been more effective?

Students themselves are not so likely to indulge in elaborate metaphorical language when they argue social issues — they usually succumb to this temptation when they write about nature — nor should they be encouraged to do so, but they should be alert to its use in the utterances of public figures and able to evaluate its contribution to the argument.

Organization

This is a long argument with many parts, whose transitions make it seem more closely organized than it really is. The following rough outline indicates how the argument proceeds.

1. background of the march in Birmingham; explanation of his imprisonment	pp. 611–615
2. definition of just and unjust laws	615–616
3. disappointment with white moderates	617–618
4. rejection of charge of extremism; defense of nonviolent action	618–620
5. disappointment with the white church leadership	620–622
6. optimism about the future	622–623

7. attack on the police use of moral means for immoral ends 623–624
8. praise for heroic demonstrators 624
9. conclusion 624–625

I Have a Dream (p. 626)
MARTIN LUTHER KING, JR.

1. Someone in the class, whether instructor or student, who can muster a compelling declamatory style, should read part of this speech aloud. If you can obtain a recording of the original speech, so much the better. There is no better way to savor the language and to gain some understanding, however limited, of the impact of this speech on its listeners. Ask students to compare, as far as possible, its effect when read and its effect when listened to. Is there a difference? (There is no doubt that the human voice, with its timbre and its capacity for emotional expression, can indicate values as effectively as words.) Students should also keep in mind that this speech was delivered before a large outdoor crowd. Would this situation influence the kind of argument King needed to make?

2. Students should be asked to consider this speech as a *written* argument. What was the purpose of this speech? How specific was King in recommending policy or actions to be undertaken by the audience? Would the speech have been more effective as argument if King had urged the enactment of specific laws and exhorted his audience to work for them?

3. Finally, students should attend to the language. Does the language enhance the impact of the argument? Or does it sometimes distract? For example, in the fourth paragraph, there is the sustained metaphor of the promissory note. But the succeeding sentences contain figures of speech involving drugs, valleys, sunlit paths, open doors, quicksand, and rocks. Are some metaphors more effective than others? If so, why?

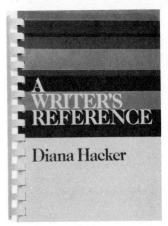

Bedford Books *of* St. Martin's Press